INTERROGATING YOUNG SUSPECTS

INTERROGATING YOUNG SUSPECTS

Procedural Safeguards from a Legal Perspective

Michele Panzavolta
Dorris de Vocht
Marc van Oosterhout
Miet Vanderhallen
(eds.)

intersentia
Cambridge – Antwerp – Portland

Intersentia Ltd
Sheraton House | Castle Park
Cambridge | CB3 0AX | United Kingdom
Tel.: +44 1223 370 170 | Email: mail@intersentia.co.uk

Distribution for the UK:
NBN International
Airport Business Centre, 10 Thornbury Road
Plymouth, PL6 7 PP
United Kingdom
Tel.: +44 1752 202 301 | Fax: +44 1752 202 331
Email: orders@nbninternational.com

Distribution for the USA and Canada:
International Specialized Book Services
920 NE 58th Ave. Suite 300
Portland, OR 97213
USA
Tel.: +1 800 944 6190 (toll free)
Email: info@isbs.com

Distribution for Austria:
Neuer Wissenschaftlicher Verlag
Argentinierstraße 42/6
1040 Wien
Austria
Tel.: +43 1 535 61 03 24
Email: office@nwv.at

Distribution for other countries:
Intersentia Publishing nv
Groenstraat 31
2640 Mortsel
Belgium
Tel.: +32 3 680 15 50
Email: mail@intersentia.be

Interrogating Young Suspects. Procedural Safeguards from a Legal Perspective
Michele Panzavolta, Dorris de Vocht, Marc van Oosterhout and Miet Vanderhallen (eds.)

ISBN 978-1-78068-299-0
D/2015/7849/83
NUR 824

With the financial support of the European Community

Sole responsibility for the contents of this publication lies with the authors and the Commission is not responsible for any use made of the information contained therein.

British Library Cataloguing in Publication Data. A catalogue record for this book is available from the British Library.

PREFACE AND ACKNOWLEDGEMENTS

This book is the result of the first part of the European Commission funded research project *Protecting Young Suspects in Interrogations: a study on safeguards and best practice*.[1] The project consists of a legal comparative study, empirical research and the merging of the legal and empirical findings, and its aim is to identify legal and empirical patterns in the procedural protection of juvenile suspects during pre-trial interrogation. The legal study underlying this volume consisted of comparative research into existing procedural safeguards for juvenile suspects during interrogation in the legal frameworks of five selected Member States of the European Union: Belgium, England and Wales, Italy, Poland and the Netherlands. The results of the empirical research, as well as the merging of the legal and empirical findings resulting in a proposal for European minimum rules and best practice on the protection of juvenile suspects during interrogation, will be published in a second volume.

The successful completion of this project has been the joint effort of a large group of people. First and foremost we would like to thank our academic partners – and in-country researchers – for their dedication to the project and the incredible amount of high-quality work they delivered: Claudia Cesari, Deborah Felice, Jackie Hodgson, Vicky Kemp, Justyna Kusztal, Joachim Meese, Vania Patanè and Barbara Stańdo-Kawecka. Comparative legal research can at times be extremely challenging because it is not easy to convey the nuances of one's own legal system outside its original language and culture. It was thanks to the large knowledge, flexibility, open-mindedness, patience and tenacity of our partners that we only experienced the positive sides of comparative research. Working with them has been an incredibly enriching experience, not only confined to legal matters.

The research and the project as a whole have also benefited enormously from the advice and assistance offered by our supporting partners: PLOT Limburg and Defence for Children who provided support in organising project events, employing social media and disseminating research findings. Thanks particularly to Maartje Berger for her useful practical information and, above all, for her passion and dedication to improving the procedural protection of children.

1 The project was funded by a Criminal Justice Action Grant of the European Commission (JUST/2011/JPEN/AG2909).

The project has benefited from the supervision of a Steering Committee, an advisory board of experts composed of leading scholars in the field of juvenile justice and criminal law coming from different jurisdictions: Prof. Ray Bull, Prof. Frieder Dünkel, Prof. Gerard de Jonge, Prof. Taru Spronken and Prof. Anette Storgaard. We thank them for their valuable guidance and constant feedback while setting up and conducting the research.

Managing and coordinating the project has been the task of the entire Maastricht project team, but three of the four members of the team (Dorris, Michele and Miet) would like to emphasise that it is in particular thanks to the outstanding daily effort of Marc van Oosterhout that everything has run smoothly and efficiently. In addition to conducting large strands of the legal and empirical research, Marc has been responsible for the many organisational and administrative tasks, ranging from setting up project meetings to managing the project website, and many others. Marc has taken up these diverse, challenging duties with the utmost positivity and perseverance and he has proven to be of inestimable value to the project.

The administration of the project was carried out by Maastricht University. Special thanks go to Diana Schabregs for her hard work in the financial management of this project, to Yleen Simonis for organising the final project conference and to the student assistants who have worked with us at different stages of the project: Jakoline Winkels, Elisabeth Pirotta and Jennifer Etoré.

We thank Kris Moeremans and the staff of Intersentia for their involvement in publishing this book.

Finally, we would like to thank the European Commission for funding this project. We truly hope that its results may contribute to the current debate on how to effectively strengthen the protection of juvenile suspects during the initial stages of criminal proceedings.

Michele Panzavolta
Dorris de Vocht
Marc van Oosterhout
Miet Vanderhallen

February 2015

CONTENTS

LIST OF ABBREVIATIONS

ASBOs	Anti-Social Behaviour Orders
CC	Criminal Code
CCP	Code of Criminal Procedure
Cost	Constitution of the Italian Republic
CPA	Child Protection Act
CPS	Crown Prosecution Service
CRC	Convention on the Rights of the Child
CWC	Child Welfare Council
C&YP	Children and Young Persons Act
DTO	Detention and Training Order
EAW	European Arrest Warrant
ECHR	European Convention on Human Rights
ECtHR	European Court of Human Rights
FME	forensic medical examiner
HR	Hoge Raad
JA	Juvenile Act
LASPO	Legal Aid Sentencing and Punishment of Offenders Act
NJ	Nederlandse Jurisprudentie
PACE	Police and Criminal Evidence Act
PNDs	Penalty Notices for Disorder
UN	United Nations
VOM	victim-offender mediation
YJA	Youth Justice Act
YOT	Youth Offending Team
YPA	Youth Protection Act

BIOGRAPHIES

Claudia Cesari

Claudia Cesari is a Professor of Criminal Procedure at the University of Macerata Law School (Italy). She graduated *magna cum laude* in criminal procedure from the University of Bologna in 1991 and obtained her PhD in criminal procedure at the same institution in 1997. Cesari served as Director of the Department of Criminal Law and Procedure at Macerata between 2007 and 2013. She now acts as Vice Director of the Law Faculty. Cesari is also Coordinator of the Centre for Studies and Research into Juvenile Justice at Macerata. Cesari's research interests include juvenile justice, rules of evidence, and diversion techniques. She teaches criminal procedure and juvenile criminal justice. Some of Cesari's most relevant recent publications include *L'irripetibilità sopravvenuta* (1999) (on an exception to the hearsay rule) and *Le clausole di irrilevanza del fatto nel sistema processuale penale* (2005) (on facts that do not warrant prosecution). Cesari has both edited and authored recent publications of the Centre for Studies and Research into Juvenile Justice.

Jacqueline Hodgson

Jacqueline Hodgson is Professor of Law at the University of Warwick (United Kingdom). She holds an LLB and PhD and has researched and written on issues within French, English/Welsh and comparative criminal justice, on the role of the criminal defence lawyer, the right to silence, the process of investigation and prosecution, terrorism, miscarriages of justice and suspects' rights. Much of her work draws upon her own externally funded empirical research and she held a British Academy/Leverhulme Senior Research Fellowship from 2009–2010. Key publications include *Custodial Legal Advice and the Right to Silence* (1993), *Standing Accused* (1994), *Criminal Injustice* (2000), *French Criminal Justice* (2005), *The investigation and prosecution of terrorist offences in France* (2006), *Suspects in Europe* (2007), *The extent and impact of legal representation on applications to the Criminal Cases Review Commission* (2009), and *Inside Police Custody* (2014). She has advised Parliamentary Select Committees and EU impact assessment studies, and her research has been relied on by the Special Immigration Appeals Commission and in European Arrest Warrant proceedings. She is an elected member of the JUSTICE Council and a Fellow of the Academy of Social Sciences. This current project on safeguards for juveniles complements her recently completed European Commission-funded project – an empirical comparative study of safeguards for suspects.

Vicky Kemp

Vicky Kemp, a Principal Research Fellow at the University of Nottingham (United Kingdom), is an experienced researcher having conducted extensive empirical studies into the criminal justice system. After having completed her doctorate at the University of Cambridge, which focused on youth justice reforms under the Crime and Disorder Act 1998, she joined the Legal Services Research Centre, an internationally recognised and influential leader in the field of access to justice research. In that role she managed a number of empirical studies, including a survey of people drawn into the criminal process and a study of youth courts, evaluating new innovative arrangements involving duty solicitors based in police stations, and was responsible for a large-scale study into the take-up of police station legal advice. Key publications include *Transforming legal aid: Access to criminal defence services* (2010), 'Children, young people and requests for police station legal advice: 25 years on from PACE' in *Youth Justice* (2011), *Bridewell Legal Advice Study: adopting a 'whole-systems' approach to police station legal advice – Interim and Final Reports* (2012 and 2013) and 'PACE, performance targets and legal protections' in *Criminal Law Review* (2014). She is a member of the International Legal Aid Group and the British Society of Criminology.

Justyna Kusztal

Justyna Kusztal (PhD) is employed as assistant professor in the Institute of Pedagogy of the Jagiellonian University in Kraków (Poland). She graduated in law and pedagogy with a specialisation in social rehabilitation at the Jagiellonian University. She obtained her PhD in 2006 in the field of pedagogy at the same institution. Her doctoral dissertation approached a comparative study of social rehabilitation systems of juvenile delinquents in Poland and Germany. She has worked in various types of research teams and is the author of approximately forty articles in the area of social prevention and rehabilitation and problems of juvenile delinquency from a Polish and an international perspective. Her interests are focused on European trends in social prevention of juvenile delinquency and criminal policy in this area.

Joachim Meese

Joachim Meese is a Doctor of law and has a Master's degree in criminology. He is a Professor at the University of Antwerp (Belgium). Joachim Meese is the author of many academic publications. His doctoral thesis, *De duur van het strafproces* (*Length of criminal proceedings*, 2006), considers the concepts of the statutes of limitations and the right to be tried within a reasonable time. This book has become a standard work in Belgium. Joachim Meese is also a lawyer, admitted to the Bar of Ghent in 1999. As a lawyer, he is a managing partner at Van Steenbrugge & Partners. He regularly participates in seminars and conferences on criminal law and criminal procedure.

Marc van Oosterhout

Marc van Oosterhout holds two degrees in law (criminal law and forensics) from Maastricht University (the Netherlands). His main research interests are in the fields of (European) criminal procedure and fundamental (suspects') rights, police proceedings and interrogation. During the course of this research project, Marc van Oosterhout was a researcher at the Department of Criminal Law and Criminology at Maastricht University. Before that he had been appointed as a researcher and tutor at the same institution. Earlier he was involved in another European project studying rights of suspects in police detention during which he conducted fieldwork in the Netherlands and Scotland. Besides empirical research, he was involved in the daily operational tasks that are required in large-scale research projects. Due to his research and operational skills, Marc has conducted legal and empirical research in the Netherlands and Belgium and is part of the project management team. He has also been responsible for social media (project website, LinkedIn and Twitter account) during the project. At present, Marc van Oosterhout is a project manager at AMBER Alert Netherlands where he is responsible for further local embedding of AMBER Alert, organising and analysing an EU regional police cooperation pilot and various other projects.

Michele Panzavolta

Michele Panzavolta is Associate Professor of Criminal Law at the University of Leuven (Belgium) and part-time Assistant Professor at the University of Maastricht (the Netherlands), where he was a Marie-Curie Fellow for a research on intelligence. He graduated from the University of Bologna (Italy) and obtained his doctorate at the University of Urbino (Italy). He was a postdoctoral fellow at the University of Bologna and a visiting scholar at the University of Cambridge. He is a qualified attorney at the Bar of Bologna and has experience as a practicing criminal lawyer in Italy. He specialises in European and international criminal law and in comparative studies on criminal law and procedure. Besides juvenile criminal justice, his research interests are in intelligence-related topics (surveillance, intelligence analysis, relationship between police and judicial bodies and intelligence services, cybercrime, *et cetera*), financial crime and asset recovery and, more generally, the protection of individual rights in criminal matters.

Miet Vanderhallen

Miet Vanderhallen is an Assistant Professor of Criminology at Maastricht University (the Netherlands) and an Assistant Professor of Psychology and Law at Antwerp University (Belgium). She holds a degree and PhD in criminology (Catholic University of Leuven, Belgium). She has conducted extensive empirical studies on various aspects of investigative interviewing, such as rapport building, suspect interviewing, legal advice, training and supervision. Miet

Vanderhallen has published many (inter)national articles and book chapters on investigative interviewing. Recently, she has participated in several EU studies on interviewing suspects, including *Procedural rights of suspects in police detention in the EU: empirical investigation and promoting best practice* (JUST/2010/JPEN/AG/1578). In addition to her research activities, she is involved in interview training programs at various police academies.

Dorris de Vocht

Dorris de Vocht is an Assistant Professor in the Department of Criminal Law and Criminology at Maastricht University (the Netherlands). She holds a degree in law (with honors) and a PhD from the same institution. In 2009 she successfully defended her doctoral thesis on the right to legal assistance in post-communist Poland. She has a special interest in procedural safeguards for suspects and defendants especially from a comparative (ECHR as well as EU) perspective. After obtaining her doctorate, she has participated in several EU-funded comparative legal studies such as *EU Procedural Rights in Criminal Proceedings* (JSL/2008/D3/002). She coordinates and teaches various bachelors and masters courses in the field of criminal (procedural) law and is a regular author in various Dutch journals and commentaries, such as *Tekst and Commentaar Strafvordering* (C.P.M. Cleiren and J.F. Nijboer, eds.). Since 2014 she is also a deputy judge with the District Court of Limburg.

Barbara Stańdo-Kawecka

Barbara Stańdo-Kawecka is Professor of Law and Head of the Department of Penitentiary Law and Policy at the Faculty of Law, Jagiellonian University in Kraków (Poland). She graduated in special pedagogy and law from the Jagiellonian University. At the same institution she obtained her PhD and defended her habilitation thesis. Her main research interests are on criminal policy, juvenile law, prison systems and penitentiary policy. She took part in several international research projects concerning juvenile justice, restorative justice and prison systems. Her past publications include chapters on juvenile justice system in Poland (in *Juvenile Justice Systems in Europe: Current Situation and Reform Developments*, 2010) and long-term prisoners in Poland (in *Long-Term Imprisonment and Human Rights*, 2014).

CHAPTER 1
INTRODUCTION

Michele PANZAVOLTA and Dorris DE VOCHT

1. THE TOPIC AND AIM OF THIS STUDY

Picture a 15-year-old at a police headquarters, sitting in front of two police officers who are confronting him about the circumstances of an alleged crime. Imagine the juvenile again when the officers read out the letter of the law and ask him a series of questions, crudely staring at him after each question, waiting for a response. Nobody could deny that such a situation is stressful and uncomfortable to say the least and that the majority of young people would most likely be scared and insecure under the circumstances. Therefore, one could argue that an adequate level of protection should be provided to the juvenile suspect in such a situation, even if at a very early stage of proceedings. But what exactly does it mean that the juvenile ought to be protected and – more specifically – how and to what extent are juvenile suspects currently protected in Europe?

This question is at the heart of the research project *Protecting Young Suspects in Interrogations,* of which this volume is part. The research project stemmed from the observation that knowledge about the level of procedural protection currently provided to juvenile suspects throughout the European Union is limited. More specifically, there is very little knowledge of what actually happens – and ought to happen – when juvenile suspects are being interrogated. The aim of this study is to fill at least part of this gap by shedding more light on the existing procedural rights for juveniles during interrogations in five selected EU Member States.

2. SETTING THE SCENE: JUVENILES AND CRIMINAL PROCEEDINGS

The picture of a suspect is somehow in natural tension with the picture of a young person. We naturally associate youth with innocence and inoffensiveness and we are thus uncomfortable every time we are confronted with an offence (allegedly) committed by a minor, to the extent that we tend either to downplay the seriousness of the crime or to forget about the immaturity of the offender.[1] Juveniles are vulnerable individuals due to their age and limited maturity – perhaps the most vulnerable category of individuals.[2] On the other hand, vulnerability is not normally the attribute we have in mind when thinking of criminal offenders.

The tension described above is at the centre of juvenile criminal law. For centuries, law- and policymakers have struggled to find the proper response to juvenile delinquency. This has proven to be a true dilemma with many different aspects to consider and even more possible answers.

It is largely acknowledged that, at least in principle, juveniles deserve to be treated separately and differently from adults when suspected of criminal behaviour. However, the ways in which a juvenile ought to be treated differ from country to country. The differences in legal traditions and structures of authority between countries[3] combine with the different approaches and philosophies regarding juvenile justice. The great diversity in current juvenile justice systems throughout the world thus comes as no surprise. Despite the many international texts 'calling for the adoption of common strategies', the national states still retain their own peculiar juvenile justice system. In other words: the common supranational framework has not prevented national juvenile justice systems from keeping or adopting different patterns of responses to the problems of youth punitive justice.[4]

---

1 Steinberg and Schwartz 2000, p. 9 ('Because we neither expect children to be criminals nor expect crimes to be committed by children, the unexpected intersection between childhood and criminality creates a dilemma that most of us find difficult to resolve. Indeed the only way out of this problem is either to redefine the offence as something less serious or to redefine the offender as someone who is not really a child').

2 Buzzelli 2008, p. 11.

3 See the traditional works of Damaška 1996 and Damaška 1997.

4 Patané 2007, p. 10: 'However, although in the last few years there have been several international texts calling for the adoption of common strategies when dealing with juvenile delinquency, the analysis carried out that the youth systems carried out by this study have, in some case, adopted different patterns of responses to the "youth justice problem", probably as a result of their philosophical underpinnings, their institutional arrangements, the operational policies and the processes involving young offenders'. In the context of this study the words 'punitive (juvenile) justice' and 'criminal (juvenile) justice' will be used in a broad sense referring to all formal responses to dealing with youth crime whether formally labelled as 'criminal' or not. This substantive approach to the terminology is inspired by the Council of Europe's Recommendation Rec(2003)20 concerning new ways of dealing with juvenile delinquency and the role of juvenile justice which defines 'juvenile justice' as 'the formal component of a wider approach for tackling youth crime'. See for a similar approach: Dünkel *et al.* 2011, p. 1539.

From a historical perspective, the concept of a separate system of justice for juveniles is a relatively recent phenomenon. The separation of juvenile justice from the 'adult' justice system first appeared in the United States where special juvenile courts were established for the first time at the end of the 19th century.[5] European countries followed this example not much later[6] and have been developing their juvenile justice systems ever since.

2.1. TYPOLOGIES OF JUVENILE JUSTICE SYSTEMS

In an attempt to find a way to explain and characterise the many differences between existing juvenile justice systems, several typologies and classificatory models have been developed. In their efforts of classification, authors generally observe the entire picture; hence, they look at both the legal situation and the sentencing practice in a particular country.[7]

Many different classifications have been suggested.[8] Some scholars, for instance, distinguish between the 'welfare', 'justice', 'corporate', 'modified justice', 'crime control' and 'participatory' models.[9] Others classify juvenile systems into 'welfare', 'justice', 'minimum intervention', 'restorative justice' and 'neo-correctionalist' models.[10] This classification of systems inevitably entails an artificial simplification of reality. It is difficult – if not impossible – to capture the many variations of each existing system by simply attaching a label to it. Furthermore, juvenile justice systems are moving objects (of research), they undergo shifts and changes that might be inspired or determined by global cultural trends.[11] Every juvenile justice system is the result of a number of different elements and components, which may point in different directions. Nevertheless classifications provide us with a valuable theoretical framework for understanding and explaining some of the diversity between countries in terms of policy, law and practice connected to dealing with juveniles in conflict with the law. Some of these labels allow us to understand how much systems combine the traditional fact-finding approach of judicial proceedings with other (non-judicial or less judicial) forms of treatment. 'Minimum intervention' models, for instance, place emphasis on diversion mechanisms and the need to avoid classic judicial proceedings wherever possible. The same is true to some extent for restorative models.

---

5 In Chicago, Illinois in 1899: see Muncie and Goldson 2006, p. 197.
6 For example in Belgium (Leuven) in 1908: Put and Walgrave 2008, p. 113.
7 Pruin 2011, p. 1545.
8 For a dense description of the classical typologies of European juvenile justice systems see: Pruin 2011, p. 1545–1549.
9 Winterdyk 2014, p. 6–8.
10 Cavadino and Dignan 2006, p. 199.
11 See in this respect Muncie and Goldson 2006.

When specifically looking at the judicial treatment of cases through the more traditional form of criminal (or in any case punitive) proceedings, the most important contrast in how juvenile suspects and defendants are dealt with is probably illustrated by the division between the 'welfare model' on the one hand and the 'justice model' on the other hand. It might be correct to argue that a modern policy of juvenile justice should overcome this stark dichotomy.[12] At the same time, this contrast remains a very powerful tool to understand the still differing approaches to juvenile judicial punitive proceedings across countries.

In a nutshell, the focus of welfare-based juvenile justice systems is on treatment, protection and rehabilitation of the juvenile (focusing on the juvenile's 'needs' in stead of his 'deeds').[13] According to the 'non punitive' welfare model, the aim is to protect the juvenile as much as possible by following an individual approach in proceedings and sentencing. From the traditional welfaristic point of view providing juveniles with 'regular' procedural safeguards is superfluous and even potentially harmful: procedural rights protection may constitute a possible risk for the informal and individualistic approach which is essential for providing the juvenile with the necessary protection (paternalistic approach). According to this line of reasoning, the risk of providing juvenile suspects and defendants with due process rights is that it will limit the discretionary powers of judges and other actors involved in juvenile proceedings to choose the right approach taking into account the specific, individual needs of the juvenile. In contrast to this approach, the justice-oriented model is based on the idea that – in principle – the juvenile could and should be held accountable for his actions and that sanctions should be proportionate to the severity of the offence. In doing so, the juvenile should be provided with the necessary legal protection (due process rights).[14]

This (inevitably simplified) dichotomy between the welfare and juvenile justice models seems to illustrate most clearly the universal dilemma in juvenile justice: whether the focus should be on punishing or protecting the juvenile. In a way, every juvenile justice system tries to find the right balance between the need for protection (education/rehabilitation) of the juvenile on the one hand and the need for punishment and proportionate sanctioning on the other. As scholars have observed, the difficult task of every juvenile justice system is to find 'the appropriate balance between humanistic benevolence, with its potential for abuse, and the safeguarding of individual liberties, with its potential for thrusting juveniles into an adversary system of justice'.[15] In this respect, the

[12] Hill 2007, p. 18.
[13] Hill 2007, p. 18 (with a preference for the label 'child care and protection system', which is considered less ambiguous than 'welfare system').
[14] The contrast between 'rights' and 'needs' has been often identified in the literature: see e.g. Archard 2007, p. 250 and Hill *et al.* 2007, p. 21.
[15] Grisso and Pomicter 1977, p. 322.

welfare and justice models may be considered as the two poles of the same continuum where '[a]t one extreme lies the system best described by the concept of *parens patriae*, with an emphasis on 'helping' the child, intervening in his or her best interest. At the other lies the more formal, legalistic system, with a due process model of restricted information flow and precise rules of adjudication'.[16]

2.2. CHANGING PHILOSOPHIES

Originally the foundation of specialised juvenile justice systems throughout the Western world was inspired to the philosophy and values of the welfare model.[17] Over time, however, many states have moved away from welfaristic values and arrangements. This has been the result of several factors. On the one hand, a blow to the most extreme forms of welfarism was delivered by the emerging culture of rights, and by the realisation that juvenile suspects needed and deserved not only care but also some kind of procedural protection.[18] As a result, there has been a gradual shift towards a more justice-oriented juvenile justice often conflicting with the traditional welfaristic principles of juvenile justice. This development is well illustrated by the experience of the United States. During the 1960s and 1970s the US Supreme Court delivered a series of landmark decisions emphasising the need for procedural protection of juvenile suspects. The first of these due process decisions of the US Supreme Court – also characterised as the 'due process revolution'[19] – was the *Kent* case,[20] later followed by other revolutionary judgements.[21] The decision in *Kent* explicitly reflected the concern that the US juvenile justice system was not living up to its expectations. In the judgement the Supreme Court's majority held 'that there may be grounds for concern that the child receives the worst of both worlds [in juvenile courts]: that he gets neither the protections accorded to adults nor the solicitous care and regenerative treatment postulated for children.'[22] With *Kent*, it was acknowledged that juvenile suspects were entitled to certain fundamental due process rights and as a consequence more procedural formalities were introduced in juvenile proceedings throughout the US.[23] Eventually, a similar trend was also seen in Europe.

16 Feld 1982, p. 549–555.
17 The origin of this philosophy is well described in Garland 1985, p. 235.
18 Hill 2007, p. 22.
19 Houle 2011, p. 90.
20 *Kent v. United States*, 383 U.S. 541 (1966).
21 Such as *In re Gault*, 387 U.S. 1 (1967) and *In re Winship*, 397 U.S. 358 (1970). For an overview of the development of the American case law on due process in cases concerning juveniles, see Feld 2013.
22 *Kent v. United States*, 383 U.S. 541, 555–556 (1966).
23 Although some scholars argue that the extension of rights to children did not happen in a fully consistent manner: Schmidt and Reppucci 2002, 87.

Another reason for departure from welfaristic arrangements in more recent times has been the rise of cultural trends favouring a more punitive approach toward juvenile delinquents, sometimes also visible in the depiction of the minor as a 'responsible person'.[24] Over the last few decades a more punitive turn has been noticeable in juvenile justice policies throughout the world. Starting from the 1980s and 1990s a 'tough on crime' trend has been visible in the US as well as in Europe.[25] Examples of this repressive policy can be found in various systems such as the United Kingdom, the Netherlands and France.[26] Even countries that had become the symbol of welfarism, such as Scotland, have not been immune from this punitive drift.[27] Some of this cultural trend still remains alive today despite the decline (more or less everywhere) of the rate of youth crime and offenders.

Nowadays, most European juvenile justice systems present a combination of elements of both welfare and justice. However, as mentioned, great variations exist as to how this combination is given shape. In general, all European countries provide for some sort of special regulations for juvenile suspects and defendants but each set of national rules is peculiar. It is noticeable, for instance, that some countries refuse to label judicial proceedings against juveniles who committed an offence as criminal proceedings, while others normally qualify them as juvenile criminal proceedings. Differences between countries exist on many points – related to substantive as well as procedural law – such as how the special rules for juveniles are codified (relevant legal sources), what kind of behaviour can lead to juvenile justice proceedings (acting in conflict with criminal law or – for example – also anti-social behaviour), relevant age categories (most importantly the minimum age of criminal responsibility), relevant authorities responsible for dealing with young suspects and offenders (law enforcement, social welfare institutions), different sanctions and the availability of alternative proceedings (diversion).[28]

---

24 Bailleau and Cartuyvels 2007, p. 13; Cavadino and Dignan 2006, p. 210 (the authors differentiate this more recent trend of 'responsibilisation' – which they term 'neo-correctionalism' – from the more classical 'justice model' in that in the latter the responsibility of children evokes their being bearer of rights compromising the procedural safeguards that are associated with the justice model, whereas in the former the responsibility of children emphasises the fact that they owe toward other, including the victim, the community and the State); Muncie and Hughes 2002, p. 3.

25 Even in countries like Japan (see Fenwick 2006, p. 151).

26 Muncie 2008, p. 111 'not only in the USA and England and Wales but throughout much of western Europe, punitive values associated with retribution, incapacitation, individual responsibility and offender accountability have achieved a political legitimacy to the detriment of traditional principles of juvenile protection and support'. For an account of the English turns between welfarism and more punitive thinking starting from the 1970s, Padfield 2002, p. 405.

27 McAra 2006, p. 134; Whyte 2007, 162.

28 See on these relevant aspects of the juvenile justice system and the different variations within Europe: Gensing 2011.

3. THE INTERROGATION OF JUVENILE SUSPECTS

While comparative research gives much attention to juvenile justice in general, less attention is usually paid to the procedure in itself and to single procedural activities, unless they highlight a specific feature of the system. Although it can hardly be said that the interrogation[29] of a juvenile suspect is an activity that characterises the entire system in one way or another, it is all but a trivial moment. After all, it is during this activity that the vulnerability of the juvenile suspect – which generally concerns all phases of the criminal process – is probably greatest. Pre-trial interrogations – most often carried out by the police – will usually constitute the juveniles' first contact with law enforcement authorities when they are in an unfamiliar and stressful situation.[30] Furthermore, it is a known fact that in most criminal justice systems the results of these first interrogations – in adult as well as in juvenile cases – can and often will be of fundamental importance for the development and the outcome of the case.[31] As will be shown later, the vulnerability of the juvenile suspect during his initial contacts with law enforcement agencies is also underlined by certain supranational juvenile justice instruments.[32]

Interrogations are also important from another perspective. It is a moment that calls into question the capacity of children to take decisions. During interrogations children are (or might be) required to make choices, for example on whether or not to exercise their procedural rights, or on whether or not to answer the questions posed, and – if so – how. Altogether, the juvenile is faced with many fundamental questions and decisions with far-reaching consequences. This raises the issue of the maturity and decisional competence of children[33] and of the best context for ensuring the exercise of such competence.

The interrogation of young suspects is thus a specific moment that deserves to be more carefully looked at in order to assess whether the vulnerability of the young suspect is duly considered and protected by the justice system. Nonetheless, despite the fact that interrogations of juvenile suspects are such a sensitive moment, little attention has so far been paid to them by the European literature. There are some valuable American studies on the topic, which show the

29 For the working definition of the concept of 'interrogation' used in this volume, see *infra* paragraph 9.4.

30 'Police interrogation is a unique social and legal context, particularly for youthful suspects, in which the role of *suspect* subjugated to the police officer's role of *interrogator* is conflated with the developmental role of *youth* subjugated to the officer's role of *adult*': Cleary 2014, p. 272.

31 Cape *et al.* 2007, p. 19–20. For a US perspective see Feld 2007, p. 222.

32 See *infra* paragraph 7.

33 For an American perspective on adjudicative competence, see Bonnie and Grisso 2003, p. 73–103; Woolard 2002, 270.

complexity and the many challenges of this confrontational moment,[34] but there is very little research available in Europe[35] and none at the comparative level. This lack of attention is even more surprising when looking at the large bulk of research carried out on the interviewing of minors as victims and witnesses.[36] The aim of the present volume is to start closing the gap in the available studies and knowledge on juvenile law and procedural protection during criminal interrogations across different jurisdictions.

4. THIS BOOK AND THE PROJECT 'PROTECTING YOUNG SUSPECTS IN INTERROGATIONS'

This book represents the first part of a larger research project financed by the European Commission under the title *Protecting Young Suspects in Interrogations.*[37] It concerns a legal comparative and empirical study that attempts to shed more light on the field of procedural rights for juveniles in the pre-trial phase and to identify legal and empirical patterns to improve the protection of juveniles. The project is the joint effort of several partners (Warwick University, Antwerp University, Jagiellonian University, Macerata University, Defence for Children and PLOT Limburg), led by Maastricht University. As mentioned above, the project stemmed from the observation that the existing level of procedural protection of juvenile suspects throughout the European Union is limited: most of the literature on juvenile justice focuses on the rules of substantive criminal law (like the threshold of criminal liability, or the type of penalties imposed) or on criminological issues related to crime treatment and sentencing but less attention has been paid to the field of procedural law for juveniles.[38]

As is clear from its title, the focus of the project is on the position of juvenile suspects during (pre-trial) interrogation. As described above, the reason for focusing on this particular procedural activity lies in the fact that these interrogations constitute a moment during which the juvenile's vulnerability is probably greatest. This is particularly true for interrogations during the

34 See *inter alia* Grisso and Pomicter 1977 and Feld 2012.

35 See for instance the UK studies of Kemp *et al.* 2011; Lingwood and Bull 2013.

36 See *inter alia* Spencer and Flinn 1993.

37 The full name of the project is *Protecting Young Suspects in Interrogations: a study on safeguards and best practice.* The project was funded by a Criminal Justice Action Grant of the European Commission (JUST/2011/JPEN/AG2909).

38 Nevertheless, some comparative studies dealing with procedural safeguards have pointed out that the position of suspects and defendants, including juveniles, throughout Europe deserves greater attention and, most likely, improvement: Spronken and Attinger 2005, Cape *et al.* 2007, Spronken *et al.* 2009, Cape *et al.* 2010 and Blackstock *et al.* 2014.

investigative stage, which usually constitute the juveniles' first contact with law enforcement authorities.

The research project consists of three parts. The first part concerns a legal comparative study into the existing legal procedural safeguards that provide protection for juvenile suspects during interrogation in five Member States that represent different systems of juvenile justice (Belgium, England and Wales, Italy, Poland and the Netherlands).[39] The second part comprises empirical research consisting of observations (analysis of audio and/or audio-visual recorded interrogations and analysis of written records of interrogations) and focus group interviews with key actors and juveniles. These two first parts are brought together in the third part which consists of a final merging of the legal and empirical findings, resulting in a proposal for European minimum rules and best practice on the protection of juvenile suspects during interrogation. In a nutshell, the project intends to contribute to the EU-wide implementation of optimal standards for effective protection of procedural safeguards for juvenile suspects during interrogation.[40]

The contributions contained in this first volume represent the legal part of the study. A second volume will contain the findings of the empirical research and the proposal for harmonisation and best practice.[41] The present volume contains the country reports of the five jurisdictions observed and a final chapter with transversal observations stemming from the analysis of the rules and safeguards applicable in the five countries. For each of the five countries a report has been drawn following a common template, with a view to grasping the features of the domestic system of juvenile punitive justice and the more specific rules connected to the interrogation of young suspects.[42] The country reports intend to describe the state of the art with regard to the protection of young suspects in interrogations in order to permit the identification of common patterns with a view to harmonising the systems and improving the protection of juvenile suspects' rights.

5. THE COUNTRIES INVOLVED IN THIS STUDY

The choice of the countries involved in this study has been made in connection with the general aim of the project. Since the project aimed to carry out in-depth

39 For an extensive work on the existing variety of European juvenile justice systems, see Dünkel *et al.* 2011. See also Patané 2007.

40 More information on the project can be found at the website www.youngsuspects.eu.

41 Vanderhallen *et al.* 2015 forthcoming.

42 The common template for writing the country reports is added as an annex to this volume. The methodology of the legal study will be further explained *infra* paragraph 9.

empirical research, it was essential to limit the choice of countries to a number that could allow a meaningful fieldwork. The selection of countries had thus to combine the need to focus on a reduced number of jurisdictions and at the same time to select a sufficiently representative sample. Five countries was considered to be an adequate compromise in order to accommodate the need for proper in-depth empirical research with that for sufficient representation of European trends. Within this number, the idea was to take a sample of states that would adequately represent the different points along the 'justice-welfare spectrum' identified above. At the same time, another concern was to ensure a sufficiently meaningful geographical divide between the countries, so as to cover different European areas (south, north-centre, east) and to include members of common law and civil law legal families. Furthermore, one more element which was taken into consideration was the need to have representatives of systems that avoid labelling punitive proceedings as criminal.[43]

In this respect, England and Wales and the Netherlands were chosen as countries that are closer to the 'justice' end of the spectrum. As mentioned, both countries have enacted reforms that mean their juvenile justice systems tend to create a starker divide between the public authority and the juvenile defendants. While England and Wales embodies the common law experience and represents the due process culture typical of the Anglo-Saxon world, the Dutch system is a representative of the continental culture of criminal justice.

Examples of a more welfaristic approach are Belgium and Poland. But while Belgium is normally considered to be a country with a strong welfaristic culture, Poland is a country where welfaristic arrangements intertwine with the neo-liberal trends of post-Soviet countries. Both countries allow 'ordinary' criminal proceedings against juveniles only in a limited set of serious cases, while they term proceedings against juveniles in conflict with the law as 'educative'.

Italy is a representative of the south of Europe, where there is a strong familial culture and in general a very lenient and tolerant approach toward juveniles. In terms of features of the system, Italy was chosen as a country in the middle of the justice-welfare spectrum. The methodology underlying the legal study will be further explained in paragraph 9.

6. HARMONISING JUVENILE SUSPECTS' RIGHTS

The reader might wonder why the choice was made to undertake a project on juvenile suspects' rights and how to improve them, and even more so why a transnational European study, aiming at identifying patterns of harmonisation

43 See *supra* paragraph 2.

and/or of uniform improvement of practice, was chosen. There are several reasons for this choice.

First, since the relationship between young people and criminal justice has always been problematic, it still offers room for further reflection and improvement. Criminal proceedings normally represent a stressful and difficult moment for everyone involved, particularly for suspects and defendants. As mentioned before, this inherent tension reaches its peak when the suspect is a juvenile since young individuals are vulnerable and deserve protection. It is extremely complicated to mitigate the harshness of criminal justice and proceedings so as to protect the young suspect.

As mentioned, European states have developed distinct models of justice for addressing the situation of juveniles who are in conflict with the law. Nevertheless, all countries have struggled and still struggle with finding an adequate balance between the needs of young suspects/defendants/offenders and society's need to address the problem of youth crime. It is for this reason that juvenile law, particularly juvenile justice, is an area where – in principle – harmonisation can be more intense and far-reaching. The field of juvenile rights lends itself to the possibility of a more profound harmonisation in that the vulnerability of children and the need to protect them is more likely to remove the reluctance and the resistance of countries to move beyond the boundaries of their national laws, and even their procedural traditions. In other words, the effort to protect juveniles can more easily overcome the national concerns of states regarding altering the shape of their national system: it can more easily defeat the traditional conservative approach of Member States when it comes to harmonisation measures.

A sign of the higher aptitude (predisposition) of juvenile law towards harmonisation is offered by several already existing supranational and international documents. At present, there are a number of supranational sources concerning the field of juvenile rights and even juvenile justice, which supplement those general international documents dealing with fundamental human rights and fair trial rights such as the UN International Covenant for Civil and Political rights and the European Convention on Human Rights (hereafter: ECHR). However, as will be discussed later,[44] the effectiveness of this supranational framework is debatable.

44 See *infra* paragraph 7.4.

7. EXISTING INTERNATIONAL AND EUROPEAN SAFEGUARDS[45]

As mentioned, the aim of the research underlying this volume is to evaluate the current standard of legal protection offered to juvenile suspects during interrogation in five EU Member States. In relation to this, it is important to see what (minimum) standards can already be derived from existing human rights instruments provided for at the international and the European level: after all, this is the existing normative framework that current juvenile justice systems have to comply with. In doing so, it is worth looking both at general human rights instruments such as the ECHR as well as conventions, rules and guidelines specifically focusing on juvenile justice. With regard to the latter category, it should be mentioned that the incorporation of specific rights of children into the administration of juvenile justice is a relatively recent development in the international law on the rights of children.[46] Since the 1980s, international standards of juvenile justice have been developed by international organisations such as the United Nations and the Council of Europe. The most important is indeed the Convention on the Rights of the Child of 1989 (hereafter: CRC) together with the accompanying (non-binding) recommendations and General Comments of the Committee on the Rights of the Child.[47]

Furthermore, the UN has adopted several soft law instruments on juvenile justice, such as the UN Standard Minimum Rules for the Administration of Juvenile Justice in 1985[48] (*Beijing Rules*), the UN Rules for the Protection of Juveniles Deprived of their Liberty of 1990 (*Havana Rules*), the UN Guidelines for the Prevention of Juvenile Delinquency of 1990 (*Riyadh Guidelines*) and the UN (ECOSOC) Guidelines on Justice in Matters involving Child Victims and Witnesses of Crime of 2005.[49] These instruments further explain the provisions of the CRC and as a result they should be read in connection to each other. In addition to the international rules stemming from the UN,[50] relevant safeguards for juveniles in conflict with the law are also provided for at the European

45 The drafting of this paragraph has benefitted from a study on supranational instruments conducted by J. Winkels in the context of the research project. The report resulting from this study is available at www.youngsuspects.eu.

46 Van Bueren 2006.

47 Such as General Comment No. 10 on Children's Rights in Juvenile Justice (CRC/C/GC/10).

48 Which was the first UN instrument on juvenile justice.

49 The latter instrument does not focus specifically on juvenile justice but applies accordingly to proceedings involving juvenile defendants when the victim is a juvenile (under the age of 18) as well.

50 In addition to the UN instruments specifically drafted in the context of the rights of children and/or juvenile justice, there are of course also more general UN rules which are of relevance for all suspects including juveniles, such as (the following enumeration is by no means meant to be exhaustive): the *United Nations Basic Principles for the Treatment of Prisoners* (1990), *United Nations Basic Principles on the Role of Lawyers* (1990), the *United Nations*

level. Within the European context, one of the main instruments of human rights protection is of course the ECHR and the accompanying case law of the European Court of Human Rights (hereafter: ECtHR).

The most relevant supranational instruments and their significance for the juvenile suspect will be discussed below. This will not be done by providing a general and comprehensive description: the main focus will be on those provisions and rules which may be of relevance for protecting juvenile suspects during interrogation.

7.1. CRC AND OTHER UN INSTRUMENTS

Of all the international and European instruments dealing with children's rights, the CRC is without a doubt the most important. This Convention – referred to by some as 'the touchstone for children's rights throughout the world'[51] – requires State Parties *inter alia* to establish special juvenile laws, procedures and institutions for children in conflict with the law, set a minimum age of criminal responsibility and adopt measures to deal with children without resorting to judicial proceedings.[52] As far as legal safeguards are concerned it should be noted that within the context of the CRC a distinction can be made between general principles underlined by the Convention – such as the best interests of the child and the dignity of the juvenile – and more specific safeguards meant to give these general principles a practical dimension. As far as these general principles and specific safeguards are (potentially) of relevance for the protection of juvenile suspects during interrogation, they will be described below. The main focus of this description is on the CRC, but when and where relevant, provisions of other UN instruments – such as the *Beijing Rules,* which preceded the CRC – will be mentioned as well.

7.1.1. General principles

The CRC contains provisions on many different aspects of the child's life including his possible contacts with the justice system. Art. 3 CRC provides that the best interests of the child should be a primary consideration in all actions concerning children.[53] In the context of the juvenile's contacts with the justice

Basic Principles on Declaration on Crime and Justice (2000) and the *United Nations Vienna Declaration on Crime and Justice* (2000). These instruments will not be discussed here.

51 Fortin 2009, p. 49.

52 For an overview see also Doek 2009.

53 See art. 3 CRC. The principle of the best interests of the child is also explicitly mentioned in rule 14 para. 2 of the *Beijing Rules*: 'The proceedings shall be conducive to the best interests of the juvenile and shall be conducted in an atmosphere of understanding, which shall allow the juvenile to participate therein and to express herself or himself freely'.

system, the most important provisions are arts. 37 and 40 CRC. According to art. 37 – concerning detention and punishment – no child shall be deprived of his liberty unlawfully or arbitrarily: arrest, detention and imprisonment shall be used as measures of last resort and for the shortest appropriate period of time. Furthermore, it is stated that every child deprived of liberty shall be treated with humanity and respect for the inherent dignity of the human person, and in a manner which takes into account the needs of persons of his or her age. In addition, juveniles should have the right to prompt access to legal and other appropriate assistance, as well as the right to challenge the legality of the deprivation of their liberty before a court or other competent, independent and impartial authority, and to a prompt decision on any such action.

The general principle of the 'dignity of the juvenile' is explicitly mentioned in art. 40(1) of the Convention. This provision deals with juvenile justice in general and guarantees *inter alia* that states should recognise the right of 'every child alleged as, accused of, or recognised as having infringed the penal law to be treated in a manner consistent with the promotion of the child's sense of dignity and worth, which reinforces the child's respect for the human rights and fundamental freedoms of others and which takes into account the child's age and the desirability of promoting the child's reintegration and the child's assuming a constructive role in society'. According to General Comment no. 10 on Children's rights in juvenile justice, the right to dignity has to be respected 'throughout the entire process, from the first contact with law enforcement agencies all the way to the implementation of all measures for dealing with the child'.[54] The Committee underlines the importance of law enforcement and other professional actors acting as role models in this respect: 'If the key actors in juvenile justice, such as police officers, prosecutors, judges and probation officers, do not fully respect and protect these guarantees, how can they expect that with such poor examples the child will respect the human rights and fundamental freedom of others?'.[55] The General Comment also stresses that respecting the child's dignity requires a certain level of specialisation: all professionals involved in the administration of juvenile justice should have knowledge on child development, the dynamic and continuing growth of children, what is appropriate to their well-being and the pervasive forms of violence against children.[56] With regard to the latter, it goes without saying that respect for the dignity of the child means that all forms of violence in the treatment of children in conflict with the law should be prohibited and prevented.[57]

---

54 General Comment on Children's rights in juvenile justice of 2007, CRC/C/GC/10, para. 13.
55 General Comment on Children's rights in juvenile justice of 2007, CRC/C/GC/10, para. 13.
56 General Comment on Children's rights in juvenile justice of 2007, CRC/C/GC/10, para. 13.
57 CRC/C/GC/10, para. 13.

The importance and impact of the juvenile's first contact with the police is stressed in the *Beijing Rules* which (*inter alia*) provide that parents should immediately be notified of the juvenile's apprehension and that all contacts between law enforcement agencies and a juvenile should be managed 'in such a way as to respect the legal status of the juvenile, promote the well-being of the juvenile and avoid harm'.[58] According to the commentary to the *Beijing Rules,* the wording 'to avoid harm' is flexible and covers many features of possible interaction such as the use of harsh language, physical violence or exposure to the environment. Furthermore, it is stressed that avoiding harm is 'especially important in the initial contact with law enforcement agencies, which might profoundly influence the juvenile's attitude towards the State and society. Moreover, the success of any further intervention is largely dependent on such initial contacts. Compassion and kind firmness are important in these situations'.[59] Looking at these provisions and considerations, the requirement of respecting the right to dignity and not causing harm when interacting with juvenile suspects is not only justified by the vulnerability of the juvenile suspect in itself but also by the 'credibility' of the juvenile justice system and the necessity of convincing the juvenile of the importance of respecting rights and freedoms of others. The *Beijing Rules* also underline the importance of specialisation of law enforcement personnel, who usually represent the juvenile's first contact with the justice system: it is stressed that police officers who frequently or exclusively deal with juveniles or who are primarily engaged in the prevention of juvenile crime should be specially instructed and trained.[60]

Another general principle to be found in the CRC relevant in the context of pre-trial interrogations concerns the right of the child to be heard: art. 12 of the Convention explicitly provides the juvenile with the right to express his views freely in all matters affecting him. In this respect, the juvenile should be provided with 'the opportunity to be heard in any judicial and administrative proceedings affecting the child, either directly, or through a representative or an appropriate body, in a manner consistent with the procedural rules of national law'. Clear, specific rules on how the interrogation of a juvenile suspect should be carried out are, however, not provided for by the CRC or any other UN instrument.[61]

58 Rule 10 of the *Beijing Rules.*

59 Commentary of Rule 10 of the *Beijing Rules.*

60 Rule 12 of the *Beijing Rules.*

61 Nevertheless, some authors feel that certain more practical minimum rules on how to conduct the interrogation can be derived from the CRC and accompanying instruments. For instance, Mijnarends argues that asking a juvenile suspect leading questions would be contrary to art. 12 CRC: Mijnarends 1999, p. 182.

7.1.2. Specific safeguards

Building upon the general principles mentioned above, the CRC provides for a number of more specific procedural safeguards, which are directly or indirectly of relevance for the juvenile suspect in the phase of pre-trial interrogation. These more specific safeguards – laid down in art. 40 para. 2 – include the right of the juvenile to:

- be presumed innocent until proven guilty according to law;
- be informed promptly and directly of the charges against him, and, if appropriate, through his parents or legal guardians;
- have legal or other appropriate assistance in the preparation and presentation of his defence;
- have the matter determined without delay by a competent, independent and impartial authority or judicial body in a fair hearing according to law, in the presence of legal or other appropriate assistance and, unless it is considered not to be in the best interest of the child, in particular, taking into account his or her age or situation, his or her parents or legal guardians;
- not be compelled to give testimony or to confess guilt;
- examine or have examined adverse witnesses and to obtain the participation and examination of witnesses on his behalf under conditions of equality;
- have the free assistance of an interpreter if the child cannot understand or speak the language used; and
- have his privacy fully respected at all stages of the proceedings.[62]

Most of these more specific safeguards are not only provided for in the CRC but have a basis in other international or European legal instruments as well. For example, the right of the juvenile suspect to have the assistance of a lawyer is codified in art. 40 para. 2 and – for children who are held in detention – in art. 37 para. d of the CRC. According to the latter provision, every child deprived of his or her liberty has the right to prompt access to legal or other appropriate assistance.[63] In addition to the CRC, the *Havana Rules* of 1990 also lay down the right to free legal aid as well as the right to communicate on a regular basis with legal advisors.[64] Furthermore, the right of the juvenile to be represented by a legal advisor or to apply for free legal aid (where it is provided for) as well as

---

[62] Many of the basic procedural safeguards provided for in the CRC can also be found in the *Beijing Rules* including *inter alia* the presumption of innocence, the right to be notified of the charges, the right to remain silent, the right to counsel and the right to the presence of a parent or guardian at all stages of the proceedings: see rule 7 of the *Beijing Rules*.

[63] CRC/C/GC/10, para. 49. With regard to 'other appropriate assistance' the General Comment on Children's rights in juvenile states stipulates that the person providing this assistance should have 'sufficient knowledge and understanding of the various legal aspects of the process of juvenile justice and must be trained to work with children in conflict with the law'.

[64] Rule 18(a) of the *Havana Rules*.

the right of parents or guardians to participate in the proceedings are explicitly mentioned in the *Beijing Rules*.[65] As will be discussed below, the right of the juvenile charged with a criminal offence to have access to legal assistance is given further shape in the case law of the ECtHR.[66]

The right to privacy is also a fundamental safeguard which is to be found in several supranational instruments. First of all, it is explicitly formulated in general terms in art. 16 of the CRC and – in the context of judicial proceedings – in the aforementioned art. 40 para. 2 CRC.[67] The latter provision regulates that the right to privacy should be protected during 'all stages of the proceedings' which obviously includes the initial contact with law enforcement authorities.[68] In the context of providing adequate protection to juvenile suspects, the right to privacy is of particular importance since it is to be expected that 'undue publicity' or the process of 'labelling' will be especially harmful when the suspect is of a young age. For that reason no information shall be published which may lead to the identification of the child because of its effect of stigmatisation and possible impact on his ability to have access to education, work housing or to be safe.[69] The right to privacy requires all professionals involved in the implementation of measures of courts or other competent authorities – which should be interpreted as referring to all relevant professional actors in juvenile justice including authorities conducting pre-trial interrogations – to keep all information that may result in the identification of the child confidential in all their external contacts.[70]

When looking at the procedural safeguards provided for in the CRC and accompanying UN legal instruments, it is clear that they mostly concern 'classic' or 'common' procedural safeguards which are applicable to adult suspects and defendants as well but are given a broader scope or extra emphasis in the context of juveniles. The right to privacy is a good example in this respect: obviously, the right to privacy should be respected as much as possible in criminal proceedings involving adult suspects as well but – due to the risks undue publicity may have for a young person who still has his whole life ahead of him and who should be given the opportunity for a fresh start – it is given extra weight in the context of juvenile suspects and defendants. One of the few – if not the only – (categories of) youth specific safeguards mentioned in the CRC concerns the right to have parents or guardians involved in the proceedings. First of all, this safeguard includes the child's right to have his parents notified of his arrest and of the charges against him. For example, art. 9 para. 4 CRC imposes a duty on states

65 Rule 15 of the *Beijing Rules*.
66 See *infra* paragraph 7.2.
67 See also rule 8 of the *Beijing Rules*.
68 CRC/C/GC/10, para. 64.
69 CRC/C/GC/10, para. 64.
70 CRC/C/GC/10, para. 66.

to provide the parents of children in detention pending trial, upon request, with the essential information concerning the whereabouts of their child.[71] The *Beijing Rules* even require that upon the apprehension (arrest) of the juvenile, his parents or guardian should be notified immediately.[72] As mentioned above, art. 40 para. 2 CRC regulates that informing the child of the charges against him should, if appropriate, take place through his parents or legal guardian. In connection to the foregoing, the child is awarded the right to stay in contact with his family during the pre-trial stage of proceedings. According to art. 37 para. c CRC every child deprived of liberty shall have the right to maintain contact with his family through correspondence and visits, save in exceptional circumstances. As stressed in General Comment no. 10 on Children's rights in juvenile justice, such exceptional circumstances should be laid down in the law and not left to the discretion of authorities.[73]

From the context of the interrogation, it is important to note that several supranational norms provide the child with a right to be interrogated in the presence of their parent or legal guardian. Obviously, the idea behind the right to have parents or guardians involved is that their presence provides the child with the necessary support and emotional assistance. On the basis of rule 7 of the *Beijing Rules*, the juvenile has the right to have a parent or guardian present at all stages of proceedings. In addition to this, rule 15 para. 2 of the *Beijing Rules* reads that parents or guardians are entitled to participate in the proceedings unless this should be denied in the interest of the juvenile. From the latter provision, it is possible to derive a right of the juvenile to be interrogated in the presence of his parents or guardians. However, this right does not seem to be absolute since it is regulated that parents and guardians may be denied participation by the competent authority if there are reasons to assume that such exclusion is necessary in the interest of the juvenile. In this respect it is important to stress that the *Beijing Rules* only refer to the interest of the juvenile as a ground for excluding parents or guardians from taking part in the proceedings, which seems to suggest that such a decision should not be based on the interest of the investigation.

7.2. ECHR AND STRASBOURG CASE LAW

The most important instrument of human rights protection on the European level is of course the ECHR, of which arts. 3, 5, 6 and 8 are of particular relevance

71 The only exception to this duty is if it is in the best interests of the child *not* to tell the parents.

72 See rule 10 para. 2 of the *Beijing Rules*. When immediate notification is not possible, the parents or guardian should be notified within the shortest period of time after the arrest. See also rule 22 of the *Havana Rules*.

73 CRC/C/GC/10, para. 87, p. 23. The right of the child to maintain contact with his family is also provided for in rule 59 (as well as rules 60 and 61) of the *Havana Rules*.

for suspects and defendants in criminal proceedings. It should be stressed that the provisions of the ECHR contain only very few explicit references to juveniles 'charged with a criminal offence'. In fact, the Convention makes specific reference to juveniles only on two occasions: in art. 6 ECHR where in the context of the right to a fair trial it is regulated that the press and public can be excluded from all or part of a trial 'where the interest of juveniles (...) so require' and in art. 5 para. 1d ECHR which provides for the detention of a 'minor for the purpose of educational supervision or his lawful detention for the purpose of bringing him before the competent legal authority'.[74] Although the main part of the case law of the European Court of Human Rights dealing with children does not concern either of these two provisions,[75] the Strasbourg Court has dealt with the issue of the protection of juvenile suspects and defendants on several occasions. It is worth mentioning that the ECtHR – when dealing with cases of juvenile applicants – often explicitly refers to the CRC which again stresses the intertwinement of the different international and European legal instruments.[76]

It should not be forgotten that important general procedural rights principles are also (and foremost) formulated by the ECtHR in cases not concerning juveniles, generally applying to all suspects irrespective of their age. It falls outside the scope of this research to provide a full overview of all these procedural safeguards, which should be awarded to suspects in the early stages of police interrogation. In a nutshell, these procedural rights – derived from arts. 5 and 6 ECHR – mainly concern: the right to free interpretation and translation, the right to information (about rights, the arrest, the accusations and the charge, and the case file), the right to legal assistance (before and during interrogation), the privilege against self-incrimination, and the right to silence.[77]

From the Strasbourg cases concerning juvenile suspects and defendants, a number of general principles can be derived. Most importantly, the ECtHR has repeatedly stressed the importance of the juveniles' ability to understand the steps of the procedure and to participate and effectively exercise his rights and benefit from the protection of privacy. This happened for the first time in the *T.*

---

74 See – within the context of the UN – also art. 14 of the Covenant on Civil and Political Rights, concerning the right to a fair trial, which explicitly refers to juveniles: 'In the case of juvenile persons, the procedure shall be such as will take account of their age and the desirability of promoting their rehabilitation' (para. 4).

75 See Kilkelly 2010, p. 248. Most of the Strasbourg case law concerning the protection of children's rights is connected to art. 8 (right to respect for private and family life) and art. 3 (the right to freedom from torture and inhuman or degrading treatment or punishment). See also: Kilkelly 1999.

76 See on the relationship between the CRC and the ECHR: Kilkelly 2001.

77 See for an overview of Strasbourg standards in this respect (*inter alia*): Blackstock *et al.* 2014, p. 6–22.

and V. v. United Kingdom cases,[78] in which the Court was confronted with the question whether the trial against two 11-year-olds accused of murder had been oppressive and unfair due to the young age of the defendants. In these cases, the Court emphasised that the proceedings against a juvenile should take 'full account of his age, level of maturity and intellectual and emotional capacities', to the extent that steps should be taken 'to promote his ability to understand and participate in the proceedings'.[79] A few years later, the ECtHR again deliberated on the matter in a case concerning a juvenile suspect with a very low IQ who was tried in an adult court and sentenced to two and a half years of detention for attempting to steal a bag from an old lady.[80] Since the Court – given the particular circumstances of the case and given the national procedures followed – was not convinced that the applicant was capable of effectively and fully participating in the proceedings, it found a violation of art. 6 para. 1 ECHR.[81]

Subsequent Strasbourg case law has followed the same lines – underlining the importance of a juvenile defendant's right to effective participation and adequate understanding – by introducing some more specific obligations for authorities in dealing with juveniles. For example, in the context of the early stages of criminal investigation and questioning by the police, the ECtHR has held that a young suspect should be dealt with having 'due regard to his vulnerability and capacities from the first stages of his involvement in a criminal investigation and, in particular, during any questioning by the police'.[82] More specifically, this obliges authorities to 'take steps to reduce as far as possible his feelings of

---

[78] ECtHR 16 December 1999 (Grand Chamber), *T. v. United Kingdom*, no. 24724/94, and ECtHR 16 December 1999 (Grand Chamber), *V. v. United Kingdom*, no. 24888/94. The cases were jointly dealt with by the ECtHR.

[79] ECtHR 16 December 1999 (Grand Chamber), *T. v. United Kingdom*, no. 24724/94, para. 84 and ECtHR 16 December 1999 (Grand Chamber), *V. v. United Kingdom*, no. 24888/94, para. 86.

[80] ECtHR 10 November 2004, *S.C. v. United Kingdom*, no. 60958/00.

[81] ECtHR 10 November 2004, *S.C. v. United Kingdom*, no. 60958/00, para. 36. In this decision the Court also stressed that it was essential for a young defendant of limited intellectual ability to be tried by a specialist tribunal: para. 35: 'The Court considers that, when the decision is taken to deal with a child, such as the applicant, who risks not being able to participate effectively because of his young age and limited intellectual capacity, by way of criminal proceedings rather than some other form of disposal directed primarily at determining the child's best interests and those of the community, it is essential that he be tried in a specialist tribunal which is able to give full consideration to, and make proper allowance for, the handicaps under which he labours, and adapt its procedure accordingly'.

[82] ECtHR 11 December 2008, *Panovits v Cyprus*, no. 4268/04, para. 67. In this case a 17-year-old boy suspected of murder had been interviewed by the police in a rather questionable manner and in the absence of any adult assistance. See also the well-known decision in the case of *Salduz* which also concerned a 17-year-old boy who was questioned without having access to a lawyer and who was subsequently convicted mainly on the basis of these statements. In comparison to the *Panovits* case, the Courts reasoning in the *Salduz* case on the importance of the right to access to a lawyer during police custody was formulated in more general wording (notwithstanding the fact that the Court explicitly stressed the fundamental

intimidation and inhibition and ensure that the accused minor has a broad understanding of the nature of the investigation, of what is at stake for him or her, including the significance of any penalty which may be imposed, as well as of his rights of defence and, in particular, of his right to remain silent. It means that he or she, if necessary with the assistance of, for example, an interpreter, lawyer, social worker or friend, should be able to understand the general thrust of what is said by the arresting officer and during his questioning by the police'.[83]

In the context of the right to legal assistance the Court stresses – in more general terms – that art. 6 ECHR requires that 'the accused be given the benefit of the assistance of a lawyer already at the initial stages of police interrogation. The lack of legal assistance during an applicant's interrogation would constitute a restriction of his defence rights in the absence of compelling reasons that do not prejudice the overall fairness of the proceedings'.[84] Furthermore, the Court considers that a waiver of the right to legal assistance requires special consideration when it is given by a juvenile: 'given the vulnerability of an accused and the imbalance of power to which he is subjected by the very nature of criminal proceedings, a waiver by him or on his behalf of an important right under Article 6 can only be accepted where it is expressed in an unequivocal manner after the authorities have taken all reasonable steps to ensure that he or she is fully aware of his rights of defence and can appreciate, as far as possible, the consequences of his conduct'.[85]

The right to effective participation in the stages of police interrogation was further reiterated in a Turkish case against a 15-year-old applicant with severe mental health problems who – according to the ECtHR – had not had an effective opportunity to participate in his trial mainly because he had not been adequately represented by a lawyer during most of the trial.[86] In a Polish case concerning a 15-year-old boy who was arrested for the murder of a 10-year-old, the ECtHR again stressed the importance of juvenile suspects having broad access to a lawyer from the beginning of proceedings. In this case the applicant had only been able to meet with his lawyer six weeks after the proceedings had begun. Because his lawyer was the first to inform him of the right to remain silent and the right not to incriminate himself, he had made self-incriminating statements without being informed of his rights. Reiterating the general principles following from earlier case law that should be taken into account when dealing with

importance of providing access to a lawyer when the person in custody is a minor (para. 60)): ECtHR 27 November 2008 (Grand Chamber), *Salduz v. Turkey*, no. 36391/02.

83 ECtHR 11 December 2008, *Panovits v. Cyprus*, no. 4268/04, para. 67.

84 ECtHR 11 December 2008, *Panovits v. Cyprus*, no. 4268/04, para. 66.

85 ECtHR 11 December 2008, *Panovits v. Cyprus*, no. 4268/04, para. 68.

86 ECtHR 20 January 2009, *Guvec v. Turkey*, no. 70337/01, para. 132.

juvenile suspects,[87] the Court found a violation of art. 6 paras. 1 and 3c ECHR, stressing that – given the applicant's age – he could not be expected to be aware of his defence rights or of the consequences of not invoking them.[88] Finally, in the context of the question of who should be considered a juvenile, it is worth noting that the ECtHR has argued in a more recent case that the reasons for which the special treatment of minors is required – such as the person's level of maturity and intellectual and emotional capacities – do not cease immediately once the legal age is reached.[89]

From this brief description of the Strasbourg case law concerning juvenile suspects and defendants – which is by no means meant to be exhaustive – it becomes clear that national justice systems when dealing with juvenile suspects are obliged to give sufficient consideration to the juvenile suspect's age and maturity in order to safeguard his ability to adequately understand and effectively participate in the proceedings. Despite the lack of express safeguards referring to children in conflict with the law, the case law of the ECtHR has developed a number of binding instructions, whose aim is to give practical dimension to the general principles of understanding and effective participation in judicial proceedings for juveniles.

7.3. OTHER COUNCIL OF EUROPE DOCUMENTS AND SOURCES

Leaving aside the ECHR, the Council of Europe has been very active in the field of juvenile rights and juvenile justice. Under the umbrella of the Council of Europe several instruments were adopted, such as the European Rules for juvenile offenders subject to sanctions or measures of 2008 and the Guidelines on Child-friendly justice of 2010 (hereafter: the Guidelines).[90] Furthermore, the Council of Europe has issued various recommendations related to juvenile delinquency and juvenile justice such as Recommendation Rec(87) 20 on social reactions to juvenile delinquency, Recommendation Rec(2000) 20 on the role of early psychosocial intervention in the prevention of criminality and Recommendation Rec(2003) 20 concerning new ways of dealing with juvenile

87 Such as ECtHR 16 December 1999 (Grand Chamber), *T. v. United Kingdom*, no. 24724/94 and ECtHR 16 December 1999 (Grand Chamber), *V. v. United Kingdom*, no. 24888/94.

88 ECtHR 2 March 2010, *Adamkiewicz v. Poland*, no. 54729/00, para. 89.

89 ECtHR 30 May 2013, *Martin v. Estonia*, no. 35985/09, para. 92, in this case, the applicant was 17 years old at the time of the commission of the offence (murder) but reached the age of 18 three weeks before his arrest.

90 Guidelines of the Committee of Ministers of the Council of Europe on child-friendly justice, adopted by the Committee of Ministers on 17 November 2010 at the 1098th meeting of the Ministers' Deputies.

delinquency and the role of juvenile justice.[91] Although the main focus of these Council of Europe instruments seems to be on how to respond to juveniles committing crimes, some of them do contain minimum rules or principles that may be of relevance for juvenile suspects during interrogation. Most importantly, some of the general principles guaranteed by the CRC and other UN instruments are also formulated on the European level. For example, in the Guidelines on Child-friendly justice, the general principles of the juvenile's best interest (including psychological and physical well-being and legal, social and economic interests of the child) and the child's dignity are reiterated.[92] With regard to the latter it is regulated that '[c]hildren should be treated with care, sensitivity, fairness and respect throughout any procedure or case, with special attention for their personal situation, well-being and specific needs, and with full respect for their physical and psychological integrity'.[93] The Guidelines explicitly require Member States 'to establish multidisciplinary approaches with the objective of assessing the best interests of children in procedures involving them'.[94]

The Guidelines also contain a further significant clarification: while affirming that the general elements of due process (such as the principles of legality and proportionality, the presumption of innocence, the right to a fair trial, the right to legal advice, the right to access to courts and the right to appeal) are equally applicable for children as they are for adults, it underlines that the principle of the child's best interest should never constitute a 'pretext' for the minimisation of such rights.[95]

With respect to the right to be heard, the Guidelines emphasise that this is 'a right of the child, not a duty'.[96] The Guidelines provide for several additional requirements regarding the right to be heard: children should be given all necessary information on how to use their right to be heard effectively[97] and professionals who interview children should interact with them with respect and sensitivity.[98] With regard to the right to information, the Guidelines require children and their parents to be informed of all their rights, especially the specific rights children have in the context of judicial or non-judicial proceedings. Equally important is the fact that the Guidelines stress that the right to information does not only concern the right to be informed on rights but also extends to information about (*inter alia*) the system and the procedure, the existing support mechanisms, the charges, the time and place of hearings, the general progress of

91 See Dünkel 2009, p. 33–44.
92 Guidelines on Child-friendly justice, para. I.1, III.B.1–4, III.C.1.
93 Guidelines on Child-friendly justice, para. III.C.1.
94 Guidelines on Child-friendly justice, para. III.B.4.
95 Guidelines on Child-friendly justice, para. III.E.2.
96 Guidelines on Child-friendly justice, para. IV.D.46.
97 Guidelines on child-friendly justice, para. IV.D.48.
98 Guidelines on Child-friendly justice, para. IV.D.57.

proceedings, the availability of protective measures and the existing mechanisms for review of decisions affecting the child.[99] Furthermore, it is provided that children should be thoroughly informed and consulted on the opportunity to have recourse to either a court proceeding or alternatives outside a court setting which information should explain the possible consequences of each option. In addition, children should be given the opportunity to obtain legal advice and other assistance in determining the appropriateness and desirability of the proposed alternatives.[100] The information provided should be adapted to the age and maturity of the child. Information on the charges must be given directly after the charges are brought and be given to the parents as well.[101] In the context of the right to legal assistance, the Guidelines require children to have access to free legal aid, under the same or more lenient conditions as adults.[102]

Several of the Guidelines are of specific relevance for the interrogation of juvenile suspects. First of all, it is regulated that whenever children are being heard or giving evidence this should preferably take place *in camera* with the presence of only those directly involved, provided that they do not obstruct children in giving evidence.[103] When apprehended, children should be provided with access to a lawyer and be given the opportunity to contact their parents or a person whom they trust.[104] Save for exceptional circumstances, parents should be informed of the child's presence in the police station, given details of the reasons why the child has been taken into custody and be asked to come to the police station.[105] Questioning of the child should only take place in the presence of a lawyer or a parent.[106] During all stages of proceedings (including questioning) language appropriate to children's age and level of understanding should be used and professionals should interact with them with respect and sensitivity.[107] As far as appropriate, interviewing rooms should be arranged in a child-friendly environment.[108] With regard to children giving evidence it is *inter alia* regulated that – when multiple interviews are necessary – they should preferably be carried out by the same person in order to ensure coherence of approach in the best interests of the child and the number of interviews should be as limited as possible and their length should be adapted to the child's age and attention span.[109]

---

99 Guidelines on Child-friendly justice, para. IV.A.1.

100 Guidelines on Child-friendly justice, para. IV.B.25.

101 Guidelines on child-friendly justice, para. IV.A.1.

102 Guidelines on child-friendly justice, para. IV.D.38.

103 Guidelines on Child-friendly justice, para. IV.A.9.

104 Guidelines on Child-friendly justice, para. IV.C.28.

105 Guidelines on Child-friendly justice, para. IV.C.29.

106 Guidelines on Child-friendly justice, para. IV.C.30.

107 Guidelines on Child-friendly justice, para. IV.D.56–57.

108 Guidelines on Child-friendly justice, para. IV.D.62.

109 Guidelines on Child-friendly justice, para. IV.D.66–67. Although it should be recalled that the focus of the relevant provision seems to be on children giving evidence as a witness, there

7.4. THE CURRENT SUPRANATIONAL FRAMEWORK: PRACTICAL AND EFFECTIVE?

The supranational rules discussed above provide for an important framework of general minimum standards for dealing with juvenile suspects and defendants. Nonetheless, the general supranational picture is affected by some deficiencies, the most important of which concerns the practical effectiveness of the existing international and European legal instruments, which is often doubted.[110]

There are two main reasons for the limited effectiveness of the existing supranational safeguards. The first reason is connected to the fact that many of the rules are of a non-binding character and – when they are binding – an effective enforcement mechanism is often missing. For example, the different Rules and Guidelines adopted by the UN are non-binding and 'only' provide for a minimum level of protection to be provided for by Member States. On the contrary, the CRC is a binding document but enforcement of its provisions is difficult due to the lack of an effective control mechanism.[111] To a certain extent, the same is true even for instruments stemming from the Council of Europe. As for the Council of Europe Recommendations, they only represent a form of soft law but their provisions are not *per se* binding and cannot be directly enforced. Some problems of effectiveness can also be raised with regard to the ECHR, despite the existence of an actual enforcement mechanism which has the ECtHR as its peak. It falls outside the scope of this study to discuss in detail the various problems connected to the effectiveness of the Strasbourg human rights regime but there seems to be consensus on the fact that the ECtHR is not always able to fulfil its role as an efficient or effective control mechanism.[112] To illustrate this, it may be recalled that the majority of the cases in which the ECtHR finds a violation of the ECHR originate in failures to comply with the Convention that have already been dealt with on earlier occasions by the Court.[113] In addition to this, previous general studies on the standard of procedural rights protection afforded to suspects across the EU have indicated that there is room for improvement and have given evidence that the ECHR human rights regime

is no reason why juveniles who are interrogated as a suspect should not be given the same protection.

110 For a recent critical account of the degree to which individual nation states receive and respond to their human rights and 'child-friendly justice' obligations: Goldson and Muncie 2012, p. 47–64.

111 For the statement that the rights accorded by the CRC are 'extensively violated throughout the world', see: Archard 2007, p. 251.

112 Some of these limitations are of a practical nature – such as the enormous backlog of cases the Strasbourg Court is confronted with – and others are more systemic such as the *ex post* nature of the application process: Blackstock *et al.* 2014, p. 22.

113 Cape *et al.* 2010, p. 13.

is not always able to make sure that national authorities pay due regard to their responsibilities in safeguarding suspect's procedural rights.[114]

The second reason for the ineffectiveness of the existing international and European legal framework may be found in the 'flexibility' of the relevant provisions: the majority of the supranational norms are formulated in a broad sense using vague concepts without clearly translating these general rules and principles into specific, binding rules on how and to what extent juvenile suspects should be protected during the different stages of criminal proceedings. As described above, the CRC and other international and European instruments introduce several fundamental principles – such as the 'dignity of the juvenile' and 'the best interest of the child' – which clearly have the objective of functioning as a guideline for how law enforcement and other relevant juvenile justice actors should act when dealing with juvenile suspects. However, because of the broad and flexible wording of these general principles, no clear standards are provided for as to how these principles should be put into practice. From the perspective of the specific topic of protecting juvenile suspects during interrogation, it should be stressed that there are only few specific supranational norms on effective protection of juveniles especially during this early phase of proceedings. As discussed above, these more specific rules are mostly laid down in non-binding instruments such as the UN Guidelines on Child-friendly justice (such as the rule that interviewing rooms should be arranged in a child-friendly environment and that interviews should preferably be carried out by the same person).[115] The safeguards provided for by the (binding) CRC and ECHR are mostly not youth-specific (right to remain silent, right to a lawyer, right to information *et cetera*) with the exception of the right to the presence of parents or guardians.

Summing up, it can be concluded that the existing international and European legal instruments do not provide the EU Member States with a clear framework of rights that – to use a standard expression of ECtHR judgements – are sufficiently practical and effective. In fact, the inadequacy of the existing supranational instruments is recognised by the EU as one of the main reasons for attempting to formulate new, more specific minimum standards dealing with juvenile suspects and defendants in criminal proceedings.[116] It is mostly

114 See *inter alia* Blackstock *et al.* 2014, p. 22. See also Spronken and Attinger 2005, Cape *et al.* 2007, Spronken *et al.* 2009, Cape *et al.* 2010 and Blackstock *et al.* 2014.

115 See *supra* paragraph 7.3.

116 See for example Recital 3 of the Proposal for a Directive on special safeguards for children suspected and accused in criminal proceedings (which will be discussed in paragraph 8.2): 'Although the Member States are parties to the European Convention for the Protection of Human Rights and Fundamental Freedoms, the International Covenant on Civil and Political Rights and the United Nations Convention on the Rights of the Child, experience has shown

for these reasons that the EU has taken up several initiatives to strengthen procedural rights which will be further discussed below.

8. HARMONISATION WITHIN THE EUROPEAN UNION

Is juvenile justice a field that lends itself to harmonisation also in the context of the European Union? The rights of children constitute indeed a priority for the Union. According to art. 3 of the Treaty on European Union (TEU), the Union shall, among other things, promote the protection of the rights of the child both within the Union and in the relations with the wider world. Furthermore, the rights of children are expressly upheld in art. 24 of the Charter of Fundamental Rights of the European Union. According to the Charter, children shall have the right to such protection and care as is necessary for their well-being, including the possibility of expressing their views freely. Furthermore, in all actions relating to children, whether taken by public authorities or private institutions, the child's best interests must be a primary consideration.

Nevertheless, from the perspective of the European Union, harmonisation is in principle not a goal in itself; it is instead a means to an end: it is the basis (or pre-requisite) for improving judicial cooperation and thus it respects the subsidiarity clause only if it is geared towards judicial cooperation. On the other hand, the expansion of police and judicial cooperation in criminal matters between the Member States brings along new needs, first and foremost a more uniform protection of the rights of suspects and defendants across the different jurisdictions. Harmonisation in the field of procedural law and safeguards is a key variable to develop and ensure a higher level of trust between Member States and, consequently, a swifter and more efficient cooperation between them. In this respect, harmonisation of procedural law and safeguards simultaneously serves two purposes of judicial cooperation. On the one hand, it ensures that cooperation procedures run more smoothly and rapidly, by reducing the likelihood of delays and refusals to cooperate. On the other hand, it decreases the

that this in itself does not always provide a sufficient degree of trust in the criminal justice systems of other Member States'. See – in the broader context of the protection of vulnerable suspects – also the Impact Assessment accompanying the Proposal for a directive of the European Parliament and of the Council on procedural safeguards for children suspected or accused in criminal proceedings, Brussels, 27 November 2013, SWD(2013) 480 final, p. 12–13: 'The current national, international and European legal framework for the protection of the rights of suspected or accused vulnerable persons in criminal proceedings in Europe is insufficient'. 'While the international instruments should be considered as a starting point (...) action at EU level will ensure more effective minimum rules for vulnerable persons, in particular for children'.

risk of a negative impact on the individuals concerned in that it minimises the differences and gaps in the protection of rights. Consequently, the harmonisation of suspects' rights constitutes a crucial step in increasing both the mutual trust between European countries and the protection of rights of individuals involved in cooperation proceedings. And if the assumption is true in general, it should be all the more so for juveniles.

Some might object that cooperation in criminal matters does not often concern juveniles. Besides the fact that quite a number of cases already concern juveniles (particularly in the context of the European arrest warrant) and that more are to be expected in the near future, the objection must be dismissed as a matter of principle. Even if there were only a few cases of cooperation involving juveniles each year, the interests at stake are still of such importance that they deserve the utmost attention from the Union. Juveniles are extremely vulnerable and punitive justice can cause them irreparable harm. The risk that uneven safeguards and gaps in the protection of juveniles may irreversibly harm the well-being and the tranquillity of the child is a serious one, which should be avoided as much as possible.

Thus, as a matter of principle, the harmonisation of procedural safeguards for juveniles should represent an absolute priority for the European Union. It is probably for this reason that children's rights in criminal proceedings are to an increasing extent also on the agenda of the EU. A sign of this can be seen in the EU Agenda for the Rights of the Child of 2011.[117] The EU Agenda for the Rights of the Child set by the European Commission aims to reinforce the full commitment of the EU to promote, protect and fulfil the rights of the child in all relevant EU policies and actions. The agenda consists of eleven concrete actions, including the tabling of a proposal for a directive on special safeguards for suspected or accused persons who are vulnerable, including children.[118] The latter initiative has been incorporated into the so-called Roadmap for strengthening procedural rights of suspected or accused persons in criminal proceedings (hereafter: the Roadmap).[119] In this Roadmap the area of procedural safeguards for juveniles and other vulnerable suspects has been identified by the EU as one of those deserving priority in the process of legal harmonisation.[120]

Before discussing the main legal initiatives the EU has – up until now – taken in this respect, it should be noted that the role of the EU is indeed different from that of other supranational organisations and so are its legislative instruments.

117 COM(2011)0060 final.

118 See *infra* paragraph 8.2.

119 Resolution of the Council of 30 November 2009 on a Roadmap for strengthening procedural rights of suspected or accused persons in criminal proceeding [2009] OJ C295/01.

120 As such it is explicitly included in the Council Roadmap for procedural safeguards: Resolution of the Council of 30 November 2009 [2009] OJ C295/01.

Not only is it the case that the rules contained in a European directive are binding for Member States, but it should also be recalled that the Union has now strong enforcement powers against non- or incorrect implementation of its rules. For example, directives need to be implemented within a certain timeframe and if a Member State does not fulfil its obligations in this respect, the European Commission may bring a case against this state, which may eventually lead to the imposition of financial penalties.

8.1. THE 'ROADMAP'

The aforementioned Roadmap is a document approved by the Council to promote several measures of harmonisation in the field of procedural rights. As mentioned above, the underlying idea is that harmonisation is needed for solving problems related to cross-border cases,[121] where some form of judicial cooperation is involved. With the initiative on procedural rights the Union also wants to portrait itself as a 'champion of fundamental rights' after the widespread criticism that the Union's action was excessively driven by a policy grounded on repression and prosecution of crimes.

The Roadmap follows previous unsuccessful attempts to legislate in the field of procedural rights and formulate common procedural safeguards for suspects and defendants in criminal proceedings. It was already in 2003 that the Commission issued a Green Paper on procedural safeguards for suspects and defendants in criminal proceedings,[122] which eventually – in 2004 – led to a proposal for a Framework Decision on certain procedural rights in criminal proceedings.[123] The Commission believed that one of the areas where common minimum standards were most needed was that of vulnerable suspects with a view to ensuring that persons who are not capable of understanding or following the proceedings receive appropriate attention. The proposal came to a stalemate after lengthy negotiations, which encountered the fierce opposition of some Member States. Even the final attempt made by the German Presidency in 2007 to substantially water down the text and reach a compromise on few basic points did not succeed.

The failure of the negotiations on the framework decision brought about a new strategic plan. In 2009 the idea of promoting procedural rights was picked up again under a new strategic framework inspired by 'a step-by-step' approach, which was formalised in the aforementioned Roadmap for procedural

---

121 As is stated by art. 82 TFEU.

122 COM(2003)75 final.

123 Proposal for a Council Framework Decision on certain procedural rights in criminal proceedings throughout the European Union, COM(2004)0328 final, 28 April 2004.

safeguards. The Roadmap consists of five measures to be enacted in a timeframe of five years (2010–2014) on the following topics: (a) the right to interpretation and translation; (b) the right to information; (c) the right to legal advice and legal aid; (d) communication with relatives, employers and consular authorities for people held in detention; (e) special safeguards for vulnerable people, plus a Green Paper on pre-trial detention.[124]

What could appear surprising is that the area of rights for vulnerable suspects was left at the bottom of the list of the legislative path envisaged by the Roadmap instead of being the top priority. In this regard, it can probably be said that the European institutions have partly underestimated the strategic importance of this area. After all, one could have expected countries to be more open to finding common solutions in the area of juvenile suspects before discussing procedural safeguards for adults. And the solutions agreed for juveniles (for example in the context of legal assistance) could have later been extended with the needed adjustments to adults. For instance, it could have probably been more sensible to place measure (e) (or, better, the juvenile related part of measure (e)) before measure (c), because this could have accelerated the negotiations of both measures. Assuming that countries have a higher propensity for overcoming their own domestic legal legislation and traditions when increasing the protection of rights of vulnerable suspects, this particular field of justice (particularly juvenile justice) most likely represents a strategic area and it could even be seen as the key for further harmonisation of procedural systems.

To date three of the Roadmap measures have been adopted: the Directive on interpretation and translation in criminal proceedings,[125] the Directive on the right to information in criminal proceedings,[126] and the Directive on the right of access to a lawyer in criminal proceedings and in European arrest warrant proceedings, and on the right to have a third party informed upon deprivation of liberty and to communicate with third persons and with consular authorities while deprived of liberty.[127] These three directives set a wide range of standards necessary for safeguarding the fairness of criminal proceedings.

From the perspective of the effective protection of juvenile suspects during interrogation, it is important to assess whether the three directives provide for any extra or specific safeguards for suspects who are vulnerable due to their young age. As far as the first Directive – on translation and interpretation –

124 The latter was issued in 2011.
125 Directive 2010/64/EU of 20 October 2010.
126 Directive 2012/13/EU of 22 May 2012.
127 Directive 2013/48/EU of 22 October 2013. In relation to the right to legal assistance the Commission Recommendation of 27 November 2013 on the right to legal aid for suspects or accused persons in criminal proceedings (2013 C-378/11) should also be remembered.

is concerned, this is not the case. This Directive does not contain any specific safeguards for young (or otherwise vulnerable) suspects. In the second Directive, on the right to information, there is explicit reference to the position of vulnerable suspects on (at least) one occasion. In general, the Directive provides that all suspected and accused persons in the EU should be informed of their rights orally and in case of arrest through a written Letter of Rights.[128] The Letter of Rights should be written in a language that the suspect or accused understands. In the Directive it is stressed that authorities should pay particular attention to persons who cannot understand the content or meaning of the information. In this respect, it is regulated that Member States are required to ensure that the information on rights[129] shall be given orally or in writing, in simple and accessible language taking into account any particular needs of vulnerable suspects or vulnerable accused persons.[130] Although the Directive makes no explicit reference to young or otherwise vulnerable suspects in the context of the Letter of Rights, it is regulated that the Letter of Rights should be drafted in simple and accessible language.[131]

In the third Directive – on access to a lawyer – there is also some explicit reference to the special position of children in criminal proceedings. In general, the Directive aims to realise in practice the right of all suspects to be advised by a lawyer from the earliest stages of criminal proceedings.[132] The importance of respecting the rights of children in this respect is highlighted in Recital 55 which states that the Directive 'promotes the rights of children' and ensures that 'suspects and accused persons, including children, are provided with adequate information to understand the consequences of waiving a right under this Directive and that such waiver is made voluntarily and unequivocally. Where the suspected or accused person is a child, the holder of parental responsibility should be notified as soon as possible after the child's deprivation of liberty and should be provided with the reasons therefor.' The latter obligation is laid down in art. 5 of the Directive where it is regulated that '[i]f the suspect or accused person is a child, Member States shall ensure that the holder of parental responsibility of the child is informed as soon as possible of the deprivation of liberty and of the reasons pertaining thereto, unless it would be contrary to the best interests of the child, in which case another appropriate adult shall be

128 Art. 3 and art. 4 para. 5.

129 Provided for under 3 para. 1.

130 Art. 3 par. 2. See also Recital 26 where it is regulated that – when providing suspects or accused persons with information in accordance with this Directive – competent authorities should pay particular attention to persons who cannot understand the content or meaning of the information, for example because of their youth or their mental or physical condition.

131 Art. 4 para. 4.

132 Blackstock *et al.* 2014, p. 29.

informed.'[133] Member States may temporarily derogate from the application of these rights under certain circumstances and on the basis of certain compelling reasons.[134] Finally, in art. 13 of the Directive on access to a lawyer, it is provided that Member States shall ensure that the particular needs of vulnerable suspects and vulnerable accused persons are taken into account in the application of the Directive.

8.2. PROPOSAL FOR A DIRECTIVE ON CHILDREN SUSPECTED OR ACCUSED IN CRIMINAL PROCEEDINGS

Following the steps of the aforementioned Roadmap, on 27 November 2013 the Commission tabled a package of three proposals aimed at strengthening the procedural rights of suspects and defendants. The package also contains a proposal on procedural safeguards for children suspected or accused in criminal proceedings (hereafter: the Proposal).[135] As is clear from its title, the Proposal deals with the largest and most important category of vulnerable suspects: juveniles.[136] In its 25 articles, the Proposal covers some of the most significant rights of juvenile suspects and defendants during criminal proceedings. They range from the right to be informed of procedural rights, to the right to be assisted by an appropriate adult and a lawyer, from the right to an individual assessment and an appropriate treatment to the protection of privacy, from the right to liberty to the right to be present in person at trial. Given the fact that – at the time of writing this chapter – the Proposal had not been adopted yet, its content will not be discussed *in extenso*. The main focus will be on the draft provisions dealing with specific safeguards, which are (or might be) of relevance for juvenile suspects during interrogation.[137] But before discussing these specific safeguards, a few words on the Proposal's scope and relevant definitions are appropriate.

The subject matter of the Directive is identified in art. 1 as 'minimum rules concerning the rights of suspects or accused persons in criminal proceedings who are children and of children subject to European arrest warrant proceedings'. 'Minimum rules' is the common expression for the provisions

133 Art. 5 para. 2.

134 See art. 5 para. 3.

135 Proposal for a Directive of the European Parliament and the Council on procedural safeguards for children suspected or accused in criminal proceedings (COM(2013)822/2).

136 It does not however address the topic of adult vulnerable defendants, which is covered by a separate recommendation, accompanying the proposal: Commission Recommendation on procedural safeguards for vulnerable persons suspected or accused in criminal proceedings (COM(2013)8178/2).

137 For a more extensive discussion of the Proposal see: De Vocht *et al.* 2014.

contained in the Roadmap directives. Clearly Member States cannot offer a lower level of protection but they are free to maintain or to enforce higher standards of protection. The scope of the Proposal is described in art. 2 using two criteria: the age of the suspect and the type of proceedings. With regard to the first, it is stressed that the Directive only covers proceedings against children who are under the age of 18.[138] With regard to the second criterion – the type of proceedings – the Proposal takes a rather restrictive approach: it applies only to criminal proceedings and European Arrest Warrant Proceedings. According to the explanatory notes attached to the Proposal, this means that the Directive does not apply to proceedings that the domestic law does not formally label as criminal.[139]

In the context of definitions, the Proposal contains only one relevant provision: in art. 3 the term 'child' is defined as 'a person below the age of 18 years'. By using this definition, the draft Directive closely follows the aforementioned main international legal instruments on children's rights, particularly the CRC.[140] The Proposal does not provide for any other definitions, which might be relevant for determining the scope and/or implementing the Directive. For example, it does not set out a definition of vulnerability[141] or of the term 'questioning'. As far as specific safeguards are concerned, the Proposal provides for a number of safeguards, which directly concern the field of (pre-trial) interrogation. These are:

1. the right to be informed of rights;
2. the right to have an appropriate adult involved;
3. the right to legal assistance;
4. the right to an individual assessment; and
5. the right to have interviews audio-visually recorded.

8.2.1. The right to be informed on rights

The right to information – laid down in art. 4 of the draft Directive – is divided into three parts. First, there is a general rule that children – as adult suspects –

---

138 Nevertheless, in accordance with art. 2 para. 3 of the draft Directive its content may also cover juveniles who turn 18 in the course of the proceedings, in which case the safeguards apply until the conclusion of the proceedings.

139 Part 3 Legal elements of the Proposal (para. 16).

140 See art. 1 of the CRC where a child is defined as 'any human being below the age of eighteen years unless, under the law applicable to the child, majority is attained earlier'.

141 Given the definition of the concept of a child, the underlying assumption seems to be that children are automatically vulnerable due to their age: Impact Assessment accompanying the Proposal for a directive of the European Parliament and of the Council on procedural safeguards for children suspected or accused in criminal proceedings, Brussels, 27 November 2013, SWD(2013)480 final, p. 12–13 and p. 18.

should be informed 'promptly' of their rights in accordance with the Directive on the right to information in criminal proceedings.[142] Second, art. 4 adjusts and supplements the list of rights of the previous Directive in relation to the juvenile suspect by making explicit reference to some of the specific rights incorporated in the Proposal. Some of these rights are 'juvenile specific', such as the right to have the holder of parental responsibility informed, the right to an individual assessment and a medical examination and the right of the holder of parental responsibility to have access to court hearings. Others are more traditional procedural safeguards, which are given a specific shape and content in connection to the needs of juvenile suspects, such as the right to a lawyer and the right to legal aid, the right to appear in person at the trial, the right to liberty and to specific treatment in detention. Third, the communication with children deprived of their liberty is regulated separately. For juvenile suspects who are arrested or detained, providing oral information is not enough: they should be given a (standardised) Letter of Rights as foreseen in the aforementioned Directive on the right to information.[143] This Letter of Rights should include the specific rights of the draft Directive.[144]

8.2.2. The right to have an appropriate adult involved

Several provisions of the Proposal are dedicated to the involvement of the holder of parental responsibility or other appropriate adult.[145] The right to an appropriate adult represents a traditional safeguard of juvenile punitive justice already found in many European juvenile justice systems. The Proposal clearly values the role of the holder of parental responsibility as a person to monitor the well-being of the child, who should ensure 'moral and psychological support and adequate guidance to the child'.[146] To this end, the holder of parental responsibility/other appropriate adult is given three rights: (a) to be given the same information the juvenile receives under art. 4; (b) to ask for a medical examination of the juvenile; and (c) to have access to hearings involving the

142 Directive 2012/13/EU.

143 Directive 2012/13/EU.

144 Art. 4 para. 2 of the Proposal.

145 The term 'holder of parental responsibility' is defined in art. 2 of the Council Regulation (EC) 2201/2003, according to which it identifies those who enjoy 'all rights and duties relating to the person or the property of a child, which are given to a natural or legal person by judgment, by operation of law or by an agreement having legal effect. The term shall include rights of custody and rights of access'. The term 'appropriate adult' obviously has a broader meaning than 'holder of parental responsibility'.

146 See in this regard the explanatory memorandum (Legal elements of the Proposal, para. 23) where the protective role of parental responsibility is explicitly stressed: 'The holder of parental responsibility is important to ensure moral and psychological support and adequate guidance to the child. The holder of parental responsibility is well placed to enhance the protection of the rights of the defence of the suspected child (e.g. to appoint a lawyer or to decide to appeal a decision)'.

juvenile. These three rights (to be informed, to ask for medical examination and to take part in court hearings) can be found in arts. 5, 8 para. 2b and 15 of the Proposal. Other than the provision on the adult's right to take part in hearings, the draft Directive does not contain any specific provisions on whether – at some point in the proceedings – the presence of an adult is mandatory. Nor are there any rules on the adult's role and function during questioning.

8.2.3. *The right to legal assistance*

In its original version, art. 6 of the Proposal grants juveniles the right of access to a lawyer, by extending to juvenile suspects the same prerogatives provided for adult suspects by the recently approved Directive on access to a lawyer.[147] There is however a fundamental difference from the regime applicable to adults: the Proposal qualifies the juvenile's right to a lawyer as a mandatory right that cannot be waived.[148] The underlying assumption seems to be that juveniles are in too vulnerable a position to make a proper waiver of their right to legal assistance. The choice to make the right of access to a lawyer a mandatory right is justified in the explanatory memorandum through reference to international documents[149] and to the ECtHR case law.[150] With regard to the latter, the reference particularly concerns the *Panovits* case, where the Strasbourg Court stated that juveniles can only waive their right to legal assistance when certain strict conditions are met.[151] As for the scope of the mandatory right to legal assistance, art. 6 para. 2 of the Proposal clarifies that it also covers the part of 'criminal proceedings that may lead to the final dismissal of the case by the prosecutor after the child has complied with certain conditions'.[152] Since the

147 Directive 2013/48/EU.

148 In the case of an adult suspect, a waiver is possible as long as it is voluntary and unequivocal and the suspect has been properly informed of his rights and of the possible consequences: see art. 9 of Directive 2013/48/EU.

149 The Guidelines of the Committee of Ministers of the Council of Europe on child-friendly justice, the *Beijing Rules*, and the 2007 UN CRC 2007 General Comment No. 10 on Children's rights in juvenile justice.

150 Explanatory memorandum (Legal Elements of the Proposal), para. 28: 'The ECtHR has repeatedly underlined the importance of assistance by a lawyer for children from the outset of the proceedings and during police questioning thereby suggesting that a waiver can represent significant risks for them'.

151 In ECtHR 11 December 2008, *Panovits v. Cyprus*, no. 4268/04, para. 68, the Court held that 'given the vulnerability of an accused minor and the imbalance of power to which he is subjected by the very nature of criminal proceedings, a waiver by him or on his behalf of an important right under Article 6 can only be accepted where it is expressed in an unequivocal manner after the authorities have taken all reasonable steps to ensure that he or she is fully aware of his rights of defence and can appreciate, as far as possible, the consequence of his conduct'. See also *supra* paragraph 7.2.

152 See also Recital 17 of the Preamble, referring to penalties imposed by or agreements reached with public prosecutors in order to divert them as soon as possible from the stigmatising effects of regular criminal proceedings.

scope of the right is determined by reference to the Directive on access to a lawyer,[153] the right to a lawyer does not apply to proceedings concerning minor offences.[154] Inextricably linked to the right to access to a lawyer is the right to legal aid which is provided for in art. 18 of the Proposal. During the deliberations on the Proposal, the right to legal assistance has been subject to changes, which have significantly reduced the scope and mandatory character of the safeguard as originally proposed. According to the current wording,[155] children should be assisted by a lawyer only (a) when they are questioned by the police, or by other law enforcement or judicial authorities, including during the trial (unless this is not proportionate taking into account the complexity of the case, the seriousness of the alleged offence or the maximum penalty at stake) or (b) when they are deprived of liberty, unless the deprivation of liberty is supposed to last only for a short period of time. According to the new art. 6a para. 2, the absence of a lawyer does not always mean that the questioning of the juvenile should be postponed: in exceptional circumstances during the pre-trial stage, the competent authorities may immediately proceed with the questioning when there is an urgent need to avert serious adverse consequences for the life, liberty or physical integrity of a person or where immediate action by the investigating authorities is imperative to prevent substantial jeopardy to criminal proceedings.

8.2.4. The right to an individual assessment

One of the most notable features of the Proposal is the right to an individual assessment as provided for in art. 7 of the Proposal. This safeguard includes that all state authorities involved shall 'ensure that the specific needs of children concerning protection, education, training and social integration are taken into account'. To achieve this, an individual assessment of each juvenile suspect will be made, taking particular account of the personality and maturity of the child and their familial and social background.[156] The assessment should be regularly updated in order to ensure that it effectively captures the present condition of the juvenile involved in the proceedings.[157] The assessment must be carried out with the direct involvement of the child and it may have a different degree of detail depending on the circumstances of the case (such as the severity of the offence). The obligation to carry out an individual assessment is not absolute: Member States may derogate from it when it is not proportionate taking into account the

---

153 Directive 2013/48/EU.

154 Art. 2 para. 4 Directive 2013/48/EU.

155 Proposal for a Directive of the European Parliament and of the Council on procedural safeguards for children suspected or accused in criminal proceedings – General approach (text resulting from the DROIPEN meeting on 5 May 2014), 2013/0408 (COD).

156 Art. 7 para. 2.

157 Art. 7 para. 6.

circumstances of the case.[158] In its original wording, art. 7 provided that the individual assessment should be carried out 'at the earliest appropriate stage of the proceedings and, at the latest, in any case before the indictment'. With the recent amendments made to the Proposal, the final part of this sentence was changed to 'at the latest, in due time for it to be taken into account by the court when sentencing',[159] which makes it possible for the authorities to postpone the individual assessment to an even later stage of the proceedings than originally foreseen (after the indictment). This change seems to imply that the individual assessment is mainly meant to help the judge during the sentencing stage and not to provide law enforcement officials with the necessary information on how to deal with the juvenile suspect during the early stages of pre-trial interrogation. Be that as it may, the current wording of art. 7 does not oblige Member States to carry out the individual assessment before any of the pre-trial interrogations.

8.2.5. The right to have interviews audio-visually recorded

From the perspective of protecting juvenile suspects when they are most vulnerable, a legal instrument dealing with procedural safeguards for juvenile suspects and defendants should pay particular attention to interrogations, especially those at the early stages of the proceedings. In the explanatory memorandum of the draft Directive, it is recognised that the questioning of children 'is a potentially risky situation where their procedural rights and dignity may not always be respected and their vulnerability may not be duly taken into account'.[160] The Proposal contains one provision dedicated to 'Questioning of children' (art. 9), which – contrary to what the quite general wording of its title seems to suggest – only concerns the safeguard of making audio-visual records of the questioning. Although audio-visual recording has the potential of constituting an important safeguard against abuse, it is striking that the Proposal does not offer further instructions or safeguards for how to conduct the interrogation of a juvenile suspect.

The original text of art. 9 of the Proposal prescribed the audio-visual recording of any questioning of children by the police or other law enforcement or judicial authority carried out prior to the indictment. Audio-visual recording was not mandatory when it would not be proportionate in light of the complexity of the case, the seriousness of the alleged offence and the potential penalty that could be imposed. In addition to this, the questioning of children should always be

158 Art. 7 para. 7.

159 Proposal for a Directive of the European Parliament and of the Council on procedural safeguards for children suspected or accused in criminal proceedings – General approach (text resulting from the DROIPEN meeting on 5 May 2014), 2013/0408 (COD). Also the word 'familial' was added to art. 7 para. 2.

160 Legal Elements of the Proposal, para. 40.

audio-visually recorded where the child is deprived of liberty, irrespective of the stage of the criminal proceedings (art. 9 para. 2). Recently, the text of art. 9 has been amended, changing the character of the safeguards from 'mandatory unless' into 'a possibility, unless'.[161] As a result of these amendments, making audio-visual recordings is only mandatory when the juvenile is deprived of his liberty and even then recording should be proportionate to the complexity of the case, the seriousness of the alleged offence and the maximum penalty at stake. In addition, it is explicitly stated that Member States may decide not to make audio-visual recordings when the questioning takes place in the presence of a lawyer. Finally, there is another 'escape' from the obligation for audio-visual recording formulated in para. 3: when it is proportionate to make audio-visual recordings but an unforeseeable technical problem renders it impossible, the police or other law enforcement authorities may question the child without an audio-visual recording if questioning of the child is imperative (a) because of an urgent need to avert serious adverse consequences for the life, liberty or physical integrity of a person; or (b) to prevent substantial jeopardy to criminal proceedings. Summing up, it is clear that the recent amendments to art. 9 of the Proposal have significantly diminished the scope and mandatory character of the safeguard.

Although at this moment in time it is too early to assess the Proposal in detail, it is safe to say that it marks an important step in the European process of attempting to achieve a higher and more homogenous level of procedural safeguards for juvenile suspects and defendants. Whether it will successfully fill the existing gap of the aforementioned legal framework in providing effective procedural protection for juvenile suspects during interrogations remains to be seen.

9. THE METHODOLOGICAL APPROACH

Doing comparative research in the field of criminal justice is a highly challenging task. Comparative methodology is one of the most intricate fields of legal theories. There is no pre-established or widely accepted theory of what comparing criminal systems means, what it is about and how it should be done. Nonetheless, it would be naïve to leave every comparative endeavour to the intuition and sensitivity of each researcher. Although it might be true that no perfect or official method exists, comparative research cannot completely do without a minimum methodological basis. And it seems sensible to proceed from the premise that every methodological approach must be tailored to the

161 Proposal for a Directive of the European Parliament and of the Council on procedural safeguards for children suspected or accused in criminal proceedings – General approach (text resulting from the DROIPEN meeting on 5 May 2014), 2013/0408 (COD).

specific needs of each endeavour. In other words, it seems appropriate to believe that the method changes depending on the goal of the study.[162]

In the case of the legal comparative study underlying the present volume, it should be recalled that it represents the first step of a more complex comparative research. Thus, the study is not only a goal in itself but it is also instrumental in the following steps of the research.[163] Hence, the methodological approach was devised taking into account the overall structure of the research.

9.1. THE FUNCTIONAL METHOD

It is often said that the comparative method for addressing issues of harmonisation is the functional method. Indeed, one of the most frequently used expressions in comparative criminal justice is 'functional equivalent'.[164] Often the functional method has been considered to be the (best) method for comparative legal research.[165] Much comparative research is about finding functional equivalents in different systems, in order to adequately compare the systems in whole or in part. The widespread success of the functional method might also depend on the very broad concept of functions,[166] which opens the door to different ways of construing the functional method.[167] In essence, the assumption of the functional method is that systems can reach similar ends in different ways. As long as a similar result and/or objective is reached, the different tools for reaching it are functional equivalents.

The functional method focuses not on rules but rather on their effects,[168] on their social functions.[169] The common function performed or the common result achieved becomes the common basis, the *tertium comparationis,* for establishing some form of equivalence (or difference) between systems.

Often the goal of comparative legal research, particularly within the field of juvenile justice, is to compare two systems as a whole, by identifying the different functions performed by the justice system. It is also the case that comparison is made between two legal tools (or provisions) that perform a common function

162 De Coninck 2010, p. 321 (remarking that the 'acknowledgement of the diversity of possible purposes of comparative legal research necessarily entails acknowledgement of at least some measure of methodological pluralism').

163 See for a description of the different parts of the research project: *supra* paragraph 4.

164 See, for instance, Reitz 1998, p. 620.

165 Zweigert and Koetz 1998, p. 34 ('The basic methodological principle of all comparative law is that of *functionality*') and Gordley 2012, p. 107–119.

166 See in this respect some of the critical remarks of Frankenberg 1985, p. 437.

167 Michaels 2006.

168 Michaels 2006.

169 De Coninck 2010, p. 323.

within a system, in order to compare approaches to dealing with the same legal problem and appreciate the pros and cons of each solution.

It should be kept in mind that the present study moves from an even more specific perspective, which is rather uncommon in the field of juvenile justice. In fact the project deals not with comparing criminal justice systems in general but with comparing a specific procedural activity within the respective systems. In doing so, the study proceeds from the common concept of interrogations and it aims to compare the rules on how to conduct interrogations of juvenile suspects. Whether interrogations perform the same functions across the different jurisdictions is part of the study, but is not the ultimate goal. The ultimate purpose of the legal part of the study is, in the first place, to identify precisely and in detail all the rules and safeguards that apply when conducting interrogations. In second instance, the purpose of the study is to identify – on the basis of the national enquiries – differences and similarities and to observe common general trends (which are termed 'general patterns').[170] In this respect it can be said that the study proceeds from the identification of the interrogation as an equivalent activity in different countries; it explores to what extent this common activity pursues a common function; it aims to find out the rules in each country, the common patterns among the different jurisdictions; and finally it aims to identify whether and to what extent commonalities and differences in values, principles, rules and safeguards would make a harmonisation effort feasible.

This does not mean that the functional approach is useless for the purposes of this study. The comparison by function remains a useful tool to evaluate the role played by rules and safeguards in the context of interrogations and to meaningfully compare them. The transversal analysis carried out in the final chapter mostly revolves around a similar exercise. There, the commonalities and differences between the five jurisdictions are evaluated in order to identify which general patterns can be extracted from them.

9.2. THE COUNTRY REPORTS AND THE COMMON TEMPLATE

As mentioned, the country reports have been drafted following a common template.[171] The structure of the template did not merely instruct the country rapporteurs to illustrate the rules for conducting the interrogations of juvenile suspects in their own country: the approach taken by the template was broader.

170 See *infra* chapter 7.

171 The common template used for drafting the country reports is added as an annex to this volume.

The underlying assumption of the template is that the function of interrogations, the applicable rules and safeguards cannot be understood in a vacuum. Procedural systems are a complex machine where each cog in the machine performs a function that can only be entirely understood within the context of the whole mechanism. It is for this reason that the template was structured to have two parts: a first part concerning the overall shape of the juvenile justice system and a second part focusing specifically on interrogations.

The first part of the country reports not only aims to offer a general picture of the domestic juvenile justice system, it also aims to offer a taste of the social context. For this reason the authors have been asked to highlight, as far as possible, some of the cultural keystones of their own system. This includes a brief history of the most salient developments of the system and a review of the literature on juveniles' needs within juvenile justice. The idea is that it is not possible to meaningfully grasp the state of the law of a country without some basic insight into the societal context. This takes into account the sociological remark connected to the importance of legal culture in the performance of comparative studies: 'the idea of legal culture points to differences in the way features of law are themselves embedded in larger frameworks of social structure and culture which constitute and reveal the place of law in society'.[172] However, it should be recalled that the study conducted in this volume remains a legal study and not a sociological study. The type of theoretical study conducted would hardly allow us to compare legal cultures in a broader sociological sense. Nonetheless, it has seemed important to have some general notion of the contextual social features in order to improve the understanding of the legal rules that are in force in each country, under the assumption that society always has some impact on how the law is shaped.

The second part of the common template goes into more detail on the rules governing interrogations. First it required the authors to map all the types of possible interrogations of their systems and to identify the function of each. As the reader will see, the interrogation of a young suspect can serve different purposes. It can have the traditional goal of discovering what happened (or, as some say, revealing the truth) and finding evidence to solve the case, particularly incriminating evidence. But interrogations can also serve to allow the suspect to defend himself (and some parts of the interrogation are provided only to that end) or to establish whether certain pre-trial custodial/coercive measures are in place (as in *habeas corpus* interrogations). Additionally, 'interrogations' of young suspects can even have the goal of uncovering the social context of the juvenile suspect and understanding more of his family/societal background (in order to undertake the proper form of social/judicial treatment).

---

172 Nelken 2001, p. 25. See also Nelken 2010 and Nelken 2012.

The template then required country rapporteurs to look closely at the rules governing the interrogation. In this respect, the interrogation activity was categorised in the common template using two criteria: firstly the logical and chronological sequence of actions that compose the interrogation; and secondly the functional criterion organised around the different safeguards and right to be protected (e.g. right to silence, legal assistance, *et cetera*).

9.3. CHALLENGES IN DESCRIBING NATIONAL LAW

Every comparative endeavour of the kind that is attempted in this study is faced with major challenges. The first is a problem of a very general, if not philosophical, nature. National reports should be mostly descriptive of the national law that is in force. But is it possible to describe the existing law at all? Or is it not the case that every description of the law entails an interpretation that makes the report a prescriptive one, stating how the law ought to be interpreted?

Second, what is the law? In countries like Italy, the term 'law' (*legge*) traditionally identifies the legal provisions in themselves, as separated by the judicial interpretation that can be given of them. In countries like England and Wales, the term 'law' encompasses case law, which shapes, integrates and supplements the statutes. In order to address this challenge, the common template was built around the methodological approach suggested by the theory of legal formants.[173]

The theory of legal formants is based on the idea that the law is not to be taken as a whole but it is rather the product of the action of different players, each of which contributes to the shaping of the overall system. Hence, 'instead of speaking of the "legal rule" of a country, we must speak instead of the rules of constitutions, legislatures, courts and, indeed, of the scholars who formulate legal doctrine'.[174] This approach does not refute the idea of unity of the law, but it invites us to consider the different elements that contribute to the shaping of the law. The function of legal formants is thus to help us (a) to consider the structure and functioning of the system and its inner flexibility more analytically, and (b) to identify the inconsistencies/contradictions which sometimes are present in different legal texts or between legal texts and judicial decisions.

The use of this theory requires that the law is broken, as far as possible, into the different layers that shape it. In other words, it is important not just to identify a legal rule, but also to identify how the legal rule came into being, i.e. through the action of which legal institution or 'player'. It thus makes a difference whether

173 Sacco 1991a, Sacco 1991b and Monateri 2012.

174 Sacco 1991a, p. 21.

the same rule is at constitutional level in one country and at subordinate level in another; whether a rule is the product of case law or the expressed decision of Parliament codified in a statute; and so on. In order to address this concern the authors were also asked to identify as much as possible the source of each rule (constitutional rule, primary legislation, secondary legislation, case law, practical instructions/guidelines, *et cetera*), so that it would be possible to understand the level at which the rule was given in each country.

The attempt to identify the specific legal domestic source of a rule is particularly important for a project that aims to identify possible patterns of harmonisation. It is a common misconception that harmonising the law is simply a matter of finding the best legal solution (or legal compromise) to deal with a common problem. This is already an oversimplification of reality. But the difficulty of harmonisation is not only in the finding of a proper common rule. Among other things, harmonisation must also be technically feasible, which means that the proposed harmonised rule must be generally compatible with the domestic system. This requires the researcher to be able to identify the conditions that would make a proposal of harmonisation incompatible with one national system (e.g. the existence of some constitutional limits; the existence of superior rules that would conflict with the proposed harmonisation, *et cetera*). It is for this reason that knowledge of a system should not only be knowledge of existing and applicable legal rules but also knowledge of how important each rule is in the system, how strong it is, how resistant it is to derogations or amendments, and so on. It is not enough to know that a certain practice or conduct is forbidden or allowed by the law: it makes a difference whether the prohibition or permission is contained in case law, in a statute or in the constitution.[175]

9.4. DEFINITIONS

Another challenge of a comparative endeavour is of course that of definitions. Legal definitions are stipulations made on the basis of a historical/traditional development or on a purely conventional basis for purposes of greater clarity. Inevitably every translation of a legal term from one language to another is in itself artificial, or rather is a new stipulation. In any case, such a translation always requires a comparative study in itself, because it is essential to ensure the best (functional) correspondence (or equivalence) possible between the original term and its translation. In principle, the authors of the country reports have been asked to look for the English translation of their national terms that was most suitable and that would best express the greatest number of shades of

[175] For example: we could easily figure a harmonised solution that overcomes the current state of the case law of a country, but a harmonised solution which would require a country to change its constitution is less likely to be accepted.

meaning of the domestic concept. It is for this reason that the choice was made not to artificially impose one uniform language (or in other words: a set of fixed definitions). However, in order to reduce the risk of misunderstandings or alterations, the authors have been asked to incorporate – in some more controversial cases – the original term between brackets, just after the translation of their national wording. It was only after the first drafts of the country reports that the editors consulted each author in order to enquire whether in some cases the translation of certain terms could be made more uniform without affecting the best understanding of the nuances of the system.

With regard to the terms mostly recurrent in this work, it is important to highlight that for the purposes of this volume the terms 'juvenile', 'young person' and 'child' are taken as synonyms to identify all minors, i.e. those who have not attained the age of maturity according to the rules in force in each country.

As for the term 'interrogation', this is probably the most complex to capture in one fixed definition. After all, this concept may have different meanings not only when comparing different national juvenile justice systems but also within a single jurisdiction. For the purpose of this legal study we chose to use a working definition of 'interrogation' referring to all pre-trial confrontations between a public authority and a juvenile suspect. The authors of the country reports were asked to offer an overview of all the kinds of interrogations present in their national systems but to devote greater attention to those types of interrogation of juvenile suspects which – in their system – are aimed at gathering evidence during the investigation stage. Nonetheless, information is also given on other types of pre-trial interrogations, by highlighting the relevant distinction in function and relevant rules. In this volume, words such as 'interview', 'questioning' or 'hearing' are sometimes used as synonyms of the word interrogation. When these words intend to refer to a situation that does not fit within the aforementioned working definition of 'interrogation', this is explicitly mentioned.

BIBLIOGRAPHY

Archard 2007
D. Archard, 'Children's Rights and Juvenile Justice', in: M. Hill, A. Lockyer and F. Stone (eds), *Youth Justice and Child Protection*, London: Kingsley Publisher, 2007, p. 250–265

Bailleau and Cartuyvels 2007
F. Bailleau and Y. Cartuyvels, 'La mise en question du modèle 'protectionnel' dans la justice des mineurs en Europe', in: F. Bailleau and Y. Cartuyvels (eds.) *La justice pénale des mineurs en Europe. Entre modèle Welfare et inflexions nèo-liberales*, Paris: L'Harmattan, 2007, p. 8–19

Blackstock *et al.* 2014
J. Blackstock, E. Cape, J. Hodgson, A. Ogorodova and T. Spronken, *Inside Police Custody – An Empirical Account of Suspects' Rights in Four Jurisdictions*, Cambridge (etc.): Intersentia, 2014

Bonnie and Grisso 2003
R.J. Bonnie and T. Grisso, 'Adjudicative Competence and Youthful Offenders', in: T. Grisso and R.G. Schwartz, *Adjudicative Competence and Youthful Offenders*, Chicago: The University of Chicago Press, 2003, p. 73–103

Buzzelli 2008
S. Buzzelli, 'Il panorama delle garanzie a protezione della "fonte fragile": il contesto europeo', in: Claudia Cesari (ed), *Il minorenne fonte di prova nel processo penale*, Milano: Giuffré 2008, p. 1–20

Cape *et al.* 2007
E. Cape, J. Hodgson, T. Prakken, and T. Spronken, *Suspects in Europe*, Antwerp: Intersentia, 2007

Cape *et al.* 2010
E. Cape, Z. Namoradze, R. Smith and T. Spronken, *Effective Criminal Defence in Europe*, Antwerp: Intersentia, 2010

Cavadino and Dignan 2006
M. Cavadino and J. Dignan (eds.), *Penal Systems. A comparative approach*, London: Sage, 2006

Cleary 2014
H.M.D. Cleary, 'Police Interviewing and Interrogation of Juvenile Suspects: A Descriptive Examination of Actual Cases', *Law and Human Behavior*, 2014, 3, 271–282

Damaška 1986
M.R. Damaška, *The Faces of Justice and State Authority*, New Haven and London: Yale University Press, 1986

Damaška 1997
M.R. Damaška, *Evidence Law Adrift*, New Haven and London: Yale University Press, 1997

De Coninck 2010
J. De Coninck, The Functional Method of comparative Law: Quo Vadis, *RabelsZ*, 2010, p. 318–350

De Vocht *et al.* 2014
D.L.F. de Vocht, M. Panzavolta, M. Vanderhallen and M. van Oosterhout, 'Procedural Safeguards for Juvenile Suspects in Interrogations: A Look at the Commission Proposal in Light of an EU Comparative Study', *New Journal of European Criminal Law*, 2014, 4, p. 480–506

Delmas-Marty and Spencer 2002
M. Delmas-Marty and J. Spencer, *European criminal procedures*, Cambridge: Cambridge University Press, 2002

Doek 2009
J. Doek, 'The UN Convention on the Rights of the Child', in: J. Junger-Tas and F. Dünkel (eds), *Reforming Juvenile Justice*, Dordrecht: Springer, 2009, p. 19–31

Dünkel 2009
F. Dünkel, 'Young People's Rights: The Role of the Council of Europe', in: J. Junger-Tas and F. Dünkel (eds), *Reforming Juvenile Justice*, Dordrecht: Springer, 2009, p. 33–44

Dünkel *et al.* 2011
F. Dünkel, J. Grzywa, P. Horsfield and Pruin, *Juvenile Justice Systems in Europe – Current Situation and Reform Developments*, Vol 1–4, Mönchengladbach: Forum Verlag Godesberg, 2011

Esin 2007
Ö. Esin, 'Methodological Aspects of Comparative Law', *European Journal of Law Reform*, 2007, vol. III, 1, p. 29–42

Feld 1989
B.C. Feld, 'The Right to Counsel in Juvenile Court: An Empirical Study of When Lawyers Appear and the Difference they Make', *Journal of Criminal Law and Criminology*, 1989, 4, p. 1185–1346

Feld 2007
B.C. Feld, 'Police Interrogation of Juveniles: an empirical study of policy and practice', *Journal of Criminal Law and Criminology*, 2006–2007, 97, p. 219–316

Feld 2012
B.C. Feld, Kids, *Cops and Confessions: Inside the Interrogation Room*, New York and London: New York University Press, 2013

Feld 2013
B.C. Feld, 'Behind Closed Doors: What Really Happens When Cops Question Kids', 23 *Cornell Journal of Law and Public Policy*, 23 (2013), p. 395–462

Fenwick 2006
M. Fenwick, 'Japan: From Child Protection to Penal Populism', in: J. Muncie and B. Goldson (eds.), *Comparative Youth Justice*, London: Sage, 2006, p. 146–158.

Fortin 2009
J. Fortin, *Children's Rights and the Developing Law*, Cambridge: CUP, 2009

Frankenberg 1985
G. Frankenberg, 'Critical comparisons: Re-thinking Comparative Law', *Harvard International Law Journal* 1985, 26, p. 411–455

Garland 1985
D. Garland, *Punishment and Welfare. A History pf Penal Strategies,* Aldershot Gower, 1985

Gensing 2011
A. Gensing, 'Jurisdiction and characteristics of juvenile criminal procedure in Europe', in: F. Dünkel, J. Grzywa, P. Horsfield and I. Pruin, *Juvenile Justice Systems in Europe - Current Situation and Reform Developments*, Vol. 4 (2nd revised edition), Mönchengladbach: Forum Verlag Godesberg, 2011, p. 1607–1648

Goldson and Muncie 2012
B. Goldson and J. Muncie, 'Towards a global 'child friendly' juvenile justice?', *International Journal of Law, Crime and Justice*, 2012, 1, p. 47–64

Gordley 2012
J. Gordley, 'The Functional Method', in: P.G. Monateri, *Methods of Comparative Law* (ed), Cheltenham: Edward Elgar, 2012, p. 107–119

Grisso and Pomicter 1977
J.T. Grisso and C. Pomicter, 'Interrogation of Juveniles: An Empirical Study of Procedures, Safeguards and Rights Waiver', *Law and Human Behavior*, 1977, 4, p. 321–342

Hill *et al.* 2007
M. Hill, A. Lockyer, F. Stone, 'Introduction: The Principles and Practice of Compulsory Intervention when Children are 'At Risk' or Engage in Criminal Behaviour, in: M. Hill, A. Lockyer and F. Stone (eds.), *Youth Justice and Child Protection*, London: Kingsley Publisher, 2007, p. 9–38.

Houle 2011
S.R. Houle, 'Juvenile Justice is Not Just Kids Stuff: the Forgotten Side of Fairness and Due Process', *Dartmouth Law Journal*, 2011, p. 86–119

Junger Tas 2006
Junger-Tas, J., 'Trends in International Juvenile Justice: what conclusions can be drawn?', in: J. Junger-Tas and S. Decker (eds.), *International Handbook of Juvenile Justice*, Berlin, New York: Springer, 2006, p. 503–532

Kemp *et al.* 2011
V. Kemp, P. Pleasence and N.J. Balmer, 'Children, Young People and Requests for Police Station Legal Advice: 25 years on from PACE', *Youth Justice* 2011, 11, p. 28–46

Kilkelly 1999
U. Kilkelly, *The child and the European Convention on Human Rights*, Aldershot (etc.): Ashgate/Dartmouth, 1999

Kilkelly 2001
U. Kilkelly, 'The Best of Both Worlds for Children's Rights? Interpreting the European Convention on Human Rights in the Light of the UN Convention of Human Rights?', *Human Rights Quarterly*, 2, 2001

Kilkelly 2010
U. Kilkelly, 'Protecting children's rights under the ECHR: the role of positive obligations', *Northern Ireland Legal Quarterly*, 2010, 3, p. 245–261

Lingwood and Bull 2013
J. Lingwood and R. Bull, 'Interviewing young adolescent suspects: When to reveal incriminating information?', *The European Journal of Psychology Applied to Legal Context*, 2013, 5, p. 141–146

McAra 2006
L. McAra, 'Welfare in Crisis? Key Developments in Scottish Youth Justice', in: J. Muncie and B. Goldson (eds.), *Comparative Youth Justice*, London: Sage, 2006, p. 127–145

Michaels 2006
R. Michaels, 'The Functional Method of Comparative Law', in: R. Zimmerman and R. Reimann, *The Oxford Handbook of Comparative Law*, Oxford: Oxford University Press, 2006, p. 339–382

Mijnarends 1999
E.M. Mijnarends, *Richtlijnen voor een verdragsconforme jeugdstrafrechtspleging: Gelijkwaardig maar minderjarig*, Deventer: Kluwer, 1999

Monateri 2012
P.G. Monateri, 'Methods in comparative Law: An Intellectual Overview', in: P.G. Monateri (ed.) *Methods of Comparative Law*, Cheltenham: Edward Elgar, 2012, p. 7–24.

Muncie and Goldson 2006
J. Muncie and B. Goldson, 'States of Transition: Convergence and Diversity in International Youth Justice', in: J. Muncie and B. Goldson (eds.), *Comparative Youth Justice*, London: Sage, 2006, p. 196–214

Muncie and Hughes 2002
J. Muncie and J. Hughes, 'Modes of Youth Governance', in: J. Muncie, G. Hughes, E. McLaughlin, *Youth Justice. Critical Readings*, London: Sage, 2002, p. 1–18

Muncie 2008
J. Muncie, 'The 'punitive' turn in juvenile justice: Cultures of control and rights compliance in western Europe and the USA', *Youth Justice*, 2008, 2, p. 107–121

Nelken 2001
D. Nelken, 'Toward a Sociology of Legal adaptation', in: D. Nelken and J. Feest (eds.), *Adapting Legal Cultures*, Oxford: Hart, 2001, p. 7–54

Nelken 2010
D. Nelken, 'Comparative criminal Justice, in: D. Nelken, *Comparative Criminal Justice*, London: Sage, 2010

Nelken 2012
D. Nelken, 'Using Legal Culture: Purposes and Problems', in: D. Nelken (ed.) *Using Legal Culture*, London: Wildy, Simmonds and Hill, 2012, p. 1–51

Padfield 2002
N. Padfield, 'Juvenile Justice', in: M. McConville and G. Wilson (eds), *The Handbook of The Criminal Justice Process*, Oxford University Press: New York, 2002, p. 403–422

Patané 2007
V. Patané (ed.), *European Juvenile Justice Systems*, Milano: Giuffré, 2007

Pruin 2011
I. Pruin, 'The scope of juvenile justice systems in Europe', in: F. Dünkel, J. Grzywa, P. Horsfield and I. Pruin, *Juvenile Justice Systems in Europe – Current Situation and Reform Developments*, Vol 4 (2nd revised edition), Mönchengladbach: Forum Verlag Godesberg, 2011, p. 1539–1582

Put and Walgrave 2008
J. Put and L. Walgrave, 'Belgium: From Protection Towards Accountability?', in: J. Muncie and B. Goldson (eds.), *Comparative Youth Justice*, London: Sage, 2006, 111–126

Reitz 1998
J.C. Reitz, 'How to do comparative law', *The American Journal of Comparative Law* 4, p. 617–636

Sacco 1991a
R. Sacco, 'Legal Formants: A Dynamic Approach to Comparative Law (Installment I of II)', *The American Journal of Comparative Law*, Vol. 39, No. 1. (Winter, 1991), p. 1–34

Sacco 1991b
R. Sacco, 'Legal Formants: A Dynamic Approach to Comparative Law (Installment II of II)', *The American Journal of Comparative Law*, Vol. 39, No. 2 (Spring, 1991), p. 343–401

Schmidt and Reppucci 2002
M.G. Schmidt and N.D. Reppucci, 'Children's Rights and Capacities', in: B.L. Bottoms, M.B, Kovera and B.D. McAuliff, *Children, Social Science, and The Law*, Cambridge University Press: Cambridge, 2002, p. 76–105.

Spencer and Flinn 1993
J. Spencer and R. Flinn, *The Evidence of Children*, London: Blackstone Press, 1993.

Spronken and Attinger 2005
T.N.B.M. Spronken and M. Attinger, *Procedural Rights in Criminal Proceedings: Existing Level of Safeguards in the European Union*, Brussels: DG Justice Freedom and Security, 2005

Spronken *et al.* 2009
T. Spronken, G. Vermeulen, D. de Vocht and L. van Puyenbroeck, *EU Procedural Rights in Criminal Proceedings*, Antwerp: Maklu, 2009

Steinberg and Schwartz 2000
L. Steinberg and G. Schwartz, 'Developmental Psychology Goes to Court', in: T. Grisso and R.G. Schwartz, *Adjudicative Competence and Youthful Offenders*, Chicago: The University of Chicago Press, 2003, p. 9–31

Van Bueren 2006
G. van Bueren, *Article 40: Child Criminal Justice*, Leiden: Nijhoff, 2006

Vanderhallen *et al.* 2015
M. Vanderhallen, M. van Oosterhout, M. Panzavolta and D. de Vocht, *Interrogating Young Suspects: Procedural Safeguards from an Empirical Perspective*, Cambridge (etc.): Intersentia (forthcoming 2015)

Whyte 2002
B. Whyte, 'Changes, Evidence, Challenges. Youth Justice Developments in Scotland', in: M. Hill, A. Lockyer and F. Stone (eds), *Youth Justice and Child Protection*, London: Kingsley Publisher, 2007, p. 139–157

Winterdyk 2014
J.A. Winterdyk, 'Introduction: Juvenile Justice in the International Arena', in: J.A. Winterdyk, *Juvenile Justice, International Perspectives, Models, and Trends*, Boca Raton: CRC Press, 2014, p. 1–24

Woolard 2002
J.L. Woolard, 'Capacity, Competence and the Juvenile Defendant', in: Bette L. Bottoms-Margaret Bull Kovera-Bradley D. McAuliff (eds), *Children, Social Science, and the Law*, Cambridge: Cambridge University Press, 2002, p. 270–298

Zweigert and Koetz 2012
K. Zweigert and H. Koetz, *Introduction to comparative law*, Oxford: Clarendon, 1998

CHAPTER 2
BALANCING THE NEED FOR PROTECTION AND PUNISHMENT OF YOUNG DELINQUENTS
Country Report Belgium

Marc VAN OOSTERHOUT and Joachim MEESE

I. THE BELGIAN JUVENILE JUSTICE SYSTEM: GENERAL OVERVIEW

1. BACKGROUND

1.1. GENERAL FEATURES OF THE SYSTEM

Belgium became a federalist state after federalisation reforms in the 1970s and 1980s. The federal state now consists of three communities: a French, Dutch and German community. This inner-communities and communities versus federal division makes for a complex model of criminal law which is somewhat difficult to describe.[1] Responses to juvenile delinquency and execution of measures are divided between the federal state and the communities, creating a complex system. Dealing with juvenile delinquency has remained a state responsibility, while the execution of measures is handled by the communities: when an educational measure is imposed on a juvenile delinquent by the juvenile judge or court, the communities are responsible for executing it.[2]

Adding to the complexity of the system are the developments in juvenile criminal justice which have recently taken place in Belgium, causing the system to veer away from a welfare-oriented towards a more hybrid system with both welfare and punitive elements.[3] Following the adoption of the Child Protection

1 Christiaens, Dumortier and Nuytiens 2011, p. 99.
2 Christiaens, Dumortier and Nuytiens 2011, p. 99.
3 Put and Walgrave 2006, p. 111–126.

Act in 1912 (hereafter: CPA)[4] and the Youth Protection Act in 1965 (hereafter: YPA)[5] there have been numerous proposals for reform to the latter, and in 2006 some major changes were indeed adopted. More recently the *Salduz* ruling by the European Court of Human Rights (hereafter: ECtHR)[6] has had an impact on Belgian criminal proceedings, leading to the enactment of the new so-called Salduz legislation.[7]

Considering the fact that federal legislation governs the national response to juvenile delinquency, this report will be written mainly from that perspective. Only where diverging rules apply in the various communities and where these rules significantly affect the treatment of juvenile suspects will they be discussed.

1.1.1. Sources of juvenile (criminal) justice in Belgium

The Belgian legal system provides for a separate system of juvenile justice. The above-mentioned acts contain separate provisions which are only applicable to juvenile suspects. Thus, as opposed to the Dutch system – where a few separate provisions are provided for in criminal (procedure) law –the Belgian system provides for a completely separate set of rules. Furthermore, this system is not labelled as 'criminal', but is seen as a youth protection system instead. In theory this is an important distinction, but the measures that can be imposed on juveniles can nonetheless be experienced by these juveniles as punitive, causing a gap between the theoretical embedding and it having a 'criminal' feel to it in practice. For the purposes of this report, the system will be referred to as 'juvenile criminal law'; the term 'juvenile justice' is considered to be too all-encompassing since it also includes juvenile civil law. Even though Belgium does have a separate system for dealing with juvenile delinquency, some rules that are applicable to adult suspects also apply to juvenile suspects, for instance the provisions on the safeguards applicable prior to and during police interrogation.[8] Before discussing these special provisions and the specifics of Belgian juvenile criminal justice, a few words on the Belgian legal sources are fitting.

In Belgian law a distinction is made between 'legislation in a narrow sense' (*wetgeving in enge zin*) and 'legislation in a broad sense' (*wetgeving in ruime zin*). The former concerns the Constitution which is drafted and can be adjusted by the federal parliament, laws/acts (*wetgeving*) enacted by the federal parliament, decrees which are enacted by the various communities as well as by the Flemish

4 Law of 15 May 1912.
5 Law of 8 April 1965.
6 ECtHR 27 November 2008, *Salduz v. Turkey*, no. 36391/02.
7 Salduz Act 2011 (Law of 13 August 2011).
8 Such as the right to legal assistance as provided for in the abovementioned Salduz Act.

and Walloon country parts,[9] and finally ordinances (*ordonnanties*) of the capital province of Brussels (*Brussels Hoofdstedelijk Gewest*) which only apply to this province. The latter encompasses both the legislation in a narrow sense as well as lower level decrees enacted by the executive powers such as the royal decree and ministerial regulations.[10] Furthermore, case law is considered to be a source of law. The highest judicial institutions are the Court of Cassation and the Constitutional Court. In the context of juvenile justice it is important to note that separate juvenile courts exist. In line with the continental legal tradition – on which the Belgian criminal law is founded – codified law is considered to be a higher source of law than case law, but interpretation of legislation through case law may have an impact on the scope and meaning of legislation. International rules stemming from treaties are directly applicable in Belgian law and form an integral part of its legislation. Thus, directly applicable provisions can be invoked in court and should be applied preferentially when they have direct effect (*directe werking*). Important examples – also in light of this report – are art. 6 of the European Convention on Human Rights (hereafter: ECHR) and art. 3 of the Convention on the Rights of the Child (hereafter: CRC). Below, the historical developments as well as the relevant legal sources – those mentioned above and the Belgian Code of Criminal Procedure (hereafter: CCP)[11] – will be further explained.

1.1.2. Underlying ideology of Belgian juvenile justice

According to legal doctrine, '[t]he Belgian juvenile justice system has always been mentioned as one of the most welfare-oriented in Europe'.[12] The underlying philosophies have been geared towards (re)education (amelioration), rehabilitation and the notion that the child should be protected. Thus, reintegration instead of punishment was the motto underlined by the CPA of 1912.[13] Instead of punishments, protective measures 'in the best interest of the child' were imposed.[14] It is important to already note at this point that juvenile suspects cannot commit crimes under Belgian law, but they can commit so-called acts defined as a crime (*een als misdrijf omschreven feit*). This distinction – which is more theoretical than practical – does have implications for possible 'punishments' of juveniles.[15] Because of this distinction and as

9 Besides being separated into three communities, Belgium is also divided into two provinces: the northern part, Flanders; and the southern part, Wallonia.

10 Statutes are published in the Official Bulletin of Acts (*Belgisch Staatsblad* – www.ejustice.just.fgov.be).

11 Law of 17 November 1808.

12 Christiaens, Dumortier and Nuytiens 2011, p. 99.

13 Christiaens, Dumortier and Nuytiens 2011, p. 100.

14 Christiaens 1999, p. 5–21.

15 As mentioned before, officially a juvenile cannot be punished, but measures are imposed. Nonetheless, these measures may be experienced as a punishment by the juvenile.

a result of the welfare model, juvenile offenders are not held to be responsible for their acts but instead these offences are seen as symptoms of underlying problems. As a result, responses to these acts defined as crimes are not based on the principle of proportionality, but on the juvenile's social context and his personality.[16] Because a juvenile offender is not punished through criminal law but rather is ameliorated through educational and/or rehabilitative measures, there is no need or place for criminal law dealing with juvenile delinquency.

1.2. BRIEF HISTORY OF AND CURRENT TRENDS IN CRIMINAL JUVENILE JUSTICE POLICY

As mentioned before, the starting point for juvenile criminal law in Belgium was the enactment of the Child Protection Act of 1912. Before this law there was no autonomous separate juvenile criminal law. Juvenile offenders were considered criminally liable when they had committed an offence and were able to understand the consequences of their actions and the criminality of it (*oordeel des onderscheids*). Then, they could be punished.[17] The existing concept of the human being was that he is a rational and reasonable being who commits acts based upon his own autonomous will.[18] This concept was also applied to juveniles and therefore they – in principle – were considered criminally liable.[19] With the enactment of the CPA this changed and juveniles under the age of 16 years were kept out of criminal proceedings, as opposed to juveniles over the age of 16 who were tried through normal criminal (procedure) law. Ffrom 1912 onwards criminal law was replaced by a system of juvenile protection and this development can be seen as a 'shift from a moral responsibility to a social responsibility'.[20] This was the first time an age-threshold for criminal liability (16 years) was set. Punishments for juveniles below the age of 16 were replaced with measures of prevention (*behoeding*), education (*opvoeding*) and retention (*bewaring*).[21] These juveniles were from then on tried by specialist courts and judges (*kinderrechtbanken en kinderrechters*). Measures could not only be imposed on juvenile offenders under the age of 16, but also on juveniles who 'were considered to be in danger because of pre-delinquent or bad behaviour'.[22] In line with the rehabilitation and welfare philosophy, Belgian juveniles were re-educated through welfare sanctions.[23] These sanctions consisted of: custody at his Majesty's pleasure (*terbeschikkingstelling*), placement of the juvenile in a

16 Christiaens, Dumortier and Nuytiens 2011, p. 100.
17 Brouwers 2007, p. 3–4.
18 Tulkens and Moreau 2000, p. 17.
19 Put 2010, p. 22.
20 Cartuyvels 2001, p. 133.
21 Brouwers 2007, p. 4.
22 Christiaens, Dumortier and Nuytiens 2011, p. 100.
23 Garland 1981, p. 29–45.

private or public facility or in a foster family, and a warning (*admonestation*).[24] All these measures could coincide with the probationary measure of liberty under surveillance (*liberté surveillé*). The CPA also introduced a specialised and unique judge, the juvenile judge. The role of this magistrate was considered to be a very paternalistic one, which was embodied in the fact that the entire criminal case concerning a juvenile – from the pre-trial stage to the execution of a sanction – was handled by the same judge. This is, as of today, still one of the key characteristics of the Belgian juvenile justice system.[25] It is also a characteristic that the Belgian system shares with the Polish system.

1.2.1. The Youth Protection Act of 1965

As is immediately apparent, there is quite a gap in time between the enactment of the Child Protection Act and the adoption of the Youth Protection Act in 1965. This does however not mean that in the meantime the CPA was considered to be without lacunas and 'problems'. Some of the issues mentioned were that the CPA had dangerously repressive elements, lacked fundamental safeguards for juveniles and that the juvenile judge was given too much power of authority and to wide a margin of appreciation in juvenile matters.[26] Aside from these more substantial criticisms, there were also questions asked about the effectiveness of the measures that could be imposed, fuelled by the fact that crime rates amongst juveniles kept rising. Eventually, these criticisms gave rise to two opposing legal movements: one advocating a restrictive interpretation of the competences of the juvenile judge, and one arguing the contrary. The latter movement prevailed and an extensive interpretation of the competence of the juvenile judge within the CPA was born.[27] With that, the Youth Protection Act entered into force on 8 April 1965. This legislation has replaced the CPA of 1912 and with that the age of criminal maturity was increased to 18 years.[28] A juvenile over the age of 16 but below the age of 18 can only be prosecuted before a 'normal' criminal court under certain specific circumstances.[29] Furthermore, it became possible to treat adult suspects – aged between 18 and 21 years old – as a juvenile in certain cases.[30] A possibility which was later abolished.

This new legislation regarding juvenile protection was designed as a wider and more positive model which needed to replace the narrow and negative model of 1912.[31] More than ever, the aim was to keep juveniles away from criminal

---

24 Christiaens, Dumortier and Nuytiens 2011, p. 100.

25 Christiaens, Dumortier and Nuytiens 2011, p. 100–101.

26 Cartuyvels 2001, p. 136.

27 Brouwers 2007, p. 4.

28 Art. 36 para. 4 YPA.

29 Art. 38 YPA. See *infra* paragraph 2.2 (part I).

30 Art. 36 YPA.

31 Put 2007, p. 1–7.

proceedings and criminal law[32] and the focus veered away from societal protection towards protection of the juvenile. The legislator still mirrored the view of a determined human being, but an explanation for deviant and delinquent behaviour was sought in the social context of the juvenile offender.[33] The judge was instructed to focus on the social surroundings of the juvenile, because he could not be held responsible for his actions when there was a lack of insight in guilt (*schuldinzicht*).[34] The central notion became 'the interest of the child'.[35] The system of the YPA drafted to facilitate this 'protection of the child' was divided into three phases: general social protection, specific social protection and judicial protection.[36] These phases were devised to be complementary to each other,[37] and even though legislation lacked a definition of what was to be understood by 'social protection', the assumption was that it meant preventive acting.[38] *Inter alia*, the third phase (judicial protection) is different in that it involved legal action against the juvenile. If social protection failed, legal action could be used as the final tool. In Title II of the YPA the possibility of legal acting is documented and underscribed by the founding of a juvenile court (*jeugdrechtbank*). This court is, as it was under the CPA of 1912, presided over by one juvenile judge. But contrary to the situation under the CPA, these judges do not act as a solely singular power, because the YPA also provided for the founding of the juvenile protection committee (*jeugdbeschermingscomité*) and the communal social services[39] which assist the juvenile judge.[40] The measures that can be imposed were similar to those of the Act of 1912: prevention, education and retention were anchored in the YPA.[41] Additionally the concept of transferral (*uithandengeving*) of the juvenile, meaning that a juvenile suspect aged between 16 and 18 years could be *transferred* to the proceedings of 'normal' adult criminal law, was adopted.[42] This is still in force.

The YPA was – similar to the CPA of 1912 – subjected to vast and persistent criticism. It was said to cause congestion of the judicial system and its institutions, and due to a lack of qualified personnel this led to problems with the legality principle.[43] According to critics, there was little to no respect for the protection of fundamental procedural rights of juvenile suspects and the law still

32 Cartuyvels 2000, p. 8.
33 Put 2007, p. 1–7.
34 De Smet, 2010, p. 7.
35 Put 2007, p. 1–7.
36 Cartuyvels 2001, p. 141.
37 Put 2010, p. 26.
38 Tulkens and Moreau 2000, p. 227.
39 For more information on actors, see *infra* paragraph 2.4 (part I).
40 Tulkens and Moreau 2000, p. 228.
41 Art. 37 YPA.
42 Art. 38 YPA. See *infra* paragraph 2.2 (part I).
43 Put 2010, p. 26.

seemed to focus on societal protection instead of protection of the juvenile.[44] Besides neglecting procedural rights, the State Council (*Raad van State*) was of the opinion that the YPA was in conflict with constitutional provisions and that 'preventing the judge from doing evil also meant preventing him from doing good'.[45] This means that the judge was too restricted in his role and powers. In the case of *Bouamar v. Belgium* the ECtHR concluded that art. 5 paras. 1 and 4 of the ECHR were breached because the juvenile was detained in remand prison on nine successive occasions and the Belgian government did not put in place appropriate institutional facilities which met the demands of security and the educational objectives of the 1965 Act.[46] The Court also took into account the fact that in the end no criminal actions were launched against Bouamar. Belgian juvenile law lacked efficiency and comprehensibility and needed to be surrounded by more safeguards.[47] Despite this strong criticism and the proposals for reform, the YPA remains the foundation of juvenile criminal law in Belgium.

1.2.2. Reform: the laws of 15 May 2006 and 13 June 2006 and sixth state reform

Similar to the time-lapse between the CPA and the YPA, it took quite a long time before the YPA was eventually reformed. Despite this extended period in which there was no reform, there had been several proposals for reform. Again there was a division noticeable between two legal movements: one advocating further de-legalisation and the other proposing further penalisation. Emphasis was placed on emancipation in the 1970s, proposing more rights for legal subjects – including juveniles.[48] In the 1980s some institutional reforms were enacted, transferring juvenile protection from a federal responsibility to a communal (*gemeenschappelijk*) duty. Only when a juvenile was prosecuted on the basis of an act defined as a crime could the judge impose federal measures, but execution of these measures remained at the level of the communities, causing difficulties in execution.[49] Additionally, in the 1980s there was a noticeable shift from social responsibility towards individual responsibility and as a result the social context in which juveniles committed offences could no longer be considered as the trigger of deviant behaviour.[50]

This led to a stricter response to juvenile offending and in the 1990s the focus was placed on a feeling of societal insecurity, resulting in a call for re-penalisation.

44 Van de Kerchove 1979, p. 16.
45 Put 2010, p. 26.
46 ECtHR 29 February 1988, *Bouamar v. Belgium*, no. 9106/80.
47 Cartuyvels 2000, p. 11.
48 Nagels, 2006, p. 31.
49 De Smet 2010, p. 11.
50 Cartuyvels 2001, p. 148.

This led to two proposals for legislation: a sanctions model and a restorative model.[51] These proposals raised some fundamental issues and formed the basis of further reforms in the 1990s. In the mid-1990s a proposal was drafted abolishing the notion of protection and constructing a model focussed on sanctioning.[52] The report which contained the proposal for reform highlighted three important aims: more attention to the victim, more responsibility placed on the juvenile offender and better procedural safeguards for juveniles.[53] As a counterbalance to this more punitive model, voices were also raised to promote the restorative model. The central notion of this model is the restoration of damages through mediation between the suspect and victim. The focus of the model is shifted from punishment for the crime towards restoration of the consequences of the offence.[54] This dichotomy aside, some reforms were introduced in the mid-1990s resulting in more procedural reform, safeguards for juvenile suspects when a measure is imposed,[55] and alignment with international rules such as the ECHR. Eventually in 2002 it became impossible to apply pre-trial detention (amongst adult detainees) to juveniles in protection proceedings.[56] However, in 2002 the so-called Everberg Act was adopted by the federal government as a response to the release of several juvenile delinquents because of the over-population of regular facilities, again making it possible to place juvenile delinquents in pre-trial detention but in a separate closed facility.[57]

In 2004 the Minister of Justice Onkelinx presented a framework note (*Kadernota*) which spurred on further reform to the Belgian juvenile criminal justice system. It proposed changes on two levels: better protection for juveniles on the one hand and stricter sanctioning of those juveniles who pose a danger to society on the other. Once again much attention was paid to the victim in criminal proceedings and juveniles were burdened with more responsibility, but at the same time more procedural safeguards were introduced in all phases of criminal proceedings.[58] This note again endured some heavy criticism, namely that it merely ornamented the YPA of 1965 and that it – wrongfully – kept the possibility of transferral of juveniles to adult criminal proceedings.[59] Besides scholarly criticism, the children's rights commission (*Kinderrechtencommissariaat*) also disapproved of the note, considering it to be

[51] Put 2010, p. 38.
[52] Decock 2012, p. 2.
[53] Put 2007, p. 4.
[54] Put 2007, p. 4–7.
[55] Put 2010, p. 36.
[56] It was previously pointed out to Belgium by the ECtHR that this form of pre-trial detention is in breach of art. 5 of the ECHR (ECtHR 29 February 1988, *Bouamar v. Belgium*, no. 9106/80).
[57] Everberg Act of 1 March 2002.
[58] Onkelinx 2007, p. 9–13.
[59] Decock 2004, p. 66.

inconsistent with important international treaties such as the CRC.[60] Despite all this, the note became an official proposal for legislation (*wetsontwerp*) in 2005, albeit with adjustments as a concession to the issues raised. This led to two laws being approved by Parliament (*Kamer*) on 15 May 2006, one of which was amended shortly thereafter. Hence the two laws entered into force: one on 15 May and the other on 13 June 2006. Subsequently these two acts became known as the Youth Justice Act (hereafter: YJA) of 2006.[61]

The law of 15 May governs the restorative element of juvenile criminal justice[62] while the law of 13 June establishes some fundamental safeguards for juvenile suspects, such as the mandatory right to legal assistance of a lawyer who is supposed to play a pivotal role in proceedings.[63] The goal of these new laws was to modernise the juvenile criminal justice system and to adhere to some developments and changes that had been made in practice.[64] The system has since incorporated elements of juvenile protection and sanctioning, or as De Smet has described it: 'juvenile protection law with a *pinch* of juvenile sanction law'.[65] He observes a narrowing of the gap between normal criminal proceedings and juvenile criminal justice, as general safeguards became applicable to juvenile suspects as well.[66] The concept of transferral was upheld, but with some slight changes to the procedure. As of 2013, this historical development that resulted in the amended version of the YPA of 1965 still constitutes the foundation of Belgian juvenile (criminal) justice. The relevant notions, procedures and safeguards which will be discussed below therefore need to be seen against this background.

Finally, it is important to note that Belgium is a country that is subject to so-called state reform. What happens during such reform, in a nutshell, is that changes are made at a constitutional level. The sixth reform has recently been enacted and this has brought about a decentralisation of power. Some powers that used to fall under federal rule have been handed over to the communities. Amongst these are juvenile proceedings, making communities responsible for prosecuting, placing and rehabilitating juveniles. It is too early to assess what the actual impact of this reform will be on juvenile proceedings.

60 Kinderrechtencommissariaat 2004, p. 67 (www.kinderrechtencommissariaat.be).
61 Put, Vanfraechem and Walgrave 2012, p. 86.
62 De Smet 2006, p. 344.
63 Onkelinx 2007, p. 9–13.
64 Put 2010, p. 41.
65 De Smet 2006, p. 342–368.
66 De Smet 2005, p. 418.

2. STRUCTURE AND MAIN CHARACTERISTICS OF THE BELGIAN JUVENILE JUSTICE SYSTEM

2.1. MINIMUM AGE OF CRIMINAL LIABILITY

Officially, in the Belgian system, there is no minimum age of criminal liability. However, legislation governing this liability is rather ambiguous. The YPA of 1965 does not formally define an age below which a juvenile cannot be held criminally responsible; rather it is seen as a responsibility of the public prosecution service which decides upon this matter through its monopoly of prosecution (*vervolgingsmonopolie*).[67] Thus, in principle it is possible that the prosecution service might decide to prosecute a very young juvenile. The only restriction written into the YPA is that juvenile measures can only be imposed on juveniles over the age of 12 years.[68] But exceptions exist and juveniles under the age of 12 can be reprimanded (*berispt*), placed under supervision of social services or subjected to educational guidance.[69] De Smet has referred to this as a 'light version of juvenile criminal law'.[70] One problem with this ambiguous cut off point as a minimum age for criminal liability is that according to international standards, such as the *Beijing Rules*,[71] states are required to have a hard minimum age. Apart from the *Beijing Rules* this demand is also formulated in the CRC which does not define the exact age, but does require states to set a clear standard where criminal liability starts and apparently this age cannot be too low.[72] These requirements are 'an obligation which needs to be fulfilled'.

2.2. DEFINITION OF JUVENILE AND RELEVANT CATEGORIES

There is a formal legal definition of 'juvenile' in Belgian criminal law. Art. 100*ter* Criminal Code (hereafter: CC) (*Strafwetboek*) states that the term 'minor' in book II means every person who has not reached the age of 18 years. In addition to this definition in the CC, the YPA of 1965 also states that: 'the juvenile court is informed of (...) claims by the public prosecution service regarding persons who are being prosecuted for an act defined as a crime, committed before the full

67 Brouwers 2007, p. 5.
68 Art. 37 YPA.
69 Dumortier and Christiaens 2006, p. 275.
70 De Smet 2008, p. 134.
71 United Nations Standard Minimum Rules for the Administration of Juvenile Justice, 29 November 1985, GA 40/33.
72 Art. 40 para. 3 sub a CRC.

age of 18 years'.[73] This corresponds to provisions of civil law which also define a person, male or female, under the age of 18 years as a minor.[74] In addition to this definition of a juvenile under Belgian criminal law, some relevant (age) categories can be distinguished which will be discussed below. These categories correspond to the possibility of transferral mentioned earlier.

2.2.1. *Transfer of the juvenile to criminal law*

Under Belgian law juveniles are *a priori* excluded from criminal law. The rationale for this exclusion is that juveniles are seen as incapable of understanding guilt and being held culpable (*schuldonbekwaam*) and therefore are not criminally liable. Even though this is the starting point, some exceptions to this rule were made when the YPA was enacted and later adapted – resulting in the YJA of 2006. This apparent need to punish some juveniles – codified in the exceptions – has been further fuelled by some high-profile crimes involving juvenile suspects in Belgium. A well-known example is the so-called case of Joe Van Holsbeeck of 2006, where two juveniles were suspected of murdering Van Holsbeeck.[75] This fuelled calls for harsher and stricter punishment of juvenile delinquents and in some cases even for treating them as adults, and according to some legal authors a moral panic was unleashed.[76]

The foremost exception to the rule that juveniles are considered *schuldonbekwaam* is the transferral of the juvenile. When a juvenile suspect is aged between 16 and 18 years, the juvenile judge can decide to transfer the juvenile to a normal correctional criminal court. Art. 57*bis* para. 1 YPA states that the judge can decide to transfer the juvenile's case to the public prosecution service in order to be tried before a special chamber within the juvenile court which will apply normal criminal (procedural) law when it deems the applicable educational measures insufficient. A perfect illustration of this mechanism can be found in the Van Holsbeeck case where the judge ruled that transferral of one of the suspects was in order, because two years of educational measures were deemed insufficient. The reasoning was that the suspect was a lost cause, because he was sunk in criminal behaviour and kept placing the blame on his co-defendant.[77] The transferral of a juvenile suspect to a normal criminal court is subject to certain requirements and special proceedings, and has consequences for the juvenile suspect, which will be briefly discussed in the next paragraph. Research prior to 2009 has shown that transferral to adult courts in Belgium is a possibility which is used only very rarely: on a national level it happens only in 1

73 Art. 36 para. 1 sub 4 YPA.
74 Art. 388 of the Belgian Civil Code (as per 19.01.1990).
75 For more information, see: Nuytiens 2006.
76 Christiaens and Dumortier 2006, p. 36.
77 Brouwers 2007, p. 15.

per cent of provisional decisions[78] and in 3 per cent of all final youth protection measures taken by juvenile judges in court.[79]

2.2.2. *Requirements of transferral*

As stipulated in art. 57*bis* para. 1 of the YPA, the juvenile must be between 16 and 18 years of age at the time of committing the act defined as a crime in order for him to 'qualify' for transferral. With the main criterion being the juvenile suspect's age, the severity of the alleged offence is – in principle – irrelevant. This has changed with the amendments formulated in the law of 13 June 2006, adding the requirement that when a juvenile has not been convicted before he can only be transferred when he is being prosecuted for a severe offence.[80] This is now codified in art. 57*bis* para. 1 of the YPA.[81]

Additionally there should be a report or findings during the court proceedings (*onderzoek ter terechtzitting*) showing that measures of education are no longer sufficient.[82] According to De Smet, the juvenile judge should in his decision on transferral only refer to the degree of maturity (*maturiteitsgraad*) of the juvenile suspect and his environment and not be influenced by possible pressure from society to punish the juvenile harshly when suspicion of a serious offence exists.[83] Nonetheless, circumstances of the offence can be put forward to support views on the personality of the juvenile – for instance the severity of the way the offence was committed – forming so-called supportive evidence (*steunbewijs*).[84]

A final requirement is that the transferral of the juvenile suspect can only be implemented when this is done through a decision which is accompanied by the reasons for said transferral (*een met redenen omklede beslissing*). Art. 50 para. 1 YPA states that in order for the juvenile judge to make the decision of transferral, an investigation into the suspect's social background (*maatschappelijk onderzoek*) – conducted by social services – has to be completed. As well as this investigation into the juvenile suspect's social context and environment, another requirement is that a psychiatrist reports on the personality of the juvenile.[85] The purpose of this report is to provide the judge with a view on the juvenile's personality and behaviour, allowing him to make an informed decision on the possible effectiveness of educational measures.[86] When these investigations have been

---

78 For more information on the provisional and final measures, see *infra* paragraph 2.3 (part I).
79 Christiaens and Nuytiens 2009, p. 131–142.
80 De Smet 2006, p. 354.
81 For an overview of the offences, see: De Smet 2006 and art. 57*bis* YPA.
82 Art. 57*bis* para. 2 YPA.
83 De Smet 2006, p. 354.
84 Dupont and Verstraeten 1988, p. 269.
85 Art. 57*bis* para. 2 YPA.
86 De Smet 2006, p. 355.

completed and the public prosecution service has summoned the juvenile suspect, the juvenile judge will take his decision regarding transferral. This decision is a final decision (*eindbeslissing*).[87] Appeal against the decision of transferral is possible, but research has shown that this possibility is not often used.[88]

2.2.3. Procedure of transferral

Transferral is accompanied by a debate before the juvenile court. The public prosecution service should formulate the request for transferral in the summons, but the juvenile judge can also decide to transfer even when the juvenile district council of the prosecution service[89] (*jeugdparket*) still believes in the effectiveness of educational measures.[90] The procedure of transferral starts with a notification to the public prosecution service by the juvenile judge. No later than three days after the medical-psychological report has reached the juvenile judge, he should pass this on to the public prosecution service.[91] They in turn have 30 days to summon the juvenile suspect and his parents for the purpose of transferral. The 30 days run from receipt of the report.[92] When the King's prosecutor (*procureur des Konings*)[93] of the juvenile district council decides to apply transferral, this should be discussed in court at the earliest possible hearing.[94] Within 30 days of this hearing, the juvenile judge has to make a decision. If an appeal is lodged the procurator-general (*procureur-generaal*) has 20 days to summon the juvenile suspect and his parents before the court of appeal (*Hof van Beroep*).[95] Following this summoning a juvenile chamber of the court of appeal has 15 days to rule on the matter.[96]

2.2.4. Consequences of transferral

Several consequences stem from an order of transferral:

- Possibility for the juvenile suspect to be summoned before the sentencing court (*vonnisgerecht*): after the case is referred to the public prosecution service, they *can* decide to summon the juvenile suspect to appear before the normal criminal court based on grounds formulated in law.[97] In line with the so-called

87 De Smet 2006, p. 354.
88 Nuytiens, Christiaens and Eliaerts 2005, p. 71.
89 This is a special department within the public prosecution service dealing with juveniles.
90 De Smet 2006, p. 356.
91 De Smet 2006, p. 356.
92 Art. 57*bis* para. 3 YPA.
93 This is the public prosecutor in first instance under Belgium criminal law.
94 De Smet 2006, p. 356.
95 Art. 57*bis* para. 3 YPA.
96 Art. 57*bis* para. 3 YPA.
97 Art. 57*bis* para. 1 YPA.

discretionary principle (*opportuniteitsbeginsel*) the decision to prosecute a (juvenile) suspect remains entirely in the hands of the prosecution.[98] Which court is then authorised to rule on the matter depends on the type of crime committed. When the crime is open to correction (*correctionalisering*) a special chamber of the juvenile court – composed of a judge of the correctional court and two specialised juvenile judges[99] – will preside over the case. Though this chamber is part of the *juvenile* court, the judges will apply normal criminal (procedural) law.[100] If the alleged offence is not open to correction, the Assize Court (*hof van assisen*), which involves a jury, will preside over the case.[101]

- Possible pre-trial detention (*voorlopige hechtenis*):[102] when transferral is decided upon, all provisional or final educational measures seize.[103] If the juvenile suspect does not attend the hearing before the juvenile judge, an arrest warrant can be requested by the prosecutor through the juvenile judge.[104] This warrant is subject to the requirements of the pre-trial detention law: it must be necessary for public safety and court proceedings can result in a correctional prison sentence of at least one year and, when punishable by less than 15 years, additional requirements are that there is a danger of recidivism, collusion, embezzling evidence or fleeing.[105] Execution of the arrest warrant is done in a closed federal centre which is a separate system for juveniles.[106]
- Possible prison sentence (*gevangenisstraf*): after transferral the juvenile suspect will be tried before an adult court[107] and when the alleged offence is proven and the juvenile suspect is found guilty, an appropriate prison sentence – not solely focussed on restoration of damages, but also inflicting suffering (*leedtoevoeging*) – can be imposed. This is not a necessity and the judge can also decide to impose a diversion measure if the juvenile suspect has shown good behaviour.[108]
- Expelling from juvenile protection: the juvenile will be subjected to ordinary criminal proceedings from the moment a final ruling on transferral has been made. This applies for all crimes listed in the indictment.[109] The only problematic issue remaining is that it is not clear at which moment these

98 Bosly and Vandermeersch 2003, p. 507.
99 Art. 78 Judicial Code (*gerechtelijk wetboek, 10 October 1967*).
100 De Smet 2006, p. 356.
101 Art. 57*bis* para. 1 YPA.
102 Normally, pre-trial detention is not applicable to juvenile suspects: Cass. 5 October 1994.
103 De Smet 2006, p. 357.
104 Art. 3 Pre-trial detention Act.
105 Art. 3 Pre-trial detention Act.
106 De Smet 2006, p. 357.
107 Of course only if the aforementioned criteria are met, such as the prosecution service deciding to prosecute.
108 Van Dijk 2005, p. 27–28.
109 Art. 57*bis* para. 5 YPA.

provisions become applicable: when the juvenile receives the indictment or at another point.[110] The juvenile judge is empowered to decide that the transferral can be executed immediately.[111]

2.2.5. *Accelerated transferral*

As well as the normal transferral procedure, there is also the so-called accelerated transferral, which allows[112] for transferral without waiting for the medical-psychological report.[113] Accelerated transferral is allowed under the following three circumstances:

- the juvenile suspect has refused medical-psychological examination;
- the juvenile has an earlier conviction for a similar crime;[114] or
- the suspect has reached the age of 18 years at the time of the indictment and committed the offence when aged 16 years or over.[115]

2.2.6. *Transferral in case of traffic infringements*

In addition to transferral after deliberation followed by a formal decision by the juvenile judge, transferral can also happen automatically when the offence involves an infringement of traffic rules. When the juvenile suspect has reached the age of 16 years and is suspected of violating the Traffic Act (*verkeerswetgeving*) he will be summoned to appear before the police court (*politierechtbank*) instead of the juvenile court.[116] Officially this is not a transferral, because transferral is not necessary, seeing as the police judge is already authorised to rule in case of traffic violations.

2.3. MEASURES FOR JUVENILES

The possible measures to be imposed on juveniles are numerous under Belgian juvenile criminal law. While still in the judicial investigative stage of the proceedings, the juvenile judge can impose provisional measures, but the power to do so has been somewhat restricted with the enactment of the laws of 2006. In accordance with art. 52 YPA the juvenile judge can – at the instigation of the prosecutor – impose some measures to extract the juvenile from his living

---

110 De Smet 2006, p. 359.

111 Art. 58 YPA.

112 The word 'allows' is used because it is an option of the juvenile judge, not a mandatory requirement.

113 Art. 57*bis* para. 2 YPA.

114 For categories of crimes, see: De Smet 2006, p. 355.

115 De Smet 2006, p. 355.

116 Art. 36*bis* YPA.

environment or measures which are supportive of his education and upbringing while awaiting trial.[117] As a provisional measure this can be in the form of 30 hours of community service, prohibition from leaving the family home, or placement in a public institution.[118] The term 'provisional' is important because it does not allow measures to be imposed which can only be effective in the long term. They should have an immediate impact. Another important issue in imposing provisional measures is that an infraction of the juvenile's rights is made at an early stage; this can conflict with the presumption of innocence.[119] Thus the YPA states that there have to be sufficiently serious indications of guilt (*voldoende ernstige aanwijzingen van schuld*).[120] The provisional measure can in no way involve a punitive element and must be necessary for the intended purpose. The Belgian Constitutional Court has found that the imposition of pre-trial measures by the same judge is in itself not unconstitutional but if the same judge has to decide on matters of guilt when deciding on pre-trial measures, it becomes problematic. Since, according to the law, some measures required indications of guilt, the Constitutional Court deleted this condition, allowing the same judge to impose pre-trial measures and also decide on the outcome of the case during the actual court proceedings.[121] Thus, the court did not introduce the obligation of a different judge at the various stages of the proceedings.[122] With the adoption of the Everberg Act in 2002 the judge can place the juvenile in the Everberg federal facility for pre-trial detention.[123]

Once at trial a wide range of measures can be imposed, but since the coming into force of the new laws of 2006 the subsidiarity principle applies, meaning that the least punitive and intrusive measure should be imposed.[124] This means – in practice – that the judge should first consider mediation or group conferencing, then a *written* project,[125] a measure of supervision, and as a last resort a custodial sentence.[126]

2.3.1. *Reprimand*

First, when the trial has led to the ascertainment that the facts (acts defined as crimes) have been committed by the juvenile, the judge can still decide to reprimand the juvenile when he establishes that the juvenile and his

117 Loop 1993, p. 30.
118 Christiaens, Dumortier and Nuytiens 2011, p. 108.
119 Art. 6 ECHR.
120 Art. 52*quater* para. 2 YPA.
121 Constitutional Court 13 March 2008, no. 49/2008.
122 Christiaens, Dumortier and Nuytiens 2011, p. 109.
123 Everberg Act 2002: this form of pre-trial detention is different from its counterpart in normal criminal proceedings.
124 Christiaens, Dumortier and Nuytiens 2011, p. 109.
125 For both, see *infra* paragraph 2.6 (part I).
126 Christiaens, Dumortier and Nuytiens 2011, p. 109.

environment cannot (or no longer) be seen as 'problematic'.[127] In practice, this will be a warning to the delinquent juvenile and his parents not to commit acts defined as crimes in the future. The reprimand leads to the abolishment of the supervision by the juvenile court.[128]

2.3.2. *Community measures*

The juvenile judge has a wide range of community measures at his disposal in order to keep the juvenile under supervision or adjust his behaviour through these measures. However, he cannot deprive the juvenile of his liberty. The first community measure is placement under the supervision of social services.[129] In practice, this measure is meant to keep the juvenile in his natural living environment – when no negative behavioural patterns have been discerned – resulting in the least impact on the juvenile's well-being. This supervision can be made conditional and the conditions can be linked to the supervision by the social services separately or cumulatively.[130]

Another measure that can be imposed is intensive educational supervision.[131] This will be imposed when regular supervision by social services is deemed insufficient. A so-called reference educator (*referentieopvoeder*) will be appointed to supervise the juvenile and his family closely and devise an educational trajectory catered to the juvenile's specific needs. Finally the juvenile can be forced to follow ambulant treatment at a psychological or psychiatric service.[132] It is important to note that not all of these measures can be imposed on juveniles below the age of 12: this category of juveniles is excluded from performing community service.[133]

In contrast to criminal proceedings, the YPA does not provide for a possibility of automatic custodial placement when the juvenile fails to properly perform the imposed measures and possibly attached conditions.[134] The juvenile judge can then decide to place the juvenile in a community facility under the resolute condition that communal service will be performed within a timeframe of six months.[135]

---

127 Art. 37 para. 2, section 1 YPA.

128 Tulkens and Moreau 2000, p. 641.

129 Art. 37 para. 2, section 2 YPA.

130 The possible conditions can be found in art. 37 para. 2*bis* YPA: (a) Attend school on a regular basis; (b) Provide a service – maximum of 150 hours; (c) Perform paid labour – maximum of 150 hours; (d) Take into account certain medical or pedagogical guidelines; (e) Attend a course on the impact of the actions; (f) Attend a sport, cultural or social activity; (g) Uphold a contact- or locational restraining order; (h) Refrain from performing certain activities; (i) Respect house arrest (*huisarrest*); and (j) Uphold another condition or specific restraint.

131 Art. 37 para. 2, section 3 YPA.

132 Art. 37 para. 2, section 5 YPA.

133 Christiaens, Dumortier and Nuytiens 2011, p. 110.

134 Art. 37*ter* para. 1 CC.

135 Art. 37 para. 2 YPA.

2.3.3. *Residential placement*

The YPA further provides some possibilities to place the juvenile in residential care. First of all, the juvenile can be placed under the supervision and in the care of a trusted person in order to extract him from his home.[136] This does not entail permanently taking away guardianship from the parents. It is just a temporary measure where housing, upbringing and education are provided away from the parental home. The biological parents remain responsible for the juvenile's upbringing.[137] Similarly, the juvenile can also be placed under the supervision of a legal corporate body (*rechtspersoon*)[138] in order to fulfil a positive achievement.[139] The juvenile can also be placed in a hospital that organises withdrawal courses.[140] Finally the YPA also classifies placement in an open or closed psychiatric facility as 'residential'.[141] It may be doubtful that placement in a closed psychiatric facility should indeed be qualified as such. Art. 43 YPA is applicable and when a juvenile suffers from mental illness the YPA does not provide a separate set of rules for placement. The law *on the protection of persons with a mental illness*[142] applies *mutatis mutandis* and the juvenile judge is now empowered to force placement in such a facility (*collocatie*).[143] Before placement, the juvenile should first be observed, but in crisis situations the prosecutor can order arrest and placement.[144] The judge can order placement for a maximum duration of two years, which has to be checked at intervals of three months and each decision is open to appeal.[145] The placement ends at the instigation and decision of the director of the institution (*diensthoofd*).[146]

2.3.4. *Custodial measures*

The most important custodial measures to be imposed are placement in an open or closed community institution. Placement in an open institution can happen in an institution as far as 'it is considered apt to provide the juvenile with decent living, education or upbringing'.[147] This can be any institution as far as they are

---

136 Art. 37 para. 2, section 7 YPA.
137 Smets 1996, p. 346.
138 Art. 37 para. 2, section 6 YPA.
139 Christiaens, Dumortier and Nuytiens 2011, p. 110.
140 Art. 37 para. 2, section 10 YPA.
141 Art. 37 para. 2, section 11 YPA.
142 Law of 26 June 1990.
143 Rom 2007, p. 203–205.
144 Art. 9 Law of 26 June 1990.
145 Arts. 22 and 30 para. 3 Law of 26 June 1990.
146 Art. 12 section 3 Law of 26 June 1990.
147 Art. 37 para. 2 section 7 YPA.

recognised by the Flemish community.[148] Preferably[149] this placement should happen in the vicinity of the juvenile's parents.[150] The juvenile can also be placed in day-care instead of a 24-hour placement.[151] The maximum duration of this placement is one year but can be prolonged.[152] Termination of the measure can also occur sooner – for instance because of good behaviour – and it can also be replaced by another measure.[153] Besides placement in a recognised institution, the juvenile can also be placed in a public community facility (*openbare gemeenschapsinstelling*). The requirements for doing so are the the juvenile is at least 12 years old and that he has committed an act defined as a crime for which the minimum possible sentence is three years.[154]

Placement in a closed institution is the most far-reaching custodial deprivation of liberty. The maximum duration is six months, which can be prolonged in the event of continuous bad or dangerous behaviour. The requirements are: a minimum age of 14 years – which can be lowered to 12 years if the juvenile suspect is suspected of having 'committed a severe attack on the life or health of a person and shows signs of extreme dangerous behaviour-[155] – and the alleged offences must be of a certain severity.[156] Some additional requirements are formulated in art. 52*quater* YPA when the placement concerns provisional placement during the pre-trial phase.[157] A provisional placement in a closed institution can last no longer than three months.

According to research done by Vanneste in 2003, custodial sentences such as placement in an institution are the central mode in sentencing practice.[158]

2.4. RELEVANT ACTORS

One of the characteristics of Belgian juvenile (criminal) justice is that it takes a multidisciplinary approach. Besides judicial authorities – such as courts, judges

148 Senaeve 1995, p. 395.
149 Meaning that, if no other possibility exists, placement can also occur in another district: Smets 1996, p. 367.
150 Smets 1996, p. 367.
151 Smets 1996, p. 345.
152 Art. 60 YPA.
153 De Smet 2007, p. 262.
154 Art. 37 para. 2, section 8 YPA.
155 Art. 37 para. 2*quater*, section 3 YPA.
156 Art. 37 para. 2*quater*, section 3 YPA.
157 These are: the juvenile shows behaviour which is dangerous to himself or others and serious reasons to believe that – once free – the juvenile will commit new acts defined as crimes, flees, tries to dispose of evidence or tries to establish secret contact with third parties.
158 In 1999, 50 per cent of sentences were of a custodial nature, of which a proportion of 26 per cent represented placement in a closed public institution (Vanneste 2003, p. 232–263).

and the prosecutions service – several non-judicial organs – such as social services and the Child's Rights Commission – are involved in juvenile criminal proceedings. These actors are discussed below.

2.4.1. *Juvenile district council (jeugdparket)*

The public prosecution service only has the power to prosecute and, due to the discretionary principle, it may decide to drop (*sepot*) the case of a juvenile suspect at any point during the (criminal) proceedings.[159] On first instance the King's prosecutor can ask the juvenile judge to impose temporary measures. This does not result in an obligation to demand measures to be imposed during the actual court proceedings (*maatregelen ten gronde*).[160] The prosecution service's freedom of judgement is meant to serve the best interests of the child. When temporary (or provisional) measures have proven to be effective, it is not in the best interests of the child to apply further measures. In executing his tasks, the King's prosecutor is assisted by assistant prosecutors who are police officials.[161]

2.4.2. *Juvenile courts and juvenile judges*

Juvenile courts are composed of chambers within the courts of first instance (*gerecht in eerste aanleg*) wherein a single judge – a specialist in juvenile law – presides over the case.[162] As mentioned before, this judge decides on all matters and at all points of the ('criminal') proceedings in the case of a juvenile suspect. Thus, in the Court of Appeal (*hof van beroep)* the case is also presided over by a single judge, as opposed to normal criminal proceedings before the correctional court (of appeal) where cases are dealt with by chambers composed of more than one judge.[163] The Supreme Court (*Hof van Cassatie*) has ruled that, considering the difference between suspects, this does not constitute a breach of the principle of equality (*gelijkheidsbeginsel*).[164] Besides ruling in matters of appeal after a court sentence on first instance, the Court of Appeal also decides on appeals brought against provisional measures.[165]

Aside from presiding over cases in juvenile protection proceedings, the 2006 reform of the YPA has also led to the establishment of special courts for dealing with juvenile suspects who have been transferred to normal criminal

---

159 Vandromme 2004, p. 181.

160 Tulkens and Moreau 2000, p. 175.

161 Art. 48 and further CCP.

162 Art. 79 Judicial Code.

163 Legislation to change this is pending, but has been met with criticism. In the future the practice might change and be more in line with 'normal' criminal proceedings.

164 Cass. 29 May 2001, *AR* P10167F.

165 Cass. 27 November 2002, *AR* P.02.1423.F.

proceedings.[166] Both on first instance and on appeal these courts are composed of one regular judge – normally a judge specialised in correctional criminal law – and two specialist juvenile judges. On first instance these judges come from the specialist juvenile courts and on appeal they are magistrates who are specially trained in dealing with juvenile suspects.[167]

As a side note, after transferral for a severe crime such as murder, the juvenile can be tried by the Assize Court. This court is comprised of one presiding judge, two additional judges (*bijzitters*) and a jury of 12 peers. Two of the judges must have been awarded the specialisation of 'juvenile magistrate'.[168] This was the subject of reform in 2009, because in 2008 the Constitutional Court ruled that the Assize Court should, when ruling on matters involving juvenile suspects, be comprised of specialised magistrates.[169] Figure 1 below gives a schematic overview of the organisation of (juvenile) courts in Belgium.

Figure 1. Schematic overview of judicial organisation in Belgium

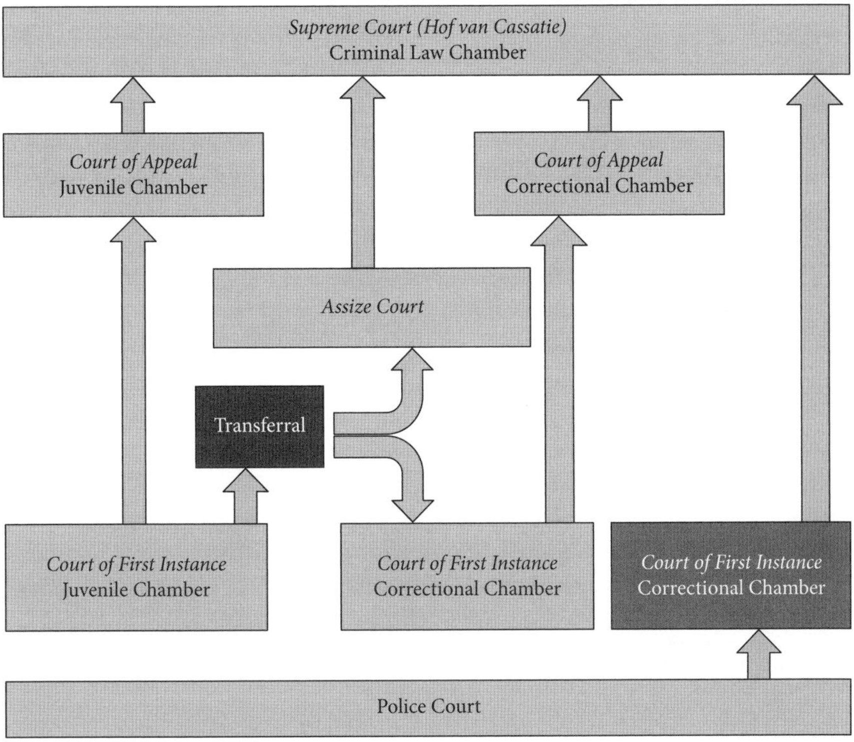

[166] See *supra* paragraph 2.2 (part I).
[167] Art. 78 Judicial Code.
[168] Art. 57*bis* para. 1 YPA and art. 119 Constitution.
[169] Constitutional Court 13 March 2008, no. 49/2008.

2.4.3. *Police forces*

The Belgian police force is divided into two main structures: the federal police and local police forces.[170] The former fall under the authority of both the Home Office Department and the Justice Department (*Federale Overheidsdienst Binnenlandse Zaken en Federale Overheidsdienst Justitie*) and are governed by the commissioner-general (*commissaris-generaal*). The federal police exercise their power throughout the entire Belgian territory. Local police forces are divided into 195 corps of which 50 cover one municipality and the remaining 145 cover more than one municipality.[171] These police forces are headed by a chief of police (*korpschef*) and some of these police forces have a special juvenile unit.[172]

2.4.4. *Specialist juvenile lawyers*

In Belgium the supervision and structure of lawyers is divided into two main bars – one for the Dutch-speaking Flemish region which covers 14 local bars, the Order of Flemish Bars[173] (*Orde van Vlaamse Balies*), and one bar for the French- and German-speaking regions, the Order of French and German Bars of Belgium (*Ordre Des Barreaux Francophones et Germanophone de Belgique*), which covers 13 local bars. The legal tasks of the bars are laid down in the Judicial Code. Belgium also has a union of specialist juvenile lawyers (*jeugdadvocaten*).[174] The juvenile lawyers' bar has provided specialist training for lawyers dealing with juveniles. These courses mostly involve both legal and practical training (roleplay) on dealing with juveniles in (criminal) proceedings. An example is the training provided by the University of Antwerp.[175] These courses are organised between lawyers without input and interaction with other actors in the field of juvenile justice. As pointed out by some scholars, training with different practitioner groups present simultaneously could lead to better training and application of juvenile justice in the long run.[176]

---

170 www.polfed-fedpol.be.

171 www.lokalepolitie.be/portal/nl/samenstelling.html.

172 Verhellen, Cappelaere and Vandekerckhove 1991, p. 52. For more information about training and specialisation of (local) police forces, see *infra* paragraph 1.3.1 (part II).

173 Since the Law of 4 July 2001 (*B.S.* 25 June 2001) the Order of Flemish bars is officially recognised and active since the framework note of 17 February 2002 (*KB* 17 January 2002).

174 www.jeugdadvocaat.be.

175 Dienst voor het Strafrechtelijk beleid, *Evaluatie Salduz-wet: Eerste tussentijdse rapport*, 1 February 2012.

176 Smets 2011, p. 221.

2.4.5. Bridging magistrates (verbindingsmagistraten)

With the enactment of the two laws in 2006[177] the role of the so-called 'bridging magistrate' was established, whose task it is to smooth out problems with respect to placement of juveniles in a juvenile detention facility. When pre-trial detention is deemed necessary after an act described as a crime, these magistrates will optimise placement when a shortage of places occurs.[178] The magistrate forms a bridge between the federal juvenile judge who decides on the measures to be imposed and the local facilities governed by the communities. The goal is to place the juvenile in a facility best equipped to fit the juvenile's needs. In practice – due to capacity issues – the decision will often be influenced by which facility has capacity instead of which facility can provide the best possible care and guidance.[179] Another task of the magistrates is to transfer youngsters who have reached the age of 18 years from a juvenile facility to a normal prison for adults.[180]

2.4.6. Social services

Social services perform several tasks throughout juvenile ('criminal') proceedings. When the juvenile judge is involved and a report on the juvenile's social context is needed in order to provide the judge with information on the most appropriate measures, social services will talk to the juvenile in order to draft this report. When talking to the juvenvile, they do not have the power to force him to cooperate.[181] Social services also provide the juvenile with guidance during the measure of supervision and they supervise and control execution of measures which have been imposed by the juvenile judge (*maatregelen ten gronde*).[182]

2.4.7. Child's Rights Commission

The Child's Rights Commission (*Kinderrechtencommissariaat*) was established in 1997 by decree of the Flemish parliament.[183] The commission is officially recognised as the spokesperson for children's rights before the Flemish parliament. The commission does not solely operate within criminal[184] or juvenile proceedings, but can nonetheless handle complaints

177 See *supra* paragraph 1.2 (part I).
178 De Smet 2006, p. 365.
179 De Smet 2006, p. 365.
180 Art. 606 CCP.
181 Smets 1996, p. 523.
182 Art. 6–21 Social Services Act 1991.
183 Child's Rights Commission decree 1997.
184 This refers to the situation where a juvenile has been transferred to normal criminal proceedings.

stemming from juvenile proceedings. The two main activities of the commission are managing a complaint line (*klachtenlijn*) and advising the Flemish parliament, the Flemish government, administrations and agencies and international governments.[185] A similar institution appears to be lacking for Wallonia.

2.5. MAIN PHASES OF THE JUVENILE 'CRIMINAL' PROCESS

The aforementioned overview introduced both *tracks* of dealing with a juvenile delinquent – under normal juvenile protection proceedings (YPA) and after transferral.[186] This section will be written in light of juvenile protection proceedings where a juvenile is suspected of committing a criminal offence. This has implications for the way in which the proceedings are structured and how the juvenile is dealt with. When the juvenile is suspected of having committed an act defined as a crime he cannot be held in pre-trial detention and he will not be punished in court. Instead (provisional) measures (see *supra* 2.3.) can be imposed, ordered by the public prosecution service and enforced by the juvenile judge.[187]

Within the Belgian criminal juvenile protection procedure there is a clear distinction between pre-trial proceedings (*vooronderzoek*) and proceedings during trial (*onderzoek ten gronde*). The former is further divided into an investigative stage (*opsporingsonderzoek*)[188] and a judicial investigation (*gerechtelijk onderzoek*).[189] The investigative stage is *supervised* by the King's prosecutor who, in cooperation with the police, is burdened with investigating crimes or, in the case of juvenile delinquency, acts defined as crimes. The judicial investigation is run by the investigative judge (*onderzoeksrechter*) and in juvenile proceedings he has to be specifically appointed to do so.[190] The *ratio legis* behind this is that juveniles require special treatment and the educational element of these proceedings should not be forgotten.[191] Figure 2 provides a schematic overview of juvenile 'criminal' proceedings.

185 www.kinderrechtencommissariaat.be.
186 Art. 57*bis* YPA.
187 Decoker and Vroman 2013, p. 62.
188 Art. 28*bis* para. 1 CCP.
189 Art. 55 CCP.
190 Art. 9 YPA.
191 Frencken 1971, p. 142.

Figure 2. An overview of stages of juvenile 'criminal' proceedings

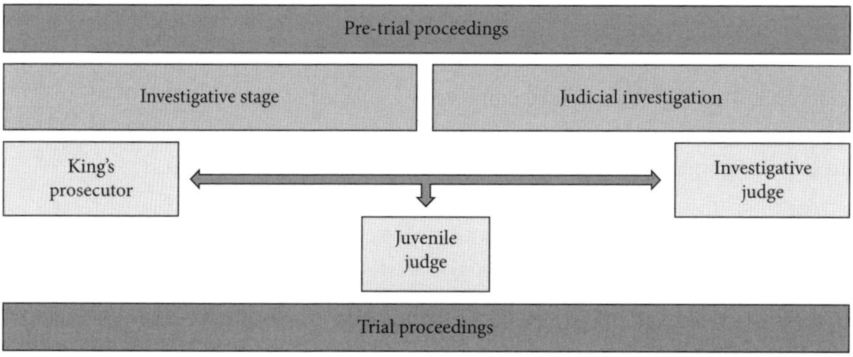

Normally, juvenile protection proceedings consist of the following main steps:

(a) Arrest by the police (*aanhouding*)[192]
(b) Interrogation (*verhoor*)
(c) Imposing provisional measures (*voorlopige maatregelen*)
(d) Summoning the juvenile to appear before the juvenile judge in court (*dagvaarding*)
(e) Court proceedings – possibility of imposing measures (*maatregelen ten gronde*)
(f) Execution of measures

The legal basis for arrest can be found in the law on pre-trial detention.[193] Police forces are only allowed to arrest a person when caught in the act (*betrapping op heterdaad*) or when they are ordered to do so by the King's prosecutor. The Salduz Act has made the provisions regarding interrogation in the Pre-trial Detention Act applicable to juveniles as well as adults.[194] This means that when a juvenile is arrested, his parents have to be informed. When a juvenile is transferred to criminal proceedings the provisions stemming from the Pre-trial Detention Act are fully applicable. This Act defines a time-limit of 24 hours for police detention – which also applies to juveniles being arrested under the YPA.[195] A similar time-limit is also documented in the Constitution.[196] The police will inform the prosecutor as soon as possible of the arrest. Only the prosecutor is empowered to order the arrest when a suspect is not *caught in the act*. The detention after arrest may last no longer more 24 hours starting from the moment a suspect is deprived of his liberty by public authorities.[197] An

192 Of course this is optional. A juvenile can also be invited to the station.
193 Law of 20 July 1990 (art. 1 and 2).
194 Berkmoes 2012, p. 120.
195 Cass. 20 December 2011, P.11.1981.N, *T.Strafr.* 2012, 450.
196 Art. 12 Belgian Constitution.
197 Art. 1 paras. 2 and 3 pre-trial detention Act.

interrogation can take place within the investigative phase when instructed by the prosecutor. On his instigation the police will interrogate the juvenile suspect and an official report (*proces-verbaal*) of the interrogation is drafted containing a reproduction of the interrogation, the start and end time, who attended, possible interruptions, rights that were conveyed[198] and other relevant circumstances.[199] The interrogation of juvenile suspects and applicable safeguards will be discussed in detail in part II of this chapter.

As mentioned before, the judge is empowered to impose provisional measures upon the juvenile during the judicial investigation. During this pre-trial phase the investigative (juvenile) judge can investigate the social situation of the juvenile suspect and is empowered to take all provisional measures needed in order to comprehend the juvenile.[200] Social services will be involved to draft a social-contextual report and a psychiatric expert will draft a medical-psychological report. When these investigations by the juvenile judge are completed, the case will be referred back to the public prosecution service (public prosecutor) who will then decide – within two months – whether or not to prosecute the juvenile, summoning him to appear in court before the juvenile judge.[201] During the juvenile court proceedings, the juvenile judge can impose measures which will thereafter be coordinated and monitored by the social services.[202] The juvenile judge thus has a far-reaching role in all stages of proceedings involving juveniles, something which is not seen as an infringement of the right to a fair trial by the ECtHR[203] or the Belgian Supreme Court.[204]

2.6. ALTERNATIVES TO IMPOSED MEASURES IN JUVENILE COURT

First and foremost it should be mentioned that the proceedings under the YPA are themselves in fact an alternative to criminal proceedings, because they are not formally classified as 'criminal' proceedings. Nonetheless, they can – and most probably will – be seen as having punitive elements by outsiders as well as by the juveniles involved. If official labels are taken out of the equation, the YPA proceedings can be considered to include 'criminal' elements such as police detention, and some alternatives to the above-mentioned measures[205] can be

198 Art. 47*bis* CCP.
199 Art. 47 para. 3 CCP.
200 Art. 50 YPA.
201 Art. 52*bis* YPA.
202 See *infra* paragraph 2.3 (part I).
203 ECtHR 24 August 1993, *Nortier v. the Netherlands*, no. 13924/88.
204 Cass. 15 June 1999, P.99.0841.N.
205 See *infra* paragraph 2.3 (part I).

seen as the alternatives to these 'criminal' proceedings. Research conducted by Vanneste in 2003 has however shown that only 19 per cent of the imposed measures were alternative sanctions and almost 50 per cent of the sentencing decisions in Belgium were of a custodial nature.[206]

2.6.1. *Disposal by the prosecutor*

After the judicial investigation has been closed, the juvenile judge refers the case back to the King's prosecutor who decides whether or not to prosecute the juvenile in all types of proceedings. Thus, this discretionary power can also result in the decision not to prosecute and simply dispose of the case. Police forces do not have this power of disposal under Belgian law, only the prosecution services. According to research, disposals occur in 70 per cent of all cases.[207] In practice the majority of these disposals are of a technical nature due to a lack of evidence or the fact that no suspect has been identified.[208]

2.6.2. *Restorative measures*

Besides some measures and alternatives to the 'sanctioning' under the YPA, some measures are also directed at restoring damages. Since the legislative reforms of 2006, the focal point in juvenile proceedings has been diverted from sanctioning measures towards the more restorative measures. This refers back to the subsidiarity principle as laid down in the new Act of 2006.[209] The three main categories of restorative measures under Belgian juvenile criminal proceedings are: mediation, group conferencing and the written project. Each of them will be briefly described below.

2.6.2.1. Mediation

The aim of mediation in juvenile cases is 'to provide an opportunity to the person who has committed an act defined as a crime, the people who exercise parental power over that person, the people who are his legal guardian as well as the victim to, through the help of an impartial mediator, collectively come to *restoration* of the relational and material consequences of that act'.[210] After the ruling by the Constitutional Court of 13 March 2008[211] the requirements for mediation (and group conferencing) are that the victim must have been identified and all participants must explicitly and without reservation agree to

---

206 Christiaens, Dumortier and Nuytiens 2011, p. 112.
207 Christiaens, Dumortier and Nuytiens 2011, p. 111.
208 Christiaens, Dumortier and Nuytiens 2011, p. 111.
209 Laws of 15 May and 13 June 2006.
210 Art. 37*bis* para. 2 YPA.
211 Constitutional Court 13 March 2008, no. 50/2008.

mediation. In its ruling the Constitutional Court abolished the requirement that the juvenile suspect was not allowed to deny the fact, because this was considered to be in conflict with the presumption of innocence.[212]

2.6.2.2. Group conferencing (herstelgericht groepsoverleg)

As a more specific form of mediation, group conferencing must be seen in the same light and with the same aim as mediation. The difference, according to the explanatory memorandum, is that group conferencing constitutes – more so than mediation – a communication process in which people from the social environments of both the juvenile suspect and the victim are involved.[213] The definition of the aim of group conferencing – laid down in art. 37*bis* para. 3 YPA – is not much different from that of mediation, but the focus seems to be more on a public confession. Restoration of material damage does not seem to be the foremost aim. Instead, the juvenile should own up to his mistakes to the victim and his social environment and strive to restore damaged relations.[214] The requirements for entering into group conferencing are the same as for mediation.

2.6.2.3. Written project

According to legal authors the so-called written project is 'surrounded by more questions than answers'.[215] It is a proposal that the juvenile makes to the juvenile judge.[216] The project can consist of an apology, following treatment for a maximum of 45 hours, participating in a mediation session or restoring damages. The same authors note that it is likely that the proposal will be drafted by the juvenile's lawyer, social services or even the juvenile court.[217] By others it is considered to be a form of self-inflicting impositions on the juveniles which otherwise would have been imposed by the juvenile court.[218]

2.7. SOME STATISTICS ON BELGIAN JUVENILE JUSTICE

In paragraph 2.3 and 2.6 (part I) several measures and alternative disposals which can be imposed by the juvenile judge have been discussed. In this paragraph some statistics in relation to these measures and out-of-court disposals will be presented.

212 Constitutional Court 13 March 2008, no. 50/2008.
213 Memorie van Toelichting, *Parl.St.* Kamer 2004–05, no. 1467/001, p. 5.
214 De Smet 2007, p. 273.
215 Christiaens, Dumortier and Nuytiens 2011, p. 109.
216 Christiaens, Dumortier and Nuytiens 2011, p. 109.
217 Christiaens, Dumortier and Nuytiens 2011, p. 109.
218 Christiaens and Dumortier 2006, p. 36.

2.7.1. *Communal service, learning projects, group conferencing and mediation*

The first set of data is based on an annual survey conducted by the *support group juvenile assistance (steunpunt jeugdhulp)*[219] which maps the restorative and constructional completions (*herstelrechtelijke en constructieve afhandelingen*). Based on a report from 2010, the figures for the four mentioned means of completion of cases (communal service, learning project, group conferencing and mediation) saw an increase between 2006 and 2010 for communal service and mediation and a decrease in learning projects. In the study, researchers combined the figures of projects from the 12 regions of Belgium. Figure 3 shows the statistics and figure 4 shows the distinction between boys and girls in 2010.

Figure 3. Statistics on completions of cases – 2006–2010[220]

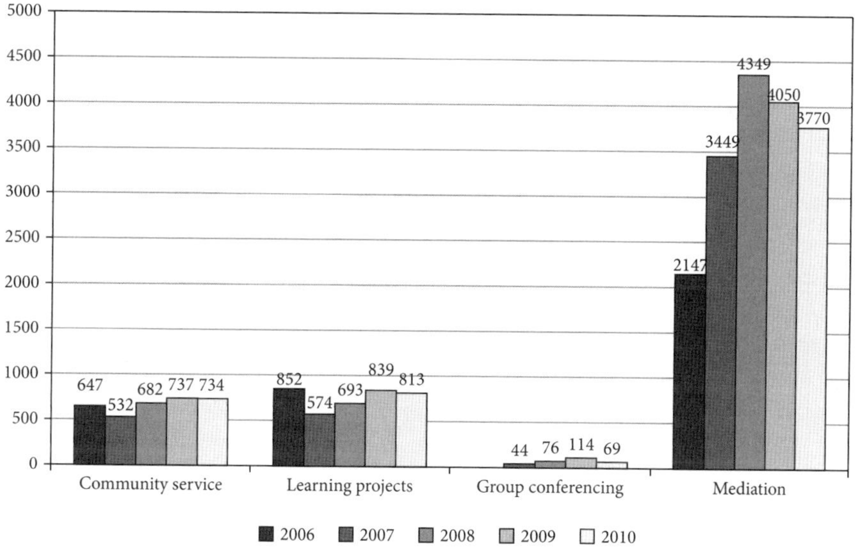

Figure 4. Closed cases – completions 2010: boys vs. girls[221]

	Community service		Learning projects		Group conferencing		Mediation		Total	
Boys	619	93.36%	633	92.27%	76	96.2%	2,816	87.53%	4,144	89.21%
Girls	44	6.64%	53	7.73%	3	3.8%	401	12.47%	501	10.79%
Total	663	100%	686	100%	79	100%	3,217	100%	4,645	100%

219 http://2013.steunpuntjeugdhulp.be/.
220 Balcaen 2010, p. 3–4.
221 Balcaen 2010, p. 5.

Figure 4 clearly shows that boys are over-represented amongst juvenile delinquents in Belgium. In the cases that were closed in 2010 by means of a restorative completion they represent roughly 90 per cent of all cases. In group conferencing in particular they represent a large proportion of 96 per cent.

A further distinction can be made between age categories of these juvenile offenders in cases completed by means of a restorative completion. It should be noted that all these figures date from 2010 and concern only the restorative completion of cases. Information on measures imposed by juvenile judges in court will be further discussed below. Figure 5 shows the distinction between ages as they are represented in the overall population of closed cases in 2010.

Figure 5. Age of juvenile suspects in 2010 – divided between the four forms of completion[222]

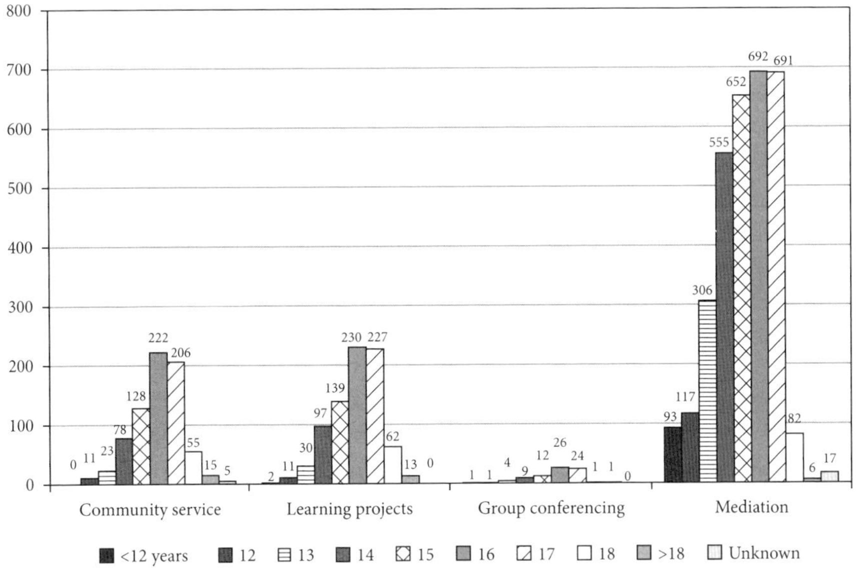

This diagram illustrates two interesting findings: that mediation is used as a form of completion far more often than the other three forms of completion[223] and that the age categories of 16 and 17 years are over-represented. As a form of completion, mediation is used about twice as often as the other three forms combined (3,211 vs. 1,633 times). Juveniles aged 16–17 were represented in 2,318 cases of a total of 4,844, which is 47.85 per cent of all cases.

222 Balcaen 2010, p. 6.

223 Figures 3 and 4 also show that mediation is the most used form of completion.

2.7.2. *Statistics on court imposed measures*

Figures from 2003 show that, if an act defined as a crime is proven, the juvenile judge opted for placement in an open institution in 26 per cent of the cases. This figure is based on a national average in Belgium, because figures from the juvenile court in Ghent in 2005 show that placement of the juvenile delinquent happened in roughly 50 per cent of all cases.[224] For those juvenile suspects placed for the first time, 24 per cent were placed in the Everberg federal institution and the remaining 76 per cent were transferred to closed community institutions.[225] For reprimands there is not much statistical data available. Research by Vanneste in 2001 has shown that supervision was imposed in 30 per cent of all cases in which a measure was imposed on juvenile suspects.[226]

2.7.3. *Statistics on juvenile crime*

Not many statistics on juvenile criminality in Belgium are available. A first attempt to map prosecution figures on a governmental level was done by Vanneste *et al.* in 2005 and published in 2007.[227] Therefore academics consider 2005 to be "reference year zero".[228] Vanneste's report on juvenile crime figures in 2005 shows that the average age of all registered juveniles was 12.5 years, but these represent both registration for delinquent behaviour (an act defined as a crime) and when a juvenile is suffering from a problematic upbringing. The average age of juveniles registered for delinquent behaviour was around 14 to 15 years.[229] In total 66,342 juvenile cases were reported at the prosecution office. Of these cases, a little over 55 per cent were registered on the basis of a criminal offence. Of all of those cases, 65 per cent represented juvenile boys. This overview changes when the boys and girls are further sub-divided between offences and problematic upbringings. Within the former boys are even more over-represented: 77 per cent boys versus 23 per cent girls. In non-delinquent situations there is hardly a noteworthy difference: 52 per cent boys versus 48 per cent girls.[230]

224 Van Welzenis 2003, p. 104.
225 Walgrave 2002, p. 232.
226 Vanneste 2001, p. 206.
227 Vanneste, Goedseels and Detry 2007.
228 Christiaens, Dumortier and Nuytiens 2011, p. 103.
229 Christiaens, Dumortier and Nuytiens 2011, p. 104.
230 Vanneste, Goedseels and Detry 2007, p. 45.

II. INTERROGATIONS

1. INTERROGATIONS OF JUVENILES IN THE PRE-TRIAL PHASE

In order to fully grasp the concept of juvenile interrogations and related issues in Belgium, some concepts and definitions need clarification. This will be dealt with in the first section of part II. Here, the focus will be on the interrogation of juveniles under the YPA. Where diverging practices exist and are relevant – for example when the juvenile suspect is transferred to normal criminal proceedings – this will be discussed separately. After the discussion of relevant concepts and definitions, an outline will be given of the procedural safeguards surrounding the interrogation of juvenile suspects and of the rules for conducting such interrogations. Part II will be rounded off with a discussion of several topics relevant to the interrogation of juvenile suspects: the results of the interrogation, possible remedies and sanctions for breaching relevant rules, the dissemination of the results of the interrogation, and the location of juvenile interrogations; finally some important comparisons will be made.

1.1. CONCEPT OF INTERROGATION: RELEVANT DEFINITIONS

When discussing the subject matter of interrogation of juvenile suspects in Belgium certain relevant definitions should be clarified. This mainly concerns, for the purposes of this report, the following concepts: (a) suspect, (b) interrogation and (c) juvenile. In addition to defining these concepts, an overview of the context in which these interrogations are situated is necessary. Therefore, notions such as (d) investigative stage and (e) criminal charge will also be discussed in this section.

1.1.1. The suspect

'The suspect is the person who is suspected of having committed a criminal offence'.[231] Under Belgian law the term suspect is often used to refer to the person against whom a criminal procedure is launched. However, several types of suspects should be distinguished, related to the stage of the criminal

[231] As mentioned before, juveniles do not commit 'criminal offences' but 'acts defined as a crime'. Belgian juvenile law does not provide for a separate definition of a juvenile suspect and thus the common definition of a suspect is applicable to juveniles as well. See also: Van den Wyngaert 2011, p. 571.

proceedings and the severity of the suspicion. Van den Wyngaert speaks of the *weight* of the suspicion in this respect.[232]

1.1.1.1. The suspect during pre-trial investigation (*vooronderzoek*)

During pre-trial investigation two terms are often used in Belgian criminal law: the suspect (*verdachte*) and the 'person charged with a suspicion' (*inverdenkinggestelde*). Belgian law does not explicitly define the term suspect in a separate provision, but the procedural rights of the suspect are tied to various weights of suspicion. The suspect is the person against whom a criminal investigation is directed which may take the form of a police investigation (*opsporingsonderzoek*) or a judicial investigation. The latter is the *suspect* against whom a formal charge (*aanklacht*) has been launched, the so-called *inverdenkingstelling,* ex art. 61*bis* CCP. This happens automatically when a judicial investigation has started against a known suspect or in the course of the investigation when the investigative judge has found serious indications of guilt.[233]

1.1.1.2. The suspect during court proceedings

During court proceedings the official terminology changes from the suspect to the defendant or the accused. When the accused or defendant is eventually convicted, the person is referred to as the convicted. The defendant refers to the suspect who is being tried in front of the police court or the correctional court.[234] A person tried before the Assize Court is also referred to as accused.[235] Proceedings before the Assize Court formally start with the formulation of the accusation[236] (*inbeschuldigingstelling*) and referral to the Assize Court by the chamber of accusation. This is a formal indictment after all the investigations are completed and all evidence is ready to be presented to the judge.[237] These definitions will only apply to juveniles when they are transferred to normal criminal proceedings. Because there is no official definition of the juvenile suspect, one can assume that similar definitions apply to juvenile suspects. Thus, when in the phase of pre-trial investigation – whether by the King's prosecutor or the juvenile judge – the juvenile will be a suspect and during the trial phase at the juvenile court he will be referred to as a defendant.

---

232 Van den Wyngaert 2011, p. 571.
233 Van den Wyngaert 2011, p. 571.
234 For the different courts, see *supra* paragraph 2.4.2 (part I).
235 Van den Wyngaert 2011, p. 572.
236 Van den Wyngaert 2011, p. 620 and further.
237 Van den Wyngaert 2011, p. 571–572.

1.1.2. *Criminal charge*

Belgian law does not officially formulate a definition of the criminal charge and when considering the charge as the moment at which a suspect is informed about the allegation, the most common and official means is the summons. To prosecute under Belgian law means 'bringing a case before the judge with the purpose of applying the criminal code' (*strafwet*), which means establishing a criminal process (*strafvordering*)[238] as defined by law.[239] In the case of adult suspects, summoning the suspect to appear in court is done through an official and direct summons (*dagvaarding*) or through an official report (*proces-verbaal*).[240] The latter is used only rarely and relates to the situation where a suspect is arrested (*aangehouden*) under arts. 1 and 2 of the Pre-trial Detention Act and where a criminal investigation has been conducted against him.[241] This summons should contain the alleged offence(s) and information about the date and time of the proceedings.[242] For juveniles the situation is different, because art. 216*quater* CCP is not applicable.

1.1.3. *Pre-trial investigation – investigative stage and judicial investigation*

The investigative stage in Belgium is defined as the *preliminary* investigation or pre-trial investigation (*vooronderzoek*) because it precedes the trial phase of criminal proceedings. The goal of this stage of criminal proceedings is to identify a possible (juvenile) suspect and to ascertain whether there are sufficient objections (*voldoende bezwaren*) against that suspect.[243] If sufficient objections exist the aim is to eventually summon the suspect before a court to come to a formal decision in the criminal case.[244] The investigative actions have a preliminary character and – in principle – thus need to be repeated during the trial phase and will then finally (*ten gronde*) be evaluated.[245] If the investigation does not result in the pinpointing of a suspect or the establishment of sufficient objection, the investigation is halted and the second stage – court proceedings – will not commence.[246] As mentioned paragraph 2.5 (part I) the investigation in the preliminary phase of criminal proceedings may take two forms: the

238 See: Van den Wyngaert 2011, p. 734.
239 Art. 28*quater* CCP.
240 Art. 216*quater* CCP.
241 Van den Wyngaert 2011, p. 742.
242 Art. 216*quater* CCP.
243 Van den Wyngaert 2011, p. 558.
244 Van den Wyngaert 2011, p. 558.
245 However, this is a theoretical depiction of the system and its requirements. As in many countries where investigations are documented in writing, the case file will serve as the basis for the court hearing.
246 De Smet 1997, p. 494.

investigative stage run by the King's prosecutor and the judicial investigation run by the investigative judge – in juvenile proceedings the juvenile judge.

1.1.3.1. The investigative stage

The investigative stage is that part of pre-trial investigations which is supervised by the King's prosecutor. With the help of his assistant officers (*hulpofficieren*), he runs these proceedings without the intervention of the investigative judge.As well as run by the King's prosecutor, the investigation at this stage is also closed by the King's prosecutor and it is he who decides on the subsequent steps and actions.[247] Following the investigation the prosecutor can decide to drop the case (*sepot*) or to summon the suspect to appear in court.[248] According to legal doctrine this form of pre-trial investigation is used in more than 90 per cent of criminal proceedings.[249]

1.1.3.2. The judicial investigation

The judicial investigation is run and supervised by the investigative judge and takes place at the instigation of the King's prosecutor.[250] In practice, the prosecutor will initiate such an investigation when it is necessary to apply means of coercion (*dwangmiddelen*) which need judicial authorisation, such as an arrest warrant, wire-tap, *et cetera*.[251] Since the enactment of the so-called Franchimont Act in 1998[252] the suspect has been offered more powers and tools to direct and steer the judicial investigation.[253]

1.1.3.3. Characteristics of pre-trial investigation

The three main characteristics of a pre-trial investigation in criminal proceedings are that it is: secret, non-contradictory (inquisitorial) and written.[254] This results in a predominantly inquisitorial character of pre-trial proceedings with some acquisitorial elements. These options of control for the suspect are only applicable during the judicial investigation, which only makes up 10 per cent of all criminal proceedings.[255] Since February 2013 it has become possible for the defence to request copies of the case file.[256] The nature of pre-

247 Van den Wyngaert 2011, p. 558.
248 Art. 216*quater* CCP.
249 Van den Wyngaert 2011, p. 559.
250 Art. 136 CCP.
251 Van den Wyngaert 2011, p. 559.
252 Law of 12 March 1998.
253 Van den Wyngaert 2011, p. 559.
254 Van de Wyngaert 2011 and Declercq 2003.
255 Van den Wyngaert 2011, p. 559.
256 Art. 21*bis* CCP.

trial investigation is first and foremost inquisitorial. The impact on the case is considered to be less severe because no judicial decisions are made and thus the suspect has, in principle, no right to refute the evidence or request certain investigations. The situation is different in judicial investigation; the suspect has a more far-reaching opportunity to ask the investigative judge to conduct specific investigative actions.[257]

The pre-trial criminal proceedings are secret for two reasons: on the one hand to prevent the investigation from being thwarted and on the other hand to avoid unnecessary publicity.[258] Only where the suspect is the direct object of the investigation will he be present and informed of the investigations conducted.[259] The other actions, which are documented in the case file, will – at this point in the proceedings – not be accessible to the suspect or his lawyer.[260] With the enactment of the Franchimont Act of 1998 a few adjustments to this inquisitorial nature were made, such as the possibility to ask for additional investigative measures.

The fact that the pre-trial phase of criminal proceedings has a written character means that all investigative actions need to be documented in an official report (*proces-verbaal*) and are added to the case file.[261] This case file will later serve as the basis for the trial proceedings. Belgian criminal law does not provide many rules on how to document and what needs to be documented in a *proces-verbaal*. *Ex officio* findings need to be documented in an official written report.[262] Besides this mandatory information which needs to be documented in the written report of the interrogation of a suspect[263] there is no formal legislation which stipulates what needs to be documented.[264] Some information, however, such as the right to remain silent, needs to be conveyed before the interrogation commences and needs to be formally recorded in the written report of the interrogation.[265]

1.1.4. Interrogation

What should be considered an interrogation is not clearly defined by Belgian law. According to legal authors there is no formal definition codified in legislation, something which the State Council (*Raad van State*) found necessary nonetheless in light of the new Salduz Act and the implications stemming

257 Art. 61*quinquies* CCP.
258 Van den Wyngaert 2011, p. 560.
259 Van den Wyngaert 2011, p. 560.
260 For more information about disclosure, see *infra* paragraph 2.5 (part II).
261 Van den Wyngaert 2011, p. 565.
262 Art. 53 CCP.
263 Art. 47*bis* CCP.
264 Bockstaele 2005, p. 403.
265 For more information, see *infra* paragraph 3 (part II).

therefrom for the right to legal assistance.[266] According to the explanatory memorandum of the Salduz Act, the Council envisaged the interrogation to be: 'a substantive interrogation related to an alleged offence with the aim of collecting evidence'.[267] Bockstaele uses a more encompassing definition which, according to him, is extracted from the Code of Criminal Law and Criminal Procedure: 'a police interrogation is a conversation between a police officer and a person who is directly or indirectly involved in events which interest the judicial authorities where questions are asked (*vraaggesprek*) and which is documented by means of an official written report with the aim of gathering all relevant information aimed at truth finding and all of this is done in a way as described by law'.[268]

Similar to the Dutch situation, there is no consistent use of the term 'interrogation' in Belgian legislation. Arts. 28*quinquies* para. 2 and 47*bis* CCP for instance use the terms *interrogation* (*verhoor*), *declaring* (*verklaren*) and *questioning* (*ondervragen*) without indicating why these terms are used in this manner. Bockstaele rightfully points out that, aside from formal legal definition and impact, these terms also have different substantive and etymological meanings. When these terms were codified in legislation members of parliament just assumed that 'the interrogation of a person is an interrogation of a person'.[269] Of course this is circular reasoning. For the purposes of this report the goal is not to come up with a definition of interrogation relevant for Belgian juvenile justice. The focus of this report will be on the interrogation which is formally documented in art. 47*bis* CCP. It can be conducted by the King's prosecutor, the investigative (juvenile) judge and the police and takes place during the (pre-trial) criminal investigation or (pre-trial) court investigation. It is used for evidence gathering and for that purpose it constitutes the most important form of pre-trial interrogation. Where other interrogations are relevant, for instance in the light of safeguards or best practice, this will be explicitly mentioned and discussed.

1.2. TYPES AND FUNCTIONS OF INTERROGATIONS

An important distinction should be made between whether or not the suspects' interrogation is mandatory. Here a clear distinction can be seen between the treatment of juvenile and adult suspects. The interrogation of an adult suspect by the investigative judge under the judicial proceedings is not a mandatory

266 Meese and Tersago 2012, p. 936.
267 Proposal for legislation, *Parl.St.* Senaat 2010–11, no.5–663/1, p. 13.
268 Bockstaele 2008, p. 22.
269 Bockstaele 2008, p. 19.

requirement laid down in the CCP.[270] Only when a warrant for detention (*aanhoudingsbevel*) is issued is there a formal legislative obligation placed on the investigative judge to hear the suspect.[271] When the sampling of cell material is ordered, there is an obligation to hear the person (suspect, witness or third party).[272] In both cases this hearing is conducted by the investigative judge in normal adult criminal proceedings or in criminal proceedings against juveniles after a transferral. Aside from these 'mandatory' hearings, the most common form of interrogations conducted in Belgian (criminal) proceedings are those conducted by the police or the King's prosecutor which are aimed at gathering evidence.[273]

On a supranational level, one can say that a child has a right to be heard in any judicial and administrative procedure when he is (in)directly affected by these proceedings.[274] This provision stemming from the CRC should allow for a minimum standard of enabling a juvenile to participate in his own (criminal) proceedings. This should be done in a manner compatible with national proceedings.[275] In Belgium this is done through the YPA in art. 52*ter*. This provision states that: 'The juvenile who has reached the age of 12 years should be heard in person by the juvenile judge before any measure is taken'.[276] A questionable implication of this procedure is that the Act speaks of juveniles over the age of 12 years while in fact juveniles under the age of 12 years can also be subjected to youth protection procedures. The CRC does not make this restriction and solely mentions a right of all juveniles to be heard in procedures which concern them. Besides the YPA, the juvenile can also claim his right under the Constitution which in art. 22*bis* states that: 'every child has the right to express his opinion in all instances that concern him; the age and ability to distinguish (*onderscheidingsvermogen*) must be taken into account'. This is more in line with the CRC, seeing as there is no threshold of age applicability. It is doubtful, however, whether the child's opinion will be taken into account, because taking into account the maturity of the juvenile might lead to that opinion being discarded.[277]

The King's prosecutor and police are empowered to interrogate juvenile suspects.[278] It is the police officer who shapes the interrogation – location,

270 Cass. 14 January 1998, *J.L.M.B.* 1999. It is however considered to be a deontological obligation of the investigative judge to do so: Declercq 2003, p. 213 and Cass. 6 January 1982, *R.W.* 1983–84, 2914.
271 Art. 16 para. 2 pre-trial detention Act.
272 Art. 90*undecies* CCP.
273 For the definition of these interrogations, see *supra* paragraph 1.2 (part II).
274 Art. 12 para. 2 CRC.
275 Art. 12 para. 2 CRC.
276 Art. 52*ter* YPA.
277 Put 2010, p. 56.
278 Van den Wyngaert 2011, p. 964.

time and breaks – and who decides on the questions to be asked. Factors that should be taken into account when asking questions are the education level, experience and demeanour of the suspect.[279] This police interrogation[280] – by far the most frequently used investigative method[281] – is considered to be the 'backbone' of the judicial case file.[282] The record of the police interrogation is one of the evidentiary materials which the juvenile judge will use to form an opinion about the allegedly committed act defined as a criminal offence by the juvenile and to come to the ascertainment of guilt, followed by the imposition of a measure. It is the task of the police to discover the truth, which is considered to be the guiding principle and ultimate goal in all tasks performed by the police.[283] The information gathered in the interrogation must be acquired in an honest, objective and legal manner.[284] Despite its important function, this form of interrogation is hardly governed by formal legislation. It is briefly mentioned in arts. 28*quinquies* para. 2 and 47*bis* CCP. For other regulations on the legal framing of interrogation techniques[285] and the documentation of the interrogation in an official report[286] one has to fall back on general principles of law and developments in case law.[287]

There is no formal legal rule in Belgian law stating when an interrogation should be conducted; in fact an interrogation can even take place several few years after a criminal offence is uncovered if it takes time for the suspect to be found.[288] Unlike the situation in for example the Netherlands, juvenile suspects in Belgium are not susceptible to pre-trial detention and thus a formal hearing by the investigative judge will in principle not take place. The juvenile should only be heard when the juvenile judge wants to impose provisional measures.[289] A suspect can however complain in court that his procedural rights have been breached when no interrogation was conducted, stripping him of the opportunity to exonerate himself by providing an alternative scenario or to provide police officials with contradictory evidence that proves his innocence. The Supreme Court has found that this can be done before the sentencing court

---

279 Van den Wyngaert 2011, p. 967.

280 For lack of a better term to define this interrogation and seen in light of the fact that it is mostly the police who conduct the interrogation, from now on this interrogation will be referred to as the 'police interrogation'.

281 Bockstaele 2008, p. 17.

282 Vermassen 1999, p. 87.

283 Van den Wyngaert 2006, p. 914 and further.

284 Bockstaele 2008, p. 17.

285 For more information on interrogation techniques, see *infra* paragraph 3 (part II).

286 For more information on the documentation in an official report, see *infra* paragraph 3 (part II).

287 Bockstaele 2008, p. 17.

288 Cass. 5 April 1996, *Arr.Cass.* 1996, no. 11.

289 See *supra* paragraph 2.3 (part I).

(*vonnisgerecht*), but it may be assumed that the same provision – a right to file a complaint – should hold for the juvenile suspect before the juvenile judge.[290]

1.3. AUTHORITIES EMPOWERED TO CONDUCT INTERROGATIONS OF JUVENILE SUSPECTS

The police interrogation is the investigative technique most commonly used by the police. Aside from police officials (and to a more limited extent the King's prosecutor), a juvenile suspect can also be heard by the juvenile judge in the judicial investigation stage of pre-trial 'criminal' proceedings. Under this section these three authorities will be further elaborated upon – specifically focussing upon the legislative bases for their empowerment to interrogate juvenile suspects and their respective training and specialisation requirements.

1.3.1. Police forces

Belgium has a long tradition of establishing specialist juvenile police units – dealing with both suspected offenders as well as possible victims. In the 1930s, with the growing understanding that juveniles need separate treatment under (criminal) law, awareness of the face that police forces needed to adapt also increased. Several attempts to establish specialist units were made. The first noteworthy attempt was made in 1935. The understanding was that 'fit preventive measures needed to be found in order to combat juvenile delinquency in Belgium'[291] and thus a ministerial commission was set up to examine these 'fit' measures, but without any actual results. Another attempt was made in 1946 at the initiative of magistrates working in juvenile justice. This proposal was not followed up until 1955 and it has taken many more years and proposals to formulate a true Belgian juvenile police. Research by Verhellen and others has shown that even in 1991 the so-called juvenile unit was not established throughout Belgium.[292] The development of specialist units therefore remains an ongoing project.

There is no formal legislative basis explaining the set of tasks which *should* be performed by specialist juvenile police units within a police force/region. For that matter there is also a very limited explanation of the police tasks in general. Art. 8 CCP only states that '[t]he police are burdened with investigating crimes, deviant acts and offences, collecting evidence and handing over perpetrators to the courts burdened with punishing these perpetrators'. The

290 Cass. 10 April 1979, *Pas.* 1979, I, 957.
291 Verhellen, Cappelaere and Vandekerckhove 1991, p. 115.
292 Verhellen, Cappelaere and Vandekerckhove 1991, p. 12.

tasks, obligations and functioning of the police are regulated in more detail in the Law on the functioning the police of 1992.[293] The specific juvenile tasks vary from region to region and a common phenomenon is that these regions also have other specialist units – for instance ones specialising in financial crime or drug offences – and when a juvenile falls within the remit of one of these units, that unit will handle the case and not the juvenile unit *per se*. The realisation and outline of these tasks are thus a responsibility of the respective police regions.

The tasks of the juvenile police must be placed within the framework of the YPA and this Act provides the police with some grounds for intervention in the case of juvenile delinquency. Because one of the founding principles of this Act is also to prevent juvenile delinquency and another is to educate juveniles, the police have the power to act pre-emptively in order to prevent acts defined as crimes committed by juveniles. Whenever such an act is uncovered, the police have a duty to report this and follow up on it.[294]

On the basis of art. 36 para. 4 YPA the juvenile court takes knowledge of the claims by the public prosecution service against those who are suspected of having committed an act defined as a crime. Seeing as the police are tasked with investigating these acts under the supervision of the King's prosecutor, they are also tasked with investigating juvenile crime. If a police zone is equipped with a specialist juvenile police unit, they are tasked with dealing with the juvenile case files, presenting a juvenile suspect to the juvenile judge and if necessary transporting the juvenile to an institution where he will be provisionally detained.[295] If the juvenile judge decides that the juvenile can remain in his normal living environment,[296] he can link some requirements to this– for instance that the juvenile is placed under house arrest or cannot contact certain persons – and he can then task the police with supervising these requirements. Another specific task of the juvenile police is to protect, care for and properly address juveniles who have been the victim of an offence. Aside from investigating crimes and caring for juvenile victims, the police have another important task, which is preventive supervision in the event of a *problematic upbringing situation* (*problematische opvoedingssituatie*). This is: '[a] situation wherein the physical integrity, the affectionate, moral, intellectual or social developmental chances of juveniles are endangered through special events, through relational conflicts or because of the circumstances in which they live'.[297] Only if this situation is complex and long-lasting and the juvenile's

293 Law of 5 August 1992.
294 Verhellen, Cappelaere and Vandekerckhove 1991, p. 52.
295 Van Welzenis and Massei 2002, p. 9–10.
296 Art. 37 para. 2*bis* YPA.
297 Art. 2 Decree 4 April 1990.

development at risk will this situation be labelled problematic.[298] In order to protect those juveniles who are endangered by such problematic upbringing, (specialist) police units will systematically check on the situation. This of course does not mean that the juvenile will never get worse or even cause the problematic situation at home. When that is the case and the juvenile is showing signs of deviant behaviour, the police may also intervene and perform pre-emptive supervision.[299]

Various police academies are burdened with education and training of police officials. In order to train these specialist juvenile police units, there are various modules within these training courses. Both the PLOT[300] *(Provincie Limburg opleiding en training)* for the Limburg region of Belgium and the OPAC[301] *(Oost-Vlaamse Politieacademie)* for East Flanders have modules on juvenile justice and how to deal with juveniles as victims and offenders. However, special legal provisions on how juvenile suspects should be interrogated do not exist on a national level. There is however a provision on interrogating juveniles as witnesses.[302]

1.3.2. The King's prosecutor

The King's prosecutor is part of the public prosecution service and the tasks and powers of this service are laid down in the Judicial Code of 1967 (arts. 137–156) which mostly defines the organisation of the public prosecution service. The King's prosecutor is empowered to interrogate juvenile suspects.[303] The legal formal foundation can be found in arts. 28*quinquies* para. 2 and 47*bis* CCP. Furthermore, the YPA also provides the public prosecution service – and thus the King's prosecutor – with the power to ask the juvenile judge to impose provisions and measures.[304] In Belgian legislation, however, no reference is made to the juvenile prosecutor.[305] To become a King's prosecutor or other magistrate with the juvenile prosecution council (*jeugdparket*), a simple appointment will suffice.[306] The fact that there is no formal documentation of the term 'juvenile prosecutor' does not mean that they do not exist and that there is no attention given to the specialist requirements for dealing with juveniles. The public prosecution service in Leuven for instance mentions the existence of a specific

298 D'Haese, 2008, p. 65.
299 Art. 13 para. 3 Decree 4 April 1990.
300 Http://plot.be/.
301 Www.opac.be/.
302 See *infra* paragraph 7.1 (part II).
303 Van den Wyngaert 2011, p. 964.
304 Art. 36 para. 4 YPA.
305 Such a reference cannot be found in, for example: the Judicial Code, the CCP, the CC, the YPA, the pre-trial detention Act or the Salduz Act.
306 Art. 8 YPA.

juvenile prosecution council and briefly specifies the tasks and structure of this specific section within the prosecution department.[307] The special council is made up of juvenile magistrates who have followed specialist training supported by a criminologist.[308] Special training can be provided through the Institution for Judicial Education (*Instituut voor Gerechtelijke Opleiding*). This institution is an independent federal organ which provides – designs and executes – integral education for magistrates and personnel of judicial organisations in order to contribute to quality justice.[309] One of the courses is a specialist training course for future juvenile magistrates. The goal of the course is to provide these future magistrates with an insight into the intricacies of dealing with juveniles and to train them in the legal aspects of juvenile justice – meaning legal training on the YPA and the inter-relationship between various laws and Acts regarding juveniles.

1.3.3. The juvenile judge

In contrast to the King's prosecutor, the YPA does formulate a requirement that the judge dealing with juvenile suspects needs to be a specialist judge. Art. 9 YPA states that: 'One or more judges appointed by the chair of the court of first instance are specially burdened with those cases which fall within the authority of the juvenile court'. The *ratio legis* of this requirement is that cases wherein the suspect is a juvenile require a special approach in which special caution should be enacted making sure the educative role of the juvenile judge is not breached.[310] This specialisation is especially interesting in light of the possibility to impose provisional measures on the juvenile ex art. 49 para. 2 YPA – taking into account that specialist considerations should be made.[311] Furthermore it is specified in the Judicial Code that, in order to fulfil the role of juvenile judge, the judge must have attended specialist training[312] which lasts six days.[313] After the training is completed, the juvenile judge will receive a certificate. This training is – when analysing the law carefully – not a mandatory requirement and there is a module on juvenile justice within the standard training that all judges have to attend,[314] but nonetheless it is recommended that *juvenile* judges also attend the specialist training.[315] Thus, the level of training may vary.

---

307 www.cass.be/parket/leuven/jeugd.html.

308 www.cass.be/parket/leuven/jeugd.html.

309 www.igo-ifj.be/nl/content/wie-zijn-wij.

310 Decoker and Vroman 2013, p. 64.

311 Decoker and Vroman 2013, p. 64.

312 For more information on this training, see *supra* paragraph 1.3 (part II) because this is the same training as is provided for the King's prosecutors.

313 Art. 259*sexies* para. 1 Judicial Code.

314 Decoker and Vroman 2013, p. 64.

315 Decoker and Vroman 2013, p. 64.

2. THE RULES FOR THE INTERROGATION OF JUVENILES: GENERAL SAFEGUARDS

The safeguards surrounding interrogations of juvenile suspects in Belgium are regulated in various sources of legislation, the most important being the Youth Protection Act (YPA), the Code of Criminal Procedure (CCP) and the newly implemented Salduz Act of 2011. The following section is devoted to the safeguards which surround the interrogation of juveniles.

2.1. THE RIGHT TO LEGAL ASSISTANCE

In general, the right to legal assistance is laid down in the Belgian constitution. The constitution does not exclude juveniles from this right and states that 'the right to social security, protection of health and social, medical and legal assistance'.[316] Aside from this national legislative basis for legal assistance, the right can also be derived from art. 6 of the ECHR.

The YPA also provides for a *generic* right to legal assistance for juvenile suspects. According to arts. 52*ter* and 54*bis* YPA, every juvenile who has to appear before a juvenile judge must be assisted by a lawyer.[317] The former states that every juvenile has a *right* to legal assistance when he is summoned to appear before the juvenile judge. The latter states that when the juvenile does not have a lawyer, a lawyer will be appointed to the juvenile *ex officio*. This right to (or obligation of) legal assistance is applicable regardless of the stage of proceedings.[318] In Strasbourg case law this mandatory legal assistance has not been deemed to be in breach of the ECHR and thus the obligation to be assisted in Belgium exists lawfully.[319] The YPA speaks of 'persons who have not yet reached the age of 18 years'. When a suspect was a juvenile at the time of committing the act defined as a crime, but has already reached the age of 18 years by the time he has to appear before the juvenile judge, this assistance is no longer mandatory.[320] Art. 52*ter* YPA does not make this distinction between above or below 18 years of age; thus an adult appearing before the juvenile judge does have the right to be assisted by a lawyer. During a judicial investigation, the juvenile suspect also has a right to legal assistance.[321] Only in exceptional circumstances and when absolutely necessary can the investigative judge (in the case of juvenile proceedings a judge

316 Art. 23 para. 2 Belgian Constitution.
317 Franchimont, Jacobs and Masset 2009, p. 878.
318 De Smet 2004, p. 1168.
319 Traest 2000, p. 6.
320 Art. 54*bis* YPA.
321 This also follows from Strasbourg case law ECtHR 15 October 2009, *Kuralic v. Croatia*, no. 50700/07.

who has had some special training) be involved in the pre-trial phase of the proceedings.[322] When the juvenile is then interrogated by the judge, the same rights surrounding legal assistance as during police interrogations apply.

2.1.1. Legal assistance during police interrogation

In Belgium legal assistance during police interrogation was for a long time dependant on the goodwill of the police.[323] The aforementioned European developments, however, resulted in the adoption of the Salduz Act in 2011.[324] This Act has brought about changes to both the CCP and the Pre-trial Detention Act.[325] With regard to persons being heard as a suspect – including juvenile suspects – a distinction is made between suspects being heard after deprivation of liberty and those who have attended the police station voluntarily. Similar to the Dutch situation, the rights of persons who are deprived of their liberty are more far-reaching than of those who have attended voluntarily. If a suspect is interrogated in relation to a criminal offence after voluntarily attending the police station, a right to legal assistance during the interrogation is not foreseen. The right to legal assistance is then restricted to the right to consult with a lawyer before the interrogation, which should be instigated by the suspect.[326] Currently, this is the legal situation, but this will have to change in the future, because it is in conflict with the Directive on the right of access to a lawyer in criminal proceedings.[327] Suspects who have attended the police station voluntarily should be informed of their right to consult a lawyer before the first interrogation commences.[328]

The right to legal assistance during police interrogation cannot be waived by the juvenile when arrested. This mandatory legal assistance is codified in the new art. 47*bis* para. 2 section 3 CCP. It states that only the adult suspect can waive his right to consultation before the first interrogation. However, the law does not distinguish between adult and juvenile suspects when they are invited to attend the police station for an interrogation – meaning that juvenile suspects are also assumed to have contacted a lawyer before the interrogation.[329] However, should the suspect explicitly ask for a consultation prior to the interrogation, then the

322 Art. 49 YPA.
323 Maes 2010, p. 76.
324 Salduz Act 2011.
325 Meese and Tersago 2012, p. 936.
326 Meese and Tersago 2012, p. 938.
327 Directive 2013/48/EU of 22 October 2013, OJ L294 on the right of access to a lawyer in criminal proceedings and in European arrest warrant proceedings, and on the right to have a third party informed of deprivation of liberty and to communicate with third persons and with consular authorities while deprived of liberty.
328 Art. 47*bis* para. 2 section 3 CCP.
329 Claeys and Decaigny 2014, p. 47–48.

police should help with arranging contact between the lawyerand the juvenile suspect.[330]

2.1.2. *Legal assistance for juvenile suspects deprived of liberty*

When a (juvenile) suspect is deprived of his liberty, he has a right to a confidential deliberation prior to the first interrogation *and* assistance during each interrogation until the interrogation by the investigative judge commences.[331] As mentioned before, juvenile suspects cannot be held in pre-trial detention, but some provisions – including arts. 1, 2, 3, 15 and 16 – of the Pre-trial Detention Act are applicable.[332] These articles govern the arrest (caught in the act) or arrest warrant (on the instigation of the King's prosecutor). These suspects 'enjoy the widest degree of protection'.[333] Their rights are formulated in arts. 2*bis*, 15*bis* and 16 of the Pre-trial Detention Act, which contain the right to consult a lawyer before the interrogation, the right to assistance during the interrogation, the right to consult again when new facts are uncovered and the right to have a trusted person (*vertrouwenspersoon*) informed of the arrest.[334] No waiver of these rights is possible for juvenile suspects. Art. 47*bis* para. 3 CCP states that suspects should be informed of these rights.

2.1.3. *Applicable period for legal assistance*

The Pre-trial Detention Act provides for a period of 24 hours during which the suspect can be deprived of his liberty in order to conduct police investigations.[335] This can be prolonged when a judicial investigation is conducted.[336] The right to legal assistance applies during this period. After being informed of the juvenile's police detention, the lawyer has two hours to attend the police station and upon arrival 30 minutes to consult with his client. In the Netherlands this means a total of two and a half hours, but according to some authors in Belgium this means 2 hours, because the 30-minute consultation should happen within these two hours.[337] The law is not exactly clear on this matter. Should the lawyer be unable to attend the police station within the allocated time, there is the option to have a confidential consultation via telephone with the duty lawyer

330 Art. 47*bis* para. 2 section 4 CCP.
331 Meese and Tersago 2012, p. 941.
332 Art. 2*bis* para. 1 sections 3 and 4 Pre-trial detention Act.
333 Art. 2*bis* para. 1 sections 3 and 4 Pre-trial detention Act.
334 Art. 2*bis* para. 1 sections 3 and 4 Pre-trial detention Act.
335 Art. 1 section 1 Pre-trial detention Act.
336 Art. 15*bis* Pre-trial detention Act.
337 Van Cauwenberghe 2011, p. 82–83.

service (*permanentiedienst*).[338] It remains to be seen whether 30 minutes for a consultation before a police interrogation is sufficient time to properly inform a suspect about the upcoming proceedings and whether this practice is not in breach of European standards.[339] The Belgian Constitutional Court ruled in February 2013 that more time should be provided when this is necessary for a fair trial.[340]

2.1.4. The lawyer's role during police interrogation

Assistance by a lawyer during police interrogation is aimed at guaranteeing the rights of the defence as far and as effectively as possible.[341] The goal of this assistance is to ensure that the right not to incriminate oneself and the right to remain silent are upheld. Furthermore the lawyer should see to it that the suspect is treated properly during the interrogation, that no coercive methods of interrogation are applied and that the suspect is informed of his rights as provided for in art. 47*bis* CCP.[342] Should the lawyer feel that these provisions are breached, he has the option to have his objections documented immediately in the written report of the interrogation.[343] The State Council (*Raad van State*) is of the opinion that the lawyer's role is sufficiently defined, especially since he can see to it that the interrogation is conducted lawfully overall (*regelmatig*).[344] This provides the lawyer with a wide range of possibilities to interject and exercise control over the interrogation. It remains to be seen what the lawyer's actual role during the interrogation is, and it will be up to courts to determine whether or not breaches of suspects' rights or lawyer's rights have occurred in this respect.[345] When the Salduz Act was proposed, the Minister of Justice wanted to make clear that the role of the lawyer during interrogation should not be seen as 'passive', because the lawyer is allowed to make remarks, for instance that the question asked is suggestive.[346] Thus the bottom line is that the lawyer should be able to actively ensure that the rights of his client are respected during the interrogation. When the proposal was submitted, restrictions were however envisaged, such as not engaging in discussions with the police officer, not talking to his client (or communicating in any other way), and not objecting to questions being posed.[347]

---

338 Art. 2*bis* para. 1 section 3 Pre-trial detention Act.
339 Spronken 2011, p. 123–135.
340 Constitutional Court 14 februari 2013, nr. 7/2013.
341 Meese and Tersago 2012, p. 946.
342 Art. 2*bis* para. 2 section 2 Pre-trial detention Act.
343 Art. 2*bis* para. 2 section 3 Pre-trial detention Act.
344 Advies Raad van State, 19 April 2011, *Parl. St.* Kamer 2010–11, no. 1279/002, p. 23.
345 Meese and Tersago 2012, p. 946.
346 Commissie voor de Justitie, *Parl. St.* Senaat 2010–2011, no. 5–663/4, p. 73.
347 Meese 2011, p. 90.

2.2. LEGAL AID

In Belgium legal aid is available in criminal proceedings.[348] The right to free legal assistance in criminal proceedings is laid down in the Pre-trial Detention Act. The rules governing legal assistance and legal aid are applicable to juveniles but legal assistance for them is always free of charge, regardless of their means.[349]

In order to handle the demand for duty lawyers in (juvenile) 'criminal' cases, a system of permanently available duty lawyers (*permanentie*) has been established. Lawyers who wish to assist juveniles during youth protection or criminal proceedings must be specialists. If they are, they will be enlisted on the duty scheme and they will rotate in shifts.[350] These shifts are managed by the supervising bars: the Order of Flemish Bars and the Order of French and German Bars of Belgium. When a juvenile is arrested or an order for an arrest is made, the public prosecution service – by virtue of the King's prosecutor – will inform the Solicitor General of a lawyer's bar (*stafhouder*), who will then appoint a lawyer to the case.[351] For the juvenile, the appointment of this lawyer is free of charge and no restrictions can be imposed.[352]

2.3. THE RIGHT TO REMAIN SILENT AND CAUTION

Stemming from European provisions, no suspect (adult or juvenile) is required to contribute to his own conviction. This principle – *nemo tenetur prodere se ipsum* – is read into art. 6 of the ECHR. Arts. 28*bis* para. 3 and 56 para. 1 CCP state that the *investigative* judge and the King's prosecutor should see to it that evidence is gathered in a proper fashion. This means, *inter alia*, without the use of pressure to extract a statement from the juvenile suspect.[353] More specifically, the revised art. 47*bis* para. 2 section 2 CCP states that a person should be informed of the fact that he has the right to remain silent. It does not say *the right to remain silent* in these exact words, but it does state that the person can *choose* to make a statement, answer the questions asked or remain silent.[354] The right to remain silent does not relieve the suspect of the obligation to reveal his identity.[355] The suspect should be notified of his right to remain silent should happen before

348 http://ec.europa.eu/civiljustice/legal_aid/legal_aid_bel_en.htm.

349 Art. 54*bis* YPA.

350 www.jeugdadvocaat.be.

351 Art. 54*bis* YPA.

352 De Smet 2010, p. 356.

353 Van den Wyngaert 2011, p. 713–714.

354 Meese and Tersago 2012, p. 938.

355 If the juvenile refuses to do so, he can be detained for 12 hours to uncover his identity: art. 34 para. 4 Police Function Act.

every interrogation. This means regardless of the seriousness of the offence[356] and also in the event that these offences do not result in a right to consult with a lawyer before interrogation or to legal assistance during interrogation.[357] Every suspect that is being interrogated should be given a leaflet (*letter of rights*)[358] in which his rights – including the right to remain silent – are explained.[359] This is not a juvenile-specific right, however.

2.4. PRESENCE OF APPROPRIATE ADULT

In Belgian law there is no formal legal provision regulating the attendance of an appropriate adult. The new Salduz Act has brought about a change in the CCP through for instance art. 2*bis* par. 3, which states that: 'Everyone who is deprived of his liberty [...] has the right to have a trusted person (*vertrouwenspersoon*) informed of his arrest by the interrogating officer or another person through use of the most suitable means of communication'. When the person deprived of his liberty is a juvenile, the parents have to be informed of detention.[360] The YPA does not formulate a right to have this trusted person attend the police interrogation. However, the fact that it is not a legal right does not exclude the fact that the police can allow a trusted person to attend the interrogation which – in practice – does happen in some cases.[361]

2.5. THE CASE FILE AND THE RIGHT TO DISCLOSURE

The foundation of a right to information during criminal proceedings – more specifically during the pre-trial phase – is laid down in international and European provisions. The CRC states in art. 40 para. 2 section b, II that: 'The [child] has a right to immediately be informed about the allegations'. The ECHR further states that no person can prepare a proper defence when he is not fully aware of the accusations against him. Art. 6 ECHR states that the suspect has the right 'to be informed promptly, in a language which he understands and in detail, of the nature and cause of the accusation against him'. The most far-reaching right to disclosure is applicable from the moment a suspect is summoned to appear before a judge. From that moment on the juvenile suspect and his lawyer have a right to full disclosure of the case file.[362] Art. 55 YPA

356 ECtHR 17 December 1996, *Saunders v. United Kingdom*, no. 19187/91.
357 Meese and Tersago 2012, p. 938.
358 Meese and Tersago 2012, p. 938.
359 Art. 47*bis* para. 4 CCP.
360 Art. 48*bis* YPA.
361 www.jongerengids.be/medium/meer-lezen/articleid/599/als-ik-als-minderjarige-een-misdrijf-pleeg-kan-de-politie-me-dan-zomaar-ondervragen.
362 Franchimont, Jacobs and Masset 2009, p. 588.

states that the parties to the proceedings and their lawyer should be informed through a summons that the case file will be deposited with the clerk of the court (*griffier*). The right to disclosure prior to the first interrogation and during the pre-trial investigation is more restricted. In literature it is stressed that the information which is provided to the juvenile before the interrogation should be understandable and the use of specialist vocabulary (*jargon*) should be avoided as much as possible.[363]

Belgian criminal procedure law does not include a generic provision of a right to disclosure before police interrogation. The only relevant provision is laid down in art. 47*bis* para. 1 CCP which states that all interrogations must commence with the conveying of the facts on which the person to be questioned shall be heard.[364] More specifically this entails a provisional (legal) description with an explanation of the connection between the suspect and the alleged offence or other compelling circumstances. This implies that no elaborate explanation of the offence has to be provided.[365] This does however not mean that this information can remain vague, because the same provision also prescribes that all elements of art. *47bis* CCP should be carefully set out in the written report of the interrogation.[366] It should be noted that the aforementioned provisions are not juvenile-specific and therefore no special consideration is given, for example, to the fact that information should be given in a child-friendly manner.

2.6. THE RIGHT TO INTERPRETATION

In Belgian legislation there is not much reference to the right to interpretation, let alone guidelines governing such a right for juveniles. Art. 47*bis* para. 1 section 5 CCP does state that: 'if the questioned person wishes to express himself in another language than that of the procedure a certified interpreter is called upon or his statements are documented in his language or he is asked to note down his statement himself. If an interrogation is conducted by means of an interpreter, his identity and capacity are mentioned'.[367]

Clearly, the provisions for effectuating assistance from an interpreter still need further development and can be considered to be under construction. The first issue that arises is the available number of interpreters. It has been noted in

---

363 De Smet 2010, p. 355.

364 The terms 'questioned' and 'heard' are used, because this also applies to witnesses who as a rule are not interrogated but heard.

365 Meese and Tersago 2012, p. 937.

366 Meese and Tersago 2012, p. 937.

367 Again this article shows the interchangeability of the terms interrogation and questioning in Belgian legislation.

the past that there is a lack of sufficient interpreters and with the enactment of the Salduz Act they are called upon more frequently than in the past, because interpretation has become a necessity during the lawyer-client consultation if the suspect speaks a foreign language.[368] The evaluation of the Salduz Act has shown that in 20 per cent of cases the suspect does not speak a language spoken in Belgium (Dutch, French and German) or English.[369] Another issue that arises is related to confidentiality. Often police forces use the same interpreter for the lawyer-client consultation before the interrogation as during the interrogation.[370] These interpreters often experience problems with their conscience, because they will be privy to information exchanged during the pre-interrogation consultation which can be portrayed differently during the actual interrogation.[371] The best solution to a problem like this might lie in providing two separate interpreters, something which should be laid down in a code of conduct for interpreters.[372] A final issue is that of the quality of interpreters. Each judicial sector works with its own list of certified interpreters and these people have been screened, but not according to similar standards. Furthermore, an annual language exam is foreseen but not mandatory in each of these sectors. The consequence is that the level of quality might vary and it is difficult to exercise proper control.[373] Belgium was obliged to implement the EU Directive on the right to interpretation and translation in criminal proceedings[374] before the end of October of 2013 but has not yet done so.

3. CARRYING OUT THE INTERROGATION

This section will be devoted to the actual carrying out of interrogations in Belgium. The focus will be on police interrogation, because this is the type of pre-trial interrogation that is most often conducted, focussing on evidence gathering and truth finding. Similar to the lack of a definition of 'interrogation' in formal legislation,[375] there is a lack of rules on how the interrogation should be conducted.[376] This lack of general rules and guidelines implies that juvenile-specific rules are also lacking. Ex art. *2bis* para. 2 section 2 of the Pre-trial Detention Act, the lawyer has to ensure that the right not to incriminate oneself and the right to remain silent are respected, that the suspect is not coerced

368 DSB, *Evaluatie Salduz-wet: Eerste tussentijdse rapport*, 1 February 2012, p. 42.
369 DSB, *Evaluatie Salduz-wet: Tweede tussentijds rapport*, 30 March 2012, p. 25.
370 DSB, *Evaluatie Salduz-wet: Eerste tussentijdse rapport*, 1 February 2012, p. 74.
371 Bottamedi 2012, p. 18.
372 Van Cauwenberghe 2011, p. 76.
373 www.tvcn.nl/nl/blog/2012/2/23/belgische-gerechtstolken-hebben-kwaliteitsnorm-nodig/.
374 Directive by the European Parliament and the Council on the right to interpretation and translation in criminal proceedings, 20 October 2010 (2010/64EU).
375 Meese and Tersago 2012, p. 936.
376 Meese and Tersago 2012, p. 946.

during the interrogation, and that the interrogation is conducted lawfully (*regelmatig*). This, in a nutshell, means that the suspect cannot be coerced into making a statement, his right to remain silent should be respected and the rules and laws should be upheld during interrogation. Problematic in this respect is defining 'coercion' or 'undue pressure'. There is no list which encompasses all forms of unlawful coercion and neither is there a definition codified in Belgian legislation.[377] The only form of unlawful/inadmissible coercion which can be identified with certainty is the use of physical force or violence, because this is in breach of art. 3 ECHR.[378] Causing bodily harm will result in a breach of the prohibition against torture.[379] The fact that police officers should refrain from the use of physical force and techniques aimed at breaking the resistance of a suspect is also laid down in the deontological code of the police and the Criminal Code. Arts. 417*bis* to 417*quinquies* CC codify these principles and art. 62 section 2 of the Police Code states that: 'no violence, molestation, or immoral acts may be used to extract information'.[380] Furthermore, interrogation techniques which in themselves do not breach the prohibition on the use of force may nevertheless be deemed improper and in breach of the right to a fair trial stemming from art. 6 ECHR.[381] There is no formal restriction on intensive and lengthy interrogations, but this can nonetheless result in a breach of the provision that evidence should be gathered in a proper and lawful manner.[382] Lying to a suspect is also not allowed, because it breaches the provision of loyal evidence gathering.[383] False promises also result in a breach of art. 6 ECHR.[384]

The above-mentioned rules are applicable to both juvenile suspects and adult suspects. There are no substantial rules on the questions to be posed to suspects – neither for adult nor juvenile suspects. Thus, when taking into account the provisions mentioned above, the content of the questions posed to juveniles can take any possible form. Another point of interest when it comes to the interrogation of juvenile suspects is the location. Belgium does not have rules which govern where a juvenile should be interrogated and normally this will be done at the police station in a similar setting as is provided for adult suspects.

The Belgian police use a standard form of interrogating – for suspects as well as witnesses – which is called the basic interrogation technique (*basisverhoortechniek*). It follows a set of prescribed phases wherein the first

377 Meese and Tersago 2012, p. 946.
378 Meese and Tersago 2012, p. 946.
379 ECtHR 28 July 1999, *Selmouni v. France*, no. 25803/94.
380 Kaderbesluit 10 May 2006.
381 And go in against the provision that evidence should be gathered fairly: art. 28*bis* para. 3 and 56 para. 1 CCP.
382 Bosly, Vandermeersch and Beernaert 2010, p. 1459.
383 Meese and Tersago 2012, p. 947.
384 Traest 1999, p. 137.

phase is meant to initiate contact between the interrogating officer and the suspect. After the introduction, the officer will pose a question that will elicit a response from the suspect, prompting him to tell a story of the events as he sees them (*vrij verhaal*). After the suspect has given his version of events, the interrogating officer(s) will examine the story and confront the suspect with evidence found and try to gather evidence and additional statements from the suspect. After that, the interrogation will be closed: the statement will be recapped, revised on the instigation of the suspect, or his client if necessary, and signed. The use of this interrogation strategy is used on juveniles as well as on adult suspects. Before the interrogation commences, the information from art. 47*bis* CCP should be provided to the suspect and the lawyer – if present – should see to it that this is done properly.

3.1. RECORDING INTERROGATIONS

The recording of interrogations through audio-visual media has long been accepted in Belgium. The Supreme Court acknowledged this in 1979.[385] In this ruling the Court decided that listening to tapes of an interrogation during the court proceedings does not infringe upon the principle that evidence should be presented verbally in court. This opened the door to a further practice of recording interrogations. The CCP was revised in 2000, adding arts. 92–101 CCP which deal with the audio-visual registration of 'interrogations' of juveniles. These situations are referred to as interrogations, but in fact only concern those situations in which juvenile victims or witnesses are *heard,* and not suspects.[386] These articles govern the recording of those hearings, but there is only one provision in the CCP that deals with the audio-visual recording of the interrogation of (juvenile) suspects.[387] According to this article, the interrogation of a suspect may be recorded.

There is thus no formal obligation codified in Belgian law to audio-visually record interrogations, neither for adult nor for juvenile suspects.[388] According to art. 112*ter* CCP, audio-visual recording is a possibility and may be ordered by the King's prosecutor. Even though this is not a mandatory requirement, the Committee of Procurators-General does recommend that interrogations are recorded in this way.[389] According to para. 1 of art. 112*ter* CCP, the King's prosecutor can order the recording of an interrogation undiminished of what is

385 Cass. 17 August 1979, *J.T.* 1980, p. 104–105.

386 For more information on the audio-visual registration of hearings of juvenile victims and witnesses, see *infra* paragraph 7.1 (part II).

387 Art. 112*ter* CCP.

388 Meese and Tersago 2012, p. 945.

389 Committee of Procurator-General *omzendbrief COL 8/2011*, 62.

defined in arts. 92–101 CCP. The suspect should be informed of this decision. In para. 2 of art. 112*ter* CCP it is stated that the interrogation will then be conducted by the King's prosecutor, the investigative judge or an appointed police officer. The latter will almost always be the case in practice. Art. 112*ter* CCP does not formulate a demand that the suspect accepts the audio-visual registration. This is different from the situation where a juvenile is heard as a witness. If this is the case, an approval to record is required.

3.2. THE WRITTEN REPORT FOLLOWING AN AUDIO-VISUALLY RECORDED INTERROGATION

Art. 112*ter* para. 3 states that: 'a written report of the interrogation is drafted after the interrogation in which, regardless of what is defined in art. 47*bis* CCP, the most important elements are described and if necessary the most relevant passages are copied'. A literal transcription of the interrogation is time consuming and should only be done if this is requested by the investigative judge, the King's prosecutor, the suspect or other parties to the proceedings.[390] Paragraphs 5 and 6 of art. 112*ter* CCP further state that the interrogation should be recorded in duplicate, should be deposited with the clerk of the court and should considered to be evidentiary materials. Finally, paragraph 7 states that the recording of the interrogation has the same evidentiary value as a witness statement.

3.3. TRANSCRIPTS OF THE INTERROGATION OF A JUVENILE SUSPECT

Art. 47*bis* CCP regulates the information that should be conveyed to a suspect – and thus also to the juvenile suspect – and some of these rights have been discussed above. Paragraph 1 states that all elements of which the suspect should be informed (that he has a right to remain silent, that his statements can be used as evidence in court, *et cetera*) 'should carefully be documented in the written report of the interrogation'. During the interrogation the suspect can use documents which he has in his possession and may *demand* that these documents are added to the written report of the interrogation or are deposited with the court's clerk.[391] The written report should furthermore document the times at which the interrogation started, if it was interrupted and when, when it recommenced after an interruption, and when it ended. It should carefully

[390] Art. 112*ter* para. 4 CCP.

[391] These can be documents, possibly already in possession or provided by the lawyer, which may prove the suspects' innocence: art. 47*bis* para. 1 section 2 CCP.

note the identity of the people who interrupted the interrogation as well as their time of arrival and departure and it should report any other special circumstances.[392] At the end of the interrogation the suspect should have the chance to read through his statement, have his statement read out to him and he should be asked if he has anything to add or change.[393] Furthermore, art. 47*bis* para. 2 section 3 CCP states that if the suspect is invited to the police station, this invitation should be added to the written report of the interrogation as well. Finally, art. 47*bis* para. 1 section 1 sub a CCP states that: 'a suspect can request that all questions asked and answers given are documented in the wordings used'. When a suspect does this, the written report should reflect this request. If this request is not made, the content of the documentation will vary from police officer to police officer.

After the interrogation, a suspect has the right to receive a copy of the written report of his interrogation free of charge and he should be informed of this right.[394] A copy is not automatically given to the suspect, but may be requested.[395] The right to request this copy exists both during the judicial investigation and during the investigative stage governed by the King's prosecutor.[396] When the interrogated suspect is a juvenile some other additional rules apply. When it is evident that the written report will be taken from him (by family members for instance) or if the juvenile cannot ensure the report is kept private (to safeguard the privacy of others), the decision to withhold the report from the juvenile may be made.[397] Art. 57 para. 2 section 4 CCP documents this possibility. The decision to withhold the written report of the interrogation from the juvenile should be added to the case file.[398] If this is the case, the juvenile still has the right to consult a copy of the written report of his interrogation, but only under the supervision of for instance his lawyer.[399] Art. 57 para. 2 section 5 CCP furthermore provides an option to provide the lawyer of the juvenile suspect with a copy of the written report of the interrogation of his client. This decision also needs documenting in the case file.[400] According to the case law of the ECtHR, providing only the lawyer with relevant information and case-related documents, instead of both the lawyer and the juvenile suspect, is not in conflict with art. 6 ECHR.[401]

---

392 Art. 47*bis* para. 1 section 3 CCP.
393 Art. 47*bis* para. 1 section 4 CCP.
394 Van den Wyngaert 2011, p. 966.
395 Van den Wyngaert 2011, p. 966.
396 Art. 57 para. 2 and 28*quinquies* para. 2 CCP.
397 Van den Wyngaert 2011, p. 967.
398 Decoker and Vroman 2013, p. 83.
399 Art. 57 para. 2 section 5 CCP.
400 Decoker and Vroman 2013, p. 83.
401 ECtHR 21 September 1993, *Kremzow v. Austria*, no. 12350/86.

4. RESULTS OF THE INTERROGATION

Whether and how pre-trial statements obtained during the interrogation of a juvenile suspect may eventually be used against him, will – unlike for example in the Netherlands – not depend on the age of the juvenile. As mentioned before, even juvenile suspects below the age of 12 may be prosecuted as long as it can be proven that they have an understanding of the wrongfulness of the actions and show they are aware of their guilt. The King's prosecutor may decide to summon these juvenile suspects before the juvenile judge as well. Belgian law does not formulate specific rules on the use of statements obtained from juveniles through police interrogations. Therefore, normal criminal procedure provisions apply. Belgian law does not provide an overview of evidentiary materials which can be used in criminal proceedings.[402] According to art. 154 CCP evidence can be supplied 'through either written reports or [other] reports (*verslagen*), or through witnesses in the absence of reports and written documents'. This is not a comprehensive enumeration and thus evidence can – in principle – be submitted by any means.[403] All investigative actions – and thus also the written reports of interrogations of juvenile suspects – are documented in written form and included in the case file. This file will serve as the basis for the (possible) conviction and sentence (in the case of juvenile proceedings: measures).[404] In the case of juvenile proceedings under the YPA, the report(s) drafted by the social services will be added to the case file as well and the juvenile judge will use these documents as the basis for his judgement.

5. REMEDIES AND SANCTIONS

One of the most striking and far-reaching effects of the Salduz Act is that evidence gathered from a juvenile suspect without respect for his Salduz rights cannot be used in evidence against him. In fact, it cannot even serve as supporting evidence.[405] However, this does not mean that this evidence cannot be used against a third person. The Supreme Court has ruled that this is not problematic.[406] Nonetheless, in the case law of the ECtHR, it is stressed that a conviction based solely or for the most part on evidence collected from a third party suspect in violation of his Salduz rights conflicts with the principles of a fair trial.[407]

---

402 Van den Wyngaert 2011, p. 1199.

403 Van den Wyngaert 2011, p. 1199.

404 Van den Wyngaert 2011, p. 1199.

405 Constitutional Court, 14 February 2013, no. 07/2013.

406 Cass. 5 September 2012, AR P.12.0418.F.

407 ECtHR 11 February 2014, *Siray vs. Turkey*, no. 29724/08.

6. DISSEMINATION OF INTERROGATIONS AND PROTECTION OF PRIVACY

In this section, three separate issues will be discussed: the right to privacy of juvenile (suspects) in general, the right to privacy in the context of ('criminal') proceedings and possible dissemination of results following these proceedings, and the fact that juvenile suspects should stand trial separately.

6.1. THE RIGHT TO PRIVACY FOR JUVENILE SUSPECTS

The right to privacy is a universal right for all persons – including adult and juvenile suspects – governed at various levels: international, European and national. A general provision for both adult and juvenile suspects stems from art. 8 ECHR. In addition to the ECHR, juveniles can also rely on international, juvenile-specific provisions stemming from the CRC.[408]

Under Belgian legislation, the right to privacy is codified in the Constitution. Art. 22 of the Belgian Constitution awards everyone 'the right to have his private life, family life respected aside from those instances restricted by requirements and specified by law'. Both the ECHR and the Belgian Constitution allow for exceptions to be made, but they must be subject to the principles of legality, proportionality and legitimacy and they must be in line with these principles.[409] The CRC does not make this exception; thus the presumption is that the right to privacy for juveniles cannot be restricted on the basis of this Convention.

6.2. TRIAL BEHIND CLOSED DOORS AND DISSEMINATION OF RESULTS OF JUVENILE PROCEEDINGS

Based on art. 6 of the ECHR, trials are public and this is considered to be a right of the suspect in order to guarantee a fair trial. Nonetheless, the article does allow for restrictions to be made to this right in 'the interest of morals, public order or national security in a democratic society, where the interests of juveniles or the protection of the private life of the parties so require, or to the extent strictly necessary in the opinion of the court in special circumstances where publicity would prejudice the interests of justice'. The Belgian Constitution also

408 Art. 16 states: 'No child shall be subjected to arbitrary or unlawful interference with his or her privacy, family, or correspondence, nor to unlawful attacks on his or her honour and reputation'. More specifically, art. 40 para. 2 section b VII CRC states that this right should be protected throughout all stages of judicial proceedings: 'To have his or her privacy fully respected at all stages of the proceedings'.

409 Van den Wyngaert 2011, p. 728–732.

foresees in a public hearing.[410] If this principle of publicity of the trial is not adhered to the sanction can be annulment of the ruling.[411] However, under the Belgian Constitution this principle of publicity of criminal proceedings can be restricted if it may cause harm to public morals or public order. The Constitution does however not provide this option in relation to the pronunciation of the actual verdict, thus the verdict will always be public.[412]

The fact that proceedings are – in principle – public in Belgium, means that the same applies to juvenile suspects; after all, art. 62 YPA states that the proceedings which need to be followed in the trial of a juvenile suspect are the same as normal proceedings applicable in the correctional criminal courts. Nonetheless, the juvenile judge can decide to let the juvenile's trial take place behind closed doors, taking into account the particularities of juvenile proceedings.[413] Furthermore, rule 14 para. 2 of the *Beijing Rules* states that: 'The proceedings shall be conducive to the best interests of the juvenile and shall be conducted in an atmosphere of understanding, which shall allow the juvenile to participate therein and to express herself or himself freely'. Taking into account this atmosphere wherein the juvenile suspect can freely express himself, the juvenile judge may decide to conduct the trial behind closed doors and allow only close relatives to attend the court hearing.[414]

Special attention must be given to art. 433*bis* CC which stipulates what is forbidden in relation to the reporting on juvenile proceedings and the dissemination of result stemming from those proceedings. This provision states that: 'publication and dissemination of the account of the debates before the juvenile court, the investigative judge and the chambers of the courts of appeal through books, press, film, radio or television or any other way is forbidden'. Furthermore, it reiterates that the actual verdict is public, although: 'only the motives and the founding section of the judicial decision, publically ruled on, are an exception to this rule'. It further states that the identity of the juvenile suspect cannot be made public. Breach of these provisions by the media may result in prison sentence ranging from two months to two years and a monetary fine of € 3003,000, or in one of the aforementioned punishments alone.[415]

Besides having to adhere to the Criminal Code, the Belgian media are also subject to their own deontological code, which also formulates the restriction

410 Art. 148 Belgian Constitution.
411 Tulkens and Moreau 2000, p. 850.
412 Franchimont, Jacobs and Masset 1996, p. 593.
413 Tulkens and Moreau 2000, p. 816.
414 Smets 1996, p. 598.
415 Art. 433*bis* CC. These fines are being multiplied by a certain value in order to counter diminishing of monetary value. At the moment this value is five and a half times the amount.

on disseminating the results of juvenile proceedings or the identity of juvenile suspects. In theory this is of course good practice, but in practice these rules are breached on a regular basis. The Child's Rights Commission has received countless reports of breaches of these provisions.[416] Nevertheless, a prison sentence or monetary fine is not often imposed. Instead, the dispute is to be resolved through mediation by the Ombudsman.[417]

6.3. A SEPARATE TRIAL FOR JUVENILES

Another way of safeguarding the privacy of juvenile suspects is by providing for a separate trial. This is in contrast to adult criminal proceedings where all co-suspects will be summoned to appear in court together. The YPA provides that juvenile co-suspects will appear before the juvenile judge separately.[418] The underlying notion of this rule is that a serene court procedure trumps other judicial considerations such as being prosecuted in public[419] and that it is not the committed offence, but rather the juvenile himself who should be the focal point of juvenile proceedings. In the case of criminal investigations regarding both adult and juvenile suspects, the separation of the cases (and the case files) will happen as soon as this separation will no longer cause harm to the pre-trial investigations.[420] If the juvenile suspect is transferred later (if his case is referred to adult criminal proceedings and the adult court) the cases can be merged again.[421]

7. RELEVANT COMPARISONS

In this section some important comparisons are made in relation to the treatment of juveniles in other proceedings and situations, such as the hearing of juvenile victims and witnesses of crimes or the questioning of the juvenile suspect by social services in order to inform the juvenile judge about the juvenile's living environment and the best measures to be imposed. A final comparison will be made between normal juvenile (protection) proceedings and the extradition of a juvenile suspect under the European Arrest Warrant (hereafter: EAW).

416 Vandekerckhove 2008, p. 351.
417 Voets 2008, p. 309.
418 Art. 48 para. 1 YPA.
419 De Smet 2010, p. 360.
420 Art. 48 para. 2 YPA.
421 Art. 48 para. 2 YPA.

7.1. RULES FOR HEARING JUVENILE WITNESSES AND VICTIMS

An entire section of the Belgian CCP is devoted to the *hearing* of juvenile witnesses and victims of crime.[422] Again, the CCP does not make a clear distinction between the use of the terms *interrogation* and *hearing*. The relevant chapter of the CCP contains arts. 91*bis* to 101 – the same provisions as art. 112*ter* CCP refers to.[423] Some significant differences become clear when examining these provisions. Unlike the interrogation of a juvenile *suspect*, the questioning of a juvenile *witness* is surrounded by more safeguards, such as the presence of an appropriate adult and the fact that the questioning should be conducted in a location specially designed for that purpose.

7.1.1. Persons attending the questioning

In principle, witnesses and victims do not have a right to be assisted during questioning under Belgian law.[424] For vulnerable witnesses and victims – including juveniles – this situation is different however. Belgian legislation shelters juvenile victims from the suspect and the contact between the two is restricted through the use of video-registration of the questioning of these juvenile victims.[425] On the basis of art. 91*bis* CCP juvenile victims of a certain category of offences[426] have a right to be assisted by an 'adult person of their choice' when they are questioned by judicial authorities. This adult person can be a *lawyer*, but also a *trusted person* (*vertrouwenspersoon*). The King's prosecutor or judge can, if the interests of the juvenile or interests of the investigation so require, refuse the presence of such a person. This refusal needs to be laid down in a decision stating the reasons for doing so (*een met redenen omklede beslissing*).[427] Aside from the possible presence of a trusted person, art. 94 CCP provides for a restrictive overview of who else can attend the questioning of a juvenile victim or witness: 'The persons who can be allowed to attend the recording are the interrogator, the person mentioned in art. 91*bis*, a member or members of the technical service and a psychiatrist- or psychologist-expert'.

7.1.2. Location and registration of the questioning

The 'interrogations' of juvenile victims and witnesses can be audio-visually recorded if the King's prosecutor orders that this should be done. This

422 Chapter VII*bis* CCP: 'Interrogation of juveniles who are the victim or witness of certain crimes'.
423 See *supra* paragraph 3 (part II).
424 Van den Wyngaert 2011, p. 980.
425 See also ECtHR 2 July 2002, *S.N. v. Sweden*, no. 34209/96 and De Smet 2010, p. 147–158.
426 For instance paedophile (sexual) crimes.
427 Art. 91*bis* CCP.

can be done in the case of severe offences or other severe and exceptional circumstances.[428] If the juvenile is under the age of 12, the King's prosecutor does not require permission to audio-visually record the questioning as art. 92 para. 1 CCP states that: 'if the juvenile is less than 12 years old, it is enough to inform them [about the recording]'. The same provision states that for juvenile witnesses and victims over the age of 12, permission to record is a requirement: 'with their permission'. These provisions both apply when the juvenile is the victim of a serious offence – as prescribed in art. 91*bis* CCP – or in other special circumstances.[429] The following articles – arts. 93–97 CCP – regulate the specifics of the interrogation, such as the fact that the juvenile can at any time ask for the questioning to be interrupted, that the questioning will be documented in an official written report and that the recording is done in duplicate and that no copies may be made of these original cassettes.[430]

Arts. 93 and 94 CCP specify who has to conduct the questioning of the juvenile victim or witness and where this should be done. According to art. 93 CCP this questioning is – depending on the phase of the proceedings – done by a magistrate of the public prosecution service, the investigative judge or a police officer. This means the questioning will be conducted by a judge or a police officer during the judicial investigation and by a police officer or (in rare cases) the King's prosecutor during the normal pre-trial investigation. Art. 94 CCP further states that: 'the recorded interrogation of the juvenile will take place in a room which is specially equipped for that purpose'. The law does not however state what these special modifications to support the questioning of this group of vulnerable victims and witnesses should be. One can assume that it needs proper recording equipment and possibly a reassuring atmosphere, but the CCP does not mention this. The recordings of the questioning can be used by the investigative or court judges, eliminating the need for the juvenile to appear in person in court and thus contributing to the protection of this category of vulnerable juvenile victims and witnesses.[431] Should the (investigative) judge nonetheless feel the need to hear the juvenile 'in person'[432] then he can order his appearance for personal questioning.[433]

---

428 Arts. 91*bis* and 92 CCP.

429 Art. 92 para. 2 CCP.

430 Claeys and Cools 2001, p. 533–564.

431 Van den Wyngaert 2011, p. 980.

432 This face-to-face questioning can also be done through the use of a video-conference ex-art. 112 to 112*ter* CCP for the pre-trial investigation and arts. 158*bis* to 158*quater* (for court proceedings in first instance) and arts. 317*quater* to 317*quinquies* (appeal) CCP during court proceedings.

433 Art. 100 CCP.

7.2. THE HEARING OF A JUVENILE SUSPECT BY SOCIAL SERVICES

As mentioned above,[434] social services perform an important task throughout juvenile proceedings: they inform the juvenile judge about the juvenile's environment and suitable measures and supervise the (provisional) measures imposed.[435] In order to report to the juvenile judge, a social worker will have to talk to the juvenile. This form of hearing the juvenile suspect is not really governed in formal legislation. What is certain though is that the service – and thus also an appointed social worker – does not have the power to force cooperation in drafting the report.[436]

Social services envisage their role as one of providing support to juveniles in need of such support, either because they are under investigation for an act defined as a crime or because they live in a problematic situation.[437] In an elaborate folder – available on the website of the social services for juveniles (*jongerenwelzijn*) – the role of social services during juvenile proceedings is explained. On page 13 the folder reads: 'the juvenile judge investigates your situation and gives social services the task to further look into your situation and to inform him about your future'.[438] An entire section of the folder – section 4 – is devoted to the role of the special counsel (*consulent*) of the social services. It informs the juvenile that it is the counsel's task to perform a judicial investigation into the juvenile's societal environment and that, in order to draft a report for the juvenile judge, the counsel will talk to the juvenile and his parents, but it does not state whether or not the juvenile has to cooperate, whether he has a right to remain silent during these talks, or what can happen with possible incriminating statements that the juvenile makes to this social services counsel.[439]

7.3. EUROPEAN ARREST WARRANT PROCEEDINGS

There are no divergent rules on interrogating juveniles in the case of EAW proceedings. Due to Belgium's intricate hybrid system of juvenile protection under the YPA and common criminal (procedure) law it is not immediately clear in which kind of cases the juvenile can be expedited in the first place. The

434 See *supra* paragraph 2.4.6 (part I).
435 Arts. 6–21 Social Services Act 1991.
436 Smets 1996, p. 523.
437 https://wvg.vlaanderen.be/jongerenwelzijn/over-ons/.
438 Folder of the juvenile social services Flanders, p. 13 (download: https://wvg.vlaanderen.be/jongerenwelzijn/assets/docs/publicaties/jongerenbrochures/jeugdrechtbank/jij_en_de_jrb_nl.pdf).
439 Folder of the juvenile social services Flanders, p. 17–20.

underlying core principle of the EAW is 'mutual recognition' and if the transfer of a Belgian juvenile national is requested, the consideration must be made whether under Belgian law the juvenile suspect would be held responsible for his (criminal) actions. If the answer to this consideration is negative, the warrant should be refused.[440] According to the EAW Act of 2003, the age of criminal responsibility is a mandatory ground for refusal (if this age has not yet been reached).[441]

The minimum age for criminal responsibility in this respect is 16 years, because under Belgian law these juveniles are not considered to be responsible for their action and are dealt with through youth protection and the YPA instead of criminal law. They cannot be subjected to criminal proceedings, not even by means of a transferral to normal criminal proceedings. This situation remains unchanged, even if extradition would be possible under the legislation of the requesting State.[442] It becomes more difficult to establish boundaries for applying the EAW to juvenile suspects aged between 16 and 18 years. First, it should be mentioned that – aside from the figure of transferral of the juvenile suspect to normal criminal proceedings – the age of criminal liability in Belgium is 18 years. Some legal authors are however of the opinion that, if the crime for which extradition is requested falls within the scope of art. 57*bis* YPA[443] the juvenile aged between 16 and 18 years can be extradited.[444] The Supreme Court, however, does not share this vision and in a decision of 2013 it ruled that – even though the provisions of art. 57*bis* YPA could be applied, this has not been the procedure in the requesting state (*in casu*: Romania) – there was no reason to examine whether art. 57*bis* YPA is applicable under EAW proceedings.[445] This seems contradictory to earlier rulings by the Supreme Court in which the extradition of a juvenile aged 16 years was accepted, because he could be transferred to adult court.[446] The requesting state *in casu* was Israel and thus it seems that extradition is possible when the juvenile is aged between 16 and 18 years and the requesting country is a non-European Union state.[447]

Finally, the same seems to apply to juveniles who have committed a traffic offence and are aged between 16 and 18 years, even though they will be automatically transferred to adult criminal proceedings. According to legal doctrine[448] and the Belgian government,[449] these juveniles should be susceptible to extradition, but in

440 Decoker and Vroman 2013, p. 89.
441 Act of 2003, *B.S.* 22 December 2003.
442 Brouwers 2007, p. 3.
443 Art. 57*bis* YPA contain the grounds for transferal.
444 Decoker and Vroman 2013, p. 90.
445 Cass. 6 February 2013, no. P.13.01/2F/2.
446 Cass. 23 August 2006, no. P.06.1119.N.
447 Decoker and Vroman 2013, p. 91.
448 Decoker and Vroman 2013, p. 90.
449 Ministerial circular letter, 8 August 2005, EAW, *B.S.* 31 August 2005.

applying the aforementioned, the conclusion must be that for these offences it can also only be done if the requesting state is not a member of the European Union.

III. CONCLUSIONS

The Belgian juvenile justice system used to be solely characterised as a protection model wherein the juvenile delinquent needed protection and rehabilitation instead of punishment. At present, Belgian juvenile justice represents an ambiguity where on the one hand juveniles are punished and on the other hand protection is the aim. However, as in many European juvenile justice systems, a tendency towards a more punitive system has been visible over the last few years. This movement towards a more punitive system is represented by the fact that although the YPA of 1965 with its welfare and protection ideologies still forms the basis for the current juvenile justice system, several punitive options have been added. The most striking change to the system (realised in 1965) is the possibility of transferral. When a juvenile is suspected of an act defined as a crime, there is the possibility to transfer this juvenile to normal criminal proceedings. This possibility was created as a response to a growing feeling of societal insecurity and a belief that juveniles had become more criminal. Thus, the current Belgian system of juvenile justice is a hybrid consisting of both protection under the YPA and punishment under normal criminal proceedings when the act committed by a juvenile requires such a response.

Additionally, the Belgian juvenile justice system has some very unique elements such as the division between the investigative stage and the phase of judicial investigation. In YPA proceedings, an investigative judge will mostly not be involved. This has consequences for the defence, because there is no formal procedure to ask for additional investigations carried out by the judge. A judicial investigation can only commence when a juvenile suspect is transferred to criminal proceedings.

The federal state of Belgium has undergone a lot of state reforms: at present, the sixth reform is still underway, wherein powers are being shifted from the central federal government to community rule. As a result of these reforms, the juvenile justice system has been subject to various changes as well. For example, as a result of the *Salduz* ruling of the ECtHR, the right to legal assistance during police interrogation has been introduced and codified under Belgian law. In the Salduz Act the special vulnerability of juveniles is emphasised and because of this vulnerability juveniles cannot waive their Salduz rights. This means that legal assistance during interrogation is mandatory for juveniles,[450] which is

450 Art. 47*bis* para. 2 section 3 CCP.

a very important aspect of juvenile protection. As for the sixth state reform, it will be interesting to see what the actual impact will be of handing over juvenile proceedings to the power and responsibility of the communities.

Belgian law does not provide for a definition of the concept of 'interrogation' but rules surrounding the juvenile suspects' interrogation are nonetheless established. For the purposes of this country report, interrogation conducted by the police with the aim of gathering evidence has been chosen as the focal point because of its great impact on the outcome of proceedings. As mentioned before, legal assistance remains mandatory for juvenile suspects during such an interrogation, unless they are invited to attend the police station. Legal assistance is free of charge. The fact that legal assistance is mandatory and free of charge is – from the perspective of procedural rights protection – one of the 'stronger' features of Belgian juvenile justice. Another strong feature is the right to be assisted by an appropriate adult, often a relative, for support. This assistance is not foreseen as including assistance during the interrogation, but it nonetheless happens in practice. In contrast, some of the 'weaker' features of the interrogation of juveniles are that audio-visual recording is not mandatory and that there are no specific rules on the actual conduct (content, duration, timing, posing of questions, *et cetera*) of the interrogation. Furthermore, the assumption that an juvenile has consulted a lawyer may lead to the acceptance of a possible non-voluntary waiver of the right to legal assistance.[451] These weaker features may be adjusted in the future, strengthening the legal position and safeguards for juveniles under the aforementioned sixth state reform.

BIBLIOGRAPHY

Advice Committee Procurator-General 2011
Committee of Procurator-General, appendix to the *omzendbrief COL 8/2011*, 23 November 2011

Advice State Council 2010
Advies Raad van State, 19 April 2011, *Parl.St.* Kamer 2010–11, no. 1279/002

Balcaen 2010
L. Balcaen, *Cijfernota HCA 2010*, 30 november 2011 (*www.steunpuntjeugdhulp.be*)

Berkmoes 2012
H. Berkmoes, 'Verhoor: Regelgeving – Consultatie en bijstand door een advocaat – Proces-verbaal – Rechten arrestanten (Salduz-wet)', *Postal Memorialis*, 2012, 1 June 2012

Bockstaele 2005
M. Bockstaele, *Processen-verbaal*, Antwerp: Maklu, 2005

451 Claeys and Decaigny 2014, p. 47–48.

Bockstaele 2008
M. Bockstaele, *Handboek verhoren 1*, Antwerp/Apeldoorn: Maklu, 2008

Bosly and Vandermeersch 2003
H.D. Bosly and D. Vandermeersch, *Droit de la procedure pénale*, Brussels: La Charte, 2003

Bosly, Vandermeersch and Beernaert 2010
H.D. Bosly, D. Vandermeersch and M. Beernaert, *Droit de la procedure pénale*, Bruges: Die Keure, 2010

Bottamedi 2012
C. Bottamedi, 'De lokale politie en de Salduz-wet. De gevolgen van het Salduz-arrest voor politie, justitie en advocatuur', *Politie J.*, 2012, 1, p. 18–19

Brouwers 2007
B. Brouwers, 'Jeugdsanctierecht in Europa: is uithandengeving een evidentie?', *Jura Falconis*, 2007–08, 1, p. 3–37

Cartuyvels 2000
Y. Cartuyvels, 'Jeugdrecht in België: wat is er veranderd?', *Orde dag*, 2000, 11, p. 7–13

Cartuyvels 2001
Y. Cartuyvels, 'De grote etappes in het Belgische jeugdrecht: continuïteit, circulariteit of breuk?', *Tijdschrift voor Jeugd en Kinderrechten* 2001, 4, p. 132–157

Christiaens 1999
J. Christiaens, 'A history of Belgium's Child Protection Act of 1912: The redefinition of the juvenile offender and his punishment', *European Journal of Crime, Criminal Law and Criminal Justice*, 1999, 7, p. 5–21

Christiaens and Dumortier 2006
J. Christiaens and E. Dumortier, 'De aanpak van jeugddelinquenten in tijden van onveiligheid', *Orde dag* 2006, 36, p. 7–13

Christiaens and Nuytiens 2009
J. Christiaens and A. Nuytiens, 'Transfer of juvenile offenders to adult courts in Belgium: Critical reflections on the reform of a moderate practice', *Youth justice*, 2009, p. 131–142

Christiaens, Dumortier and Nuytiens 2011
J. Christiaens, E. Dumortier and A. Nuytiens, 'Belgium', in: F. Dünkel, J. Grzywa, P. Horsfield and I. Pruin, *Juvenile Justice Systems in Europe – Current Situation and Reform Developments*, Vol 1 (2nd revised edition), Mönchengladbach: Forum Verlag Godesberg, 2011, p. 99–129

Claeys and Cools 2001
L. Claeys and B. Cools, Audiovisueel verhoor van kinderen, in: G. Vermeulen (ed.), *Strafrechtelijke bescherming van minderjarigen*, Antwerp: Maklu, 2001, p. 31–48

Claeys and Decaigny 2014
C. Claeys and T. Decaigny, 'Consultatie en bijstand bij het politieverhoor van minderjarige verdachten', in: *Een leidraad voor het politioneel verhoor van minderjarigen in het kader van de Salduz-wet. Verslagboek studiemiddag, Tijdschrift voor Jeugd en Kinderrechten*, 2014, p. 37–49

Commission for justice 2010
Commissie voor de Justitie, *Parl.St.* Senaat 2010–2011, nr. 5–663/4

De Smet 1997
B. de Smet, *De hervorming van het strafrechtelijk vooronderzoek in België*, Antwerp: Intersentia, 1997

De Smet 2004
B. De Smet, 'Verschillen tussen straf(proces)recht en jeugdbeschermingsrecht', *Rechtskundig Weekblad,* 2004–2005, p. 1161–1172

De Smet 2005
B. De Smet, 'Het wetsontwerp-Onkelinx van 14 juli 2005. Kleine stappen in de richting van jeugdsanctierecht', *Rechtskundig Weekblad,* 2005–2006, 11, p. 414–418

De Smet 2006
B. De Smet, 'De strafprocedure voor minderjarigen na de wetten van 15 mei 2006 en 13 juni 2006: Jeugdbeschermingsrecht met een vleugje jeugdsanctierecht', *Rechtskundig Weekblad,* 2006–07, p. 342–368

De Smet 2008
B. De Smet, 'Het nieuwe jeugdrecht gewikt en gewogen door het Grondwettelijke Hof', *Rechtskundig Weekblad,* 2008–2009, p. 130–141

De Smet 2010
B. De Smet, *Jeugdbeschermingsrecht in hoofdlijnen,* Antwerp: Intersentia, 2010

De Valkeneer 2005
C. De Valkeneer, *Manuel de l'enquête pénale*, Brussels: Larcier, 2005

Declercq 2003
R. Declercq, *Beginselen van Strafrechtspleging*, Mechelen: Kluwer, 2003

Decock 2004
G. Decock, 'Bescherming à la française: reflecties op de kadernota Onkelinx', *Tijdschrift voor Jeugd en Kinderrechten,* 2004, 2, p. 66–71

Decock 2012
G. Decock, 'Beschermen, straffen, herstellen. Twintig jaar nadenken over het sanctioneren van jongeren', in: G. Decock and J. Put (eds.), *Jeugdsanctierecht gewikt en gewogen. Toets van wetgeving en praktijk aan de principes van het jeugdsanctierecht*, Brussels: Larcier, 2012, p. 1–7

Decoker and Vroman 2013
J. Decoker and F. Vroman, Het gerechtelijk onderzoek met minderjarige verdachten: het mijnenveld ontruimd, *Tijdschrift voor Strafrecht,* 2013, afl. 2, p. 62–103

Defrancq and Decock 2009
R. Defrancq and G. Decock, 'Het recht op bijstand van een advocaat voor minderjarigen vanaf het eerste politieverhoor', *Tijdschrift voor Jeugd en Kinderrechten,* 2009, 3, p. 254–257

D'Haese 2008
W. D'Haese, *Politionele jeugdzorg*, Antwerp: Maklu, 2008

Dumortier and Christiaens 2006
E. Dumortier and J. Christiaens, 'De nieuwe wet op de jeugdbescherming. Krijtlijnen van een ambigue hervorming', *Tijdschrift voor Jeugd en Kinderrechten*, 2006, p. 273–280

Dupont and Verstraeten 1988
L. Dupont and R. Verstraeten, *Handboek Belgisch Strafrecht*, Leuven: Acco, 1988

Franchimont, Jacobs and Masset 2009
M. Franchimont, A. Jacobs and A. Masset, *Manuel de procédure pénale*, Brussels: Larcier, 2009

Frencken 1971
E. Frencken, Le role dévolu au judge d'instruction, *Ann.dr.* 1971, p. 141–156

Garland 1981
D. Garland, 'The birth of the welfare sanction', *British Journal of Law and Society*, 1981, 8, p. 29–45

Green Paper European Commission 2003
Green Paper from the Commission, *Procedural Safeguards for Suspects and Defendants in Criminal Proceedings throughout the European Union*, COM (2003) final, 19 February 2003

Kinderrechtencommissariaat 2004
(G)een 'nieuw' jeugdrecht? Opmerkingen vanuit het Kinderrechtencommissariaat op de kadernota van minister Onkelinx betreffende de hervorming van de wet op de jeugdbescherming, *Tijdschrift voor Jeugd en Kinderrechten*, 2004, 2, p. 132–135

Loop 1993
R. Loop, 'Prestations éducatives ou philanthropiques', *Journal du droits des jeunes*, 1993, 126, p. 785–791

Maes 2010
K. Maes, Verhoor van de minderjarige door de politie, *Tijdschrift voor Jeugd en Kinderrechten*, 2010, 1, p. 75–76

Meese 2011
J. Meese, De advocaat in de hoek. Enkele korte bedenkingen over de rol van de advocaat bij het verhoor en bij de sanctieregeling van de Salduz-wet, in: E. Michaux, P. Tersago, M. Vanderhallen and G. Vervaeke (eds.), *Het Salduz-arrest: tussen uniform en toga. De gevolgen van het Salduz-arrest voor politie, justitie en advocatuur*, Brussels: Politeia, 2011, p. 89–99

Meese and Tersago 2012
J. Meese and P. Tersago, 'Het recht voor elkeen die wordt verhoord op consultatie van en bijstand door een advocaat na de Salduz-wet van 13 augustus 2011', *Rechtskundig weekblad*, 2011–2012, 21, p. 934–952

Ministerial Circular Letter 2005
Ministerial circular letter, 8 August 2005, EAW, *B.S.* 31 August 2005

Nagels 2006
C. Nagels, 'De jongere, de delinquent en de sociale reactie op jeugddelinquentie', *Orde dag*, 2006, 36, p. 29–34

Nuytiens, Christiaens and Eliaerts 2005
A. Nuytiens, J. Christiaens and C. Eliaerts, *Ernstige jeugddelinquenten gestraft? De praktijk van de uithandengeving*, Ghent: Academia Press, 2005

Nuytiens 2006
A. Nuytiens, 'Rien ne va plus! Een kritische reflectie op de onverwachte (en ondoordachte?) facelift van de uithandengeving', *Tijdschrift voor Jeugd en Kinderrechten*, 2006, 281, p. 281–290

Onkelinx 2007
L. Onkelinx, 'Ontstaansgeschiedenis, krachtlijnen en beginselen van de nieuwe Jeugdwet', in: J. Put and M. Rom (eds.), *Het nieuwe jeugdrecht*, Brussels: Larcier, 2007, p. 9–13

Put and Walgrave 2006
J. Put and L. Walgrave, 'Belgium: From Protection Towards Accountability?', in: J. Muncie, B. Goldson (eds.): *Comparative Youth Justice*, London: Sage, 2006, p. 111–126

Put 2007
J. Put, Het nieuwe jeugdrecht: een terugblik naar de toekomst, in: J. Put and M. Rom (eds.), *Het nieuwe jeugdrecht*, Brussels: Larcier, 2007, p. 1–7

Put 2010
J. Put, *Handboek jeugdbeschermingsrecht*, Bruges: Die Keure, 2010

Put, Vanfraechem and Walgrave 2012
J. Put, I. Vanfraechem and L. Walgrave, 'Restorative Dimensions in Belgian Youth Justice', *Youth Justice*, 2012, p. 83–100

Rom 2007
M. Rom, Geesteszieke minderjarigen, in: J. Put and M. Rom (eds.), *Het nieuwe jeugdrecht*, Brussels: Larcier 2007, p. 183–214

Service for criminal policy 2012
Dienst voor het Strafrechtelijk beleid (DSB), *Evaluatie Salduz-wet: Eerste tussentijdse rapport*, 1 February 2012

Service for criminal policy 2012
Dienst voor het Strafrechtelijk beleid (DSB), *Evaluatie Salduz-wet: Tweede tussentijds rapport*, 30 March 2012

Senaeve 1995
P. Senaeve, *Inleiding tot het jeugdbeschermingsrecht*, Leuven: Acco, 1995

Smets 1996
J. Smets, Jeugdbeschermingsrecht, *A.P.R.* Ghent: Story-Scientia, 1996

Smets 2011
L. Smets, 'Opleiding verhoortechnieken in het post-Salduz tijdperk: naar een universele nationale training?', in: M. Bockstaele, E. Devroe and P. Ponsaers, *Salduz-bijstand van advocaten bij verhoren*, Antwerp/Apeldoorn: Maklu, 2011, p. 209–222

Spronken 2011
T. Spronken, 'Advocaat bij politieverhoor: de gevolgen van de zaak Salduz in Nederland', in: E. Michaux, P. Tersago, M. Vanderhallen and G. Vervaeke (eds.), *Het Salduz-arrest: tussen uniform en toga. De gevolgen van het Salduz-arrest voor politie, justitie en advocatuur*, Brussels: Politeia 2011, p. 123–135

Traest 1999
P. Traest, De bewijswaarde van een politieverhoor, in: S. van Elchingen (ed.), *Het politieverhoor*, Kessel-Lo, C.P.S. 1999, p. 129–146

Traest 2000
P. Traest (ed.), *Perspectieven uit de recente rechtspraak in strafzaken*, Ghent: Mys & Breesch 2000, p. 101–113

Tulkens and Moreau 2000
F. Tulkens and T. Moreau, *Droit de la jeunesse: aide, assistance, protection,* Brussels: Larcier, 2000

Van Cauwenberghe 2011
K. van Cauwenberghe, 'De nieuwe wet: de oplossing of…?', in: E. Michaux, P. Tersago, M. Vanderhallen and G. Vervaeke (eds.), *Het Salduz-arrest: tussen uniform en toga. De gevolgen van het Salduz-arrest voor politie, justitie en advocatuur*, Brussels: Politeia, 2011, p. 75–88

Van de Kerchove 1979
M. van de Kerchove, 'l'Evolution du droit des mineurs et les fonctions d'un tribunal de jeunesse', in: Centre d'étude de la délinquance juvénile, Fonction sociale du tribunal de la jeunesse, Brussels: C.E.D.J. 1979, 16, p. 15–35

Van den Wyngaert 2006
C. van den Wyngaert, *Strafrecht, strafprocesrecht en internationaal strafrecht*, Antwerp: Maklu, 2006

Van den Wyngaert 2011
C. van den Wyngaert, *Strafrecht & strafprocesrecht in hoofdlijnen*, Antwerp/Apeldoorn: Maklu, 2011

Van Dijk 2005
C. van Dijk, 'De uithandengeving naar Amerikaans model: adult time for adult crime? Realiteit, retoriek of symboliek', *Panopticon,* 2005, p. 151–166

Van Welzenis and Massei 2002
I. van Welzenis and A. Massei, Dossier: jeugdbrigade, *Sociaal welzijnsmagazine*, 2002, 5, p. 9–12

Van Welzenis 2003
I. van Welzenis, '*Jeugddelinquentie: Wat verstaan we eronder, waar komt het vandaan en wat doen we eraan?*', Mechelen: Kluwer, 2003

Vandekerckhove 2008
A. Vandekerckhove, 'Minderjarigen, media en (gebrek aan) privacy', *Tijdschrift voor Jeugd en Kinderrechten,* 2008, 5, p. 350–353

Vandromme 2004
S. Vandromme, 'De afsluiting van het gerechtelijk onderzoek in jeugdzaken', *Tijdschrift voor Jeugd en Kinderrechten*, 2004, 178, p. 178–184

Vanneste 2001
C. Vanneste, De beslissingen genomen door de parketmagistraten en de jeugdrechters ten aanzien van delinquente minderjarigen, *Departement Criminologie van het NICC*, Brussels, 2001, p. 193–202

Vanneste 2003
C. Vanneste, 'Les logiques décisionnelles des magistrats du parquet et des juges de la jeunesse à l'égard des mineurs délinquants', *Revue de Droit pénal et de Criminologie* 2003, 85, p. 232–263

Vanneste, Goedseels and Detry 2007
C. Vanneste, E. Goedseels and I. Detry, Onderzoek met betrekking tot de productie en wetenschappelijke exploitatie van cijfergegevens aangaande jeugddelinquentie en jeugdbescherming (Eerste onderzoeksrapport: Analyse van de instroom op de jeugdparketten voor het jaar 2005), Brussels: NICC, 2007

Verhellen, Cappelaere and Vandekerckhove 1991
E. Verhellen, G. Cappelaere and A. Vandekerckhove, *Politie en jeugd: een inventarisstudie omrent de relatie politie - minderjarigen*, Bruges: Van den Broele, 1991

Verhoeven and Stevens 2013
W.J. Verhoeven and L. Stevens, *Rechtsbijstand bij politieverhoor. Evaluatie van de Aanwijzing rechtsbijstand politieverhoor in Amsterdam-Amstelland, Groningen, Haaglanden, Limburg-Zuid, Midden- en West-Brabant en Utrecht*, The Hague: Boom Lemma Uitgevers, 2013

Vermassen 1999
J. Vermassen, 'Verhoren: de ruggengraat van het gerechtsdossier', in: Kessel-Lo, *Het politieverhoor*, Politeia-C.P.S. 1999, p. 87–101

Voets 2008
F. Voets, 'Namen (niet) noemen: journalistiek beroepsethiek en berichtgeving over jongeren', *Tijdschrift voor Jeugd en Kinderrechten*, 2008, 5, p. 307–310

Walgrave 2002
L. Walgrave (ed.), *Van kattenkwaad en erger: Actuele thema's uit de jeugdcriminologie*, Leuven - Apeldoorn: Garant, 2002, p. 44–59

CHAPTER 3

ENSURING 'APPROPRIATE' PROTECTIONS FOR YOUNG SUSPECTS

Country Report England and Wales

Jacqueline HODGSON and Vicky KEMP

I. THE JUVENILE JUSTICE SYSTEM IN ENGLAND AND WALES: GENERAL OVERVIEW

1. BACKGROUND

1.1. GENERAL FEATURES OF THE SYSTEM

The juvenile justice system in England and Wales has emerged on an *ad hoc* basis over the past hundred years, as part of the broadly adversarial criminal justice system in place. Criminal procedure in England and Wales is rooted in the adversarial, party-based tradition; the police enjoy a high level of investigative autonomy and there is no pre-trial supervisory role of the prosecutor or other judicial officer. While the 1908 Children Act established the principle of dealing with juveniles separately from adults, a range of different approaches have been adopted to the problem of young people and crime. Within the contemporary system, referred to as the 'youth justice system', there is a specialist criminal court which deals with defendants aged under 18 years but there is no separate system of justice for juveniles. Instead, the law relating to children and young persons in the criminal justice system is based on an adaption of the rules that apply to adults.

The main sources of law and principles dealing with youth justice and the criminal justice system comprise statute, procedural rules and international standards – including the European Convention on Human Rights (hereafter:

ECHR) – and to a lesser extent, EU law.[1] There are also civil law interventions available in relation to the offending behaviour of juveniles.

1.1.1. Statute

While there is the specialist youth court dealing with defendants aged under 18 years, the law relating to children and young people is not to be found in one statute; instead a series of statutes are relevant. The most important pieces of legislation which established the rules in relation to juveniles are the Children and Young Persons Acts of 1908, 1933, 1963 and 1969, together with the Bail Act 1976, Magistrates' Courts Act 1980, Police and Criminal Evidence Act 1984, Prosecution of Offences Act 1985, Criminal Justice and Public Order Act 1994, Crime and Disorder Act 1998, Powers of Criminal Courts (Sentencing) Act 2000, Anti-Social Behaviour Act 2003, Criminal Justice Act 2003 and the Legal Aid Sentencing and Punishment of Offenders Act 2012.

1.1.2. Procedural rules

The Criminal Procedural Rules 2005 established an overriding objective of the criminal justice process, which is that criminal cases should be dealt with justly. This includes, amongst other things, recognising the rights of a defendant, particularly those under art. 6 ECHR. Other rights include acquitting the innocent and convicting the guilty, dealing with the prosecution and defence fairly and dealing with cases efficiently and expeditiously.[2]

1.1.3. International standards

In England and Wales there are various international standards that apply to children and young people drawn into the criminal justice system. The ECHR, for example, was ratified by the United Kingdom in 1951 and the Convention on the Rights of the Child (hereafter: CRC) was ratified in 1990. This means that relevant legislation and practice in the criminal justice system needs to conform to the principles set out in these two Conventions. In addition, under the Human Rights Act 1998 it is unlawful for any public authority, including a court, to act in a manner which is incompatible with a Convention right.

There are other standards for children and young people involved in the youth justice system, which have been adopted by the United Nations (hereafter:

1 The common law is also an important source of criminal law, but not specifically concerning juveniles.

2 Criminal Procedure Rules (UK SI 2005 No. 384). These procedural rules are examined further below when considering more generally principles within the criminal justice system.

UN). These include the UN Standard Minimum Rules for the Administration of Juvenile Justice (1985: '*the Beijing Rules*'); the UN Rules for the Protection of Juveniles Deprived of their Liberty (1990: '*the Havana Rules*'); and the UN Guidelines for the Administration of Juvenile Delinquency (1990: '*the Riyadh Guidelines*'). As found more generally within the youth justice system, however, there are tensions within these Conventions due to the potential for conflict between 'just deserts' and 'welfarist' imperatives.[3]

The CRC is the most ratified of all international human rights instruments, but without sanctions being imposed for breaches of those rights, it has also been found to be the most violated. In relation to England and Wales, for example, the UN Committee on the Rights of the Child has highlighted many failings, particularly concerning the low age of criminal responsibility (at 10 years) and for using the youth justice system to target non-criminal behaviour and other social problems.[4] There have also been concerns raised by the European Commissioner for Human Rights over disproportionate sentences, increases in the use, and length of, custodial sentences and insufficient respect for the rule of law.[5]

In an exchange between the UN Committee and the Labour government in the late 1990s, it could be seen how the CRC, and other Conventions, could be flouted. This dispute involved the UN Committee being critical of government in England and Wales for intensifying modes of intervention into the lives of children and young people aimed at preventing crime under the Crime and Disorder Act 1998. In response, the government had claimed that early intervention is an entitlement and that such pre-emptive policies contribute to "the right of children to develop responsibility for themselves".[6] Thus, as Muncie and Goldson point out, the government in England and Wales was to appropriate a discourse of rights, which was to justify degrees of authoritarianism that were far removed from UN intentions.[7]

1.1.4. European Union (EU) law

The EU is increasingly active in the area of police and judicial co-operation, which includes joint investigations, evidence sharing and the extradition of accused and convicted individuals. More recently, the need for greater harmonisation of the procedural safeguards provided to suspects, including those who are the subject of these EU measures, has been recognised. Directives

---

3 Put and Walgrave 2006 and McAra 2010, p. 291.
4 UN Committee on the Rights of the Child 2008.
5 European Commissioner for Human Rights 2005.
6 UK Government 1999.
7 Muncie and Goldson 2006, p. 38.

are now in place guaranteeing the right to interpretation and translation,[8] the right to information[9] and the right to legal assistance.[10] In November 2013, the Commission adopted additional procedural safeguards, including a draft Directive on special safeguards for children. This would include some provisions already in place in England and Wales – such as the presence of a parent or appropriate adult – but also some new safeguards, such as a provision on mandatory legal assistance.

The 2009 Lisbon Treaty confirms that ECHR rights constitute general principles of EU law, and EU criminal law measures and their implication at the domestic level must be interpreted in accordance with fundamental rights. However, EU measures in criminal law and justice have less of an impact in England and Wales because the UK government managed to negotiate an opt-out to the Lisbon Treaty under Protocol 21, which extends to legislation amending existing measures which are binding upon the United Kingdom; instead participation is to be decided on a case-by-case basis.[11] The UK must decide to 'opt in' to measures such as the recent procedural safeguards, for them to have any legislative effect in England and Wales. To date it has opted in to the Directives on the right to translation and interpretation and on the right to information, but not on the right to legal assistance. It has also announced that it does not intend to opt in to the three draft Directives currently being debated, concerning the presumption of innocence, the right to legal aid, and safeguards for children.

1.1.5. Civil law

The civil law is relevant in relation to youth justice when dealing with anti-social behaviour. In particular, the Crime and Disorder Act 1998 introduced a number of orders addressing criminal behaviour through the civil law. This includes anti-social behaviour orders (ASBOs), a civil order which can be applied for in respect of anyone aged 10 years and older (including adults) when their behaviour is thought likely to cause alarm, distress or harassment.[12] The orders last for a minimum of two years, and any breach constitutes a criminal offence, which carries a maximum sentence of six months if dealt with in the youth court and five years in the Crown Court. There have been serious concerns raised over the impact of ASBOs on children and young people, particularly over the minimum order being in force for so long; the evidential basis on which the orders are issued; the number of prohibitions imposed being excessive; the

8 Directive 2010/64/EU.

9 Directive 2012/13/EU.

10 Directive 2013/48 EU.

11 See further Ormerod 2011, p. 18–21.

12 The Anti-Social Behaviour Act 2003 was to further extend the powers available under an ASBO.

number of orders breached; and the proportion receiving a custodial sentence for breach.[13]

There was also introduced under the civil law the child safety order, which can be imposed by a family proceedings court on a child below the age of criminal responsibility (10 years) who is considered to be 'at risk' of offending. Intended as a protective measure, the order places the child under the supervision of a social worker or a member of the youth offending team for a period up to 12 months. A breach of requirements can lead to a care order being imposed, which is reminiscent of the welfare interventions required for juveniles before being abolished under the 1989 Children Act.

The 1998 Crime and Disorder Act also introduced parenting orders under the civil law. These orders can require guidance or counselling sessions once a week for up to 12 weeks, and can be imposed on parents whose children are subject to a child safety order, an anti-social behaviour order or a sex offender order. The maximum penalty for breach of a parenting order is £1,000.

1.2. BRIEF HISTORY OF AND CURRENT TRENDS IN JUVENILE JUSTICE POLICY

An historical approach is helpful in seeking to understand the contemporary system of youth justice in England and Wales. This is not only a history of young people and crime but also one of social control. In addition to changes in the criminal law, police and prosecution system, therefore, it is also important to consider developments in welfare. It was due to an increased awareness of the different needs of juveniles and adults that the Children and Young Persons Act (hereafter: C&YP) 1908 first established juvenile courts. These courts were to deal with both offenders and neglected and destitute children, thus combining 'justice' and 'welfare' responses. From the outset, therefore, conflict and ambivalence were embedded within the concept of the juvenile court.[14]

By the early twentieth century the development of criminological science, known as positivism, was to become influential. Conceptions of the offender were to change as they came to be perceived as diseased or dysfunctional in nature, requiring individualised treatment responses from psychiatrists, psychologists and social workers, designed to meet the offender's needs.[15] 'Justice' on the other hand, was represented by agencies of the police and

13 European Commissioner for Human Rights 2005: par. 108–120 and Morgan and Newburn 2012, p. 513. ASBOs are considered further below.

14 For further details of the juvenile justice system in England and Wales see Gelsthorpe and Kemp 2014.

15 O'Brien 1995.

magistrates who tended to hold classical conceptions of the offender operating under their own free will, independent of moral agents. Thus, punishment rather than treatment was considered to be the best way to deal with juvenile offenders.

The 1933 C&YP Act formally required the court to have regard to 'the welfare of the child' when dealing with child offenders. The juvenile court was to act in *loco parentis*, which meant adjudicating on matters of family socialisation and parental behaviour, even if no crime had been committed. While the 1933 Act meant that the role of the 'welfare' agencies was dominant, the 'justice' agencies were prepared to work cooperatively alongside them. This led to the expansion of the juvenile justice system as it came to deal with both deprived and depraved children, concentrating on either their needs or deeds.

Tensions between notions of 'welfare' and 'justice' were to come to the fore in the 1969 C&YP Act. The intention of the Act was to adopt a 'welfare' approach which was to include diverting children from the juvenile courts (by increasing the age of criminal responsibility from 10 to 13 years)[16] and by imposing restrictions on the prosecution of those aged 14 to 17 years. The 1969 Act was not implemented in full, principally due to the two main political parties holding very different conceptions of young people and crime. According to Bottoms, this led to a dual system of justice, bringing together two ideologically opposed models of 'welfare' and 'justice,' which continue to lie at the heart of the problem of our contemporary youth justice system.[17]

By the early 1970s the welfare approach came to be criticised for extending the net of social control by drawing non-offenders into the juvenile justice system. There was also evidence emerging that rehabilitative efforts were having no appreciable effect on reducing offending.[18] In the 1980s, in England and Wales, across Europe and in the United States there was an explicit revival of traditional crime control values – which led to a more punitive juvenile justice system. The Conservative Government's Criminal Justice Act 1982 was to hit at the root of the social welfare perspective underlying the 1969 Act. Instead of 'welfare' the rhetoric was targeted at young 'thugs' who were said to be in need of a 'short, sharp shock' and so the number of secure places for juveniles was to be increased. However, alongside the requirement for harsher and more punitive penalties there were adopted diversionary strategies, particularly police cautioning for less serious offences. Thus, a process of bifurcation, or a 'twin-track approach' was occurring.[19]

The 1989 Children Act was to represent a major structural alteration in the law concerning the welfare of juveniles. The most important change was the cessation of the use of the care order as a disposal available to the court in

16 The age of criminal responsibility had been raised from 8 to 10 years in the 1963 C&YP Act.
17 Bottoms 1974.
18 Martinson 1974.
19 Bottoms 1977.

criminal proceedings, and the removal of the offence condition in proceedings that justified state intervention into the life of a family. Instead of the juvenile courts dealing with children in 'need', new rules provided for the transfer of care proceedings to the renamed family proceedings court. There were also changes with the 1989 Act requiring 17-year-olds to also be dealt with in the newly named 'youth court'.

The 1990s were seen to take a punitive turn following the well-publicised urban disturbances of 1991 and the moral panic over persistent young offenders, particularly following the abduction and murder of two-year-old James Bulger in 1993 by two 10-year-old boys. With sensationalised media reports, both nationally and internationally, this event was to trigger a moral panic that led to widespread moral outrage and concerns that the youth justice system was failing to protect the public.[20] Custody was once more promoted as the key means to prevent offending through Conservative slogans of 'prison works'. In relation to persistent young offenders there was introduced in 1993 a new custodial sentence known as the 'secure training order'. After having been in opposition for 18 years, the newly elected Labour Government in 1997 made reform of the youth justice system a priority.

The Crime and Disorder Act 1998 which followed was described as a 'comprehensive and wide-ranging reform programme'.[21] The legislation appears to favour punishment to signal society's disapproval of criminal acts and deter offending. At the same time, it was to remain faithful to its commitment to be 'tough on crime, tough on the causes of crime' by referring at times to social factors which contribute to crime, and by proposing to prevent re-offending through an interventionist, welfare approach reminiscent of interventions in the 1960s and 1970s. The Act also contains provisions that underline support for the government's belief in restorative justice principles.

The 1998 Act set out a managerial framework for youth justice, which included the setting up of the national Youth Justice Board and multi-agency Youth Offending Teams (hereafter: YOTs) based in each local authority area.[22] There was a wide range of interventions introduced by the 1998 Act, both out-of-court and in court, which required a 'stepwise' or 'progressive' approach to reoffending. Not surprisingly, the Crime and Disorder Act 1998 was to have the desired effect of increasing the number of children and young people drawn into the formal youth justice system. However, subsequently there were changes made which were intended to introduce more flexibility when dealing with young offenders both in and out of court.

---

20 Concerns were raised that the police were using 'multiple cautions' instead of sending persistent offenders to court (though this practice was never as widespread as believed – see Evans and Wilkinson 1990).

21 Home Office 1997, p. 1.

22 The composition of YOTs is discussed below.

In 2008 an Independent Commission on Youth Crime and Anti-Social Behaviour was set up with a remit to establish a blueprint for an effective, humane and sustainable approach to youth crime and anti-social behaviour based on clear principles and sound evidence. The blueprint for reform is contained in *A New Response to Youth Crime*,[23] which sets out nine main recommendations for reform. These include reducing the number of cases brought to court as well as the number of young people taken into custody, increasing the use of restorative conferences and requiring resources to be targeted more towards prevention.

The general election in 2010 resulted in a hung parliament with no one political party gaining an overall majority in the House of Commons. For the first time since the Second World War a coalition government was formed, here between the Conservatives and the Liberal Democrats. In this current time of austerity, the priority for the Coalition Government is to tackle the deficit. This has led to budget cuts being imposed on all criminal justice agencies. In addition, in the Legal Aid, Sentencing and Punishment of Offenders Act 2012, there are measures designed to introduce a more flexible approach to juvenile offenders. These include, for example, increased opportunities for diverting juveniles from court and also adopting a more flexible approach to court sentences, designed to reduce the number of juveniles sent to custody. However, the 2012 Act also adopts a punitive measure through the introduction of a new offence of 'knife crime', which is an offence of 'threatening with an article with blade or point or offensive weapon in public or on school premises'. This new offence is intended to have a deterrent effect with a mandatory minimum sentence of four months being required for 16- and 17-year-olds.[24] Once again, therefore, there can be seen to be a process of bifurcation with a shift towards diversionary policies but, at the same time, with the adoption of harsher and more punitive penalties.

1.3. GENERAL PRINCIPLES OF NATIONAL JUVENILE LAW AND JUVENILE CRIMINAL JUSTICE

In England and Wales, there is no written penal code, criminal procedure code or definitive statement of the principles of criminal justice. Instead, as Ormerod explains, the criminal law has developed over many centuries, and the purposes of those who have framed it, and those who have enforced it, have undoubtedly been many and varied.[25] Criminal justice is about society's formal response to crime. In the absence of a penal code, there are some important principles that guide criminal justice procedure as well as the rule of law.

23 Smith 2010.
24 There is a maximum custodial sentence of four years for this offence.
25 Ormerod 2011, p. 4.

There had been a distinction under the common law when dealing with children between the ages of 10 and 14 years as they were presumed not to possess the necessary knowledge to have a criminal intention. This common law presumption of *doli incapax* was rebuttable by the prosecution after calling evidence to show that the child knew what he or she was doing was seriously wrong in the criminal sense. However, this defence came to be seen as anachronistic and it was abolished under the Crime and Disorder Act 1998.[26]

The most important statute governing the investigation of crime and the rights of suspects held in custody is the Police and Criminal Evidence Act (hereafter: PACE) 1984. The Act set out the grounds for police powers to stop and search people, to make arrests, as well as to provide access to legal advice for people arrested by the police on suspicion of having committed an offence. There are detailed Codes of Practice, with Code C setting out the requirements for the detention, treatment and questioning of non-terrorism related suspects in custody. The main concession in Code C in relation to juveniles (aged 10 to 16 years) is that the police must arrange for them to have an appropriate adult.[27] This mandatory safeguard is also required for detainees who have mental health problems and/or learning disabilities. For suspects (or their parents when acting as appropriate adults) who do not understand English, PACE requires that the police arrange for an interpreter during interrogations, and for the translation of essential documents in order that the suspect can exercise their right of defence.[28]

The criminal justice system operates within an adversarially-rooted framework for both adults and juveniles. However, under section 37(1) of the Crime and Disorder Act 1998 the principal aim of the youth justice system is to prevent offending and section 37(2) requires 'all persons and bodies carrying out functions in relation to the youth justice system to have regard to that aim'. It is difficult to see how defence practitioners are required to comply with this requirement when acting to protect the legal rights of young suspects and defendants.

When examining a brief history of the juvenile justice system above, it is evident that criminal justice principles can vary over time. A good example of how fluctuations in policy and practice can influence non-prosecution decisions, including the suspect's age, can be seen in changes to the Crown Prosecution Service (hereafter: CPS) Code of Practice. In the first Code, for example, the objective was to divert juveniles from court if at all possible and, it was stated, '[p]rosecution should always be regarded as a severe step'.[29] The revised Code further encouraged diversion of young suspects, stating that prosecution should

26 See Fionda 2001.

27 A recent change to PACE means that 17-year-olds are also now required to have an appropriate adult. The role of the appropriate adult is considered further below.

28 PACE Code of Practice C, para. 13.

29 CPS 1986.

only be used as a last resort.[30] A new Code in 1994 was to reflect the changing political mood towards young offenders. The requirement then was that 'Crown Prosecutors should not avoid prosecuting simply because of the defendant's age', a statement which was reiterated in the next version of the Code.[31] However, in the latest Code, age is once again re-asserted as an important factor, which should influence a non-prosecution decision. Indeed, in promoting a different approach to juveniles it states:

> 'The criminal justice system treats children and young people differently from adults and significant weight must be attached to the age of the suspect if they are a child or young person under 18. The best interests and welfare of the child or young person must be considered including whether a prosecution is likely to have an adverse impact on his or her future prospects that is disproportionate to the seriousness of the offending. Prosecutors must have regard to the principal aim of the youth justice system, which is to prevent offending by children and young people. Prosecutors must also have regard to the obligations arising under the United Nations 1989 Convention on the Rights of the Child'.[32]

It is evident therefore that diversionary policies and practices are shaped by changing political influences, rather than on principles based on differences of age.

1.4. MODELS OF JUVENILE JUSTICE IN ENGLAND AND WALES

The youth justice system in England and Wales is based on an adversarial criminal justice system within which suspects and defendants are considered to be innocent until proven guilty. The burden of proof is on the prosecution to prove beyond reasonable doubt that the defendant is guilty.

There are various typologies that can be used to classify the youth justice system in England and Wales. When examining a brief history of juvenile justice above, it was noted that throughout much of the twentieth century there were tensions between the competing paradigms of 'welfare' and 'justice'. With a concentration on management in the criminal justice system from the 1980s, Winterdyk classified England and Wales as having a 'corporatist model'.[33] Following the 1998 Crime and Disorder Act, and other legislation, new paradigms of 'restoration' and 'actuarialism' are also seen to be dominant in the youth justice system. For example, restoration can be seen in restorative justice

---

30 CPS 1992.
31 CPS 1994 and CPS 2010.
32 CPS 2013a, para. 4.12(d).
33 Winterdyk 2002.

where interventions seek to involve both the victim and offender in seeking to address the harm caused by the offence and/or their offending behaviour. The actuarial model focuses on the management of crime through a calculation of the 'risk' of reoffending when deciding on appropriate interventions. It is evident, therefore, that while relevant typologies can be identified, there is no single classification that would effectively bring together these competing paradigms.[34]

There are difficulties in seeking to adopt a single classification because, as McAra points out, a central tension which lies at the heart of the youth justice systems is the requirement to meet the needs of the troubled and vulnerable young offender at the same time as meeting the needs of society.[35] While the aim of any reform, first and foremost, should be to reconcile such tensions, she notes that such reform is always to be constrained by the broader social, cultural and political environments within which the youth justice system operates. A major factor influencing reform of the system in England and Wales has been the political context within which policy decisions have been made. With a broad political consensus between the two main political parties following the Second World War, for example, this was to break down in the 1970s as the parties came to hold different conceptions of social order and the appropriate response to juvenile offenders. The Conservatives effectively promoted themselves as the Party of 'law and order' and after having spent 18 years in opposition, the Labour Party wanted to shake off its image of being 'soft on crime'. In published reports the Labour Party in opposition set out its proposal to improve the effectiveness of the youth justice system by 'preventing, deterring and punishing youth crime'.[36]

Because of the broader social, cultural and political environment within which a youth justice system is located, therefore, the capacity for reform is to be constrained. At present the Coalition Government are concerned with financial imperatives, which can be seen to be influencing changes in the youth justice system as well as the criminal justice process more widely. Instead of the interventionist approach adopted following the reforms of the 1998 Crime and Disorder Act, there can be seen a shift towards what Cavadino and Dignan describe as a 'minimal intervention' model.[37] However, at the same time as diversionary policies are aimed at reducing the number of young offenders coming into court and custody, new measures have been introduced which require a tough line to be taken with serious and persistent offenders.[38]

While such typologies are useful in identifying differences in youth justice systems, they can be insufficient in reflecting the vastly different trajectories of youth justice. As Muncie points out, such classificatory models can fail to

---

34 See further Winterdyk 2014.

35 McAra 2010.

36 Home Office 1997, p. 2.

37 Cavadino and Dignan 2006, p. 201.

38 The introduction of the new sentence of 'knife crime', for instance.

do justice either to the ways in which systems are always in a state of change themselves or to the various ways in which broad trends can be 'challenged, reworked, adapted or resisted at the local level'.[39]

1.5. THE TREATMENT OF JUVENILES IN CRIMINAL PROCEEDINGS

The youth justice system provides only few additional protections to children and young people drawn into the criminal process. Indeed, apart from the mandatory requirement for an appropriate adult, and a separate youth court, juveniles are treated in the same way as adults within the criminal process. When arrested and detained by the police, for example, the questions asked by a custody officer are the same for juveniles as they are for adults. This means that at the age of 10 a child is asked if they are dependent on alcohol and/or drugs; girls at that age are also to be asked if they could be pregnant. There is no mandatory requirement for children, or other vulnerable suspects, to have legal advice in the police station, even when being dealt with for very serious offences.[40]

There are some additional protections in relation to age with the taking of fingerprints, photographs and non-intimate samples, as the police have to have the consent of a parent/appropriate adult for those aged 10 to 14 years.[41] For those aged 14 to 18 years, the consent of the suspect is also required. The police do have the power to take fingerprints, photographs and non-intimate samples, such as hair (other than pubic hair) or nail samples, without consent in cases where a suspect has been arrested for a recordable offence.[42] Intimate samples, such as blood, semen, urine and saliva can only be taken by a doctor or other registered health care professional on the authority of at least the rank of inspector. Such samples can only be taken with consent, which, in the case of juveniles, as noted above is the same as that required when dealing with non-intimate samples. If consent is refused the suspect must be warned that their refusal may harm their case if it comes to trial.[43]

At court there have been attempts to make the youth court more informal, and for magistrates to engage more positively with young defendants. Indeed, as a consequence of the ruling of the European Court of Human Rights (hereafter:

39 Muncie 2008, p. 117.

40 The remedy for a vulnerable person being interviewed without legal advice in relation to very serious cases would be for the lawyer to challenge the admissibility of the interrogation evidence at trial (S. 76 and 78 of PACE are the two main exclusionary evidential rules).

41 See PACE Code of Practice D for the rules relating to the taking of fingerprints, photographs and intimate and non-intimate samples.

42 Recordable offences include all but the most trivial offences.

43 PACE Code of Practice D, para. 6.3.

ECtHR) in the case of *T v. United Kingdom* and *V v. United Kingdom*,[44] a Practice Direction was issued.[45] The Direction encouraged judges to ensure that all those concerned in proceedings understood what is happening and that they sought to increase the level of engagement with young people and their parents. This included recommendations that the court should explain the proceedings to a young defendant, remind legal representatives of their continuing duty to explain each step of proceedings, and to ensure, so far as practicable, that the trial is conducted in language that the defendant can understand. The Direction also requires steps to be taken to minimise the formality of young defendants' Crown Court trials (for example, require the barristers in court to remove their wigs and gowns) and to enhance their participation, which guidance was also extended to the youth court.[46] From earlier research findings it was evident that such steps were required. In a study that included 37 interviews with young people who had experience of the youth justice system, for example, proceedings in court were generally not understood, and instead 'passed in something of a blur'.[47]

It seems from more recent findings that not a lot has changed. In Lacey's study, for example, which included interviews with 58 young defendants, while YOTs are required to provide information to juveniles, and their parents/carers, prior to coming into court, many respondents reported receiving little or no information or support.[48] This left the juvenile, and their parent/carer feeling anxious and confused. In addition, Lacey found that the atmosphere of the courtroom, and what was described as the 'unapproachable nature of the judges and magistrates' was to have an effect on the extent to which children felt able to talk in court. Having confirmed their name and entered their plea of 'guilty', most respondents said they felt it was inappropriate to speak further in court; instead this was seen to be the role of their solicitor. Deterring juveniles from speaking up in court, Lacey notes that '[t]here was also an assumption on the part of the young people that they did not know how to speak to the "judge" and that they might act out of turn'.[49] Similar issues were highlighted in a Criminal Justice Joint Inspection of youth court work and reports, where YOTs were found not to engage sufficiently with young people and their parents/carers in court, or to help them understand what was happening.[50]

While youth courts are required to be less formal courtrooms in seeking to meet the needs of juvenile defendants, this is not always the approach adopted

44 ECtHR 16 December 1999, *T v. United Kingdom*, no. 24724/94 and *V v. United Kingdom*, no. 24888/94.

45 Practice Direction (Crown Court: Trial of Children and Young Persons) [2001] 1 Cr. App. R. 483.

46 See Home Office and Lord Chancellor's Department 2001 and Youth Justice Board 2002 and 2003.

47 Hazel *et al.* 2002, p. 12.

48 Lacey 2012.

49 Lacey 2012, p. 129.

50 Criminal Justice Joint Inspection 2011a.

by presiding magistrates. In the Joint Inspection, for example, it was found that some of those responsible for sentencing young defendants had mixed feelings about how informal a youth court should be. In particular, '[t]hey wanted the court to have appropriate authority and for the experience to be memorable for the young person'.[51]

2. STRUCTURE AND MAIN CHARACTERISTICS OF THE JUVENILE JUSTICE SYSTEM IN ENGLAND AND WALES

2.1. MINIMUM AGE OF CRIMINAL LIABILITY

The minimum age of responsibility in England and Wales is 10 years, which means that persons under that age cannot be guilty of any offence.[52] They cannot be arrested and interrogated as a suspect when under 10 years of age, although they can be interviewed by the police as a potential witness in a case.[53] As noted above, there had been a legal presumption of *doli incapax*, which assumed that children aged under 14 years did not know the difference between right and wrong and were therefore incapable of committing an offence. This was a rebuttable presumption if the prosecution could satisfy the court that the child knew that what they were doing was seriously wrong. The presumption of *doli incapax* was abolished by section 34 of the Crime and Disorder Act 1998, which means that juveniles aged 10 years and above are now treated as adults in the criminal justice system.

The UN Committee on the Rights of the Child has consistently criticised England and Wales for its low age of criminal responsibility.[54] Nevertheless, in the case of *T v. United* Kingdom and *V v. United Kingdom*[55] the ECtHR ruled that the age of 10 could not be said to be so young as to differ disproportionately from the age limit followed by other European States.

2.2. DEFINITION OF JUVENILE AND RELEVANT CATEGORIES

The definition of a 'juvenile' varies in relation to a range of different activities. For example, a juvenile cannot buy a pet until they are 12 years or older, do a

51 Criminal Justice Joint Inspection 2011a, p. 28.

52 Section 50 of the C&YP Act 1933 set the minimum age of criminal responsibility at 8 years. This was increased to the current age of 10 by section 16 of the C&YP Act 1963.

53 See CPS 2011 and CPS 2013b.

54 UN Committee on the Rights of the Child 2008.

55 ECtHR 16 December 1999, *T. v. United Kingdom*, no. 24724/94 and *V. v. United Kingdom*, no. 24888/94, [2000] 2 All ER 1024 (Note).

newspaper delivery round from 13 years onwards, and consent to sex until they are 16. With the consent of their parents a 16–year-old can get married but they are not allowed to drive a motor vehicle until they are 17. In relation to suspects arrested and detained by the police, as well as defendants taken to court, the legal definition of a 'juvenile' is now those aged between 10 and 17 years inclusive (Criminal Justice Act 1991).[56] Within the category of 'juveniles' there tends to be a distinction drawn between children aged between 10 and 13 years, and young people, aged between 14 and 17 years. Up until April 2013, PACE had defined juveniles as those aged 10 to 16 years – with 17-year-olds being treated as adults. However, following a successful judicial review in the case of *Regina v. Cousins-Chang*[57] it was held that treating 17-year-olds as adults was unlawful. Accordingly, juveniles are now defined as those aged 10 to 17 years, which means that 17-year-olds are required to have an appropriate adult when detained by the police.[58]

When juveniles are dealt with in the youth justice system there are age restrictions concerning certain types of criminal sanctions. These differences are explored further below when considering court sentences and out-of-court penalties.

2.3. RELEVANT ACTORS

The relevant actors within the criminal process include the youth offending team, the police, the Crown Prosecution Service, the judiciary, defence solicitors and appropriate adults.

2.3.1. Youth Offending Team (YOT)

YOTs comprise social workers and probation officers, who have historically worked with young offenders, police officers, representatives from education and health and a YOT manager. The role of the YOT is wide-ranging as it includes both preventive work with children and young people 'at risk' of offending, as well as with their parents; those receiving an out-of-court disposal which requires an assessment and intervention; and also supervising offenders subject to court orders and those who are released from custody.

56 In the context of safeguarding the welfare of children, this also includes 17-year-olds. See Department for Children, Schools and Family 2010.

57 R. (Cousins-Chang) v (1) Secretary of State for the Home Department and (2) The Commissioner of Police of the Metropolis [2013] EWHC 982 (Admin).

58 This requirement has been recognised by the police, although Code of Practice C of PACE has yet to be amended to this effect (see Association of Chief Police Officers 2013).

2.3.2. *Police*

The police are the competent authority to deal with investigations into alleged criminal offences and the gathering of evidence. For the most part, the procedures are the same for juveniles and adults. It is the police who are responsible for undertaking interrogations with juveniles and for making charging decisions – although the CPS are required to make decisions in relation to more serious and complex offences. There is no requirement for the police to be specialised when dealing with juvenile suspects, although there are specialists within child protection teams who deal with children as victims of crime.

2.3.3. *Crown Prosecution Service (CPS)*

As with adult offenders, when a decision to charge has been taken, the case is passed from the police to the CPS. A prosecutor will review the case file, liaise with the police concerning any additional evidence required, and prosecute the case in court. Within the CPS there is an appointed 'youth offender specialist' (YOS)[59] whose role is to review case files involving young defendants, to make all major decisions in relation to those files and to provide training locally to other prosecutors in dealing with young offenders. The YOS will also make regular appearances in the youth court (but not all youth court cases are dealt with by the YOS) and provide training to other prosecutors in dealing with young offenders.

2.3.4. *Judiciary*

The judiciary sitting in youth court cases will either be a district judge (who is an experienced criminal lawyer) or a lay magistrate. A judge deals with cases in the Crown Court. There is training provided for the judiciary which will involve issues relating to juvenile defendants and witnesses.[60] For lay magistrates a specialised training course has to be completed before they are allowed to preside over cases in the youth court. Both district judges and magistrates gain experience of working with juveniles by regularly sitting in the youth court. There are not a sufficient number of cases sent up to the Crown Court to enable judges to become specialised in juvenile cases.

2.3.5. *Defence solicitors*

Defence solicitors can represent the legal interests of children and young people at both the pre-charge investigative stage and also at court, in the same way

---

59 The YOS is required to have undertaken a youth offender training course.

60 The Judicial College is responsible for training judges and for oversight of the training of magistrates.

that they deal with adults. Suspects have the right to free and independent legal advice when detained in police custody and also when interviewed by the police on a 'voluntary' basis.[61] Police station legal advice can be provided by criminal solicitors or accredited legal representatives.[62] The accreditation scheme for duty solicitors and non-solicitors includes training on the special treatment of juveniles and other vulnerable persons investigated by the police. The scheme has been found to help improve the quality of legal advice and assistance provided to those held in police custody.[63] However, recent research suggests that the quality of legal advice has declined, at least in some stations, particularly where legal advisers have been excluded from custody suits.[64] In particular, in a recent in-depth study of one large police station where the defence had been excluded, a key finding was the passive and non-adversarial way in which the majority of legal advisers engaged in the pre-charge process.[65] Such criticisms are reminiscent of issues raised in earlier research studies.[66]

In a large scale study of suspects arrested and detained in police custody in 2009, 45 per cent were found to request legal advice, and around 35 per cent received such advice.[67] There was the same request rate for juveniles aged 10 to 17 years as for adults at 45 per cent,[68] but there were variations depending on age. For instance, there was a similar request rate for those aged 16–17 years and also 14–15 years, at 46 and 45 per cent respectively, compared to just 39 per cent of those aged 10 to 13 years. With such a young and vulnerable age group it is of concern that they are the least likely of any age group to request legal advice. It seems that this is because at such a young age their parents, or other carer, tend to take on the role of the appropriate adult and they are not as aware of the importance of having legal advice as are the professional and voluntary services.[69]

If prosecuted, both adult and juvenile defendants have to apply for a representation order to obtain the services of a publicly funded lawyer. Both have to pass the 'interests of justice' test before legal aid will be granted, with

61 Section 58(1) of PACE and of Practice C, para. 3.21.
62 There is an assessment and training programme for legal advisers through which they gain accreditation to provide legal advice. As a probationary trainee they can provide legal advice for up to twelve months before gaining accreditation.
63 Bridges and Choongh 1998.
64 Kemp 2010, p. 5 and Kemp 2013a, p. 201.
65 Such passivity on the part of some legal advisers within an adversarial system of justice was seen to undermine clients' legal protections – see Kemp 2013b, p. 20.
66 McConville and Hodgson 1993 and McConville *et al.* 1994.
67 This was based on a sample of over 30,000 custody records drawn from 44 police stations in four police force areas – see Pleasence *et al.* 2011. The previous large-scale study was based on custody records drawn from the mid-1990s and the request rate for legal advice at that time was 40 per cent and 34 per cent received advice – see Bucke and Brown 1997.
68 Bucke and Brown (1997) found that the request rate for juveniles at 41 per cent was slightly higher than that for adults at 39 per cent.
69 Kemp *et al.* 2011, p. 38.

the same test being applied to adults and juveniles.[70] There is also a financial test that has to be applied, although those in full-time education – up to 16 years – are exempt. For 17-year-olds who are in employment the financial test is the same as it is for adults. While defence solicitors are not required to have any special training when dealing with children and young people, some do tend to specialise by routinely dealing with cases in the youth court.

2.3.6. Appropriate adults

There is a mandatory requirement for vulnerable suspects, which includes juveniles and those with a learning disability or mental health problem, to have an appropriate adult present in police custody. The necessity for this mandatory protection arose out of a miscarriage of justice case, known as the 'Confait Affair'. This case involved the death of Maxwell Confait, where two juveniles and an 18-year-old, who had the mental capacity of a 13-year-old, were wrongly convicted of murder. This miscarriage of justice led to the setting up of the Royal Commission on Criminal Procedure,[71] which recognised that the welfare needs of vulnerable suspects meant that they were particularly susceptible to coercion and suggestion.[72] The protection of requiring an appropriate adult was subsequently incorporated into Code of Practice C (Code C) of PACE 1984. While parents or carers tend to act as the appropriate adult, the Crime and Disorder Act 1998 gave the YOTs the statutory responsibility for ensuring the provision of an appropriate adult service for juveniles (under 17 years) when parents or carers were not available.

The role of appropriate adults is to advise, support and assist vulnerable detainees in the police station, which now includes all children and young people under 18 years of age. When a juvenile is investigated by the police, the appropriate adult is required to look after their welfare, to explain police procedures and to provide them with information about their rights and to ensure that these are safeguarded, and to facilitate communication with the police.[73] Parents, a guardian or carer can take on this role in relation to children and young people but in cases where this is not possible they can be assigned a practitioner working in the YOT, social services or a volunteer sourced from the local appropriate adult volunteer network.[74] It is not the role of the appropriate adult to provide the juvenile with legal advice, but Code C, para. 6.5A requires them to consider whether legal advice from a solicitor is required. If the juvenile indicates that they do not want advice, the appropriate adult does have the right to ask for a solicitor to attend if they consider this to be in the best interests of

70 The test can include the nature of the offence and the risk of custody.
71 Royal Commission on Criminal Procedure 1981.
72 Sanders and Leng 1991.
73 See the Guide for Appropriate Adults (Home Office 2013).
74 Medford *et al.* 2003 and Pierpoint 2008.

the young suspect – although this does not mean that the suspect has to have legal advice if he or she is adamant that they do not want a solicitor.[75] Research studies have found that YOT workers acting as appropriate adults do encourage the detainee to obtain legal advice, and many volunteer schemes have adopted a policy of requesting legal advice as a matter of course.[76]

The effectiveness of appropriate adults has been questioned in earlier empirical research.[77] Some studies highlight that they often tend to be untrained and do not always appreciate the legal significance of police questions and procedures. Family members and friends are most likely to contribute to the interview (both appropriately and inappropriately) but more generally, the presence of an appropriate adult was seen to have an important effect: it was associated with less interrogative pressure and a more active legal adviser role.[78]

2.4. MAIN PHASES OF THE JUVENILE CRIMINAL PROCESS

In 2010–2011 there were a total of 1,360,451 arrests in England and Wales, of which 15.5 per cent (210,660) were juveniles.[79] Thus, while 10- to 17-year-olds accounted for 15.5 per cent of all arrests they were 10.7 per cent of the population in England and Wales.[80] Having made an arrest it is generally police practice to bring the suspect into police custody. Unfortunately there are no statistics that highlight the proportion of suspects who are arrested and detained by the police, although it is anticipated that this continues to be the majority of all juveniles who are interrogated by the police. This is despite Art. 37 of the UN Convention of the Rights of the Child, which states that arrest and detention 'shall be used only as a measure of last resort'.

Following the making of an arrest there are various steps taken in the criminal process.

2.4.1. Arrest and detention

Just as with an adult suspect, having made an arrest the police are required to identify themselves, tell the suspect that they are being arrested, for what crime, and to explain why it is necessary to make an arrest. The police also have to caution the suspect, which is to advise them that they have the right to remain

75 Code of Practice C, Note 6.5A.

76 Appropriate adults, particularly specialist independent appropriate adults, have been found to be influential in increasing request rates for legal advice (Brookman and Pierpoint 2003).

77 For a review of earlier research see Hodgson 1997.

78 Medford *et al.* 2003.

79 This is the latest period for which data is available.

80 Ministry of Justice 2013.

silent but, as noted below, adverse inferences at trial can be made if the suspect later seeks to rely on evidence which was not mentioned during the police interview. When brought to the police station it is the responsibility of a custody officer to determine whether or not there are sufficient grounds on which to authorise the suspect's detention. This requirement tends to be satisfied on the basis that further investigations are required, particularly the interrogation of the suspect.

Having authorised the detention of a suspect in relation to non-terrorism offences, in relation to both juveniles and adults, the police generally have 24 hours in which to detain suspects without charge, although an extension of a further 12 hours can be authorised by the police.[81] After 36 hours, the police have to apply to the magistrates' court for a warrant of further detention. The overall maximum period of detention that can be authorised in this way is 96 hours.[82]

There is a PACE Code C requirement that a juvenile shall not be placed in a police cell unless no other secure accommodation is available and the custody officer considers it is not practicable to supervise them if they are not placed in a cell.[83] While the police might try to deal with juvenile suspects differently, such as placing them in a cell with a glass door within the custody suite, the lack of alternative accommodation in custody suites tends to mean that they are frequently held in police cells. With juveniles being required to have an appropriate adult present during the interrogation, this can sometimes have the perverse effect of extending their time in police custody.[84] For juvenile suspects arrested in the early evening or during the night, for example, they can be held in custody due to the lack of availability of an appropriate adult and the interrogation having to be delayed until the following day.[85] In 2008 and 2009 it was found that approximately 53,000 juveniles aged 10 to 16 years inclusive were held overnight in police cells.[86]

2.4.2. *Legal rights under PACE*

When suspects are booked into police custody the custody officer first asks them a set of questions concerning their welfare, including an assessment of the risk of being detained. The next set of questions deals with a suspect's three legal

81 PACE section 42(1). An extension has to be authorised by a superintendent or a more senior police officer.

82 PACE section 43(1).

83 Code of Practice C, para. 8.8. The Code also states that juveniles will not be held in cells with adult suspects.

84 See Kemp *et al.* 2012, p. 742.

85 Appropriate adult services are provided either directly by the YOT or by a voluntary (or private) sector agency on their behalf. This tends to be operated on a rota basis but not providing cover at night-time: Criminal Justice Joint Inspection 2011b, p. 26 and Skinns 2011.

86 Of those, four were children under the age of criminal responsibility, 1,674 were aged 10 and 11 years and 11,540 were children under the age of 14 years: Skinns 2011.

rights. The first right informs them that they can have someone informed of their arrest, and for juvenile suspects the police must inform their parents (or carer) of their detention. The second right advises them that they have access to free and independent legal advice and the third right is that they can consult the PACE Codes of Practice. If the suspect and/or their appropriate adult are unable to speak English then the police are required to obtain the services of an interpreter.

As mentioned before, as the appropriate adult is not always available when suspects are first brought into custody their legal rights have to be repeated later on by the custody officer in the presence of the appropriate adult. It seems that police practice in some stations is to wait until the police are ready for the interrogation before contacting the appropriate adult and asking them to attend.[87] This can be problematic, particularly if legal advice has been declined, as it is unlikely that the suspect would be persuaded to change their mind, and risk further delay while waiting for the solicitor to attend at the station. Securing their release from custody has been found to be an important priority for many suspects. Research has found that this leads them to decline legal assistance in some instances, as they believe, or are told by the police, that requesting a lawyer will delay things and result in a lengthier period of detention.[88]

It seems that it is also the practice of legal advisers to wait until the police are ready to conduct the interrogation before attending at the station.[89] While such an approach is more convenient for legal advisers, it can be to the detriment of their clients. This is because solicitors tend to be accepting of the police timetable, including in cases with unduly long delays. It also means that solicitors tend to concentrate on the interrogation rather than the wider issues concerning their client's detention.[90] Accordingly, the following criticism made by the Criminal Justice Joint Inspection of appropriate adults can also be said to apply to the defence: 'The role of the appropriate adult had evolved over time to become increasingly focussed on process rather than safeguarding the interests of the child and promoting their welfare'.[91]

2.4.3. Charging and bail decisions

Having conducted their investigations, the police (or the CPS in relation to serious and complex cases) then have to decide whether to take 'no further

87 Criminal Justice Joint Inspection 2011b, p. 31 and Kemp 2013a, p. 198. This would appear to be contrary to PACE which requires that legal advice should be available 'as soon as practicable' following an arrest (Code of Practice C, para. 3.15).

88 See Blackstock *et al.* 2014 and Kemp 2013a, p. 198.

89 With solicitors receiving a fixed fee for providing legal advice it can be more efficient and cost effective for them to wait until the police interview before getting involved in cases (Kemp 2013, p. 196).

90 Kemp 2013a.

91 Criminal Justice Joint Inspection 2011b, p. 5.

action', impose an out-of-court penalty or to take the case to court, either by charging the juvenile or issuing a summons. If the police decide to conduct further investigations the suspect can be bailed to return to the police station at a later date.[92] It is also a matter for the police (or the CPS) to decide whether a suspect who has been charged should be bailed to court or held in police custody until the next available court date.[93] Statistics indicate that there are around 5,000 juveniles per year for whom police bail was refused.[94]

For juveniles under 17 years, if bail is denied by the police, section 38 of PACE requires that they should generally be transferred to local authority accommodation.[95] However, there are exceptions allowed where the custody officer considers it impracticable to arrange for a transfer. In addition, in the case of juveniles aged 12 to 16 years, they can be held in police custody if there is no secure accommodation available and/or other local authority accommodation would not be adequate to protect the public from serious harm. When a joint inspection team examined this issue, there were criticisms of the police for not routinely collecting this information.[96] Instead, a sample of 49 cases was examined where juveniles had been held in custody after charge. It was found that in nearly two-thirds of cases (33), local authority accommodation was not sought.[97] In the following comment there were criticisms made of both the police and appropriate adults for allowing juveniles to remain in police custody until their court appearance:

> 'Whatever the intentions behind the legislation, we found that the procedure didn't really consider the needs of the children and young people (...) Overall, the lack of clarity about both the role of the appropriate adult and the arrangements whereby a child or young person could be transferred to local authority accommodation meant that children and young people were spending longer in an unsuitable and potentially detrimental environment than was needed. The system put in place to protect their interests was not working.'[98]

2.4.4. Court proceedings

When dealt with at court a juvenile must have a parent or appropriate adult accompany them. An important difference in the youth court is that proceedings

---

92 Certain conditions can be attached to bail, such as a condition of residence or a curfew. There can also be a condition not to associate either with the victim, witnesses and/or co-accused.

93 This would normally involve an overnight stay in police custody, although if charged late on a Saturday a suspect would tend to be held until Monday morning.

94 That was approximately 5,000 per year during 2008/09 and 2009/10: Skinns 2011.

95 Under section 21(2)(b) of the Children Act 1989 every local authority must provide accommodation for children whom they are requested to receive under section 38 of PACE.

96 Criminal Justice Joint Inspection 2011b.

97 In 67 per cent of those 49 cases the Inspectors assessed that local authority non-secure accommodation would have been suitable: Criminal Justice Joint Inspection 2011b, p. 40.

98 Criminal Justice Joint Inspection 2011b, p. 5.

are conducted in private whereas members of the public can be present in the adult courts.[99] The youth court, and the adult magistrates' court, is presided over either by a district judge or three lay magistrates. There is also a legally trained court clerk who can assist the district judge/magistrates with the proceedings.

In most youth courts, juvenile defendants will be allowed to sit outside of the dock, usually with a parent or their appropriate adult. If produced from custody, they will be in the secure dock. The youth court operates in very similar ways to the adult court, although in an attempt to be less formal, advocates tend to remain sitting when addressing the court (instead of standing as required in the adult court), and address young defendants by their first name, rather than their surname. Magistrates are also encouraged to engage with the young defendant when imposing a sentence, by asking them if they want to add anything to what has already been said.[100] However, as noted above, it seems that little has changed as the formality of the youth courts still deters juveniles from speaking when being dealt with in the youth court. YOTs were also criticised for failing to engage with juveniles at court.

At court the charge (or indictment in the Crown Court) is put to the juvenile who either pleads guilty or not guilty. In the event of a 'guilty' plea, which occurs in the majority of cases, the magistrates can proceed to sentence, although there may be an adjournment if a pre-sentence report is required (which is prepared by the YOT). A trial is dealt with in the youth court in the same manner as other proceedings, that is, either with a district judge sitting alone or with a bench of three lay magistrates. The role of the district judge/magistrates is to decide on the basis of the evidence presented if, beyond reasonable doubt, the defendant was guilty or not guilty.

While most cases involving juveniles will be heard in the youth court, they can be dealt with in the adult court (either magistrates' court or Crown Court) if jointly charged with an adult.[101] In cases involving more serious offences being dealt with by the Crown Court which jointly involve an adult and a juvenile, the court must only send the juvenile to the Crown Court for trial with an adult where it is necessary in the interests of justice to do so.[102] Factors to be taken into account include the ages of the adult and young person, their respective roles in the commission of the offence, the likely plea, whether there are existing charges in the youth court, the need to deal expeditiously with the case in the youth

---

99 The media can be present in the youth court but there are reporting restrictions concerning the identity of the juveniles concerned.

100 Youth Justice Board 2002 and 2003.

101 Juveniles jointly charged with adults can be dealt with summarily in the magistrates' adult court under section 51 Crime and Disorder Act 1998.

102 If the juvenile is convicted in the adult court or pleads guilty, the adult court will usually send the juvenile's case back to the youth court for sentence. If the adult pleads guilty or his case is discharged and the juvenile pleads not guilty then their case may be sent back to the youth court for trial.

court, and the likely sentence upon conviction. Other matters with which the juvenile is charged, and which meet the requisite conditions, may also be sent up to the Crown Court (under section 51(5) and (6) of the Crime and Disorder Act 1998). Once a juvenile is validly committed to the Crown Court with an adult they must be tried in the Crown Court, even if the adult pleads guilty. However, the juvenile can be remitted to the youth court if there is no longer an indictable offence against the adult and the juvenile has not been arraigned (i.e. asked to enter a plea), unless the remaining offence is a grave crime which requires a Crown Court trial.[103]

In the Crown Court there is a judge who deals with cases on his/her own if the defendant enters a plea of guilty, but in cases involving a contested trial there is a jury of twelve members of the public who are required to determine issues of fact. The only concession when dealing with children in the Crown Court tends to be the removal of wigs by advocates and the judge. In the case of the two boys mentioned above, who were aged 11 when on trial for the murder of James Bulger, an additional step taken was the raising of the dock so that they could view the proceedings.[104] However, the ECtHR held that these steps were insufficient and that the trial was in violation of art. 6 ECHR, which guarantees the right of an accused to participate effectively in his criminal trial. In particular, with the trial taking place in open court, in front of an interested media and hostile public gallery, this was found to have the effect of intimidating and inhibiting the defendants, which was held to be incompatible with allowing them to participate effectively in their trial.

When being dealt with at court for serious offences young defendants can be remanded into secure accommodation, although concerns were raised over too many juveniles being remanded, particularly when a significant proportion went on to receive a non-custodial sentence.[105] Indeed, in 2010 the Prison Reform Trust noted that three quarters of juveniles remanded by the magistrates' court, and one third by the Crown Court, were subsequently acquitted or given a community sentence.[106]

The issue of juvenile remands has been addressed by sections 91–107 of the Legal Aid Sentencing and Punishment of Offenders Act (hereafter: LASPO) 2012. The Act aims to reduce the use of secure remand for children and young people, and to simplify the complex remand arrangements into a 'single remand

---

103 There are very serious offences involving juveniles which can be sent up to the Crown Court for sentence, which are examined further below.

104 ECtHR 16 December 1999, *T. v. United Kingdom*, no. 24724/94 and *V. v. United Kingdom*, no. 24888/94, [2000] 2 All ER 1024 (Note); (1999) 30 EHRR 131; 7 BHRC 659.

105 There are approximately a quarter of juveniles in custody on remand: 620 in 2005–2006 and 477 in 2011–2012: Ministry of Justice 2013.

106 Prison Reform Trust 2011.

framework'.[107] Before remanding a young person in custody the court now has to make sure that one of two conditions are met: the seriousness of the offence must be either a violent or sexual offence, or one that, if committed by an adult, is punishable with a sentence of imprisonment of 14 years or more, or secondly, that there is a 'realistic prospect' of the young defendant receiving a custodial sentence – due to the young person having a history of committing offences or absconding while on remand. The 2012 Act also provides that 17-year-olds can be remanded in secure children's homes or secure training centres, and not just young offender institutions. A court can impose conditions on a child remanded to local authority accommodation that are similar to those which can be imposed on a juvenile remanded on bail, such as electronic monitoring.

2.5. COURT SANCTIONS FOR JUVENILES

There have been changes to court sanctions available for juveniles over recent years. The 1998 Crime and Disorder Act, for example, introduced a number of new orders with the intention of encouraging the court to adopt a more interventionist approach when dealing with young offenders. These included curfew orders, rehabilitation orders and action plan orders. The courts could also impose community sentences, such as community rehabilitation orders and community punishment orders (previously probation orders and community service orders respectively). The Youth Justice and Criminal Evidence Act 1999 introduced the 'referral order' to be used with most first time offenders. Subsequently, in an attempt to rationalise the various court orders the Criminal Justice and Immigration Act 2008 introduced the 'youth rehabilitation order'.

The number of sentences imposed by the courts on juveniles has declined significantly over recent years: 94,870 in 2001–2002 and 59,335 in 2011–2012 – a reduction of 37 per cent. In part, such a decrease is due to a number of systems being put in place to try and divert young people from entering into the youth justice system and also from court. In relation to adults there has been little change in the number of court sentences imposed over the same period of time.[108]

In relation to juvenile offenders, as noted above, the 1998 Crime and Disorder Act required the courts to adopt a more interventionist approach and this led to new community sentences being made available to the courts. The 'referral order' was used with the majority of those being dealt with at court for the first-time.[109] Under this order the juvenile is required to attend a youth offender panel

---

107 This includes transferring the costs of keeping a young person on remand to local authorities, as an incentive to use remand more sparingly. These provisions came into force in April 2013.

108 There was a slight reduction with 1,240,126 adult offenders sentenced in 2001–2002 compared to 1,213,630 in 2011–2012: Ministry of Justice 2013.

109 A referral order was to be imposed unless the offence was so minor as to warrant a discharge or so serious that custody was considered to be appropriate.

(made up of two members of the local community and an advisor from a YOT) and agree activities to be carried out under a contract. These can include making reparation to the victim or the wider community, as well as a programme of activity designed to prevent further offending.[110] This new court order was seen to have the potential to be 'the jewel in the crown in New Labour's youth justice reform panoply', but it seldom led to the active participation of victims.[111]

With the courts required to impose a referral order when dealing with the majority of juvenile first-time entrants into court, the intention was to displace the courts use of discharges and fines.[112] As shown in figure 1, the referral order was to have the desired effect.

Figure 1. Discharges, fines and referral orders imposed on juveniles in court from 2001 to 2012[113]

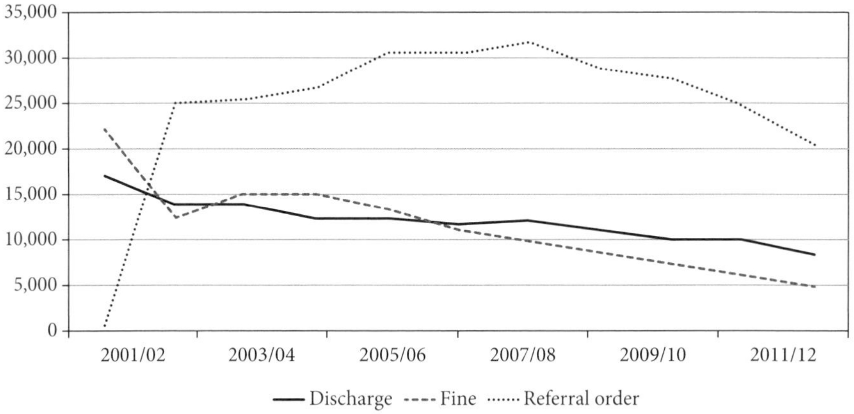

The steady reduction in the number of referral orders imposed from 2007 reflects the decline more generally in the number of cases coming into court. However, following implementation of the LASPO Act 2012 it is to be expected that the courts use of these three court sanctions will increase. In particular, the Act now encourages magistrates to discharge or fine juveniles in cases where it is proportionate to do so. They also have flexibility in appropriate cases to repeatedly use a referral order.

So far as community sentences are concerned, as noted above there were a number of orders available to the courts prior to the 1998 Act which also included a combined community rehabilitation and punishment order together with supervision orders and attendance centre orders. The Crime and Disorder

110 The activities can last for between three months and a year.

111 Morgan and Newburn 2012, p. 519.

112 There is both an 'absolute' and a 'conditional' discharge available to the court. It is the parent who is responsible for payment of a fine imposed on a child aged under 16 years.

113 All criminal statistics are drawn from Ministry of Justice 2013.

Act introduced a number of new sentences. In addition to those mentioned above, it introduced the drug treatment and testing orders and the sex offender orders. Subsequently, the new 'youth rehabilitation order' has replaced these different orders by providing a generic sentence in which there is available to the court a menu of 18 requirements that can be attached to this order to provide different types of intervention as required.[114] A member of the YOT is required to supervise the young offender placed on a youth rehabilitation order, which can be imposed for any time between six months and three years. If the order is breached the young offender can be re-sentenced for the original offence. A maximum fine of £2,500 can also be imposed.

Set out in figure 2 are the number of community sentences imposed between 2001 and 2012.[115] Also shown are the number of youth rehabilitation orders and custodial sentences imposed on juveniles.

Figure 2. The number of community sentences, youth rehabilitation orders and sentences of custody imposed on juveniles from 2001 to 2012

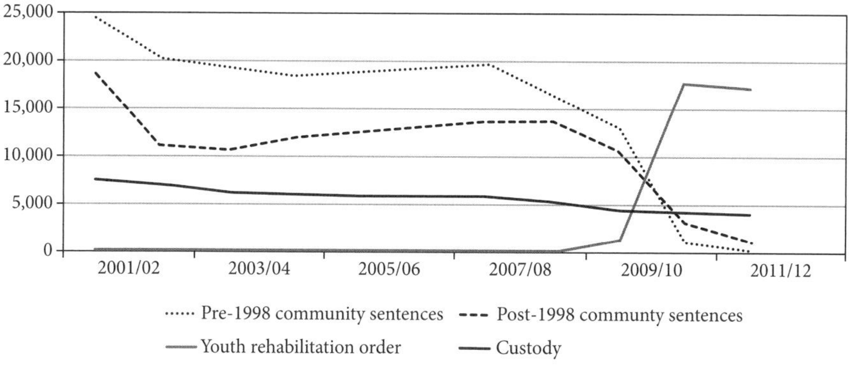

Introduction of the referral order in 2002 is likely to have been the cause of the sharp reduction in the number of community sentences from 2001/02. Similarly, the decline in pre- and post-1998 community sentences from 2008 is evidently due to the new youth rehabilitation order.

The number of custodial sentences is also included in figure 2, which shows a gradual decline in the use of custody since 2001/02. The Crime and Disorder Act 1998 introduced the new 'detention and training order' (hereafter: DTO), which is the main custodial sentence available for 12- to 17-year-olds.[116] The DTO can

114 These include, for example, a curfew, supervision, unpaid work, electronic monitoring, drug treatment, mental health treatment, education requirements and restorative justice.

115 The community sentences are shown as those which had been available prior to the 1998 Act and the new orders introduced by the Act.

116 The 1998 Act had provided for this order to be imposed on 10- and 11-year-olds, but it has only been implemented with juveniles aged 12 years and older. The DTO replaced the secure training order for juveniles.

be imposed for between four and twenty-four months – with half of the order being served in custody and the other half in the community. The number of DTOs imposed by the courts over the past decade has declined by around a half – from 6,915 in 2001–2002 to 3,482 in 2011–2012. While there has been a gradual reduction in the courts' use of custody, it is anticipated that the new offence of 'knife' crime, commented on above, is likely to have an effect on increasing the number of juveniles receiving a DTO. This is due to the deterrent effect of the mandatory minimum sentence of four months required for 16- and 17-year-olds.[117]

There are other custodial sentences shown in figure 2. Under sections 90–92 of the Powers of Criminal Courts (Sentencing) Act 2000, for example, juveniles can be sentenced to custody for very serious offences, such as homicide, and also 'grave' offences, which include firearms and various sexual offences, robbery, residential burglary and handling stolen goods.[118] In 2001–2002 there were 570 juveniles who were sentenced under these provisions and 381 in 2011–2012 – a reduction on the previous year of 33 per cent. There are also 'extended' and 'indeterminate' sentences, which can be given for the protection of the public under sections 226(3) and 228 of the Criminal Justice Act 2003. In 2005–2006 there were 135 such sentences compared to 62 in 2011–2012.[119]

The provisions under the 2003 Act have now been abolished by the LASPO Act 2012 and instead there has been introduced a new 'extended sentence', to be used when there is found to be a significant risk to members of the public of serious harm occasioned by an offender of specified offences.[120] The new 'extended sentence' requires that the court impose a custodial term of at least four years. A juvenile would serve two-thirds of the custodial term before being released on an extended licence of up to five years for violent offences, eight years for sexual offences.

As noted above, the civil law is sometimes used to adopt risk-based initiatives, which were intended to make juveniles responsible for their offending behaviour. In relation to 'anti-social behaviour orders' (hereafter: ASBOs), for example, a breach of the order can be dealt with in the youth court as a criminal offence. From 2000 to 2011 there have been a total of 21,749 ASBOs imposed by the courts, 8,160 of which were on juveniles (38 per cent). There can be seen to be variations in the use of ASBOs for juveniles, rising from 62 orders imposed in 2000, when first introduced, rising to a peak in 2005 of 1,581, and then a decline

117 All sentences and the new offence of 'knife crime' offence were implemented in December 2012.

118 This means juveniles can be detained for a longer period than the normal maximum of 24 months, which is available under the DTO, if being dealt with for very serious offences.

119 These sentences are available in relation to certain violent and sexual offences where the offender is defined as 'dangerous'.

120 See sections 123–5 of LASPO.

to 375 in 2011.[121] Also, as commented on above, concerns were raised over the potential criminalising effect of ASBOs. This was also the view of the Home Affairs Committee when it commented on the breach rate of ASBOs by juveniles being high at 68 per cent, with custody being used as a sanction in 38 per cent of cases.[122] Thus, as the Committee notes, the use of ASBOs does not seem to have been effective in changing behaviour in most cases. There are proposed reforms to ASBOs currently before Parliament under the Anti-Social Behaviour, Crime and Policing Bill. This includes expanding the definition of anti-social behaviour from that which causes 'alarm, distress or harassment' to 'conduct capable of causing nuisance or annoyance'. Instead of seeking to curtail the courts use of ASBOs, therefore, the new broader definition is likely to have the effect of widening the type of behaviour which can be brought under an order.[123]

2.6. ALTERNATIVES TO CRIMINAL PROCEEDINGS

There were a total of 46,328 juveniles receiving a criminal sanction by way of an out-of-court disposal in 2011–2012. The 1998 Crime and Disorder Act had introduced a new final warning scheme for juveniles as an alternative to a police caution, which continues for adult offenders.[124] The final warning scheme effectively gave juveniles two opportunities for an out-of-court disposal prior to charge by way of a reprimand or warning.[125] If convicted at any time, the suspect was not eligible for either reprimand or warning and instead the police decision was either to take no action or to charge. A final warning would initiate a referral to the YOT for an assessment of what intervention may be required to reduce the likelihood of reoffending.

The rigidity of this 'stepwise' approach to out-of-court disposals had been criticised for criminalising some juveniles inappropriately and also for bringing minor and trivial offences into court unnecessarily.[126] Some flexibility was introduced in 2005, when the police were allowed to impose 'penalty notices for disorder' (hereafter: PNDs) when dealing with 16- and 17-year-olds. Shown in

---

121 Ministry of Justice 2013.

122 Compared to 52 per cent for adults. See Home Affairs Committee 2013, para. 36.

123 This is a concern of many children's specialists and practitioners who have argued that the new definition could lead to ASBOs being imposed on children for simply playing outdoors (Play England 2013).

124 A police caution is a formal warning that is given to a person admitting an offence as an alternative to prosecution.

125 A juvenile's eligibility for a reprimand or warning under the scheme depended on the seriousness of the offence. For a first offence the police decision was limited to imposing either a reprimand, warning or charge. Only one reprimand was allowed for a first offence and generally one warning, although a second warning could be imposed if the offence had been committed two years later.

126 Kemp *et al.* 2002.

figure 3 below are the numbers of juveniles receiving a reprimand and warning from 2001 to 2012, and also the number of PNDs from 2005. The number of out-of-court disposals was seen to reach its peak in 2006/07. Indeed, in that year a total of 152,269 offenders received an out-of-court disposal. Together with the 94,583 juveniles who received a court sentence in 2006/07, this means that 62 per cent of those receiving a criminal sanction had been diverted from court. This compares to 44 per cent in 2011/12 when 59,335 juvenile offenders received a court order and 46,328 an out-of-court penalty.

When considering these changes in the police use of out-of-court disposals it is important to examine other influences in the criminal justice system. In particular, in 2002 a police performance target was introduced which had the effect of significantly increasing the police use of out-of-court disposals, particularly in relation to minor offences committed by juveniles.[127] The target was revised in 2007 to encourage the police to focus on more serious offences, and it was abandoned altogether in 2010.

Figure 3. Reprimands, final warnings, conditional cautions and penalty notices for disorder for juveniles from 2001 to 2012

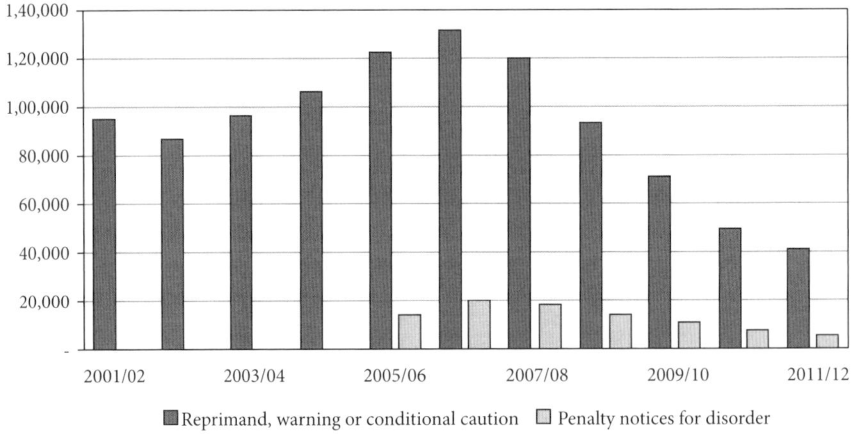

The LASPO Act 2012 abolished the final warning scheme and the police are no longer allowed to use PNDs for juveniles. Instead a simplified and more flexible approach has been adopted, with three main out-of-court disposals for juveniles. These include 'community resolution', 'youth cautions' and 'youth conditional cautions'.[128] The disposal decision for out-of-court penalties is to be based on the seriousness of the offence, the previous offending history and the likelihood of compliance – the views of the victim can also be taken into account. Community resolution involves an informal response after the juvenile has admitted the

127 See CPS 2002, Office for Criminal Justice Reform 2010 and Morgan and Newburn 2012, p. 515.
128 These new sanctions came into force in April 2013.

offence and agrees to participate in activity based on resolving the offence, including restorative justice. Youth cautions and youth conditional cautions are formal disposals that do not have to be used in a set order. On the contrary, there is no limit on the number of youth cautions or youth conditional cautions and these disposals can be imposed in cases where a juvenile has previously been convicted.

When imposing a youth caution the police are required to notify the YOT.[129] In relation to the youth conditional caution the conditions that can be attached must have one or more of the following objectives: rehabilitation – to help modify the behaviour of the young offender, serve to reduce the likelihood of re-offending or help to reintegrate them into society; reparation – conditions which serve to repair the damage done either directly or indirectly by the young offender; and punishment – unpaid work or a financial penalty which punishes the young person for their unlawful behaviour.

The police decide whether or not a youth caution or youth conditional caution is appropriate and these are issued by a police officer in the presence of the juvenile and their appropriate adult. A Crown prosecutor can also consider imposing a youth conditional caution as an alternative to court in cases where the young person has been charged. These disposals are formally recorded and may be cited in court if the young person reoffends in the future. Non-compliance with the conditions attached as part of the youth conditional caution may result in prosecution for the original offence. As the youth caution and youth conditional caution are intended to be used as an alternative to prosecution, there are legal criteria which have to be met. In addition to admitting the offence, the police/CPS need to ensure that there is sufficient evidence to obtain a realistic prospect of conviction, and that it is not considered to be in the public interest to prosecute. There is no requirement for the young person to consent to receiving a youth caution, although such consent is required for the youth conditional caution.

II. INTERROGATIONS

1. INTERROGATIONS OF JUVENILES IN THE PRE-TRIAL PHASE

1.1. CONCEPT OF INTERROGATION: RELEVANT DEFINITIONS

Having set out a general outline of the juvenile justice system in England and Wales in the first part of this report, the second part will – first of all – examine

[129] For a first youth caution the YOT will use their expertise to determine whether there is the need for an assessment and intervention. An assessment is required for second and subsequent youth cautions.

more specifically definitions concerning the interrogation of juvenile suspects. The rules concerning the interrogation of suspects are the same for both adults and juveniles, although an appropriate adult is required in cases involving juveniles and other vulnerable suspects.

1.1.1. *Arrest and detention*

Once the police receive a report that a crime has been committed the usual response is to arrest a suspect, gather evidence and conduct an interrogation. It is at the end of the investigation that the police, or the CPS, decide whether or not the suspect should be charged. In the past, the position at common law had been that the police would first make their enquiries and an arrest would be made immediately before a suspect was charged. With PACE granting the police time, facilities and powers to conduct interrogations, the police station has now become the focal point of the investigation in many cases.[130] This means that instead of the police gathering evidence before making an arrest, which could make the need for an interview redundant, the practice is to arrest early on so that the interrogation has become an essential part of the police investigation.[131] The process is the same for both adults and juveniles.

1.1.2. *The interrogation*

The police are allowed to detain suspects in order to question them. For the purpose of an interrogation PACE refers to the interview as: 'the questioning of a person regarding their involvement or suspected involvement in a criminal offence or offences which, under para. 10.1, must be carried out under caution'.[132] Code C of PACE, para. 10.1, states that a person must be cautioned when there are grounds to suspect them of having committed an offence and before any questions are put to them. At the commencement of the interview, PACE provides that the suspect should be reminded of their right to remain silent and their continuing right to legal advice.[133] PACE also requires that the police must not interrogate juveniles, or adults with mental health problems, in the absence of an appropriate adult.

There are restrictions on the extent to which the police can use informal exchanges taking place between the police and a suspect as providing admissible

130 In *Holgate-Mohammed v Duke* [1984] 1 All ER 1054, it was accepted that the primary purpose of arrest is to enable detention and so interrogation at the police station, where a confession is more likely to be forthcoming.

131 Section 37 of PACE requires that a custody officer shall determine whether there is sufficient evidence against a suspect to charge when first brought into custody. However, suspects tend to be detained on the basis that there needs to be an interrogation: Sanders *et al.* 2010.

132 Code of Practice C, para. 11.1A.

133 Code of Practice C, para. 11.4.

evidence in court. In the case of *R. v. Absolam,*[134] for example, it was upheld by the Court of Appeal that the questioning of a suspect in the charging room by the custody officer did not amount to an interrogation, particularly as the suspect had not been read his rights prior to the questioning. Accordingly, the conviction was quashed. PACE requires that in cases where the police seek to rely on a significant statement or silence prior to police questioning, that this is put to the suspect at the commencement of the interrogation.[135]

In legal terms, in addition to establishing whether or not the suspect admits or denies the allegation, a key aim of the interrogation is to establish evidence of the suspect's thought processes at the relevant time (the *mens rea* of the offence). The interrogation is not, therefore, a 'search for the truth'. As Baldwin explained, 'the idea that police interviewing is, or is becoming, a neutral or objective search for truth cannot be sustained, because any interview inevitably involves exploring with a suspect the detail of allegations within a framework of the points that might at a later date need to be proved'. Instead, interrogations need to be seen as mechanisms directed towards the 'construction of proof'.[136] Or, as McConville *et al.* put it, as 'social encounters fashioned to confirm and legitimate a police narrative'.[137]

The police interrogation of a suspect, either adult or juvenile, is not mandatory, although the police seem to value the questioning of suspects, particularly when an admission is forthcoming. This is because the police are primarily judged on how successful they are in 'catching criminals' and bringing them to justice.[138] Confessions represent an efficient means of resolving cases, relieving the police of gathering additional evidence. An admission made during the interrogation can also lead to a quick 'guilty' plea at court or the recording of an out-of-court disposal (where an acceptance of guilt is required). In addition, during the interview the police can seek to obtain information about other offences and/or offenders. The police cannot interrogate juveniles below the age of 10 years. If the police have responded to complaints concerning the behaviour of a child below the criminal age of responsibility they can refer them to the YOT or to the local authority social services department for a child safety order to be considered.

1.1.3. 'Voluntary' interviews

There is a difference between interrogations depending on whether or not an adult or juvenile suspect has been arrested. In cases where the police

134 [1988] 88 Cr. App. Rep. 332.
135 Code of Practice C, para. 11.4. A significant statement is one which appears capable of being used in evidence against the suspect, an admission of guilt, for example. A significant silence is a failure or refusal to answer a question or answer satisfactorily when under caution.
136 Baldwin 1993, p. 327.
137 McConville *et al.* 1991, p. 79.
138 Sanders *et al.* 2010, p. 257.

believe it is not necessary to arrest a suspect in order to conduct an interview, the interrogation can take place on a 'voluntary' basis, but with the same legal protections applying. That is, the suspect has to be cautioned prior to the commencement of the interrogation, advised that they have the right to independent legal advice, and be told that they are free to leave the interview, unless they are subsequently arrested.[139] Juvenile suspects are also required to have an appropriate adult present in the interrogation. The 'voluntary' interview can take place at the juvenile's home, their place of education, or in a police station – but outside of the custody suite, generally in an interview room with equipment available to facilitate the recording of the interview.

1.1.4. Mediation and diversion

When responding to minor offences or anti-social behaviour the police can impose a 'community resolution'; delivered with or without the use of restorative justice techniques. This is an informal response in cases where the offence is admitted but the police do not need to conduct an interrogation. There are other forms of diversion from court where juvenile suspects are required to be interrogated by the police. As noted above in relation to the youth caution and youth conditional caution, for example, there are legal requirements which have to be met, such as an admission and sufficient evidence to obtain a realistic prospect of conviction, which criteria can be satisfied if the offence is admitted during the interrogation.[140]

1.2. TIMING OF INTERROGATIONS AND THE PRE-CHARGE PROCESS

There is no precise moment when the suspect has to be interrogated but this usually takes place following an arrest and prior to the charging decision. Having made an arrest and detained a suspect in custody, the police can either interrogate them straightaway, or otherwise gather evidence before conducting an interview. In cases where the police gather evidence prior to the interrogation, there can be long delays with suspects waiting in police cells. Indeed, during the first period of detention suspects were found to be held in police custody on average for nine hours; almost seven and a half hours for juvenile suspects.[141]

---

139 Code of Practice C, para. 3.21. If arrested, the police officer has to bring a suspect before a custody officer.

140 The other criterion involves the public interest test.

141 Further analysis of the dataset was used to identify the average time juveniles were held in police custody during the first detention period. In addition, a sub-sample of 300 custody records were analysed in one police station where additional information had been extracted manually. The records included all suspects who had requested legal advice and the average

Having interrogated the suspect, the police, or the CPS in relation to more serious and/or complex cases, then have to decide whether to continue with their investigations or decide that there is sufficient evidence to make a charging decision.[142] In some cases the suspect can be required to return to the police station at a later date while police enquiries are ongoing. If the suspect is charged, they will either be bailed to attend court at a future date, or otherwise held in police custody until the next available court date.

1.3. AUTHORITIES EMPOWERED TO CONDUCT INTERROGATIONS OF JUVENILE SUSPECTS

The police are empowered to carry out the interrogation of juvenile suspects. Police investigators can become specialised when dealing with certain types of offences, such as homicide, sexual offences, robbery and drugs. There is police training provided in relation to interrogation techniques, but there is no requirement for police investigators to be specialists when dealing with juvenile suspects. Neither prosecutors nor the judiciary are competent authorities to carry out the interrogation of either adult or juvenile suspects within an adversarial system of justice.

There is no formal way of regularly assessing the capacity of juvenile suspects to be interrogated. However, if the police are concerned that a suspect has a mental health problem, or are told that this might be the case, then certain action has to be taken. In relation to adult suspects this involves arranging for an appropriate adult to be involved, a protection which is already required for juveniles. The police must also contact a doctor, usually a forensic medical examiner (hereafter: FME),[143] who will carry out an assessment, although a psychiatrist can act as the FME when mental health issues are involved.[144] The FME will advise the police about whether the suspect is well enough to be questioned about the offence, and also to remain at the police station. In some cases the FME will arrange for a mental health assessment, in which case a psychiatrist would evaluate whether the suspect is fit to be interviewed, or if they require admission to hospital, or to be released from custody.

There are no special rules for the interrogation of 'extra-vulnerable' juveniles. Indeed, this category does not exist in England and Wales, although in addition

time from arrest to the interrogation was 7 hours and 37 minutes. It should be noted that there are longer delays in cases where there is an interview and legal advice has been requested. See Kemp *et al.* 2012, p. 740.

142 If the case requires a CPS decision, there is a delay while the evidence is faxed, or otherwise sent electronically, to the prosecutor who makes the charging decision.

143 Qualified doctors are available on 'call' to provide assistance to the police. When called to the police station they are referred to as the 'FME'.

144 Ventress *et al.* 2008.

to their young age, a juvenile with mental health problems would be considered as particularly vulnerable. As mentioned before, if there are concerns over the mental health of the suspect then the police will arrange for a medical assessment to ascertain whether they are fit to be interviewed and/or held in detention. There is no role within the adversarial criminal justice system for medical experts, social workers, or YOT members to be involved in the interrogation of a juvenile suspect, unless acting as their appropriate adult.

2. THE RULES FOR THE INTERROGATION OF JUVENILES: GENERAL SAFEGUARDS

There are legal safeguards for those arrested and questioned by the police, including the right to publicly funded legal advice, the right to remain silent, to have an appropriate adult and, if required, an interpreter.

2.1. THE RIGHT TO LEGAL ASSISTANCE

Under section 58(1) of PACE all suspects have an 'unequivocal' right to consult with a solicitor free of charge and privately at any time. There is also the associated requirement that the police inform suspects of this right (Code C, para. 3.1).[145] The suspect is first advised of their right to free and independent legal advice when booked into police custody (Code C para. 3.1(ii)). If legal advice is requested the police telephone through to the Defence Solicitor Call Centre, which routes the request for legal advice. In case of certain summary offences the request is routed through to CDS (Criminal Defence Services) Direct, which is a call centre providing telephone-only advice.[146] However, the suspect is entitled to a solicitor of their choice being present if the police conduct an interrogation in such cases.

The suspect can delay their request for legal advice until just prior to the police interrogation, when they are reminded by the police of their right to legal advice.[147] If legal advice is requested at this stage, the interrogation has to be delayed while the solicitor is contacted and either speaks to the suspect over the telephone and/or attends at the police station to be present during the interrogation. If legal advice is requested the suspect can speak to an adviser over

---

145 Suspects also have a right to independent legal advice when interrogated by the police on a 'voluntary' basis and, if requested, the police have to arrange for a legal adviser to attend (Code of Practice C, para. 11.2).

146 Detainees who have been arrested after having breached their bail conditions and also those arrested on warrant, having failed to attend a court hearing are also routed to CDS Direct.

147 Code of Practice C, para. 11.2.

the telephone or, as is more common practice, the legal adviser will wait until the interrogation before advising their client at the police station.

Suspects have the right to a lawyer being present during the interrogation, although there may be occasions when a lawyer decides not to attend and instead provides advice over the telephone. Legal advisers are encouraged to be present during the interrogation when dealing with juveniles or other vulnerable suspects, even when dealing with minor matters which have not been routed to CDS Direct.[148]

When attending at the police station the solicitor will first meet with the police investigators to discuss details of the alleged offence and, if provided, to consider what evidence has been disclosed by the police against their client.[149] The solicitor will then meet with their client privately to discuss the strength of the prosecution case and to take their client's instructions before advising them on how to approach the interrogation.[150] The suspect may be advised to speak, to be silent, or to give a prepared written statement, which the lawyer will note down.[151] A difficulty may arise for the solicitor if the appropriate adult also wants to be present during this private consultation. Of particular concern will be issues of confidentiality, with the consultation being subject to 'legal privilege' but with the appropriate adult not being subject to these rules.[152] It is a matter for the solicitor and their client to decide whether the appropriate adult should be present; PACE requires that a suspect should have the opportunity to consult privately with a solicitor in the absence of the appropriate adult.[153]

The solicitor's role in the police station is to protect and advance the legal rights of their client.[154] This means that the solicitor is to ensure that the interrogation is conducted fairly and in accordance with PACE and the Codes of Practice, which seek to protect the suspect from unnecessary pressure and distress. PACE recognises that on occasions this may require the solicitor to give advice that has the effect of the client avoiding the provision of information which could strengthen the prosecution case. In addition, it is recognised that the solicitor is allowed to intervene in order to seek clarification; or to challenge

148 Ashford *et al.* 2006, p. 160. There is also higher fixed fee payable for legal advisers who attend at the station and provide face-to face legal advice.

149 Under the Criminal Procedure and Investigations Act 1996 the police investigator is not under an obligation to reveal to the defence any or part of the evidence prior to the interrogation.

150 Code of Practice C para. 3.1(ii) provides suspects with the right to consult privately with a solicitor while held in custody.

151 For the most recent empirical data on custodial legal advice, see Blackstock *et al* 2014, chapters 6 and 7.

152 'Legal privilege' protects confidential discussions between a solicitor and their client, provided that the communication is for the purpose of seeking and receiving legal advice.

153 Code of Practice C, Note 1E.

154 There is no legal source which outlines the responsibility of legal advisers in the police station. However, there are comprehensive and practical guides, which cover the solicitor's role, including defending young people. See Ashford *et al.* 2006.

an improper question to their client, or the manner in which it is put; to advise their client not to reply to particular questions; or if they wish to give their client further legal advice.[155]

From the defence perspective, as stressed in legal literature, the solicitor is required to intervene in the interrogation to ensure that the police do not use complex language, or ploys designed to elicit responses through leading questions, multiple questions and/or hypothetical questions. The solicitor also needs to be alert to any signs that the young suspect may be susceptible to any veiled threat by the police, which might not be immediately obvious, and to ensure that the interrogation is not conducted in an oppressive manner. In addition, the objective for the solicitor in the interview is to ensure that the young suspect 'does his best in the interview', irrespective of whether or not they respond to questions put by the police, and to keep an accurate record of the interview.[156]

If legal advice has been requested, and the solicitor wishes to attend, the police can only proceed with an interrogation in their absence if an urgent interview is required and a delay could involve a serious risk or harm to evidence, persons or property. This has to be authorised by an officer of at least the rank of superintendent.[157] Under the same provision, PACE also allows the police to proceed with an interrogation in cases where a solicitor, including a duty solicitor, has agreed to attend but they are delayed and awaiting their arrival would cause unreasonable delay to the process of investigation. In addition, if legal advice has been requested but the suspect changes their mind about wanting a solicitor present in the interrogation, the interview can proceed if authorised by an inspector. The inspector's involvement is to ensure that the suspect has not been put under pressure by the police not to have a solicitor. After having spoken to the suspect and the solicitor requested, if satisfied that the suspect has made an informed decision, the inspector can authorise that the interrogation continues without a solicitor present.[158]

Suspects are entitled to request a solicitor but having legal advice is never mandatory. If juveniles decline legal advice there is no power to make an *ex officio* appointment. Indeed, while the appropriate adult can request a solicitor to attend at the police station on the suspect's behalf, it is the suspect who has to make the decision about whether or not to have legal advice. It is interesting to reflect that children as young as 10 to 13 years old are responsible for deciding whether or not to have a solicitor, even though at such a young age they are unlikely to understand the role of a solicitor and how this could assist them when in police custody.

155 Code of Practice C, Note 6D. For an empirical account of the lawyer's role during police interrogation of the suspect, see Blackstock *et al.* 2014, chapter 8.

156 See Ashford *et al.* 2006, p. 164 to 165 and Cape 2011.

157 PACE, section 58 and Code of Practice C, para. 6.6.

158 Revised Code of Practice C, para. 6.6.D(i).

2.2. LEGAL AID

Legal aid is available to provide free access to legal advice for all suspects held in police custody. Access to legal aid is structured around suspects either requesting their own nominated solicitor[159] or otherwise requesting the services of the duty solicitor. The duty solicitor scheme comprises local defence practitioners who take their turn on a rota to provide legal advice at the police station. Those providing cover under the duty solicitor scheme have to be experienced criminal practitioners. There is no special qualification required for defence solicitors when dealing with juveniles, although some practitioners tend to specialise in such cases by regularly dealing with young clients.[160]

2.3. THE RIGHT TO REMAIN SILENT

Under common law, suspects interrogated by the police had a right to remain silent without any adverse inferences later being drawn in court. In the late 1980s, there were concerns raised by the police that the right to silence was adversely impacting on the conviction rate.[161] While this issue was examined by the Royal Commission on Criminal Justice, with the majority agreeing that the suspect's right to remain silent should continue,[162] this decision was ignored by government, which went on to legislate the Criminal Justice and Public Order Act 1994.[163] The court can now draw adverse inferences from silence if defendants seek to rely on evidence in court, which they did not mention to the police when questioned. Accordingly, while suspects can refuse to answer some or all of the questions put by the police in the interrogation, solicitors have to advise their clients about the potential for adverse inferences to be drawn later on in court.

It is an important decision, therefore, for solicitors to advise their clients about whether or not to respond to some or all of the police questions put to them in the interrogation. The advice will depend, to some extent, on what evidence the police disclose to the defence prior to the interview. However, as noted above, the police are under no obligation to disclose evidence to the

---

159 The choice of a publicly funded solicitor is restricted to those working for solicitors' firms who hold a General Criminal Contract with the Legal Aid Agency.

160 While there is no form of specialisation in juvenile criminal law, there is a Children Law Accreditation Scheme run by the Law Society. This scheme includes practitioners who deal with family and public law cases, rather than criminal cases involving juveniles.

161 Sanders *et al.* 2010, p. 272. There was no clear evidence of an impact on the conviction rate and in fact, very few people exercised their right to silence; of those who did, they often later answered questions and even went on to plead guilty. See McConville and Hodgson 1993 and Leng 1993.

162 Royal Commission on Criminal Justice 1993, Recommendations 82 and 83.

163 See sections 34, 36 and 37.

defence prior to the interrogation. Nevertheless, in the case of *R. v. Imran and Hussain*,[164] it was noted that if the police disclose little or nothing to the solicitor, then it is likely that the suspect will be advised to remain silent. While the police are encouraged to provide some evidence to the defence, in the above case Lord Bingham of Cornhill stated: 'It is totally wrong to submit that a defendant should be prevented from lying by being presented with the whole of the evidence against him prior to the interview.' This point of view was later re-affirmed in the case of *Thirwell v. R.*[165]

If the police do not disclose to the solicitor whether or not they have any evidence, the solicitor might assume that there is no evidence and, on the basis of protecting their client from self-incrimination, they are likely to advise them to remain silent. The solicitor's advice of what the client should say in the police interview is also informed by other factors. This includes not only whether or not the police have any evidence, but also the admissibility of such evidence, and whether or not their client has a defence and/or alibi.[166] With solicitors being aware of how clients, particularly vulnerable clients, can get drawn into answering questions during an interrogation, there is the option for them prior to the interrogation to assist the juvenile by preparing a written statement, setting out the issues the defence wishes to raise, and this can then be read out by the lawyer during the interrogation.

While suspects have the right to remain silent during an interrogation, they do not have the right to absent themselves from police questioning. If the suspect, or their solicitor, advises the police that they will remain silent, it is common practice for the police to go through the process of asking questions, as this will assist in constructing the prosecution case. The suspect can refuse to answer all questions or otherwise be selective in refusing to answer one or more questions.

In cases where the suspect has remained silent during the interview, and there is insufficient evidence to charge, the police decision has to be to take 'no further action'. Accordingly, there can be a positive outcome for the suspect in making no comment. However, in cases where the police have strong evidence, the advice to remain silent during the interrogation can be detrimental to the client. At court, for example, adverse inferences can be drawn if the suspect seeks to rely on evidence that was not mentioned during the interrogation. In addition, without an admission, the suspect is not eligible for an out-of-court disposal, which can be used in some cases as an alternative to prosecution. The extent to which lawyers are able to canvass such possibilities with the client will depend to some extent on the police disclosing sufficient information of the evidence against the suspect.[167]

164 [1997] Crim L.R. 754.
165 [2002] EWCA Crim. 286.
166 See Cape 2011.
167 See Blackstock *et al.* 2014, chapter 7.

Within an adversarial system of justice there is a presumption of innocence and the burden of proof is on the prosecution to prove that the suspect is guilty 'beyond reasonable doubt'.[168] There is also the related 'privilege against self-incrimination' which has given suspects the right to remain silent during police interrogations. While there is a relationship between the two, the concepts are not synonymous.

2.4. RIGHT TO INFORMATION: POLICE CAUTION

As soon as an officer has reasonable grounds to suspect that someone has committed an offence, they should be cautioned and any questioning following the caution must be conducted as an official interrogation with the attendant safeguards set out in PACE. If this is not done, the interrogation may be inadmissible as evidence in court. Only in exceptional circumstances may the police conduct an 'urgent' interview without cautioning the suspect, but the admissibility of the evidence can be questioned later on in court. Before the commencement of an interrogation the police are required to caution the suspect.[169] The only difference for juveniles when cautioning suspects is that this has to be done in the physical presence of the appropriate adult. If they are not present when the suspect is first cautioned then this has to be repeated in their presence before the start of the interrogation.[170]

The police investigator has to caution a suspect before asking them questions about an offence on each occasion the suspect is interrogated.[171] The caution has to be given verbally by a police officer in the following terms: 'You do not have to say anything. But it may harm your defence if you do not mention when questioned something which you later rely on in court. Anything you do say may be given in evidence'.[172] As the caution includes the qualification to the right to remain silent, this can make it difficult for people – especially juveniles – to understand. In a study undertaken by Clare *et al.*, for example, they found that only a small proportion of a group of students and the 'general population' were able to explain all three sentences of the caution correctly.[173] While another group of police officers had a better understanding of the caution, only half of this group were able to explain correctly the three sentences comprising the caution. If a suspect does not appear to understand the caution in the interrogation, the person giving it is required to explain it in their own words.[174]

---

168 See Blackstock *et al.* 2014.
169 Code of Practice C, para. 11.1A.
170 Code of Practice C, paras. 10.11A and 10.12.
171 Code of Practice C, para. 10.
172 Code of Practice C, para. 10.5.
173 Clare *et al.* 1998.
174 Code of Practice C, Note 10D.

2.5. PRESENCE OF APPROPRIATE ADULT

It is mandatory for a juvenile suspect to have an appropriate adult present when they are interrogated by the police.[175] When they are first brought into custody the custody officer must seek to ascertain from the suspect the identity of the person responsible for their welfare. They then have to inform them as soon as practicable of the arrest and why the suspect has been detained.[176] If the appropriate adult is not the juvenile's parent or guardian, they too must be informed of the basis on which the suspect has been detained and asked to attend at the station in order to see them.[177] With long delays often occurring between the police gathering evidence and the interrogation, the practice of appropriate adults, as noted above, seems to be to wait until the police are ready to proceed before attending at the station.

PACE requires that appropriate adults must be present when juveniles are interrogated but this right can be waived if an urgent interview is required. As noted above in relation to the involvement of a solicitor, the police can proceed with an interrogation in the absence of an appropriate adult if waiting for them could involve a serious risk or harm to evidence, persons or property.[178] An officer of the rank of superintendent or above has to authorise that the interrogation can proceed in the absence of an appropriate adult. If the circumstances which require an urgent interview are no longer relevant then the interview will cease.

There are situations where a person is unable to act as the appropriate adult because this could be in conflict with the interests of the child. This would include circumstances where the appropriate adult is involved as a victim or other witness in the alleged offence, or where the juvenile has admitted the offence to them.[179] In addition, a juvenile's parent should not be asked to be the appropriate adult if they are estranged and the child expressly objects to their presence. While intended as a safeguard for juveniles, parent(s) acting as an appropriate adult can undermine other legal protections for young suspects. In particular, it seems that a commonly held view among suspects is that legal advisers are the main cause of delays.[180] Accordingly, a parent or guardian might discourage the juvenile from having a solicitor if they perceive that this would lead to a delay. In addition, it can be difficult for a lawyer to maintain the suspect's right to remain silent, if the parent is angry at their child's perceived

175 Code of Practice C, para. 11.1A.

176 Code of Practice C, para. 3.13.

177 Code of Practice C, para. 3.15.

178 Code of Practice C, para. 11.15.

179 Code of Practice C, Note 1B. In addition, in cases where a social worker, or other YOT member, has been appointed as the appropriate adult, but the juvenile had earlier admitted the offence, another appropriate adult should be appointed in the interest of fairness.

180 Blackstock *et al.* 2014 and Kemp 2013a.

wrongdoing and is urging them to tell the police what happened. This situation helps to highlight the potential conflict in the roles of the appropriate adult and the legal adviser.

If an appropriate adult is present at an interrogation, PACE requires that they are to be informed that they are not expected to act simply as an observer and their presence is to advise the juvenile being questioned; to observe that the interview is being conducted properly and fairly; and to facilitate communication with the juvenile being interviewed.[181] As noted above, research has shown that appropriate adults are of variable effectiveness, but this is perhaps not surprising given that parents and family members are generally untrained and do not always appreciate the legal significance of police questions and procedures.

2.6. THE RIGHT TO INTERPRETATION AND TRANSLATION

When a suspect is first brought into police custody the police are responsible for making sure appropriate arrangements are in place for accessing suitably qualified interpreters for people who are deaf or do not understand English.[182] If the suspect is unable to understand English the custody officer will contact 'Language Line' in order to book them into custody. This provides a three-way conversation over the telephone that enables the custody sergeant to ask the suspect questions, which the interpreter then translates, and the suspect's response to the interpreter is then fed back to the custody officer.[183] Any notices received by the suspect, including the notice of their legal rights, has to be translated into the language spoken by them.[184] When the suspect is to be interrogated by the police it is the responsibility of the police to arrange for an interpreter to be present in the interview.[185]

In cases where a legal adviser is involved, they have to decide whether the interpreter arranged by the police for the interrogation can also act as the interpreter when they take instructions and advise their client. The Law Society's Practice Note suggests that in most cases the interpreter arranged by the police will be suitable for this purpose, although there are certain circumstances in which this may not be so.[186] The Practice Note also highlights the importance

---

181 Code of Practice C, para. 11.17.

182 Code of Practice C, para. 13.1.See Blackstock *et al.* 2014, p. 148 for details of interpretation and translation services in England and Wales.

183 Language Line has available interpreters who can cover over 200 different languages.

184 Code of Practice C, Note 3B.

185 If possible, interpreters should be drawn from the National Register of Public Service Interpreters (NRPSI), the Council for the Advancement of Communication with Deaf People (CACDP) or the Directory of British Sign Language/English (Code of Practice C, para. 13.1).

186 This includes, for example, where the interpreter is known to the suspect, or if the offences are of a particularly sensitive and/or serious nature. See Law Society 2012.

for solicitors to confirm with the interpreter that they are bound by their Code of Conduct so as to ensure the confidentiality of the communication between the solicitor and their client during the private consultation.

3. CARRYING OUT THE INTERROGATION

Whenever a suspect is interrogated by the police they must be informed of the nature of the offence about which they are to be questioned.[187] The juvenile does not have a right to access the police case file but, as noted above, when considering the suspect's right to remain silent during the interrogation, the police investigators first meet with the solicitor and discuss what evidence they have in the case. With the police being under no formal obligation to disclose all, or even some, of the evidence, the extent to which information is disclosed by the police is likely to influence what is said by the suspect in the interrogation.

3.1. RECORDING POLICE INTERROGATIONS

PACE requires that an accurate record be made of the police interview. Police custody suites contain one or more interview rooms where suspects are formally questioned and the interrogations are tape recorded or, increasingly, digitally recorded. The recorded interview needs to include the place of the interview, the time it begins and ends, the time the record was made (if different), any breaks in the interview and the names of all those present.[188] At the end of the interview there is a master tape (or disc), which is sealed with a label, which has to be signed by the maker of the tape; those present in the interrogation are also invited to sign the label.[189] In the case of 'voluntary' interviews taking place outside of police custody, if no recording equipment is available contemporaneous handwritten notes can be made of the interrogation.[190] These have to be signed by the officer making the record and those present are also invited to check whether the notes provide an accurate record and, if so, they are invited to sign the interview to that effect.[191]

There are duplicate copies made of the interrogation, one copy of which is kept by the police and the other is available for the defence on request once instructed by the suspect. The record of the interrogation is not transcribed unless the suspect is charged with an offence. If charged, the police will then

[187] Code of Practice C, para. 11.1A.
[188] See Code of Practice C, Note 11.7.
[189] Code of Practice C, paras. 11.7(b), 11.9 and 11.11.
[190] Code of Practice C, para. 11.7(c).
[191] Code of Practice C, paras. 11.9 and 11.11.

provide a written summary of the interrogation, made after listening to the tape and this, together with the taped interview (if not provided before) will be included as part of the evidence disclosed to the defence.

3.2. QUESTIONS AND INTERROGATION TECHNIQUES

There are no specific rules for the police when posing questions to juvenile suspects or on specific interrogation techniques. The presumption of innocence is connected to the right of a suspect to remain silent and not to incriminate themselves. In the case of *Saunders v. United Kingdom*[192] the ECtHR held that if methods of coercion or oppression are used to procure self-incriminating statements, which are subsequently used in a prosecution, the suspect's right to a fair trial under art. 6 ECHR will have been breached. The extent to which police questioning could be oppressive or unfair was considered above when examining the role of solicitors in the police interrogation.

There are certain types of offences where the police might explore with the juvenile during the interrogation family and/or cultural background issues. In cases involving sexual abuse, for example, it may be pertinent for the police to ask certain questions about such issues if relevant to the offence(s) being investigated. Similarly, when dealing with offences of violence arising out of family relationships, the police may ask questions in order to understand better the family and/or cultural issues involved.

3.3. DURATION OF INTERROGATIONS

There are no rules which restrict the length of time a suspect can be interrogated, or how often. However, due to the vulnerability of juvenile suspects, long and/or repeated interrogations could later be challenged at court as having been oppressive. While there is no rule which states that a juvenile cannot be interviewed at night-time, it seems that this does not often happen, for two main reasons. First, PACE requires that in any 24-hour period of time the suspect has a continuous period of at least eight hours of rest, free from any questioning, which is usually during the night-time.[193] Second, and as noted above, appropriate adults are not always available during the night, which means that the interview has to be delayed.

As noted above, in addition to the police investigators and the juvenile suspect being involved in the interrogation, an appropriate adult must also be present and, if requested, a legal adviser, unless an urgent interview is

192 [1997] 23 EHRR 313 (68–9).

193 Code of Practice C, para. 12.2.

required. If a juvenile suspect is interviewed in the absence of an appropriate adult and subsequently charged, it is a matter for the defence lawyer at court to consider whether the grounds for an emergency interview existed and whether the requisite authority was obtained.[194] If not, the admissibility of the police interrogation, or part thereof, could be challenged. There is no PACE requirement for a solicitor to be present in the interrogation, although if legal advice is requested a solicitor is likely to be involved.

4. OUTPUTS OF THE INTERROGATION

The statements obtained by the police during the police interrogation can be used to inform the charging decision. In particular, what is said, or not said, could determine whether the police/CPS decide to take no further action, impose an out-of-court penalty, summons or charge. The main purpose of the statements obtained by the police is that these can be admitted as evidence at court. If the juvenile defendant at court pleads 'not guilty', then the statements can be used in examination and cross-examination. As noted above, if the defendant remains silent during the interrogation, then adverse inferences could be drawn if they seek to rely on evidence that they might reasonably have advanced at the time of the interrogation. If the juvenile is charged and remanded in custody by the court, then the statements could also be used either by the prosecution or the defence in a bail application.

When suspects make a confession during the interrogation, the statement can assist when seeking to achieve maximum credit for an early guilty plea at court. The guidance set down by the Sentencing Guidelines Council recommends that there should be a one-third discount if there is a guilty plea entered at the first opportunity.[195] However, in the case of *Caley and Others v. R.*[196] the Court of Appeal considered a number of cases which involved discounts for guilty pleas. It was held that an admission in the interrogation is a mitigating factor and not an 'indication of a guilty plea' for the purpose of gaining credit. The first reasonable opportunity for an admission to be made in order to achieve the maximum credit was held to be at the defendant's appearance in the magistrates' court when a plea is invited, rather than a confession made in the police station. A confession during the interrogation is also relevant when considering the

194 More generally, section 78 of PACE gives the courts discretion to exclude from a criminal trial evidence which has been obtained unfairly.

195 This then reduces to a one-quarter discount after the trial date is set and a one-tenth discount for a guilty plea just prior to, or after the trial has commenced. It is expected that these guidelines will be followed unless there is a good reason to depart from them. If not, this can be the basis of an appeal. See Sentencing Guidelines Council 2007.

196 [2012] EWCA Crim. 2821.

potential imposition for an out-of-court disposal, as this requires the offence to be admitted, without which the suspect could instead be charged.

5. REMEDIES AND SANCTIONS

The main remedy available for a breach of PACE safeguards (for all suspects) is to challenge the admissibility of the evidence obtained during the interrogation in court. It is evident that the provisions of the 1984 PACE Act are law, and have to be followed, but a breach of the Act is not a criminal offence. It also seems that there has been no sanction imposed in a civil case arising out of a breach of PACE. The only possible formal sanction against the police for a breach of PACE is disciplinary action. However, as Zander points out, 'such proceedings are as rare as hen's teeth'.[197]

So far as the PACE Codes of Practice are concerned, section 67(11) of the Act provides a sanction for a breach of the Codes in that the court can take this into account when determining whether or not the statements should be admissible in court. Breaches of the Codes have led to the ruling of evidence as being inadmissible, as well as convictions being overturned. Convictions have been quashed, for example, where the defendant was not told required information, not given access to a solicitor, not cautioned, or an appropriate adult was not involved when required. It is a matter for the court to determine whether a breach of the Code is condoned or otherwise used to exclude evidence or overturn convictions. The Notes for Guidance included in the Codes of Practice are not technically part of the Codes but these are often referred to by the courts when considering whether or not there has been a breach of the Code. The Notes, therefore, are for the guidance of not only police officers but also others, including judges.

6. DISSEMINATION OF INTERROGATIONS

The interrogation of the juvenile cannot generally be disseminated outside of the actors involved in the criminal proceedings. While there is a general rule that the administration of justice must be done in public, there is an exception where proceedings involve juveniles. In the youth court, for example, proceedings are held in private, although section 47 of Children and Young Persons Act 1933 includes a specific exception for representatives from the media to be present. While the media are entitled to observe youth court proceedings they are prohibited from publishing the name, address or school or any other matter

197 Zander 2012, p. 713.

that is likely to identify a person under 18 as being concerned in the proceedings (section 49 of the 1933 Act).[198] Crown Court proceedings involving juveniles are held in open court. There is no automatic restriction on reporting proceedings in the Crown Court, but the court may direct that the same restrictions apply as in the youth court.

7. LOCATIONS OF INTERROGATIONS

The interrogation of juvenile suspects is generally conducted in the police station where they are detained. Instead of booking suspects into custody who have attended for a pre-arranged appointment, the police are encouraged to interview them outside of the custody suite on a 'voluntary' basis. Special locations/ facilities for the interrogation of juvenile suspects are not provided. However, there are special interview arrangements when taking a witness statement from a juvenile, particularly in sexual cases or where there was violence or neglect or a child has been abducted. In such cases the interviews are conducted by police officers or social workers who have been trained to work with children, and they can use a specially equipped room in order to record on video what children under the age of 17 have to tell them.

8. INTERVIEWING JUVENILES AS VICTIMS AND WITNESSES

Guidance published by the Ministry of Justice considers preparing and planning for interviews with witnesses, decisions about whether or not to conduct an interview, and decisions about whether the interview should be video-recorded or whether it would be more appropriate for a written statement to be taken following the interview.[199] Vulnerable witnesses are defined by section 16 of the Youth Justice and Criminal Evidence Act 1999 (as amended by the Coroners and Justice Act 2009). Children are defined as vulnerable by reason of their age.

When dealing with a child as a vulnerable witness, the guidance suggests that they should have the support of someone who is independent of the police. Similar to the role of the appropriate adult, this support could be provided by a friend or relative. The guidance also states that specialist training should be developed to interview witnesses with particular needs, including child witnesses, traumatised witnesses and witnesses with a mental disorder or learning disability; including working with intermediaries. While juvenile

[198] These automatic reporting restrictions may be lifted in certain circumstances, such as when it might be in the public interest to do so.

[199] Ministry of Justice 2011.

suspects can experience similar problems, there is no requirement for specialist training of police investigators in relation to their interrogations. A video-recorded interview of a child witness can serve as evidence gathering for use in the police investigation and in criminal proceedings, particularly in relation to allegations of child abuse and sexual offences. The police can video-record the interrogation of a juvenile suspect but such facilities are not generally available in police stations and so instead the interviews tend to be taped or digitally recorded.

There can be an application made to court for 'special measures' to assist vulnerable witnesses, either prosecution or the defence, to give evidence in court. The 'special measures' are a series of provisions that help vulnerable and intimidated witnesses give their best evidence in court and help to relieve some of the stress associated with giving evidence. These include screens being made available in the court which shield the witness from the defendant when giving evidence. There can also be set up a live link, which enables a witness to give evidence during the trial from outside the courtroom, through a televised link. In cases involving sexual offences or intimidation by someone other than the accused, a vulnerable witness can give evidence in private, with members of the public and the press being required to leave the court (except for one named person to represent the press). Where there is a video-recorded interview with a vulnerable witness before the trial, this could be admitted by the court as the witness's evidence-in-chief. The court can also appoint an intermediary to deal with examination of a witness, to assist them in giving their evidence at court. The intermediary is allowed to explain questions or answers so far as is necessary to enable them to be understood by the witness or the questioner, but without changing the substance of the evidence. It is the defence lawyer who provides such assistance for juvenile defendants at court.

The protections for interviewing child witnesses are wide-ranging and detailed. This includes both the video-recording of interviews and requiring a multi-agency approach to be adopted when dealing with complex and sensitive issues.[200] Such protections are not generally extended to the interrogations of juvenile suspects.

III. CONCLUSIONS

There is an ambivalence within juvenile justice as a system that is designed to punish wrongdoing, but also to protect the vulnerable. In recent times, the emphasis has moved further away from welfare and towards punishment, in line with the wider law-and-order rhetoric of successive governments. The boundaries between those committing offences and those needing protection is

200 Ministry of Justice 2011.

often unclear and overlapping. There is, however, a complex system of support and intervention from YOTs who work with young people who are at risk of criminal offending, as well as those who have been charged and convicted. A range of measures has also been introduced that increases parental responsibility for the actions of children, including a mixture of criminal and civil law orders.

From the initial investigation through to the courtroom hearing, the criminal process must balance sometimes competing interests. When the suspect is a young person, their status as a vulnerable person whose psychological and moral culpability is very different from that of an adult means that their status as an accused must be understood differently from that of an adult. Procedure in the youth court is less formal than in the adult court and the language and appearance of prosecutors, lawyer and judges is adapted to be less intimidating. A range of diversion measures has been introduced, diverting juveniles away from prosecution as well as imprisonment. However, penal policy is often political, rather than being based on evidence of the importance of age, development and moral culpability of young people, and as such, is subject to constant change.

There are also special protections required when detaining and questioning a juvenile suspect in police custody – principally, the requirement to have an appropriate adult present. The presence of an independent adult to ensure that the young person understands the process and to act as an additional check on police behaviour is an important safeguard. However, whilst the appropriate adult may be a trained and experienced criminal justice professional, they may also be a volunteer (with varying degrees of training) or simply the suspect's parent. This means that there will inevitably be inconsistency in the kinds of safeguarding that the appropriate adult can provide.

Although many police officers are trained to interview juvenile suspects, this is not mandatory. Overall, the detention procedure for juveniles (who may be as young as 10 years old) does not differ from that of adults in significant ways. This contrasts with the care taken over young witnesses, whose vulnerability defines their reliability and credibility more strongly than is the case for juvenile suspects. Balancing the welfare, support and crime prevention needs of young people with the interests of society in seeing sanctions administered to those who have harmed the victims of crime is a difficult equation.

BIBLIOGRAPHY

Ashford *et al.* 2006
M. Ashford, A. Chard and N. Redhouse, *Defending Young People,* London – Legal Action Group, 2006

Association of Chief Police Officers 2013
Association of Chief Police Officers, *Judicial Review - the Treatment of 17 Year Olds in Custody.* Letter from Assistant Chief Constable Dawn Coley to all Chief Constables, Heads of Criminal Justice and Heads of Crime, dated 13 June, 2013

Baldwin 1993
J. Baldwin, 'Police Interview Techniques: Establishing Truth or Proof?', *British Journal of Criminology,* 1993, 33/3, p. 325–352

Blackstock *et al.* 2014
J. Blackstock, E. Cape, J. Hodgson, A. Ogorodova and T. Spronken, *Inside Police Custody: An Empirical Account of Suspects' Rights in Four Jurisdictions*, Cambridge - Intersentia Ltd, 2014

Bottoms 1974
A. Bottoms, 'On the Decriminalisation of the English Juvenile Court', in R. Hood (ed.), *Crime, Criminology and Public Policy*, London - Heinemann, 1974

Bottoms 1977
A. Bottoms, 'Reflections on the Renaissance of Dangerousness', *Howard Journal,* 1977, 16(2), p. 70–96

Bridges and Choongh 1998
L. Bridges and S. Choongh, *Improving Police Station Legal Advice*, London - Blackstone, 1998

Brookman and Pierpoint 2003
F. Brookman and H. Pierpoint, 'Access to Legal Advice for Young Suspects and Remand Prisoners', *The Howard Journal of Criminal* Justice, 2003, 42/5, p. 452–470

Bucke and Brown 1997
T. Bucke and D. Brown, *In Police Custody: Police Powers and Suspects' Rights under the Revised PACE Codes of Practice (Research Study 174),* London - Home Office, 1997

Cape 2011
E. Cape, *Defending Suspects at Police Stations*, London - Legal Action Group, 2011

Cavadino and Dignan 2006
M. Cavadino and J. Dignan, *Penal Systems: A Comparative Approach,* London - Sage, 2006

Clare *et al.* 1998
I. Clare, G. Gudjonsson and P. Harari, 'Understanding of the Current Police Caution (England and Wales) Among Suspects in Police Detention', *Journal of Community and Applied Social Psychology,* 1998, 8/5, p. 83–93

Criminal Justice Joint Inspection 2011a
Criminal Justice Joint Inspection, *Not Making Enough Difference: A Joint Inspection of Youth Offending Court Work and Reports*, 2011a. Available at: www.justice.gov.uk/downloads/publications/inspectorate-reports/hmiprobation/Court_Work_and_Reports_ Thematic_Report-rps.pdf

Criminal Justice Joint Inspection 2011b
Criminal Justice Joint Inspection, *Who's Looking Out for the Children? A Joint Inspection of Appropriate Adult Provision and Children in Detention after Charge,* 2011b. Available at: www.justice.gov.uk/downloads/publications/inspectorate-reports/hmipris/thematic-reports-and-research-publications/whos-looking-after-children.pdf

Crown Prosecution Service 1986
Crown Prosecution Service, *Code for Crown Prosecutors,* London – CPS, 1986

Crown Prosecution Service 1992
Crown Prosecution Service, *Code for Crown Prosecutors,* London – CPS, 1992

Crown Prosecution Service 1994
Crown Prosecution Service, *Code for Crown Prosecutors,* London – CPS, 1994

Crown Prosecution Service 2002
Crown Prosecution Service, *Narrowing the Justice Gap,* London – CPS, 2002

Crown Prosecution Service 2010
Crown Prosecution Service, *Code for Crown Prosecutors,* London – CPS, 2010

Crown Prosecution Service 2011
Crown Prosecution Service, *Safeguarding Children as Victims and Witnesses,* 2011. Available at: www.cps.gov.uk/legal/v_to_z/safeguarding_children_as_victims_and_witnesses/

Crown Prosecution Service 2013a
Crown Prosecution Service, *Code for Crown Prosecutors,* London – CPS, 2013

Crown Prosecution Service 2013b
Crown Prosecution Service, *Youth Offenders,* 2013. Available at: www.cps.gov.uk/legal/v_to_z/youth_offenders/

Department for Children, Schools and Family 2010
Department for Children, Schools and Family, *Working Together to Safeguard Children: A Guide to Inter-agency Working to Safeguard and Promote the Welfare of Children,* Nottingham – DFCS, 2010

European Commission for Human Rights 2005
European Commissioner for Human Rights, *Report by Mr Alvaro Gil-Robles, Commissioner for Human Rights, on his Visit to the United Kingdom, 4–12 November 2004,* Strasbourg – Council on Europe, 2005

Evans and Wilkinson 1990
R. Evans and C. Wilkinson, 'Variations in Police Cautioning Policy and Practice in England and Wales', *Howard Journal,* 1990, 29/3, p. 155–176

Fionda 2001
J. Fionda, 'Crime and Disorder Act 1998: New Labour, Old Hat: Youth Justice and the Crime and Disorder Act 1998', *Criminal Law Review,* 1990, 1, p. 36–47

Gelsthorpe and Kemp 2014
L. Gelsthorpe and V. Kemp, 'Juvenile Justice: England and Wales' in J. Winterdyk (ed.), *Juvenile justice: International perspectives, models, and trends,* Boca Raton, FL: CRC Press – Taylor and Francis

Hazel *et al.* 2002
N. Hazel, A. Hagell and L. Brazier, *Young Offenders' Perceptions of their Experiences in the Criminal Justice System,* London – Policy Studies Institute, 2002

Hodgson 1997
J. Hodgson, 'Vulnerable Suspects and the Appropriate Adult', *Criminal Law Review,* 1997, 11, p. 785 –795

Home Affairs Committee 2013
Home Affairs Committee, *Twelfth Report: The Draft Anti-social Behaviour Bill: Pre-legislative Scrutiny,* London – TSO, 2013

Home Office 2013
Home Office, *Guidance for Appropriate Adults,* 2013. Available at: https://www.gov.uk/government/publications/guidance-for-appropriate-adults

Home Office 1997
Home Office, *Tackling Youth Crime,* London – HMSO, 1997

Home Office and Lord Chancellor's Department 2001
Home Office and Lord Chancellor's Department, *Good Practice Guide 'The Youth Court 2001 – the Changing Culture of the Youth Court,* London – Home Office, 2001

Kemp 2010
V. Kemp, *Transforming Legal Aid: Access to Criminal Defence Solicitors,* 2010. Available at: http://eprints.nottingham.ac.uk/27833/1/Kemp%20Transforming%20CD%202010.pdf

Kemp 2013a
V. Kemp, '"No Time for a solicitor": Implications for Delays on the Take-up of Legal Advice', *Criminal Law Review,* 2013, 3, p. 184–202

Kemp 2013b
V. Kemp, *Bridewell Legal Advice Study: Final Report,* 2013. Available at: http://eprints.nottingham.ac.uk/27834/1/Kemp%20BLAST%20Final%20Report.pdf

Kemp *et al.* 2002
V. Kemp, A. Sorsby, M. Liddle and S. Merrington, *Assessing Responses to Youth Offending in Northamptonshire* (Research Briefing 2), London – NACRO, 2002

Kemp *et al.* 2011
V. Kemp, P. Pleasence and N. Balmer, 'Children, Young People and Requests for Police Station Legal Advice: 25 Years on from PACE', *Youth Justice,* 2011, 11/1, p. 28–46

Kemp *et al.* 2012
V. Kemp, N. Balmer and P. Pleasence, 'Whose Time is it Anyway? Factors Associated with Duration in Police Custody', *Criminal Law Review,* 2012, 10, p. 735–571

Lacey 2012
L. Lacey, *Youth Justice in England and Wales: Exploring Young Offenders' Perceptions of Restorative and Procedural Justice in the Referral Order Process* [Doctoral Thesis], London – London School of Economics and Political Science, 2012

Law Society 2012
Law Society, *Practice Note: Use of Interpreters in Criminal Cases*, 2012. Available at: www.lawsociety.org.uk/advice/practice-notes/interpreters-in-criminal-cases/

Leng 1993
R. Leng, *The right to silence in police interrogation: a study of some of the issues underlying the debate*, London – HMSO, 1993

Martinson 1974
R. Martinson, 'What Works?' – Questions and Answers about Prison Reform', *The Public Interest*, 1974, 35, p. 22–54

McAra 2010
L. McAra, 'Models of Youth Justice' in D. Smith (ed.), *A New Response to Youth Crime*, London – Willan Publishing, 2010

McConville *et al.* 1994
M. McConville, J. Hodgson, J., L. Bridges and A. Pavlovic, *Standing Accused: The Organisation and Practices of Criminal Defence Lawyers in Britain*, Oxford – Clarendon Press, 1994

McConville *et al.* 1991
M. McConville, A. Sanders and R. Leng, *The Case for the Prosecution: Police Suspects and the Construction of Criminality*, London – Routledge, 1991

McConville and Hodgson 1993
M. McConville and J. Hodgson, *Custodial Legal Advice and the Right to Silence*, London - HMSO, 1993

Medford *et al.* 2003
S. Medford, G. Gudjonsson, and J. Pearse, 'The Efficacy of the Appropriate Adult Safeguard During Police Interviewing', *Legal and Criminological Psychology*, 2003, 8/2, p. 253–266

Ministry of Justice 2013
Ministry of Justice, *Youth Justice Statistics 2011/12 England and Wales* (including supplementary tables), London – Ministry of Justice, 2013

Ministry of Justice 2011
Ministry of Justice, *Achieving Best Evidence in Criminal Proceedings: Guidance on Interviewing Victims and Witnesses, and Guidance on Using Special Measures*, London – Ministry of Justice, 2011

Morgan and Newburn 2012
R. Morgan and T. Newburn, 'Youth Crime and Justice: Rediscovering Devolution, Discretion and Diversion?' in M. Maguire, R. Morgan and R. Reiner (eds.), *The Oxford Handbook of Criminology* (5th edition), Oxford – Oxford University Press, 2012

Muncie 2008
J. Muncie, 'The 'Punitive' Turn in Juvenile Justice: Cultures of Control and Rights Compliance in Western Europe and the USA', *Youth Justice,* 2008, 8/2, p. 107–121

Muncie and Goldson 2006
J. Muncie and B. Goldson, 'England and Wales: The New Correctionalism' in J. Muncie and B. Goldson (eds.), *Comparative Youth Justice,* London – Sage, 2006

O'Brien 1995
P. O'Brien, 'The Prison on the Continent: Europe, 1865–1965', in N. Morris and D. Rothman (eds.), *The Oxford History of the Prison: the Practice of Punishment in Western Society,* New York – Oxford University Press, 1995

Office for Criminal Justice Reform 2010
Office for Criminal Justice Reform, *Initial Findings from a Review of the Use of Out-of Court Disposals,* 2010.
Available at: www.justice.gov.uk/downloads/publications/moj/2011/out-of-court-disposals-june2011.pdf

Ormerod 2011
D. Ormerod, *Smith and Hogan's Criminal Law (13th edition),* Oxford – Oxford University Press, 2011

Pierpoint 2008
H. Pierpoint, 'Quickening the PACE: The Use of Volunteers as Appropriate Adults', *Policing and Society,* 2008, 18(4), p. 397–410

Play England 2013
Play England, *Letter to the Times on the Anti-Social Behaviour, Crime and Policing Bill,* dated 16 July, 2013. Available at: www.playengland.org.uk/news/2013/07/letter-to-the-times-on-the-anti-social-behaviour,-crime-and-policing-bill.aspx

Pleasence *et al.* 2011
P. Pleasence, V. Kemp and N. Balmer, 'The Justice Lottery? Police Station Advice 25 Years on from PACE', *Criminal Law Review,* 2011, 1, p. 3–18

Prison Reform Trust 2011
Prison Reform Trust, *Innocent until Proven Guilty: Tackling the Overuse of Custodial Remand,* London – Prison Reform Trust, 2011

Put and Walgrave 2006
J. Put and L. Walgrave, 'Belgium: From Protection towards Accountability', in J. Muncie and B. Goldson (eds.), *Comparative Youth Justice,* London – Sage, 2006

Royal Commission on Criminal Procedure 1981
Royal Commission on Criminal Procedure, *Report* (Cmnd 8092), London – HMSO, 1981

Royal Commission on Criminal Justice 1993
Royal Commission on Criminal Justice, *Report* (Cmnd 2263), London – HMSO, 1993

Sanders *et al.* 2010
A. Sanders, R. Young and M. Burton, *Criminal Justice,* Oxford – Oxford University Press, 2010

Sanders and Leng 1991
A. Sanders and R. Leng, *The Case for the Prosecution*, London – Routledge, 1991

Sentencing Guidelines Council 2007
Sentencing Guidelines Council, *Reduction in Sentence for a Guilty Plea: Definitive Guideline Revised*, London – Sentencing Guidelines Secretariat, 2007

Skinns 2011
L. Skinns, *The Overnight Detention of Children in Police Cells*, London – Howard League for Penal Reform, 2011

Smith 2010
D. Smith, *A New Response to Youth Crime*, Cullompton – Willan Publishing, 2010

UK Government 1999
UK Government, *Convention on the Rights of the Child: Second Report to the UN Committee on the Rights of the Child by the United Kingdom*, London – HMSO, 1999

UN Committee on the Rights of the Child 2008
UN Committee on the Rights of the Child, *Concluding Observations: United Kingdom of Great Britain and Northern Ireland* (49th session), 2008. Available at: www2.ohchr.org/english/bodies/crc/docs/AdvanceVersions/CRC.C.GBR.CO.4.pdf

Ventress *et al.* 2008
M. Ventress, K. Rix and J. Kent, 'Keeping PACE: Fitness to be Interviewed by the Police, *Advances in Psychiatric Treatment*, 2008, 14, p. 369–381

Winterdyk 2002
J. Winterdyk, *Juvenile Justice Systems: International Perspectives* (2nd edition), Toronto – Canadian Scholars' Press, 2002

Winterdyk 2014
J. Winterdyk, *Juvenile justice: International perspectives, models, and trends*, Boca Raton, FL: CRC Press – Taylor and Francis

Youth Justice Board 2002
Youth Justice Board, *Young Defendants Pack: Scoping study*, London – Youth Justice Board, 2002

Youth Justice Board 2003
Youth Justice Board, *Making it Count in Court (2nd edition)*, London – Youth Justice Board, 2003

Zander 2012
M. Zander, 'If the PACE Codes are Not Law, Why Do They Have to be Followed?', *Criminal Law and Justice Weekly*, 2012, 176, p. 713–714

CHAPTER 4

BETWEEN RESPECTING 'TRADITIONAL' SAFEGUARDS AND MODERN NEEDS OF PROTECTING JUVENILES

Country Report Italy

Claudia CESARI

I. THE ITALIAN JUVENILE JUSTICE SYSTEM: GENERAL OVERVIEW

1. BACKGROUND

1.1. GENERAL FEATURES

In Italy, the juvenile justice system is kept separate from the adult justice system. First of all, a special law is dedicated to it (d.P.R. 22 September 1988, No. 448, hereafter: d.P.R. 448/88) and its provisions define a quite original model of criminal proceedings. Secondly, the judicial organisation is partly independent. Juvenile courts (*tribunali per i minorenni*) are distinct bodies, composed of magistrates who are exclusively dedicated to juvenile justice (criminal and civil); they are also located in different places from regular courts, in order to avoid contact between juveniles and adults involved in criminal proceedings. Attached to each juvenile court is a juvenile office of public prosecutors (*procura della repubblica*), also composed of specialised personnel, which only deals with juveniles both in civil and criminal proceedings. On a higher level of judicial organisation, separation is less strong. Each Court of Appeal has a specialised 'section' (*sezione*) dealing with juvenile justice matters, but it is located in the same place and belongs to the organisation of the Court; its magistrates are assigned exclusively to this section only if the number of the cases dealt with is sufficient; otherwise they can also work in other sections.

As mentioned before, the separation of the juvenile criminal justice system from the adult system is mainly due to the different sources of law in the area of criminal procedure. Criminal proceedings against adult suspects are governed by the Code of Criminal Procedure (hereafter: CCP). However, the rules of the CCP only have a subsidiary role in juvenile proceedings, in that a special law is dedicated to the rules on criminal proceedings against juveniles (d.P.R. 448/88), supplemented by another set of special rules dedicated to more specific and practical aspects (d.lgs. 28 July 1989 No. 272, hereafter: d.lgs. 272/89, containing rules for application and coordination of the d.P.R. 448/88). These statutes provide for a distinctive model of process, with formalities, hearings, measures and a range of decisions of its own. The proceedings are mainly focused on the goal of protecting the juvenile from the stressful impact of the criminal justice system and on offering him psychological support and educational treatment, whenever possible, tailoring the institutional response to criminal behaviour to his specific needs. Such principles naturally shape a type of proceedings where the position of the suspect, the role of the persons around him, the functions of the main actors (judge, defence lawyer, public prosecutor), the object of judicial ascertainment and the consequences of the decisions are very different from those in ordinary proceedings. These peculiar provisions, though, do not govern every aspect of the proceedings, but only the crucial areas where it seems more important to provide the young suspect with a totally different approach. The parts of the criminal process that are not governed by the special rules fall under the application of the Code of Criminal Procedure applicable to adult suspects and offenders. The method of combining the general and the special legislation is described by art.1 d.P.R. 448/88, as follows: in the proceedings against juveniles, the rules of the d.P.R. 448/88 must be applied first, and the ones of the code shall be observed only unless the separate legislation prescribes anything specific.

It must be observed that real autonomy is granted to the juvenile criminal justice system only in the area of criminal procedure. The rules regarding juveniles in the criminal field are actually much more original than those in other areas of the system. Rules on criminal offences and sanctions for juveniles are still governed by the regular Criminal Code (hereafter: CC) and have never received any special attention from the legislator. No effort was ever made to define new forms of sanctions or alternative measures for young offenders.[1] The Italian Constitutional Court quashed some of the provisions that were more obviously in conflict with the protection of juvenile offenders, for example by forbidding life imprisonment for juveniles,[2] but criminal legislation as a whole still ignores the special needs of young offenders. This

1 Ever since, Italian doctrine has been stressing that this issue should not be delayed any more: see, among others, Palermo Fabris 2011, p. 37 and Siracusano 2009, p. 202.

2 Corte cost. n. 164/1994.

problem is also noticeable with regard to the penitentiary system. Art. 79 of the prison law (l. 26 July 1975, No. 354) states that implementation of criminal sanctions for juveniles is regulated according to the same rules as provided for adults until a special law is passed. Since then, though, no such law has been approved and the penitentiary discipline remains one common to both adult and juvenile offenders. The Constitutional Court has often reminded the legislator that special rules for juveniles should be introduced[3], and meanwhile quashed the clauses of prison law that were radically in contrast with the special needs of re-education, individualisation and the flexibility of criminal response granted to juveniles.[4] Nevertheless, the legislator still remains silent on this issue.[5]

Italy has a statutory legal system, according to the continental European tradition, and all the above-mentioned sources are statutory legislation. At the top of the hierarchy of legal sources lies the 1948 Constitution of the Italian Republic (hereafter: Cost.), some principles of which have quite an important role in the field of juvenile justice and protection of juveniles in general. The fundamental provision in the field of juvenile justice is art. 31 para. 2 Cost., according to which the Italian Republic must protect children and young people, promoting disciplines that can be useful to achieve this goal. This rule has often been used to justify derogations to general provisions in favour of juveniles (also in the area of criminal proceedings) because of their special status and in order to grant them special protection. In relation to criminal justice, it is also important to remember that the Italian Constitution was significantly changed in 1999 (l. cost. 23 November 1999, No. 2), when principles of fair trial were 'translated' in the text of art. 111 from international sources, such as art. 6 of the European Convention on Human Rights (hereafter: ECHR). In doing so, the legislator chose to implement the ECHR principles at a constitutional level, but preferred to rewrite them instead of simply including in the Constitution a reference to the Convention; this is why the Italian constitutional text departs on several points from the Convention. The inclusion of the fair trial principles in the constitutional framework, however, was an important turning point for the Italian criminal justice system and, as those principles are generally applicable to any kind of criminal proceedings including against juveniles, they are now a necessary point of reference for interpretation and application of basic safeguards in favour of the juvenile suspect. A juvenile suspect must be guaranteed not only the presumption of innocence and the right to defence, but also the more detailed fair trial requirements in art. 111 paras. 3, 4 and 5 Cost. (for example, the right of the accused to face the prosecution's witnesses, the right of the

---

3 See Corte cost. n. 125/1992.

4 Among others, Corte cost. n. 109/1997, n. 450/1998, n. 403/1997, n. 436/1999.

5 Italian doctrine is very critical about this permanent gap in the juvenile justice system: see Bouchard 2011, p. 701, Caraceni 2010, p. 295, Coppetta 2010b, p. 251 and Ruggeri 2009, p. 241.

accused to be informed of the charges, and the right of the accused to be assisted by an interpreter). In recent times, ECHR provisions have gained greater impact due to an amendment to the Constitution (art. 117) and a couple of decisions of the Constitutional Court.[6] As a consequence, the ECHR provisions, as interpreted by the European Court of Human Rights (hereafter: ECtHR), do not prevail over constitutional rules, but they are superior to statutes; hence, when a statute is in conflict with the EHCR, it must be interpreted and applied by judges in coherence with the latter and, if this is not possible, it may be declared constitutionally void.

In Italy case law is not a source of law. Judgements of higher courts or previous decisions of other judges are not binding; they have only an indirect, persuasive influence on future cases, due to the 'cultural authoritativeness' of the courts and the practical fact that higher courts decisions (especially those of the Court of Cassation in its full composition – *sezioni unite*) assert 'principles of law'.[7] Nevertheless, in the field of juvenile justice, case law is quite influential. As the legislator chose to give juvenile judges broad discretionary powers, rules of law in this area of legislation are much less precise than in other sectors of the criminal justice system. This implies that very often the duty of giving a precise meaning to definitions, rules and conditions, is entrusted to judicial decisions, both of lower and higher courts. In the juvenile criminal system, the actual contents of many rules will often be found to a greater extent in judicial application and interpretation than in legislative texts. This, of course, creates a situation of uncertainty that may sometimes collide with the principles of legality and equality (arts. 3 and 25 Cost.), often at stake in this area of the system.

Juvenile justice legislation is also made more complicated by the connections it has with different areas of the legal system. Civil law, for example, can be very influential in juvenile criminal proceedings, both in an indirect and in a direct way. Civil law is indirectly relevant in the identification of specific support persons, such as parental authority holders, when parents lose such authority or when it is suspended. Furthermore, civil law can be directly relevant in criminal proceedings – during both the preliminary hearing and trial – since the judge can deliver temporary civil decisions for the protection of the juvenile suspect whenever it is necessary and urgent (art. 32 para. 4 and 33 para. 4 d. P.R. 448/88). In this respect, the effort to make criminal proceedings an occasion to have a complete overview of the juvenile's life and environment, in order to support his personal development and developmental process, is quite clear.

---

6 Corte cost. n. 348/2007 and n. 349/2007.

7 This means that they give an interpretation of law that is expected to be confirmed and kept steady in time, so that any decision that might be in conflict with such an interpretation later on should consequently be annulled by the Supreme Court itself.

1.2. HISTORY AND CURRENT TRENDS

The first two decades of the 1900s were crucial for the development of the juvenile justice system in Italy. From 1908 onwards,[8] some administrative acts and the results of ministerial commissions appointed to draft reform projects on juvenile justice progressively enacted the first stages of a specialised judicial and procedural system for juvenile suspects and offenders. On these occasions, 'modern' solutions for juvenile criminal justice were suggested, such as hearings *in camera*,[9] alternative measures based on work or educational treatment instead of detention, and specialist judges.[10] The first structural reform in this field, however, was made in the 1930s.

First of all, in the 1930 Criminal Code the age of criminal liability was raised from 9 to 14 and the age of maturity in the field of criminal justice was lowered from 21 to 18. It also introduced a new type of extinction of the offence, only for juveniles, namely the 'judicial pardon' (*perdono giudiziale*), which allowed the judge, despite the ascertainment of culpability, to dismiss the case for minor offences and if it was to be expected that the suspect would not break the law any more. In the cultural atmosphere of criminal law that at the time clearly aimed at retribution, this derogation in favour of juveniles was certainly meaningful.[11] The real cornerstone of the legal reforms in the field of juvenile criminal justice, however, was the r.d.l. of 20 July 1934, No. 1404 (hereafter: r.d.l. 1404/34), which set up a special court for juveniles and a few original procedural rules. This law – still partly in force – introduced for the first time the concept of a specialist judge for juveniles. Not only did the new provisions establish a separate body of magistrates dealing exclusively with juveniles in civil, administrative and criminal matters, but it also introduced specialist lay judges to sit on the panel, in order to bring different competences (biology, psychiatry, psychology, criminal anthropology, pedagogy) into judicial decisions involving juveniles. Special proceedings were not provided for, but some important differences were nonetheless enacted. Art. 11 r.d.l. 1404/34, for example, obliged the juvenile courts to perform 'special inquiries' aimed at verifying the social and moral environment of the juvenile and his family. Nevertheless, the rest of the juvenile criminal system (except for the clauses mentioned above) was not changed or separated from the law applicable to adults and, generally, it

8 See the act issued by the Minister of Justice, V.E. Orlando on 11 May 1908, recommending, for example, that cases about juvenile offenders should be assigned normally to the same judges, or that, when dealing with juvenile suspects, not only their culpability, but also their family and environment should be taken into account.

9 Finally, it was the 1913 Criminal Code that regulated that trials with juvenile defendants should be held *in camera*.

10 Patanè 2009c, p. 2.

11 The discipline was aimed, according to the explanatory report of the bill, at 'saving young lives from perdition'.

was deeply influenced by the repressive ideology of that time. In fact, despite the 'revolutionary' choices made by r.d.l. n. 1404/34, in practice there was widespread use of administrative measures to control and punish, more than educate, juveniles who were deemed to be behaving 'irregularly'; this was done without the restrictions and safeguards that criminal proceedings may offer.

After the 1934 reform, the system remained untouched for a long time. After the breakdown of Fascism, the approval of the Republican Constitution (1948) created a slow but progressive change in the cultural approach to juvenile justice and to juvenile suspect's rights. Based on the protection of fundamental rights of individuals, the Constitution pushed the system towards a different philosophy on the institutional response to offences committed by juveniles, whereby juveniles are considered not only as passive objects of protection, but also as citizens, persons entitled to rights and powers. In particular, such principles as substantial equality (art. 3 Cost.), education as the main goal of criminal sanctions (art. 27 para. 3 Cost.), and protection of juveniles (art. 31 para. 2 Cost.), were combined into a basic legislative framework, which created a new vision of the system. As a result it began to be understood that the juvenile, as a person with individual needs, must be treated in an individual way, different from an adult offender; more specifically, that he has a stronger need to be supported and re-educated, and that the entire criminal justice proceedings should at all stages be based on this effort to assure the youngster's social reintegration. Even the punitive function of criminal sanctions loses importance and can be subordinated to the main goal of educating the young offender.[12]

In the 1970s, the reform of the structure of local authorities and social services (d.P.R. 24 July 1977, No. 616) also changed the legislative and cultural background of juvenile justice. Social services were moved from the national to the local level, and social assistance organisation and competences were transferred from the state to the regional and municipal administrations, including the assistance and support of minors involved in judicial proceedings. This made it easier to support juveniles in their natural environment and with the involvement of the community they belong to, as local social services can be in direct contact with the juvenile and his family.[13]

It took quite a long time to see a really thorough reform of the system of juvenile justice. The right occasion came when a new Code of Criminal Procedure was approved in 1988. Following the radical change in criminal procedure, a separate law for juvenile criminal proceedings was approved, with a new model of criminal proceedings for juvenile suspects (d.P.R. 448/1988). According to the law, which delegated drawing up the rules[14] for a new model

---

12 See *infra* paragraph 2.5 (part I).

13 See Corte cost. n. 287/1987: Patanè 2009c, p. 9.

14 In Italy, legislative powers belong to the Parliament, but the government has the power to adopt legislative decrees (*decreti legislativi*), that must be drafted observing the principles and criteria contained in a specific delegation law (*legge delega*), approved by the Parliament

for juvenile proceedings to the government, juvenile criminal procedure had to be shaped according to the principles of the new code, with adjustments made according to the individual juvenile's particular psychological conditions, maturity and educational needs (art. 3 para. 1 l. 16 February 1987, No. 81). Other guidelines set out in the aforementioned law were respect for the accusatorial style and respect in criminal proceedings for fundamental principles of human rights recognised by the Italian Constitution and international Covenants. In the field of juvenile justice, these references led to a model based both on accusatorial principles and respect for basic safeguards for the suspect in criminal proceedings, and on the individual safeguards granted to juveniles by international charters and documents. In Italy, essential points of reference were the UN *Beijing Rules* and the Rec. 87/20, which inspired the main derogations from the structure of the proceedings for adults and the most original solutions. Following these guidelines, for example, diversion mechanisms were introduced, the role of social services and parents was redefined and strengthened, and specialisation of personnel dealing with juveniles was increased.

Except for criminal procedure, however, the system of juvenile justice altogether did not change much. The Criminal Code was ignored by republican legislative reforms and the system of sanctions for juveniles is still derived from the adult one: sanctions for juveniles are reduced, and there are some special favourable provisions conceived for them,[15] but no structural change was made to the framework of measures applicable to young offenders. No original solutions were introduced in the penitentiary system either: thus, the model for implementation of sanctions and the set of alternative measures to detention are the same for juveniles and adults.[16]

At the moment, the tendency in criminal politics in the field of juvenile justice can be described, first of all, on a legislative level, as showing (after a period of 'emergency' that led to a government bill inspired by a sort of 'zero tolerance', which was not passed)[17] an increasing interest in the need to complete and harmonise the system. So, there are draft acts on the introduction of a penitentiary system for juveniles, a special set of sanctions and measures dedicated to juveniles only (with a reduction of custodial measures), and the redefinition of competences and the shape of juvenile courts (to be converted

(art. 76 Cost.). This is the method normally used to reform wide areas of the legislation in force, such as the codes.

15 See *infra* paragraph 2.5 (part I).

16 Only the Constitutional Court cancelled the most evident inconsistencies of the system, eliminating some clauses that collided with basic principles of juvenile justice, such as forms of automatic exclusion of convicted juveniles from alternative measures (that limited discretionary powers of judges in order to assure individualised solutions) or sanctions that did not offer any educational opportunity (such as life imprisonment). See above, footnotes 3 and 4.

17 P.d.l. n. 2501/02. For a comment, see *Il processo penale dei minori: quale riforma per quale giustizia*, Giuffrè, 2004.

into 'family courts' or specialist sections of ordinary courts).[18] In practice, however, the greatest interest is in deflation, probation and diversion techniques in general, as well as studying their impact on the speediness of trials and their ability to address recidivism. Court practice also shows a tendency towards implementing mediation (which is not explicitly regulated by law in Italy), which is increasingly considered a useful tool of diversion and education of the juvenile, and is used in spite of the permanent legislative inertness on this issue.

1.3. FUNDAMENTAL PRINCIPLES

The ideology of Italian juvenile criminal justice is rooted in a mixture of purposes, where traditional goals are combined with the need to protect and support the young suspect in order to facilitate his growth and re-education. From this point of view, criminal proceedings must first of all ascertain the defendant's criminal responsibility for the alleged offence, but this is perceived as not being enough. On the one hand, the proceedings are seen as a complex and painful mechanism that could harm the natural development of juveniles, reducing their opportunities of socialisation and growth; hence the proceedings must be structured in a way that limits these side-effects. On the other hand, criminal proceedings are seen as a valuable occasion to activate an early educational and support strategy. So, in the Italian system, there is a clear effort to balance modern goals within the 'classical' framework of criminal proceedings. This creates a certain ambiguity in juvenile criminal procedure,[19] since it is a hybrid of the welfare and justice models. With criminal proceedings being like those for adults, aimed at ascertaining guilt and determining the appropriate punishment, they must respect the principles of fair trial and have the same basic structure. Nevertheless, the juvenile justice system has many specific, original features, based on a welfare model and aimed at the protection and education of the juvenile, providing measures that apparently do not need the same amount or type of safeguards. Obviously, the problem with this coexistence of approaches is that principles and goals may sometimes collide. This is the case, for example, with disciplines which are intended to be favourable for the juvenile, where the presumption of innocence could in practice be underestimated, such as probation or dismissal for irrelevance of fact. Both these forms of diversion require that the juvenile is considered guilty, but they are taken at a stage of the proceedings when guilt has not been fully proven. Moreover, these results should be based on the juvenile's consent that allows the pre-trial adoption of decisions implying guilt, even if it is not proven

18 See p.d.l. n. 3910/10, p.d.l. 5165/12, d.d.l. 2441/10, d.d.l. 595/13.

19 Pepino 1989, p. 10.

beyond any reasonable doubt; nevertheless, the law does not make it clear that this is the case.[20]

In general, criminal proceedings against juveniles in Italy are based on the same basic principles as the adult criminal justice system found in the Italian Constitution and international covenants. Therefore, it shares with ordinary criminal proceedings the same general principles and safeguards, such as the presumption of innocence, fair trial clauses, accusatorial style, participation of the parties in the production of evidence, the right to defence, and the inviolability of personal freedom. It is widely recognised that the purpose of protection of juveniles can never imply lower standards of the general safeguards assured to individuals in the criminal justice system.[21] However, juvenile proceedings also have many original features, which essentially rely on three basic principles: specialisation, minimum harm and individualisation.

The 'principle of specialisation' implies that anyone involved in the institutional response to the offence should have specific 'bent, preparation and experience'.[22] This goal is pursued both by recruiting personnel with specific skills and ensuring that bodies and personnel that work in this field are not given tasks other than those related to juveniles, which allows them the time to develop significant experience. Moreover, in criminal proceedings against juveniles there is an effort to involve personnel who do not professionally belong to the justice system, but who boast a different kind of competence, such as lay judges or social services personnel.[23] Consequently, magistrates are specialists and panels are composed of professional judges and lay judges; part of the judiciary police is attached to juvenile courts and staffed only by specialist personnel; even defence lawyers – if appointed by the court – must have specific experience and competence in the field of juvenile justice. The high rate of specialisation in juvenile criminal proceedings is also confirmed by the constant involvement of social services personnel, from the very start of the investigation: it is actually a basic rule of d.P.R. 448/88 that the social services can be involved at any stage of the proceedings, a provision that can be set aside only exceptionally.

The second pillar of the juvenile system is based on the so-called 'principle of minimum harm' (*principio di minima offensività*). The underlying assumption is that criminal proceedings always put the vulnerable personality of the young defendant in jeopardy. From this perspective, the legislator made a true effort to reduce this potential harm, both 'softening' the forms of intervention that directly affect the juvenile suspect's quality of life (for example coercive measures) and granting the juvenile specific safeguards aimed at reducing the amount of stress caused by the proceedings. Corollaries of this principle are the

---

20 See *infra* paragraph 2.4 (part I).

21 Larizza 2004, p. 86.

22 These words are frequently used in legislation, to define the skills of specialist personnel: see, for example, art. 5 d.P.R. 448/1988 or art. 4, 6, 7 d.lgs. 272/1989.

23 See *infra* paragraph 2.2 (part I).

effort to avoid any labelling (*destigmatizzazione*) and to use custodial measures only exceptionally, as an *extreme measure* (*decarcerizzazione*). In relation to the former, hearings in juvenile courts are always held *in camera*. Only defendants aged 16 years and over can ask for a public trial, and the court will only allow it when it is deemed in the best interests of the juvenile (art. 33 paras. 1–2 d.P.R. 448/88). In relation to the second effort, the system of provisional limitations of liberty is crucial: in fact, it is entirely aimed at avoiding useless stress, preventing contact with adult criminals, avoiding unnecessary detachment from the family and ensuring continuity of a normal educational process.

Finally, a third cornerstone of the juvenile justice system is the 'principle of individualisation' (*principio di individualizzazione*), according to which every decision taken during the proceedings must be tailored to the subjective features and needs of the juvenile involved.[24] This puts the defendant at the very heart of the proceedings, as every decision, every strategy, every intervention bound to have an effect on the suspect's life is focused on their specific needs and potential. The immediate expression of this principle is art. 9 d.P.R. 448/88, which obligates both prosecutors and judges to collect information on the personal, family and social life of the young suspect; such information shall concern not only the present features of the juvenile's environment, but also the strengths and potential he might rely on in order to promote his growth and development. On the basis of this personality and social assessment, the juvenile prosecutor and judge are expected to adopt the most suitable solutions in the juvenile's best interest.

In the Constitution, the fundamental provision in the field of juveniles' legislation is art. 31 para. 2, according to which the Italian Republic must 'protect' children and young people and promote specific laws aimed at achieving this goal. Combined with art. 3 Cost., where the principle of equality is ratified, it implies the necessity of offering the juvenile the shelter of special safeguards and stronger protection, in order to assure effectiveness of formal rights: even if these are formally granted to the juvenile suspect, the natural vulnerability of juveniles could in practice eliminate the protection provided by law.[25] Together with art. 27 para. 3 Cost. – on the rehabilitative function of punishments – art. 3 and art. 31 Cost. also justify a more intense effort to ensure that criminal sanctions for juveniles have re-socialising the juvenile offender as a priority. In its case law, the Constitutional Court has often referred to such clauses in order to grant juveniles special treatment, even if this means departing radically from the rules for adults. Over the years, the Court has established a set of principles that can be considered the stable basis of the constitutional

---

24 For a wider perspective, see Patanè 1999.

25 An important decision in this perspective, for example, was made on the right of the 'parental authority holder' (parent or guardian) to be informed and intervene during proceedings, which the Court recognised in 1975: see Corte cost. n. 99/1975.

system of juvenile justice.[26] According to the Court's case law, the main goals of criminal justice for juveniles are re-education and re-socialisation. From this perspective, a specialist judge for juveniles is necessary; automatic application of measures, of any kind, is forbidden, as every decision affecting the juvenile must be tailored in his best interests and must be discretionary; and the juvenile must be protected from the stressful and labelling effects of the proceedings. This implies *inter alia* that the interest in having a speedy trial is stronger for juveniles and that custody must be used only in extreme cases, as detention endangers the possibilities of re-socialisation for juveniles. In general, against the background of this procedural ideology, there is the 'revolutionary' idea that for juveniles the purpose of re-socialisation must prevail over the need for punishment traditionally satisfied by criminal sanctions.[27]

2. STRUCTURE AND MAIN CHARACTERISTICS OF THE ITALIAN JUVENILE JUSTICE SYSTEM

2.1. THE JUVENILE

In Italy, nobody can be punished if they are 'unable to understand and to want' (*incapace di intendere e di volere*) at the moment they committed the crime (art. 85 CC). The expression describes the condition of persons who are incapable of understanding the meaning of their own actions, of distinguishing right from wrong and of assessing their behaviour in that regard. In such cases, applying a criminal sanction and trying to re-socialise offenders who have no control over themselves and are in no condition to understand the meaning of the offence they are responsible for and of the consequent punishment would be of no use. Children belong to this group of people up to the age of 14, meaning that below the age of 14 they are not held responsible for their actions and this presumption is not rebuttable (art. 97 CC). Once it is verified that the defendant is younger than 14, a dismissal must be delivered immediately, at any stage of the proceedings (art. 26 d.P.R. 448/88). Beyond the age of 14 and up to the age threshold of 18, juveniles must be proven responsible to be subject to criminal sanctions. They are punishable only if there is evidence that they are able to understand and to want their actions (art. 98 CC); if their 'criminal maturity' cannot be fully determined,[28] the judge must deliver a decision of acquittal as

---

26 Larizza 2004, p.88.

27 Corte cost. n. 168/1994, for example, abolished life imprisonment for juveniles, because life detention can have no educational goal and offers no perspective of re-socialisation to the offender, while the role of punishment that penalties for adults maintain, for juveniles must withdraw before the need of re-education and can never prevail.

28 Evidence of criminal maturity of the suspect is usually given by social services reports or expert witnesses.

soon as possible, but not before the preliminary investigations are closed (for example, the juvenile can be acquitted at the end of the preliminary hearing).

'Young adults' (young persons aged over 18) do not receive special consideration in the Italian criminal justice system, except for the enforcement of criminal sanctions. In the latter case, juvenile courts and magistrates are competent to deal with convicts until they have reached the age of 25 (art. 3 para. 2 d.P.R. 448/88), in order to avoid any contact between the youngster and the adult criminal system. Moreover, any kind of measure limiting freedom (provisional measures, sanctions, safety measures, *et cetera*) must be enforced in the forms provided for juveniles until the defendant or convicted juvenile is 25 years old (art. 24 para. 1 d.lgs. 272/89).[29]

The term 'juvenile' is used in the special law on criminal proceedings in a comprehensive way, normally being applicable to a person who was a juvenile at the time of the offence, even if he has reached the age of majority during the proceedings. Consequently, the special clauses of juvenile proceedings are frequently applied to people over 18, unless they are clearly connected to needs of protection that young adults do not have.[30] Different characteristics that may produce increased vulnerability of the juvenile, such as gender or ethnic background, are not taken into consideration, unless they imply a specific requirement for protection generally provided by law, such as the assistance of an interpreter if the suspect does not speak or understand Italian. This does not mean that, in practice, special categories of juveniles are not important in the system, as, for example, the number of foreign youngsters involved in criminal proceedings makes up an increasing proportion of juvenile suspects.[31]

2.2. RELEVANT ACTORS

Persons and bodies involved in juvenile proceedings in Italy are identified and shaped with the aim of understanding the juvenile's needs, protecting and supporting him, and not interfering negatively in the educational effect the proceedings could offer.[32]

---

[29] This legal rule was changed by L. 11 August 2014, n. 117, which raised the previous age threshold of 21 to 25: however, the rule provides that the ordinary forms of enforcement for adults apply, if the juvenile is older than 21 and there are special reasons of security, also taking into account the educational goals of the measures applied.

[30] For example, psychological and affective support provided for by art. 12 d.P.R. 448/1988 is considered applicable only to suspects who are still juveniles at the time of the proceedings: parents' support is not granted to the suspect once he has come of age.

[31] There are no data available on the number of foreigners involved as suspects in criminal proceedings. Available percentages are only partial, but still meaningful. For example, 50.3 per cent of juveniles who entered in first reception centres between 2006 and 2014 were foreigners (source: Ministry of Justice – Department of juvenile justice).

[32] See on the 'principle of specialisation': *supra* paragraph 1.3 (part I).

Magistrates dealing with juveniles are specialists, whatever their role in the proceedings is. First of all, juvenile courts are established at a district level. Attached to each juvenile court is a juvenile prosecutor's office. Both prosecutors and judges assigned to juvenile courts have exclusive functions (that is, they cannot be assigned to different courts or have other duties at the same time: art. 3 d.lgs. 272/89). Specialisation in the Court of Appeal has been ensured with the creation of a specific chamber that deals only with juveniles, although its members can also be assigned to different duties if the workload so requires (art. 4 d.lgs. 272/89). The specialisation of judging panels is strengthened by the presence of lay judges, chosen from among citizens with special characteristics (art. 2 r.d.l. 1404/34). They must be older than 30, representative of both genders, experts on social assistance and specialists in at least one meaningful scientific area (biology, psychiatry, criminal anthropology, pedagogy or psychology).[33] They enrich the panel with their knowledge in fields other than the law, which can help to make a full evaluation of the juvenile and his background. Their presence in panels differs depending on the type and role of the body they take part in: the judge for preliminary investigations always sits alone and is always a professional magistrate; in preliminary hearings the panel is composed of three members, two of whom are lay judges; the trial chamber is composed of a panel of four, two of whom are lay judges; and in the chamber for juveniles of the Court of Appeal, the panel of five members is composed of three professionals and two lay judges (50, 50 *bis*, 58 r.d. 30 January 1941, No. 12). The composition of the panels reflects the importance and quality of the decisions they are entrusted to take. For example, the reason why the majority of the panel in the preliminary hearing is composed of lay judges is that diversion decisions are normally adopted at this stage of the proceedings and such measures are based on the best interests of the child and his educational needs.[34] Specific training on legal issues regarding juveniles, family problems, and problems of adolescence and growing up must be provided to both professional and lay judges by the Ministry of Justice in cooperation with the magistrates' national representative body (*Consiglio superiore della magistratura*) (art. 5 d.lgs. 272/89).

Police staff dealing with juveniles must also be specialists. Therefore special sections of judiciary police are attached to juvenile courts and report directly on the juvenile prosecutor (art. 5 d.P.R. 448/1988).[35] Such police sections are staffed only by specialist personnel who have specific talents, experience

---

33 Data illustrate that lay judges are often chosen beyond those criteria, as 4 per cent of them have a degree in law, 30.7 per cent in 'social sciences', 11.7 per cent in medicine and and 5.7 per cent in 'human sciences'. In general, 40.2 per cent of lay judges have competences which are not mentioned in the legal requirements (data referred to 2014, source: Ministry of Justice – Department of juvenile justice).

34 Grasso 1994a, p. 331 and Pansini 2011, p. 631.

35 This does not mean that a special juvenile police exists: the staff of such police services works for juvenile prosecutors and courts, but still belongs to ordinary police bodies.

and education (art. 6 para. 2 d.lgs. 272/89); training is provided by police administration together with Ministry of Justice (art. 6 para. 3 d.lgs. 272/89). In practice, however, policemen dealing with juveniles at the time of their arrest, when the juvenile's first clash with the judicial system occurs, are not necessarily specialists.

The principle of specialisation in juvenile criminal proceedings is also implemented through the constant involvement of social services personnel. It is actually a basic rule of d.P.R. 448/88 that social services are involved in the proceedings at any stage, save for exceptional situations, and their role is often crucial, both for the support they give the suspect and for the reports they draft for the Court. The services that judges and prosecutors rely on are, first of all, those provided by the state administration, which depend directly on the Minister of Justice. Furthermore, the law allows and sometimes explicitly sets out the intervention of local social services (art. 6 d.P.R. 448/1988), which depend on local authorities (regional councils or town administrations). For example, after a youngster's pre-trial arrest, the police must immediately inform justice administration social services; probation-related activities, on the other hand, need the cooperation of local authority social services.

Like adult defendants, juveniles have the right to be assisted by a lawyer. They may appoint any lawyer, even if he is not specifically qualified or specialised. Specific qualification, however, is required for the appointment of duty lawyers by the court or prosecutor. Local bar associations must keep a list of lawyers specifically qualified in the field of juvenile criminal law-and related matters (social, psychological and educational) (art. 11 d.P.R. 448/1988; art. 15 d.lgs. 272/1989). Inclusion in the list of qualified lawyers is given to advocates who regularly practise before juvenile jurisdictions or to those who attend professional upgrade courses on juvenile law and developmental age-related matters. Training of lawyers on legal issues regarding juveniles and evolving age issues is provided by specific courses organised by bar associations of cities where the juvenile courts reside, together with the President of the Court and the Prosecutor (art. 15 para. 4 d.lgs. 272/1989).

2.3. MAIN PHASES OF THE PROCEEDINGS

Juvenile courts have jurisdiction over alleged offenders who were under 18 when the crime was committed (art. 3 d.P.R. 448/88). This means that the court maintains its jurisdiction and has to apply the special procedure rules of d.P.R. 448/88 for juveniles, even if the defendant in the meantime, or during the proceedings, has reached the age of 18.The main steps of criminal proceedings for juveniles are the same as in ordinary proceedings against adults: preliminary investigations – preliminary hearing – trial.

Preliminary investigations start when the prosecutor or the police receive the information that a crime has been committed. In Italy, the prosecutor is a magistrate who directs the investigation (*pubblico ministero*). Access to this career is through an exam which is the same as the exam for judges; so the public prosecutor is not elected, nor is he a lawyer. The prosecutor is responsible for conducting investigations and is solely responsible for the investigative strategy, as there is no such thing in Italy as an instructing judge. The prosecutor also has the power to request provisional measures limiting the personal freedom of the suspect. The police depend on the prosecutor and receive directives from him; over the years, though, the police have been given wider powers, and can carry out autonomous investigations without or outside the prosecutor's orders or indications. At the investigative stage, the only judicial figure involved is the judge for preliminary investigations (*giudice per le indagini preliminari*), whose main task is to adopt decisions on measures that can affect fundamental rights or liberties (for example, measures of interception or provisional detention).

In Italian criminal proceedings for juveniles, the system of coercive provisional measures departs quite significantly from the one applicable to adults, being aimed at causing the least harm to juveniles and not interrupting their psychological growth and educational progress. According to this perspective, the main features of the system are the exceptional use of custodial measures, graduality and flexibility of the measures, broad discretionary judicial powers, and the involvement of social services in providing assistance to and control of juveniles who must undergo such measures. There are three forms of provisional arrest (*misure precautelari*): the suspect can be arrested (*arresto*), provisionally 'held' in custody (*fermo*) and 'accompanied' to the police station (*accompagnamento*). When juveniles are caught in the act of committing a serious offence (punishable with a maximum penalty of no less than nine years' imprisonment) or immediately thereafter, the police can arrest them. While arrest for adults in Italy can be compulsory or discretionary, the arrest of juveniles is always discretionary (art. 16 d.P.R. 448/88). For less serious crimes (punishable with a maximum statutory penalty of at least five years) the juvenile can be brought (*accompagnato*) to the police station and kept there no longer than twelve hours, in order to be returned to his parents or caretakers and taken home (art. 18 *bis* d.P.R. 448/88). The juvenile can also be 'stopped' provisionally (*fermato*) on the public prosecutor's order, when there is strong suspicion of guilt (if the crime is punishable with a maximum statutory penalty of no less than nine years' imprisonment and a minimum penalty of at least two years) and there is a serious risk that he might flee (art. 17 d.P.R. 448/88). In none of these cases will the juvenile be taken to prison. The arrested juvenile is brought to 'first reception centres' (*centri di prima accoglienza*) or to 'public or authorised communities' (*comunità pubbliche o autorizzate*). These facilities are specifically designed for juveniles and managed by specialist staff; they also have a family-like structure, have few residential guests and no adult prisoners, and are small in size (arts. 9 and 10 d.lgs. 272/89). Furthermore, the young suspect is entitled to the same rights as adults (under art. 13 Cost.), such as the right to be brought before a judge: within 48 hours from arrest, the prosecutor must ask the judge to confirm the arrest and within the following 48 hours a hearing *in camera* must be held and the judge will decide whether the arrest was lawful. The young age of the arrestee requires a higher level of guarantees than for adults, so as to soften the hard impact of the measure. Thus, parents or persons with parental authority receive immediate notice of the arrest; social services are also quickly informed of the arrest and can promptly offer the juvenile their assistance (art. 18 d.P.R. 448/88).

Even more unique are the solutions adopted in Italian legislation in the field of pre-trial coercive measures for juveniles, where the system is quite original and very different from the adult model. The procedure is similar, as coercive measures are issued by the proceeding judge (normally the judge for preliminary investigations) at the prosecutor's request, but only if there is a serious suggestion of the suspect's culpability and the danger that, if left free, he might corrupt evidence, flee or commit other crimes. For juveniles, however, the prerequisites are stricter, as these measures can be applied only in the case of crimes punishable with no less than a maximum statutory penalty of five years (nine, for custody). Furthermore, specific measures are provided, on the grounds of avoiding custody as far as possible and trying different kinds of solutions, that can be enforced in the life environment of the young suspect. That is why legislation provides original measures, such as 'prescriptions' (*prescrizioni*), home custody (*permanenza in casa*), residential care (*collocamento in comunità*), and, as an extreme solution, custody (*custodia cautelare*).

Pre-trial coercive measures
Prescriptions
Home custody
Residential care
Custody

When prescriptions are imposed, the juvenile is ordered to undertake specific activities in relation to study or work or activities that are otherwise useful for their education (art. 20 d.P.R. 448/88). Home custody is a coercive measure that compels the juvenile to stay at home and not leave it unless authorised by the judge, in order to undertake educational activities, such as attending school or going to work (art. 21 d.P.R. 448/88). Even a 'custodial' measure, like residential care, has none of the features of detention: the juvenile is taken to the aforementioned 'community', a small institution with specialist staff (psychologists and social assistants), a family-like atmosphere and no features of prisons, where they have to fulfil educational requirements (art. 22 d.P.R. 448/88). Custody is the most traditional measure and it is carried out in detention centres; it may be adopted only if strictly necessary (art. 23 d.P.R. 448/88). Whenever such measures are deemed necessary, the judge shall choose the least 'intrusive' measure, that is the one which does not interrupt the educational progress of the juvenile (art. 19 d.P.R. 448/88). This should mean that in practice custody is used in quite a low number of cases. However, data indicate the opposite, as prescriptions are used in 13.4 per cent of cases, home custody in 24.1 per cent, and residential care in 33.9 per cent, while custody still makes up a high proportion at 28.3 per cent of the measures applied.[36] It is also important to stress that, whatever measure is ordered, the juvenile is entrusted to social services, which then have to 'support and control' (art. 19 para. 3 d.P.R. 448/88) the young suspect.

At the end of investigations, the prosecutor decides whether to charge the suspect or to drop the case, according to criteria established by law (as he has no discretionary power in deciding whether or not to prosecute). If he decides not to prosecute, he asks the preliminary investigations judge to 'place the case on file' (*archiviare*) that is to drop the case without bringing a charge. If he decides to prosecute, he has to send to the suspect the 'information of investigations closing' (*avviso di chiusura delle indagini*) and allow full disclosure of the investigation file;[37] therefore, the suspect has one more occasion to defend himself/herself, for example by asking to be interrogated or by producing evidence (art. 415*bis* CCP). If a charge is brought, the prosecutor lodges a request for trial (*richiesta di rinvio a giudizio*) and a preliminary hearing (*udienza preliminare*) is held before a judge (*giudice dell'udienza preliminare*) in order to determine whether there is sufficient evidence to go to trial: if not, the case is dismissed (*sentenza di non luogo a procedere*); if so, it is sent to trial by the judge with a decree (*decreto che dispone il giudizio*). In juvenile proceedings, the preliminary hearing is quite important, as it was conceived to allow the judge to achieve early conclusion of proceedings as often as possible (that is, to adopt as many dismissals as possible). Preferably, the diversion mechanisms should be used at this stage, so the hearing must ensure that the smallest number of proceedings result in a trial. This is why the judge of the preliminary hearing has a wide range of decisions at its disposal, with a number of alternatives that are unknown in adult criminal proceedings. In fact, the preliminary hearing can lead, not only to a dismissal for insufficient evidence of guilt or to a decree that sends the case to trial, but also to: a probation order, a dismissal for irrelevance of fact, a dismissal based on the defendant being immature (not liable), a judicial pardon and a conviction

[36] Data refer to decisions issued by juvenile judges for preliminary investigations in 2012 (source: Ministry of Justice – Department of juvenile justice).

[37] The file is deposited in the prosecutor's office and kept at disposal of the defence, so that it can read and copy its contents.

to a substitutive measure (art. 32 d.P.R. 448/1988). This is why the preliminary hearing is often described as a form of 'special proceedings', a kind of diversion technique itself, and certainly a way to ensure minimum harm is done the young suspect and very quick resolution of the proceedings.[38] Preliminary hearings are always held *in camera* and require the full participation of the parties and the subjects of the proceedings (art. 31 d.P.R. 448/1988). It is not only the defendant and public prosecutor who take part in it: the holder of parental responsibility is summoned, and must appear at the hearing;[39] the victim is summoned and may be questioned if necessary; social services that supported the juvenile during the investigation are summoned and can be heard by the judge about the juvenile's personality; parents (if different from the parental care holder) have the right to participate to give the juvenile affective support (art. 12 d.P.R. 448/1988). It should be noted that, in the Italian juvenile justice system, a civil action for damages that occurred as a consequence of the crime is not allowed within the context of criminal proceedings. So the victim of a crime that was committed by a juvenile must claim damages through a separate civil procedure (art. 10 d.P.R. 448/1988). This derogation from ordinary rules was introduced in order to avoid the presence in the proceedings of a person who would fight to obtain a conviction and be an obstacle to diversion and educational solutions.[40]

The trial is held according to the adversarial model: the parties introduce evidence and directly examine and cross-examine witnesses; the investigation file is only known by the parties and in general its contents cannot be used as evidence, except when it is absolutely impossible to reproduce the contents at trial with the contribution of the defence lawyer and the prosecutor (for example, when a witness suddenly died or a relevant object was destroyed or in the case of search and seizure). The participants in the hearing, at this stage, are the same as for the preliminary hearing: so, under the same conditions and with the same goals, the holder of parental authority, the victim, social services, the parents and, of course, the defendant, along with his lawyer, and the prosecutor will be summoned. There are only a limited number of special rules for a trial before juvenile courts. First of all, the hearing is held *in camera*; the only exception is when a defendant who is over 16 years old asks for a public trial and the court deems that publicity is in his best interests (art. 33 para. 1, 2 d.P.R. 448/1988). Moreover, the examination of the juvenile (if he is still under 18 at the time of the trial) is made by the judge, also with questions proposed by the parties (art. 33 para. 3 d.P.R. 448/1988): the aim of this clause is to protect the defendant from the harshness of cross examination, which might be psychologically stressful,

---

38 Grasso 1994b, p. 347, Palomba 2002, p. 241, Pansini 2011, p. 630 and Sfrappini 2009, p. 436.

39 If the holder of parental responsibility does not appear in court, he can be given a fine from € 25 to € 516.

40 Bronzo 2009, p. 108–111. The derogation from the general principles (which in Italy allow the victim to claim for civil damages descending from the offence into the criminal proceedings) was considered justified and sensible by Corte cost. n. 433/1997.

allowing only the judge to conduct a 'soft' examination.[41] At the end of the trial, the defendant can be convicted only if his responsibility is proven beyond any reasonable doubt; if not, he will be acquitted. The verdict must be reasoned and can be appealed by both the defendant and the prosecutor. The parental authority holder is also entitled to lodge an appeal, with the same powers as the juvenile (art. 34 d.P.R. 448/1988).

In Italy there are various forms of 'summary trial' or, so to speak, alternatives to the ordinary structure of the proceedings, following the typical sequence of: investigations – preliminary hearing – trial. These 'alternative proceedings' are governed in the CCP and are applicable in the proceedings for adults (art. 438–464 CCP). These 'special' proceedings are: summary trial (*giudizio abbreviato*), plea bargain (*patteggiamento*), immediate trial (*giudizio immediato*), direct trial (*giudizio direttissimo*) and proceeding by decree (*procedimento per decreto*). Summary trial can be held at the request of the defendant and implies that he is judged – without going to trial – at the preliminary hearing, using as evidence the investigation file; in the event of conviction, the sentence is diminished by one third. A plea bargain simply allows the defendant and prosecutor to propose a sentence they both agree on and that is diminished up to one third of the sentence applicable to the committed crime; the initiative can be taken during investigation or during the preliminary hearing and, if accepted by the judge, results in the immediate closing of the proceedings with a decision. Immediate trial and direct trial are both decided by the public prosecutor and make it possible to avoid a preliminary hearing, in order to go directly to trial. The first one is based on 'manifest evidence of culpability' and it is allowed only if the suspect was interrogated on such evidence; the second one is based on arrest *in flagrante delicto* or on confession to a magistrate during interrogation. The last form of alternative proceedings are the ones by decree, a short and bureaucratic form of deciding provided for offences punishable only with pecuniary sanctions. In such cases, the prosecutor can simply ask the judge for a decree of conviction, that, if delivered, is notified to the defendant and can be opposed by him: if the defendant lodges his opposition, the decree is overruled and the case comes to trial; if not, the decree becomes definitive and the defendant receives his benefits (first of all a serious reduction in sentence, up to half the minimum sanction established by law for the offence).

Not all of these alternatives are allowed in juvenile proceedings. Plea bargains and proceeding by decree are simply inapplicable (art. 25 para. 1 d.P.R. 448/88). In fact, they were considered too bureaucratic and impossible to explain properly to juveniles. Moreover, the legislator argued that showing a juvenile that one can 'bargain' on crimes or avoid the consequences of his deeds simply by paying a fine and without even appearing in court would be pedagogically inappropriate and send the wrong message to the juvenile. Summary trial is applicable with

[41] Mazza, in Cesari 2008, p. 211.

no conditions. Immediate and direct trial, on the contrary, are allowed on two conditions: if the special speediness of trial cannot prejudice the educational progress of the juvenile; and if affective and psychological support can be granted to him in spite of the acceleration of the procedural pace (art. 25 para. 2, 2 *bis*, 2 *ter* d.P.R. 448/88).

2.4. THE ALTERNATIVES: DIVERSION MECHANISMS

As a rule, every offence in Italy entails conducting criminal proceedings. This is a result of the fact that prosecution is mandatory and the information about a crime will therefore always start an investigation, led by the public prosecutor. This means that, in general, there are no forms of diversion entrusted to administrative authorities or police forces. In juvenile criminal proceedings, however, there are two different kinds of diversion, with and without probation: dismissal for 'irrelevance of fact' (*irrilevanza del fatto*) (art. 27 d.P.R. 448/1988) and suspension of the proceedings with a probation order (*messa alla prova*) (art. 28, 29 d.P.R. 448/1988, art. 27 d.lgs. 272/89). In 1988, these solutions pioneered diversion techniques into Italian criminal justice, as nothing similar had been ever done before, except for probation during the enforcement of detention. Even if such alternatives to ordinary proceedings normally always have a positive impact on the speediness of trials, in the juvenile system they are basically inspired by the principle of minimum harm. They clearly show a connection with the Rules of Beijing and Rec(87)20, which pushed the 1988 legislator to find ways to expel the juvenile from judicial proceedings –as far as possible and as soon as possible – in order to support quicker and more effective re-socialisation.

Dismissal for irrelevance of fact allows the judge to recognise the offender's guilt and, nevertheless, to deliver a sentence of acquittal, without any further consequence: the crime was committed by the defendant, but the state gives up the punishment and closes the proceedings as soon as possible. Three concurrent circumstances must occur to deliver a dismissal decision for irrelevance of fact: (a) the tenuity of the criminal behaviour; (b) the fact the crime is 'occasional' in the offender's life; and (c) the potential harm to the offender's education caused by the further development of the proceedings. Irrelevance of fact can be declared at any stage of the proceedings: during investigations, during the preliminary hearing, and even as an outcome of the main trial.[42] During the preliminary hearing the defendant's consent is needed, while apparently this condition is not required by law for dismissal during the investigations; there

42 Cesari 2009, p. 320 and p. 329–331. The possibility of this kind of acquittal in trial was stated by Corte cost. n. 149/2003.

is a widespread opinion, though, that it should be as such at every stage before trial.[43]

Probation can be ordered only during the preliminary hearing or during the main trial (never during investigations). There is only one condition for delivering a probation order: the need to evaluate the juvenile's personality after completing the probation programme, a broadly discretionary evaluation,[44] mainly based on reports from social services covering the juvenile's personality and social background. As probation requires the young offender's cooperation, it cannot be ordered for someone who is unwilling to undertake it; furthermore, it sometimes includes prohibitions and limitations on personal liberty, so it cannot be imposed on someone who has not been convicted yet. That is why the suspension of proceedings to perform a probation programme is thought to require the defendant's consent, even if the law does not explicitly indicate the suspect's consent as a prerequisite for the probation order.[45] The law is also totally silent on the need to ascertain the defendant's guilt for the crimes they were charged with, before they undergo a probation programme; nonetheless, it is common opinion, widely shared by courts, that the ascertainment and declaration of the defendant's guilt is an unexpressed prerequisite of the probation order.[46] When a probation order is made, the process is suspended and remains on standby for the term the judge fixed for the programme. During this time the offender is entrusted to social services, who draft the program first (art. 27 d.lgs. 272/89), and then observe, support and supervise the prescribed activities (art. 28 d.P.R. 448/1988). At the end of the term established for probation, social services draft a report on the results of the probation. If the offender fulfilled the requirements of the programme and his personality showed a positive change, the process will be finalised with a decision of acquittal: a successful probation extinguishes the crime (art. 29 d.P.R. 448/1988). Otherwise, the proceedings start again from the stage it stopped at.

In practice, diversion techniques are used less often than the legislator hoped, at the time they were introduced. In respect of the outcomes of preliminary hearing, dismissal for irrelevance of facts covers about 13.7 per cent and extinction of the offence for a successful probation about 15.6 per cent. This result is even lower when it comes to trial, where successful probation covers

43 This conclusion could be reached already, interpreting the law according to other general principles, in some authors' opinion (Coppetta 2011a, p. 596–597 and Patanè 2002, p. 3414–15) or it might be only a result of the Constitutional Court's intervention, according to others (Cesari 2009, p. 308 and Vigoni 2004, p. 2165).

44 Cesari 2009, p. 347, Coppetta 2011b, p. 611, Sergio 2005, p. 119 and Pepino 1997, p. 483.

45 See in general and for complete references, Cesari 2009, p. 356–359. It must be stressed, anyway, that the Constitutional Court has denied the consent of the juvenile as a necessary prerequisite for probation (Corte cost. n. 125/1995). In practice, the juvenile's consent to probation is considered of fundamental importance by juvenile judges.

46 Corte cost. n. 125/1995. In doctrine, among many others, reference can be made to: Cesari 2009, p. 347, Coppetta 2011b, p. 611 and Palomba 2002, p. 414.

about 6.3 per cent of the final decisions and data about irrelevance of fact are not even available.[47]

The Italian system does not provide for any structured form of victim-offender mediation (hereafter: VOM), neither in the adult nor in the juvenile justice system. Although the opportunity and, in compliance with Council of Europe prescriptions,[48] the necessity of introducing a specific discipline for mediation are vigorously disputed, in scientific as well as political circles, at this moment legislation still considers mediation as a marginal tool, that can be used only for reconciliation by Justices of peace or as a point of probation programmes for adults.

Nevertheless, practitioners have been progressively developing some new strategies aimed at performing VOM, when juveniles are involved in the crime. As meeting the victim is considered educationally useful and sometimes crucial for starting a true re-socialisation process, margins for mediation were progressively found in the legislation. The options normally used to perform VOM are: acquittal for irrelevance of fact and a probation order. In both cases, in fact, a successful mediation offers the chance of early finalisation of the proceedings. The common practice of mediation, as it has been performed in juvenile courts over the last decade[49], starts when the judge or (as it is more frequent) the prosecutor refers the case to social services, in order to try and check whether a successful mediation is possible. Social services then contact the offender and the victim, to determine whether there is a chance for dialogue; if so, they promote a series of meetings where the two parties can be face to face. If the mediation succeeds, the social worker who presided over drafts a concise report on the outcomes of mediation and sends it to the prosecutor or to the judge. If mediation is deemed successful, the prosecutor asks for acquittal for irrelevance of fact during the investigations and the proceedings can immediately be concluded. Another way to practise mediation in the Italian juvenile system is probation, since mediation can be a meaningful part of probation programmes. Art. 28 d.P.R. 448/88 explicitly provides that the judge who orders probation can give specific prescriptions about restorative activities and reconciliation with the victim: it is quite easy to connect a real mediation

---

47 Data refering to 2012 (source: Ministry of Justice – Department of juvenile justice).

48 See Recommendation No. R (99) 19 of the Committee of Ministers to Member States concerning mediation in penal matters.

49 The practice of mediation was first adopted by some juvenile courts (like Turin's), where practitioners were more willing to experiment with new solutions in criminal justice for juveniles. Later on, other courts followed this example and coordinated social services in the practice of mediation in criminal proceedings. As the law does not say much on this issue, the proceedings described here simply are the result of the steps that are usually made, in practice, in a mediation process: it must be kept in mind, however, that no law prescribes that mediation should have this structure. Although there can be some differences from court to court, the steps made in mediation in criminal proceedings remain quite alike all over Italy. See on this issue: Mestitz 2004.

process to these conditions that can even be a crucial part of the programme. Afterwards, if mediation succeeds, it can be regarded as a positive outcome of probation, so that the crime is extinguished and the process is concluded with an acquittal. This option makes it possible to perform mediation at an intermediate stage of the proceedings, such as preliminary hearing or trial: the process is suspended and stands by, waiting for the mediation process to develop. In practice, acquittal for irrelevance of fact is the favourite option for performing mediation, because it allows an immediate outcome of the process.[50]

In summary, it is clear that, in practice, mediation is performed quite often, but always on the borderline of the current (inadequate) legal framework and social assistance practices that have been developing a sort of 'material' procedure. It is certainly an important issue for future reforms.

2.5. THE SET OF SANCTIONS

As to sanctions, youngsters do not benefit from youth-specific measures, and share the same type of punishments as adults. They are entitled, however, to a special treatment as to the gravity of sanctions they can be submitted to. If convicted, they are given a reduced penalty (art. 98 CC). In practice, however, except for this basic rule, the system of sanctions for juveniles is not original, quite complicated and not always rational. An overview of the set of sanctions applicable to juveniles in Italy can be drafted as follows:

Sanctions	Safety measures	Substitutive sanctions
Detention	Supervised liberty	Semi-detention
Fine	Residential care	Controlled liberty
		Pecuniary sanction

In the Italian system of sanctions, there is a so-called 'double track' (*doppio binario*), which means that responsibility for the crime can lead to a double form of consequences: penalties (primarily inspired to retribution for the offence) and 'safety measures' (*misure di sicurezza*) (aimed at social reintegration) (arts. 199–235 CC). These can be applied together, penalties being enforced first, or separately, as safety measures may be applied even when the offender is acquitted (for example, for not being criminally liable and even if under 14).

Ordinary criminal sanctions in Italy are: life imprisonment, detention and fine. Life imprisonment for juveniles was cancelled by a Constitutional Court

50 This kind of solution severely forces the rule of law, as acquittal for irrelevance of fact is only possible for criminal behaviours that appeared unserious from the start and could not be used for offences that became irrelevant afterwards, through the positive effect of mediation. Only a free interpretation of law lets the practitioners use art. 27 d.P.R. 448/88 as a way to certify a successful mediation and, actually, a key to introduce a discipline still inexistent.

decision in 1994 which declared unlawful art. 17 CC as far as it allowed juveniles to be given life sentences. Detention and fines are applicable to juveniles, but, if applied, they are reduced. For juveniles, safety measures include 'supervised liberty' (*libertà vigilata*) and residential care (*riformatorio giudiziario*), both disciplined by d.P.R. 448/88 in a way that prevents their use as forms of detention. The first implies that juveniles must abide by specific requirements about study, work or other educational activities or that they cannot leave the family home without the authorisation of a judge. Residential care takes place in a 'community' (*comunità*), that is a facility hosting no more than ten juveniles, who attend an educational programme, under the supervision of specialist staff. Communities are public or private and authorised by local bodies. The conditions under which a safety measure can be applied are: that the juvenile actually committed the crime (whether he is convicted or not for it) (art. 202 CC); and that the juvenile is considered 'socially dangerous' (art. 203 CC) as there is a serious risk that he might commit violent crimes or crimes related to terrorism or criminal organisations (art. 37 d.P.R. 448/88). In any case, the severity of the offence and the moral status of the juvenile's family must be taken into account (art. 224 CC).[51] The duration of safety measures is undetermined, because only the minimum duration is established by law; they are revoked when a personality assessment states that the person is not socially dangerous any more. Safety measures are applied by the juvenile court, together with the conclusive decision, but can also be applied provisionally, during the proceedings (art. 205–206 CC, art. 37, 39 d.P.R. 448/88).

In order to reduce the use of detention for juveniles as much as possible, the law also provides for a range of 'substitutive sanctions' (*sanzioni sostitutive*). These are: 'semi-detention' (*semidetenzione*); 'controlled liberty' (*libertà controllata*) and 'pecuniary sanction' (*pena pecuniaria*). The first one obliges the convicted person to spend no less than ten hours per day in a 'semi-detention institution', a special facility where integration with external community must be assured (art. 11 d.lgs. 272/89). Under the second, the person is entrusted to social services for a re-socialising program. The third one involves the payment of a fine. The first two are applicable to juveniles when the sentence does not exceed two years; the fine can be substituted for a sentence of no more than six months.[52] The decision to convert the detention with such a measure is taken after the evaluation of the juvenile's personality, study or work needs, social and family conditions (art. 30 d.P.R. 448/88). This wide range of alternatives to detention was judged to be positive by scholars, and it is in fact possible to convert detention into different forms of penalty even for offences of medium severity, allowing the judge to find the best solution in the interests and according to the individual needs of the juveniles.

For petty offences, penalties are different both for adults and juveniles, belonging to the discipline for the justice of peace (d.lgs. 28 August 2000, n. 274),

[51] The decision about social dangerousness is considered broadly discretionary and based on too vague conditions: see Panebianco 2004, p. 117.

[52] Panebianco 2004, p. 126 and Siracusano 2009, p. 213.

which provides a separate and special range of sanctions: home detention, social work and fines. So when the proceedings concern an offence belonging to the competence of the justices of peace but the alleged offender is a juvenile, the case is dealt by the juvenile court, but the sanctions available are the ones provided by the law on justice of peace criminal proceedings.

The Criminal Code also provides for some kind of 'merciful discipline' for juveniles, aimed at giving a juvenile who has committed an offence for the first time a second chance: this measure is called 'judicial pardon' (*perdono giudiziale*). When the crime is committed by a person younger than 18 and the judge deems that the crime would merit a sentence of a maximum of two years of imprisonment, the offender can be pardoned if the court expects that he will not commit any more offences (art. 169 CC and art. 19 r.d.l. 1404/34). This means that the offender will not be punished, and also that he will not be sent to trial or, if already summoned to court, that he will be acquitted. The pardon, however, can be awarded only once, as it presumes that the juvenile is not socially dangerous and the crime was an occasional mistake that the state can overcome to promote easier reintegration into society. The legislator intended that this measure would be used rarely after the criminal proceedings reform of 1988: new diversion techniques, in fact, were intended to replace it, offering solutions with a deeper educational impact.[53] Nevertheless, judicial pardon is still an important option in practice, as it still makes up about 15.9 per cent of decisions adopted in preliminary hearings by juvenile judges.[54]

II. INTERROGATIONS

1. INTRODUCTION

The approach of the Italian legislator when drafting the 1988 reform on juvenile criminal justice was to provide juvenile suspects with at least the same safeguards as the adult suspect and, at the same time, to add more special safeguards, connected with the individual needs and characteristics of juveniles involved in judicial proceedings. So, first of all, during the preliminary phase of the proceedings, the young suspect is afforded the same regime of protection and the same rights of any suspect, according to the international principles that recognise that the juvenile, due to his vulnerability, must never be in a worse situation than an adult suspect would be.[55] Furthermore, the juvenile has a

---

53 Judicial pardon had been used for a long time as a kind of 'automatic' solution for petty offences, in order to avoid detention for episodes of illicit behaviour that were not serious or that in practice could be spontaneously reabsorbed in the juvenile's environment: see Ciavola 2009, p. 172.

54 Data referring to 2011 (source: Ministry of Justice – Department of juvenile justice).

55 In general, on this issue: Giostra 2005.

higher standard of protection, granted by special safeguards, which take into account his naturally weaker position. The juvenile's immaturity, lower level of education, psychological fragility and undefined personality structure naturally put the suspect in an weaker position before the prosecutor and, in general, in the proceedings, so they need to be counterbalanced by a surplus of safeguards. These enriched safeguards, of course, may not solve every problem. On the one hand, it must be verified whether the regular safeguards provided for the juvenile are, considering the special circumstances of his position, really effective. On the other hand, one might also wonder whether the additional safeguards offered by the system are adequate or sufficient.

2. GENERAL FEATURES OF INTERROGATIONS OF JUVENILES DURING INVESTIGATIONS

2.1. CONCEPT OF INTERROGATION

The word 'interrogation' (*interrogatorio*) covers the same situations for juvenile and adult suspects, meaning the questioning of a suspect by a magistrate (public prosecutor or judge) in the pre-trial phase, with the specific safeguards provided for by arts. 64 and 65 CCP.[56] It must be distinguished from the concept of 'summary information' (*sommarie informazioni*), which is used, on the one hand, for the statements obtained from the suspect by the police, with a lower level of safeguards (art. 65 CCP is not applied in that case), and, on the other hand, for witness statements collected by the police or the public prosecutor during investigations. Practitioners often use the expression 'audition' (*ascolto*) to describe situations where the juvenile is heard by anybody (magistrates, police, social services) within or during proceedings. The term, alien to the official legal discourse, is taken from the methodology of social workers, and evokes an 'empathetic' way of listening to the juvenile, leaving him the freedom to express his emotions, needs and opinions. It is more frequently used for contacts with the juvenile that take place in contexts where the role of social services is crucial, such as during the enforcement of a probation programme; but not exclusively,[57] as sometimes the term defines an approach that implies emotional involvement or psychological openness of the person that leads the audition towards the needs of the juvenile. The problem with this definition is that it might encompass a mode of interviewing which is in violation of the safeguards established for the suspect's interrogation.[58] Of course,

---

56 See *infra* paragraph 2.3 (part II).

57 See Turri 1998, p. 39, according to whom the audition of the juvenile suspect in the hearing about irrelevance of fact must be considered 'a *listening to* without interrogating'.

58 Mazza 2008, p. 215–216, for example, stresses such risks, but also deems that during preliminary hearings the juvenile can simply be 'heard' (as the law literally says) and this operation might be 'informal', because being 'heard' is not the same as being 'interrogated'.

it might be easy to say that, in theory, only the adversarial method of questioning requires safeguards to be respected, while the protective attitude and methods of an audition do not need such formalities. Nevertheless, such a view is dangerous: it is difficult, within an audition, to distinguish declarations made spontaneously from ones made by the suspect after questioning; it might also be difficult to discern which part of the juvenile's statements simply express needs, feelings and emotions (and can be used only to offer appropriate support to the juvenile), and which part is connected with issues of criminal responsibility (and can be used to decide upon it). In fact, since in juvenile proceedings the personality assessment is crucial for the outcome of the case, it is impossible to say if and to what extent the juvenile's statements in an 'informal' audition have an influence on the final decision and the measures applied.

2.2. CONCEPT OF INTERROGATION IN RELATION TO CONCEPT OF CHARGE

Either way, the technical definitions of 'interrogation' and 'summary information' are only used to define activities to obtain the suspect's statements during the pre-trial stage of proceedings, that is before a charge is formally brought and, after that, during the preliminary hearing. In Italy, a 'charge' (*accusa*) is brought only at the end of preliminary investigations, and introduces the stage of preliminary hearing (for more serious crimes) or of trial (for lesser offences) with a formal prosecution. From that moment on, the charge has defined features, and cannot be withdrawn or (except for peculiar situations) changed. Before that moment, there is technically no 'charge', but only a sort of 'temporary accusation', a 'hypothesis of charge', that the results of the investigations should confirm or not. Until that stage, the person against whom the proceedings are carried out is a 'suspect' (*indagato*) and only after that does he become a 'defendant' (*imputato*). So the questioning of a defendant after the charge and during the preliminary hearing is still defined as an 'interrogation', but it is led by the judge of the preliminary hearing and is performed before the trial and after the closing of the investigations.

2.3. DIFFERENT FORMS OF QUESTIONING THE SUSPECT: 'INTERROGATION' AND 'SUMMARY INFORMATION'

There are many occasions when, during investigations, the suspect can or must be interrogated. Depending on the occasion, the function of the interrogation partly changes: interrogation, in fact, has multiple goals, from self-defence to gathering elements of evidence against the suspect, but each goal prevails over the others depending on the kind of interrogation and on the specific stage or occasion in which it is carried out. Of course, the person conducting the interrogation also changes, depending on the stage of the proceedings and on the specific activity the interrogation is connected to.

During investigations, police forces can question the suspect, both on their initiative and on the public prosecutor's behalf. In the first case, there are special safeguards for the act (called 'summary information'): the suspect must not be under arrest and the presence of a lawyer is compulsory, unless the declarations are obtained in the place where the crime was committed and immediately thereafter (but if the lawyer is not present, the declarations cannot be recorded and used during the proceedings) (art. 350 CCP). The purpose of the act is to collect useful information for the investigations. In the second case, the act is called an 'interrogation', as it carried out on the prosecutor's behalf and according to the same rules and safeguards concerning the correspondent act when performed personally by the prosecutor; in fact, such safeguards are partly strengthened, as the suspect must be free and the lawyer's presence is compulsory (art. 370 CCP).

The public prosecutor can interrogate the suspect on different occasions, always with the goal of collecting information that might be useful for the investigation, that is, to decide whether or not to bring a charge against the defendant. That is why the public prosecutor's interrogation has a prevailing investigative function. In general, the prosecutor can carry out the suspect's interrogation during the preliminary phase whenever he deems it useful, and can choose to do so at any stage of the proceedings, simply by inviting the suspect to present himself to the prosecutor's office (art. 364–375 CCP). Moreover, when the suspect is arrested, the prosecutor can interrogate him (art. 388 CCP). If the person is submitted to a provisional coercive measure, though, the prosecutor's interrogation cannot precede the one carried out by the judge (art. 294 para. 6 CCP). Lastly, at the end of investigations, when the suspect is informed that the preliminary phase is being closed and asks to be interrogated, the public prosecutor must invite him to be questioned. If the request was made in time, such an interrogation is mandatory and, differently from other forms of interrogations conducted by the prosecutor, it has a defensive aim, as it offers the suspect an opportunity to explain to the prosecutor why the case should be dropped (art. 415 *bis* CCP). The prosecutor can carry out the interrogation(s) in person or delegate it to the police.

As explained above, during investigations the judge does not collect information for the proceedings, but his duty is only to oversee fundamental rights which might be infringed by the criminal proceedings. Thus, the suspect's interrogations by a judge are usually connected to cases of deprivation of personal liberty and have a prevailing defensive goal. So, the judge interrogates the arrested suspect to ensure that he is heard on the subject of the legal basis of his arrest. In fact, when an urgent measure of arrest is adopted (for example, arrest *in flagrante delicto* or after the juvenile was 'accompanied' to police station), within 48 hours the prosecutor shall lodge a request for the validation of the arrest by the judge; a hearing must be held within the next 48 hours. During this hearing, the suspect, if present, must be interrogated by the judge for preliminary investigations (art. 391 CCP). Furthermore, when a provisional coercive measure should be applied during investigations, the public prosecutor files a request for it and the judge for preliminary investigations orders the measure. Afterwards, the suspect must be interrogated by the judge within five days (in case of custody, 10 days for lesser measures), otherwise the measure loses efficacy; after the interrogation, though, the measure can be revoked, confirmed or changed (art. 294 CCP). Art. 299 CCP also provides for a 'defensive' interrogation whenever there is a request to withdraw or substitute the coercive measure that was first applied. After the stage of investigations where the preliminary hearing is held, the judge for preliminary hearing can of course interrogate the defendant if he asks for it or consents; the purpose of interrogation at such a phase is to offer the judge information so that he can decide whether to deliver a sentence of acquittal or send the case to trial (art. 421 CCP).

There are also two cases of 'spontaneous' statements (*dichiarazioni spontanee*), given by the suspect to the police or to the public prosecutor, without any questions being posed to the suspect. Obviously, their aim is defensive, but there is no prohibition on using such elements against the suspect. First of all, voluntary declarations can be collected by the police during preliminary investigations (art. 350 CCP): they must be transcribed, but the suspect's statements cannot be used in trial. Furthermore, according to art. 374 CCP, the public prosecutor can also receive spontaneous statements from the suspect during preliminary investigations; the suspect can attend the prosecutor's office to offer voluntary statements. Nevertheless, after the suspect attended his office, the prosecutor can inform the suspect of the provisional charges, thus turning the act into a formal interrogation, with all the related consequences in terms of method, safeguards and use in the proceedings.

All the kinds of interrogation or questioning mentioned above are applicable both for juvenile and adult suspects. For juveniles, though, there can be other situations where they can be questioned, even if such activities are not labelled as interrogations by law. Art. 9 d.P.R. n. 448/1988, first of all, provides that collecting information about the juvenile's personality and background is compulsory for the judge and the public prosecutor. Not only does the clause not explain how such elements must be gathered, but it also authorises 'hearing' experts or people who know the juvenile, 'without any formality'. Thus there is no legal limitation as to the procedural means that can be used, so that questioning the juvenile directly is not forbidden and the interview can be done during investigations. Normally such interviews are performed by social service staff, and this is why the act cannot be technically termed as an 'interrogation' and is not surrounded by any safeguards. Given the lack of safeguards, it would be appropriate to think that the statements can only be used for social enquiry purposes and not as evidence of responsibility and that social services could not ask questions about the fact or the responsibility of the suspect. Nevertheless, it must be admitted that such a distinction might be difficult in practice. The suspect could be easily induced to give statements about his involvement in the alleged offence, and these statements could turn out to be crucial for the outcome of the proceedings, since every decision about the juvenile must be based on the results of the social and psychological assessment. In any case, if a magistrate questions the suspect in order to gain information about his personality or background, safeguards of the interrogation should be applied, if the results of the interview will probably be used in the proceedings. According to a convincing opinion, in fact, art. 9 para. 2 d.P.R. n. 448/1988 could be construed so as to allow the prosecutor to avoid formalities whenever the interview is limited to give the magistrate the opportunity to better understand the information about the juvenile and be aware of the personal and social background of the juvenile; if the magistrate instead wants to use such information in the criminal proceedings, 'formalities' become necessary and the ordinary forms and safeguards of the acts must be applied.[59] For the case of an interview with a suspect, this implies that the audition, whenever the prosecutor wants to use its results during the investigation, must be considered and treated as an interrogation, with all the applicable set of safeguards.

Other cases of declarations obtained from the suspect and not formally identified as interrogations, can be found in the system of diversion techniques. Art. 27 d.P.R. n. 448/1988 provides a form of interrogation carried out by the judge for preliminary investigations: during the hearing on dismissal for 'irrelevance of fact', which takes place at the preliminary phase, the suspect must be 'heard' if he appears before the judge. Despite the ambiguity of the text of the law, this should be listed as a case of interrogation whenever questions are posed to the juvenile defendant, whereas statements given on such an occasion can be used by the judge to evaluate the prerequisites of dismissal for the fact being irrelevant (including the defendant's culpability, the material gravity of the fact, and the fact that the illicit behaviour can be considered occasional).[60] Another possible time to collect statements from the suspect is during probation, because art. 28 d.P.R. n. 448/1988 and art. 27 d.lgs. n. 272/1989 provides that the juvenile can be heard, even 'informally', to test how successful the probation program is. The interview is carried out by the judge of probation (this may be the judge for preliminary hearing, at a pre-trial stage), that is, in practice, the president of the panel or, more frequently, one of the lay judges,

59 Reynaud 1994, p. 94–95.
60 Cesari 2009, p. 325.

on the president's behalf. In this case, too, the problem is that the law makes it possible to avoid formalities and safeguards (including the assistance of a lawyer or even of parents) for statements from which elements could be gathered in order to establish if probation is successful or not and about the subsequent outcomes of the proceedings. Furthermore, if a probation order is withdrawn and the proceedings go on, final decisions would be taken by the same judge who carried out the 'informal' interview, during which the suspect could have given any kind of statement on any relevant issue. In this case, too, a solution could be that any statements released 'without formality' could not be used in the proceedings (even before trial); so, whenever the judge wants to use statements in the proceedings as a basis to deliver a decision, forms and safeguards of interrogations should be used.

Finally, it must be stressed that in mediation practices, the juvenile is usually heard by the mediator (a social services staff member), first of all in order to gain consent to mediation, but also to verify whether there is any controversy over the charges: only if the suspect does not object to the charge is mediation considered possible. These first contacts are often made without legal assistance and they are about criminal responsibility, so it may be a problem if the suspect's statements could be used in the proceedings. As in Italy there are no provisions on mediation in juvenile criminal proceedings, these problems are quite important, as mediation is often used by juvenile courts according to local social services protocols. One should think that, given the lack of rules on forms and limits of this way of collecting declarations, they could not be used at all in the proceedings, but it is obvious that a clear legal rule on this issue is increasingly necessary.

2.4. ASSESSMENT OF THE JUVENILE'S CAPACITY TO BE INTERROGATED

There are no rules on the ascertainment of the capacity of the suspect to be interrogated. During the proceedings, only age can be assessed, as juveniles under 14 years old are not criminally liable. Above this threshold the suspect can always be interrogated, unless he is mentally ill. In fact, if there is the possibility that, due to illness, the suspect is not able to consciously take part in the proceedings, this must be verified; if so, the proceedings are suspended (art. 70 CCP). Thus, children under the minimum age of liability must immediately be acquitted. When a doubt is raised about their age, the judge must ascertain whether they are younger than 14, and when it is proven so, or doubt on this point remains, the case is dismissed. Therefore, in theory, normally there should not be any interrogations of juveniles under 14 years of age. It is true, though, that the law does not forbid the interrogation of juveniles under the age of 14: so, until the proceedings are formally closed with an acquittal, questioning the suspect is still possible[61] and should be considered an interrogation, with the subsequent safeguards. In practice, juvenile judges do interrogate juveniles under the age of 14, even during proceedings bound to be closed at an early stage for the lack of criminal liability of the suspect.

3. THE RULES FOR THE INTERROGATION OF JUVENILES: GENERAL SAFEGUARDS

As far as basic safeguards are concerned, the legal provisions for juveniles are the same as provided for adults. Moreover, there are no distinct rules for different categories of juveniles. Actually in the Italian system, juveniles are, first of all, granted the same level of safeguards as adult suspects and only in addition to that do they receive special assistance or protection, considering their vulnerability and weakness due to an immature age. More specifically, juveniles benefit fully from the enriched set of safeguards that the Italian legislator introduced in July 2104, regarding the right of the suspect to be completely and clearly informed of all his rights during the proceedings.[62] In the following description, the ordinary set of safeguards will be outlined: any rule that is particular to juveniles will be specifically underlined.

3.1. THE RIGHT TO LEGAL ASSISTANCE

The implementation of the right to a lawyer is the product of different safeguards. First of all, such a right is strictly connected to the information that is given to the suspect about the proceedings and the right (and need) to appoint a defence lawyer. This information, of course, is important and must be ensured, first of all, when the suspect is questioned or summoned for an interrogation. Obviously, the ability of a young suspect to understand this information is of paramount importance, and the effectiveness of the safeguards mainly depends on the clarity and efficacy of the contents of the advice given and on the way it is made.

3.1.1. Information on the right to legal assistance

In general, the public prosecutor must send the suspect a so-called 'safeguard information' (*informazione di garanzia*) at the moment of the first act that

61 Actually, the interrogation (or the 'audition') of the juvenile in such cases is quite normal, since the proceedings to realise an early acquittal are complicated: it implies criminal action, a special hearing *in camera* and the ascertainment of culpability. So, it cannot be avoided that the juvenile is heard at some stage of this process. In general, about such discipline, see Renon 2011, p. 574–578,.

62 See D.lgs. 1 July 2014, n. 101.

entails the right to assistance of a defence lawyer (art. 369 CCP). This advice is written and informs the suspect that proceedings against him have been started, specifying the legal provision that he is supposed to have violated, the place and date of the alleged offence, and the invitation to appoint a defence lawyer. If the suspect has not appointed a lawyer yet, he is also given another advice, a written information regarding not only the different aspects of the right to a lawyer (compulsory character of legal assistance, right to appoint a lawyer, right to legal aid, right to interpretation and translation), but also the name, address and telephone number of the lawyer appointed by the prosecutor (art. 369 *bis* CCP). This specific information is, in any case, given before the invitation to appear for an interrogation held by the prosecutor and, at the latest, when the investigations are formally closed.

Whenever the suspect is questioned or the first contact with judicial or police authorities occurs, advice concerning the right to appoint a defence lawyer must be given. So, when the suspect is arrested *in flagrante delicto* by the police, he must immediately be informed in writing, clearly and in a language that he understands, about the right to appoint a lawyer; immediate information about the arrest is also given to the already appointed lawyer (art. 386 CCP). When a pre-trial coercive measure is applied, the officers who arrest the suspect must inform him straight away, by means of a specific written act, about the right to a lawyer (art. 293 CCP) and then immediately inform the appointed lawyer of the arrest. Afterwards, the order that applies the pre-trial measure has to be deposited and the defence lawyer should be informed of the deposit. In both cases (arrest and pre-trial measure), if the suspect does not appoint a lawyer, an *ex officio* appointment must be done and the information about the arrest is given to the so called 'duty solicitor' (*difensore d'ufficio*). If the suspect is not detained and the public prosecutor wants to question him, he must send the suspect a written invitation to appear (art. 375 CCP) three days beforehand. The invitation has to be served to suspects who do not have a lawyer yet, together with the information on the right to be assisted by a duty lawyer if the suspect has no counsel yet, and must contain a rough description of the fact as it emerges from the investigation developed until that moment.

3.1.2. The right to consultation of a lawyer

In order to ensure that the defence strategy is prepared in a timely and adequately manner, the right to appoint a lawyer is accompanied by the suspect's right to consultation and to receive appropriate advice. If the suspect is free, there are obviously no limitations on the lawyer-client consultation. If the suspect is in pre-trial custody, the right to consult a lawyer is granted by art. 104 CCP from the very beginning of the coercive measure. Only exceptionally, during the preliminary investigation, can the prosecutor ask the judge to prohibit defendant-lawyer consultations for no longer than five days. In any case, such an order can be adopted only on specific and exceptional grounds (e.g. danger of corruption of evidence) and must explain the reasons why the judge decided so. In the case of arrest *in flagrante delicto* or to prevent escape, the right to consultation with the lawyer is assured immediately after the arrest; the prosecutor, though, can directly impose the aforementioned prohibition on consultations until the arrested person is brought to the judge (that is, approximately 48 hours after the arrest). The right to consultation is set out explicitly and in detail, in order to ensure that the suspect can talk to his lawyer before the interrogation, as this is also seen as a mean of self-defence, and consequently implies a previous consultation between the suspect and his lawyer. Consultations are held in the place where the suspect is in custody, and the defence lawyer has a specific right of access to such places to talk with his client (art. 36 d.lgs. 28 July 1989, No. 271, hereafter: d.lgs. 271/89). For juveniles, this means that the lawyer normally talks to the juvenile in the special facilities where they are kept after arrest, such as first reception centres or communities.

3.1.3. *The right to have a lawyer present during interrogation*

As the assistance of a lawyer is crucial during interrogation, the defence lawyer must be kept informed of any occasion in which the suspect may be questioned. Prior to the summary information, for example, the police must give the lawyer prompt notice of the act (art. 350 para. 3 CCP). In the case of a prosecutor's interrogation, the lawyer must be informed at least 24 hours prior to the act (art. 364 para. 3 CCP). When there is a risk of prejudice in the collection of evidence, the prosecutor has the option to carry out the interrogation in advance, but the lawyer has the right to be notified promptly (art. 364 para. 5 CCP). Such previous information is aimed at allowing the lawyer to be present at the interrogation and must be given in time to allow the lawyer to arrive and attend the act. The presence of the lawyer is in some cases compulsory (and a condition for the validity of the interrogation), and in some cases allowed but not necessary. The police interrogation cannot take place without the presence of a lawyer (art. 350 para. 4 CCP), while the interrogation made by the public prosecutor, in principle, can take place without the defence lawyer (art. 364 para. 1–4 CCP), provided that he was informed in a timely manner that the interrogation would take place. The lawyer participating in the interrogation has the right to give the suspect advice about the opportunity to answer or not to answer all or some of the questions; he is allowed to make applications, comments and remarks which have to be recorded (art. 364 para. 7 CCP).

3.1.4. *Appointment of a lawyer ex officio and legal aid*

In any case of interrogation, when the suspect has not exercised his right to appoint a lawyer, an *ex officio* lawyer must be appointed (art. 350 paras. 2, 4 and art. 364 para. 2 CCP). The juvenile suspect and defendant who should be considered indigent, according to predetermined legal criteria, is granted legal aid. Specific provisions on this subject matter are contained in d.P.R. 30 May 2002, No. 115, about judicial expenses, where conditions to obtain this kind of support are established in general, for both adult and juvenile suspects. Legal aid is granted to the defendant whose family gross income is lower than € 10,628.16 per annum, taking into consideration the incomes of all cohabitants. Legal aid is assured in relation to defendant's appointed lawyer and *ex officio* lawyer and it covers all the phases and actions of the proceedings, and connected proceedings. The information on legal aid is given with the written information on legal assistance (art. 369 *bis* CCP), served prior to the first act (as interrogations) which imply the right to be assisted by a lawyer. In general, legal aid has to be requested by a written application where the applicant (the suspect) declares the existence of the legal prerequisites to obtain it; when these prerequisites are verified, legal aid is granted, the defendant can appoint the lawyer and the lawyer's expenses and fees are paid by the state. In order to provide a stronger protection for juveniles, the law provides that, if the juvenile does not appoint a lawyer and accepts being assisted by an *ex officio* appointed lawyer, legal aid is consequential and there is no need to apply for it. This means that the defence lawyer appointed *ex officio* to a juvenile, is paid directly by the state, on a presumption of indigence of the juvenile who did not appoint him personally; only afterwards are the juvenile and his family asked to give evidence of their low income and, if that income exceeds the legal limit, the sums paid to the lawyer will be claimed back from the juvenile by the state. This way, it is deemed that defence activity for juveniles who do not appoint a lawyer will be more continuous and effective.[63] There are two problems, though, arising from this construction. The first is that there is no specific rule about the possibility that the juvenile comes of age before the end of the proceedings; so the appointed lawyer could be paid according to the special system for juveniles only for the activities carried out up to that point, while he should make the ordinary request to obtain legal aid after that point. This kind of treatment denies the young adult the same special safeguards of the juvenile, simply for reaching the 18 years of age threshold, which normally does not automatically imply a meaningful increase of income; this is why case-law on this point is divided[64] and it would be preferable to admit that legal aid conceded to a juvenile in his proceedings is offered according to the same special regime until the proceedings are closed, even if the juvenile reaches 18 years meanwhile. Another problem is related to specialisation of the lawyer: when legal aid is granted to the suspect, the lawyer can be appointed only from among

63 Presutti 2011b, p. 445.

64 Cass., 20 June 2007, M., in *Cassazione penale*, 2009, p. 2006, denies this special safeguard with regard to legal aid to the juvenile who came of age during the proceedings. In contrast to this, Cass., 3 April 2008, P.G. in c. A., in *Rivista penale*, 2009, p. 766, considers the age of the suspect irrelevant in this perspective.

those lawyers included in a specific list of 'lawyers for legal aid'. When a duty solicitor is appointed in juvenile proceedings, the choice is limited to another list of lawyers, specialised in juvenile and family matters. So, the two lists are different and this implies that the juvenile who is granted legal aid might not always receive the assistance of a specialised lawyer. There is, of course, the possibility to do so, but the system is quite complicated and not always rational, so that in doctrine there are voices in favour of an intervention of the legislator to reshape it.[65]

3.2. THE RIGHT TO REMAIN SILENT

The right to remain silent is a crucial component of the right to defence and has the purpose of ensuring that the defendant is not compelled to collaborate in the ascertainment of his responsibility for the alleged offence. It also is a measure to grant the privilege against self-incrimination. This right entails, first of all, that the defendant may refuse interrogation or to answer single questions (art. 64 para. 3b CCP). Moreover, if the suspect decides to answer questions, he is allowed to lie to the police and judiciary authorities, with the only prohibition on slandering someone else. The right to silence is always granted, in any kind of investigating or trial interrogation, whether carried out by the judge, the prosecutor or the police (art. 64 CCP), and it is effective from the very beginning of the interrogation.

If a suspect is summoned for an interrogation, he has only two obligations. The first one is to present himself to the authorities (arts. 350 CCP and 650 CC, art. 375 para. 2d CCP). In case of unjustified absence, the prosecutor may ask the judge to order the coercive attendance of the suspect to the interrogation, and specific caution about such coercive power must be given to the suspect in the invitation to appear for the interrogation (art. 375 para. 2d CCP). Moreover, during the interrogation, the suspect must answer questions about his identity (name, surname, place and date of birth),[66] which information is not covered by the right to remain silent. Besides that, the suspect has no other obligation, being allowed to choose whether or not to answer the questions, to keep silent during the whole interrogation or to tell the truth or not about any issue he is questioned about. The exact limits on the right to remain silent, however, are subject to debate, as doctrine is divided upon the question whether identity data are irrelevant from the point of view of the defence, so that the suspect can be justly compelled to give complete and truthful declarations about such issues. In fact, there are dissenting opinions, according to which these matters are sometimes relevant for the defensive strategy, so that in such cases they should

65 Presutti 2011b, p. 446, 449 and Sechi 2006, p. 193.
66 See Corte cost., 6 May 1976, n. 108.

be covered by the right to remain silent like any other relevant fact for the defence case.[67] The point is quite important for juvenile proceedings, as in this context, for example, age is always relevant to obtain a favourable treatment, if not an immediate acquittal; the date of birth, in this perspective, could never be considered something that the juvenile suspect could be compelled to answer (truthfully). In addition to these data, Italian law provides that during the first act where the suspect is present (including an interrogation), judicial authority must ask him other information, for example about other criminal proceedings against him or previous convictions, and also about his social, family and personal life conditions. This further information is deemed to be excluded from the notion of 'identity data' and subsequently should be covered by the right to remain silent.[68] This opinion is particularly convincing when applied to the system of juvenile justice, where such issues are a crucial part of judicial ascertainment and a condition to deliver most decisions.

It is necessary to remember that in Italy, with l. 1 March 2001, No. 63, the structure of the right to remain silent was partially changed, as the right was limited in order to assure the right of confrontation of suspects who were accused by other persons submitted to criminal proceedings. Thus the law provided that, in general, a suspect who gives information about someone else's responsibility for an offence cannot invoke his own right to remain silent on such facts, being compelled to answer (and answer truthfully) on them ever since. In theory, the reform is based on the principle of responsibility, and implies that if a person accuses someone else of an offence, he cannot withdraw, if the accused person and his defence lawyer want to confront him. In practice, though, the discipline on this point is quite complicated and difficult to understand and apply, so that the exact borders of what is covered by the right to remain silent and what is not are quite vague. Naturally, these difficulties are even more serious in juvenile proceedings, where the suspect has fewer cultural and intellectual tools to manage the technicalities of the criminal justice system and oversee the implications of his behaviour in proceedings. Within this context, it is clear how much the effectiveness of the right to remain silent depends on the existence and quality of previous information on the scope and contents of this right, given to the suspect.[69]

Apparently, the right to remain silent is applicable in each and every contact between the suspect and police or magistrates (public prosecutor or judge) during the proceedings. However, there is no mention of it as far as contacts between the suspect and social services are concerned. The problem is that such 'dialogues' or 'auditions' are often held in an informal way, and the risk is high that the juvenile suspect is 'softly' forced to make statements, give information

[67] See Mazza 2008, p. 201 for this opinion and more references on the issue.
[68] Kostoris 1992, p. 78.
[69] See *infra* paragraph 3.3 (part II).

or even to confess. In theory, the right to remain silent should be considered a direct effect of the right to defence, and therefore a general principle of the system; this means that the right to remain silent should be operational at every stage, on every occasion of the proceedings where the suspect is questioned, whoever carries out the audition, including social services staff. In practice, though, the area of social and personal inquiry is a sensitive and dangerous one from the perspective of the right to remain silent and the privilege against self-incrimination.

There is no explicit legal provision on the consequences of exercising the right to remain silent. The suspect is only informed that, in case of silence, the proceedings will carry on anyway (art. 64 para. 3b CCP). Refusal to answer questions is documented in the interrogation transcript (art. 65 para. 3 CCP). In theory, no detrimental effect could spring from the suspect's silence on his position, as silence is granted to the accused person as a fundamental right in the proceedings and a basic profile of the right to defence. Nonetheless, in practice the suspect's non-collaborating behaviour is often taken into consideration in juvenile proceedings, where broad discretionary powers are given to the judge to deliver decisions and adopt measures that are based on evaluation of the juvenile's character and his behaviour. It is meaningful, that part of case law tried to consider the confession, for example, as a prerequisite to probation. This opinion was hotly debated, and opponents correctly recalled that the right to remain silent does not allow submitting a favourable measure to the defendant's cooperation to the ascertainment of responsibility.[70] Nevertheless, the debate on this issue shows how much the collaboration of the juvenile may in practice be crucial in order to obtain diversion decisions, such as probation, or forms of immediate acquittal, such as judicial pardon.[71]

3.3. THE RIGHT TO BE INFORMED ON RIGHTS

The efficacy of rights granted by law to the suspect is widely dependent on whether he is actually aware of them. This is even more important when a juvenile suspect is involved in criminal proceedings, as he must be given the exact perception of the nature, contents, limits and consequences of such rights and their exercise and such purpose is particularly difficult to achieve with a young person.

---

70 In general, about this issue, see Cesari 2009, p. 349–350.

71 Such decisions, moreover, must be based also on the proven responsibility of the defendant for the alleged offence: so, it happens frequently that, in order to avoid the difficulties of producing evidence against the suspect, judges try to simplify and shorten the proceedings using the short cut of a confession as a condition for a probation order or other diversion decision.

In general, caution must precede the interrogation; it should be given orally and should be specifically documented in the interrogation record (art. 64 CCP). The suspect must be informed that:

- he has the right to legal assistance and to appoint a lawyer;
- he has the right to refuse to answer questions, but, if he does, the proceedings will go on anyway;
- he has the obligation to answer questions about identity;
- any statements can be used against him; if he makes statements about criminal liability of other persons he could be called to give evidence as a witness about their culpability.

No ritual *formula* for informing the suspect of the aforementioned rights is imposed.[72] It is only necessary that the content of the rights as listed is clearly communicated and understood by the suspect, whatever the words used by the proceeding authority to caution him. The actual contents of the rights, though, might be quite difficult to understand, especially for a juvenile, so it is crucial that the warnings are explained in simple language and in detail to the young suspect. It must be considered an obligation for the proceeding authority to verify that the suspect did really understand the meaning of the advice on every point. This is true in general, but for juveniles it is a consequence of the rule that obliges the judge to explain to the juvenile suspect the meaning of the procedural activities in which he takes part (art. 1 para. 2 d.P.R. n.448/1988). Actually, the provision literally refers only to the judge, but it can be extended also to the police and the prosecutor, with respect to the advice given before an interrogation. The aim of the rule is to put the suspect in a position to understand the proceedings and consciously determine his behaviour in it, so it is a principle that must be applied on this occasion too.[73] The rule requires the police and prosecutor to make a particular effort to assure full comprehension of the warnings, with the help of the defence lawyer if necessary. The involvement of the latter could also be insufficient, though, and the proceeding personnel could also ask for the help of supporting figures that are involved in the act,[74] such as the suspect's parents or social service personnel, in order to define the appropriate means of cautioning in accordance with the age and the maturity of the juvenile. Social services staff are in particular involved in such acts exactly in order to ensure good communication, as a sort of 'driving belt', between the judicial authority and the juvenile. Even an expert (psychologist, childhood or adolescence psychiatrist) could be involved, if necessary to assure comprehension of the

72 Cass., 20 November 2002, Falcicchio, in *Archivio della nuova procedura penale*, 2003, p. 21 and 388.
73 Mazza 2008, p. 193.
74 See *infra* paragraph 4.2 (part II).

advice, provided that he is appointed by defence and is considered part of the defence staff.[75] The physical presence of an expert is not forbidden, of course, but it must be stressed that it is neither imposed nor legally provided for. The expert is a figure that is taken into consideration for the assistance of juvenile witnesses during trial (art. 498 para. 4 CCP) or, due to a very recent reform, for summary information collected from juvenile witnesses by the police, the defence lawyers, the public prosecutors, during investigations for sexual abuse (arts. 351, 362, 391 *bis* CCP). It is not considered at all, on the contrary, for juvenile suspects, for whose protection only 'psychological' and 'affective' support is granted by assuring the presence of social service and parents by the juvenile's side, while there is no specific concern about the problems of communication between him and the proceeding bodies. From this perspective, in fact, the lawyer's assistance and parental (and social services) support were probably thought to be sufficient. Since this might not always be true, however, one might suggest that the law should provide for the possible intervention of an expert in favour of the juvenile suspect, whenever it appears necessary during the interrogation and the interrogating official or the defence lawyer deem this additional support to be useful.

The way advice on the suspect's rights is given is crucial not only as to the words used and clarity of the message given, but also as to the general manners and attitude of the authority that carries out the interrogation. It must be kept in mind that, in Italy, the advice is simply the information of the rights the suspect is entitled to and is not a threatening, an admonition or a question.[76] So, also the voice, the intonation, the general attitude of the operating judge, police officer or prosecutor should never evoke anything different than the effort of giving information, creating a 'fair play atmosphere' and putting the juvenile in the position to understand what is going on and consciously determine his choices in his own best interests.[77] For example, nothing in the way the advice is made can ever suggest that the suspect is compelled to cooperate with the authorities or that silence could cause him negative consequences; also a caution should never even sound as a question or be posed in an interrogative form, so as not to give the impression that an effort or a commitment is required from the suspect.[78]

Of course, in order to control whether such forms of undue pressure have occurred, a proper documentation of the interrogation and its prior cautions

---

75 See Mazza 2008, p. 193, who stresses the risk that the expert is appointed by the judicial authority and behaves consequently in a direct relationship with the juvenile but not in his exclusive interest. For a different view, see La Placa 2006, p. 1121, according to whom the expert should be appointed by the proceeding judge, as an impartial support figure.

76 Mazza 2008, p. 194. In general, see Grevi 1972, p. 318.

77 Mazza 2008, p. 196.

78 Mazza 2008, p. 200.

should be granted. Italian case law is sometimes superficial on this point,[79] but in juvenile proceedings the appropriate forms of documentation of such safeguards are fundamental. So, it must be stressed that the previous advice must be specifically documented[80] and, also, that it would be necessary to adopt very faithful techniques of documentation in order to verify afterwards how the caution was made.[81]

In order to avoid confusion, and establish the correct basis to communicate and exchange information, caution on rights must be given at the beginning of each interrogation. If more than one interrogation is performed, the advice must be repeated on every occasion. The first caution can never absorb the following ones, because the suspect might easily be pushed to think that his rights ceased to be effective after the first time or simply forget or underestimate their relevance: and this might happen even more easily when the suspect is a juvenile.[82] This is why doctrine is very critical of the Italian case law allowing the interrogating authority not to repeat the caution when the interrogation is interrupted and delayed to another session.[83] A very young suspect might, in the second part of the audition, not remember or be uncertain about his rights.[84]

Although in Italy the suspect, when interrogated, has no obligation to give truthful statements, being allowed to lie, no caution on this has to be given. The absence of such an obligation was criticised, as the possibility of lying is considered as a profile of self-defence. Therefore, it was suggested in doctrine that the officer, prosecutor or judge who carries out the interrogation can give the suspect additional information on the right of not telling the truth.[85] It is understandable, however, that no such advice is normally given, especially to the juvenile suspect, as it would be difficult to explain to a juvenile why ethically incorrect behaviour like lying must be considered a legitimate (and sometimes even advisable) option. This is also why such information – which the suspect will normally receive from his lawyer – should be given by the defence lawyer in an appropriate way.

No warning is provided for before the auditions that social services personnel might carry out with the juvenile suspect, even when – as normally happens – this audition is carried out without the presence of parents or the lawyer. Such auditions are not defined as interrogations, so the specific safeguards disciplined in art. 64 CCP are not applicable. This should be balanced by the

---

79 See Cass., 19 June 1992, Capasso, in *Rivista penale*, 1993, p. 1292, according to which the absence of the caution in the transcription does not matter, if it is documented that the suspect said 'I want to answer' at the beginning of the interrogation.

80 Doctrine esteems that the single words used to make the caution should be transcripted: Mazza 2008, p. 198, and, in general, Grevi 1972, p. 331–332.

81 See also *infra* paragraph 5.2 (part II).

82 Mazza 2008, p. 196.

83 Cass., 22 April 2004, Bisognano, CED 230341.

84 Mazza 2008, p. 197.

85 Mazza 2008, p. 200.

fact that statements given by the suspect on such occasions cannot be used in trial, but in practice things might be very different. Declarations of the juvenile could be narrated in the social report that the social services personnel writes for the judge and, in this way, be reported to the court and indirectly used, as these drafts are normally considered documents, and used as evidence in judicial proceedings. Anyway, the statements may influence the social service decisions and its proposals to the judge, which are often crucial for the juvenile's access to diversion or probation proceedings. Moreover, nobody could say how much pressure applied upon the juvenile on these occasions can influence his behaviour before the prosecutor or the judge in the subsequent activities of the proceedings. In any case, it is forbidden to testify or ask questions on declarations given by the suspect during the proceedings (art. 62 CCP), including the acts that in juvenile proceedings are carried out by social service personnel.

Finally, it must be reiterated that caution is excluded in case of spontaneous statements, to which art. 64 CCP is considered not to apply.[86] The problem is that in practice it can be quite difficult – especially when the suspect is a juvenile – to establish whether the statements were really spontaneous or some sort of undue pressure was applied. In general, anyway, as soon as a question is asked, declarations given afterwards cannot be considered spontaneous anymore; they actually turn into an interrogation and, before carrying it out, the caution must be given.

As mentioned before, it must be added that in July 2014, the Italian criminal procedural law was revised in order to adhere to the level of safeguards established in Directive 2012/13/EU on the right to information in criminal proceedings.[87] According to these changes in Italian legislation the suspect (juveniles included) must be given a specific letter of rights, listing their rights, on specific occasions such as the implementation of pre-trial coercive measures and the provisional arrest. The rights that must be listed in the letter are numerous and include: the right to be informed of the accusation, the right of access to a judge within the term established by law, the right to appoint a lawyer, the right of access to relevant materials of the proceedings, the right to interpretation and translation, the right to access to urgent medical assistance and the specific right to use the means of appeal provided for by the law. Among the rights listed in the letter there are also some crucial ones for the protection of minors in the first steps of the proceedings, such as the right to inform the family of his detention, the right to remain silent, and the right to be interrogated (both in the case of provisional arrest and pre-trial coercive measure) by a judge. The judge himself must, on the first contact with the arrestee, control whether the caution about these rights has been given and if it was complete: if not, he must

86 Cass., 27 June 2008, Vanese, CED 241466; Cass., 20 January 2010, Capozzi, CED 246590.

87 The national law implementing Directive 2012/13/EU is D.lgs. 1 July 2014, n. 101, which reformed arts. 293, 294, 369, 369 *bis*, 386, 391 CCP.

give the caution or complete it. This task, therefore, is given to the judge who conducts the first interrogation of the juvenile suspect after pre-trial custody has been applied.

Another important detail of this kind of caution is the fact that it is must be written in a 'clear and precise form' and in a language that the suspect understands. This is going to be particularly important for minors, as – according to the intention of the legislator – the way in which the caution is given must be clear enough to make the rights really and fully understood by the suspect. This goal is harder to achieve for minors and should imply special attention for and effort in drafting the letter of rights: after all, the Directive 2012/13/EU itself provides that, in drafting the information about rights in a simple and accessible language, 'particular needs of vulnerable suspects' must be taken into account.[88]

3.4. INFORMATION ON THE CHARGES

Before being asked any questions, the suspect must know what he is accused of, and on which elements the allegations against him are based. Thus, before the interrogation starts, charges must be communicated to the suspect in a 'clear and precise form', together with the elements collected against him at that point of the investigation (art. 65 para. 1 CCP). In addition, in the so-called 'invitation' to be interrogated (*invito a presentarsi*) – the written act that invites the suspect to present himself to judicial authority in order to be questioned – the charges must be 'summarily described'. The suspect is also informed of the sources of evidence against him, unless this might prejudice the investigations (art. 65 para. 1 CCP). Some kinds of interrogation, however, have a different regime, with a higher or lower standard of protection. Sometimes, when an interrogation is performed, the defence is already aware of some or all the results of the investigations (for example, in the interrogation after a coercive measure was applied or when the interrogation is asked by the suspect after investigation was closed). Sometimes, art. 65 CCP is not applicable, and such information is not given at all: this is the case of summary information collected by the police, prior to which only the general caution about the suspect's rights is given (art. 350 para. 1 CCP). When this information must be given, it should be complete and be given to the suspect at the beginning of the interrogation. If an interrogation is carried out giving the suspect fragmentary data (for example, about elements against him) and delaying the moment when he has a precise vision of evidence against him, the accused is not aware of his situation and his right of defence cannot be effective. Nonetheless, the practice of delay and incompleteness of information about the

88 Directive 2012/13/EU art. 3.2.

charges during the interrogation is considered admissible,[89] even if it is severely criticised by doctrine, especially when the suspect is a juvenile and can easily be puzzled or manipulated by the interrogating authority.[90] From this same perspective, it must be stressed that information about the accusation might be given in practice by a simple (and quick) reference – made by the proceeding judge or prosecutor – to previous written acts where the charges were described (for example, the order to apply a coercive pre-trial measure). Such a tricky practice should be avoided, as it is obvious that real understanding of the charges is not ensured that way, especially when the interrogated person is a juvenile. On the contrary, the interrogation is a very delicate moment and should be based on consciousness of the charges, and on fair play: in this respect it is important to show the juvenile suspect, at this important step of the proceedings, that the authority handles the act correctly and that the officials are trustworthy.[91]

With the aforementioned reform of July 2014, the right to information on the charges and the right to access the acts the arrest is based on, are specifically listed in the letter of rights which is given to the suspect at the moment of the arrest (both in case of provisional arrest and pre-trial custody). Therefore, as soon as he is arrested, the juvenile suspect will also be informed of such rights in a 'clear and precise form' and in a language that he understands. No doubt, of course, the real efficacy of this caution will mostly depend on the way it is given in practice, in order to make sure that such rights (the content of which may be difficult to understand) are really made clear to the juvenile suspect.

3.5. THE RIGHT TO INTERPRETATION AND TRANSLATION

Additional important safeguards are provided for foreign suspects or for suspects who do not speak or understand the language used in the proceedings. These safeguards are important for juveniles as well, given the fact that a relevant part of juveniles involved in criminal proceedings is now composed of foreign juveniles. Moreover, given the vulnerability of the juvenile suspect, ignoring the language of the process puts him in an even more difficult position. When the juvenile suspect does not understand the language of the proceedings the feelings of alienation and bewilderment that he normally has when coping with criminal proceedings are most likely increased and may cause a lower ability to manage the procedural behaviour and defensive choices.

In general, from the beginning of the procedure, a suspect who cannot speak or understand the Italian language has the right to free assistance of an

89 Cass., 23 November 2000, Magaddino, in *Archivio della nuova procedura penale*, 2001, p. 344.
90 Mazza 2008, p. 207.
91 Mazza 2008, p. 209.

interpreter during hearings and procedural activities in which he takes part and in order to understand what he is accused of (art. 143 para. 1 CCP, as recently reformed by d.lgs. 4 March 2014, n. 32). This safeguard is also granted at a constitutional level by art. 111 para. 3 Cost., in accordance with the safeguards provided for in the ECHR[92] and the suspect must be informed about it specifically with the letter of rights which he receives when being arrested or when undergoing a coercive measure.

This right is also operational for written acts, such as the 'safeguard information' (art. 143 para. 2 CCP),[93] but it has always been recognised as fundamental for oral activities,[94] such as interrogation. This opinion is now supported by the new art. 143 CCP, which explicitly provides for the right to an interpreter even for the consultation with the lawyer: it would be illogical to grant the assistance of an interpreter for the dialogue between the suspect and his lawyer and not for the questioning of the suspect by the authorities. The above-mentioned rule is applicable for the entirety of the proceedings, including the stage of preliminary investigations and the acts performed by the police and the public prosecutor[95] and this opinion seems to be confirmed by the new text, where several rules directly refer the safeguard of the interpreter's assistance to activities which are performed at the preliminary stage. For example, a specific right to be assisted by an interpreter (for free) has been recognised for the suspects who do not understand Italian and are in custody or under arrest, in order to communicate with the defence lawyer (art. 104 para. 4 *bis* CCP). When an interrogation is carried out and the suspect is not Italian (for whom the knowledge of the language is presumed), art. 143 CCP imposes that the proceeding magistrate verifies that he understands Italian and, if not, an interpreter is appointed. The burden of proof about the fact that the foreign citizen does not understand the language is not on the suspect, as the proceeding authority must verify the linguistic competence, independently from any request from the suspect (art. 143 para. 4 CCP).[96] If doubts remain about

92 Sau 2010, p. 158–160.

93 The new art. 143 CCP lists various acts that should be translated: among these, however, some relevant acts – in the perspective of defence – do not appear. This is the case for the invitation to appear for interrogation (art. 375 CCP), for which translation can perhaps be considered possible, but not compulsory (applying to the prosecutor the new art. 143 para. 3 CCP, which actually refers to the 'judge', and provides for the possibility of translating all the acts that are considered essential for the defendant to be aware of the crime he is charged of). In any case, we could say that this act, too, ought to be translated in order to respect the right to a defence.

94 Sau 2010, p. 178.

95 Corte cost. n. 10/1993.

96 This opinion had been already stated in the case law of the Court of cassation (Cass., Sez. Un., 24 September 2003, Zalagaitis, in *Cassazione penale*, 2004, p. 1563, Cass., Sez. Un., 23 June 2000, Jakani, in *Cassazione penale*, 2000, p. 3255), as before it was deemed that not knowing Italian had to be proven or at least declared by the defendant in order to obtain the interpreter's assistance. Obviously, in this way, the right to an interpreter was ineffective

the real citizenship and linguistic competence of the suspect,[97] the right to an interpreter's assistance should also be granted.

The audition ought to be totally conducted with the assistance of the interpreter, so that every step of it is translated and the suspect can be aware of the exact contents of warnings, information and questions asked or received. Of course, caution about the rights of the suspect given before the interrogation must be given in the language understood by the suspect, because otherwise it is totally ineffective.

4. THE RULES FOR INTERROGATION OF JUVENILES: SPECIAL SAFEGUARDS

4.1. SPECIALISATION OF AUTHORITIES

The first specific safeguard that the Italian juvenile justice system provides, is specialisation of the authorities, bodies and persons, who are faced with the juvenile suspect during the proceedings. Specialisation of actors should be guaranteed in juvenile proceedings especially on the most sensitive occasions, such as the interrogation. This goal is achieved whenever the interrogation is conducted by a juvenile magistrate: the judge for preliminary investigations and the public prosecutor dealing with juveniles belong to a separate and specialised body that in principle assures competence and correct behaviour. Yet this is not the case with police officers. There are specialist police offices attached to each juvenile court, who are normally in charge of supporting the juvenile prosecutor during investigations. But, in practice, as such police staff do not work 'on the beat', the first intervention in the case of a crime or offence committed by juveniles is made by ordinary police officers: thus, arrest and summary information made immediately after the crime was committed, are dealt with by police officers who belong to ordinary police forces and are not specialised at all. Given this circumstance, which is often criticised by doctrine,[98] this suggests that in Italy appropriate training and specific guide lines should be offered to all police force personnel, in order to assure that in any case the juvenile, during his first contact with the criminal justice system, is heard by someone who knows how to manage the special situation, interests and needs of the suspect.

---

for juveniles: it is hard to imagine a juvenile being able to declare or prove such a point and require to be assisted.

97 This is quite frequently the case when dealing with migrant juveniles, with no documents or adult relatives.

98 Bouchard 1995, p. 146, Cibinel 1994, p. 61 and Presutti 2011a, p. 433.

4.2. THE RIGHT TO PRESENCE OF AN APPROPRIATE ADULT AND SOCIAL SERVICE PERSONNEL

A typical specific safeguard that the Italian system grants to juvenile suspects is the presence of an appropriate adult throughout the proceedings and on specific (more important or delicate) occasions. This kind of safeguard is specifically provided for juveniles and is aimed at strengthening their position, as the context of the proceedings might be too stressful and confusing for them. It is clearly an effect of the 'principle of minimum harm'. Moreover, the juvenile suspect's immaturity can, as a matter of fact, undermine his ability to defend himself and to understand the choices that must be made in the proceedings; this is why further support is granted to ensure that an adult figure shares with the defendant such choices and manages strategies together with him, as without this support, defence may be ineffective. On these premises, in Italy two different kinds of supporting figures are provided to the juvenile suspect: some of them are aimed at assuring him adequate affective and psychological protection; some of them have the purpose of putting an adult as a point of reference to implement and support the right to defence.

Under the first perspective, art. 12 d.P.R. n. 448/1988 grants the juvenile the right to affective and psychological support at any stage of the proceedings. So, when the juvenile suspect's presence is needed, parent(s) must also be present at his side and it is compulsory for the proceeding authority to provide for their presence. Alternatively, where parents are deceased, absent or in a condition of conflict of interests with the juvenile, their place can be taken by another appropriate adult, chosen by the juvenile and authorised by the judicial authority. This person could be anyone (including a teacher, a relative, a priest and so on), provided that the juvenile has a relationship of affection and trust with him. In addition to the persons already mentioned, the presence of social services personnel is also provided (art. 12 para. 2 d.P.R. 448/1988). A specific communication is given to social services and parents (or other persons), in order to make their presence by the juvenile's side possible (art. 17 d.lgs. n. 272/1989). Apparently, though, there is no legal obligation to give the juvenile specific information on his right to be assisted by an appropriate adult. These provisions are apparently applicable only for acts performed by judicial authorities, as police investigations are not explicitly mentioned in art. 12. If the legal rules are interpreted this way, this means that summary information collected from the suspect by the police might be carried out without the presence of social services or parents. It may be possible, actually, to interpret art. 12 as applicable to police, too, as the law provides that the juvenile must be granted psychological and affective assistance at any stage of the proceedings (so, one could say, during police investigations, too). Nevertheless, the law is not clear on this crucial point and might leave the juvenile without full protection in the early stages of proceedings where stronger protection is needed as the first contact with the proceedings is the most challenging and stressful.

The role of the people involved in the proceedings to give the juvenile support, is to grant and protect psychological balance and serenity of the suspect in the highly stressful environment of the criminal process. Parents (or somebody else, when parents are not available) are expected to give the juvenile the necessary loving support to face a complicated situation, where people representing institutions are strangers, often perceived as hostile by the juvenile.[99] Social services personnel provide psychological support (in this case, based on specialist competences) to the juvenile, offering a kind of intermediation between the juvenile suspect and the criminal proceeding's main characters and activities.[100] Under art. 12 para. 3 d.P.R. 448/1988, the judge and the prosecutor can forbid the participation of the 'appropriate adults' to an act,[101] whenever it would be in contrast with the interest of the juvenile or for serious procedural needs. These criteria are actually quite vague,[102] because it is undetermined what kind of interests of the juvenile could justify the exclusion of parents or other persons, and the interests of the efficiency of the proceedings is also a very broad and undefined notion. In practice, judicial authorities have a very broad discretion in establishing whether allowing the presence of supporting figures at the acts or not.

As follows from the foregoing, when a juvenile is interrogated, other persons and subjects should be present by his side: not only the ones who grant the juridical profile of the defensive activity (the defence lawyer and an interpreter, if the juvenile does not speak Italian, or an expert, when technical or scientific evidence must be given), but also parents (or, alternatively, other persons close to the juvenile) and social services. All these persons, save for the lawyer and the interpreter, can be excluded by the judge or the public prosecutor, in the best interests of the juvenile or due to special needs of the proceedings. Furthermore, it should be stressed that these persons cannot ask questions during the interrogation and it is forbidden for them to make signs of approval/disapproval to questions or answers when the interrogation is being performed (art. 364

---

99 This goal can be considered the logical basis and inspiration for the legal rule, but it is not specifically explained or described by law, except for the definition of 'affective and psychological support'. Anyway, there is no provision about the preparation or information of the parents or other persons about their role in the proceedings, whatever the act they are summoned to be present in or informed of.

100 This does not imply that social services may ever interfere with defence strategies, as their role is not one of supporting defence or collaborating with the juvenile's lawyer. Social services, instead, are involved in the case by appointment by a magistrate's (prosecutor or judge) and they cooperate with the judicial authority.

101 The law does not mention the police. This may be read as a confirmation of the fact that appropriate adults must not participate in police activities, or, on the contrary (and preferably), that the police has no power to exclude the juvenile's parents or other support persons or personnel from any act.

102 Sfrappini 2009, p. 132.

para. 7 CCP). They cannot intervene, with the exception of the lawyer. The judge or the public prosecutor, in any event, may allow social services personnel to explain to the juvenile the meaning of the activities performed or explain the questions he was asked.

The legal rule about the presence of an appropriate adult and of social service does not specify for which acts it is necessary. The law refers in general to any kind of act where the presence of the juvenile is requested (art. 12 D.P.R. n. 448/88). This includes, for example, not only all interrogations and hearings, but also the taking of fingerprints or photographs. Nevertheless, the criteria that justify exceptions to this rule are, as already said, wide; in particular, an act can be done without these persons when it is deemed necessary for the proceedings, which is interpreted also as need for speediness. As such acts are normally done quickly at the beginning of the proceedings and considered urgent, the rule might easily find an exception on such occasions. A special safeguard is provided for collecting biological samples or for medical examination of juveniles (independently of their role in the proceedings, apparently). As consent of the person submitted to this kind of examination is requested, the parent or holder of parental authority, who can be present during the act or exam, should give their consent (art. 72 *bis* disp.att. CCP). The safeguard is similar to the one provided for in art. 12 D.P.R. n. 448/88, but it is not identical and is in some ways inconsistent with it. The rule, in fact, provides that the consent is given by the parent not in addition, but in substitution of the juvenile's, which collides with the principle that juveniles – if they are not only children – are able to choose whether or not to give their consent; above 14 years old, they are certainly considered perfectly able to express their consent within criminal proceedings. Moreover, the assistance of the adults protecting the juvenile is described as optional and not compulsory, depending on the choice of parents or holders of parental authority; but this is not fully consistent with the need of the juveniles, in their best interests, of always being supported by the persons they trust and love most, when coming in contact with criminal proceedings. Nonetheless, one might believe that, when such examinations or data collections are done in relation to a juvenile suspect, the special safeguards of art. 12 D.P.R. n. 448/88 shall be applied in all cases.

4.3. THE RIGHT TO SPECIAL ASSISTANCE IN ORGANISING THE DEFENCE

Under the aforementioned second perspective, in addition to affective and psychological support, the juvenile is granted a special kind of assistance to efficiently organise and manage his defence. This is the goal pursued by the involvement of the 'parental responsibility holder' (*esercente la responsabilità genitoriale*): serving as an 'integration of self-defence'.[103] The holder of parental authority can be the parent, or a different person with parental responsibility if the parents are absent, deceased or their authority was suspended or cancelled. In such a case, this person can be a lawyer or a different carer (for example, the person responsible for a specialised facility, such as a Community, the juvenile was entrusted to), or also a representative of institutions (for example, the mayor of a little town or village). His role consists of supporting the juvenile in organising his defence in the proceedings, helping in the appointment of the lawyer and cooperating with him in defining the defence strategy: so, for example, in deciding whether to accept to answer an interrogation or to invoke the right to remain silent, or in explaining and preparing the juvenile for it. This person also explains the options and consequences of defence choices to the juvenile and is sometimes responsible for the juvenile's behaviour (for example, during coercive measures, when prescriptions are given to the juvenile, or home arrest is adopted). The holder of parental responsibility is often heard during the preliminary phase with respect to relevant outcomes, such as irrelevance of facts (art. 27 d.P.R. n. 448/1988) or the adoption of prescriptions like a pre-trial measure (art. 20 d.P.R. n. 448/1988). The implementation of this safeguard is granted in general by a specific duty to inform the parental authority holder about the most important moments of the proceedings. So, the carer must receive, first, the 'safeguard information', given about the existence of the proceedings as soon as an act that requires the lawyer's assistance is performed; second, he must be informed of any hearing held during the proceedings (art. 7 d.P.R. 448/1988). This information is a condition of validity of the subsequent acts and aims at assuring the timely involvement of the person legally responsible for the juvenile in the proceedings and at times during which preparation of defence and awareness of procedural choices are needed.

This kind of safeguard, however, is not detailed and sometimes it appears insufficient. First of all, there is no legal provision requiring the juvenile to be informed of his right to be assisted by the holder of parental responsibility. This kind of assistance is also not clearly defined by law as to its scope and – especially when the parent and the holder of parental authority are the same person – is in practice often confused with affective support. Moreover, the right of the parental responsibility holder to be informed is not clearly connected to a right of participating in the acts he is informed of, so that he might for example receive information about the proceedings if the prosecutor decided to summon the suspect for an interrogation (and the proceedings were not known to the suspect before), but without being able to assist at the interrogation itself: he could only prepare the juvenile for the performance and discuss it with the lawyer in advance. Furthermore, no information is provided on specific acts, even though they may be very important from a defensive point of view. This is true for the

103 Presutti 2011b, p. 454.

interrogation, as the parental authority holder must not receive any specific communication about it (unless it is connected with the general information about the existence of the proceedings); in such a case, this person is not entitled to be informed personally in advance, nor to be present during the audition (unless it is done in the preliminary hearing). His presence actually is allowed only if the holder of parental authority is the juvenile's parent, in order to assure affective assistance; but if there is no parent and the person legally responsible for the juvenile is someone else, he has no right to participate in the interrogation. The fact that the parental responsibility holder does not have to be informed beforehand of the interrogation is certainly a gap in Italian legislation,[104] and one can only hope it will be remedied by the legislator or the Constitutional Court. Furthermore, the information given to the legally responsible person about the proceedings is not complete, as, for example, this person does not have to be advised of the closing of the investigations. This is seen as another serious hole in the net of safeguards, as the aim of such advice is to implement a defence and one of the main opportunities given on such occasion to the suspect is the interrogation or the spontaneous declarations that he might ask for; but, again, the holder of parental responsibility is not directly informed of it.[105]

4.4. PRESENCE OF EXPERTS AND THE INTERROGATION OF JUVENILE WITNESSES

Normally experts are not present during acts performed in the juvenile suspect's presence, except those of social services staff and only within the limits of psychological assistance, as art. 12 d.P.R. n. 448/1988 provides. In contrast to this, the use of experts for the audition of juvenile witnesses is governed in all criminal proceedings, if examined during trial (art. 498 para. 4 CCP). In fact, the questioning of juvenile witnesses has been arranged in detail in Italy as far as trial evidence is concerned, but it has been ignored for many years when it comes to the audition of juveniles during investigations. Only recently, with l. 1 October 2012, No. 172, were a few rules on the audition of juvenile witnesses during the preliminary phase introduced. The new provisions bind defence lawyers, public prosecutors and judiciary police to ensure the assistance of an expert in children's psychiatry or psychology, when collecting declarations of a juvenile witness (whether or not victim of the crime) in proceedings dealing with sexual offences or slavery. The new rules, however, do not provide specific sanctions for violations and, although it may in theory be held that, in certain cases, breaching the rule could make evidence invalid, in practice it is most likely

104 Patanè 2009a, p. 86.
105 Patanè 2009a, p. 87.

that no sanctions are deemed applicable. Thus, it can be said that the system still has serious weaknesses on this issue.

5. CARRYING OUT THE INTERROGATION OF A JUVENILE SUSPECT

The way in which the interrogation is carried out in practice is particularly important to ensure the effectiveness of the safeguards formally granted by law. In Italy, there are general rules aimed at establishing a climate of fair play and respect for the suspect, in order to avoid undue pressures and physical and moral violence. The suspect must always be made aware of his position and of the consequences of his choices, and he should be free to make decisions in this respect (for example, about the opportunity of using the right to remain silent). A juvenile suspect, of course, benefits from the same general protection. The framework can be described as follows and mostly concerns all forms of interrogation. Differences between the interrogation of the prosecutor on the one hand and the interrogation by the police on the other will be stressed when and where relevant.

5.1. METHODS OF INTERROGATION

The suspect participates in the interrogation in a state of physical and moral freedom. First of all, the rule is that the suspect takes part in the interrogation freely, except when specific measures must be adopted to prevent the risk of escape or violence (art. 64 para. 1 CCP). For juveniles, the use of such precautions (such as handcuffs) should be considered exceptional and is actually very rare.

Secondly, there is a general prohibition on using any methods or instruments that might interfere with or compromise the suspect's 'moral liberty' (*libertà morale*), that is self-control and ability to remember or evaluate facts (art. 64 para. 2 CCP). This rule is a specific expression of a general principle of the system, established by law for any kind of evidence collection from a person (art. 188 CCP). Breaching this rule implies that the information gained in this manner is not admissible. In Italy the rule can be used as a shelter against inappropriate methods of carrying out the juvenile suspect's interrogation: in fact, it does not only forbid the use of instruments like narco-analysis or lie detectors but also, more widely, any kind of vexatious behaviour.

It should be stressed that, in Italy, there are no specific rules or limits on the methods of interrogating a juvenile suspect; for example, no time limit is established by law. Thus, the juvenile could be interrogated several times, by the same or by different subjects or authorities; interrogations at night are not forbidden; interrogations might even go on for several hours. Nevertheless, one might say that, with the juvenile being a vulnerable person, interrogations that take too long or questioning during the night could be considered forms of undue pressure, which could undermine the young suspect's self-control and make the interrogation invalid.[106]

There are no specific rules on the way questions should be posed to a juvenile suspect during an interrogation. There are rules of this kind provided generally for trial examination of witnesses and defendants: for example, leading questions are forbidden in direct examination during trial (art. 499 para. 3 CCP), and a victim of sexual offences cannot be questioned about his sexuality or private life (art. 472 para. 3 *bis* CCP). Except for these rules, however, no limits are established on the kind of questions that can be asked during the suspect's interrogation, especially during the investigation. Thus, questions can be asked about the juvenile's family or social/cultural background, in order to gain information on these matters. Such questions can be asked by social services,[107] by the police and by the prosecutor or the judge himself. In theory, while collecting information in this way, no question about the juvenile's responsibility for the offence should be asked, and the juvenile's statements about it should have no influence on the verdict. Nevertheless, it should be stressed that information on the juvenile's personality and his background can in fact heavily influence the outcomes of proceedings (e.g. as to probation, irrelevance of fact, judicial pardon). In theory, leading questions are not forbidden during investigations in Italy; nonetheless, captious or deceptive questions should be considered inadmissible.[108]

5.2. RECORDING OF THE INTERROGATION

Normally, the interrogation is simply recorded by transcript. When the interrogation is carried out by the prosecutor, transcripts are made by judicial administration personnel (such as secretaries of prosecutors) or a police officer. When the judge conducts the interrogation, transcripts are made by the administrative personnel of his office. The transcript should be drafted during the interrogation or immediately afterwards, if a contemporary documentation is impossible. In the written transcription it should be mentioned whether statements were made to answer a question and, if so, the question should also be recorded. The defence lawyer, if present at the interrogation, can check

---

106 Such methods are actually considered forbidden by doctrine even when the suspect is an adult: see Mazza 2004, p. 110–111.

107 All this information can be used as evidence, whoever collected it, of the juvenile's character and background, on the occasion that such information is relevant (choice of coercive measures, access to diversion, judicial pardon, *et cetera*).

108 Mazza 2004, p. 109.

immediately whether the transcription is correct and suggest different words or expressions to use, to assure a correct recording. Once the document is completed, the defence lawyer can only read (or listen to or watch) the contents: transcripts and tapes are lodged in the prosecutor's office within three days and are kept there for five days, so that the defence can examine and make a copy of them (art. 364 CCP).

It should be noted that only a reproduction of contents by technologically advanced means can ensure faithful documentation of the act. Italian law provides that, if the transcription is not verbatim, audio recording must be added (art. 134 para. 3 CCP). Unfortunately, the Italian practice for interrogations was quite superficial: using the waiver admitted by law in case of 'temporary unavailability of technological means' (art. 140 para. 1 CCP), judges and prosecutors normally documented interrogations summarily, with no added audio recording. This is why a special provision was added by l. 8 August 1995, No. 332, imposing videotaping or, alternatively, audio taping, when the interrogated suspect is in detention or custody and the interrogation is not carried out in a hearing (art. 141 *bis* CCP). If the judicial offices lack the technological facilities or trained personnel, an expert shall be appointed to make the recording, but the method of documentation must be used regardless. This reform was certainly necessary, as a faithful documentation is a deterrent to forms of violence or undue pressure upon the suspect on occasions where he is in a particularly weak condition, such as detention: conditions that are even more difficult to manage for a juvenile. Nevertheless, the safeguard is not complete. On the one hand, it is applicable only to acts that are defined formally as 'interrogations': for example, it is not applicable to spontaneous statements.[109] On the other hand, the rule operates only if the suspect is 'in detention', which refers only to custodial measures, such as provisional custody in an institution or safety measure; the juvenile suspect in probation or home detention, for example, is not entitled to this safeguard.[110] The practical result of this regulation is that some of the most delicate moments of contact between the juvenile suspect and his interrogator or authorities are still documented by written transcription or, at most, audio recording. The special protection rule allows the prosecutor or judge to choose between different means, and this implies that videotapes remain an exception.[111]

109 Conti 1995, p. 2434, Mazza 2004, p. 162, Cass., 20 May 1998, Alfano, in *Cassazione Penale*, 2000, p. 645, Cass., Sez. Un., 25 March 1998 and D'Abramo, in *Diritto penale e processo*, 1999, p. 75.

110 Cass., Sez. Un., 25 March 1998 and D'Abramo, in *Diritto penale e processo*, 1999, p. 78.

111 This point seems particularly difficult for the Italian legislator to face, if one considers that the recent reform to give application to the Lanzarote Covenant simply ignored the problem: while the Covenant specifically establishes the possibility of videotaping the information collected from a juvenile victim of sexual abuse, l. 172/12, the Italian legislator did not change the code on this issue, so that videotaping is still a possibility, but never compulsory. Nevertheless, it must be stressed that Court of Cassation stated that a juvenile's statements

There are no other specific safeguards offered to juveniles during interrogations, considering their special position. More specifically, there are no rules on the interrogation of juveniles in detention or custody, except the rule on the necessity of videotaping or audiotaping the interrogation. There is also no specific rule on the interrogation of juveniles who might be considered 'extra-vulnerable' (this category is not recognised by law). However, there are particular safeguards for suspects who in practice can be considered extra-vulnerable, such as foreigners: as already mentioned, for example, the right to be assisted by an interpreter if the defendant does not speak Italian. Finally, no specific rules are provided for the interrogation of juveniles in the legal rules on the European arrest warrant.

5.3. LOCATION OF THE INTERROGATION

Interrogations of juveniles are usually carried out in police stations or in juvenile prosecutor offices. The juvenile prosecutor offices are kept separated from the adult offices and as a rule, the two categories of suspects cannot come into contact. In police stations, however, there are generally no special facilities for juvenile suspects. Juveniles can also be interrogated in detention centres, but only in the special ones that host juveniles: in general, the first interrogation after arrest is usually done in a first reception centre or in a community, special facilities where juveniles are brought after arrest and where assistance from social services and specialist staff is assured.

6. RESULTS OF THE INTERROGATION

Statements made by the juvenile during the interrogations can be used at any stage and for any purpose of the preliminary phase, such as the adoption of coercive measures, dismissal for irrelevance of fact, and, of course, the final decisions by the prosecutor at the end of investigations whether to prosecute or not. The results of the interrogation can also be used in summary proceedings – closing the criminal proceedings at the early stage of preliminary hearing – and for the outcomes of the preliminary hearing itself (for example, for a probation order). In trial, as a rule, the results of the interrogations are not suitable evidence. However, they can be used to cross-examine the defendant. In this case, if the previous statements are used by a party to confront the defendant

can be judged to be credible only if the expert who conducted the audition fully documented the act with adequate methods, such as videotaping (Cass., 26 June 2006, in *Rivista penale*, 2007, p. 595). So, in practice, juvenile victims' statements during investigations (especially in sexual offences proceedings) are normally videotaped.

in the examination, they can be used as evidence against him, if they had been given to the judge, public prosecutor or the police (on behalf of the prosecutor) with the safeguard of the defence lawyer's assistance (art. 503 CCP). The same happens if the defendant does not appear in court or refuses to be examined in trial (art. 513 CCP): previous statements given during interrogations with full legal safeguards can be read and used as evidence.

A confession is only legally relevant as a prerequisite for 'direct proceeding' (*giudizio direttissimo*), where admission of facts by the defendant justifies a simplified procedure that takes the proceedings directly to trial, avoiding a preliminary hearing. Otherwise, a confession has no legal relevance as evidence. If the suspect admits his responsibility, the information is only one of the results of the investigations that should be verified. If a confession is given in trial (or the admission of facts stated during an interrogation is repeated in trial as evidence: see above), it is considered one of the elements of evidence that judges can base their decision upon. Nevertheless, a confession is often considered, in practice, by juvenile courts as a prerequisite for diversion: this is the case, in particular, with respect to probation orders, where judges deem that opportunities of re-socialising the suspect are demonstrated by his regret for the offence committed; in this perspective, a confession is considered to be crucial.

The text of an interrogation generally cannot be published, but the summarised contents of it can, if the precise text of the declarations is not exactly reproduced. It is forbidden to spread via the media or disseminate in any form any information that might lead to the identification of the juvenile suspect (art. 13 d.P.R. n. 448/1988).

7. REMEDIES AND SANCTIONS

In Italy, the consequences of breaching the safeguards provided for the interrogation of juveniles are different depending on the rule that was violated. Normally, such breaches imply that the interrogation is inadmissible, the degree to which depending on the safeguard and the gravity of the breach: the breach means that the act is sometimes inadmissible as evidence (*inutilizzabilità*), sometimes wholly void (called an 'absolute nullity' by Italian law) and sometimes partially void (called an 'intermediate nullity'). In all these cases, the breach can be declared by the judge (even if the defence did not raise any claim). The judge can declare that the interrogation is wholly void or inadmissible as evidence at any stage of the proceedings and in such cases there are no remedies. If the interrogation is only partially void, the judge must declare it before delivering the decision on first instance unless the irregularity has been remedied in the meantime, for example, with the defence accepting the effects of the irregular act. Once these breaches have been declared by the judge, the invalid interrogation cannot be used as a basis for any kind of decision during the proceedings, nor can it be used as evidence in trial. Depending on the kind of safeguard that was violated, the consequences are:

- If the suspect was not previously informed of his right to remain silent: the interrogation is inadmissible as evidence;
- If the suspect was not previously informed that any statement might be used as evidence against him: the interrogation is inadmissible as evidence;
- If the suspect was not previously informed about his right to be assisted by a lawyer: the interrogation is partially void;
- If the lawyer's assistance is compulsory (e.g. at interrogation by the police) and the lawyer is not present: the interrogation is wholly void;
- If the lawyer is not previously informed of the interrogation (or receives too short notice of it): the interrogation is partially void;
- If the holder of parental authority is not informed of the proceedings and of the right of the suspect to be assisted by a lawyer: the interrogation is partially void;
- If parents or social services are not present at the interrogation: no specific sanction is explicitly provided by law (this implies that only disciplinary measures could in theory be applied to the responsible authority that carried out the interrogation); in doctrine, nevertheless, somebody believes that the case could be considered as a violation of right to defence, and consequentially the interrogation is considered partially void;[112]
- If the suspect does not speak Italian and is not assisted by an interpreter: the interrogation is partially void.

During the interrogation, the defence lawyer can issue requests, claims and observations, including a claim for breach of a safeguard.

III. CONCLUSIONS

In Italy, the legal framework for the interrogation of juvenile suspects generally offers an adequate set of safeguards, providing for both defensive rights and psychological and educational support. The landscape of the rules on this issue, however, also shows some critical aspects, under different perspectives. On the one hand, some safeguards seem to be granted in general, but are not implemented to a satisfactory level in the context of the interrogation of juvenile suspects. On the other hand, there are very delicate issues which the legislator

112 Patanè 2009b, p. 76. Case-law, however, reflects the opposite viewpoint, stating that violations of the rule on affective and psychological assistance involve no procedural sanction whatsoever (see Cass., 5 January 2006, R., in *Archivio della nuova procedura penale*, 2007, 135).

has simply ignored and which – as a result – are left to the choices made on a case-by-case basis by practitioners.

In relation to safeguards not being implemented to a satisfactory level, it seems, for example, that the role of the holder of parental responsibility should be specified and strengthened by law. The juvenile's carer is in fact involved in the proceedings at some crucial stages, but the interrogation is not one of them: the carer is not informed about it beforehand or allowed to participate. Given the importance of the act, it is surprising that the law does not make the role of the holder of parental authority more precise. It is certainly a point which the Italian legislator should take into consideration soon. Similar observations can be made about the problem of recording interrogations. It is true that Italian legislation provides for many ways to record the interrogation and the most complete and reliable ones (such as videotaping) can be used in practice. Nonetheless, videotaping as a method for recording interrogations is used in practice only rarely, and the lack of appropriate technology, together with the broad discretion to choose from among the different tools, mean that interrogations are normally simply recorded by transcript. This method, however, is insufficient, and it would be necessary for the law (and the organisation of the judiciary) to provide for a clear duty of videotaping the juvenile's interrogations, in order to adequately control the effectiveness of the safeguards on a case-by-case basis.

In relation to the issues which the legislator has ignored, one can think for example of the fact that no rules or guidelines are provided for how juvenile suspects should be interrogated in practice. For example the location, the manner of posing questions, and the hours and duration of the interrogation simply are not regulated by law. This suggests that an effort should be made to regulate such important aspects either by law or at least with a set of methodological guidelines able to compel the officials conducting the interrogation to respect a few common minimum standards for the protection of the juvenile suspect.

BIBLIOGRAPHY

Bouchard 1995

M. Bouchard, *Processo penale minorile*, in *Digesto delle discipline penalistiche*, X, Utet, 1995

Bouchard 2011

M. Bouchard, 'L'esecuzione penale e le misure penitenziarie', in E. Palermo Fabris and A. Presutti (eds.), *Diritto e procedura penale minorile*, Milan: Giuffrè, 2011, p. 701–738

Bronzo 2009

P. Bronzo, 'Art. 10', in G. Giostra (ed.), *Il processo penale minorile. Commento al D.P.R. 448/1988*, Milan: Giuffrè, 2009, p. 107–122

Caraceni 2010
L. Caraceni, 'Magistratura di sorveglianza e giurisdizione rieducativa minorile', in M.G. Coppetta (ed.), *L'esecuzione penitenziaria del minorenne nelle carte internazionali e nell'ordinamento italiano*, Milan: Giuffrè, 2010, p. 295–348

Cesari 2008
C. Cesari (ed.), *Il minorenne fonte di prova nel processo penale*, Milan: Giuffrè, 2008

Cesari 2009a
C. Cesari, 'Art. 27', in G. Giostra (ed.), *Il processo penale minorile. Commento al D.P.R. 448/1988*, Milan: Giuffrè, 2009, p. 293–339

Cesari 2009b
C. Cesari, 'Art. 28', in G. Giostra (ed.), *Il processo penale minorile. Commento al D.P.R. 448/1988*, Milan: Giuffrè, 2009, p. 341–396

Cesari 2012
C. Cesari (ed.), *Le limitazioni alla libertà personale del minore imputato*, Milan: Giuffrè, 2012

Chiavario 1994
M. Chiavario (ed.), *Commento al codice di procedura penale, Leggi collegate*, I, *Il processo minorile*, Turin: Utet, 1994

Ciavola 2009
A. Ciavola, 'Il perdono giudiziale', in A. Ciavola and V. Patanè, 'La specificità delle formule decisorie minorili', in E. Zappalà (ed.), *La giurisdizione specializzata nella giustizia penale minorile*, Turin: Giappichelli, 2009, p. 170–178

Cibinel 1994
D. Cibinel, 'Art. 5', in M. Chiavario (ed.), *Commento al codice di procedura penale, Leggi collegate*, I, *Il processo minorile*, Turin: Utet, 1994, p. 59–62

Conti 1995
G. Conti, 'Le modalità di documentazione dell'interrogatorio nel nuovo art. 141 *bis* c.p.p.', in *Cassazione penale*, 1995, p. 2433–2436

Coppetta 2010a
M.G. Coppetta, 'La legge di ordinamento penitenziario del minorenne: una riforma improcrastinabile', in *Studi in onore di Mario Pisani*, vol. III, *Diritto processuale penale*, Rome: La Tribuna, 2010, p. 3–24

Coppetta 2010b
M. G. Coppetta (ed.), *L'esecuzione penitenziaria del minorenne nelle carte internazionali e nell'ordinamento italiano*, Milan: Giuffrè, 2010

Coppetta 2011a
M.G. Coppetta, 'Il proscioglimento per irrilevanza del fatto', in E. Palermo Fabris and A. Presutti (eds.), *Diritto e procedura penale minorile*, Milan: Giuffrè, 2011, p. 590–606

Coppetta 2011b
M.G. Coppetta, 'La sospensione del processo per messa alla prova', in E. Palermo Fabris and A. Presutti (eds.), *Diritto e procedura penale minorile*, Milan: Giuffrè, 2011, p. 607–627

Di Nuovo and Grasso 2005
S. Di Nuovo and G. Grasso, *Diritto e procedura penale minorile. Profili giuridici, psicologici e sociali*, Milan: Giuffrè, 2005

Giostra 2005
G. Giostra (ed.), *Per uno statuto europeo dell'imputato minorenne*, Milan: Giuffrè, 2005

Giostra 2009
G. Giostra (ed.), *Il processo penale minorile. Commento al D.P.R. 448/1988*, Milan: Giuffrè, 2009

Grevi 1972
V. Grevi, "Nemo tenetur se detegere". *Interrogatorio dell'imputato e diritto al silenzio nel processo penale italiano*, Milan: Giuffrè, 1972

Grasso 1994a
L. Grasso, 'Art. 31', in M. Chiavario (ed.), *Commento al codice di procedura penale, Leggi collegate*, I, *Il processo minorile*, Turin: Utet, 1994, p. 328–345

Grasso 1994b
L. Grasso, 'Art. 32', in M. Chiavario (ed.), *Commento al codice di procedura penale, Leggi collegate*, I, *Il processo minorile*, Turin: Utet, 1994, p. 345–359

Kostoris 1992
R.E. Kostoris, 'Art. 21', in M. Chiavario (ed.), *Commento al nuovo codice di procedura penale, La normativa complementare*, vol. I, *Norme di attuazione*, Utet, 1992, p. 75–80

La Placa 2006
A. La Placa, *Il ruolo dell'imputato minorenne nel dibattimento*, in *Indice Penale*, 2006, p. 1107–1153

Larizza 2004
S. Larizza, 'I principi costituzionali della giustizia penale minorile', in A. Pennisi (ed.), *La giustizia penale minorile: formazione, devianza, diritto e processo*, Milan: Giuffrè, 2004, p. 85–95

Mazza 2004
O. Mazza, *L'interrogatorio e l'esame dell'imputato nel suo procedimento*, Milan: Giuffrè, 2004

Mestitz 2004
A. Mestitz, *Mediazione penale: chi, come, dove, quando*, Rome: Carocci, 2004.

Palermo Fabris 2011
E. Palermo Fabris, 'Evoluzione storica e recenti tendenze del sistema penale minorile, in E. Palermo Fabris and A. Presutti (eds.), *Diritto e procedura penale minorile*, Milan: Giuffrè, 2011, p. 3–49

Palermo Fabris and Presutti 2011
E. Palermo Fabris and A. Presutti (eds.), *Diritto e procedura penale minorile*, Milan: Giuffrè, 2011

Palomba 2002
F. Palomba, *Il sistema del processo penale minorile*, Milan: Giuffrè, 2002

Panebianco 2004
G. Panebianco, 'Il minore reo', in A. Pennisi (ed.), *La giustizia penale minorile: formazione, devianza, diritto e processo*, Milan: Giuffrè, 2004, p. 97–163

Pansini 2011
C. Pansini, 'Udienza preliminare', E. Palermo Fabris and A. Presutti (eds.), *Diritto e procedura penale minorile*, Milan: Giuffrè, 2011, p. 629–658

Patanè 1999
V. Patanè, *L'individualizzazione del processo penale minorile: confronto con il sistema inglese*, Milan: Giuffrè, 1999

Patanè 2009a
V. Patanè, 'Art. 7', in G. Giostra (ed.), *Il processo penale minorile. Commento al D.P.R. 448/1988*, Milan: Giuffrè, 2009, p. 71–87

Patanè 2009b
V. Patanè, 'L'intervento dell'imputato minorenne nelle varie fasi del procedimento', in E. Zappalà (ed.), *La giurisdizione specializzata nella giustizia penale minorile*, Turin: Giappichelli, 2009, p. 59–92

Patanè 2009c
V. Patanè, 'Origini storiche e percorsi legislativi', in E. Zappalà (ed.), *La giurisdizione specializzata nella giustizia penale minorile*, Turin: Giappichelli, 2009, p. 1–16

Pazè 1989
P. Pazè (ed.), *Codice di procedura penale minorile commentato*, in *Esperienze di giustizia minorile*, n. sp., Rome: Istituto poligrafico e Zecca dello Stato, 1989

Pennisi 2010
A. Pennisi (ed.), *La giustizia penale minorile: formazione, devianza, diritto e processo*, Milan: Giuffrè, 2004

Pepino 1989
L. Pepino, 'Art. 1', in P. Pazè (ed.), *Codice di procedura penale minorile commentato*, in *Esperienze di giustizia minorile*, n. sp., Rome: Istituto poligrafico e Zecca dello Stato, 1989, p. 9–17

Presutti 2011a
A. Presutti, 'Gli organi della giustizia minorile', in E. Palermo Fabris and A. Presutti (eds.), *Diritto e procedura penale minorile*, Milan: Giuffrè, 2011, p.401–436

Presutti 2011b
A. Presutti, 'La posizione del minore', in E. Palermo Fabris and A. Presutti (eds.), *Diritto e procedura penale minorile*, Milan: Giuffrè, 2011, p. 437–478

Renon 2011
P. Renon, 'L'obbligo di immediata declaratoria di imputabilità', in E. Palermo Fabris and A. Presutti (eds.), *Diritto e procedura penale minorile*, Milan: Giuffrè, 2011, p. 573–589

Reynaud 1994
G. Reynaud, 'Art. 9', in M. Chiavario (ed.), *Commento al codice di procedura penale, Leggi collegate*, I, *Il processo minorile*, Turin: Utet, 1994, p. 79–101

Ruggeri 2009
S. Ruggeri, 'La disciplina penitenziaria', in E. Zappalà (ed.), *La giurisdizione specializzata nella giustizia penale minorile*, Turin: Giappichelli, 2009, p. 241–260

Sau 2010
S. Sau, *Le garanzie linguistiche nel processo penale*, Cedam, 2010

Sechi 2006
P. Sechi, *Il patrocinio dei non abbienti nel procedimenti penali*, Giuffrè, 2006

Sergio 2005
G. Sergio, 'Discrezionalità e messa alla prova nel processo penale minorile', *Minori giustizia*, 2005, n. 4, p. 117–125

Sfrappini 2009
P. Sfrappini, 'Art. 31', in G. Giostra (ed.), *Il processo penale minorile. Commento al D.P.R. 448/1988*, Milan: Giuffrè, 2009, p. 435–444

Siracusano 2009
F. Siracusano, 'La sanzione penale nei confronti dell'imputato minorenne', in E. Zappalà (ed.), *La giurisdizione specializzata nella giustizia penale minorile*, Turin: Giappichelli, 2009, p. 201–228

Turri 1998
G. Turri, 'L'audizione nel processo penale del minore indagato', in *Minori giustizia*, 1998, f. 4, p. 38–54

Vigoni 2004
D. Vigoni, *L'ambito della declaratoria per irrilevanza del fatto: dalle indagini al giudizio d'appello*, in *Cassazione penale*, 2004, p. 2161–2166

Zappalà 2009
E. Zappalà (ed.), *La giurisdizione specializzata nella giustizia penale minorile*, Turin: Giappichelli, 2009

CHAPTER 5

PROTECTING JUVENILE SUSPECTS IN A PEDAGOGICAL BUT PUNITIVE CONTEXT

Country Report the Netherlands

Marc van Oosterhout and Dorris de Vocht

I. THE DUTCH JUVENILE JUSTICE SYSTEM: GENERAL OVERVIEW

1. BACKGROUND

1.1. GENERAL FEATURES OF THE SYSTEM

The Dutch legal system provides for a separate system of criminal justice for juveniles. However, there are no separate codes dealing with juvenile criminal (procedure) law. The general rule is that provisions of 'adult' criminal law apply to juveniles as well unless specific diverging rules are formulated. Such diverging rules can be found in the general Criminal Code (hereafter: CC) and the general Code of Criminal Procedure (hereafter: CCP) which both have the status of statutory legislation.[1] Before going into these special provisions and the specifics of Dutch juvenile criminal justice, a few words on Dutch legal sources are fitting. In Dutch law a distinction is made between 'legislation in a formal sense' (*wetgeving in formele zin*) and legislation in 'a material sense' (*wetgeving in materiele zin*). The former consists of legislation (laws and bylaws) made by the central government together with Parliament (*Staten-Generaal*) and is the most important source of legislation. The latter consists of rules made by other government agencies (not the central government and Parliament) such as ministerial regulations and circulars.[2] Case law is also considered to be

1 See arts. 77a-77h CC and arts. 486–505 CCP.
2 Statutes are published in the Official Bulletin of Acts (*Staatsblad*).

a source of law. In this respect, judgements of higher courts serve as guidance for lower courts, with judgements of the Dutch Supreme Court (*Hoge Raad*, hereafter: HR) having most authority.[3] However, in line with the continental legal tradition, codified law is considered to be a higher source of law than case law. With respect to the hierarchy of national and international rules, art. 94 of the Constitution is important. This provision states that statutory provisions that are incompatible with international rules of law do not apply. Furthermore, the Dutch Constitution contains some general principles – such as the right to liberty and the right to legal assistance, which are relevant in criminal proceedings – but no youth-specific provisions. Since it is not allowed for the judiciary to test laws and treaties against the constitution and since there is no constitutional court in the Netherlands, the direct influence of the Constitution on criminal (procedure) law is limited.

The above-mentioned special provisions provided for in the CC and the CCP – both legislation in a formal sense – are applicable to juveniles between the ages of 12 and 18 and in certain cases to adolescents between the age of 18 and 23.[4] The main principle underlying these specific provisions is the best interests of the child, which is illustrated by the fact that – at least in theory – juvenile criminal (procedure) law aims at re-education of the juvenile and follows a pedagogical approach. In line with these principles, the regulation is characterised by a strong focus on out of court settlement and different (often less severe) sanctions than in case of adults.

The CC and CCP are certainly not the only relevant sources of law dealing with juvenile delinquency. Relevant rules can also be found in – for example – instructions of the public prosecution service (*aanwijzingen Openbaar Ministerie*).[5] These instructions do not have the status of law but according to administrative law the prosecution service has to follow the instructions and may deviate from them only in special circumstances. For many years the prosecution policy in juvenile cases has been heavily influenced by the Instruction on the effective settlement of juvenile criminal cases (*Aanwijzing effectieve afdoening strafzaken jeugdigen*).[6] Moreover, there are several legal

---

3 Important cases are published in (among others) the weekly periodical *Nederlandse Jurisprudentie* (hereafter: *NJ*) and on the Internet (www.rechtspraak.nl).

4 This age category used to be 18–21 but was recently broadened with the realisation of a separate criminal law for young adults (*adolescentenstrafrecht*). This law entered into force on 1 April 2014 (*Staatsblad* 2013, 485). See on different age categories of juvenile suspects: *infra* paragraph 2.2 (part I).

5 The Board of Prosecutors General (*College van Procureurs Generaal*) may give instructions to the members of the prosecution service concerning their tasks and powers in relation to the administration of criminal justice and other statutory powers: Tak 2008, p. 50.

6 *Staatscourant* 2011, 10941. See also the Directive on juvenile criminal proceedings (*Richtlijn voor strafvordering jeugd*), *Staatscourant* 2011, 19253. Both instructions have recently

regulations relevant for the position of juveniles in detention, such as the Youth Custodial Institutions Act (*Beginselenwet Justitiele Jeugdinrichtingen*) and Youth Custodial Institutions Regulations.

It should be stressed that the Dutch legal system does not provide for one juvenile (protection) law but makes a clear distinction between juvenile civil law on the one hand and juvenile criminal law on the other.[7] Of fundamental importance for juvenile protection in the Netherlands is the so-called Youth Care Act (*Wet op de Jeugdzorg*) of 22 April 2004. Despite the formal distinction between civil and criminal law, in practice both fields of law are very much intertwined in the sense that juveniles who show problematic (criminal) behaviour will often be faced with civil measures – such as a youth care order or a placement under supervision – as well as interventions based on criminal law at the same time.[8] Also illustrative of the interrelationship between civil and criminal law are the so-called combined court sessions (*combi-zittingen*) during which juvenile judges in some court districts simultaneously decide on matters of civil law as well as criminal law in individual cases. In addition, ongoing civil proceedings – for example on the withdrawal of parental custody of (one of) the parents of the juvenile suspect or on the measure of placing the juvenile under supervision – are legal grounds for temporarily suspending criminal proceedings against the juvenile suspect.[9] Finally, many organisations active in juvenile criminal law – such as the Child Welfare Council (*Raad voor de Kinderbescherming*) and Youth Care (*Bureau Jeugdzorg*)[10] – play an important role in juvenile civil law as well.

1.2. BRIEF HISTORY OF AND CURRENT TRENDS IN JUVENILE JUSTICE POLICY

The basis of the current Dutch system of child protection and juvenile criminal law can be found in the so-called Children Acts (*Kinderwetten*) of 1905, which were composed of three acts: one concerning criminal law, one on administrative law and one on civil law.[11] At that time, the main focus of the legislator was on

(March 2014) been replaced by a new instruction on criminal proceedings for juveniles and adolescents, including sentencing guidelines Halt (*Richtlijn en kader voor strafvordering jeugd en adolescenten, inclusief strafmaten Halt*), *Staatscourant* 2014, 8284.

7 Nevertheless, over the last few decades the introduction of one uniform juvenile law has repeatedly been suggested.

8 For many years juveniles placed in detention centres under civil law – a measure allowed with the authorisation of a juvenile judge – were accommodated in the same institutions as juveniles placed under criminal law. Since 1 January 2010 this is no longer allowed.

9 Art. 14a CCP.

10 See *infra* paragraph 2.3 (part I).

11 Van Kalmthout and Bahtiyar 2011, p. 911.

protection and correction of children who committed crimes.[12] In the decades following 1905 the legislative framework concerning juvenile justice has been the subject of numerous changes and reforms. One of the main reasons for the many reforms is the fact that the focus in Dutch juvenile criminal policy is – as in many other countries – constantly changing. In fact, this focus is more subject to change than is the case in adult criminal policy. This can be explained by the fact that juvenile criminal law focuses more on (special) prevention than on retribution. Therefore, it is a government's responsibility to continuously invest in the development of young people and in an effective juvenile justice policy.[13]

According to the dominant model on the European continent, the Dutch juvenile justice system represents a combination of punishment and protection in which the interest of the juvenile is the first matter of importance. As mentioned before, traditionally the Dutch criminal juvenile justice system is pedagogically oriented and has a strong emphasis on protection and (re)education. Nevertheless, part of it is also aimed at retribution, which explains the fact that juveniles who have committed a crime can not only be given a measure but could face a punishment as well. The Dutch juvenile justice system is qualified by some experts on comparative juvenile justice as an example of the so-called 'modified justice model' in which responsibility and the protection of society reflect a legalistic approach and mitigated accountability and special needs of young offenders reflect welfare elements.[14]

From an historical point of view, it should be stressed that – since approximately 1950 – the Dutch system mainly resembled the welfare approach (or so-called protection model), with its main characteristics being minimal intervention in the best interests of the child and large numbers of cases being dismissed and/or dealt with through out-of-court settlement. During the 1980s – in line with a European trend – the climate changed and the 'soft' protection model was increasingly criticised. Eventually this resulted in a shift towards a more repressive, justice-oriented model with less emphasis on protection, care and treatment and a greater focus on the juvenile's individual (criminal) responsibility. This shift to a more repressive criminal juvenile justice policy has been particularly noticeable since 1995 when Dutch juvenile criminal law was extensively revised resulting *inter alia* in harsher punishments. The drastic revision of 1995 was mainly based on the presumption that juveniles are nowadays more mature and are able to bear more individual responsibilities. Although the revision of 1995 did indeed 'harshen' the juvenile sanction system, it should be mentioned that – from a European comparative perspective –

---

12 De Jonge and Van der Linden 2013, p. 50–54.

13 De Jonge and Van der Linden 2013, p. 3.

14 Pruin 2011, p. 1546, Winterdyk 2002, Hartjen 2008, p. 88 and Muncie 2008, p. 117.

punishments applicable to juveniles in the Netherlands might still be considered rather mild. This is also because of the fact that the maximum sentences (maximum duration of juvenile detention) are hardly ever applied in practice. Over the last two decades, many different governmental policy programs have been presented mainly focusing on prevention, the effective cooperation of institutions and actors in juvenile criminal justice and a more individualistic approach to juvenile offenders.[15]

Most recently, two of the main points of interest for the current Dutch government – known for its rather tough-on-crime policy – are (*inter alia*) dealing with juvenile gangs and the realisation of a separate criminal law for young adults (*adolescentenstrafrecht*).[16] Also important are the current trends in speeding up proceedings and the expansion of prosecutorial powers to deal with cases out of court.[17]

The many legislative changes and shifts of focus in Dutch criminal justice policy paint a complex picture and it is felt by some that not enough time is taken to reflect on the actual needs of juvenile delinquents.[18] Some Dutch juvenile law experts are of the opinion that juvenile criminal law in the Netherlands has become more repressive over the last ten years although criminality seems to be rather stable.[19]

1.3. GENERAL PRINCIPLES OF NATIONAL JUVENILE LAW AND JUVENILE CRIMINAL JUSTICE

As mentioned before, general rules of criminal procedure are (in principle) applicable in juvenile cases unless specific rules state otherwise. As a result, regular criminal proceedings in juvenile cases do not differ much from criminal proceedings in adult criminal cases – this is especially true for the pre-trial stage. Nevertheless, as will be explained later on, the majority of juvenile cases are dealt with out of court. With regard to substantive criminal law the most 'juvenile-specific' part concerns the available sanctions, which are completely different from the punishments and measures available for adults.[20]

---

15 See for example the report of the Commission of Montfrans (*'Met de neus op de feiten'* 1994, containing 30 recommendations on how to approach juvenile delinquency, the report of State Secretary Kalsbeek with more specific recommendations on dealing with juvenile delinquency (*'Vasthoudend en effectief'* 2002), the policy programme *'Jeugd Terecht'* (2003–2007) aimed at preventing (re)offending of juveniles (*Programma Aanpak Jeugdcriminaliteit – Jeugd Terecht, handreiking jeugdstrafrecht*, Ministry of Justice 2004) and more recently the programs *'Aanpak Jeugdcriminaliteit'* and *'Veiligheid begint bij voorkomen'*.

16 The *adolescentenstrafrecht* which entered into force on 1 April 2014 (*Staatsblad* 2013, 485).

17 See for different forms of out of court settlement or diversion *infra* paragraph 2.6 (part I).

18 De Jonge and Van der Linden 2013, p. 74–75.

19 Weijers 2011, p. 30.

20 See *infra* paragraph 2.5 (part I).

Some general principles and distinguishing features of Dutch criminal procedure (law) are worth mentioning here because of their influence on everyday criminal justice – in adult as well as juvenile cases. First of all, one important characteristic of Dutch criminal procedure is the fact that there is a strong focus on pre-trial investigation. Although, according to the CCP, the emphasis of criminal proceedings lies at the trial, in reality truth-finding is done at the pre-trial stage.[21] This is also closely connected to a second characteristic of Dutch criminal justice, which concerns the limited practical importance of the principle of immediacy. Since the Dutch Supreme Court accepted hearsay evidence in written form, witness statements may be used as evidence in court via written statements of investigative officials.[22] As a result, hearing witnesses in the trial phase of proceedings is rather the exception than the rule. To a certain extent, this is also true for statements of suspects: statements made during the pre-trial stage – to a police officer, prosecutor or investigating judge – may be used as evidence in court as long as these written statements are read out at the trial. Nevertheless, since juveniles – unlike adult suspects – are obliged to appear in court, it is more likely that the suspect will give a statement at the trial as well. Finally, it should be highlighted that according to the discretionary principle (*opportuniteitsbeginsel*) the public prosecutor has wide discretionary powers to decide whether or not to prosecute.[23] The Dutch public prosecution service has a monopoly over prosecutions and makes use of its hierarchical structure to pursue a coordinated policy. This enables the prosecution service to determine systematically what cases should be brought to trial, and what sentences the courts should be asked to impose.[24] The police and the prosecutor have many possibilities to deal with cases out of court, which are widely used in practice both in adult as well as in juvenile cases.[25]

2. STRUCTURE AND MAIN CHARACTERISTICS OF THE DUTCH JUVENILE JUSTICE SYSTEM

2.1. MINIMUM AGE OF CRIMINAL LIABILITY

In the Netherlands the minimum age of criminal liability is set at 12. When applying this minimum, the age of the juvenile at the moment of committing the alleged offence is decisive, even when proceedings start after the juvenile

---

21 Tak 2008, p. 29.

22 Hoge Raad 20 December 1926, *NJ* 1927, 85.

23 It should be noted that – as a result of a complaint of an interested party (*rechtstreeks belanghebbende*) the decision not to prosecute could be overruled by a higher court. See arts. 12–13a CCP.

24 Tak 2008, p. 47.

25 See *infra* paragraph 2.6 (part I).

has turned 18. From a European comparative perspective a minimum age of 12 is rather low: it is the lowest age acceptable according to the Committee on the Rights of the Child.[26] Worldwide, the average minimum age of criminal liability is 12.[27]

2.2. DEFINITION OF JUVENILE AND RELEVANT CATEGORIES

There is no formal legal definition of a juvenile (suspect or defendant) in Dutch criminal law. According to the aforementioned age limits anyone above 12 and under the age of 18 – and in some cases even until the age of 21 – can be subjected to juvenile criminal law. Relevant age in this respect is the age of the juvenile at the time of committing the alleged offence. According to civil law a juvenile is anyone who has not reached the age of 18.[28]

In addition to the minimum age of criminal liability, several relevant (age) categories can be distinguished. First of all there is the group of juveniles below 12 years of age: the so-called '*12-minners*'. This category is exempted from criminal prosecution[29] but can, however, be the object of criminal investigation or subjected to civil law measures. The CCP clearly states which investigative methods can be applied against juveniles under the age of 12. This list contains some rather intrusive police powers such as making the juvenile stand still in order to ask for his identification (stop), arrest the juvenile, bring him to a police station for questioning, hold him at the police station for a maximum of six hours (or nine hours between midnight and 9 am) and search his house for the purpose of arrest or the seizure of goods.[30] In addition, there are far-reaching possibilities to strip-search a juvenile below 12. First of all, the juvenile who is 'stopped' may be strip-searched by a police officer when it is deemed necessary for identification purposes.[31] Furthermore, in case of arrest, strip-searching the body, clothes and searching *in* the body is possible under the same conditions as applicable to adults.[32] Since a juvenile under the age of 12 cannot be prosecuted, his statements made during interrogation cannot be used against him. However,

---

26 See Cipriani 2009, p. 108 and UN document CRC/C/GC/10 (General Comment No. 10, Committee on the Rights of the Child), para. 32.

27 Cipriani 2009, p. 108.

28 See art. 233 of Book 1 of the Dutch Civil Code. According to this provision maturity can also be reached by marriage or registered partnership. Until 1986 maturity under civil law was reached at 21.

29 Art. 486 CCP excludes juveniles under the age of 12 from prosecution.

30 Art. 487 CCP.

31 Art. 55b jo. art. 487 CCP.

32 Art. 56 jo. art. 487 CCP.

they can be used against other (co-)suspects[33] and – in addition to this – the statements of the juvenile may be a reason for applying intrusive civil law measures.[34] In a nutshell, it is fair to say that the wide possibilities to use police powers against juveniles under 12 is not properly counter-balanced by youth-specific procedural safeguards for this particular age category.[35]

Secondly, there is the group of 12- to 18-year-olds to whom – in principle – all ('adult') investigative methods may be applied,[36] including for example the so-called special investigative methods (*bijzondere opsporingsmethoden*) such as observation and the recording of confidential communication as well as the taking of DNA material against the will of the juvenile.[37] As mentioned in the Instruction on the effective settlement of juvenile criminal cases, police and prosecution should exercise restraint when dealing with 12- and 13-year-olds. That this is not always the case in practice is illustrated by a judgement of the court of appeal of Amsterdam of October 2010.[38] In this case a 12-year-old boy was prosecuted for possessing an alarm-gun, which he found with a friend during scouting activities. They had repeatedly asked their supervisors whether they thought the gun was real and the answer had consequently been no. Not much later the boy was arrested, searched and held at the police station for over five hours – all under quite severe conditions. Partly because of this 'heavy approach' in such a light case concerning a young child, the Court of Appeal decided to bar the prosecution service from prosecuting the case.[39]

Within the age category of 12- to 18-year-olds, juveniles aged 16 and 17 have a separate status. When a defendant was 16- or 17 years old at the time of the offence and the court deems it appropriate given the seriousness of the crime, the personality of the juvenile or the circumstances of the case, he may decide to apply adult sanctions.[40] It should be noted that this applicability of adult criminal law only applies to sentences – the juvenile will still be tried according to the rules of juvenile criminal procedure law. If the juvenile court does decide to apply adult criminal law to a juvenile, it is not possible to impose a prison sentence for life. However, in theory, it is possible to give a juvenile a 30-year prison sentence (the maximum temporary prison sentence according to Dutch

---

33 See on this matter also the Supreme Court decision of 17 June 2003, *NJ* 2003, 611, *LJN* AF7925 from which it is clear that arresting and interrogating a suspect below the age of 12 is not in itself an example of 'abuse of powers' (only) because the suspect himself cannot be prosecuted.

34 De Jonge and Van der Linden 2013, p. 176–180.

35 See *infra* paragraph 2.1 (part II).

36 Art. 488 CCP.

37 Respectively arts. 126g, 126l, 151b and 195d of the CCP.

38 Court of Appeal Amsterdam 7 October 2010, *LJN* BZ1001.

39 See also *infra* paragraph 5 (part II).

40 For a discussion of juvenile sanctions see *infra* paragraph 2.5 (part I).

criminal law).[41] Art. 77c CC provides a mirror image of art. 77b CC and offers the court the possibility to apply juvenile sanctions to 18-, 19-, 20-, 21- and 22-year-olds when he deems it appropriate given the personality of the offender or the circumstances of the case.[42] Both the possibility of art. 77b as well as art. 77c are not often applied in practice.[43]

With regard to the relevance of gender within the Dutch juvenile justice system – in a nutshell – it should be noted that statistics show an increase in the number of female juvenile suspects heard (for example between the years 1995 and 2005, an increase of 93 per cent can be seen). Although current statistics show a growing number of offending (juvenile) girls, according to experts the problem is manageable and does not require specific measures or policies.[44] Another important category within the group of juvenile suspects concerns young migrants (such as juveniles of Moroccan and Caribbean origin) who seem to be overrepresented in the statistics on juvenile criminal behaviour.[45] The alleged 'trouble' caused by these ethnic minorities – especially in large cities – is a much-debated subject in politics and the media. Several special forms of intervention have been developed for certain ethnic groups.

2.3. RELEVANT ACTORS

One general characteristic of juvenile law is that it has a strong multidisciplinary approach. Besides the regular judicial authorities there are several non-judicial organs involved in juvenile criminal proceedings.

In practice, a fundamental role in dealing with juvenile crime is played by the police and the prosecution service.[46] Within the Dutch police there is a long history of specialisation in juvenile cases (in fact the longest of all actors involved in the juvenile criminal process): it dates back to 1918 – the year in which the first bureau *'zeden- en kinderpolitie'* was founded in Rotterdam.[47] However, formally, the Law on the Police Force (*Politiewet*) does not require establishment of specialist units and since a reorganisation of the Dutch police in 1994 many police regions 'lost' their specialist youth departments.[48] It is now up to the

41 Some experts are of the opinion that this may conflict with the Convention on the Rights of the Child. See De Jonge and Van der Linden 2013, p. 109.
42 As mentioned before, the age category for applying juvenile sanctions to adolescents has recently been broadened from 18–21 to 18–23.
43 Weijers 2011, p. 162–163.
44 De Jonge and Van der Linden 2013, p. 12–15.
45 De Jonge and Van der Linden2013, p. 22–29.
46 See *infra* paragraph 2.6 (part I).
47 Uit Beijerse and Dubbelman 2011, p. 170.
48 Uit Beijerse and Dubbelman 2011, p. 170–171.

regional police force to decide on this matter, and for example in Maastricht there are only a few police officers who are appointed as youth officers.

In Dutch criminal proceedings special status is awarded to the so-called assistant prosecutor (*hulpofficier van justititie*). The assistant prosecutor is a senior police officer with some extra powers. Most of these powers are awarded to the assistant prosecutor for situations in which seeking the permission of the public prosecutor would cause undue delay.[49] For example, the assistant prosecutor may decide to detain the suspect at the police station. It should be noted that the assistant prosecutor is a member of the police force and not the prosecution service.

The ultimate responsibility for all aspects of criminal investigation lies with the prosecution service (*Openbaar Ministerie*). It is the public prosecutor's task to ensure that the police observe all statutory rules and procedures. In practice, the police deal with most (adult) cases without prior consultation with the prosecutor except in more important criminal cases.[50] In juvenile cases, regular consultations – at least every two weeks – between police, public prosecutors and Child Welfare Council are held to discuss all criminal cases involving juvenile suspects (*Justitieel Casus Overleg*). Within the prosecution service specialist prosecutors are appointed to deal with juvenile cases (*jeugdofficieren*). This form of specialisation is not required by law but derives from the power awarded to the chief prosecutor to appoint special prosecutors. Coordinating juvenile prosecutors are appointed at district court level (*arrondissementsparket*).[51]

At the court level, juvenile cases are dealt with by specialist juvenile judges. The juvenile judge – introduced to the Dutch legal system in the 1920s – in principle acts as a single judge. In more severe and/or complex cases, juvenile cases will be heard by a court composed of three judges.[52] The juvenile judge acts as an investigating judge (*rechter-commissaris*) as well as a trial judge. As of 1 January 2013 the role of the investigating judge in Dutch criminal procedure has changed substantially. One of the main changes concerns the abolishment of the preliminary judicial inquiry (*gerechtelijk vooronderzoek*) as a separate phase of pre-trial investigation. The goal of the reform is to affirm the status of the investigating judge as an independent observer of the legitimacy and efficiency of pre-trial proceedings. In juvenile cases, the main tasks of the investigating judge are *inter alia* deciding on detention on remand (*bewaring*), deciding on the

---

[49] Tak 2008, p. 92.

[50] Tak 2008, p. 43–44.

[51] The coordinating juvenile prosecutor is president of the *Arrondissementaal Platform Jeugdcriminaliteit* and part of the national Platform *Jeugd Openbaar Ministerie*. See Uit Beijerse and Dubbelman 2011, p. 170–172.

[52] Art. 495 CCP, one of them has to be a specialist juvenile judge.

legitimacy of arrest and police custody (art. 59a CCP) and fact-finding (hearing suspects and witnesses).

At district court level, special chambers are installed for dealing with juvenile crime. Within the organisation of Dutch (adult and juvenile) criminal justice, cases are heard by criminal sectors of courts at three levels. The first instance level consists of the district courts (*rechtbanken*) and the second level is the court of appeal (*gerechtshof*). There are 11 district courts and four courts of appeal. The highest level is the Supreme Court (*Hoge Raad*) in The Hague.[53] Most juvenile judges specialise in criminal as well as civil juvenile law and some of them practice both fields of law at the same time. Research shows that juvenile judges often are relatively inexperienced judges.[54] As mentioned before, in some court districts combined court sessions (*combi-zittingen*) are held during which matters of both civil and criminal law are decided upon simultaneously in one individual case.

Providing legal assistance to juveniles who are suspected of having committed a criminal offence is the task of professional lawyers (*advocaten*). Once admitted to the Bar, all lawyers are in principle allowed to defend juveniles. However, the rules are somewhat stricter when it comes to early legal aid funded by the state (*piket*). In the last few years, a tendency towards specialist juvenile defence lawyers seems to be developing. In 2006 a union of specialist juvenile lawyers (*Vereniging van Nederlandse Jeugdrechtadvocaten*) was founded.[55]

The main non-judicial organ active in Dutch juvenile criminal proceedings is the Child Welfare Council (hereafter: CWC) (*Raad voor de Kinderbescherming*). This organisation carries out many different tasks in juvenile criminal cases such as: (1) offering assistance to juveniles after arrest (early intervention system), (2) providing information on the juvenile to the prosecutor (and the judge) and (3) offering advice to the Minister of Justice on the execution of certain sentences.[56] The early intervention system (1) provides that every juvenile who is arrested will be interviewed by a social worker as soon as possible after arrest.[57] The CWC is not obliged to visit the juvenile and will consider the necessity of a visit on a case-by-case basis. When an official of the CWC visits the juvenile and draws up a report on the personality and the environment of the juvenile on the basis of this visit, the prosecutor is obliged to take notice of the content of

53 Tak 2008, p. 55.
54 Verberk and Fuhler 2006.
55 www.vnja.nl.
56 Art. 77v para. 4 CC.
57 See also art. 491 CCP para. 1: the police has to inform the Child Welfare Council immediately of police custody (*inverzekeringstelling*) of a juvenile.

the report before ordering detention on remand (*voorlopige hechtenis*).[58] When the juvenile is summoned to appear in court the prosecutor is obliged to request the CWC to draw up a full report on the juvenile and his social context which is done by social workers.[59] CWC officials can be present at trial. Statements made by the juvenile to the CWC official may in principle not be used as evidence against the juvenile. However, the official might be heard as a witness during the trial. When, in such a case, the official does not invoke the right to testimonial privilege, there is no reason why the statement may not be used as evidence in court.[60] Finally, the CWC also has a leading role in providing for youth probation (through Youth Care) as well as in the execution of community service and educational orders.

Another important non-judicial actor is the Youth Probation Services (*Jeugdreclassering*) forming an integral part of every regional Bureau for Youth Care (*Bureau Jeugdzorg*). They are *inter alia* involved in the execution phase of several sentences (mostly behavioural measures).

Finally, the Children's Ombudsman (*Kinder Ombudsman*) is worth mentioning. Although this institution – which was introduced in the Netherlands in 2011 – will not be involved in ongoing criminal proceedings against juveniles, it has an important role in dealing with the observance of children's rights also in case of criminal prosecution.[61] For example, in 2012 the Children's Ombudsman published a critical report on the position of juveniles in police detention with special attention to their opportunities to speak to their parents.[62]

2.4. MAIN PHASES OF THE JUVENILE CRIMINAL PROCESS

In the Netherlands the majority of juvenile criminal cases will not reach the trial phase. In fact, the same is true for adult criminal cases but the variety and importance of alternative ways of dealing with crime has an even stronger emphasis in juvenile law than in adult law.[63] When regular court proceedings are

---

58 Art. 491 para. 2 CCP. De Jonge and Van der Linden 2013, p. 197–203.

59 Art. 494 CCP.

60 As was recently pointed out by the Supreme Court in Hoge Raad 25 September 2012, *LJN* BX4269. See also De Jonge and Van der Linden 2013, p. 197–199.

61 For more information: www.dekinderombudsman.nl.

62 See 'Bezoek van ouders aan minderjarigen in politiecellen, Rapport over een klacht over het regionale politiekorps Gelderland-Midden te Arnhem en signalen over het regionale politiekorps Utrecht te Utrecht', 13 February 2012, 2012/017, KOM001/2012, available at: www.dekinderombudsman.nl/ul/cms/fck-uploaded/documents/Kinderombudsmanrapport0001-2012.pdf.

63 See for a discussion of the different diversion mechanisms and out-of-court settlement *infra* paragraph 2.6 (part I).

followed, criminal proceedings will to a great extent resemble the proceedings in adult criminal cases and will consist of the following main steps:

1. Arrest (*aanhouding*)
2. Interrogation (*verhoor*)
3. Drawing up of an official report (*proces-verbaal*)
4. Referral of the case to the prosecutor
5. Summoning of the juvenile (*dagvaarding*)
6. Court proceedings
7. Execution of the sentence

In a nutshell, the criminal process consists of three phases: the pre-trial phase, the trial phase and the execution phase. With regard to deprivation of liberty during the pre-trial phase the following measures can be distinguished:

a. Arrest by the police[64] (*aanhouding*)
b. Police detention (*ophouden voor onderzoek*)
c. Police custody (*inverzekeringstelling*)
d. Detention on remand (*voorlopige hechtenis*)

After arrest – which is allowed under the same conditions as applicable to adults[65] – the juvenile will be brought to the police station. He can be held there for six hours (or in theory 15 when the hours between midnight and 9 am are included). This phase is referred to as police detention (*ophouden voor onderzoek*). When the suspicion concerns a criminal offence for which detention on remand is not allowed, the police detention may be extended for another six hours (or – again – 15 when nightly hours are included). During police detention different kinds of investigative measures (*maatregelen in het belang van het onderzoek*) may be taken, such as the taking of photographs and fingerprints, the obligation to take part in a line-up and placement in a cell for observation.[66] Again, it should be stressed that the police can – as a rule – use the same coercive and investigative methods on juveniles as on adults. With regard to the place of detention during police detention, it is important to note that the juvenile will normally spend this time at the police station. During the day this can be done in a separate, closed room (*ophoudkamer*), which has a more friendly character than a normal police cell.[67] There is, however, much criticism of the detention of juveniles in Dutch police stations. See on this matter the Report *'Een "paar nachtjes" in de cel' (Spending a Couple of Nights in a Police Cell)* by

64 Or the (assistant) prosecutor.
65 See arts. 53 and 54 CCP.
66 See art. 61a CCP.
67 De Jonge and Van der Linden 2013, p. 183–191.

Defence for Children.[68] One of the main points of concern highlighted in the report is the fact that child friendly cells or facilities are rare in Dutch police stations, that juveniles are kept in police cells for too long and that there are not enough alternatives for detaining juveniles in police cells. Since the Defence for Children's report drew attention to the matter, some initial steps have been taken to draw up a National Protocol for the Treatment of Juveniles in Police Cells. This has eventually taken the form of a list of measures aimed at improving the treatment of juveniles at the police station which was introduced by the police in 2013.[69] The figure below indicates how many juvenile suspects are interrogated by the police and taken in police custody on a yearly basis:

Figure 1. Number of juvenile suspects interrogated and in police custody[70]

Indicators	2009	2010	2011	2012	2013
Total number of juvenile suspects interrogated by the police	54,048	50,969	46,477	41,601	34,772
Total number of juvenile suspects in police custody	8,059	9,234	8,240	7,603	6,963

In the case of suspicion of a criminal offence for which detention on remand is allowed, following the police detention the juvenile may be kept at the police station for another three days. This is the phase of police custody (*inverzekeringstelling*).[71] Police custody can only occur when necessary in the interests of the investigation and may – when there is a matter of urgency (and as matter of exception) – be extended for another three days. During police custody the juvenile will – as a rule – still be staying at the police station.[72] Furthermore, the police custody may be spend at 'any place the judge seems fit' (*elke daartoe schikte plaats*).[73] For example, this could be the home of the juvenile.

A very important moment in the pre-trial stage is the appearance (*voorgeleiding*) of the juvenile before the investigating judge. This should happen within three days and 15 hours of the arrest.[74] During the *voorgeleiding* the investigating judge examines the lawfulness of the arrest and decides on the detention to follow.

68 Report written by Berger and Van der Kroon 2011.

69 One of the measures (14 in total) entails that the police – when dealing with a juvenile – should take due regard of his age. See for a list of the measures (in Dutch): www.defenceforchildren.nl/p/148/Politie_voert_landelijk_maatregelen_in_voor_minderjarigen_in_politiecellen/mo233-m80.

70 Statistics taken from Annual Report Children's Rights (Jaarbericht Kinderrechten) published by Defence for Children and Unicef 2014, available at www.defenceforchildren.nl/images/20/3489.pdf.

71 Arts. 57 and 58 CCP.

72 See art. 59 para. 6 CCP.

73 De Jonge and Van der Linden 2013, p. 191–192.

74 Art. 59a CCP.

After the expiry of police custody, detention on remand may follow. As mentioned before, according to Dutch criminal procedure detention on remand consists of three types of detention: *bewaring*, *gevangenhouding* and *gevangenneming*. The decision on *bewaring* is taken by the investigating judge. In cases concerning juveniles this should be a juvenile judge.[75] For adults as well as juvenile suspects, the maximum term for this form of detention is 14 days. It is the explicit obligation of the investigating judge to check whether there is a possibility to suspend the *bewaring* (with certain conditions).[76] In practice this possibility to suspend under conditions is used quite often. Again, *bewaring* may be 'executed' at any place the judge seems fit.[77] Normally this will be a youth detention centre: as soon as detention on remand (*bewaring*) starts, the juvenile should leave the police station and be brought to a juvenile detention centre. However, due to capacity problems, practice has been that juveniles have stayed at the police station for a longer period of time – even during *bewaring*. Since 2002, this practice has been given a legal basis.[78] According to this legal provision the legal maximum terms for which juveniles can be held at a police station are nine days and 15 hours (below 16 years old) and 16 days and 15 hours (16 and 17 years old). Since the available places in juvenile detention centres have considerably increased over the last few years, one may expect that in the near future this rule will have only limited practical importance.

In summary, it is important to stress that decisions on police detention (*ophouden voor onderzoek*), police custody (*inverzekeringstelling*) and detention on remand (*voorlopige hechtenis*) are covered by the same rules and conditions as are applicable to adult suspects: the CCP does not provide for any youth-specific criteria in this respect. The way in which detention on remand is applied to juveniles in the Netherlands is a matter of concern for the Committee on the Rights of the Child.[79] One important youth-specific aspect of detention on remand is the strong focus on conditional suspension. As mentioned before, the judge who decides on detention on remand has the obligation to consider the possibility of suspending the detention (immediately or within a certain period of time).[80] In practice this possibility is very often used and raises concerns from the point of view of the presumption of innocence. The main reason for this concern is the fact that – in many cases – the suspension is not aimed at

---

75 Art. 492 CCP.

76 Art. 493 para. 1 CCP.

77 Art. 493 para. 3 CCP.

78 Art. 15 Youth Custodial Institutions Act (*Beginselenwet Justitiele Jeugdinrichtingen*).

79 Para. 77, UN Document CRC/C/NLD/CO/3 (Concluding Observations of the Committee on the Rights of the Child: The Kingdom of the Netherlands, 30 January 2009). See for a critical view on the Dutch practice also: Van den Brink 2012.

80 See also art. 493 para. 6 CCP and art. 2 Decision of 22 January 2008 on the implementation of possibilities to have an impact on the behaviour of juveniles who have committed criminal acts (*Besluit gedragsbeinvloeding jeugdigen*), *Staatsblad* 2008, 23.

providing an alternative to detention on remand but primarily used to facilitate early interventions with regard to the juvenile's behaviour.[81]

The legal position of juveniles in juvenile detention centres (*justitiele jeugdinrichtingen*) is regulated in separate regulations (Youth Custodial Institutions Act and regulations deriving from it). This comprehensive legal framework is in sharp contrast to the lack of specific rules and safeguards for juveniles who are detained outside juvenile detention centres, for example at the police station.[82]

As soon as the prosecutor has decided to bring a case to court and summons the juvenile, the trial phase starts. In this respect, it is important to mention that in 2012 the Ministry of Justice launched a new nationwide program called 'ZSM' (*Zo Snel Mogelijk* – As Soon As Possible). The main goal of this program is to deal with 'bulk' crime – by juvenile as well as adult suspects – as swiftly and efficiently as possible by improving cooperation between police, public prosecution service and other relevant actors. In practice, following the ZSM model means that a decision on how to settle a criminal case is taken as soon as possible after arrest of a (juvenile) suspect.[83] For the juvenile, it could mean he will be sent home with a summons shortly after arrest. From the point of view of procedural safeguards, the ZSM model can be criticised. For example, following the ZSM speedy proceedings in juvenile cases may have a negative impact on the juvenile's opportunity to prepare his defence. In addition, it may result in there not being enough time for the prosecutor to acquire the necessary information on the personality of the juvenile and his social context from the Child Welfare Council.[84]

The juvenile suspect is obliged to appear in court.[85] Since 1 January 2011, the obligation to appear in court has applied to parents as well.[86] Research shows that communication with juveniles during court sessions could (seriously) be improved, especially when it comes to juveniles below the age of 14.[87] In principle, court sessions with juvenile suspects will be held behind closed doors.[88] Under certain conditions the judge may decide to have the court session in public.[89] The judgement will always be delivered in public.[90]

---

81 See on this matter (providing an insight in the opinion of juveniles, their parents and practitioners on this issue): Van den Brink 2013. See also Uit Beijerse 2009, p. 323.

82 See Berger and Van der Kroon 2011.

83 For more information, see the factsheet ZSM on the website of the Ministry of Justice and Security: www.om.nl/onderwerpen/zsm/.

84 De Jonge and Van der Linden 2013, p. 191–192.

85 Art. 495a CCP.

86 Art. 496a CCP.

87 Rap and Weijers 2011.

88 Art. 495b CCP.

89 Art. 495b para. 2 CCP.

90 Art. 462 CCP.

2.5. SANCTIONS FOR JUVENILES

As in adult criminal law, the juvenile sanction system follows a two-track approach with sentences on the one hand and measures on the other. Traditionally, sentences are aimed at punishment/retribution while measures are focused on the safety of society, restoration of the old situation or treatment of the offender.

The special sanctions for juveniles can be found in art. 77a-77h CC. These provisions provide for a great variety of sanctions and because of the wide possibility to combine the many different sentences the juvenile sanction system is rather complex. The available juvenile sanctions are:

Principal sentences:

- Juvenile detention (with a maximum depending on the age of the juvenile)
- Community service (*taakstraf*) (introduced in 1995)
- Educational order (*leerstraf*)
- Fine (monetary penalty)

Additional sentences:

- Forfeiture of seized goods
- Denying the right to drive motor vehicles

Measures:

- Placement in a juvenile institution for treatment (*Plaatsing in Instelling Jeugdigen – PIJ*)
- Measure for improving conduct (*Gedragsbeinvloedende Maatregel – GBM*) (introduced in 2008)
- Dispossession of dangerous goods (*onttrekking aan het verkeer*)
- Dispossession of criminal gains
- Reparation of damages
- Judicial restraining order (*rechterlijk gebieds- of contactverbod*) (since 2012)[91]

In principle all combinations of sentences and measures are possible.[92] This should allow the judge to decide which sanction fits the needs of the juvenile best. Despite

---

91 Currently, there is a draft law pending introducing a new measure, which will oblige the juvenile to go back to school and get a diploma (*maatregel terbeschikkingstelling aan het onderwijs*).

92 Art. 77g CC.

the large discretionary power to deliver 'tailor made' sentences, Dutch juvenile justice faces a rather high percentage of recidivism. For example, approximately 60–70 per cent of juveniles sent to youth detention reoffend, and this number is even higher for juveniles who are sanctioned with a measure.[93] Over the last few years, juvenile detention has been applied less often. As a result of this development, a number of juvenile detention centres have been closed.[94] Community service is the sanction which is most often used. A fine – on the contrary – is not often applied in practice. Generally it is believed that judges fear that parents will pay the fine and that as a result the sanction will have no effect on the juvenile.[95] The Dutch juvenile justice system provides for many different education programs for the purpose of educational orders. They may vary per court district.[96] The relatively new measure for improving conduct (GBM) aims at re-education of the juvenile and allows the court to order him to complete an extramural behavioural program for a period of 6–12 months (to be extended once).

As is the case in adult criminal law, conditional sentences are quite often used. The sanction is then imposed with the condition that the juvenile will not commit a new criminal offence within a specific period of time and will 'obey' certain specific conditions related to the behaviour of the juvenile (such as a ban on visiting certain places).[97] The wide variety of available special conditions – aimed at having an impact on the behaviour of the juvenile – is an important characteristic of the Dutch juvenile criminal justice system.[98] The public prosecution service monitors whether the juvenile complies with the special conditions.

Although it is not a sanction as such, it should be mentioned that under Dutch criminal law there are rather wide possibilities to store DNA of convicted juveniles. On the basis of a law enacted in 1995 (Act on DNA research on convicted persons – *Wet DNA-onderzoek bij veroordeelden*, in force since 1 February 1995) a person who is convicted of a felony (*misdrijf*) for which detention on remand may be applied, will be ordered by the prosecutor to give cell material, which will be used to form a DNA profile. This profile is stored in the national database of the Dutch Forensic Institute (*Nederlands Forensisch Instituut – NFI*) and will be used for investigation purposes. The aforementioned obligation to give cell material also applies to juveniles when they are sent to youth detention, given community service or placed in a juvenile institution for

93 Vlaardingenbroek 2011, p. 62.
94 De Jonge and Van der Linden 2013, p. 111–112.
95 De Jonge and Van der Linden 2013, p. 113–115.
96 De Jonge and Van der Linden 2013, p. 119–120.
97 Van Kalmthout and Bahtiyar 2011, p. 928.
98 See also the Decision of 22 January 2008 on the implementation of possibilities to have an impact on the behaviour of juveniles who have committed criminal acts (*Besluit gedragsbeinvloeding jeugdigen*), *Staatsblad* 2008, 23.

treatment.[99] Over the last few years, the number of DNA profiles of juveniles in the national database has increased substantially.[100] The wide possibility to take and store DNA material in juvenile cases is being criticised in academic literature and by NGOs.[101] According to Defence for Children this part of Dutch practice conflicts with the Convention on the Rights of the Child (hereafter: CRC).[102]

2.6. ALTERNATIVES TO CRIMINAL PROCEEDINGS

As mentioned before, in juvenile cases, the principle of subsidiarity is key. In principle, this means that a juvenile who is suspected of a criminal offence will not face normal court proceedings unless there are compelling reasons for it.[103] In line with the aforementioned principle, the Dutch juvenile criminal justice system provides for various possibilities of diversion or out-of-court settlement. The wide use of possibilities to deal with a case out of court is seen as one of the characteristics of the Dutch juvenile justice system focusing on the best interests of the child.

Although the public prosecutor has full responsibility for the prosecution policy, in juvenile cases decisions on how an individual case should be dealt with are taken in close consultation with other relevant actors such as the police, the Child Welfare Council and Youth Probation Services. For this purpose, in each district consultation meetings are regularly held: this concerns the aforementioned Judicial Case Consultation (*Justitieel Casusoverleg*). Normally, a case will be referred to Judicial Case Consultation within seven days of the first interrogation of the juvenile.[104]

Most out-of-court settlements are decided upon by either the police or the public prosecutor. In this respect the police has the following possibilities:

- Unconditional dismissal/warning
- Conditional dismissal: compensation of damages or apologies
- Conditional dismissal: fine (art. 74c CC)
- Special form of conditional dismissal: Halt-disposal (art. 77e CC)

99 Art. 1 para. 1 sub d and para. 2 of the Act on DNA research on convicted persons.

100 In 2012 the total number of juveniles of whom DNA is stored in the database increased from 17,313 to 20,281 (total number of persons – both juveniles and adults – in 2012 was 157,864). See Yearly Report DNA database for criminal cases 2012 (*Jaarverslag 2011 van de DNA-databank voor strafzaken*), Dutch Forensic Institute, Ministry of Justice and Security, Den Haag april 2012.

101 See for example: Ingelse 2008 and Moerman 2010.

102 See www.defenceforchildren.nl/p/21/1754/mo89-mc21.

103 The principle of subsidiarity is also expressed in arts. 37 and 40 of the CRC.

104 Van Kalmthout and Bahtiyar 2011, p. 930.

In the near future, the possibility of conditional dismissal on the basis of art. 74c CC will be replaced by the police disposition (*Politie Strafbeschikking*).[105] The Halt disposal is often used in practice and therefore deserves some particular attention.

With the public prosecutor's permission the police may refer a juvenile to this specific diversion program called Halt (short for *Het ALTernatief* – 'the alternative').[106] This way of dealing with a case is only possible for certain specific (mild) offences such as shoplifting or vandalism and – very importantly – if the juvenile admits to having committed the crime. The juvenile will receive a written proposal to follow a Halt program. What is important in this respect is the fact that the police have to inform the juvenile that he is not obliged to accept the Halt proposal and to explain the possible consequences of not participating. The juvenile will receive this information in writing as well. If the juvenile accepts the Halt proposal, a written 'contract' has to be signed. For juveniles between the 12 and 16 years old, written consent will also have to be given by his or her legal *guardian* (*wettelijk vertegenwoordiger*). In principle, the juvenile does not have a right to *ex officio* legal assistance by a lawyer during these 'deliberations'. However, since the *Salduz* case of the European Court of Human Rights (hereafter: ECtHR) and the Dutch Instruction on legal assistance during police interrogation (*Aanwijzing rechtsbijstand politieverhoor*)[107] which entered into force on 1 April 2010, this situation has changed for a certain category of juveniles. According to the aforementioned instruction, juveniles below the age of 16 cannot waive their right to consult a lawyer before the first interrogation during which the possibility of Halt will have to be formally discussed and assessed. This means that a lawyer will have to be consulted – even in the relatively mild cases which can be dealt with through a Halt dismissal – before the juvenile may be interrogated. It should be noted, however, that the foregoing only applies to juveniles below the age of 16 who have actually been arrested, which will – given the 'mild' character of criminal cases eligible for Halt-referral – in practice be rather the exception than the rule.[108] How the Halt dismissal is shaped may vary.[109] When the program is successfully completed, no official report of the case will be sent to the prosecutor and the juvenile will not have a criminal record. If Halt is not an option – or is not carried out satisfactorily – the police send the official report to the prosecutor.

---

105 See art. 257b CCP.

106 The first Halt bureau in the Netherlands was set up in 1981. It obtained formal legal basis in the Criminal Code in 1995 (art. 77e CC). In practice, over 16,000 juvenile cases are dealt with through Halt. For more information see: www.Halt.nl.

107 *Staatscourant* 2010, 4003.

108 See *infra* paragraph 2.7 (part II).

109 For example it may take the form of community service, fulfilling some sort of pedagogical learning order (*leeropdracht*), a conversation between the juvenile and his parents, making apologies to the victim or repairing the damages. Regardless of the form chosen, the Halt disposal may amount to a maximum of 20 hours: art. 77e para. 4 CC. See De Jonge and Van der Linden 2013, p. 94–96.

The options open to the prosecutor are the following:

- Unconditional dismissal
- Conditional dismissal (for example: *transactie*)
- Prosecutorial disposition (*strafbeschikking*)
- (Referral of the case to court)

Currently the *transactie* and the *strafbeschikking* are applied simultaneously, with the latter being available in only a small amount of cases. In the near future, the former will be fully replaced by the latter. In the course of deciding on the best way of dealing with a case, the prosecutor may decide to invite the juvenile and his parents or guardian to his office for a 'hearing' which will – as a rule – take place without legal assistance (a so-called TOM hearing – short for *Transactie Openbaar Ministerie* – or TOMMIE when it concerns juveniles). A *transactie* is possible in the case of criminal offences which a maximum six-year prison sentence. This way of dealing with a case can take different forms with different conditions such as payment of a fine, compensation of damages, performing community service and following directives of Youth Care. Although the wide powers of the prosecution services to settle cases have since long been a point of concern from the point of view of legal protection, in 2008 they were even further broadened through the introduction of the so-called prosecutorial disposition (*strafbeschikking*). The prosecutorial disposition enables the prosecution to impose sentences and orders without intervention of a court. Like the *transactie*, the prosecutorial order can take different forms such as payment of a fine and performing community service (which for juveniles may amount up to 60 hours). The prosecutorial order has been applicable to juveniles since 1 March 2011. It differs from the transaction in the sense that, in principle, the prosecutor may impose the prosecutorial order without the consent of the juvenile: the sentence becomes final unless the juvenile objects to it. In the latter case, a trial hearing will have to take place.[110] However, in certain cases – for example when the prosecutor wants to impose community service – the juvenile has to be heard by the prosecutor beforehand, during which the juvenile has to declare that he is willing to fulfil the obligations of the disposition. In certain cases, at this moment the juvenile will have to be informed of his right to request the appointment of a lawyer. This information should be provided at the latest at the start of the hearing (art. 257c para. 1 CCP).[111]

In summary, the majority of juvenile criminal cases are dealt with out of court by the police or the prosecutor. In practice, the most important alternative ways

110 Tak 2008, p. 89.

111 As a rule, the Child Welfare Council will be involved in case of a prosecutorial disposition (by informing and advising the prosecution services). Also, a defence lawyer will be involved *ex officio* in the case of community service of over 20 hours (art. 489 para. 1 sub a CCP). See De Jonge and Van der Linden 2013, p. 105–106.

of settling a juvenile case are Halt or the *transactie*/prosecutorial disposition (*strafbeschikking*).[112]

Finally, it should be mentioned that mediation is not a formal part of the Dutch juvenile (criminal) justice system: it only takes place on an experimental basis. Therefore, whether and how mediation is organised may differ significantly per court district. For example, in Maastricht there is a somewhat different practice than elsewhere in the Netherlands. Where in other districts mediation is organised at the level of the courts and mediation is initiated and conducted by independent mediation firms, in Maastricht it is organised at the level of the public prosecution service. Hence, the district secretary of the public prosecution service is entrusted with mediation. This means, in practice, that a public prosecutor will present a case to the secretary who will then deliberate with both the (juvenile) suspect and victim(s) and find out their stance towards and willingness to cooperate in a mediation procedure. In theory, a complaint filed by the victim and a suspect (willing to cooperate) can be enough to start the mediation procedure: the suspect does not even have to be interrogated by the police.[113] Normally, a suspect will have admitted guilt to the offence or at least taken full responsibility for his actions and shown a willingness to cooperate in the procedure.[114]

II. INTERROGATIONS

1. INTERROGATIONS OF JUVENILES IN THE PRE-TRIAL PHASE

1.1. CONCEPT OF INTERROGATION: RELEVANT DEFINITIONS

After the general outline of the Dutch juvenile criminal justice system, the second part of this report will focus – more specifically – on the interrogation of juvenile suspects and the relevant safeguards provided for in the Dutch legal framework. In order to understand the scope and function of pre-trial 'interrogation' in the Netherlands, several general criminal procedural concepts such as 'suspect', 'charge', 'investigative stage' and finally 'interrogation' need clarification.

112 For statistics see www.halt.nl. (click '*jaarberichten*' below the heading '*over Halt*').
113 Although this can be the case in theory, in practice the suspect is 'normally' interrogated by the police before mediation commences.
114 See also Wolthuis 2012, p. 354. For the applicable safeguards during mediation see *infra* paragraph 2.7.5 (part II).

1.1.1. Suspect

The notion of 'suspect' (*verdachte*) is of fundamental importance in Dutch criminal procedure. Firstly, because it is a status which entails certain fundamental procedural rights, such as the right to remain silent. Secondly, because it makes it possible for investigative authorities to use certain coercive investigative methods against the person concerned such as arrest. According to Dutch law, a 'suspect' is someone 'against whom, given facts and circumstances, a reasonable suspicion of guilt in relation to a criminal offence exists'.[115] Thus, the definition of a suspect is closely linked to the existence of the 'reasonable suspicion of guilt' against a particular person. Art. 27 para. 1 CCP holds three elements relevant for the qualification of a suspect: (a) the existence of a criminal offence, (b) the existence of a reasonable suspicion of guilt which (c) must be based on facts or relevant circumstances.[116]

The scope of art. 27 para. 1 CCP is further developed in case law. In general, it can be said that the Dutch courts take a rather stringent approach in deciding whether a 'reasonable suspicion' exists. The criterion used is that there should be a substantiated and individualised suspicion.[117]

In the context of definitions, it is important to note that Dutch criminal procedure law does not use the term 'accused' (*aangeklaagde* or *beschuldigde*): during the trial stage the term 'suspect' (*verdachte*) still applies.

1.1.2. Charge – first formal allegations towards a suspect

Dutch legislation does not provide for a formal definition of 'charge'. When considering the *charge* as the moment at which a suspect is (or should be) officially informed of the allegations against him, the most formal modality in Dutch criminal procedure is considered to be the official summons (*dagvaarding*) which the public prosecutor will send to the suspect when he decides to prosecute the case.[118] The main part of the summons is the so-called *tenlastelegging* in which the allegations are described, including a reference to the relevant provisions of the codes and/or statutes that the suspect is said to have breached. This summoning of the suspect will – as a rule – happen at the end of the pre-trial stage in criminal proceedings.[119]

---

115 Art. 27 para. 1 CCP.

116 This is the 'material' definition of the term suspect. Art. 27 para. 2 CCP also contains a 'formal' definition: the person against whom a prosecution is started also qualifies as a 'suspect'. See: Corstens 2011, p. 75.

117 It should be noted that Dutch case law accepts that judgments based on experience of police officers (*ervaringsoordelen*) form the basis of a suspicion. See *inter alia* HR 14 January 1975, *NJ* 1975, 207.

118 Art. 258 para. 1 CCP.

119 The official summons usually marks the start of the trial phase.

Before receiving the official summons, the arrested suspect will be informed of the charges on different occasions during pre-trial proceedings. Normally, the suspect will be verbally informed upon arrest on the reasons for doing so. This obligation to inform arrested suspects of the reasons for their arrest is currently not laid down in Dutch legislation but follows from art. 5 para. 2 of the European Convention on Human Rights (hereafter: ECHR). This situation is expected to change in the near future with the implementation of the Directive on the right to information in criminal proceedings.[120] In addition, when a suspect is brought before the assistant public prosecutor he will again be informed about the allegation(s). Furthermore, if he is taken into police custody the (juvenile) suspect will receive a written order containing the relevant articles of the criminal code or other statute(s). In this phase, the suspect will, as a rule, not be provided with more information than the articles of the applicable legal provisions. For example, there is no obligation to inform the suspect of the existing evidence.[121]

1.1.3. Investigative stage

Under Dutch law, criminal proceedings usually start with an 'investigation' (*opsporingsonderzoek*).[122] A legal definition of 'investigation' has been lacking in Dutch criminal proceedings until 2000 when a definition was introduced in art. 132a CCP. New legislation on investigative measures – *the law on special investigative measures*[123] – brought about the anchoring of the definition in the Code of Criminal Procedure. Since the introduction of the law on *terrorist crimes*[124] the definition of 'investigation' has evolved into the following – rather broad and ambiguous – wording: 'Investigation must be seen as the examination in relation to criminal offences under the authority of the public prosecutor with the aim of taking criminal procedural decisions.'[125] This is a formal definition of investigation as an activity and not so much as a separate stage of criminal proceedings.

1.1.4. Interrogation

There is no legal provision in Dutch law providing for a definition of 'interrogation'. The concept is defined in case law as 'all questions stated to a person – who is considered a suspect – concerning his involvement in an alleged

120 Directive 2012/13/EU of May 2012.
121 Prakken and Spronken 2007, p. 167.
122 Corstens 2011, p. 243.
123 Wet bijzondere opsporingsbevoegdheden, 25 May 1999, *Staatsblad* 1999, 245.
124 Wet ter verruiming van de mogelijkheden tot opsporing en vervolging van terroristische misdrijven, 20 November 2006, *Staatsblad* 2006, 580.
125 Art. 132a CCP.

criminal offence'.[126] According to Dutch case law, the nature of the questions is the decisive factor, not where the questioning takes place. Some questions asked by the police of a (potential) suspect, however, do not fall under the definition of an interrogation, for example questions aimed at the identification of the suspect.

The concept of interrogation mentioned above needs to be viewed separately from the 'hearing of the suspect as a party in the proceedings'. The latter reflects the opportunity for the suspect to put forward his perceptions and position in relation to the possible enactment of certain impeding measures.[127] Therefore, this does not constitute a 'material interrogation' conducted to retrieve evidence or information but is a form of hearing that provides the defence with an opportunity to express their views.[128] In Dutch legislation, this distinction is not consistently made: the words 'hearing' (*horen*) and 'interrogating' (*verhoren*) are often used as synonyms.[129]

Another important distinction is the difference between statements which are given 'spontaneously' on the hand and statements given during interrogation on the other. According to the Dutch Supreme Court a spontaneous declaration in the back of a police van – made during transport to the police station – does not constitute an 'interrogation'.[130] In this case the suspect told the arresting officers that 'he had done something terrible' at a specific location. Thus, when a suspect wishes to spontaneously make a statement, this does not constitute an 'interrogation' and these statements can be used in evidence without the suspect being warned beforehand.[131]

Finally, it should be noted that when talking about *interrogation* as mentioned in the CCP, this relates to all interrogations concerning both adult as well as juvenile suspects.

In conclusion one can say that in Dutch criminal (procedural) law there are not many definitions which relate to fundamental concepts such as *suspect, charge, investigation* and *interrogation* in a clear and precise manner. Irrespective of the fact

126 HR 2 October 1979, *NJ* 1980, 243.

127 Remmelink 1966, p. 311–321.

128 In the context of this report, these hearings will be referred to as 'formal interrogations'.

129 See for example art. 29 CCP which stipulates: 'In all cases in which someone is *heard* as a suspect, the *interrogating* public servant'. See on the different types of interrogation and – more specifically the distinction between formal and material (or case related) interrogation *infra* paragraph 1.2 (part II).

130 HR 15 May 2012, *LJN* BU8773.

131 It is questionable whether this is in line with the ECHR. In recent case law the ECtHR has held that informal questions asked of a suspect do constitute an interrogation (ECtHR 20 September 2012, *Titarenko v. Ukraine*, no. 31720/02). According to the ECtHR the deciding factor seems to be whether or not the officers pose questions. When doing so, the suspect needs to be warned. If however the suspect starts confessing voluntarily, without questions asked, this can be documented in an official transcript (*proces-verbaal*) and used as evidence.

that some legal definitions do exist, these are often vague and ambiguous, leaving room for interpretation by the Dutch courts. It is for this reason that the Supreme Court has been highly influential in further defining some of these concepts.

1.2. TYPES AND FUNCTIONS OF INTERROGATIONS

1.2.1. Different types of interrogations

Under Dutch law there is a wide variety of pre-trial 'interrogations' applicable to juvenile suspects. In general, two main types of interrogations can be distinguished: 'material interrogations' or 'case-related interrogations' on the one hand and 'formal interrogations' on the other.[132] The 'case-related' interrogations primarily aim at obtaining evidence and may be conducted by police officials (investigative officers or the assistant public prosecutor), public prosecutors and (juvenile) judges.[133] In practice, a juvenile suspect will – as a rule – be interrogated for the first time by an investigative police officer, at the police station in an interrogation room. This police interrogation can – and for the purpose of this report will – be considered the *most important interrogation in relation to evidence gathering*, first of all because it is the most common in practice and second of all because of the impact the (results of this) interrogation may – and most often will – have on the outcome of criminal proceedings. As mentioned before, the police interrogation is not bound to a specific location, nor is it formally necessary to arrest the (juvenile) suspect before interrogating him.[134] The determining factor is whether questions are being asked in relation to the alleged criminal offence. The goal of the aforementioned interrogation is truth finding and therefore – in an ideal situation – the objective should not be to extract a confession, but to have the suspect shed light on the alleged offence should he be willing and able to do so.[135]

The category of formal interrogations which allow the defence to express their view and/or enable the authorities to ascertain whether prolonging deprivation of liberty is in line with the principles of proportionality and subsidiarity can be further subcategorised in four categories:

1. Appearance before the (assistant) public prosecutor: art. 53 and 54 CCP.
2. Appearance before the (assistant) public prosecutor before the decision on police-detention is made: art. 57 CCP.

---

132 See also *supra* paragraph 1.1 (part II).
133 Art. 29 CCP.
134 Although interrogating a suspect after arrest is the most common way in practice.
135 Amelsvoort *et al* 2007, p. 25.

3. Appearance before the investigative judge (*habeas corpus* proceedings): art. 59a CCP.
4. Appearance before the investigative judge before the decision on pre-trial detention is made: art. 60 CCP.

Formally, the interrogations mentioned under 3 and 4 are separate: the *habeas corpus* proceedings are held to ascertain the lawfulness of the deprivation of liberty and the procedure under art. 60 CCP is to decide whether the suspect should be placed in pre-trial detention. Even though both procedures are regulated separately, in practice they often coincide.

1.2.2. Formal interrogations

After being arrested a juvenile suspect will be brought before the (assistant) public prosecutor who 'hears' the suspect.[136] In practice, he will inform the suspect of his procedural rights (right to remain silent and right to legal assistance) and ask him about the circumstances of the arrest and the alleged offence. The goal of the appearance before the (assistant) public prosecutor is to verify the lawfulness and acceptability of the arrest and to ascertain whether prolongation of deprivation of liberty is necessary. When – later on in the proceedings – detention on remand is ordered, the (assistant) public prosecutor will again hear the suspect and inform him about this remand.[137] Finally, the investigative judge can hear juvenile suspects[138] on two occasions in the criminal process. Firstly, during the *habeas corpus* proceedings[139] and secondly during the hearing in which the decision on pre-trial detention is made.[140]

In Dutch criminal proceedings, the formal interrogations – offering the juvenile suspect an opportunity to put forth his view on his treatment and/or the proceedings – are mandatory. After a suspect is arrested, he *must* be presented before the (assistant) public prosecutor who hears the suspect. After the police interrogation the suspect *must* also be heard by the (assistant) public prosecutor again before deciding on police custody (*inverzekeringstelling*). The same applies for the *habeas corpus* hearing by the investigating judge. Although the material police interrogation is – from the point of view of evidence gathering – the most important form of interrogation, information can be gathered during these formal

136 Arts. 53 para. 3 and 54 para. 3 CCP. As mentioned before, the assistant public prosecutor is a police official who serves as the 'extension' of the public prosecutor. Although his role is to assist the prosecutor, he is nonetheless a police officer and he is not part of the public prosecutions department.
137 Art. 57 CCP.
138 In juvenile proceedings, the investigative judge is a specialised juvenile judge.
139 Art. 59a CCP.
140 Art. 60 CCP.

interrogations as well. Therefore, the juvenile suspect will have to be warned before every interrogation – irrespective of whether it is a formal or a material interrogation. When statements are spontaneously given during an interrogation – material or formal – nothing prevents the interrogating officer from documenting it in an official document and submitting the statements as evidence.[141] Sufficient and adequate procedural safeguards should therefore be applicable during all these interrogations, which – as will be discussed later on – is not always the case.

Following the aforementioned, the most common chronologic sequence of the earliest phase of police interrogation in a 'normal' criminal case will be: (1) bringing a suspect before the (assistant) public prosecutor, (2) a case-related interrogation by an investigative police officer and if the suspect is kept in (police) detention longer, (3) again a hearing by the (assistant) public prosecutor, and finally (4) a hearing before the investigative judge.

1.2.3. Material interrogations

With respect to material interrogations, there is no pre-ordered and precise moment in criminal proceedings at which a juvenile suspect should be interrogated. In practice a suspect will be transported to the (nearest) police station – to be heard – following his arrest.[142] The CCP does prescribe a six-hour timespan (or 15 hours when the hours between midnight and 9 am are included) during which preliminary investigations should be conducted.[143] Following transportation, the (assistant) public prosecutor will hear the suspect and inform him of his procedural rights and verify whether the arrest was lawful (this constitutes a formal interrogation as mentioned above). If this is the case and he sees a need for detention for investigative purposes, police detention will be ordered. During police detention, the suspect will be interrogated for the first time. Following that first (and possibly more) interrogation(s), the decision for further detention is made. If needed, police custody (*inverzekeringstelling*) can be ordered after the first six (or 15) hours of police detention. When police custody is ordered, the (assistant) public prosecutor will inform the suspect of this decision. In practice this is done rather quickly by visiting the suspect in his cell and talking to him.

In comparison to formal interrogations, material (case-related) interrogations are in theory not mandatory. Nonetheless, the police interrogations – aimed

---

141 See *infra* paragraph 4 (part II).

142 Art. 61 para. 1 CCP. This is another example of the inner changeability of the terms 'hearing' and 'interrogation' in Dutch formal legislation.

143 Art. 61 para. 1 CCP. The term of six hours does not start from the moment of arrest, but from the moment the (assistant) public prosecutor has ordered police detention (*ophouden voor onderzoek*).

at acquiring information – are said to be at the heart of criminal proceedings because in each case the rationale is that the suspect holds the answers to questions only he can answer.[144] Because of this predisposition towards interrogating every suspect, this becomes a sort of self-fulfilling prophecy – resulting in the fact that in principle every suspect *is* interrogated, irrespective of the amount of technical or tactical evidence available and notwithstanding his vulnerability due to young age. Because the police perceive the material interrogation to be of great importance, juvenile suspects are – just like adults – (almost) always interrogated. In this respect, the main consideration seems to be whether the juvenile holds key information for the investigation, whether it be incriminating for himself or other (co-)suspects.[145] There is no legal obligation to formally assess whether the 'benefits' of interrogating the juvenile suspect outweigh possible 'costs' in the sense of damage done to the juvenile's (psychological) wellbeing.

In figure 2 a schematic overview is provided to summarise the different types of pre-trial interrogations in Dutch criminal proceedings, indicating their purpose, the competent authority, the relevant moment in proceedings and the applicable legal provision(s).

Figure 2. Schematic overview of types of interrogations in the Netherlands

Type of 'interrogation'	**Competent authority**	**Purpose**	**When in procedure**	**Legal provision(s)**
Voorgeleiding **(formal)**	(Assistant) public prosecutor	Ascertain lawfulness of arrest and need for prolongation of deprivation of liberty	As soon as possible after arrest	Arts. 53 and 54 CCP
Police interrogation **(material)**	Police officers	Evidence gathering	After arrest and the *voorgeleiding*	Art. 29 CCP
Police custody hearing **(formal)**	(Assistant) public prosecutor	Information about remand and procedure	After the first police interrogation	Art. 57 CCP
Habeas corpus hearing **(formal)**	Investigative judge	Ascertain lawfulness of deprivation of liberty	Within 3 days and 15 hours after arrest	Art. 59a CCP
Pre-trial detention hearing **(formal)**	Investigative judge	Deciding on pre-trial detention	As soon as possible when the prosecutor deems remand necessary	Art. 60 CCP

144 Bockstaele 2008, p. 283.

145 See on this matter also the judgment of the Supreme Court of 17 June 2003, *NJ* 2003, 611, *LJN* AF7925 *supra* paragraph 2.1 (part I).

1.2.4. Other forms of 'interrogation'

Although the focus of this report will be on material pre-trial police interrogations, a broader definition of interrogation will be utilised in this section since other forms of 'interrogations' and hearings as described above can prompt interesting findings from the point of view of procedural safeguards as well. First of all there are the prosecutorial hearings during which the public prosecutor hears the juvenile suspect in relation to out-of-court disposals such as Halt or the prosecutorial disposition (*strafbeschikking*).[146] There are no separate rules of criminal procedure regulating this category of (more informal) hearings. Secondly, there are several hearings conducted by other authorities than the police, prosecutor or investigative judge which are not focussed on evidence-gathering but are nonetheless worth mentioning. The first situation being that wherein the Child Welfare Council (*Raad voor de Kinderbescherming*) hears the juvenile suspect[147] when the decision on the juvenile's detention on remand has to be taken.[148] When the CWC decides that a juvenile suspect in detention should be visited by a social worker, this civil servant can then draft a report in relation to the early help (*vroeghulp*) proceedings. The public prosecutor is obliged to take this report into consideration when requesting a juvenile suspect's detention on remand.[149] The social services servant will talk to the juvenile in order to draft the report for the public prosecutor. This 'hearing' of the juvenile does not constitute an interrogation in the sense of the CCP. However, it is used to assess the juvenile suspect's inherent criminal risk factors and the likelihood that he will relapse into criminal actions. In principle, whatever a juvenile says to the social worker in relation to the facts of which he is suspected – as well of the report drafted by the social worker – cannot be used as evidence. Nonetheless, the Supreme Court has recently ruled that when the social worker is called into court as a witness and he does not excuse himself from his obligation to give a statement under art. 218 CCP, the statements then made can be used as evidence in the criminal case against that juvenile.[150]

The juvenile suspect can additionally be heard in the course of mediation proceedings. In this context the case file is often very succinct. In theory, a complaint filed by the victim and a suspect (willing to cooperate) can be enough to start the mediation procedure. Thus, the suspect does not even have to be interrogated by the police.[151] In practice, the juvenile suspect has most likely

---

146 See *supra* paragraph 2.6 (part I).

147 Not in all cases because there is no obligation, thus the CWC decide on a case-by-case basis whether they attend the police station.

148 Art. 491 para. 1 CCP: the CWC is informed of the decision to remand in detention.

149 Art. 491 para. 2 CCP.

150 HR 25 September 2012, *LJN* BX4269.

151 Although this can be the case in theory, in practice the suspect is 'normally' interrogated by the police before mediation commences.

been interrogated and the objective of the mediation process is to – through dialogue between suspect and victim – come to disposal of the criminal offence and redemption of damages. Before starting the mediation procedure, it needs to first be established whether parties are willing to cooperate. Thus, in theory a suspect can admit to having committed the offence, but show an unwillingness to cooperate in any form of mediation. What is not clear is whether this statement can be used in evidence. According to legal doctrine and European restorative justice regulations, this should not be the case, for all (confessional) statements made during mediation procedures.[152] Recommendation R(99)19 by the Council of Europe states that 'participation in mediation should not be used as evidence of admissions of guilt in subsequent legal proceedings'[153] and the explanatory memorandum further states that an acceptance of facts does not constitute a legal confession of guilt.[154] This holds for both statements made during the actual mediation process or during the preliminary inquiries. Furthermore, in the Netherlands, the mediation procedure is considered to be confidential.[155]

1.3. AUTHORITIES EMPOWERED TO CONDUCT INTERROGATIONS OF JUVENILE SUSPECTS

In this paragraph the specialisation and training of authorities that can be burdened with interrogating juvenile suspects will be discussed. Whereas in part I (paragraph 2.3) the relevant actors in juvenile criminal proceedings have been described in general, here the focus will be solely on those actors actively involved in case-related pre-trial interrogations and their training or specialisation.

1.3.1. Police forces

With regard to interrogating juvenile suspects and qualification of investigative authorities it should first be mentioned that there is no formal basis for specialisation. Carrying out an interrogation is considered to be one of the generic tasks of a police officer and there is no provision that makes a distinction between juvenile or adult suspect. This is true for all police officers, regardless of their internal status – *ergo*, both uniformed officers on the beat as well as detectives who interrogate juveniles. Aside from this distinction in internal

---

152 Lauwaert 2008, p. 110.

153 Council of Europe, Recommendation no. R(99)19 of the Committee of Ministers to Member States Concerning Mediation in Penal Matters, Strasbourg 15 September 1999.

154 Explanatory Memorandum to Recommendation no. R(99)19 of the Council of Europe.

155 Wolthuis 2012, p. 355–356. For safeguards applicable during mediation proceedings, see *infra* paragraph 2.7.5 (part II).

roles, another division is made in levels of education and training. At all levels there is special attention paid to interrogating, but only for level four- and five-trained officers is there a separate module on juveniles (*module 'jeugd'*).

Aside from this generic education for police officers, the Dutch police academy also provides separate training for specific tasks.[156] These courses are not accessible for all police officers, but require a certain level of existing training.[157] Although there is attention to the interrogation of juvenile suspects within the academy, this is not a separate module,[158] but part of a larger package. The interrogation of juvenile suspects is included in the module 'interrogation of vulnerable suspects' (*Verhoor Kwetsbare Verdachten – VKV*). One requirement for participation in this training package is possession of the certificate on 'hearing juvenile or mentally disabled witnesses' (*Horen Jonge of verstandelijk beperkte Getuigen – HJG*). In order to acquire the HJG certificate, an officer must be an experienced sexual crime detective and must have taken the course. When all these requirements are met and the officer completes the VKV training package accordingly, he will become a certified interrogator of vulnerable suspects, thus not solely specialised in interrogating juveniles. Again, it should be stressed that this certification is in no way a requirement for interrogating juvenile suspects.

1.3.2. Public prosecutor

The public prosecutor is at the head of each criminal investigation. As part of the public prosecution service – which is governed by the Board of Prosecutors General – he heads the investigation as a delegate. Under Dutch criminal law, the public prosecution service has a prosecution monopoly.[159] Therefore, officially, all actions taken against a suspect in a criminal investigation are mandated by the public prosecutor.[160] Due to this role of supervision of a criminal investigation, the public prosecutor is in reality too busy to exercise investigative tasks personally. With regard to formal taskw, such as informing a suspect about his procedural rights and assessing the lawfulness of the arrest, he can delegate these to the assistant public prosecutor – who officially is a police officer. As mentioned before,[161] the actual interrogation of suspects is, as a rule, carried

156 For a more in depth overview of training provided, we refer to the website of the police academy: https://www.politieacademie.nl/Pages/Welkom.aspx.
157 Thus, most uniformed police officers will not qualify for these specialist trainings.
158 This module should not be confused with the module juveniles for the generic education of all police officers.
159 Art. 8 CCP.
160 Art. 9 para. 1 CCP.
161 See *supra* paragraph 1.2 (part II).

out by police officers. Nevertheless, prosecutors do have the power to interrogate juvenile suspects themselves.[162]

So-called Juvenile Criminality Platforms (*Platform Jeugdcriminaliteit*)[163] exist at district level of the public prosecution service. Each of these platforms has a coordinating *juvenile* public prosecutor and per district a number of *juvenile* public prosecutors are installed. In 2011 there were 56 of these juvenile public prosecutors in the Netherlands.[164] This is not legally documented, but is a matter of internal organisation per region.

It should be noted that the term 'juvenile public prosecutor' is not recognised by law. A public prosecutor can hold a specialisation in juvenile cases, but will not be formally certified as such. In this respect, the function of juvenile public prosecutor differs from other specialisations such as – for example – the TGO[165] officer who needs to possess certain qualifications in order to be appointed as such.[166] In order to become a juvenile public prosecutor, one can apply for the role or be invited into it. From that moment on, the prosecutor can start specialising. Through the Training and Study Centre for the Judiciary (*Studiecentrum Rechtspleging – SSR*)[167] prosecutors can enrol in courses on juvenile criminal justice, but this is not a requirement for becoming a specialised prosecutor. As well as courses given by the SSR,[168] prosecutors can also outsource for other relevant courses, for instance through universities.

1.3.3. Juvenile judges

In the Netherlands juvenile criminal proceedings are dealt with by specialist judges. According to the CCP, the investigative judge who acts in a case involving a juvenile suspect is a specialist judge.[169] Besides this specialisation in dealing with juveniles, the investigative judge is also an experienced criminal law judge.[170] On the basis of art. 53 of the Law on the Judicial Organisation (*Wet op de Rechterlijke Organisatie*), the board of District Courts appoint certain judges who are specifically burdened with juvenile cases. However, this special

162 Art. 29 CCP.
163 *Arrondissementale Platforms Jeugdcriminaliteit* (APJs).
164 Uit Beijerse and Dubbelman 2011, p. 172.
165 TGO is short for: *Team Grootschalige Onderzoeken* (Team Large-scale Investigations) which deals with high-end/exposure/impact crimes.
166 For an extensive report on the qualifications of TGO officers: Voortgangsrapportage 2008, openbaar ministerie, implementatie programma versterking opsporing en vervolging, May 2008, available at: www.om.nl.
167 www.ssr.nl.
168 For instance 'Theme day Youth' and 'Licence Vignette Prosecutor Juveniles'.
169 Art. 492 CCP.
170 De Bruijn 2011, p. 203.

appointment does not guarantee that the judges are specialised in criminal and civil (juvenile protection) law. In practice, court districts have different approaches to this matter. For instance, in Roermond juvenile judges handle both criminal and juvenile protection cases. In Maastricht on the other hand civil law and criminal law matters are not dealt with by the same juvenile judge: civil law specialist judges deal with juvenile protection cases and criminal law judges handle juvenile criminal cases. Currently, the judiciary is working on equalising this divergent practice as much as possible.

Juvenile judges are also trained through a central training centre for the judiciary (*Studiecentrum Rechtspleging – SSR*).[171] Before a juvenile judge handles juvenile criminal cases in court he must have attended a five-day course organised by the SSR. Each year the judge is expected to reserve 30 hours of his allocated study time to keep up-to-date on developments in juvenile law.

2. THE RULES FOR THE INTERROGATION OF JUVENILES: GENERAL SAFEGUARDS

2.1. RELEVANT LEGAL SOURCES AND SCOPE

Before discussing the various procedural safeguards applicable during the interrogation of a juvenile suspect, a few words on the relevant legal sources and the general scope of the safeguards are appropriate. It should be noted that the procedural safeguards surrounding interrogations of juvenile suspects are regulated on various (legal) levels with only a few safeguards explicitly mentioned in statutory law (the CCP).[172] Some safeguards, such as the right to legal assistance or the right to disclosure do have a legal basis in statutory law, but are rather minimal or out-dated. For example, the formal legislative basis for legal assistance is out-dated, because a temporary Instruction on legal assistance during police interrogation by the Board of Prosecutors General is valid at the moment.[173] This instruction will be replaced eventually by new formal legislation which was launched in February 2014.[174] Other safeguards, such as recording of interrogations of juvenile suspects, are regulated through material legislation: the Instruction on Audio and Video Recording of Interrogations of Victims, Witnesses and Suspects (*Aanwijzing auditief en audiovisueel registreren van verhoren van aangevers, getuigen en verdachten* – hereafter Instruction

---

171 Although not exclusively. Judges can also outsource for courses at universities for instance.
172 These safeguards apply to all interrogations, as opposed to just the first police interrogation.
173 *Staatscourant* 2010, 4003. See *infra* paragraph 2.2 (part II).
174 Wijziging van het Wetboek van Strafvordering en enige andere wetten in verband met aanvulling van bepalingen over de verdachte, raadsman en enkele andere dwangmiddelen 13, February 2014 (www.justitie.nl).

AVR).[175] Besides *formal* and *material* legislation, the safeguards applicable during interrogation in the Netherlands are also provided for by European instruments such as the ECHR.

Below, different relevant safeguards, such as the right to legal assistance, the right to remain silent and the right to be assisted by an appropriate adult will be discussed. For similar reasons as stipulated *supra* paragraph 1.2 (part II), the focus of this discussion will be on the material, case-related pre-trial police interrogation. Where diverging safeguards in other forms of interrogations exist and are relevant, this will be dealt with in the final paragraph of this section.

Finally, it should be stressed that the safeguards described below in principle only apply to juveniles of 12 years and older. As mentioned before,[176] it can be said that the wide possibilities to use investigative powers against juveniles under the age of 12 are not adequately counter-balanced by youth-specific procedural safeguards for this particular age category. Since the youth-specific provisions provided for in the CCP[177] only apply to juveniles who have reached the age of 12, no explicit rules exist on – for example – the obligation of police officers to inform a juvenile suspect below the age of 12 of his right to remain silent.[178] Also, there is no legal regulation of the right to legal assistance for juveniles younger than 12. The limited legal protection that is offered to juveniles below the age of 12 mainly concerns the fact that they should be interrogated in the presence of an adult (parent or guardian) and that this interrogation should take place in a child-friendly location. However, these requirements follow from instructions of the public prosecution service[179] and are not laid down in statutory law.

2.2. THE RIGHT TO LEGAL ASSISTANCE

Until recently, there was no formal right to legal assistance prior to or during the first police interrogation in Dutch criminal proceedings. As follows from a European procedural safeguards survey carried out in 2009, the Netherlands

175 *Staatscourant* 2010, 11885.

176 See *supra* paragraph 2.1 (part I).

177 Art. 486–505 CCP.

178 Despite the absence of an explicit legal obligation, it is generally recognised in Dutch legal doctrine that juveniles below the age of 12 should be informed of the right to remain silent. See for example De Jonge and Van der Linden 2013, p. 178–179. Furthermore, in art. 40, para. 2 under *iv* CRC it is safeguarded that states shall not pressure a child into making a statement. This means that no statements can be retained from the juvenile by force.

179 Respectively the instruction on legal assistance during police interrogation (*Staatscourant* 2010, 4003) and the instruction on Audio and Audio-visual Registration of Interrogations of Victims, Witnesses and Suspects (*Staatscourant* 2010, 11885). See on the audio-visual registration of interrogations *infra* paragraph 3.7 (part II).

was one of the few EU Member States where such a right was not legally provided for.[180] After some noteworthy miscarriages of justice, the Schiedammer Park murder case[181] being the most influential, the Dutch Ministry of Justice decided in 2008 to launch a pilot on legal assistance during police interrogation.[182] During this pilot, lawyers were allowed to assist their clients during interrogation, but only in severe cases mostly concerning adult suspects. Within the context of the pilot, the role of the lawyer was limited: his assistance during interrogation could not go beyond passive attendance.[183] While the pilot was still underway, national developments where caught up by the ECtHR landmark decision in the *Salduz* case reinforcing the importance of the right to legal assistance for (especially juvenile) suspects in the early phase of police interrogations.[184] This ground-breaking development meant that the Dutch authorities could not afford to await the outcomes of the aforementioned pilot. Although there was (and to a certain extend still is) much debate on the exact scope of the *Salduz* decision and its implications for Dutch criminal procedure, the Supreme Court soon made clear that changing the law was necessary. In his decision of 30 June 2009 the Supreme Court stipulated as a general rule that an *arrested* suspect has the right to consult with a lawyer *before* the first interrogation. According to the Supreme Court, the right to be assisted by a lawyer *during* interrogation can only be enforced by juvenile suspects. Furthermore, the Supreme Court stressed that arrested suspects should be informed about these rights.[185] Following the Supreme Court's decision and the filling of the 'legal gap' resulting from it, the Board of Prosecutors General issued an instruction which was meant to temporarily serve as the basis for this legal assistance: the aforementioned Instruction on legal assistance during police interrogation.[186] In line with the 2009 decision of the Supreme Court, the instruction makes a clear distinction between *a right to consultation* and *a right to legal assistance during police interrogation*. This distinction is especially relevant in the case of juveniles,

[180] Spronken *et al.* 2009, p. 50–52.

[181] The suspect in the *Schiedammer Park* murder case had been sentenced to 18 years' imprisonment and *terbeschikkingstelling* (*TBS*) for the murder of a young girl and the attempted murder of a young boy. In 2004 he was acquitted after a revision hearing at the Supreme Court, because the DNA found on the body matched that of the actual perpetrator who had confessed to the murder prior to the revision hearing. See also HR 7 September 2004, *LJN* AQ9834.

[182] Pilot raadsman bij politieverhoor verdachte, 1 May 2008 – 1 May 2010, executed in Amsterdam-Amstelland and Rotterdam-Rijnmond.

[183] For more information on the pilot, see the summary of the report of Stevens and Verhoeven 2010, p. 157.

[184] ECtHR 27 November 2008, *Salduz v. Turkey*, no. 36391/02. In following decisions the ECtHR has further shaped the right to legal assistance in general and for juvenile suspects in particular. See for example: ECtHR 11 December 2008, *Panovits v. Cyprus*, no. 4268/04 and ECtHR 24 September 2009, *Pishchalnikov vs. Russia*, no. 7025/04.

[185] HR 30 June 2009, *NJ* 2009, 349 and HR 9 November 2010, *LJN* BN7727.

[186] *Staatscourant* 2010, 4003.

which will be further explained in the coming paragraphs. The instruction remains valid until it is replaced by formal legislation. As mentioned above, draft legislation on access to a lawyer in the phase of police interrogation is currently pending.[187]

2.2.1. The right to consult with a lawyer before interrogation

At present, it is explicitly stated in the CCP that a (juvenile as well as an adult) suspect has the right to be assisted by a duty or chosen lawyer. However, the CCP does not clarify the scope of the right nor does it specify from which moment onwards the suspect should be able to effectuate the right.[188] This lacuna with regard to Strasbourg requirements has temporarily been filled through material legislation – the aforementioned instruction on the right to legal assistance during police interrogation. According to this instruction, the juvenile suspect has a right to consult with a lawyer from the moment he is arrested and he should be informed of this right accordingly.[189] This informing of the suspect will in practice happen after arrest by the arresting officer(s) and when he is brought before the (assistant) public prosecutor (*voorgeleiding*). At present, a debatable issue in Dutch practice is that the instruction clearly limits the scope of the right to consultation (and presence) of a lawyer to the situation of 'arrest'. According to the Supreme Court the so-called Salduz rights are – in principle – not applicable to those suspects who have not been arrested but have attended the police station under a different statute.[190] From the Dutch case law it is clear that this (limitation of Salduz rights to situations of arrest) in principle also applies to juvenile suspects.[191] Thus, a (juvenile) suspect who has 'voluntarily' attended the police station can claim use of his so-called 'Salduz rights' before the interrogation, but there is no formal obligation for authorities to inform the juvenile of these rights.[192]

The aforementioned restriction of Salduz rights to situations of arrest is questionable in light of the aforementioned Strasbourg case law and recent EU legislation, because – with regard to the applicability of Salduz rights – these sources seem to make no distinction between arrested and voluntarily attending suspects.[193] In this respect it is important to note that some lower Dutch

---

187 Wijziging van het Wetboek van Strafvordering en enige andere wetten in verband met aanvulling van bepalingen over de verdachte, raadsmand en enkele andere dwangmiddelen, 13 February 2014 (www.justitie.nl).

188 Art. 28 para. 1 CCP.

189 *Staatscourant* 2010, 4003.

190 HR 30 June 2009, *NJ* 2009/349 and HR 12 June 2012, *LJN* BW7953.

191 See for example: HR 10 June 2013, *LJN* BW7953.

192 Bartels 2011, p. 132.

193 Directive on the right of access to a lawyer in criminal proceedings (Directive 2013/48/EU of October 2013). When referring to 'Salduz rules' or 'Salduz rights', this means the right to legal assistance prior to and during the first police interrogation for (juvenile) suspects.

courts have already ruled that safeguards for juvenile suspects – such as the right to legal assistance – should apply when the suspect has presented himself voluntarily as well. An example is a case of the Maastricht court in which it was stressed that the effectuation of 'Salduz rights' should not be linked to a particular moment in time or an official criminal procedural label (especially the moment of arrest), but to the question whether or not a juvenile is 'suspected' of having committed a criminal offence and whether or not he is questioned in relation to that particular offence.[194] Furthermore, Dutch courts have ruled that special circumstances can also give rise to the applicability of Salduz rights irrespective of whether or not the suspect is arrested.[195] These exceptions seem to be more in line with Strasbourg case law wherein a more material criterion is used to define application of Salduz rights. The decisive factor seems to be whether a suspect is in fact restricted in his freedom of movement.[196] According to the ECtHR it is important whether there is a significant limitation of a suspect's *freedom of action*.[197]

Under material law and pending (draft) formal legislation, the right to consult with a lawyer prior to the first police interrogation for *arrested* suspects will become a universal right for both adult and juvenile suspects. A new article (28c para. 1) will be introduced in the CCP stating that: 'the arrested suspect will be given the opportunity to consult for 30 minutes[198] with his lawyer prior to the first interrogation.'

2.2.2. *The right to legal assistance during interrogation*

As mentioned, following the 2009 decision of the Supreme Court and the corresponding instruction on legal assistance during police interrogation, currently all juvenile suspects have a right to be assisted by a lawyer during police interrogation.[199] With regard to the possibility of waiving the right to legal assistance the instruction issued by the public prosecution service creates a distinction between different age categories of juveniles. This means that not all juvenile suspects can waive their right to legal assistance in all cases.[200] Like the

---

194 District Court Maastricht 15 July 2010, *LJN* BN2406.

195 For instance mental disability and the severity of the crime (District Court Arnhem 12 August 2011, *LJN* BR4163) and the fact that the attendance cannot be labelled 'voluntarily' due to the circumstances of the case (District Court Zwolle-Lelystad 2 November 2010, *LJN* BO9852). This line of reasoning has been affirmed by the Supreme Court (HR 12 June 2012, *LJN* BW7953).

196 HR 12 June 2012, *LJN* BW7953.

197 ECtHR 18 February 2010, *Zaichenko v. Russia*, no. 39660/02, para. 48.

198 More information on these 30 minutes for the first consultation will be provided below in this paragraph.

199 HR 30 June 2009, *NJ* 2009/349 and *Staatscourant* 2010, 4003.

200 This distinction will be dealt with in the next paragraph.

obligation to be informed about the right to consult with a lawyer prior to the first police interrogation, the juvenile suspect should be informed of his right to legal assistance *during* the interrogation.[201]

2.2.3. *Waiver of the right to legal assistance*

In the instruction on legal assistance during police interrogation several situations (connected to different age categories) with regard to waiver should be distinguished. In principle, juvenile suspects – aged between 12 and 17 years old – can waive the right to legal assistance, but two exceptions to the rule are applicable.[202] First, juveniles aged between 12 and 15 years can only waive legal assistance in so-called category C offences for which pre-trial detention cannot be applied.[203] Juveniles aged between 16 and 17 years on the other hand cannot waive this right when suspected of a serious crime (a so-called category A offence).[204] In this respect it should be noted that the instruction containing the aforementioned rules does not have the status of law. Therefore, it is up to the judge to assess each case on its merits to see whether it should have been possible for the juvenile to waive the right to legal assistance.[205]

In a new article 28d para. 1 of the draft law implementing the Directive on access to a lawyer in criminal proceedings it is merely stated that a lawyer can be allowed to attend the interrogation when requested so by the suspect.[206] Regardless of whether or not this consultation should be considered to be 'mandatory legal assistance', the Board of Prosecutors General – in a commentary to this proposed legislation – foresees a practice in which the lawyer advises the juvenile suspect on the possible consequences of a waiver and 'it is expected that as a rule the lawyer will subsequently attend the interrogation'. Obviously, in practice, many factors at play may cause the juvenile suspect to still waive his right to assistance *during* the interrogation, after this consultation. In accordance with provisions and requirements for waiver as formulated in Strasbourg case law, the waiver must be clear, unequivocal and with insight in the possible consequences thereof.[207] The instruction does not mention these requirements.

---

201 *Staatscourant* 2010 nr. 4003.

202 So-called category C offences of the public prosecution service's instruction on the right to legal assistance during police interrogation.

203 *Staatscourant* 2010, 4003.

204 Referred to as: 'consultation right'.

205 De Jonge and Van der Linden 2013, p. 186–187.

206 Draft law 'Implementatie van richtlijn 2013/48/EU van het Europees Parlement en de Raad van 22 October 2013 (PbEU L294)', February 2014 (www.justitie.nl).

207 See ECtHR 11 December 2008, *Panovits v. Cyprus*, no. 4268/04, and ECtHR 24 September 2009, *Pishchalnikov v. Russia*, no. 7025/04.

In the aforementioned instruction it is regulated that, when a juvenile suspect waives his right to consult with a lawyer before the police interrogation, he also waives his right to assistance during the interrogation. This implication has to be conveyed to the suspect by the investigative officer and needs to be documented in an official report.[208] When a juvenile suspect has waived his right to legal assistance, but wishes to withdraw this decision later on, assistance should be facilitated.[209] Waiving the right to legal assistance does not affect the right to have a trusted person present during the interrogation. From the case law of the Supreme Court it is clear that the presence of a trusted person during interrogation is considered to provide some sort of compensation for the absence of a lawyer.[210] In addition, the case law shows that a juvenile suspect cannot successfully complain about lack of legal assistance *during* interrogation when he nor his lawyer have indicated after consultation that the presence of a lawyer was requested.[211] However, in another case, the Supreme Court has also held that the fact that a defence lawyer does not indicate that he would like to be present during the interrogation may not be considered an unequivocal waiver by the juvenile.[212]

2.2.4. Duty legal assistance

As stipulated in the CCP, each suspect has the right to be assisted by a lawyer of his own choosing or an appointed (*toegevoegde*) *duty* lawyer.[213] The appointment of a duty lawyer is governed by art. 40 CCP and is effectuated by the Dutch Legal Aid Board (*Raad voor Rechtsbijstand*).[214] The Board was founded by the Minister of Justice in order to provide legal assistance for suspects who do not have prior representation.[215] Under authority and supervision of the Legal Aid Board, duty-lawyer offices (*piketcentrales*) provide a duty lawyer when the request comes in. Before the *Salduz* ruling by the ECtHR and the enactment of the temporary instruction by the public prosecution service, legal assistance became applicable from the moment police custody was ordered.[216] The new instruction has changed this, now providing for legal assistance before the first interrogation and in some cases also legal assistance for juvenile suspects during

208 *Staatscourant* 2010, 4003.
209 *Staatscourant* 2010, 4003.
210 HR 10 June 2013, *LJN* BW7953. This decision also underlines that the Salduz-rules – in principle – only apply to juveniles who have been arrested. In this case the juvenile had visited the police station voluntarily together with his mother.
211 HR 19 February 2013, *NJ* 2013, 146. In this particular case the juvenile was interrogated (only) in the presence of his mother. See on the right to have an appropriate adult present *infra* paragraph 2.4 (part II).
212 HR 21 January 2014, ECLI:NL:HR:2014:133.
213 Art. 28 para. 1 CCP.
214 www.rvr.org.
215 www.rvr.org/nl/about_rvr.
216 Art. 41 CCP.

the interrogation.[217] When a juvenile suspect wishes to be assisted by a lawyer – before and/or during the first interrogation – and he does not choose one, an appointed lawyer will be provided.[218] Arranging this is the responsibility of the police, who have to inform the corresponding duty-lawyer office immediately upon arrest that the suspect has requested legal assistance from a duty lawyer. The Legal Aid Board will be contacted and a (duty) lawyer will be provided to the juvenile suspect. These boards are however out of office between the hours of 8pm and 7am. When the request is received, the appointed lawyer has two hours to arrive at the police station to assist his newly appointed client.[219] This means that the police have to wait to interrogate the suspect until these two hours have passed. A duty lawyer scheme is applicable, and when requested a duty lawyer will assist the suspect during police custody. These provisions apply to all suspects and no distinction is made between juveniles and adults.

2.2.5. Ex officio appointment of (duty) lawyers

Ex officio appointment of a lawyer is possible on the basis of art. 41 CCP. It states that: 'a lawyer shall be provided by the Legal Aid Board to a suspect who does not have a lawyer, when his detention on remand is ordered'.[220] This procedural provision applies to those circumstances after the (first) police interrogation is conducted. As mentioned above, this *ex officio* appointment of a lawyer refers to the old situation as it was before the *Salduz* ruling.

2.2.6. Specialisation of lawyers

Although some lawyers have specialised in assisting juvenile suspects, until recently there were no official qualifications on providing (duty) legal assistance in juvenile criminal cases. Since July 2013, specialisation requirements for lawyers assisting juveniles in (criminal) proceedings apply. These specialist qualifications devised by the Dutch Legal Aid Board apply to lawyers who wish to assist juveniles in all legal areas, including criminal law.[221] In short the requirements for assisting juvenile suspects in criminal proceedings are the following: the lawyer requesting a specialist certificate[222] is supposed to have done 12 duty cases within the previous two years of which at least one was a juvenile criminal law case and one a warrant case placement in a closed centre

217 This is unofficially called Salduz duty legal assistance.
218 Only when the (juvenile) suspect is suspected of a category A or B offence will the appointment of a *duty* lawyer be free of charge; further information on the costs of legal assistance will be provided under the heading 'the right to legal assistance of juvenile suspects'.
219 *Staatscourant* 2010, 4003.
220 Art. 41 para. 1a CCP.
221 The requirements can be found on the website of the Dutch Legal Aid Board (www.rvr.org).
222 And enlistment on the specialist juvenile duty lawyer scheme.

for juvenile care. The lawyer is required to possess at least three years of relevant professional experience including (a) three years as a sworn lawyer or (b) less than three years as a sworn lawyer, but with working experience in other relevant institutions such as the public prosecution department. The lawyer has to possess 12 educational points in the field of juvenile law. These conditions apply to normal circumstances wherein the lawyer has been working as a sworn lawyer for at least last three years. When this is not the case, the previous conditions apply, plus an additional requirement: a declaration of attendance (*meeloopverklaring*) meaning that the lawyer can prove that he has accompanied (an)other lawyer(s) to juvenile cases (often the patron).[223] Besides these specialist requirements, there is a Dutch organisation of juvenile lawyers (*vereniging nederlandse jeugdrechtadvocaten*) which acts as a consortium specialised in assisting juvenile suspects in legal proceedings.[224]

2.2.7. The right to legal aid for juvenile suspects

In certain circumstances the appointment (*toevoeging*) of a *duty* lawyer is free of charge.[225] Under current formal and material legislation, a dualist system of legal aid is applicable. Under the CCP legal assistance is free of charge when a lawyer is appointed (*ex officio*) if an order for police custody is made.[226] Simultaneously, on the basis of the instruction of the Board of Prosecutors General, legal assistance is free of charge in the in so-called category A and B offences.[227] When suspected of a category C offence, legal assistance can be provided, but the costs incurred are the responsibility of the suspect. The government also finances the appointment of a chosen lawyer when the lawyer is part of the duty lawyer scheme.

2.2.8. Informing the (juvenile) suspect of legal assistance and legal aid

The aforementioned instruction on legal assistance during police interrogation formulates specific rules on informing suspects about their right to legal assistance free of charge. Under the heading 'Informing the suspect of the consultation right' (*Informeren van verdachte over het recht op consultatiebijstand*) the following is mentioned: 'Every arrested suspect who is transported to a police station for interrogation shall be informed about his right to consult a lawyer prior to his first interrogation by the police. (...) The

[223] This declaration should at least attest to the fact that the lawyer has (a) attended three juvenile criminal court hearings and (b) three warrants of placement in closed juvenile centre court hearings.

[224] www.vnja.nl.

[225] See the Law on Legal Aid (*Wet op de Rechtsbijstand*).

[226] Art. 40 CCP. See also arts. 41 and 43 CCP for the *ex officio* appointment of lawyers in the event of pre-trial detention.

[227] *Staatscourant* 2010, 4003.

suspect shall also be informed that exercising his right to consult with a lawyer is free of charge in category A and B offence and that he will have to bear the costs in category C offences.'[228] These provisions apply to both adult and juvenile suspects. For juvenile suspects there are specific provisions formulated on the right to legal assistance during interrogation. The instruction reads: 'The police must also inform the arrested juvenile suspect that he has a right to legal assistance by a lawyer (...) during the interrogation. (...) The suspect shall be informed about that exercising the right to assistance during interrogation is free of charge in category A and B offence; in category C offences on the other hand he will have to bear the costs of assistance.'[229]

2.2.9. Juvenile suspect-lawyer consultations

The instruction on legal assistance during police interrogation provides the juvenile suspects with the right to have a 30-minute consultation before the first interrogation. What is unclear, is whether 30 minutes is sufficient to provide adequate time for preparation of the defence and a proper consultation with a client. Nonetheless, this 30-minutes rule will presumably be adopted in statutory legislation since it is written in a new article 28c para. 1 of the CCP.[230] Even though one might find this time limit arbitrary and dubious, recent research by Stevens and Verhoeven[231] evaluating the aforementioned pilot on legal assistance of 2008 has shown that on average the first consultation lasted no more than 18 minutes.[232] This finding was roughly replicated in another study where researchers found that in the Netherlands the first consultation lasted on average 15 minutes.[233]

2.2.10. The role of the lawyer during interrogation

On the basis of the instruction on legal assistance during police interrogation, the role of the lawyer during police interrogation is meant to be passive. During the pilot on legal assistance of 2008, the lawyer had to sit behind his client, was not allowed to make eye contact or intervene and was solely there to ensure that the interrogation was conducted in a lawful way, i.e. to check that the interrogating officers refrained from excessive coercion and asking leading questions.[234] At present, the instruction on legal assistance during police

228 *Staatscourant* 2010, 4003.
229 *Staatscourant* 2010, 4003.
230 Draft law 'Implementatie van richtlijn 2013/48/EU van het Europees Parlement en de Raad van 22 October 2013 (PbEU L294)', February 2014 (www.justitie.nl).
231 Stevens and Verhoeven 2013.
232 Stevens and Verhoeven 2013, p. 190.
233 Blackstock *et al.* 2013, p. 313.
234 Protocol Pilot legal assistance during suspect police interrogation (*pilot raadsman bij politieverhoor verdachte*), 1 May 2008 – 1 May 2010, conducted in Amsterdam-Amstelland and Rotterdam-Rijnmond.

interrogation formulates the role of the lawyer during police interrogation as follows: 'the lawyer shall act in a reserved manner to make sure the progress of the interrogation is hindered in the least possible way and to make sure he does not influence the interrogation. Primarily, the role of the lawyer is to see to it that unlawful coercion imposed on the juvenile suspect is refrained from. Considering the vulnerable position of the juvenile suspect, the lawyer shall have the opportunity to verify whether his juvenile client understands the questions posed and whether he understands the documentation of the interrogation. Furthermore, lawyers are not allowed to disrupt the interrogation by, for instance talking on the phone or standing up. Lawyers who violate these rules can be removed from the interrogation room'.[235]

2.3. THE RIGHT TO REMAIN SILENT

A suspect has the right to remain silent when being interrogated. This fundamental right is laid down in formal legislation in art. 29 CCP: 'the suspect is not obliged to answer questions'.

2.3.1. Informing the (juvenile) suspect of the right to remain silent

Art. 29 para. 1 CCP also includes the obligation for authorities to refrain from putting any form of pressure on the suspect. In Dutch criminal procedure the right to remain silent is universal to all suspects, juvenile as well as adults. Before each interrogation all suspects should be informed of their right to remain silent. This obligation is laid down in art. 29 para. 2 CCP which prescribes that the interrogating officer should start the interrogation by informing the (juvenile) suspect of his right to remain silent. There is no standard formula for how to provide this information to the suspect, neither for juvenile nor for adult suspects.[236] In practice, officers will inform a suspect of the fact that the suspect is not obliged to answer the questions asked and some will check that the suspect understands what this means. There is, however, no legal obligation to do so. The use of different – more child-friendly – wording when informing a juvenile suspect of the right to remain silent and checking whether the juvenile has understood the (scope of the) caution is not prescribed by law. With regard to foreign (juvenile) suspects, it should be stressed that the caution will be given in their native tongue through the use of an interpreter.[237]

---

235 *Staatscourant* 2010, 4003 (Besluit inrichting en orde politieverhoor). Draft law: 'Implementatie van richtlijn 2013/48/EU van het Europees Parlement en de Raad van 22 October 2013 (PbEU L294)', February 2014 (www.justitie.nl).

236 See on the information on the right to remain silent also *infra* paragraph 2.6 (part II).

237 For the provisions regulating the use and role of interpreters, see *infra* paragraph 2.5 (part II).

2.3.2. *Possible consequences of exercising the right to remain silent*

In Dutch criminal proceedings no adverse inferences can be drawn from remaining silent. However, when all evidence flagrantly points towards the suspect and he has not provided a reasonable counter-explanation (providing an alternative scenario which fits the evidence obtained, but do not gear towards his participation in a criminal offence), the judge can draw his conclusions from that and the fact that the suspect remained silent can then be used as evidence in court.[238] In this respect, the Supreme Court has ruled that 'this does not entail that the judge, in case a suspect does not provide a reasonable negating explanation for the fact which, on its own or seen in light of other evidentiary material should be seen as giving cause to the conviction that he has committed the offence, cannot use such occurrence in his consideration'.[239] Finally, it should be noted that the caution and the right to be cautioned is not a right that can be waived. All suspects, including juveniles, will have to be formally cautioned before an interrogation and waiving it is not a possibility.[240] If the suspect has not been cautioned, statements given can – in principle – not be used as evidence.

2.4. PRESENCE OF APPROPRIATE ADULT

The appropriate adult – as such – is a notion that is absent from Dutch juvenile criminal proceedings. When referring to the concept of an 'appropriate adult' this should be considered in light of the legal provisions applicable in for example England and Wales where a scheme of social workers who act as appropriate adults is applicable.[241] In the Netherlands, however, such a scheme is non-existent and no reference to appropriate adults is made in formal legislation such as the CCP.

Current material legislation in the Netherlands does however provide the juvenile suspect with a right to be assisted by a so-called 'trusted person' (*vertrouwenspersoon*).[242] This trusted person most often will be a relative (parent, sibling) or close friend of the juvenile suspect. In addition to this, the police should inform a family member or member of the household as soon as

---

238 Nevertheless, using the right to remain silent in itself cannot be considered to give cause (*redengevend*) to the proven conviction (*bewezenverklaring*), because it does not prove anything. It can, however, be taken into account in the evidentiary decision.

239 HR 3 June 1997, *NJ* 1997, 584.

240 Even if the suspect will point out that he does not wish to be cautioned, the interrogating officer will do so anyway, because of the possible implications of absence of the caution to the usability of the evidence gathered in the interrogation.

241 With the establishment of the PACE act in 1984, the concept was introduced. The scheme of social workers is governed by the UK Home Office in a set of guidance rules.

242 *Staatscourant* 2010, 4003.

possible on the arrest of the juvenile.[243] According to the CCP the parents or legal guardian of a juvenile suspect should also be informed of their legal right to visit their child at the police station.[244] According to the instruction on legal assistance during police interrogation, the right to be assisted by a trusted person is applicable from the moment the juvenile suspect is interrogated. The instruction stipulates that the juvenile suspect should be informed of his right to be assisted by a trusted person during the interrogation.[245]

The right to have a trusted person present can be seen as a supportive right during interrogation. Important to note is that when a juvenile suspect exercises his right to legal assistance during interrogation, his right to be assisted by a trusted person is automatically annulled. The instruction states: 'The trusted person can only attend the interrogation if no lawyer is present'.[246] Furthermore the instruction states that: 'it is preferred that legal assistance during interrogation is provided by a lawyer. Nonetheless, the [juvenile] suspect is free to ask for assistance of a trusted person instead of a lawyer'.[247] The public prosecution service has thus formulated a condition wherein the hierarchical level of the lawyer supersedes that of the trusted person. Presumably, this is strongly connected to the fact that – in the past – negative experiences with parents being present during interrogation have been recorded. For example, cases in which parents embezzled evidence after the interrogation or parents who demonstrated disturbing behaviour during interrogation. In its post-Salduz decision of 2009 the Supreme Court has not stipulated the aforementioned order of rank between the lawyer and the trusted person.[248] For that reason, legal authors have questioned whether this practice will hold, because it is evidently not in line with the intentions of the Supreme Court.[249] In the future the right to be assisted by a trusted person will most likely become formally legislated. Thus, in the explanatory memorandum of the new draft law on implementation of the Directive on legal assistance (PbEU L294) it is stated that the juvenile suspect has the right to be assisted by a trusted person, but that the assistance from a lawyer should be priority.

2.4.1. Procedure for arranging for and requirements of a trusted person

The instruction on legal assistance during police interrogation prescribes that '[w]hen the suspect indicates that he does not want a lawyer, but a trusted person

243 Art. 27 Duty Instruction police (*Ambtsinstructie politie*).
244 Art. 490 CCP. See De Vocht 2012, p. 371.
245 *Staatscourant* 2010, 4003.
246 *Staatscourant* 2010, 4003.
247 *Staatscourant* 2010, 4003.
248 HR 30 June 2009, *NJ* 2009, 349, para. 2.6.
249 Stevens and Verhoeven 2013, p. 80.

to attend the interrogation, he should provide the police with details (name, address, telephone number) so that the intended person can easily be reached'.[250] When his presence is requested, the trusted person has – like the requested lawyer – two hours to arrive at the police station. The trusted person should meet certain requirements: he must be an adult, form part of the inner circle of the suspect and he cannot be evidently involved in the alleged offence.[251] Even if the trusted person does not speak Dutch, the police are not obliged to provide an interpreter.[252]

The right to be assisted by a trusted person is clearly a right bestowed upon the juvenile: it is up to the juvenile to choose and to decide. One can assume that, when involved, a lawyer might consult with the juvenile suspect and discuss possible implications of the presence of a trusted person whose presence might not be in the best interest of the juvenile. However, the juvenile will ultimately be the one who decides. The instruction explicitly states that the trusted person 'does not have an independent right to be present during the interrogation. He can only attend if the juvenile explicitly states that he wants the trusted person to do so'. The instruction does refer to the situation wherein the presence of the trusted person can be contradictory to the interest of the investigation.[253] The contact between a juvenile suspect and his parent or guardian may only be restricted in certain limited circumstances.[254] Based on art. 50 para. 2 CCP, limitation is possible if there is a reasonable suspicion that contact will lead to the juvenile being informed of circumstances which he should, in the interests of the ongoing investigation, remain oblivious to. Another reason may be that contact between a parent/guardian and the juvenile suspect is presumed to be used to obstruct the truth finding.

2.4.2. Role and task of the trusted person

In the instruction there are no provisions or rules on the role and task of a trusted person in interrogations. Obviously, the rationale behind allowing assistance of a trusted person is that he can be of moral support to the vulnerable juvenile suspect. Thus, his role in the interrogation is most likely 'to be of assistance and support to the juvenile suspect'. In contrast, the instruction does formulate explicitly what the trusted person *cannot* do, namely interrupt the interrogation, make contact with the suspect and disturb the interrogation.[255] If the trusted

250 *Staatscourant* 2010, 4003.
251 *Idem.*
252 Stevens and Verhoeven 2013, p. 81. For more information on the right to interpretation, see *infra* paragraph 2.5 (part II).
253 Stevens and Verhoeven 2013, p. 81.
254 Art. 490 CCP jo. 50 CCP.
255 *Staatscourant* 2010, 4003.

person acts in conflict with these guidelines, he can – like when the lawyer does so – be expelled from the interrogation.[256]

2.4.3. Waiver of the right to be assisted by a trusted person

The instruction does not explicitly state that the juvenile suspect can waive his right to be assisted by a trusted person, but it does however provide the juvenile suspect with a right to waive his (general) 'right to assistance during interrogation'.[257]

2.5. THE RIGHT TO INTERPRETATION AND TRANSLATION

Until recently, the juvenile suspect only had a legal right to interpretation during hearings and interrogations by the investigative judge and during court investigations.[258] The right to interpretation during police interrogation was not laid down in national law but could be derived from European rules.[259] This lack of a legal basis for the right to interpretation during police interrogations resulted in a gap between European requirements set out in ECtHR case law[260] on the application of art. 6 para. 3 sub e ECHR[261] and – ultimately – the Directive on the right to interpretation and translation in criminal proceedings[262] on the one hand and Dutch legislation on the other. The Board of Prosecutors General has tried to bridge this gap by issuing a temporary instruction on access to interpreters and translators during police investigation in 2008.[263] The Dutch legislator has recently adopted formal legislation regulating the right to interpretation and translation.[264] This law has entered into force on 1 October 2013. As a result of this new law, a new art. 27 para. 4 CCP states that: 'a suspect who does not speak Dutch at all or very well is allowed to be assisted by an interpreter'.

According to the newly adopted formal legislation, assistance by an interpreter will be called for when the suspect does not speak Dutch at all or sufficiently

256 *Staatscourant* 2010, 4003.
257 *Staatscourant* 2010, 4003.
258 Art. 191 and 275 CCP.
259 See Prakken and Spronken 2007, p. 166.
260 For example: ECtHR 19 December 1989, *Kamasinski v. Austria*, *NJ* 1994, 26.
261 And also art. 14 para. UN Convention on Civil and Political Rights 1966.
262 EU Directive on the right to interpretation and translation in criminal proceedings, 20 October 2010, 2010/64/EU.
263 *Staatscourant* 2008, 116.
264 *Staatscourant* 2013, 85 (law of 28 February 2013 implementing EU Directive 2010/64/EU by the European Parliament and the Council regarding the right to interpretation and translation in criminal proceedings (PbEUL 280)).

well.[265] It is prescribed that the interrogating officer will contact the interpreter.[266] During the preliminary investigation this can be done verbally, and in other circumstances this is done in writing. It is problematic that the law does not provide formal criteria to assess the suspect's ability to understand and speak Dutch. The law only obliges the interrogating officer to contact an interpreter.

With regard to the right to translation the new law provides for certain documents to be translated as soon as possible (*zo spoedig mogelijk*). The newly added para. 7 to art. 59 CCP reads that the suspect 'will be informed in writing as soon as possible in a language that he understands about the suspected offence'. This obligation is related to the order for police custody (*bevel tot inverzekeringstelling*), which means that there is no formal obligation for the police to provide for translation of documents prior to the first interrogation. However, upon request, the suspect should also be provided with a translation of documents relevant to his defence.[267]

2.6. THE RIGHT TO INFORMATION

In general, a suspect's right to information is twofold and concerns the right to information on rights (including procedural safeguards) as well as the right to information on the content of the case (charges and available evidence). Furthermore, a third part of the right to information may be distinguished which could be of particular importance for juveniles: the right to be informed of the general contents and sequence of proceedings. Starting with the latter: there is no legal obligation for the interrogating authorities to inform juveniles of the features of the (juvenile) criminal process and – more specifically – the role of the interrogation therein. The other two aspects of the right to information will be discussed below.

2.6.1. The right to be informed of rights

With respect to the right to be informed on rights it should be stressed that – as mentioned before – the CCP provides for an explicit legal obligation to inform the (juvenile) suspect of his right to remain silent.[268] The information on the right to remain silent should be repeated before every interrogation. With respect to the right to legal assistance it should be noted that – according to the instruction

265 New para. 4 to art. 23 CCP.
266 New para. 2 to art. 29a CCP.
267 Newly added art. 32a CCP.
268 Art. 29 para. 2 CCP.

on legal assistance during police interrogation – every (juvenile) suspect should be informed of his right to consult a lawyer and of the right to have a lawyer present during interrogation. However, the instruction does not prescribe the way in which this information should be provided.[269] From case law it is clear that police officers are obliged to ensure that the juvenile is informed of his right to legal assistance and that he has a reasonable understanding of the possible consequences of the position he takes in the proceedings. In addition, the police have to make it possible for the juvenile to able to effectuate his right to legal assistance during interrogation.[270] The aforementioned information is – in principle – provided orally. Since 2010 there is also a written folder ('You have been arrested and taken to the police station – which rights do you have?') but at present there is no legal obligation to provide this folder to juvenile suspects.[271]

As from the 1st of January 2015, there is a provision in a new art. 27c CCP which prescribes that before their first interrogation suspects should be informed orally as well as in writing of certain fundamental rights including the right to remain silent, the right to interpretation and translation, the right to have someone informed of his arrest and the right to have access to the case file. With the entry into force of this new provision, the obligation of police officers to inform (juvenile) suspects of their procedural rights will have a much stronger legal basis. Furthermore, the juvenile suspect should – according to the instruction on legal assistance during police interrogation – also be informed of his right to be assisted by a trusted person (*vertrouwenspersoon*) during the interrogation.[272]

2.6.2. *The right to be informed of the case*

Based on art. 30 para. 1 CCP the suspect can request disclosure of the case file during the investigative stage. This request needs to be addressed to the public prosecutor and should be agreed to after the first interrogation after arrest. If the prosecutor fails to do so, the suspect can ask the investigative judge to set a time limit in which the prosecutor should accommodate the previous request.[273] Regardless of whether there has been a request for disclosure, some documents can be withheld from the suspect if the prosecutor deems this is necessary in light of the ongoing investigation.[274]

269 See *supra* paragraph 2.2.8 (part II).
270 Court of Appeal Arnhem 21 April 2010, *LJN* BM1937.
271 The folder is available at www.rijksoverheid.nl.
272 *Staatscourant* 2010, 4003.
273 Art. 30 para. 2 CCP.
274 Art. 30 para. 3 CCP.

Art. 31 CCP formulates categories of documents to which access cannot be restricted, including the written records of a suspect's interrogation.[275] These provisions are not particular to juvenile suspects and are therefore applicable to adults as well.

Furthermore, there is no explicit provision in formal legislation that requires disclosure of documents relevant for the assessment of the lawfulness of the arrest. The Dutch Bar Association has criticised the fact that the moment at which the right to disclosure is enforceable is not linked to a certain procedural moment, such as the determination of the pre-trial status.[276] Regardless of this lack of procedural anchoring, Dutch courts have recognised the importance of this disclosure and found that it cannot be withdrawn from the defence when it is essential.[277] The right to access to procedural documents is a right that is bestowed upon the suspect. The lawyer has a related right according to art. 51 CCP. Even though the lawyer's right is derived from the suspect, on occasion his right may be broader, because the public prosecutor can – as mentioned before – limit the suspect's access to investigative information.[278] This access can be further restricted by limiting a suspect's access to his lawyer, preventing them from discussing the investigation.[279] In that case, a lawyer is not limited in the right of access to the file, but he is not allowed to discuss its contents with the client.[280]

Because disclosure during the investigative stage is in not an unconditional right and the formal legislative regulations are ambiguous, building a defence prior to the first police interrogation is a difficult endeavour. Often, the (juvenile) suspect will have restricted information to share and discuss with his lawyer during the consultation. This practice is criticised in Dutch legal literature and seen as a tool used by the police to prevent the suspect from adjusting his statement in light of the information gathered by the police.[281, 282]

---

275 Art. 31 sub a CCP.

276 See *Preadvies van de Adviescommissie Strafrecht Inzake Herziening regels betreffende de processtukken in strafzaken*, p. 2.

277 District Court Haarlem 24 August 2006, *Nieuwsbrief Strafrecht* 2006, 359; District Court Maastricht 4 May 2006, *Nieuwsbrief Strafrecht* 2006, 319.

278 Art. 30 para. 2 CCP.

279 Art. 50 para. 2 CCP. A suspect does have a right to consult a different lawyer, because the fundamental right to legal assistance cannot be restricted. Furthermore, the limiting of access between a lawyer and his client rarely happens.

280 Franken and Röttgering 2009, p. 283–284.

281 Franken and Röttgering 2009, p. 241.

282 Overcoming this marginal disclosure in practice proves to be difficult. Requests for disclosure should go through the investigative judge. An enforcement measure – after normal procedure of objection – can be to ask the court for a temporary injunction in summary proceedings against the State (*kort geding*). It is problematic that whilst this procedure is pending, the suspect can – and most often will – be interrogated.

2.7. RELEVANT SAFEGUARDS IN OTHER 'INTERROGATIONS'

The safeguards mentioned above, were discussed in light of material (case-related) police interrogations. Although the police interrogation can be considered to be the most important pre-trial interrogation, some different practices surrounding safeguards in other (mostly formal) 'interrogations' deserve to be mentioned here.[283]

2.7.1. The caution in formal interrogations – voorgeleiding and habeas corpus hearing

Officially the (assistant) public prosecutor 'hears' the suspect during the *voorgeleiding* and assesses the lawfulness of arrest and the need for further detention. Because this is a hearing and not an interrogation, there is no formal requirement to caution the suspect. In practice, however, the (assistant) public prosecutor will also ask the suspect about the arrest and the alleged offence and will – therefore – caution the suspect, even in the absence of a formal requirement to do so simply because at this point the suspect can make incriminating statements.[284] If a suspect *spontaneously* confesses, the (assistant) public prosecutor can document this in an official written document (*proces-verbaal*) which can serve as evidence later on in court.[285] What is unclear is whether such statements made by suspects are indeed made voluntarily. Research has shown that in practice some assistant public prosecutors might ask questions that elicit (confessional) statements by suspects.[286]

During the *habeas corpus* hearing a suspect also has the right to remain silent. Even though this hearing does not have an investigative (evidence gathering) goal and therefore does not constitute an interrogation in the strict sense of art. 29 CCP, a broad interpretation should nonetheless be adopted, meaning that the suspect should be cautioned in advance.

2.7.2. Legal assistance during Halt deliberations

It is important to stress that – according to the CCP – the juvenile in principle does not have a right to *ex officio* legal assistance of a lawyer during Halt deliberations. However, as mentioned before, this situation has changed for juveniles below the age of 16 in 2010. With the entrance into force of

283 On the difference between material and formal interrogations, see *supra* paragraph 1.2 (part II).
284 This was also found by Verhoeven and Stevens 2013, p. 172–173.
285 Art. 339 para. 1 sub 5 jo. art. 344 para. 1 sub 2.
286 Blackstock *et al.* 2013, p. 242–243.

the instruction on legal assistance during police interrogations (*aanwijzing rechtsbijstand politieverhoor*) on 1 April 2010, juveniles between the age of 12 and 15 years old who have been arrested cannot waive their right to consult a lawyer before the first interrogation – during which formally the possibility of Halt will have to be discussed and assessed. This means that the juvenile will have to wait for his lawyer to arrive. This might cause problems when a lawyer is not available to come to the station right away – for example when the juvenile was arrested late at night. In practice, it could mean that the juvenile will have to spend more time at the police station than he would have before 1 April 2010. In Dutch literature, this is highlighted as one of the counter effects of strengthening the right to legal assistance of juvenile suspects after *Salduz*.[287]

2.7.3. *Legal assistance during the prosecutorial disposition hearings*

In certain cases of prosecutorial dispositions – for example when the prosecutor wants to impose community service – the juvenile has to be heard by the prosecutor beforehand during which hearing the juvenile has to declare that he is willing to fulfil the obligations of the disposition.[288] At this moment the juvenile will have to be informed of his right to request the appointment of a lawyer. This information should be provided at the latest at the start of the hearing (art. 257c para. 1 CCP). If a prosecutorial disposition will exceed 20 hours of community service or the amount of € 115, a lawyer will be appointed *ex officio* (art. 489 para. 1 a and b CCP).

2.7.4. *Legal assistance during habeas corpus and pre-trial detention hearing*

During the *habeas corpus* hearing the (juvenile) suspect also has a right to be assisted by a lawyer on the basis of art. 59a para. 3 CCP. Similarly, the suspect has a right to be assisted by the investigative judge during the hearing in which the decision on detention on remand is taken (ex-art. 63 para. 4 CCP).

2.7.5. *Safeguards during mediation proceedings*

When a juvenile suspect and his victim(s) enter into mediation proceedings, some (procedural) safeguards apply. Because the mediation procedure is seen as a dialogue between parties in the (criminal) 'conflict' it is preferred that only the parties attend. This preference is connected to the fact that lawyers might have a negative impact on the mediation. Irrespective of this preference, both victim(s) and suspect have a right to legal assistance during the procedure and according to some authors it is even recommendable that the juvenile is assisted by a lawyer

287 Quint 2011.
288 See also *supra* paragraph 2.6 (part I).

during these proceedings.[289] There is no formal basis for this form of legal assistance in Dutch law, but it can be read into a broad interpretation of art. 6 ECHR.[290] Furthermore, juvenile suspects have to be assisted by a trusted person, normally one or both of the parents. Finally the right to remain silent needs to be mentioned. Because mediation is seen as a dialogue and the suspect's willingness to cooperate is checked in advance, the suspect is expected to fully cooperate. This does not mean that the suspect is devoid of the right to remain silent or – even worse – that he has an obligation to speak, but obviously remaining silent can have a detrimental effect on the outcome of mediation.

3. CARRYING OUT THE INTERROGATION

Similar to the lack of provisions in formal and material legislation defining what an interrogation is, there are no formal guidelines, rules or provisions on how to carry out the interrogation with suspects.[291] More specifically, there are (also) no separate rules on interrogating *juvenile* suspects. As discussed before,[292] there is little training on this matter, leaving it mainly up to the interrogating officials to decide which rules to follow when interrogating a juvenile suspect. This is in sharp contrast to the questioning of juvenile witnesses and victims: for the latter two categories, specific rules and training and manuals are available.[293]

3.1. THE USE OF COERCION

The most important procedural norm on how to conduct interrogations is the safeguard against coercion set down in art. 29 CCP. This article prohibits obtaining statements from suspects against their free will. The equivalent to coercion is 'undue pressure', a term which is not defined by (formal or material) law. Whether improper pressure has indeed been applied, is for the court to decide on a case-by-case basis. The threshold for defining the pressure to be 'undue' is rather high in the Netherlands. Incidentally, a court will disapprove of a certain, specific interrogation method. This was the case in the 'famous' case concerning the so-called Zaandam interrogation tactics (*Zaanse*

289 Wolthuis 2012, p. 356.

290 See also Lauwaert 2008, p. 154–156 on the right to legal assistance during mediation and recommendation R(99)19 by the Council of Europe.

291 As mentioned before, only art. 29 CCP is devoted to the suspect interrogation. See also Corstens 2011, p. 264.

292 See *supra* paragraph 1.3 (part II).

293 An example is: Dekens and Van der Sleen 1997. The Dutch police academy pays special attention to questioning juvenile witnesses and victims. See more extensively on this matter *infra* paragraph 7 (part II).

verhoormethode) which were declared inadmissible by the Supreme Court.[294] Furthermore, providing intentionally misleading information such as saying that the victim died as a result of the criminal offence is considered to be improper.[295] Promises, trickery and gifts in exchange for cooperation are also not allowed.[296] On the contrary, emotional pressure that does not exceed certain boundaries[297] is allowed.[298] In addition, confusing, leading, repetitive or high cognitive load-creating questions are allowed under certain circumstances.[299] Building additional pressure by interrogating several times is also not in breach of art. 29 CCP.[300] Using evidence or telling the suspect that cooperation will lead to the end of pre-trial detention are also permissible during interrogations.[301] Finally, telling the suspect that he could go home after confessing, in such a way that detention was not used as a threat, has been found admissible by the Supreme Court.[302] Using improper compulsion or improper interviewing methods during interrogation might result in exclusion of evidence but in practice this rarely happens. One of the few examples of improper interrogation methods resulting in exclusion of evidence is a decision of the Maastricht District Court concerning a case of a 15-year-old suspect who wanted to rely on his right to remain silent but was nevertheless interrogated in an intrusive manner for seven and a half hours without any breaks, during which the attitude of the police had been intimidating (in this case, yelling in the suspect's face and slamming the table with a flat hand).[303]

Also worth mentioning in this respect is a report of the National Ombudsman on a case in which police officers had asked the juvenile suspect questions during interrogation about the content of the consultation with his lawyer. In this report the Ombudsman stressed that interrogating officials are never allowed to ask the suspect any questions on conversations with his lawyer since this may result in some kind of pressure, especially when the suspect is a juvenile.[304]

In addition to the foregoing, it should be noted that there are no norms which define the time during the day at which a suspect can (or should) be interrogated, the number and duration of the interrogation(s) or other conditions for that

---

294 HR 13 May 1997, *NJ* 1998, 152. The Zaandam interrogation tactics consisted of the (threat of) using physical force, exercising strong psychological pressure and the abuse of authority to intimidate. See also Boksem *et al.* 2011.

295 HR 22 September 1998, *NJ* 1999, 104.

296 Jörg 2012, commentary on art. 29 CCP.

297 What these boundaries are exactly is not clear and will be determined by courts on a case-by-case basis.

298 Examples might be: showing the picture of a victim or appealing to moral responsibility.

299 Spronken 2013, commentary to art. 29 CCP.

300 Jörg 2012, commentary on art. 29 CCP.

301 Jörg 2012, commentary on art. 29 CCP.

302 HR 19 April 1988, *NJ* 1989, 15.

303 District Court Maastricht, 27 October 2009, *LJN* AR4661. See also Blom 2010, p. 19.

304 Report of the National Ombudsman, 28 June 2011, 194.11.

matter that regulate the interrogation. Finally it is worth mentioning that the interrogating officials are not legally obliged to read out the charges to the (juvenile) suspect before the interrogation commences.

3.2. NUMBER, DURATION AND STRUCTURE OF INTERROGATIONS

In the Netherlands there is little statistical information available on the amount and duration of interrogations and at which stage during the criminal proceedings they are conducted. However, the legal assistance pilot has led to the availability of some empirical data.[305] Because there are no statutory limits as to how long an interrogation may last – the only limitation might be that courts consider the excessive duration to have caused impermissible pressure – durations of interrogation may vary widely. An important manual on interrogations recommends that, should the interrogation last for a long time, breaks should be taken for rest, food and drink.[306] A study of 168 interrogations in relation to serious offences showed that, on average, the interrogation lasted for 1.43 to 3.59 hours.[307] In comparison, interrogations in less serious cases tend to be much shorter. In the same study, the authors found cases in which suspects were interrogated five times. On average suspects were interrogated three times before being presented to the investigative judge for the first time.[308]

3.3. TIMING OF THE INTERROGATION

There is no pre-ordered and fixed moment within criminal proceedings during which a juvenile suspect should be interrogated. As mentioned before[309] in normal circumstances the juvenile suspect will be transported to the police station for interrogation following an arrest. Should the juvenile then request legal assistance, this will have to be provided for. The Legal Aid Board will be contacted and a (duty) lawyer will be provided to the juvenile suspect. These boards are out of office between the hours of 8pm and 7am. Therefore, an interrogation usually cannot take place during these hours if the juvenile suspect has requested the assistance of a lawyer. If a juvenile suspect waives his right to legal assistance, there is no (formal and material) provision preventing interrogations at night. Additionally, the CCP stipulates that a suspect can be

305 See *inter alia* Stevens and Verhoeven in 2010 and 2013. The project *Inside Police Custody: An Empirical Account of Suspects' Rights in Four Jurisdictions* also provides valuable insights into police interrogations in practice: Blackstock *et al.* 2014, p. 383–373.
306 Amelsvoort *et al.* 2007, p. 226.
307 Stevens and Verhoeven 2010, p. 94.
308 Stevens and Verhoeven 2010, p. 45.
309 See *supra* paragraph 1.1 (part II).

held for questioning for a maximum of six hours; during these six hours it is assumed that a suspect is interrogated for the first time. The time at night, between midnight and 9am can be added to the maximum of six hours, providing for a possible total duration of 15 hours of police detention.[310] Because these night hours are excluded by formal law from the six hours for interrogating, normal practice has evolved accordingly and thus almost no interrogations are conducted by night.

3.4. ASSESSMENT OF FITNESS FOR INTERROGATION

There is no formal legal obligation for interrogating authorities to assess whether an adult or juvenile suspect is 'fit' to be interrogated. When a juvenile is under the age of 12, the decision to interrogate in a special child-friendly interrogation studio (*kindvriendelijke verhoorstudio*) might be taken, but under normal circumstances a child will be deemed fit for interrogation. Nonetheless, as is the case with adult suspects, when a suspect appears to be suffering from a (mental) illness or temporary intoxication (alcohol and/or drugs), the decision can be made to wait or have a doctor check on the suspect and examine him in light of possible interrogation.

3.5. RULES ON POSING QUESTIONS TO JUVENILE SUSPECTS AND STRUCTURE OF INTERROGATIONS

There are no separate rules specifying which type of questions should (not) be posed to juvenile suspects. A widespread and commonly used interrogation method in the Netherlands nowadays is the standard interrogation strategy (*standaard verhoorstrategie – SVS*).[311] This method is described in depth in the aforementioned interrogation manual.[312] In short the SVS is based on the tactical approach to make unwilling suspects cooperate by using soft psychological pressure to reduce the suspect's psychological resistance to telling the truth.[313] It is based on the assumption that the suspect is the actual perpetrator and that by use of a standardised interrogation strategy he can be nudged towards cooperation.[314]

The SVS is divided into three parts: the 'initial contact', the 'person-orientated interrogation' and the 'case-related interrogation'. This structure is similarly

310 Art. 61 CCP. See *supra* paragraph 2.4 (part I).
311 Ponsaers 2001, p. 82.
312 Amelsvoort *et al.* 2007.
313 Amelsvoort *et al.* 2007, p. 243–292.
314 Stevens and Verhoeven warn of the risk of this predisposition: Stevens and Verhoeven 2010, p. 51.

used in cases concerning both juvenile and adult suspects. Therefore, there is no obligation to invest more time into inquiring about the social circumstances, background or living situation of the juvenile suspect. Research shows that, in most cases, the interrogating officers adhere to the SVS.[315] In conclusion it can be said that in the Netherlands there are no formal rules governing the interrogation and furthermore a distinction between juvenile and adult suspects regarding attitude, structure and use of certain types of questions is not made.

3.6. LOCATION OF JUVENILE INTERROGATIONS

Where the interrogation of juvenile suspects should take place is not prescribed by law. Usually the juvenile suspect will be interrogated in an interrogation unit at the police station which is also used for interrogating adult suspects. As mentioned before, in certain cases, the interrogation may take place in a special child-friendly interrogation studio: this mainly concerns juvenile suspects below the age of 12[316] and situations in which the police considers it appropriate to conduct the interrogation in a child-friendly environment (for example because a juvenile between the age of 12–18 is especially vulnerable because of his mental capacities). There are several of these child-friendly studios available in the Netherlands – for example in Eindhoven – which are mainly dedicated to interviewing juvenile witnesses.

3.7. AUDIO AND AUDIO-VISUAL RECORDING OF INTERROGATIONS OF JUVENILE SUSPECTS

In 2010 the instruction on Audio and Audio-visual Recording of Interrogations of Victims, Witnesses and Suspects (hereafter AVR instruction) was adopted by the Board of Prosecutors General.[317] The AVR instruction distinguishes between audio and audio-visual recording of interrogations and also specifies when one or the other is mandatory. Audio registration is mandatory when (a) a victim has died, (b) the crime is punishable by a sentence of 12 years or more, (c) the punishment is less, but there is serious bodily harm, or (d) the crime is a sexual offence punishable by a sentence of eight years or was committed in a dependant relationship. The interrogation needs to be audio-visually recorded when it involves a vulnerable person and it meets the requirements for mandatory

315 Stevens and Verhoeven, 2010. It should be stressed that the study only concerned serious offences and thus the adherence to the SVS might be induced due to the seriousness of the offence.
316 In more severe cases in which audio-visual registration is prescribed, see hereafter.
317 *Staatscourant* 2010, 11885.

audio registration. According to the instruction, juveniles under the age of 16 are considered to be vulnerable persons. Furthermore the instruction also states that juveniles under the age of 12 years, who are vulnerable, should have their interrogations audio-visually recorded. The instruction also requires that this should happen in a so-called child-friendly interrogation room (*kindvriendelijke verhoorstudio*). It remains unclear, because the instruction is rather ambiguous on the matter, whether this interrogation setting should always be used when the juvenile is younger than 12 years or whether this is only the case when the requirement 'severity of the alleged offence' is met.[318] The instruction does not clarify who decides on recording in the mandatory cases, because in these cases it is not optional. However, the public prosecutor may decide to make an audio or audio-visual record of an interrogation if he sees a need.

The recordings of the interrogations are deposited with the authority (*instantie*) who ordered and conducted the interrogation. These recordings will be disposed of when they are no longer required for the purpose of the interrogation. If the investigations have led to a conviction, this is from the moment the verdict has become irrevocable (*onherroepelijk*).[319] Based on the legislative reform on a suspects' right to disclosure (reformed arts. 30–34 CCP) and based on the new art. 27c para. 3 sub d CCP, a suspect has the right to receive a copy of these recordings and he should be informed of this right. This right to a copy of the interrogation is a right the lawyer has as well (art. 51 CCP).

3.8. TRANSCRIPTS OF THE INTERROGATION OF A JUVENILE SUSPECT

Art. 29 para. 3 CCP contains the obligation to use the suspect's own wording in the official records (*proces-verbaal*) of the interrogation. In practice though, it seems that as a rule the wording of the interrogating officer is used.[320] There is no explicit legal provision providing the suspect and his lawyer with the right to check the content of the written record of the interrogation or to make remarks. Even though this is not formally documented, in practice this does happen. The standard forms used during interrogation include a section that states that the suspect and, if present, his representation agrees with the content of the document. In order to come to this conclusion, the suspect and his lawyer will be asked and given the chance to read through the document.[321] Afterwards, the suspect will be asked to sign the written record of interrogation, a formality that

318 *Staatscourant* 2010, 11885.
319 *Staatscourant* 2010, 11885.
320 Spronken 2013, commentary to art. 29 CCP.
321 Brouwer 2009, p. 201–202.

is not always fulfilled, because some suspects will refuse. This does not have an impact on the evidentiary value of the record.

4. OUTPUTS OF THE INTERROGATION

Whether and how pre-trial statements obtained during interrogation of a juvenile suspect may eventually be used will depend on the age of the juvenile. A juvenile under the age of 12 can – as mentioned before – be interrogated by the police but cannot be prosecuted. However, his statements can be used as evidence against co-suspects (above 12) or form the basis of civil law interventions against the juvenile himself. Statements obtained from a juvenile aged between 12 and 18 can be used throughout the entire criminal proceedings, i.e. to base further investigations upon, to establish the need for further (police) detention, and in the trial phase as possible evidence against the suspect. With regard to the evidentiary value of pre-trial statements made by the suspect, a few words on Dutch evidentiary law – which apply to adult as well as juvenile suspects – are appropriate. In this respect it is important to note that the Dutch system is ruled by two basic principles: first of all, the judge may only decide that the offense charged is proven, if he is 'convinced' (*overtuigd*) of it. Secondly, the judge must base this decision on a minimum amount of legal evidence. 'Legal' in this respect means that the CCP prescribes which sources of evidence are admissible. Statements made by the accused concerns one of these sources of evidence (see arts. 339 and 341 CCP).[322] Formally, statements made by the accused as one of the sources of evidence (mentioned in art. 341 CCP) only relate to statements made during trial. This does not mean, however, that pre-trial statements have no evidentiary value: on the contrary. Statements made before trial can be used as evidence but then fall under another category of legal sources: written documents (art. 344 CCP – this category is divided into several subcategories, normally the pre-trial statement of the suspect will be an 'official report (*proces-verbaal*)). Generally, the judge is free to use the statement made by the suspect before trial, for example because it differs from the statement made during trial or because – for any other reason – no statement was made during trial. What is also important to note is the fact the judge is bound by so-called minimum evidence rules. One of these rules is that the suspect cannot be found guilty only on the basis of a statement made by the suspect. At least one other source of evidence is needed. However, as pointed out in Dutch literature, in practice the added value of these minimum rules is limited.[323]

322 Borgers and Stevens 2010, p. 1.

323 Borgers and Stevens 2012, p. 2: 'minimum evidence rules tend to have minimum explanations as well'.

As mentioned before, the Dutch juvenile justice system provides for many different alternatives to regular criminal proceedings. Some of these alternative settlements require the consent of the juvenile and – in some cases – also a formal admittance of guilt. For example, the Halt diversion program can only be followed in case the juvenile admits having committed the crime: the juvenile will have to sign a written contract in this respect. Since official criminal proceedings might follow when the juvenile does not carry out his Halt obligations, the statements made in these early stages of proceedings might become relevant later on. As for procedural safeguards, it should be recalled that the juvenile in principle does not have a right to *ex officio* legal assistance of a lawyer during these Halt deliberations. However, with the entrance into force of the aforementioned Instruction on legal assistance during police interrogation (1 April 2010) this situation has changed for juveniles below the age of 16 who have been arrested: since a juvenile aged between 12 and 15 cannot waive his right to consult a lawyer before the first interrogation – during which formally the possibility of Halt will have to be discussed and assessed – the juvenile will have to wait for his lawyer to arrive.[324]

In the case of a prosecutorial disposition (*strafbeschikking*), statements of the juvenile do not have to be decisive. Formally, the prosecutorial disposition contains the affirmation of guilt but this does not mean that a confession of the juvenile is needed. If the juvenile does not protest the disposition within the legal time limit (*verzet*) it means that he does not object to the affirmation of guilt.

Finally it should be mentioned that in theory the outcome of (formal) police interrogations might influence the occurrence and content of mediation proceedings (as far as admittance of guilt and taking responsibility for actions is concerned). However this does not always have to be the case. In fact, it might even occur that mediation proceedings start without prior (formal) interrogations by the police.

5. REMEDIES AND SANCTIONS

Obviously, effective protection of the juvenile during interrogation requires that he and/or his representative has adequate opportunities to enforce the applicable rules and safeguards. Whether breaching the relevant rules and safeguards has consequences will to a certain extent depend on the status of the rule, i.e. the legal source it is laid down in, and on how specific the rule is. As described in this report, there are not many procedural safeguards connected to interrogating

[324] See on this matter also *supra* paragraph 2.7 (part II).

suspects written down in law in a formal sense (statutory law). Furthermore, most of the applicable rules which do have a basis in the CCP, such as the right to remain silent, concern rules and safeguards which are applicable to adults as well and do not have any youth specific counter parts.

In principle, it is up to the trial judge to decide whether procedural safeguards were violated and – if so – what the consequence of this violation should be. Of course, the juvenile, his parent and/or lawyer may raise this issue at any earlier stage of proceedings – for example already during the interrogation – but whether there indeed has been a breach and (if so) what the consequences of it should be, will mostly be dealt with at trial. The legal framework according to which the trial judge will decide on the consequences of the breaching of procedural rules during pre-trial investigation is laid down in art. 359a CCP. In this provision it is stated that if the breach can no longer be remedied and the legal consequences of the breach are not apparent from statutory law, the court may rule that

(a) the severity of the punishment will be decreased in proportion to the breach, or
(b) the results of the irregular investigations may not be used as evidence, or
(c) in cases of severe violation of procedural rules – the prosecution will be declared inadmissible (*niet ontvankelijkheid Openbaar Ministerie*).[325]

The specific sub-rules and conditions for the several possible 'sanctions' are specified in Dutch case law.[326] Art. 359a CCP concerns the breach of written as well as unwritten rules of any kind such as the right to remain silent, the right to be protected from undue pressure during interrogation and the right to interpretation/translation. Breaches of the ECHR may also be brought up in this context and 'count' as a breach of procedural rights under the heading of art. 359a CCP.[327]

Given the discretionary power the judge has according to art. 359a CCP and the possibility to choose – according to the rules laid down in case law – which sanction is most suitable in an individual case, it is hard to predict beforehand which breach will be followed by which sanction. For example, not informing a suspect of his right to remain silent may lead to exclusion of evidence but according to relevant case law this will depend on whether the suspect's interest or defence was harmed. If this is not the case – for

325 See for a translation into English of the entire provision: Borgers and Stevens 2010, p. 2.
326 Most important in this respect is the judgment of the Supreme Court of 30 March 2004, *NJ* 2004, 376. More recently the Supreme Court has delivered an important judgment on the scope and content of art. 359a CCP in HR 19 February 2013, *LJN* BY5322.
327 Borgers and Stevens 2010, p. 3.

example because the suspect repeated his confession after being informed of his rights – the breach will not have to be remedied.[328] To give another example, using improper compulsion or improper interviewing methods during interrogation might result in exclusion of evidence, but this hardly ever happens.[329] Generally, it can be said that the most severe sanction of barring the prosecution service from prosecuting (*niet ontvankelijkheid*), will only be chosen in the most extreme cases of 'serious breaches of principles of due process, through which the suspect's right to a fair trial has been harmed purposefully or with severe negligence'.[330] According to Blom, barring the prosecution service for irregularities in conducting the interrogation happened only once in the years 1995–2010. This case concerned a suspect with limited mental capacity.[331]

Finally, it should be noted that there are certain categories of breaches in which the aforementioned judicial 'freedom' to decide which sanction is most suitable is limited. An important example concerns violations of Salduz rules. According to the Dutch Supreme Court, following the ECtHR case law in this respect, not offering a suspect the opportunity to consult a lawyer before his interrogation and (in the case of a juvenile) not allowing him to have a lawyer present during the interrogation will have to result in exclusion of the evidence which was obtained before a lawyer was consulted (or in the absence of a lawyer) as well as any evidence obtained as a direct result of it.[332]

Besides complaining about the breach of procedural safeguards within the context of criminal proceedings, it is of course also possible to file an official complaint with the police. If this complaint is not dealt with to the satisfaction of the complainant, the complaint can be directed to the National Ombudsman. As mentioned before, since 2011, there is an Ombudsman specialised in juvenile matters: the Children's Ombudsman. Occasionally, the Ombudsmen also decide in matters concerning police conduct.[333] As a result of such a complaint, the

---

328 Borgers and Stevens 2010, p. 12. See also HR 16 April 2013, *NJ* 2013, 310 where the Supreme Court stresses that 'as a rule' not informing a suspect of the right to remain silent (in this case a juvenile) should result in the exclusion of evidence 'unless' the court decides that the suspect was not harmed in his defence. This makes clear that the discretionary power of the judge in deciding which sanction of art. 359a CCP is most suitable is very limited in cases concerning a breach of the right to remain silent.

329 See *supra* paragraph 3 (part II).

330 These criteria have been developed by the Supreme Court in 1995 (so-called *Zwolsman* case, HR 19 December 1995, *NJ* 1996, 249) and have been applied in Dutch case law ever since.

331 Court of Appeal Amsterdam, 29 April 2005, *LJN* AT5549. See also Blom 2010, p. 19–20.

332 Supreme Court 30 June 2009, *NJ* 2009, 349.

333 See for an example the report of the Children's Ombudsman on the position of juveniles in police detention with special attention for their possibilities to speak to parents mentioned *supra* paragraph 2.3 (part I).

(Children's) Ombudsman might contact the relevant authorities immediately or write a report on the complaint with recommendations on how similar situations should be dealt with in the future.

6. DISSEMINATION OF RESULTS OF INTERROGATION AND PROTECTION OF PRIVACY

Generally, in line with the international human rights standards as laid down in – for example – art. 16 and 40 para. 2 under bVII of the CRC, rules on protecting the privacy of juvenile suspects are even stricter than in the case of adults. Illustrative in this respect is the rule that juvenile trials should – in principle – be held behind closed doors.[334] According to the aforementioned rules of the CRC the juvenile's privacy should be protected at all stages of criminal proceedings, including pre-trial investigation. There are, however, no youth-specific rules in statutory law on the dissemination of the results (such as official transcripts) of the interrogation.

As a rule, transcripts of the juvenile's interrogations form part of the case file (*processtukken*) and during pre-trial proceedings it is up to the public prosecutor to decide who may have access to such documents.[335] Access can be given to the suspect and his defence lawyer, and under certain conditions also to the victim.[336] During pre-trial proceedings the defence may be denied access to certain documents; however, they should always have unlimited access to (*inter alia*) transcripts of the suspect's interrogations.[337] According to rules of professional ethics, defence lawyers are not allowed to hand copies of (parts of the) case file over to the media.[338] This rule applies to adult as well as juvenile cases.

Although it does not directly concern the content of the interrogation, it should be noted that in Dutch legal literature there is criticism on the stigmatising and labelling effect of a certain mechanism in the juvenile process – more specifically, the growing tendency to register juveniles who show signs of problematic behaviour and to share information between the different actors in the juvenile justice system (police, prosecution service, Child Welfare Council, *et cetera*) causes concern with respect to the protection of privacy.[339]

---

334 See *supra* paragraph 2.4 (part I).

335 In art. 30–34 CCP. The suspect and his lawyer have unlimited access to transcripts of the suspect's interrogations.

336 Art. 51b CCP. The victim may have access to those files which could be 'of relevance' to him.

337 See on disclosure of the case file also *supra* paragraph 2.6.2 (part II).

338 Rule 10 para. 2 of the Rules of Conduct of Advocates 1992.

339 See on this matter De Jong-Kruijf and Bruning 2010.

7. RULES FOR HEARING JUVENILES AS WITNESSES AND VICTIMS

Some general rules for hearing witnesses can be found in the CCP. In a nutshell, these rules concern the fact that the witness is obliged to appear in court (when summoned by a trial judge or an investigating judge – witnesses are not obliged to make a statement to the police), that he has the obligation to answer questions unless he can revoke the right to testimonial privilege, and that he has to swear an oath or take a vow before being heard by a (investigative) judge. However, since juvenile witnesses are – as a rule – heard in the pre-trial stage by the police and not at trial, these provisions of the CCP have only limited meaning for hearing juveniles as witnesses. The CCP contains hardly any provisions on this specific subject matter. One of the few statutory rules dedicated to hearing child witnesses can be found in art. 216 para. 2 CCP in which it is stated that a juvenile witness below the age of 16 who is being heard by a (investigative) judge does not have to take an oath but will be encouraged to tell the truth. As a result, juveniles under the age of 16 cannot be held liable for perjury. There is no legal provision in statutory law on the right of (juvenile) witnesses to have a lawyer (or appropriate adult) present during interrogation. Nor is it explicitly mentioned in the CCP that the right which applies to suspects not to be compelled to make statements (*pressieverbod*) is applicable to witnesses as well.

As mentioned before, as a rule, a juvenile witness will not be heard at trial but at the pre-trial stage by a police officer (in some cases by interrogators especially trained for interviewing juvenile witnesses – see below) or by the investigative judge. Rules and safeguards covering these hearings can be found in several instructions – such as the instruction on the investigation and prosecution of sexual abuse[340] and the instruction on audio and audio-visual recording of interrogations of persons making declarations, witnesses and suspects[341] These instructions contain quite detailed rules on how the juvenile should be treated before and during the interrogation as a witness. Before mentioning these rules, it should be noted that not all juveniles will be heard as a witness in special child-friendly interrogation studios. In cases in which audio-visual recording is prescribed by the instruction on audio and audio-visual recording of interrogations of persons making declarations, witnesses and suspects, hearing the witness in a child-friendly studio is obligatory. In other cases, the public prosecutor may decide that it is necessary. In practice, mostly juveniles between ages 4–13 are heard in a studio: juveniles above the age of 12 will – as a rule – be heard by regular police officials unless interrogation in a special child-

340 Aanwijzing opsporing en vervolging inzake seksueel misbruik, *Staatscourant* 2010, 19123.

341 Aanwijzing auditief en audiovisueel registreren van verhoren van aangevers, getuigen en verdachten, *Staatscourant* 2010, 11885.

friendly studio is deemed necessary because of the particular vulnerability of the juvenile. Children below the age of 4 can only be heard by behavioural experts (such as psychologists).[342]

In the case of a studio interrogation, certain extra rules and safeguards apply: parents need to give their permission (unless recording the interview is mandatory) and the juvenile as well as his parents should be thoroughly prepared for the interrogation. Parents should be instructed to inform their child of what he can expect. The information provided to the child beforehand contains – *inter alia* – the status of the person who is going to hear him, the fact that the conversation will be video-taped and what will happen with this tape, on what subject the interrogator would like to focus, that the child is free to say anything he wants and that is not a test.[343] If the parents are unfit to inform their child, the police officer will do this himself. There are also leaflets with information on the interrogation studio. Parents cannot be present during the interrogation but will be informed of the course of the interrogation during and after.[344] Interrogations conducted in child-friendly studios are conducted by officials/detectives who have had special training (so-called 'studio interrogators' who make up a small, specialist group of experienced interrogating officials).[345] Usually, the studio interrogator will not be involved in the investigation in the case in which the juvenile is interrogated: his only task is to interrogate the juvenile. He will be informed by the police officer handling the case of the level of development of the juvenile (his ability to communicate, *et cetera*) and other information relevant for the interrogation.[346] Interrogations conducted in a studio will be recorded and kept in a safe.

According to the Instruction on the investigation and prosecution of sexual abuse, there are special requirements for the training/education of officials who hear juveniles aged between 12–18 years old as witnesses in sexual crime cases.

In summary, it is clear that – although formal statutory law does not provide for many youth-specific safeguards – there is specific regulation dealing with the specific needs of juvenile witnesses. In particular, juveniles below 12 are – at least in theory – offered quite extensive protection when they are interrogated in

---

342 In cases in which audio-visual registration is prescribed by the Instruction on audio and audio-visual registration of interrogations of persons making declarations, witnesses and suspects hearing the witness in a child-friendly studio is required. In other cases, the public prosecutor may decide that it is necessary.

343 Maijenburg 2006, p. 20.

344 Maijenburg 2006, p. 20.

345 They should have followed the course 'Hearing Young and Mentally Impaired Witnesses' (*Horen Jonge en Verstandelijk Beperkte Getuigen – HJG*) – a course which is only available for certain certified police officers.

346 Maijenburg 2006, p. 19.

a special child-friendly studio. The rules on how to prepare the juvenile for the interrogation and how to assess the capability of the juvenile to make a statement and the necessity of the interrogation seem to provide important safeguards. It is also clear that specialisation and education of the interrogating officials are better provided for than in the case of the interrogation of juveniles as suspects.

III. CONCLUSIONS

Over the last few decades the emphasis of the Dutch juvenile criminal justice system has shifted from a predominantly welfare-oriented approach to a more justice-oriented model with a greater emphasis on the juvenile's individual criminal responsibility. In a nutshell, present day Dutch juvenile criminal proceedings may be characterised as punitive but with a pedagogical approach and a strong focus on protection and (re)education. The principle of subsidiarity is key, meaning that following regular court proceedings should be the exception to the rule and in relation to this many different possibilities of diversion and out-of-court settlement are provided for.

The legal framework of juvenile criminal justice in the Netherlands is fragmented. Relevant provisions of substantive and procedural criminal law are to be found in several different legal sources such as the criminal codes (statutory law) and secondary legislation (such as instructions of the public prosecutions office). Although the system is formally separated from civil law, in practice both fields of law are very much intertwined when it comes to dealing with juveniles.

With regard to the pre-trial stage of criminal proceedings it is striking to see that juvenile suspects are mostly treated in the same way as their adult counterparts. For example, the rules for arrest and following (police and pre-trial) detention are governed by the same rules as those applicable to adults. The most important (case-related) interrogations are carried out by the police in virtually the same way as interrogations of an adult suspect. Although several types of training and education are available to the police, there is no formal guarantee that the interrogation of a juvenile suspect is carried out by a police officer who has received any kind of specific training in this respect. Certain social welfare organisations such as the Child Welfare Council (*Raad voor de Kinderbescherming*) are involved in pre-trial criminal proceedings dealing with juvenile suspects but they are not involved in the actual interrogation.

With respect to the procedural protection of the juvenile suspect during interrogation, it can be concluded that the position of the juvenile suspect resembles the position of the adult suspect in many ways. The main applicable procedural safeguards – the right to legal assistance, the right to remain silent, the right to interpretation and translation and the right to be informed (of rights as well as of the case) – have to a large extent the same scope and content as the safeguards applicable to adult suspects. The safeguard of involvement of an appropriate adult – one of the few youth-specific procedural safeguards to be found in other EU Member States – is only of relative importance in the Dutch system. Currently, the juvenile suspect does have a right to request the presence of a so-called 'trusted person' during interrogation but invoking this right implies that a lawyer cannot be present. Only with regard to the right to legal assistance can some meaningful youth-specific derogations, which are directly influenced by the Salduz doctrine, be found. These mainly concern the fact that the right to legal assistance in the phase of police interrogation in some instances cannot be waived and that the right to the assistance of a lawyer also includes the right to have a lawyer present during interrogation. Further changes of these regulations are expected in the near future, with changes to the CCP pending. These developments in the context of the right to legal assistance should definitely be considered as an improvement of the legal protection of juvenile suspects during interrogation. The same is true for the expected legal changes of the right to information (broadening the legal obligation to inform suspects on several important procedural rights upon arrest). Nevertheless, what still seems to be missing is a (legal) answer to the question *how* juveniles should be informed of their rights. There are – for example – no rules on the wording to be used in the case of a juvenile suspect and whether (and how) interrogating officials are obliged to make sure that the juvenile has understood the content and scope of the rights of which he is informed. In addition to this, there are virtually no rules on how the interrogation of a juvenile suspect should be conducted. For example, there are no rules or guidelines on the number or duration of interrogations, on how to pose questions to juveniles or on the assessment of the juveniles' capability to be interrogated. To a certain extent, this seems to be in contrast with the – more youth-specific – protection offered to juvenile witnesses during interrogation.

In conclusion, it is fair to say that the youth-specific character of the Dutch juvenile justice system seems to be much more emphasised in matters of substantive law (such as sanctions) and during the trial stage than in the early – but important – phases of police interrogations. As mentioned above, the lack of clear youth-specific rules not only concerns the applicable procedural safeguards but also concerns the regulation of how to carry out the interrogation. In both fields, there is still ample room for improvement.

BIBLIOGRAPHY

Amelsvoort *et al.* 2007
A. Amelsvoort and I. Rispens, *Handleiding verhoor*, Den Haag: Reed Business, 2007

Bartels 2011
J.A.C. Bartels, *Jeugdstrafrecht*, Deventer: Wolters Kluwer Business, 2011

Berger and Van der Kroon 2011
M. Berger and C. van der Kroon, *'Een 'paar nachtjes' in de cel'. Het VN-Kinderrechten verdrag en het voorarrest van minderjarigen in politiecellen (Spending a Couple of Nights in a Police Cell. The UN Convention on the Rights of the Child and custody in police cells)*, a study conducted by Defence for Children, Leiden, 2011

Blackstock *et al.* 2014
J. Blackstock, E. Cape, J Hodgson, A. Ogorodova and T. Spronken, *Inside Police Custody: An Empirical Account of Suspects' Rights in Four Jurisdictions*, Cambridge (etc.): Intersentia, 2014

Blom 2010
T. Blom, *Vormen verzuimd tijdens het politieverhoor*, inaugural address University of Amsterdam delivered at 13 October 2010, Amsterdam: Vossiuspers, 2010

Bockstaele 2008
M. Bockstaele, *Handboek verhoren 1*, Antwerpen-Apeldoorn: Maklu, 2008

Boksem *et al.* 2011
J. Boksem et al, *Strafprocesrecht*, Den Haag: Boom Juridische Uitgevers, 2011

Borgers and Stevens 2010
M.J. Borgers and L. Stevens, The Use of Illegally Gathered Evidence in the Dutch Criminal Trial, *Electronic Journal of Comparative Law* 2010–3, vol. 14, available at: www.ejcl.org

Brouwer 2009
D.V.A. Brouwer, De verklaringen van de verdachte en getuigen in het proces-verbaal van de terechtzitting, *Delikt en Delinkwent*, 2009, 3/16, p. 201–202

Cipriani 2009
D. Cipriani, *Children's Rights and the Minimum Age of Criminal Responsibility – a Global Perspective*, Surrey – Burrington: Ashgate, 2009

Corstens 2011
G.J.M. Corstens, M.J. Borgers, *het Nederlandse strafprocesrecht*, Kluwer Deventer, 2011

De Bruijn 2011
M. de Bruijn, Rechter commissaris, kinderrechter en meervoudige kamer, in: I. Weijers and F. Imkampt, *Jeugdstrafrecht – In internationaal perspectief*, Den Haag: Boom Juridische Uitgevers, 2011, p. 201–220

De Jonge and Van der Linden 2013
G. de Jonge and A.P. van der Linden, *Jeugd en Strafrecht*, Deventer: Kluwer, 2013

De Jong-Kruijf and Bruning 2010
M. de Jong-Kruijf and M. Bruning, Mark of Cain op het voorhoofd van de jeugdige verdachte? Over stigmatisering en privacy in het jeugdstrafrecht, *Proces,* 2010–4, p. 223–237

De Vocht 2012
D.L.F de Vocht, Europese procedurele waarborgen voor de jeugdige verdachte: over kwetsbaarheden en te nemen hindernissen, in: J. Claessen and D. de Vocht (eds.), *Humaan strafwerk. Liber Amicorum Gerard de Jonge,* Nijmegen: Wolf Legal Publishers, 2012

Dekens and Van der Sleen 1997
K.M.K. Dekens and J. van der Sleen, *Handleiding het kind al getuige, Theorie en praktijk van het verhoor,* Den Haag: VUGA Uitgeverij, 1997

Franken and Röttgering 2009
S. Franken and A. Röttgering, De raadsman in het vooronderzoek, in: T. Prakken and T. Spronken (eds.) *Handboek verdediging,* Deventer: Kluwer, 2009, p. 201–296

Hartjen 2008
C.A. Hartjen, Youth, Crime and Justice: A Global Inquiry, New Brunswick, N.J.: Rutgers University Press, 2008

Ingelse 2008
H.C. Ingelse, DNA-afname bij veroordeelde minderjarigen: moet dat zomaar mogen?, *Tijdschrift voor Familie en Jeugdrecht,* 2008, 88, p. 208–2014

Jörg 2012
N. Jörg, Commentary to art. 29 CCP., in: A.L. Melai & M.S. Groenhuijsen et al. (eds.), *Het Wetboek van Strafvordering* (supl. 162). Deventer: Kluwer, 2012

Lauwaert 2008
K. Lauwaert, *Herstelrecht en procedurele waarborgen,* Antwerpen: Maklu, 2008

Maijenburg 2006
T. Maijenburg, Verhoren van jonge getuigen door de politie. Zorgvuldigheid is het sleutelwoord, Tijdschrift voor de Rechten van het Kind, *Tijdschrift voor de Rechten van het Kind,* 2006–2, p. 18–20

Moerman 2010
D. Moerman, DNA-afname bij jeugdigen: noodzakelijk in een democratische samenleving? *Proces,* 2010, 3, p. 165–176

Muncie 2008
J. Muncie, The 'punitive' turn in juvenile justice: Cultures of control and rights compliance in western Europe and the USA, *Youth Justice,* 2008–2, p. 107–121

Prakken and Spronken 2007
T. Prakken and T. Spronken, The Investigative Stage of the Criminal Process in the Netherlands, in: E. Cape, J. Hodgson, T. Prakken and T. Spronken, *Suspects in Europe. Procedural Rights at the Investigative Stage of the Criminal Process in the European Union,* Oxford: Intersentia, 2007, p. 155–179

Prakken and Spronken 2009
T. Prakken and T. Spronken (red.), *Handboek verdediging*, Deventer: Kluwer, 2009

Pruin 2011
I. Pruin, The scope of juvenile justice systems in Europe, in: F. Dünkel, J. Grzywa, P. Horsfield and I. Pruin, *Juvenile Justice Systems in Europe – Current Situation and Reform Developments*, Vol 2 (2nd revised edition), Mönchengladbach: Forum Verlag Godesberg, 2011, p. 1539–1582

Quint 2011
R. Quint, Salduz-rechtspraak risico voor Halt-jongeren, *Nederlands Juristen Blad*, 2011/569, p. 677–678

Rap and Weijers 2011
S. Rap and I. Weijers, *De jeugdstrafzitting een pedagogisch perspectief – De communicatie tussen jeugdrechter en jeugdige verdachte*, Raad voor de Rechtspraak, Research Memoranda, 2011, 2

Remmelink 1996
J. Remmelink, *Het verhoor in strafzaken*, RM Themis, 1966

Spronken *et al.* 2009
T. Spronken, G. Vermeulen, D.L.F. de Vocht and L. van Puyenbroek, *EU Procedural Rights in Criminal Proceedings*, Antwerpen: Maklu, 2009

Spronken 2013
T.N.B.M. Spronken, Commentary to art. 29 CCP, in: C. Cleiren, J.H. Crijns and M.J.M. Verpalen, *Strafvordering, Tekst & Commentaar*, Deventer: Kluwer, 2013

Stevens and Verhoeven 2013
W.J. Verhoeven and L. Stevens, *Rechtsbijstand bij politieverhoor. Evaluatie van de Aanwijzing rechtsbijstand politieverhoor in Amsterdam-Amstelland, Groningen, Haaglanden, Limburg-Zuid, Midden- en West-Brabant en Utrecht*, Den Haag: Boom Lemma Uitgevers, 2013

Stevens and Verhoeven 2010
W.J. Verhoeven and L. Stevens, *Raadsman bij politieverhoor. Invloed van voorafgaande consultatie en aanwezigheid van raadslieden op de organisatie en wijze van verhoren en de proceshouding van verdachten*, WODC, 2010

Tak 2008
P.J.P. Tak, *The Dutch Criminal Justice System*, Nijmegen: Wolf Legal Publishers, 2008

Uit Beijerse 2009
J. uit Beijerse, De nieuwe regeling van de schorsing van de voorlopige hechtenis bij jeugdigen in het licht van de onschuldpresumptie, *Proces*, 2009, 88, p. 314–325

Uit Beijerse and Dubbelman 2011
J. uit Beijerse and L. Dubbelman, De politie en het Openbaar Ministerie in jeugdstrafzaken, in: I. Weijers, De leeftijdsgrenzen, in: I. Weijers, en F. Imkampt, *Jeugdstrafrecht – In internationaal perspectief*, Den Haag: Boom Juridische Uitgevers 2011, p. 169–186

Van den Brink 2012
Y.N. van den Brink, De onschuld voorbij? Over de toepassing van voorlopige hechtenis ten aanzien van minderjarige verdachten in Nederland, *Tijdschrift voor Familie- en Jeugdrecht*, 2012, 1, p. 5–11

Van den Brink 2013
Y.N. van den Brink, Geschorst onder voorwaarden. Meningen van jeugdige verdachten, ouders en jeugdreclasseerders, *Delikt en Delinkwent*, 2013, 26, p. 270–290

Van Kalmthout and Bahtiyar 2011
A. van Kalmthout and Z. Bahtiyar, The Netherlands, in: F. Dünkel, J. Grzywa, P. Horsfield and I. Pruin, *Juvenile Justice Systems in Europe – Current Situation and Reform Developments*, Vol 2 (2nd revised edition), Mönchengladbach: Forum Verlag Godesberg, 2011, p. 911–956

Verberk and Fuhler 2006
S. Verberk and K. Fuhler, *De positionering van de jeugdrechter*, Den Haag: Raad voor de Rechtspraak, 2006

Vlaardingenbroek 2011
P. Vlaardingenbroek, De samenhang tussen het jeugdstrafrecht en het civiele jeugdrecht, in: I. Wijers and F. Imkamp, *Jeugdstrafrecht in internationaal perspectief*, Den Haag: Boom Juridische Uitgevers, 2011, p. 53–71

Weijers 2011
I. Weijers, De leeftijdsgrenzen, in: I. Weijers and F. Imkamp, *Jeugdstrafrecht – In internationaal perspectief*, Den Haag: Boom Juridische Uitgevers, 2011, p. 153–168

Weijers and Imkamp 2011
I. Weijers and F. Imkamp, *Jeugdstrafrecht – In internationaal perspectief*, Den Haag: Boom Juridische Uitgevers, 2011

Winterdijk 2002
J. Winterdijk (ed.), *Juvenile Justice Systems: International Perspectives*, 2nd edition, Toronto: Canadian Scholars Press

WODC 2010.
WODC, *Criminaliteit en rechtshandhaving 2009*, 2010

Wolthuis 2012
A. Wolthuis, *Herstelrecht, een kinderrecht. Voorstellen voor integratie van herstel in het hart van het jeugdstrafrecht*, Den Haag: Boom Lemma Uitgevers, 2012

CHAPTER 6

PROCEDURAL COMPLEXITY WITHIN A WELFARE APPROACH

Country Report Poland

Barbara Stańdo-Kawecka and Justyna Kusztal

I. THE POLISH JUVENILE JUSTICE SYSTEM: GENERAL OVERVIEW

1. BACKGROUND

1.1. MAIN SOURCES OF POLISH CRIMINAL AND JUVENILE LAW

In 1989, Poland experienced a radical change to its political, social and economic system. With the collapse of the communist system in that year, the Republic of Poland re-emerged as an independent and democratic state bound by the rule of law. Poland has been a member of the United Nations since 1945 and it has been a party to the UN International Covenant on Civil and Political Rights since 1977. The United Nations Convention against torture and other cruel, inhuman or degrading treatment or punishment was ratified by Poland in 1989, and in 2005 Poland also ratified the Optional Protocol to this Convention. Since 1991 Poland has also been a member of the Council of Europe. In the same year it ratified the Convention on the Rights of the Child (hereafter: CRC), two years later the European Convention on Human Rights (hereafter: ECHR), and in 1994 the European Convention for the Prevention of Torture. In May 2004, it entered the European Union.

As in many other post-communists countries, significant reforms to the criminal justice system were carried out in Poland during the 1990s. After the totalitarian state had collapsed in 1989, there was a broad political consensus on the need for liberalisation and rationalisation of criminal policy. As a result, in the early and mid-1990s many changes were introduced to the Codes of 1969: the Criminal Code (hereafter: CC), the Code of Criminal Procedure (hereafter: CCP) and the Code of Execution of Sentences. These changes were aimed at adjusting Poland's criminal law to international standards and making it more humane, liberal and rational.[1]

On 2 April 1997 the new Constitution of the Republic of Poland was enacted.[2] Under this Constitution, the sources of Polish law are divided into two categories: universally binding law and locally binding law. According to art. 87 of the Constitution, the universally binding sources are, leaving aside the Constitution, statutes enacted by parliament (*ustawa*), ratified international agreements (*ratyfikowane umowy międzynarodowe*) and regulations (*rozporządzenia*) issued only by those organs that are expressly mentioned in the Constitution. The latter have to be issued on the basis of specific authorisation laid down in a statute and with the purpose of implementing that statute.

After publication in the official legal bulletin (*Dziennik Ustaw*), ratified international agreements become a part of the domestic legal system and may be applied directly, providing that they contain self-executing norms. Ratification is within the competence of the President of the Republic of Poland. However, some international agreements are ratified by the President only if Parliament has passed a statute giving its consent to the ratification.[3] Only an international agreement ratified with the prior consent of Parliament can take precedence over a statute if the latter is incompatible with the agreement. Legislation passed by an international organisation is also applied directly and takes precedence in the event of a conflict with statutes where this is provided for in the agreement setting up that organisation and which is ratified by Poland (art. 91 of the Constitution).

The Constitution prohibits torture as well as cruel, inhuman and degrading treatment or punishment and corporal punishment (art. 40). Art. 41 of the Constitution obliges the legislator to ensure that every form of deprivation or restriction of liberty shall have a clear legal basis, and ensures court examination of the legality of deprivation of liberty. Additionally, section 3 of this provision contains the right of an arrested person to be informed without delay of the reasons for his arrest as well as the guarantee that deciding on detention on remand is the exclusive domain of the court. Art. 45 of the Constitution ensures

---

1 Stańdo-Kawecka and Krajewski 2010, p. 700–701.

2 *Konstytucja Rzeczypospolitej Polskiej*, 2 April 1997, Official Legal Bulletin 78, pos. 483 with later amendments.

3 Among such international agreements requiring prior consent expressed in a statute enacted by parliament are those concerning fundamental issues, for example peace, political or military arrangements, citizens' freedoms, rights and responsibilities or membership of international organisations.

the right to fair and open adjudication without undue delay by an appropriate, independent and impartial court. Art. 42 establishes several other constitutional safeguards, such as the principles of non-retroactivity of the criminal law and the presumption of innocence.[4] Section 2 of the same provision ensures the right to defence by stating: 'All persons against whom criminal proceedings have been conducted have the right to defence at every stage of proceedings. They may in particular choose a defence lawyer, or, on principles defined by statute, avail themselves of an *ex officio* lawyer'.

In the Constitution, there are no specific rules on the protection of juveniles. The term 'juvenile' (*nieletni*) is used in both criminal and juvenile law. Within the context of criminal law it refers to a person who has violated the criminal law while below the age of criminal majority set at the age of 17. In juvenile law a 'juvenile' is not only a juvenile offender but also a person below the age of 18 who displays problematic behaviour other than acting in conflict with criminal law. Some provisions concerning the protection of the rights of the child are included in the Constitution. According to the Family and Guardianship Code, a child (*dziecko*) remains under parental responsibility until the age of civil majority (*aż do pełnoletności*).[5] The age of civil majority in Poland is set at 18.[6]

According to art. 72 of the Constitution, Poland shall ensure the protection of the rights of the child. Everyone shall have the right to demand that public authorities defend children against violence, cruelty, exploitation and actions which undermine their moral sense (*demoralizacja*). The same article (section 2) states that a child deprived of parental care shall have the right to care and assistance provided by public authorities. Public authorities and persons responsible for children, in the course of establishing the rights of a child (*w toku ustalania praw dziecka*), shall consider and, as far as possible, give priority to the views of the child (section 3). Art. 72 section 4 of the Constitution provides the legal basis for the establishment of an Ombudsman for Children. The Ombudsman for Children was appointed for the first time in 2000.[7] His main tasks include safeguarding the rights of the child as defined in the Constitution, the CRC and other provisions of law, while respecting the responsibilities, rights and duties of parents.

4 Mozgawa and Szumski 2000, p. 87–88.

5 See art. 92 of the 1964 Family and Guardianship Code (*Ustawa – Kodeks rodzinny i opiekuńczy*), 25 February 1964, Official Legal Bulletin 9, pos. 59 with later amendments.

6 Exceptions refer to women who marry with the consent of the guardianship court while being at least 16 years of age: they are treated as adults under civil law. See art. 10 of the 1964 Civil Code (*Ustawa – Kodeks cywilny*), 23 April 1964, Official Legal Bulletin 16, pos. 93 with later amendments.

7 The 2000 Act on the Ombudsman for Children is available in English: www.brpd.gov.pl/uploadfiles/ustawa_o_rpd_en.pdf.

The main (binding) sources of criminal law are to be found in statutory law. The 1997 Criminal Code, Code of Criminal Procedure and Code of Execution of Sentences came into force on 1 September in 1998. In comparison with the previous codes of 1969, they introduced a number of changes stemming from Poland's international commitments. However, those changes have had little impact on Polish juvenile law, which differs significantly from adult criminal law and is regulated in a separate statute: the Juvenile Act (*Ustawa o postępowaniu w sprawach nieletnich*) of 1982.[8] Amendments introduced to the Juvenile Act (hereafter: JA) after 1989 have not changed its fundamental assumptions arising from the welfare approach to juveniles.

1.2. HISTORICAL DEVELOPMENT OF JUVENILE LAW

At the very beginning of the twentieth century, when the movement towards separation of the juvenile justice system from the adult justice system emerged in the United States, Canada, and part of Europe, Poland was not an independent country. In 1919, one year after having regained independence, a legislative commission was set up in Poland in order to prepare drafts of both criminal and civil laws. Issues concerning the juvenile justice system were heavily disputed in a subdivision of the legislative commission for the reform of criminal law. As a rule, members of the commission shared the opinion that children who had violated criminal law should not be treated as 'little adults' and they should not be subjected to the same penalties as adult offenders. The greatest matter of controversy, however, concerned the criminal responsibility of juveniles. Some members of the commission suggested that penalties containing elements of retribution and repression should be totally excluded from the catalogue of reactions towards juvenile offenders and replaced with educational or correctional measures. Other members of the commission preferred a system under which penalties could be imposed on juvenile offenders acting with discernment (*rozeznanie*), namely with the ability to understand the meaning of the act and direct their behaviour.[9]

The different assumptions concerning the juvenile justice system emerging from the legislative commission were discussed with French, Austrian and Swiss academics. After these international consultations a draft act on juvenile courts was prepared by the legislative commission in 1921. It contained a sort of compromise between supporters of radical orientation, who insisted on applying only educational and correctional measures to juveniles, and the more moderate

8 Juvenile Act (*Ustawa o postępowaniu w sprawach nieletnich*), 26 October 1982, Official Legal Bulletin, 35, pos. 228 with later amendments.

9 See also Stańdo-Kawecka 2010, p. 991–992.

scholars, who did not want to abandon all elements of criminal responsibility for juvenile offenders.[10] For financial reasons the 1921 draft of the separate act on juvenile courts was not enacted. Most of its provisions were eventually included in the 1928 Code of Criminal Procedure as well as in the 1932 Criminal Code.

1.2.1. The approach to juvenile offenders in the codes of 1928 and 1932

The Code of Criminal Procedure of 1928 introduced separate juvenile courts[11] as well as separate proceedings in juvenile cases. The most important feature of proceedings in juvenile cases was the dominant role of the juvenile judge. Under this Code, during the preparatory stage of proceedings in juvenile cases, the juvenile judge served as an investigating judge who subsequently took part as a trial judge in the final stage of proceedings. The procedure did not provide for separation of functions of investigation and adjudication. During the preparatory proceedings the juvenile judge might order a probation officer, a member of the patronage of juveniles, the police or a private trustworthy person to conduct particular investigative actions (*wykonanie poszczególnych czynności dochodzeniowych*). The juvenile judge who conducted the interrogation of the juvenile suspect, as well as of witnesses, in the preparatory proceedings was authorised to make formal written records (*protokoły*) which constituted evidence and could be read or disclosed at the main hearing (*na rozprawie*). Hearings were closed to the public, and features of adversarial trial were strongly limited, as were the powers of the prosecution service.[12]

The 1932 Criminal Code contained a separate chapter with provisions on substantive law concerning juveniles. The age of criminal majority according to the Code was 17. According to the Code a 'juvenile' was a person who committed an act prohibited by criminal law while below the age of 17. Unlike the 1921 draft act on juvenile courts, in 1932 the legislator decided not to include pre-delinquent children who displayed problematic or immoral behaviour in the juvenile justice system. Responses to juvenile offending depended on the age of juveniles as well as their ability to understand the meaning of the act and control their behaviour (discernment). Juveniles who committed an offence below the age of 13, as well as those who committed an offence without discernment after their 13th birthday but prior to their 17th, were treated as not criminally responsible. Only educational measures (reprimand, supervision of parents or another trustworthy person or institution, and placement in a state or private educational institution) could be imposed on them. Juveniles aged between 13 and 16 years who had

10 *Komisja Kodyfikacyjna Rzeczypospolitej Polskiej* 1921, p. 12.

11 In practice before World War II juvenile courts were set up only in some of the biggest cities: see Korcyl-Wolska 2004, p. 30.

12 Taracha 1988, p. 118–119.

committed an offence with discernment were as a rule sentenced to placement in a correctional institution (*zakład poprawczy*) for an unspecified time.[13] The enforcement of the placement in a correctional institution could be conditionally suspended by the court. Juveniles placed in correctional institutions could be institutionalised until the age of 21 but it was possible for them to be granted conditional release earlier. According to the prevailing opinion of scholars, the placement of a juvenile in a correctional institution under the 1932 Criminal Code was a specific penalty, *quasi*-penalty or educational penalty that replaced 'ordinary' prison sentences provided for adult offenders and combined some retributive elements with a predominantly rehabilitative goal.[14]

Provisions of the 1932 Criminal Code, as well as of the 1928 Code of Criminal Procedure that had regulated the juvenile justice system, were replaced with a separate act on juveniles in 1983 when the 1982 JA entered into force. This Act was enacted after more than 30 years of disputes and discussions about a new way to regulate responses to juvenile offences.[15]

1.2.2. The Juvenile Act of 1982

Soon after World War II the idea appeared in Polish literature on juvenile law that responses to juvenile criminal behaviour should be separated from criminal law and that a uniform educational system should be introduced to deal with both juveniles who infringed the criminal law and those who behaved in other unacceptable ways. Initially, work on the reform of juvenile law was pending together with work on new criminal codifications. In 1956 it was decided to regulate all matters relating to juvenile delinquents in a separate statute. Preparing the draft of such a statute turned out to be very difficult because of different views presented by lawyers, teachers, psychologists and criminologists. As a result of this controversy, the Criminal Code, the Code of Criminal Procedure and the Code of Execution of Sentences passed in 1969 did not introduce new provisions concerning juvenile offenders. Subsequently, provisions of the former Criminal Code of 1932 and the Code of Criminal Procedure of 1928 on dealing with juvenile offenders remained in force.

In the following years, about a dozen projects on separate statutes on juveniles were prepared not only within the Ministry of Justice, but also under the responsibility of the Ministry of Education. Finally, the Juvenile Act was passed

---

13 It was also possible to impose educational measures on juveniles aged 13–16 who acted with discernment if the court – based on the circumstances of the offence, the juvenile's character or the conditions of his life and environment – deemed that it was useless to place them in a correctional institution.

14 Stańdo-Kawecka 2007, p. 278–280.

15 Kobes 2011, p. 70–71.

in 1982.[16] In comparison with criminal codification of the 1920s and 1930s, the 1982 JA introduced a significantly stronger welfare, paternalistic and protective approach. The paternalistic and protective features are visible in the definition of a 'juvenile', the procedure applied in juvenile proceedings, the catalogue of measures provided for juveniles, and the criteria used for choosing the most adequate measure.

However, shortly after the adoption of the JA, the way proceedings in juvenile cases were regulated met with criticism. What was particularly criticised was the creation of a kind of conglomerate of civil procedure, criminal procedure and procedural provisions contained in the JA which caused serious problems in practice. As an example of the lack of synchronisation of procedural rules it was indicated that the family judge applied provisions of the Code of Civil Procedure during the explanatory (preparatory) proceedings in juvenile cases while the police acted pursuant to provisions of the Code of Criminal Procedure when collecting and preserving evidence. As a result, the rights of interrogated suspects and witnesses were narrower or wider at different stages of the same case depending on whether the interrogation was conducted by a family judge or the police.[17]

1.2.3. Developments after 1982

After the collapse of the communist system in 1989 it was believed that a fundamental reform of adult criminal law was necessary to make Polish criminal law and criminal policy more humane, liberal and rational.[18] At the same time the juvenile law regulated by the 1982 JA was – and in the opinion of many scholars still is[19] – considered to be modern, liberal and rational and for that reason it did not attract much attention. In the last ten years, different drafts for new juvenile acts have been prepared by different commissions set up by the Ministry of Justice, but all met with criticism for a variety of reasons.[20] It was only in 2013 that the government sent a draft extensive amendment to the 1982 JA to Parliament. The draft aimed at implementing the judgement of the European Court of Human Rights (hereafter: ECtHR) in the *Adamkiewicz v. Poland* case.[21] In this judgement, the ECtHR held that combining various functions by the same family judge at both the preparatory and adjudicatory stage was contrary

16 On the history of enactment of the Juvenile Act of 1982 see Rdzanek-Piwowar 1993, p. 207–220.

17 Strzembosz 1984, p. 79.

18 Stańdo-Kawecka 2002, p. 421–423.

19 Bojarski 2009, p. 278.

20 The draft juvenile act prepared in 2003–2006 was criticised mainly because of its procedural provisions being too formalistic while the draft prepared in 2006–2007 was met with criticism for being too repressive. For more information see Marek 2009, p. 389–390.

21 ECtHR 2 March 2010, *Adamkiewicz v. Poland*, no. 54729/00.

to the right to an impartial tribunal. The ECtHR stated that there was a violation of this right in the situation in which the same family judge first conducted the evidence-gathering procedure, then decided to refer the case to the adjudicatory stage and ruled in the same case as president of the trial bench.

An amendment to the 1982 JA was adopted by Parliament on 30 August 2013.[22] The amendment (hereafter: 2013 amendment to the JA) has been in force since 2 January 2014. Generally, the legislator abandoned the division of juvenile proceedings into preparatory and court (adjudicatory) stages. Under the amended JA, juvenile cases are dealt with by a family court through unified court proceedings in which a separate preparatory stage is not distinguished. As a rule, proceedings in juvenile cases are regulated by the Code of Civil Procedure modified by the JA, but there are also exceptions when provisions of the Code of Criminal Procedure apply, for example in matters related to the collection and preservation of evidence by the police as well as the appointment and functions of a defence lawyer. The 2013 amendment did not alter the dominant role of the family judge in juvenile cases. It is still possible that the same family judge who functions as a family court composed of one judge first gathers and preserves evidence of a 'punishable act'[23] and then, on the basis of evidence gathered by himself, adjudicates in the case. In such cases the impartiality of the family court may still be questioned.

1.3. GENERAL PRINCIPLES OF JUVENILE LAW

In the science of juvenile (criminal) law there are different typologies of juvenile justice models.[24] A clear division of countries according to these typologies or models is not possible, because juvenile justice systems usually combine elements of different models. The juvenile justice system established in Poland in the 1920s and 1930s was based on a compromise between the welfare and justice approach. The notion of a 'juvenile' under the 1932 Criminal Code was limited to persons who violated the criminal law while being below the age of criminal majority. Responses provided for juvenile offending were strongly influenced by the welfare ideology and consisted mainly of educational measures. Penalties were almost totally excluded from the catalogue of responses to juvenile offending. The only *quasi*-penalty (educational penalty) was placement of a juvenile in a correctional institution. Under the 1928 Code of Criminal Procedure the procedure in juvenile cases was different from adult criminal proceedings, but as a matter of fact it was still a modified criminal procedure.

---

22 See *Ustawa o zmianie ustawy o postępowaniu w sprawach nieletnich oraz niektórych innych ustaw*, 30 August 2013, Official Legal Bulletin 2013, pos. 1165.

23 See *infra* paragraph 2.3.2 (part I).

24 Pruin 2010, p. 1519–1520.

In comparison with the criminal codifications of the 1920s and 1930s, the 1982 JA strengthened the welfare approach, including the paternalistic, protectionist role of the juvenile judge. First of all, in 1982 the legislator returned to the idea discussed already in the 1920s that the juvenile justice system should cover not only juveniles who committed an act prohibited by criminal law but also children who were 'in danger of becoming offenders' because they display other problematic or immoral behaviour. As a result, 'juveniles' in the meaning of the 1982 JA are not only perpetrators of 'punishable acts' committed after having reached the age 13 but before the age of 17, but also persons under 18 who show problematic behaviours not prohibited by criminal law, referred to by the legislator as signs of 'demoralisation'.

According to criminal law, offenders are punished for offences (*przestępstwo*), including fiscal offences (*przestępstwo skarbowe*).[25] Under the 1982 JA juveniles are not punished, but measures are imposed on them for 'punishable acts' and/or signs of 'demoralisation'. 'Punishable acts' mean acts prohibited by criminal law, like offences, fiscal offences and certain petty crimes (contraventions). In 1982 the legislator chose a different term in order to stress that the goal of proceedings in juvenile cases was no longer to establish the culpability of a juvenile. Unlike the 1932 Criminal Code, the criterion of a juvenile acting with or without discernment was abandoned because it was found to be irrelevant to the choice of the most adequate measure(s).

Another important change which was introduced by the 1982 JA consisted in the creation of family courts.[26] The 1928 Code of Criminal Procedure provided for special juvenile courts dealing exclusively with persons below the age of criminal majority who violated criminal law. After World War II the jurisdiction of those special courts was gradually extended and cases concerning the deprivation of parents of their parental responsibility or limitation of that responsibility were transferred from civil courts to these special courts. In 1982 the legislator decided to establish family courts as special departments of district courts and entrust them with a broad category of different cases concerning families, including interventions in parental responsibility and proceedings in juvenile cases.[27] Like the French concept of the same name, a family judge should deal with different

---

25 In Poland, criminal responsibility for fiscal offences, such as for example tax offences, has been regulated by the separate Code on Fiscal Offences of 1999.

26 The concept of special local or administrative commissions on juveniles, found in many other communist countries, had been rejected in Poland after long discussion in the 1970s, because such commissions were found not to be able to provide juveniles and their families with the necessary and appropriate procedural rights and safeguards. For more information on the local and administrative commissions dealing with juveniles in communist and post-communist countries, see Kanev *et al.* 2010, p. 134, Pergataia 2001, p. 190–195 and Sakalauskas 2010, p. 877–878.

27 Grześkowiak, Krukowski, Patulski and Warzocha 1991, p. 11–14.

cases related to the same family, such as divorce, separation and interventions in the parental responsibility, adoption, domestic violence and other offences against the family, as well as juvenile cases. The underlying assumption of the reform was that the same family court, and also the same family judge, should deal with different problems faced by the same family in order to give consistent judgements based on his extensive knowledge of this family.[28] Broad powers initially conferred on the family courts by the 1982 JA were reduced in the following years by transferring divorce cases to regional courts and by transferring adult criminal cases related to offences against the family to criminal courts.

The revised concept of courts dealing with juvenile cases resulted in changes to procedural issues. In 1982 the legislator introduced a 'hybrid' procedure in juvenile cases which combined procedural provisions contained in the JA with elements of both civil and criminal procedure.[29] In line with the welfare approach, educational, medical and correctional measures are to be imposed on juveniles not in the name of punishment, but in the name of their protection and re-socialisation. Fundamental principles of dealing with juveniles under the 1982 JA include the principle of acting in the best interests of the juvenile[30] as well as the principle of individualisation which requires that measures should be tailored to the individual needs of a juvenile.[31] The JA does not provide for the principle of proportionality in reaction to the circumstances of the offence. The juvenile justice system created by the 1982 JA has been considered non-punitive, protective and educational.[32] Since 1982 juvenile law has not been considered to be criminal law and proceedings in juvenile cases have not been treated as criminal proceedings.[33]

2. STRUCTURE AND MAIN CHARACTERISTICS OF THE POLISH JUVENILE JUSTICE SYSTEM

2.1. MINIMUM AGE OF CRIMINAL LIABILITY

The Polish juvenile justice system does not recognise the concept of the age of criminal liability for juveniles. The rule is that the minimum age of criminal responsibility is the same as the age of criminal majority: 17 years of age at the time of the alleged offence. Juvenile offenders below the age of 17 at the time of the offence are considered not to be criminally responsible with some exceptions specified in the Criminal Code and the JA.

28 Patulski 1985, p. 18.
29 Stańdo-Kawecka 2010, p. 1008–1013.
30 Art. 3 para. 1 JA.
31 Art. 3 para. 2 JA.
32 Grześkowiak, Krukowski, Patulski and Warzocha 1991, p. 11.
33 Światłowski 2009, p. 407–408.

The lowest age of criminal majority has been fixed at 17 years at the time of the offence in art. 10 para. 1 of the 1997 Criminal Code. Juveniles suspected of having committed an offence below the age of 17 can only exceptionally be held criminally liable for their actions. According to art. 10 para. 2 of the aforementioned Code, such a person may be held criminally responsible provided that he is suspected of having committed one of the most serious crimes enumerated in this provision[34] at the age of 15 or 16 and provided that the circumstances of the offence and the offender, the level of his maturity and the ineffectiveness of educational or correctional measures justify directing the case to an adult criminal court.

Perpetrators who are suspected of having committed an offence while being 17 years of age are from the point of view of criminal substantive and procedural law treated as adult offenders. They are dealt with by ordinary criminal courts according to procedure provided for adults. Only exceptionally will the ordinary criminal court apply educational, medical or correctional measures instead of penalties to an offender who committed a non-serious offence (*występek*) at the age of 17 if the circumstances of the case and the degree of development of the perpetrator, his personal characteristics and condition justify it.[35] In practice, courts use this possibility only on very rare occasions.

Juveniles who are 15 or 16 years old when they commit one of the most serious offences and who are exceptionally criminally responsible on the basis of art. 10 para. 2 CC are also tried by ordinary criminal courts according to common criminal procedure, but the preparatory proceedings will be different from adult cases provided that the proceedings start before the accused reached the age of 18.[36] Art. 10 para. 3 CC provides rules concerning the mitigation of punishment imposed on those 15- or 16-year-old juveniles who are tried as adults by criminal courts. Pursuant to art. 54 para. 2 CC, life imprisonment is excluded for offenders who were below 18 years of age at the time of the offence.

Provisions of the 1997 Criminal Code regulating the minimum age of criminal majority raise controversy over their compliance with the CRC. Art. 1 of this Convention states that a 'child' means any human being below the age of 18 unless, under the law applicable to the child, majority is attained earlier. In its General Comment No. 10, the Committee on the Rights of the Child drew

34 Among crimes enumerated in art. 10 para. 2 CC there are such crimes as attempts on the life of the President of Poland, homicide, serious bodily injury, causing catastrophe, abduction of a vessel or aircraft, rape under aggravating circumstances, aggravated assault on a public official, hostage-taking and robbery.

35 Art. 10 para. 4 CC.

36 On differences concerning the preparatory proceeding see art. 18 para. 2 JA.

attention to the fact that the upper age limit for the application of the rules of special juvenile justice – both in terms of special procedural rules and in terms of rules for diversion and special dispositions – should apply for all children who at the time of an offence have not reached the age of 18.[37]

Exceptionally, penalties provided for adults can also be imposed on juveniles by family courts. Before the 2013 amendment to the JA a family court was authorised to impose a penalty (including imprisonment) instead of placement in a correctional institution on a juvenile who committed a 'punishable act' prohibited by the criminal law, like an offence or fiscal offence, while at least 13 years of age, so long as the juvenile was at least 18 years old at the time of the court judgement and placing the juvenile in a correctional institution would not be advisable.[38] This possibility to 'replace' the placement in a correctional institution with a penalty was removed by the 2013 amendment to the JA. However, it is still possible for a family court to impose a penalty on a juvenile who in the course of juvenile proceedings was placed in a correctional institution but reached 18 years of age before the judgement came into force. When choosing to issue a penalty instead of enforcement of the correctional measure, the family court is obliged to mitigate the punishment. The duration of imprisonment or the penalty of liberty limitation cannot exceed the period remaining until the juvenile turns 21.[39] The specific 'change' of the placement in a correctional institution for a penalty on the basis of art. 94 of the JA has been criticised due to lack of consistency with substantive criminal law, and particularly due to concerns relating the legality principle (*nulla poena sine culpa).*[40]

2.2. DEFINITION OF JUVENILE AND RELEVANT CATEGORIES

In line with fundamental ideas of the welfare approach, the notion of a 'juvenile' has been broadly defined by the JA. According to art. 1 of this Act, the term 'juveniles' covers:

(a) (alleged) perpetrators of 'punishable acts' (*czyn karalny*) committed after having reached the age of 13, but before 17 years of age;
(b) persons under 18 who show signs of problematic behaviour not prohibited by criminal law, referred to by the legislator as 'signs of demoralisation' (*przejawy demoralizacji*); and

[37] Committee on the Rights of the Child 2007, p. 11–12.
[38] See art. 13 JA before the 2013 amendment.
[39] See art. 94 JA.
[40] Stańdo-Kawecka 2007, p. 322–324.

(c) persons to whom educational or correctional measures are enforced until the person is 18 or 21 years of age.

In the JA the notions of 'offence' (*przestępstwo*) or 'petty crime' (*wykroczenie*) are not used. Instead the legislator has chosen the term 'punishable act' (*czyn karalny*) in order to stress that children below 17 years of age are as a rule not mature enough to be held criminally responsible for their acts. 'Punishable act' is defined in art. 1 para. 2 point 2 of the JA and means an action or omission prohibited by criminal law as an offence (*przestępstwo*), fiscal offence (*przestępstwo skarbowe*) or selected petty crime (*wykroczenie*).

In Polish criminology such terms as 'juvenile offences' (*przestępstwa nieletnich*) or 'juvenile offenders' (*nieletni przestępcy*) are commonly used. In the meaning of criminal substantive law a juvenile who committed a 'punishable act' did not commit an 'offence' because, as will be explained later on, during juvenile proceedings his culpability is not determined. In fact, the difference between the notions of a 'punishable act' and an 'offence' is connected with determination of guilt in the meaning of criminal substantive law. In adult criminal law the determination of the guilt of the perpetrator is the necessary precondition for punishment.[41] The JA does not require culpability (*zdolność do zawinienia*) of juvenile offenders to be determined, or even that they act with discernment (*rozeznanie*) as was the case under provisions of the 1932 Criminal Code. Measures are applied to juveniles according to their needs and irrespective of a finding of guilt in the meaning of criminal substantive law.[42]

The notion of 'demoralisation' is not defined by the JA. Art. 4 of the JA only enumerates some examples of types of behaviour or circumstances which are treated as signs of 'demoralisation': violation of the principles of community life, commission of a prohibited act, truancy, use of alcohol or drugs, running away from home, prostitution and association with criminal groups.

'Punishable acts' may be committed only by juveniles who are at least 13 years of age. It should be noted that there is no minimum age limit for juveniles showing signs of 'demoralisation'. The commission of an act prohibited by criminal law as an offence or petty crime by a juvenile under the age of 13 may be exclusively considered as a sign of 'demoralisation' and does not constitute a 'punishable act' under the JA. The same applies to petty crimes (*wykroczenia*) which are not enumerated in art. 1 para. 2 point 2 of the JA; those who commit such petty crimes when below 17 years of age may be dealt with by family courts only because of signs of 'demoralisation'.

41 See art. 1 CC.

42 Zoll 2009, p. 194–196.

In the commentary to the JA 'demoralisation' has been defined as a state or process that is characterised by negative attitudes and behaviour of a juvenile in relation to the fundamental norms and principles of conduct required by society.[43] Undoubtedly, provisions concerning juveniles who show signs of 'demoralisation' are intended to provide family courts with a broad discretion in initiating state intervention in accordance with the basic principles of the paternalistic 'child savers' ideology.[44] First of all, they allow family courts to impose on children who behave in an unacceptable way, but did not infringe criminal law, the same educational and medical measures (with the exclusion of correctional measures) as is possible in the case of juveniles acting in conflict with provisions of criminal law. The most severe category of measures provided for by the JA, that is correctional measures, applies exclusively to juvenile perpetrators of 'punishable acts' prohibited by criminal law as offences or fiscal offences.

2.3. PROCEEDINGS IN JUVENILE CASES

Not only is substantive law concerning responses to juvenile offending different from substantive criminal law, but also the procedure in juvenile cases differs significantly from regular criminal procedure. As mentioned earlier,[45] in legal literature the opinion is widely shared that under the 1982 JA the procedure in juvenile cases should not be considered a kind of special criminal procedure but rather as a procedure *sui generis*. Some procedural issues concerning juvenile cases have been fully or partially regulated in the 1982 JA. In procedural matters which are not regulated by the JA the law as a rule requires provisions of civil procedure, and only exceptionally criminal procedure, to be applied. As a result, proceedings in juvenile cases are a 'hybrid', involving a combination of the JA with the provisions of the Code of Civil Procedure or the Code of Criminal Procedure in matters which are not regulated by this Act. The 2013 amendment to the JA introduced important procedural changes to proceedings in juvenile cases. In order to explain these changes, procedural issues before the amendment will first be discussed.

2.3.1. Structure of juvenile proceedings before the 2013 amendment

Before January 2014, the key principle in juvenile proceedings was formulated in art. 20 of the JA. This provision stated that in juvenile cases provisions of the Code of Civil Procedure applied accordingly. At the same time, it

43 Grześkowiak, Krukowski, Patulski and Warzocha 1991, p. 9.
44 Krajewski 2006, p. 159.
45 See *supra* paragraph 1.3 (part I).

enumerated exceptions to this rule in which case provisions of the Code of Criminal Procedure were applicable. The latter provisions (with the adjustments introduced by the JA) applied with regard to the following matters:

(a) the collection and preservation of evidence by the police;
(b) the appointment and tasks of a defence lawyer; and
(c) correctional proceedings.

It should be added that the JA did not regulate clearly which procedure applied in the stage of implementation of imposed measures.[46]

There were three main stages of juvenile proceedings: explanatory proceedings, court proceedings and enforcement proceedings.

2.3.1.1. Explanatory proceedings

According to art. 21 para. 1 of the JA it was the family judge who instigated the proceedings if there was a suspicion of the existence of circumstances which indicated that the juvenile showed signs of 'demoralisation' or committed a 'punishable act'. In 1982, the legislator assumed that family courts would be informed by citizens and members of institutions and organisations working with children about juveniles showing problematic behaviour and suspected of having committed a 'punishable act'.[47] It also believed that family courts should not be passively waiting for such information but should actively look for it through cooperation with state institutions and social organisations that worked with children and families.[48]

The involvement of the police and public prosecutors in juvenile cases was very limited. According to arts. 37 and 39 of the JA the police were competent to collect and preserve evidence of 'punishable acts', including conducting the interrogation of a juvenile suspect, in urgent cases. 'Urgent cases' referred to cases in which it was necessary to collect and preserve traces and evidence of crimes against loss or damage before the formal commencement of the proceedings by a family judge.[49] The police had no discretionary powers; on the contrary, they were obliged to immediately report every juvenile case to a family judge after having collected and stored the necessary evidence in urgent

46 Korcyl-Wolska 2001, p. 51.
47 See art. 4 JA according to which everyone has a duty to inform the parents, a guardian, the school, a family court, the police or any other competent authority about circumstances indicating 'demoralisation' of a juvenile. Everyone who has learned about a punishable act committed by a juvenile has the obligation to inform the police or the family court.
48 Patulski 1985, p. 21.
49 See art. 308 CCP.

cases. Research on police activities in juvenile cases revealed that there was a large discrepancy between the assumptions of the juvenile law and practice. In practice, in most cases concerning 'punishable acts' it was not the family court but the police who were first informed about juvenile offending.[50] In many cases the police did not report juvenile offences to a family judge immediately after collecting the evidence in urgent cases, but rather they only did so after having made further investigations.[51]

In explanatory proceedings, it was the task of the family judge to gather information concerning the juvenile and his educational, health and welfare situation. The family judge who conducted the explanatory proceedings 'listened to' (*wysłuchiwał*) the juvenile, his parents or guardian and, where appropriate, other persons. The legislator did not use such terms as 'suspect', 'suspected person' or 'accused'. Instead, the JA consistently used the term 'juvenile'. In accordance with art. 33 of the JA the main object of the explanatory proceedings was to determine whether there was evidence of the juvenile showing signs of 'demoralisation' or of a 'punishable act', as well as to determine whether there was a need for the family court to impose educational, medical or correctional measures on the juvenile.[52]

According to art. 37 of the JA before the 2013 amendment, the family judge in the course of the explanatory proceedings could order the police or the probation officer to perform some activities, such as preparing a social inquiry report by the probation officer or collecting certain evidence by the police, including the interrogation of a juvenile. Pursuant to arts. 25 and 25a of the JA, if necessary a family court could refer a juvenile to a family diagnostic-consultative centre, another specialist centre or an expert, in order to be diagnosed or put under psychiatric observation in a health institution for a period not exceeding six weeks.

Generally, the explanatory proceedings in juvenile cases were based on the provisions of the Code of Civil Procedure. With regard to the collection and storage of evidence by the police and the appointment and functions of a defence lawyer, however, the provisions of the Code of Criminal Procedure were to be followed. The explanatory proceedings had to be dropped by the family judge if there was no evidence that the juvenile committed a 'punishable act' or showed signs of 'demoralisation'. Unlike preparatory proceedings in adult cases, which are based on the principle that – as a rule – all crimes should be prosecuted, the family judge who conducted the explanatory proceedings could at any time

50 Czarnecka-Dzialuk, Drapała and Więcek-Durańska 2011, p. 86–87.
51 Korcyl-Wolska 2001, p. 425–426.
52 Art. 33 JA before the 2013 amendment.

drop the juvenile case unconditionally following the principle of opportunity. This could happen when the judge was of the opinion that the imposition of educational or correctional measures would serve no purpose, in particular when such measures had already been imposed on the juvenile in a previous case. Furthermore, at that stage of proceedings, the family judge could refer the case to a mediation program and drop the explanatory proceedings as a result of an agreement reached between the victim and the juvenile.

Apart from discontinuing the proceedings the family judge could take one of the following decisions when the explanatory proceedings had been completed:

(a) to refer the case to the school attended by the juvenile or a social organisation to which he belonged, if the judge was of the opinion that the educational measures available to the school or organisation were adequate;
(b) to refer the case to the family court for adjudication; or
(c) to refer the case to the public prosecutor who brought the accusation to the criminal court if in the course of the explanatory proceedings circumstances came to light of the involvement of the juvenile in a very serious crime listed in art. 10 para. 2 CC.[53]

The public prosecutor dealt with juvenile cases at the stage of preparatory proceedings only exceptionally:

(a) if the case concerned a 15- or 16-year-old (alleged) perpetrator of one of the most serious crimes and it was referred to the public prosecutor by the family judge in order to bring the accusation to the criminal court;
(b) in particularly justified cases, if the juvenile was suspected of having committed an offence together with an adult perpetrator and the interests of the juvenile did not preclude a combined investigation by the public prosecutor; after completing the investigation the juvenile case as a rule should be separated and referred to the family court;
(c) if the juvenile was under the age of 17 at the time of the alleged 'punishable act', but had reached 18 years of age at the time of the instigation of proceedings which in such a case were governed by provisions of criminal procedure.

53 It happened in exceptional cases: in 1999–2009 the overall number of cases transferred to public prosecutors oscillated between 207 and 332 comprising 0.2–0.3 per cent of all cases dealt with by family judges in explanatory proceedings. For more information, see Ministry of Justice 2010, p. 11.

2.3.1.2. Court (adjudicatory) proceedings

After completion of the preparatory proceedings by a family judge, the judge could decide to refer the case to adjudication. When referring the case to this stage, it was up to the family judge to decide on the type of court proceedings to be followed. Depending on the decision taken by the family judge, juveniles could be adjudicated by family courts in one of the following court proceedings:

(a) care-educational proceedings; or
(b) correctional proceedings.

The main difference between these two proceedings was related to the provisions governing procedural issues. As a rule, care-educational proceedings were governed by the provisions of the Code of Civil Procedure. However, there had been some legislative modifications to the rules of civil procedure specified by the JA. In these proceedings the family court composed of a single family judge dealt with the case during a court sitting (*posiedzenie*). The final court verdict given in care-educational proceedings was a so-called order (*postanowienie*).

In correctional proceedings the family court was also composed of a single family judge[54] but he dealt with the case in a more formalised way during a main hearing (*rozprawa*) governed by the Code of Criminal Procedure with some modifications specified in the JA. A juvenile had to have a defence lawyer in correctional proceedings.[55] Additionally, in cases concerning serious 'punishable acts' the public prosecutor had to attend the hearing.[56] The latter, however, did not bring an accusation and acted simply as a person safeguarding the public interest. The judgement of the family court when placing the juvenile in a correctional institution took the form of a sentence (*wyrok*). However, it was not a sentence to a penalty but a sentence on the imposition of a correctional measure. Thus, under the JA depriving a juvenile of his liberty by placing him in a correctional institution did not constitute a 'conviction' but was treated as detention of a juvenile for the purpose of educational supervision in the meaning of art. 5 para. 1d of the ECHR.

Juvenile cases concerning signs of 'demoralisation' were adjudicated exclusively in care-educational proceedings. On this category of juveniles, only educational

---

54 The initial version of the 1982 JA regulated that in correctional proceedings the family court was composed of one family judge and two lay persons, but these provisions were changed in 2007. See *Ustawa o zmianie ustawy – Kodeks postępowania cywilnego, ustawy – Kodeks postępowania karnego oraz o zmianie niektórych innych ustaw*, 15 March 2007, Official Legal Bulletin 112, pos. 766.

55 See art. 49 JA before the 2013 amendment.

56 See art. 51 para. 3 JA before the 2013 amendment.

or medical measures could be imposed by family courts. In cases concerning 'punishable acts', after completion of the explanatory proceedings the judge had to decide on the type of adjudicatory proceedings and choose between care-educational proceedings and correctional proceedings. As may be seen from figure 1, the fundamental criterion for determining the applicable type of adjudicatory proceedings in juvenile cases concerning 'punishable acts' was the anticipated need to apply (a) particular measure(s) in the juvenile's case. If the family judge after conducting the explanatory proceedings was of the opinion that there were grounds for placing the juvenile in a correctional institution, he referred the case to correctional proceedings. According to statistical data from the Ministry of Justice, only 1.4–2.0 per cent of cases arising from 'punishable acts' were referred to such proceedings in the years 1999–2009.[57]

Figure 1. Type of adjudicatory proceedings in juvenile cases before the 2013 amendment to the JA

Grounds for initiating proceedings in juvenile cases	Age category	Type of proceedings at the court stage	Applicable or applied measures
Punishable act	At least 13 years of age and below 17 years of age at the time of the alleged act (save for major crimes devolved to ordinary criminal courts)	Care-educational or correctional proceedings depending on the anticipated measures	Educational, medical or correctional measures, exceptionally also a penalty instead of a correctional measure if the juvenile was at least 18 at the time of judgement
Signs of 'demoralisation'	Below 18 years of age	Only care-educational proceedings	Only educational or medical measures

According to arts. 45 and 53 of the JA before the 2013 amendment, court sessions and hearings (*posiedzenia i rozprawy*) in juvenile cases were not public, unless public sessions and hearings were justified on educational grounds. In the commentary to the JA it was explained that 'educational grounds' meant that the course of the court hearing would have an educational influence on juveniles and adults observing it.[58] Due to lack of empirical studies it is impossible to determine whether and how these public hearings were carried out in practice.

2.3.1.3. Principles of criminal procedure in correctional proceedings

The law provided for different types of proceedings in juvenile cases due to 'punishable acts' at the court stage because it was thought that older juveniles

57 Ministry of Justice 2010, p. 11.
58 Grześkowiak, Krukowski, Patulski and Warzocha 1991, p. 136.

who faced the most serious measure of placement in a correctional institution deserved to be protected by a higher standard of procedural safeguards as provided for under civil procedure law. Additionally, in the course of correctional proceedings the family court could in exceptional cases impose a penalty provided for adults instead of placement in a correctional institution if the juvenile had reached 18 years of age at the time of the court ruling and the court considered placement inadvisable. This exceptional possibility to 'replace' the correctional measure with a penalty also reinforced the need to provide this category of juveniles with a higher standard of procedural safeguards.[59] On the other hand, care-educational proceedings based on civil procedure enabled family courts to deal in a less formalised way with juveniles showing signs of 'demoralisation' as well as those alleged perpetrators of 'punishable acts' for whom educational or medical measures were considered sufficient.

In legal literature on juvenile law it was stressed that even in correctional proceedings principles of criminal procedure applied only to a limited extent. According to Kmiecik, the principle of formalism took a different form in juvenile justice because proceedings in juvenile cases did not require very detailed procedural forms due to the need to provide family judges with highly flexible methods of educational influence.[60] Procedural formalism suppressed and limited the interaction between the parties, in particular between the family judge and the juvenile. As a result, the dominant directive on interpretation of juvenile law had to be the principle of non-formalism because a far-reaching limitation of formalism enabled the family judge to make sincere and direct contact with the juvenile.[61] The same author suggested that informing the juvenile of his right to remain silent could be a sign of excessive formalism. Instead, the family judge should by gentle persuasion try to encourage the juvenile to provide explanations. This approach had a significant psychological and educational effect.[62] He also pointed out that due to the lack of potential opponents to a juvenile in juvenile cases the proceedings were adversarial only to a very limited extent. The use of traditional adversarial hearings (cross-examination) was considered impossible in the absence of any opposing party, as well as undesirable for psychological and educational reasons.[63]

The principle of the presumption of innocence was also controversial in juvenile cases for many reasons. The JA required the court to establish that the juvenile committed a 'punishable act' or showed 'signs of 'demoralisation'. It did not require the court to establish the culpability of the juvenile in the usual sense of substantive criminal law. In juvenile cases the presumption of innocence could

59 Patulski 1985, p. 24.
60 Kmiecik 1988, p. 104.
61 Kmiecik 1988, p. 107.
62 Kmiecik 1988, p. 109.
63 Kmiecik 1988, p. 115.

only be understood as the presumption that the juvenile neither committed any alleged 'punishable act' nor showed signs of 'demoralisation' until these acts and such behaviour were proven in the course of court proceedings.[64] What made the matter more complex was the fact that during the explanatory (preparatory) proceedings in juvenile cases the family judge was expected to predict what measures should be applied to the juvenile in order to determine the proper type of court proceedings (care-educational or correctional). As a result, during the explanatory proceedings the court's final decision had to be anticipated, which could be problematic from the point of view of the presumption of innocence.[65]

2.3.2. *Structure of juvenile proceedings since the 2013 amendment*

As a result of the 2013 amendment to the JA, the division of juvenile proceedings into separate explanatory (preparatory) and adjudicatory (court) stages has been abandoned and replaced with a unified court proceeding conducted by a family court composed of a single family judge. According to art. 15 para. 1 of the amended JA, proceedings in juvenile cases are conducted by a family court unless other special provisions apply. Special provisions related to exceptional situations in which juveniles are judged by ordinary criminal courts remained unchanged. There are only two stages of juvenile proceedings: court proceedings (*postępowanie przed sądem*) and enforcement proceedings (*postępowanie wykonawcze*). Court proceedings in juvenile cases aim at determining whether the juvenile committed a punishable act or whether there are circumstances indicating his 'demoralisation' and if there is a need to apply measures provided for by the JA.[66] According to art. 32b para. 1 of the JA, in the course of court proceedings data are collected which refer to the juvenile, his educational, health and material conditions and 'other evidence is conducted' (*przeprowadza się inne dowody*). The legislator seems to emphasise the need to collect extensive information on the personality and living conditions of a juvenile while putting in second place other evidence, namely evidence related to the alleged 'punishable act' or other problematic behaviours.

The procedure in juvenile cases still is a 'hybrid' procedure. Some procedural issues are regulated by the amended JA. In matters not regulated by the JA provisions of the Code of Civil Procedure appropriate for care proceedings (*przepisy Kodeksu postępowania cywilnego właściwe dla spraw opiekuńczych*) apply accordingly.[67] Apparently, the intention of the legislator has been to make juvenile proceedings much more similar to civil care proceedings related

64 Nowikowski 2009, p. 361: decision of the Polish Supreme Court (*postanowienie Sądu Najwyższego*), 13 June 2002, V KKN 275/01.

65 Korcyl-Wolska 2004, p. 206–210.

66 See art. 21a JA.

67 See art. 20 par. 1 JA.

to children in need of care. Exceptionally, provisions of the Code of Criminal Procedure apply in matters specified by the JA, for example with regard to the gathering, preserving and conducting of evidence by the police, the appointment and actions of a defence lawyer, and dealing with seized objects in the course of the proceedings. Additionally, provisions of the Code of Criminal Procedure shall apply in juvenile proceedings with regard to interrogation and other activities aimed at the gathering of evidence (*czynności dowodowe*) with the participation of juvenile victims or witnesses.[68] The previous division of adjudicating proceedings into care-educational and correctional proceedings has been abandoned. The latter proceedings were mainly governed by the Code of Criminal Procedure. As a result of these changes, the scope of application of the Code of Criminal Procedure in juvenile proceedings has been significantly reduced.

2.4. PROVISIONAL MEASURES

According to art. 40 of the JA before the 2013 amendment, a juvenile suspected of committing a 'punishable act' who had reached 13 years of age could be detained in a special police institution for children (*policyjna izba dziecka*) if there were grounds for fearing that he might hide or destroy evidence, or if it was impossible to establish his identity and the detention in a police institution was necessary due to the circumstances of the case. Police institutions for children were and still are subordinated to the Ministry of Interior and Administration. In 2013 there were 16 such institutions, usually one in every province (*województwo*). According to police statistics 8,578 juveniles were placed in these institutions in the year 2012,[69] including juveniles arrested for escaping from juvenile institutions such as a youth educational centre, correctional institution or youth detention centre.[70] Detailed rules on the stay of juveniles in police institutions for children, including the catalogue of their rights, were specified in a regulation (*rozporządzenie*) issued by the Minister of Interior and Administration[71] as well as an order (*zarządzenie*) issued by the Chief Police Commander.[72]

---

68 According to art. 20 par. 2 JA, in juvenile cases, victims and witnesses under the age of civil majority (*osoby małoletnie*) shall be interrogated by applying provisions of the Code of Criminal Procedure which provide for a special mode of interrogation of such persons in certain cases.

69 *Komenda Główna Policji 2013, Koncepcja PID*, available at: www.policja.pl/pol/kgp/biuro-prewencji-i-ruch/wydzial-konwojowy/policyjne-izby-dziecka.

70 Juveniles who left juvenile institutions without permission could be placed in police institutions for juveniles for a maximum of 5 days. See art. 40 par. 7 JA before the 2013 amendment.

71 *Rozporządzenie Ministra Spraw Wewnętrznych i Administracji w sprawie szczegółowych zasad pobytu nieletnich w policyjnych izbach dziecka*, 21 January 2002, Official Legal Bulletin 10, pos. 104 with later amendments.

72 *Zarządzenie nr 134 Komendanta Głównego Policji w sprawie metod i form wykonywania zadań w policyjnej izbie dziecka*, 30 October 2012, Official Journal of the Police Headquarters 27, pos. 59 with later amendments.

If a juvenile was detained in a special police institution, his parents or guardian had to be immediately notified. The police were also obliged to inform the competent family court within 24 hours of the arrest.[73] If within 72 hours of the arrest no decision on provisional measures had been issued by the family judge, the juvenile had to be released immediately and transmitted to the custody of his parents or guardian.

During explanatory proceedings provisional measures could be applied to juveniles by a family court. These measures ranged from the supervision of a juvenile by a probation officer, other trustworthy person, a workplace or a youth organisation, to placement in a youth educational centre, foster family or health institution.[74] Generally, provisional measures were similar to educational and medical measures imposed on juveniles by family courts after adjudicating the case. In some cases specified by art. 27 of the JA the placement of a juvenile in a youth detention centre (*schronisko dla nieletnich*) could be ordered as a provisional measure: when circumstances had come to light that recommended placement in a correctional institution and additionally there were grounds for fearing that the juvenile might flee or destroy evidence, or if it was impossible to establish the juvenile's identity. Exceptionally a juvenile could also be placed in a youth detention centre if there were circumstances that recommended placement in a correctional institution and he was suspected of committing one of the most serious offences.[75]

The 2013 amendment did not introduce significant changes to provisions concerning provisional measures. Currently, the same preliminary measures as before the amendment are applied to juveniles by family courts in unified court proceedings. As far as the detention of juveniles in police institutions for children is concerned, the legal grounds for such detention are also the same as before January 2014.[76] However, the catalogue of rights of a juvenile detained in a police institution for children has been clarified and expanded. According to the current wording of the JA, the juvenile must be immediately informed of the reason for his arrest and informed of his rights, including the rights to legal assistance, to refuse to give explanations or answer particular questions and to lodge a complaint with the family court for activities violating his rights. The juvenile should be immediately interrogated. If he so requests, the police must enable him to establish contact with a parent, guardian or lawyer.[77] Another important change introduced by the 2013 amendment consists of determining by law the maximum length of stay in a police institution for children after the family court has decided on the application of a preliminary measure. A juvenile

---

73 See art. 40 para. 5 JA before the 2013 amendment.
74 Art. 26 JA before the 2013 amendment.
75 Art. 27 para. 2 JA before the 2013 amendment.
76 See art. 32g para. JA.
77 See art. 32g para. 3 JA.

may stay in a police institution for children for no longer than five days after the court's decision on provisional placement (in a youth educational centre, foster family, health institution or youth detention centre) was announced to him.[78]

As a rule, juveniles cannot be detained in remand prisons (*areszt śledczy*) for adult suspects. However, under art. 18 para. 2 of the JA, a juvenile of at least 15 years of age at the time of the offence may, in exceptional cases, be temporarily placed in a remand prison (*tymczasowo aresztowany*) provided that there are grounds for sentencing him to a penalty provided for adults under art. 10 para. 2 CC and provided placement in a youth detention centre would not be sufficient. According to Polish prison statistics, in 2012 (as of 31 December) six persons aged 15–16 were detained on remand in detention facilities for adults.[79]

2.5. RELEVANT ACTORS

According to the 1982 JA, the Polish juvenile justice system is based on the concept that the central role in juvenile proceedings is played by the family court. Originally, the JA provided for separate departments (*wydziały rodzinne i nieletnich*) in district courts (*sądy rejonowe*). Their jurisdiction covered family and juvenile cases. In 2013 the Act on the organisation of common courts[80] was amended. Under this amendment, separate departments competent in family and juvenile cases may be set up within district courts but it is not obligatory.[81] If such separate departments are not established within a district court, juvenile cases are dealt with by judges from the civil department. In regional courts (*sądy okręgowe*) which function among others as courts of appeal from judgments given at first instance by district courts, juvenile cases are always dealt with by civil departments.[82]

In legal literature it has been stressed that family judges should have extensive knowledge of pedagogy, psychology and sociology. However, the current system of training of candidates for the profession of judge does not include courses in psychology or other social sciences.[83] In practice, the profession of a family judge in comparison with criminal or civil judges is perceived as less prestigious.[84]

---

78 See art. 32g para. 8 JA.

79 Ministry of Justice, Central Administration of Prison Service 2013, p. 14.

80 *Ustawa – Prawo o ustroju sądów powszechnych*, 27 July 2001, Official Legal Bulletin 98, pos. 1070 with later amendments.

81 *Ustawa – Prawo o ustroju sądów powszechnych*, art. 12 para. 1a.

82 *Ustawa – Prawo o ustroju sądów powszechnych*, art. 16 para. 1.

83 Arczewska 2007, p. 20–21.

84 Arczewska 2007, p. 19–20.

There is no specialisation in juvenile justice among public prosecutors and defence lawyers. The first category of actors is involved in dealing with juvenile cases only to a limited extent. In exceptional cases – more specifically cases concerning offences committed by a juvenile together with an adult – they may conduct the investigation (*śledztwo*) in a juvenile case provided that certain legal conditions are fulfilled.[85] The public prosecutor also brings an indictment to the criminal court in cases in which a juvenile is exceptionally criminally liable as an adult on the basis of art. 10 para. 2 CC. In the 'normal' course of juvenile proceedings regulated by the JA the public prosecutor is party to the proceedings but his tasks and powers in this inquisitorial process are limited.

Furthermore, no specialisation in juvenile proceedings is required for defence lawyers. They rarely take part in juvenile proceedings. Research carried out by Czarnecka-Dzialuk, Drapała and Więcek-Durańska revealed that in 2004–2008 defence lawyers participated in only 4 per cent of cases which related to 15- and 16-year-old juveniles who were judged before family courts in care-educational proceedings for serious punishable acts.[86] In correctional proceedings[87] the participation of defence lawyers was mandatory, but the share of the latter proceedings in the total number of adjudicatory proceedings was very small[88] and defence lawyers were often passive actors in these proceedings.[89] This passivity seems to be for two reasons. The first is connected with the commonly accepted opinion that the family judge acts in the best interest of a juvenile so there is no need to interfere with his activities. The second refers to a limited level of knowledge of juvenile law among lawyers because this branch of law is neglected in the academic study of law as well as during subsequent training for the legal professions.

With regard to the police, a 2010 order issued by the Chief Police Commander (*Komendant Główny Policji*) on methods and forms of performing tasks in the field of counteracting juvenile demoralisation by the police provides for special units for 'juveniles and pathology' (*komórki do spraw nieletnich i patologii*) at different levels of the organisational structure of the police.[90] Special training for policemen on different aspects of dealing with juveniles have been organised by

85 Art. 16 JA.

86 Czarnecka-Dzialuk, Drapała and Więcek-Durańska 2011, p. 109.

87 Correctional proceedings were abolished by the 2013 amendment to the JA. See *supra* paragraph 2.3.2 (part I).

88 In the period 1999–2009 only 1.4–2.0 per cent of cases dealt with in the explanatory proceedings due to 'punishable acts' were referred to correctional proceedings: see Ministry of Justice 2010, p. 11.

89 Czarnecka-Dzialuk, Drapała and Więcek-Durańska 2011, p. 109.

90 *Zarządzenie nr 1619 Komendanta Głównego Policji w sprawie metod i form wykonywania zadań przez policjantów w zakresie przeciwdziałania demoralizacji i przestępczości nieletnich oraz działań podejmowanych na rzecz małoletnich*, 3 November 2010, Official Journal of the Police Headquarters 11, pos. 64.

the Police Training Centre (*Centrum Szkolenia Policji*). These special courses are provided mainly for policemen who work in units for 'juveniles and pathology' and police institutions for children.[91] Probation officers also specialise as either probation officers for adults or family probation officers. The latter *inter alia* perform tasks connected with the preparation of social inquiry reports in juvenile cases and the implementation of educational measures imposed on juveniles which consist of the supervision of a juvenile by a probation officer.[92]

3. SANCTIONS FOR JUVENILES

With a few exceptions mentioned above, no penalties provided for adults can be imposed on juvenile offenders. The catalogue of sanctions applied to juveniles contains a wide range of educational, medical and correctional measures. All educational and medical measures may be applied both to juveniles who have committed 'punishable acts' whilst between the age of 13 and 16 and to juveniles below the age of 18 who display problematic behaviour (signs of 'demoralisation'). Correctional measures, however, may be imposed only on juveniles who have committed 'punishable acts' that are prohibited by criminal law as offences or fiscal offences, after reaching the age of 13 but prior to reaching the age of 17.

When choosing between educational, medical and correctional measures, the family court should take into account the interests of the juvenile, the need to achieve positive changes in his personality and behaviour as well as the need to encourage and support proper fulfilment of his parents' or guardians' functions.[93] As regards correctional measures, some additional factors should be taken into consideration, such as the high degree of the juvenile's antisocial attitudes ('demoralisation') and the circumstances and the nature of the act as well as the (expected) ineffectiveness of educational measures.[94]

3.1. EDUCATIONAL MEASURES

The catalogue of educational measures includes:

(a) a reprimand;
(b) supervision by parents, a guardian, a youth or other social organisation, a workplace, a trustworthy person or a probation officer;

91 Witkowski and Kuć 2007.
92 On the tasks of the probation service in Poland see Wilamowska 2008, p. 807–808.
93 Art. 3 para. 1 JA.
94 Art. 10 JA.

(c) applying special conditions, such as redressing the damage, apologising to the victim, performing unpaid work for the benefit of the victim or the local community, taking up school education or a job, taking part in educational or therapeutic training, avoiding specific locations, refraining from the use of alcohol and other intoxicants;
(d) a ban on driving;
(e) forfeiture of objects gained through the commission of a punishable act;
(f) placing the juvenile in a youth probation centre;
(g) placing the juvenile in a professional foster family;
(h) placing the juvenile in a suitable institution or organisation providing education, therapy or vocational training; and
(i) placing the juvenile in a youth educational centre.[95]

3.2. MEDICAL MEASURES

Medical measures may be applied to juveniles who are suffering from mental deficiency, mental disease, some kind of mental disorder or from an alcohol and/or drug addiction. These measures involve placing the juvenile in a psychiatric hospital, other suitable health care institutions, a social welfare institution or a suitable youth educational centre.[96] Both educational and medical measures are applied to juveniles for an indeterminate period of time. As a rule, these measures will come to an end when the juvenile reaches the age of 18, but in some cases their duration may be extended to his 21st birthday.[97] The family court that has imposed educational measures may change, revise or repeal them at any time if it is deemed advisable for educational purposes.[98] In case medical measures are enforced, the family court evaluates at least every six months, on the basis of medical reports, whether the juvenile needs to stay longer in a suitable health care institution or a social welfare institution.[99]

3.3. CORRECTIONAL MEASURES

Correctional measures consist of suspended or unsuspended placement of a juvenile in a correctional institution. Such institutions are subordinated to the Ministry of Justice, but they do not form part of the prison system. Similar to other categories of measures, the correctional measures are applied for an indeterminate period of time. The juvenile placed in a correctional institution

95 Art. 6 JA.
96 Art. 12 JA.
97 Art. 73 para. 1 JA.
98 Art. 79 para. 1 JA.
99 Art. 80 JA.

can stay there no longer than up to 21 years of age,[100] although he may be granted conditional release earlier.[101]

In practice the number of juveniles on whom educational, medical or correctional measures were imposed due to 'punishable acts' has recently been relatively stable.[102] In the years 2000–2011 it oscillated between 23–28 thousand (figure 2).

Figure 2. Juveniles judged by family courts in the years 1984–2011[103]

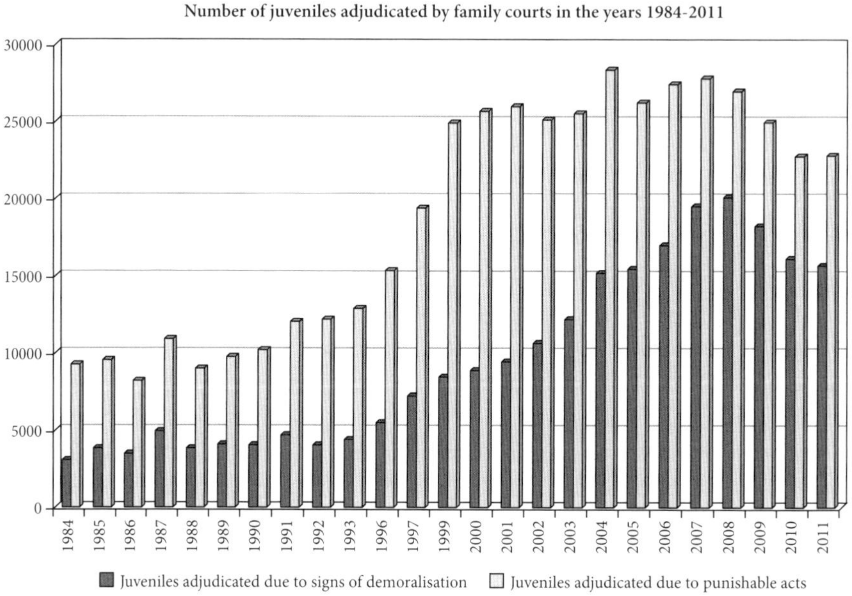

Since the entrance into force of the JA, educational measures have formed the vast majority of court dispositions for juvenile perpetrators of 'punishable acts'. Over the last few years the most frequently applied educational measures have been a reprimand and supervision by a probation officer (figure 3).

---

100 Art. 73 para. 1 JA.

101 Art. 86 JA.

102 The Ministry of Justice publishes two sets of data: on judgements given in first instance and enforceable judgements (*prawomocne orzeczenia*). In this chapter statistical data on enforceable judgements in juvenile cases are used which differ significantly from data on decisions given in first instance. In juvenile proceedings the latter decisions are very rarely challenged by parties and changed or repealed by the court of higher instance. Thus, significant differences in these two sets of data in juvenile cases are difficult to explain. See on this matter: Czarnecka-Dzialuk and Wójcik 2011, p. 873–874.

103 Data come from: Central Statistical Office, *Statistical Yearbook of the Republic of Poland (Rocznik Statystyczny Rzeczypospolitej Polskiej; before 1990: Rocznik Statystyczny)*, Warsaw, yearly publication. Data for the years 1994, 1995 and 1998 are not available.

Figure 3. Imposition of educational measures on juveniles for punishable acts in the years 1984–2011[104]

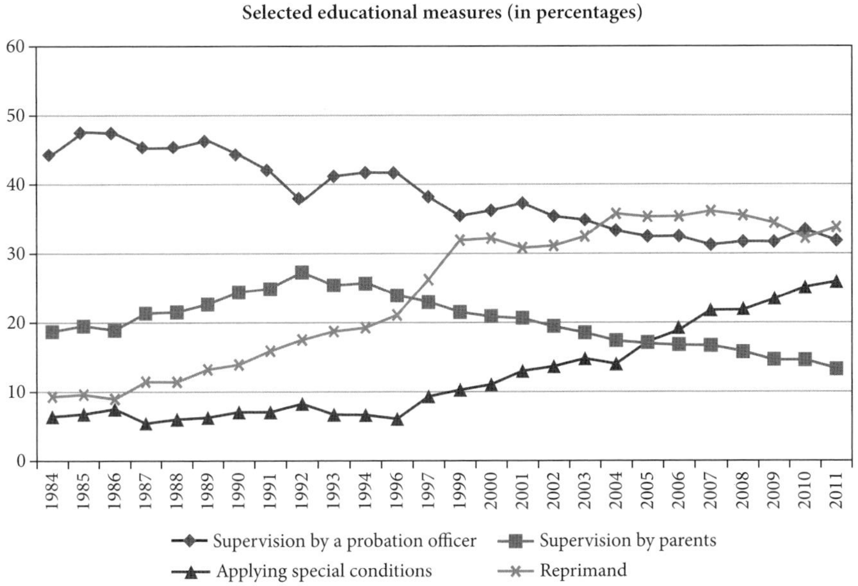

Correctional measures that involve suspended or unsuspended placement of a juvenile in a correctional institution are relatively seldom applied. Since the year 2000, suspended and unsuspended placement in a correctional institution has been imposed on 3–5 per cent of juveniles in court for 'punishable acts' (figure 4). In 1984 family courts decided to impose the placement in a correctional institution (suspended and unsuspended) on about one in five of juveniles adjudicated due to 'punishable acts'.[105] As a result of a steady decline in the use of correctional measures in 2011 they were imposed on 3 per cent of juvenile offenders. The drop in the use of correctional measures since 1984 related both to suspended and unsuspended placement of juveniles in correctional institutions. In 2011, 259 juvenile perpetrators of 'punishable acts' were immediately placed in correctional institutions, or 1.1 per cent of all juvenile offenders whose cases were judged.[106]

104 Data come from: Central Statistical Office, *Statistical Yearbook of the Republic of Poland (Rocznik Statystyczny Rzeczypospolitej Polskiej; before 1990: Rocznik Statystyczny)*, Warsaw, yearly publication. Data for the years 1995 and 1998 are not available.

105 These data refer to judgements given by family courts in first instance: see Szumski 1990, p. 156–159.

106 Central Statistical Office 2013, p. 167.

Figure 4. Number and proportion of correctional measures imposed on juvenile offenders in the years 2000–2011[107]

Year	Total number of juveniles adjudicated due to 'punishable acts'	Juveniles on whom correctional measures (suspended and unsuspended) were imposed	
		Number	Percentage
2000	25,667	1,173	4.6
2001	25,976	1,144	4.4
2002	25,111	1,280	5.1
2003	25,521	1,259	4.9
2004	28,342	1,322	4.7
2005	26,228	1,158	4.4
2006	27,419	1,075	3.9
2007	27,790	1,026	3.7
2008	26,957	927	3.4
2009	24,953	870	3.5
2010	22,758	882	3.9
2011	22,807	691	3.0

4. DIVERSION

Art. 21 para. 2 of the JA forms the legal basis for diversion without intervention. Pursuant to this provision, the family court may at any time drop the juvenile case unconditionally if in the opinion of the court the imposition of educational or correctional measures would serve no purpose, in particular when such measures has already been imposed on the juvenile in a previous case.[108] As for diversion *with* intervention, this may involve victim-offender mediation or referring the case to a school or a social (non-governmental) organisation.

Victim-offender mediation programmes were introduced in Poland in 1995, firstly within the juvenile justice system and only on an experimental basis. Eventually, mediation in juvenile cases was legally regulated in 2000 through amendments to the JA. According to art. 3a of the JA, which was added in 2000, the family court, acting on the initiative or with the consent of both the juvenile and the victim, may at any stage of the proceedings transfer the case to mediation by an institution or a trustworthy person. Results of the mediation

107 Data come from: Central Statistical Office, *Statistical Yearbook of the Republic of Poland (Rocznik Statystyczny Rzeczypospolitej Polskiej)*, Warsaw, yearly publication.

108 Before the 2013 amendment to the JA the family judge was authorised to decide on discontinuation of explanatory proceedings on the principle of expediency.

shall be reported to the court by the institution or trustworthy person, and they are taken into consideration when deciding on the case. It is also possible for the family court[109] to drop the proceedings at an early stage if the mediation is successful.

Before the 2013 amendment to the JA, the decision on referring the case to the school attended by the juvenile or a social organisation to which he belonged in order to avoid formal adjudication was taken by the family judge who conducted the explanatory proceeding.[110] The family judge could take such a decision if he was of the opinion that the educational influence of the school or organisation was adequate. After the 2013 amendment it is the family court that may take the decision on the basis of art. 32j of the JA. Under the amended provisions the consent of a juvenile is needed for such diversion.

Notwithstanding the aforementioned legal basis, the number of mediations in juvenile cases has been very limited: in recent years only between 250 and 350 juvenile cases were referred to mediation per year.[111] It seems that under the paternalistic and protective welfare approach, family courts have been showing moderate interest in victim-offender mediation and other forms of diversion because the entire juvenile justice system is perceived as aiming at diverting juveniles from criminal proceedings.

II. INTERROGATIONS

1. LISTENING TO (*WYSŁUCHANIE*) AND INTERROGATION OF (*PRZESŁUCHANIE*) A JUVENILE

In juvenile proceedings there are two different modes of questioning a juvenile in order to determine if he has committed a 'punishable act': *wysłuchanie* and *przesłuchanie*. In this chapter *wysłuchanie* has been translated as 'listening' while for *przesłuchanie* the term 'interrogation' has been used.

In Polish law there is no single definition of 'interrogation' (*przesłuchanie*). This term has been used in provisions of both the Code of Civil Procedure and the Code of Criminal Procedure with regard to the questioning of different persons (parties, witnesses, experts) by different authorities (the police, public prosecutors, courts) at different stages of proceedings. The Code of Civil

109 By a family judge before the 2013 amendment to the JA.

110 See art. 42 para. 4 JA before the 2013 amendment.

111 Ministry of Justice 2013. See also, Stańdo-Kawecka 2010, p. 1011.

Procedure regulates the interrogation of parties, witnesses and experts in civil proceedings.[112] In criminal proceedings persons who are suspected or accused of committing an offence are interrogated by the police, public prosecutors, other organs conducting the preliminary (pre-trial) proceedings or by the court at the stage of the court proceedings. 'Interrogation' in criminal proceedings also refers to witnesses testifying in a criminal case[113] as well as experts questioned in matters related to an expert opinion prepared by them[114] or persons who prepared a social inquiry report.[115]

According to Polish law, 'listening' to participants of proceedings (*wysłuchanie*) is typical for civil non-litigious proceedings.[116] The aim of listening to participants is to enable them to present their positions on the subject matter.

1.1. LISTENING TO (*WYSŁUCHANIE*) A JUVENILE BEFORE THE 2013 AMENDMENT

As mentioned above,[117] the legislator of 1982 assumed that most information concerning the alleged 'punishable acts' or signs of 'demoralisation' displayed by juveniles would be received directly by the family courts. Subsequently, the family judge should institute the explanatory (preparatory) proceedings on the basis of this information. The aim of these proceedings was to determine whether there were circumstances indicating the juvenile's 'demoralisation', and in cases concerning 'punishable acts' whether the juvenile committed the alleged unlawful act. Another aim of the explanatory proceedings was to determine whether there was a need to apply the juvenile measures provided by the JA.[118] Lack of such a need resulted in the decision on discontinuation of the explanatory proceedings taken by the family judge.[119]

In the course of the explanatory proceedings the family judge listened (*wysłuchiwał*) to the juvenile, his parents or guardian and – if needed – other persons. The rules applicable to such listening were those of the Code of Civil Procedure with the adjustments provided by the JA.[120] The essence of a family judge listening to a juvenile lies in receiving statements or explanations from the

---

112 See *Dział III. Dowody* (*Unit III. Evidence*) of the Code of Civil Procedure.
113 See art. 177 para. 1a CCP.
114 See art. 200 para. 3 CCP.
115 See art. 214 para. 6 CCP.
116 See art. 514 Code of Civil Procedure.
117 See *supra* paragraph 2.3.1 (part I).
118 Art. 33 JA before the 2013 amendment.
119 Art. 21 para. 2 JA before the 2013 amendment.
120 Art. 20 JA before the 2013 amendment.

juvenile on the subject.[121] In legal literature it was stressed that an important aim of this kind of listening, although not an aim articulated *expressis verbis* by the legislator, was also to establish a personal relationship between the family judge and the juvenile in order to initiate the educational influence on the latter and to obtain information on the personality of the juvenile and his living conditions.[122]

The JA did not require the family judge to listen to the juvenile in the course of the explanatory proceedings in the presence of his parents or guardian. Authors of commentaries to the JA stressed that it was the family judge who made the decision on how to listen to the juvenile.[123]

By referring to the rules of civil procedure, the JA did not oblige the family judge to inform the juvenile of the right to refuse to give statements or explanations.[124] Statements made by a juvenile during the listening were treated as evidence resulting from the interrogation of parties in the meaning of the Code of Civil Procedure.[125]

The family judge who conducted the explanatory proceedings could order a probation officer to carry out certain actions (such as preparing a social inquiry report). He could also order the police to carry out certain actions, including the interrogation of a juvenile.[126] Theoretically, the possibility of ordering a probation officer and/or the police to carry out certain actions constituted an exception to the rule that it was the family judge who conducted the whole explanatory proceedings.[127] At the same time, in Polish literature on the juvenile justice system it was stressed that some actions aimed at the collection of evidence, such as for example the search of a home, required experience and knowledge in the field of forensic techniques and could be carried out only by the police.[128] It should be added that provisions of civil procedure do not regulate some evidence gathering activities which are typical in criminal proceedings.

---

121 Korcyl-Wolska 2004, p. 94.

122 Strzembosz 1984, p. 95–96.

123 Grześkowiak, Krukowski, Patulski and Warzocha 1991, p. 85 and Gaberle and Korcyl-Wolska 2002, p. 120.

124 Under the rules of civil procedure, participants in the civil proceedings are obliged to testify the truth. They may refuse to answer to a question if the testimony could expose them or their close relatives, to criminal responsibility, shame, or serious and immediate damage to property as well as if the testimony might be connected with breaching of professional confidentiality.

125 Korcyl-Wolska 2004, p. 94.

126 Art. 37 para. 2 JA before the 2013 amendment.

127 Gaberle and Korcyl-Wolska 2002, p. 169.

128 Taracha 1988, p. 123.

Art. 20 of the JA stipulated[129] that in matters concerning the appointment and functioning of a defence lawyer, provisions of the Code of Criminal Procedure applied. Thus, it was the Code of Criminal Procedure (art. 84) which enabled defence lawyers to be present while the family judge listens to a juvenile. In the explanatory proceedings a juvenile could have a defence lawyer appointed by his parents or guardian. In some cases the assistance of a lawyer was mandatory, namely if the interests of a juvenile and his parents or guardian were in conflict,[130] or when the family court had applied the temporary measure of placing a juvenile in a youth detention centre (*schronisko dla nieletnich*).[131]

Under art. 37 para. 2 of the JA, the family judge could order the police to arrest and bring a juvenile to court in order to listen to him. Art. 40a of the JA[132] authorised the police acting on a family court order to arrest and place a juvenile in a police institution for children (*policyjna izba dziecka*) for a period necessary to perform actions (*czas niezbędny do wykonania czynności*), but not exceeding 48 hours.

1.2. LISTENING (*WYSŁUCHANIE*) TO A JUVENILE AFTER THE 2013 AMENDMENT

After the amendment of 2013 the form of questioning of a juvenile called *wysłuchanie* has been retained. In the current unified court proceedings the family court listens (*wysłuchuje*) to the juvenile and his parents or guardian.[133] Art. 19 of the JA stipulates (as was also the case before the 2013 amendment) the circumstances under which listening (*wysłuchanie*) to a juvenile by the family court should take place. Pursuant to this article, during the listening the juvenile should be ensured full freedom of expression. In addition to this, the listening should be conducted in 'conditions similar to natural' (*w warunkach zbliżonych do naturalnych*). Undoubtedly, conditions most similar to natural are in the juvenile's family home. This phrase could be understood as an indication that the legislator preferred the listening to a juvenile to take place in a less formal setting, namely in his home or school. Repeated listening to a juvenile on the same circumstances or circumstances already established by other evidence and not raising doubts should be avoided in the light of the same article.

The difference between the previous and amended version of the JA lies in provisions concerning the rights of a juvenile to defence and to refuse

[129] See art. 20 JA before the 2013 amendment.
[130] Art. 36 para. 1 JA before the 2013 amendment.
[131] Art. 49 JA before the 2013 amendment.
[132] Art. 40a JA before the 2013 amendment. This provision was introduced to the JA in 2011.
[133] Art. 32b para. 2 JA.

explanations. Since January 2014 provisions of the JA clearly state that a juvenile has the right to defence as well as to refuse to give explanations or answer particular questions. He should be instructed about these rights before both being listened to (*wysłuchanie*) by a family court and before his interrogation (*przesłuchanie*) by the police.[134] The JA does not require the family court to listen to a juvenile only in the presence of his parents or guardian. Parents or guardians are parties to proceedings in juvenile cases and because of that they may take part in them, but their presence is not obligatory. If the juvenile has a (chosen or appointed *ex officio*) defence lawyer, certain provisions of the Code of Criminal Procedure form the legal basis which enables him to be present during the listening to the juvenile by the family court.

1.3. INTERROGATION BY THE POLICE IN 'URGENT CASES' BEFORE THE 2013 AMENDMENT

In 1982 the legislator took into account that in some cases the information on an alleged 'punishable act' committed by a juvenile might initially be received by the police and it might be necessary to gather and preserve evidence immediately by the police, for example in the event of a juvenile caught by the police in *flagrante delicto*. For that reason, arts. 37 and 39 of the JA allowed the police (and state authorities acting under specific statutory authorisation)[135] to collect and preserve evidence of 'punishable acts', including the interrogation of a juvenile suspect, in urgent cases (*w wypadkach niecierpiących zwłoki*), before the formal proceedings were instigated by the family judge.[136] As mentioned earlier, 'urgent cases' referred to cases in which it was necessary to collect and preserve traces and evidence of crimes against loss or damage.[137] The collection and preserving of evidence of 'punishable acts' in urgent cases, including the interrogation of a juvenile, were governed by provisions of the Code of Criminal Procedure. Art. 308 para. 5 CCP provides that actions in urgent cases may be taken no longer than within five days from the first action.

1.3.1. Safeguards applicable during interrogation by the police

According to the applicable provisions of the Code of Criminal Procedure, a juvenile suspected of committing a 'punishable act' who was interrogated by the police in urgent cases, that is before the instigation of the explanatory proceeding by a family judge, had to be informed about the allegation: more

134 Art. 18a JA.
135 On state authorities acting under specific statutory authorisation and having the same powers as the police, see art. 312 CCP.
136 See arts. 37 and 40 JA before the 2013 amendment.
137 Korcyl-Wolska 2004, p. 88.

specifically, according to art. 308 para. 2 of the Code of Criminal Procedure, the interrogation had to start by informing the juvenile of the content of the allegation. Furthermore, under art. 300 a juvenile should – before the first interrogation – also be informed about:

(a) his rights and duties, including the duty to undergo examinations and the right to give explanations, to refuse to give explanations or to refuse to answer particular questions;
(b) his right to submit requests for taking evidence;
(c) his right to request an interrogation with the participation of a defence lawyer; and
(d) his right to provide explanations in writing.[138]

Such instruction (*pouczenie*) should be handed over in writing and confirmed by the juvenile with his signature.[139]

Polish criminal proceedings are based on the principle *nemo tenetur se ipsum accusare* (no one is required to testify against himself), and particularly the suspect (accused) has no such obligation. This principle is clearly formulated in art. 74 para. 1 CCP, which states that the suspect (accused) is neither obliged to prove his innocence nor has the obligation to provide evidence against himself.[140] There are, however, some exceptions to this principle, precisely determined by the law; for example, the suspect is obliged to undergo external examination of the body and other examinations not involving interference with the integrity of the body.[141] The same provisions applied (and still apply) to a juvenile interrogated by the police.

In art. 39 the JA stated *expressis verbis* that the interrogation of a juvenile should take place in the presence of his parents and/or guardian or a defence lawyer. Only if it was not possible to provide their presence during the interrogation, should a teacher, a representative of the social service (a family support centre) or a social organisation for education and re-socialisation of juveniles be present. In the literature on juvenile law it was stressed that the interrogation of a juvenile by the police in the absence of persons mentioned in the art. 39 of the JA constituted a serious breach of procedural rules; resulting in the fact that the formal written record (*protokół*) of the interrogation should not be taken into account by the court.[142]

---

138 Korcyl-Wolska 2004, p. 95–96 and Gaberle and Korcyl-Wolska 2002, p. 172–173.
139 See art. 300 CCP.
140 For more information see Świda, Ponikowski and Posnow, 2008, p. 306.
141 Art. 74 para. 2 CCP.
142 Gaberle and Korcyl-Wolska 2002, p. 171.

The interrogation of a juvenile had to be recorded in writing, which meant that a formal written record (*protokół*) has to be made.[143] According to art. 147 CCP, procedural actions which are recorded in writing could also be recorded by means of video or audio recording. Persons participating in the procedural actions should be informed of this before the video or audio recording is started. Detailed provisions on video or audio recording, as well as the way to store such records, are included in a regulation (*rozporządzenie*) issued by the Minister of Justice.[144] Generally, audio and video records should be stored in accordance with provisions concerning the way to store material evidence (*dowód rzeczowy*). In legal literature it was pointed out that video or audio recording in juvenile cases is permissible provided that the well-being of a juvenile did not preclude this.[145] In practice, video or audio recordings of the interrogation of a juvenile by the police are made only exceptionally.

1.4. INTERROGATION BY THE POLICE IN 'URGENT CASES' AFTER THE 2013 AMENDMENT

As was the case before the 2013 amendment, the JA still regulates mainly court proceedings in juvenile cases. It contains only a few rules on the interrogation of a juvenile suspect by the police in 'urgent cases' or in cases in which the family court ordered the police to interrogate a juvenile suspect after instigation of court proceedings.

Art. 32e of the JA allows the police to collect and preserve evidence in 'urgent cases' (*w wypadkach niecierpiących zwłoki*), before the formal proceedings are instigated by the family court. Nevertheless, according to the amended provisions of the JA, the police are authorised to collect and preserve evidence not only of 'punishable acts' but also of signs of 'demoralisation'. A 'punishable act' may be committed only by a juvenile of at least 13 years of age. There is no minimum age limit for showing signs of 'demoralisation'. As a result of the 2013 amendment the police have been granted powers to collect and preserve traces and evidence of signs of 'demoralisation' against loss or damage before formal instigation of juvenile proceedings by the family court, including powers to interrogate juveniles below 13 years of age. On the basis of art. 32e para. 2 of the JA, the family court may in the course of juvenile proceedings order the police to undertake certain activities, including the interrogation of a juvenile,

143 See art. 143 para. 1 CCP.

144 *Rozporządzenie Ministra Sprawiedliwości w sprawie rodzaju urządzeń i środków technicznych służących do utrwalania obrazu lub dźwięku dla celów procesowych oraz sposobu przechowywania, odtwarzania i kopiowania zapisów*, 14 September 2012, Official Legal Bulletin, pos. 1090.

145 Gaberle and Korcyl-Wolska 2002, p. 173–174.

irrespective of whether the proceedings were instigated because of a 'punishable act' or signs of 'demoralisation'.

Police powers to interrogate a juvenile before the instigation of proceedings by a family court are limited to 'urgent cases'. Generally, it is the decision of the police if in a certain case it is necessary to interrogate a juvenile in order to collect and preserve traces and evidence of 'punishable acts' or signs of 'demoralisation' against loss or damage. The amended JA (art. 32g para. 3) imposes on the police the obligation to interrogate a juvenile immediately only if he is temporarily detained in a police institution for children. If such temporary placement is not applied and there is no 'urgent' need to interrogate a juvenile, the police must refer the case to the family court without interrogating him. It should be noted, however, that police files may contain not only formal written records (*protokoły*) of interrogations but also informal notes (*notatki urzędowe*) concerning for example the reason for the police intervention, the description of the place of an alleged 'punishable act' or signs of 'demoralisation', and information on what a juvenile said at that place. Court proceedings in juvenile cases as a rule are governed by civil procedure which does not provide for such restrictions on evidence as is the case of criminal procedure. In comparison with criminal procedure the principle of immediacy is strongly limited in juvenile proceedings. On the basis of art. 32p of the JA the family court is authorised to read different formal written records (*protokoły*) as well as other documents prepared by different authorities (*wszelkie dokumenty urzędowe*) if in his opinion direct conducting of evidence during the court sitting or hearing is not necessary. As a result, informal notes (*notatki urzędowe*) made by the police on what a juvenile said without being informed about allegations and instructed on his rights could be treated by the family court as evidence.

1.4.1. Rules on carrying out the interrogation

According to the amended JA, the interrogation of a juvenile by the police – including the instruction on his rights and the way to document the interrogation – is still mainly regulated by the Code of Criminal Procedure.[146]

Basic rules on the interrogation in criminal proceedings are included in art. 171 CCP. According to these rules, which also apply to the interrogation of a juvenile, the police should enable the juvenile to freely express himself on matters related to the purpose of the interrogation. After enabling the juvenile

---

146 Similarly to the JA before the 2013 amendment, art. 20 para. 1 of the amended JA regulates that the collection and preservation of evidence of 'punishable acts' or 'demoralisation' by the police, including the interrogation of a juvenile suspect by the police, are – as a rule – governed by provisions of the Code of Criminal Procedure.

to do so, the police could ask additional questions. During the interrogation of a juvenile the police are not allowed to ask questions which suggest the answer.[147] It is also not allowed to influence the interrogated juvenile by using coercion or unlawful threat as well as to use hypnosis and chemical or technical means having influence on his mental processes.[148]

There are no regulations concerning the maximum duration of the interrogation of a juvenile by the police. After being interrogated, the juvenile is released and transferred into the custody of his parents or guardian. Only under specific circumstances determined by the JA may the interrogated juvenile be placed in a police institution for children (*policyjna izba dziecka*).[149] In that case the police have the obligation to inform the family court of the placement no later than 24 hours after the arrest. The juvenile has to be released immediately on an order of the family court or if there is no need to continue his placement. Furthermore, he has to be released if within 48 hours of the family court being informed of his arrest no court decision on temporary measures is announced to him.

After collecting and preserving evidence in urgent cases the police are obliged to immediately refer the case to the family court who decides whether there are grounds for instigation of juvenile proceedings due to signs of 'demoralisation' or a 'punishable act'.

The rules of criminal procedure concerning the interrogation of a juvenile by the police in 'urgent cases' also apply in cases in which the family court orders the police to interrogate the juvenile after instigation of proceedings.

1.4.2. Right to an appropriate adult

Art. 32f of the amended JA provides that the interrogation of a juvenile by the police shall be conducted in the presence of parents having parental responsibility or a guardian or in the presence of a defence lawyer. Only if it is not possible to provide the presence of at least one of these persons should the police provide the presence of a person close to the juvenile indicated by him or a representative of the school attended by the juvenile, the welfare authorities or a social (non-governmental) organisation working with juveniles. What is interesting is the fact that according to the amended JA the interrogation of a juvenile by the police should be conducted in 'circumstances similar to natural' (*w warunkach zbliżonych do naturalnych*), and if needed in his place of residence.

---

147 Asking questions which suggest answers has been forbidden by art. 171 para. 4 CCP. See Korcyl-Wolska 2004, p. 97.

148 See art. 171 para. 5 CCP.

149 See art. 32g JA.

The legislator prefers interrogations of juveniles by the police to take place outside a police station, which seems to be wishful thinking.[150]

1.4.3. Other safeguards applicable during interrogation by the police

Most of the safeguards applicable to a juvenile during his interrogation by the police did not change after the 2013 amendment to the JA. As was also the case before the amendment, a juvenile interrogated by the police in 'urgent cases' or on the basis of an order issued by a family court has to be informed about the allegations. A juvenile should – before the first interrogation – also be instructed about:

(a) his rights and duties, including the duty to undergo examinations and the right to give explanations, to refuse to give explanations or to refuse to answer particular questions;
(b) his right to submit requests for taking evidence;
(c) his right to request an interrogation with the participation of a defence lawyer; and
(d) his right to provide explanations in writing.[151]

The interrogated juvenile should confirm with his signature that he received such instruction (*pouczenie*) in writing.[152]

2. RIGHT TO A DEFENCE

According to Polish law, it is a constitutional principle that every person against whom criminal proceedings are conducted has the right to a defence, including the right to choose a defence lawyer or to be assisted by an *ex officio* defence lawyer, at every stage of the proceedings.[153] The right to be assisted by an *ex officio* defence lawyer does not include an absolute right to legal assistance free of charge. The Constitution ensures the right to be assisted by an *ex officio* defence lawyer according to principles set out in a statute (*na zasadach określonych w ustawie*). More specifically, it is the Code of Criminal Procedure that sets out rules concerning mandatory assistance by a defence lawyer as well as legal assistance free of charge.

150 See art. 32f JA in connection with art. 19 JA.
151 The same provisions of arts. 300 and 308 para. 2 CCP apply as before the 2013 amendment to the JA.
152 See art. 300 CCP.
153 Art. 42 section 2 of the Constitution.

According to Polish legal doctrine, proceedings in juvenile cases regulated by the JA are not considered 'criminal' proceedings. As a result, the above-mentioned constitutional principle does not apply to juvenile cases. The juvenile's right to defence is regulated by provisions of the JA and the Code of Criminal Procedure. The later Code applies only in matters concerning the appointment and functioning of a defence lawyer unless the JA regulates these issues in another way.

2.1. RIGHT TO A DEFENCE BEFORE THE 2013 AMENDMENT

Provisions of the JA before the 2013 amendment did not mention *expressis verbis* the juvenile's right to a defence. However, the juvenile, as well as his parents or guardian, were parties to the proceedings[154] and were authorised to take certain actions such as participating in court sittings and main hearings, having access to the case file, choosing a defence lawyer and requesting evidence or bringing appeals.[155]

With regard to the right to legal assistance, pursuant to provisions of the JA before the 2013 amendment, a juvenile could have a defence lawyer chosen by him or his parents or guardian at both stages of proceedings: the explanatory stage as well as adjudicating stage.[156] In some cases specified by the JA, the assistance of a defence lawyer was mandatory which meant that the president of the court appointed an *ex officio* defence lawyer (*obrońca z urzędu*) if the juvenile did not have a lawyer of his own choice (*obrońca z wyboru*). The assistance of a defence lawyer was mandatory in juvenile cases:

(a) if the interests of a juvenile and his/her parents or guardian were in conflict;[157]
(b) if the temporary measure consisting of the placement of a juvenile in a youth detention centre (*schronisko dla nieletnich*) was applied by the family court;[158]
(c) in care-educational proceedings if there was a need to apply medical measures to a juvenile;[159] and
(d) in correctional proceedings[160] which took place when the family judge was of the opinion that correctional measures should be applied to the juvenile.

154 See art. 30 para. 1 JA before the 2013 amendment.
155 For more information on the rights of a juvenile and his parents or guardian as a party to proceedings see Gaberle and Korcyl-Wolska 2002, p. 149–152.
156 See arts. 36 and 44 JA before the 2013 amendment.
157 Art. 36 para. 1 JA before the 2013 amendment.
158 Art. 49 JA before the 2013 amendment.
159 Art. 47a JA before the 2013 amendment.
160 Art. 49 JA before the 2013 amendment.

In accordance with art. 20 of the JA[161] the appointment and tasks of a defence lawyer were governed by provisions of the Code of Criminal Procedure. Under art. 83 para. 1 of this Code, which applied in juvenile cases, a juvenile could appoint a defence lawyer independently only if he was at least 18 years of age,[162] which was very rare in proceedings for punishable acts. In such proceedings art. 76 CCP applied, according to which a legal representative or caregiver could appoint a defence lawyer for a juvenile. In cases in which assistance of a defence lawyer was mandatory and the president of the court appointed an *ex officio* defence lawyer because the juvenile did not have a lawyer of his own choice the decision on the costs of this mandatory defence was taken by a family court in a final judgement.[163] Before the 2013 amendment, juveniles were deprived of the right to request an appointment of legal assistance free of charge in cases in which they and their parents were not able to cover such costs.

2.1.1. Right to legal assistance during listening to a juvenile by a family judge

In the course of explanatory proceedings the family judge who conducted it requested the president of the court to appoint an *ex officio* defence lawyer (*obrońca z urzędu*) if the juvenile did not have a lawyer of his own choice (*obrońca z wyboru*) and the assistance of a defence lawyer was mandatory. Mandatory legal assistance was provided for in the course of the explanatory proceedings only if the interests of a juvenile and his/her parents or guardian were in conflict as well as when the juvenile was temporarily (provisionally) placed in a youth detention centre.

Defence lawyers, chosen or appointed *ex officio*, were entitled to be present during the listening to a juvenile (*wysłuchanie*) by a family judge in the explanatory proceedings as well as during the listening to a juvenile by a family court at the adjudicatory stage on the basis of provisions of the Code of Criminal Procedure which applied in matters concerning actions of defence lawyers in juvenile cases.[164]

2.1.2. Right to legal assistance during interrogation of a juvenile by the police

As mentioned earlier, the collection and preservation of evidence of 'punishable acts' in urgent cases, including the interrogation of a juvenile, were governed by provisions of the Code of Criminal Procedure. In light of these provisions, the juvenile had to be instructed before the first interrogation about his right to the assistance of a defence lawyer (*prawo do korzystania z pomocy obrońcy*).[165]

---

161 See art. 20 JA before the 2013 amendment.

162 The age of 18 is the age of civil majority which means the juvenile has full capacity to enter into civil contracts: see also Gaberle and Korcyl-Wolska 2002, p. 167.

163 See art. 32 JA before the 2013 amendment.

164 Art. 20 JA before the 2013 amendment.

165 Art. 300 CCP.

At the request of the juvenile he had to be interrogated with the participation of a defence lawyer chosen by him or his parents or by a guardian. However, if the chosen lawyer (*ustanowiony obrońca*) would not appear, his absence did not inhibit the interrogation.[166] The Code of Criminal Procedure did not contain regulations on how long the police should wait for the chosen defence lawyer before starting the interrogation. Of course, the juvenile had the right to refuse to give explanations as long as his lawyer was absent.

When the interrogation of a juvenile by the police was ordered by the family judge in the course of the explanatory proceeding, a defence lawyer (chosen or appointed *ex officio*) was entitled to be present on the basis of provisions of the Code of Criminal Procedure which applied in matters concerning actions of defence lawyers in juvenile cases.[167]

2.1.3. Violation of the right to defence in the case of Adamkiewicz v. Poland

In the case of *Adamkiewicz v. Poland*[168] the ECtHR found a violation of art. 6 para. 3(c) of the ECHR because of the fact that the applicant's right to a defence had been considerably curtailed during the explanatory proceedings. The defence lawyer chosen for the juvenile by his parents made several unsuccessful requests to meet the juvenile who was arrested by the police and was then placed in a youth detention centre (*schronisko dla nieletnich*) by the family judge. It was only approximately six weeks after the arrest of the juvenile when the chosen defence lawyer had the first meeting with the juvenile, during which the latter was informed of his right to remain silent and not to incriminate himself.

Establishing the violation of art. 6 para. 3(c) ECHR, the ECtHR considered Adamkiewicz to be someone 'charged with a criminal offence' in the meaning of this article. Thus, this judgment of the ECtHR is contradictory to the view established in Polish legal doctrine that juvenile proceedings, including correctional proceedings, did not qualify as criminal proceedings but rather as *sui generis* proceedings. The judgment did not cause many discussions on these matters, which seems to indicate that juvenile law has been marginalised in Polish legal literature.

2.2. RIGHT TO DEFENCE AFTER THE 2013 AMENDMENT

Since the amendment of 2013, the JA explicitly states that the juvenile has the right to defence, including the right to legal assistance. He should be instructed

166 Art. 301 CCP: see also Posnow 2009, p. 417–420.
167 Art. 20 JA before the 2013 amendment.
168 ECtHR 2 March 2010, *Adamkiewicz v. Poland*, no. 54729/00.

about these rights before interrogation by the police or before listening to him by the family court.[169] The appointment and tasks of a defence lawyer are still governed by the Code of Criminal Procedure.[170] Provisions of the JA concerning a mandatory defence have been changed, among other reasons because of the abolition of correctional proceedings in which the juvenile was obliged to have a lawyer. According to the amended JA the assistance of a defence lawyer is mandatory in situations in which:

(a) the interests of the juvenile and his parents or guardian are contradictory;
(b) the juvenile is deaf, dumb or blind;
(c) there is a justified doubt whether the juvenile's state of mental health allows him to participate in the proceeding or defend himself in reasonable way (*prowadzić obronę w sposób samodzielny oraz rozsądny*); or
(d) the juvenile has been placed in a youth detention institution.[171]

The legislator seems to assume that as a rule juveniles are able to defend themselves in a reasonable way and that the assistance of a defence lawyer in juvenile proceedings is necessary only in exceptional cases, for example because of the juvenile's mental state.

Mandatory legal assistance includes mandatory physical presence during interrogation or listening to a juvenile. In cases in which defence is mandatory and the juvenile has no chosen defence lawyer (appointed by him or his parents or guardian) the president of the court appoints an *ex officio* defence lawyer from the list of lawyers in a certain region. It is not clearly regulated by the JA what the police should do in situations in which a juvenile has no chosen lawyer and there are grounds for a mandatory defence (for example because of doubts as to his mental health) at the stage of collecting and preserving evidence by the police in 'urgent cases', namely before the instigation of proceedings by a family court. The police can choose to transfer the case to a family court without interrogation of the juvenile or to inform the president of the court of the need to appoint mandatory defence lawyer for the juvenile and adjourn the interrogation.

Another change in provisions of the JA with regard to the right to legal assistance in juvenile proceedings concerns the request to appoint an *ex officio* lawyer when the juvenile and his parents or guardian are not able to pay the costs of a chosen lawyer. This possibility did not exist before the 2013 amendment to the JA. After the amendment, in cases in which the assistance of a defence lawyer is not mandatory and the juvenile does not have a defence lawyer of his choice he may

169 Art. 18a JA.
170 Art. 20 para. 1 JA.
171 Art. 32c paras. 1 and 2 JA.

ask the president of the court to appoint an *ex officio* lawyer provided that he and his parents demonstrate that they are not able to cover the costs of a chosen lawyer without detriment to the necessary maintenance of themselves and the family. In such a situation the president of the court is given a large discretionary power. He will only appoint an *ex officio* lawyer if he is of the opinion that the participation of the lawyer is needed (*jeżeli udział obrońcy w sprawie uzna za potrzebny*).[172]

Although the legal right to defence also covers the stage of pre-trial (police) interrogation, there are indications that juveniles are often interrogated without the assistance of a lawyer. It follows from a recent report of the European Committee for the Prevention of Torture and Inhuman and Degrading Treatment or Punishment that juveniles in police custody are still often interviewed and asked to make statements and sign documents without the presence of a lawyer (or another trusted adult) in flagrant violation of the relevant Polish legislation.[173]

3. RIGHT TO AN INTERPRETER AND TRANSLATION OF DOCUMENTS

Before the 2013 amendment, the JA did not contain provisions on the right of a juvenile to an interpreter or translation of documents. The situation did not change after this amendment. The lack of such provisions in the JA does not mean that juveniles are deprived of these rights. The Act on organisation of common courts[174] states that the official language in proceedings before Polish courts is Polish.[175] At the same time it provides for the right to the assistance of an interpreter (free of charge) for persons who do not speak Polish sufficiently well. Providing the assistance of an interpreter free of charge has been considered one of the safeguards included in the right to access to court. This safeguard has been given a broad scope and covers not only translation of the oral part of the proceedings, but also ensures translation of documents for persons who do not have sufficient understanding of the Polish language. In juvenile cases the decision to grant the assistance of an interpreter is taken by the family court which conducts the proceedings. According to provisions

172 Art. 32c para. 3 JA.

173 Council of Europe: Committee for the Prevention of Torture, Report to the Polish Government on the visit to Poland carried out by the European Committee for the Prevention of Torture and Inhuman or Degrading Treatment or Punishment (CPT) from 5 to 17 June 2013, 25 June 2014, CPT/Inf (2014) 21, available at: www.refworld.org/docid/53aa83ed4.html.

174 *Ustawa – Prawo o ustroju sądów powszechnych*, 27 July 2001, Official Legal Bulletin 98, pos. 1070 with later amendments.

175 *Ustawa – Prawo o ustroju sądów powszechnych*, art. 5.

of civil procedure, depriving a juvenile who does not speak Polish sufficiently well of the right to assistance of an interpreter or of the right to translation of documents is grounds for annulment of the proceedings by the court of higher instance because the party to the proceedings was deprived of opportunity to defend his rights.[176]

The JA states that in matters related to collection and preservation of evidence by the police in urgent cases, namely before formal instigation of proceedings by a family court, provisions of the Code of Criminal Procedure apply. The latter Code contains several detailed provisions concerning the suspect's right to an interpreter and translation of documents. According to art. 204 of the Code an interpreter should be called if there is a need to interrogate a person who does not speak Polish sufficiently well. The same should be done if there is a need to translate a document or to enable the suspect to know the content of the evidence which is presented. In the light of these provisions it is the obligation of the police to provide a juvenile interrogated by them in urgent cases with the assistance of an interpreter free of charge if the juvenile does not speak Polish sufficiently well.[177]

4. EUROPEAN ARREST WARRANT CASES

There are no special rules applicable to the interrogation of juveniles in European arrest warrant cases. According to art. 607k para. 2 CCP, the person against whom a European arrest warrant has been issued is interrogated by a public prosecutor who then refers the case to a competent court. The implementation of the European arrest warrant shall be refused, *inter alia*, if the person concerned is not criminally responsible under Polish law for offences constituting the basis for the warrant because of his age.[178]

5. REMEDIES AND SANCTIONS

According to art. 41 of the JA before the 2013 amendment, it was the task of a family judge to supervise the actions of the police in urgent cases, that is before the formal instigation of the explanatory proceedings. A juvenile and other persons whose rights were infringed by the police were entitled to bring a complaint to the family judge. After formal instigation of the explanatory

---

176 Art. 379 Code of Civil Procedure.

177 For more information on the scope and implementation of the right to assistance of an interpreter in criminal proceedings free of charge see Witkowska 2014, p. 34–38.

178 Art. 607p para. 1 point 4 CCP.

proceedings, a juvenile and other parties to the proceedings, as well as other persons (for example persons whose home was searched), could file a complaint against actions infringing their rights in the course of this proceeding.[179] Such complaints (*zażalenia*) were dealt with by family courts. In cases in which the complaint referred to actions taken by a family judge, this judge was excluded from dealing with it.[180]

After the 2013 amendment to the JA, the possibility of lodging complaints has remained unchanged to a large extent. What is different is the fact that actions of the police are supervised not by a family judge but by a family court (composed of a single judge). A juvenile and other persons whose rights were infringed by the police before formal instigation of proceedings may bring a complaint before the family court.[181] Pursuant to art. 31a of the JA, parties to unified court proceedings in juvenile cases and other persons are entitled to bring complaints about any action that violates their rights (*zażalenie na czynności naruszające ich prawa*) before the family court. A complaint that the rights of a juvenile have been infringed by a family court is dealt with by the same family court, but the family judge who performed the action complained of is excluded from examining the case. In small district courts in which there is only one judge specialising in juvenile proceedings, such complaints have to be dealt with by other judges without such specialisation.

Before the 2013 amendment to the JA, a juvenile and his parents or guardian were parties to juvenile proceedings and they retained the same status after the amendment. As parties to the proceedings they are entitled to lodge appeals against decisions of the court of first instance to the court of second instance (regional court).

A comprehensive analysis of all the possible legal implications of obtaining evidence (directly or indirectly) in violation of both civil and criminal procedural rules falls outside the scope of this contribution. Generally, according to the Code of Civil Procedure, if the party to the proceedings was deprived of the opportunity to defend his rights on first instance this is grounds for annulment of the proceedings (*zachodzi nieważność postępowania*) by the court of second instance.[182] The court of second instance has certain discretionary powers to state whether a breach of procedural rules resulted in depriving the party of the opportunity to effectively defend his rights.

179 Art. 38 JA before the 2013 amendment.
180 Gaberle and Korcyl-Wolska 2002, p. 170.
181 Art. 32i JA.
182 Art. 379 Code of Civil Procedure.

Before the 2013 amendment to the JA some appeal proceedings were governed by criminal procedure. According to the latter, the implications of obtaining evidence while violating procedural rules depend on the type of violation. For example, if the police influenced the explanations given by a juvenile suspect by using coercion or illegal threat,[183] the written record of the interrogation (*protokół*) cannot be used as evidence in court proceedings.[184] If a juvenile was interrogated by the police in the absence of parents, a guardian, a lawyer or persons specified by juvenile law,[185] different opinions on the legal implications of such a breach of procedural rules have been expressed in the criminal procedure and jurisprudence doctrine. In 1990 the Supreme Court stated that explanations obtained from a juvenile in such a situation could not constitute evidence in court proceedings.[186] This opinion has been shared by some authors.[187] However, according to the prevailing view reflected in case law, the absence of persons who according to juvenile law should be present during a police interrogation does not automatically exclude the written record of such an interrogation (*protokół*) as evidence: this will depend on the circumstances of the case.[188]

In practice, it seems that parties to juvenile proceedings file appeals only very rarely.[189] Research carried out by Korcyl-Wolska revealed that neither the parties nor the defence lawyer (if he had participated in the proceedings) acted to control the rulings of family courts in cases involving juveniles.[190] Such conclusions were confirmed by research conducted by Czarnecka-Dzialuk, Drapała and Więcek-Durańska.[191] Because of the limited number of appeals lodged in juvenile proceedings there is also limited case law of higher courts with respect to violation of juveniles' rights.

Juveniles also have the right to make complaints to the Ombudsman, as well as the Ombudsman for Children. Furthermore, they may bring complaints to international bodies acting in the field of the protection of human rights. So far, the ECtHR has dealt with juvenile cases against Poland rather exceptionally.

---

183 See art. 171 para. 5 CCP specifying which interrogations are prohibited by law.

184 See Ruling (*postanowienie*) of the Supreme Court, 3 December 2003, V KK 99/03.

185 See art. 39 JA before the 2013 amendment and art. 32f after this amendment.

186 Judgement of the Supreme Court, 22 March 1990, I KR 18/90.

187 See Górecki and Stachowiak 2007, p. 127–128.

188 Judgement of Appellate Court in Kraków, 5 February 1998, II AKa 9/98: Ruling (*postanowienie*) of the Supreme Court, 26 May 2000, I CKN 675/00: see also Bieńkowska and Walczak-Żochowska 2003, p. 162.

189 Korcyl-Wolska 2001, p. 353.

190 Korcyl-Wolska 2001, p. 354.

191 Czarnecka-Dzialuk, Drapała and Więcek Durańska 2011, p. 127.

6. INTERROGATION OF A JUVENILE WITNESS IN CRIMINAL AND JUVENILE PROCEEDINGS

The Code of Criminal Procedure does not provide for a special mode of interrogation for all juvenile witnesses (below 18 years of age). As a rule, they are interrogated according to the general rules for hearing witnesses.[192] Exceptionally, art. 189 CCP states that a witness below 17 years of age shall not swear to tell the truth. Additionally, art. 171 para. 3 of this Code states that in cases in which the interrogated person is below 15 years of age evidentiary actions (*czynności dowodowe*) involving him should be, as far as possible, carried out in the presence of a legal representative or caregiver. Art. 192 para. 2 CCP also applies to juvenile witnesses and authorises a court or public prosecutor to order the interrogation of a witness with participation of an expert in medicine or psychology if there are doubts concerning the mental state and/or mental development of a witness.

Over the last few years amendments were introduced to the Code of Criminal Procedure in order to regulate special circumstances of the interrogation of juvenile witnesses in cases concerning selected offences. To some extent special circumstances concerning the interrogation of these witnesses depend on their age at the time of the interrogation as well as whether they are a victim of the alleged offence.

In line with art. 185a para. 1 CCP, in cases concerning offences against freedom (for example human trafficking), sexual offences and offences against the family, injured persons below 15 years of age are interrogated as witnesses only once during the whole proceedings. Repeated interrogations may take place only exceptionally, at the request of the accused if he did not have a defence lawyer during the first interrogation of the victim or if new important circumstances come to light. Even in the course of the preparatory proceedings the interrogation takes place during a court session in the presence of an expert in psychology. The court session takes place in or outside the court building in specially adapted premises. Art. 147 para. 2a CCP requires such interrogations to be audio and video recorded. Pursuant to art. 185c CCP, victims of specific sexual offences are interrogated as witnesses largely in the same way as mentioned above, regardless of their age. As a result, this article also provides for special protection during their interrogation as witnesses for juveniles above 15 years of age who are victims of certain sexual crimes. The same special mode of interrogation applies in certain cases to witnesses below 15 years who are not victims.[193]

---

192 Kwiatkowska-Darul 2007, p. 195.

193 Art. 185b para. 1 CCP.

With respect to witnesses who have reached 15 years of age but are below the age of 18, they are interrogated at a distance by using technical devices which enable audio and video transmission in cases concerning violent or sexual offences or offences against the family if there is justified fear that direct presence of the suspect during the interrogation could embarrass the witness or negatively influence his mental state.[194]

According to empirical research published in 2011, in practice one third of interrogations of witnesses below 15 years of age which concerned special circumstances determined by the Code of Criminal Procedure had been video or audio recorded.[195] Recent amendments to the Code of Criminal Procedure, which significantly broadened the protection of juvenile witnesses in cases concerning selected offences, will hopefully contribute to positive changes in practice in this respect.

Before the 2013 amendment, the JA provided for special provisions concerning the interrogation of a juvenile suspect by the police, but it did not contain any provisions on interrogation of juvenile witnesses in juvenile proceedings. Pursuant to art. 20 para. 2 of the amended JA, evidentiary activities (*czynności dowodowe*) with the participation of juveniles (persons below 18 years of age) other than juvenile suspects should be conducted in accordance with respective provisions of the Code of Criminal Procedure. Thus, since 2 January 2014, provisions of the Code of Criminal Procedure apply in juvenile proceedings with the aim of protecting juvenile witnesses in cases concerning selected offences.

III. CONCLUSIONS

Poland is probably one of the last European countries in which juvenile law has been strongly influenced by the welfare approach. Not only is its substantive law on responses to juvenile offending different from common (adult) criminal substantive law, but also the proceedings in juvenile cases differ significantly from regular criminal proceedings. Penalties provided for adult offenders are almost totally excluded from the catalogue of responses to juvenile offending. Measures applied to juvenile offenders as well as to juveniles who show signs of other problematic behaviour intend to protect the best interests of the juvenile and should be tailored to his individual needs. However, since empirical research on the matter is lacking, it is not possible to assess how effective these measures are in practice in reducing re-offending as well as in supporting the development of a juvenile.

---

194 Art. 185b para. 2 CCP.

195 Trocha 2011, p. 21–23.

What is rather unique in the context of Europe, is the very complex and unclear proceedings in juvenile cases creating a mixture of regulations included in the JA and provisions of both civil and criminal procedure. The aim of this 'hybrid' procedure introduced by the 1982 JA was to enable family judges to deal with juvenile cases in a less formalistic way than required by criminal procedure law and, at the same time, to provide juveniles with some basic procedural rights. In 1982 the legislator took the position that providing juveniles with procedural rights was particularly important in cases in which it was possible to impose on them the most severe measure (placement in a correctional institution). As a result, adjudicatory proceedings were divided into care-educational and correctional proceedings and the latter were governed – as a rule – by rules of criminal procedure.

In 2013 correctional proceedings were abolished by the amendment to the JA. In doing so, the legislator assumed that unified court proceedings based mainly on civil procedure would provide juveniles with a sufficient level of protection of their rights. This assumption, however, is highly controversial. Even if measures are imposed on juveniles according to their needs, the primary condition for their application is determining in fair proceedings that the juvenile committed the alleged act that is prohibited by criminal law or that he behaved in another problematic way. In proceedings regulated by the JA there are some doubts over the fairness of dealing with juvenile cases.

The JA mainly regulates court proceedings in juvenile cases and contains only a very few provisions on the stage preceding the instigation of court proceedings. This is especially problematic since, in practice, most juveniles suspected of acting in conflict with the law or behaving in another problematic way do not have their first contact with the law with a family court but rather with the police. As regards the stage of dealing with juveniles before the institution of court proceedings, the legislator determines the conditions for a temporary placement of juveniles by the police in police institutions for children and also indicates that the police are allowed to undertake evidence gathering activities in 'urgent cases', including the interrogation of a juvenile, which is governed by the Code of Criminal Procedure. A juvenile interrogated by the police in 'urgent cases' has the same rights as provided for adult suspects by the Code of Criminal Procedure. However, court proceedings in juvenile cases are mainly governed by civil procedure which does not provide certain restrictions on the use of evidence typical for criminal procedure, such as a ban on reading during the court hearing informal notes (*notatki urzędowe*) concerning activities which required preparation of official written records (*protokoły*).[196] In accordance with art. 32p of the amended JA, the family court is authorised to read all official documents (*dokumenty urzędowe*) during the hearing, if in the court's opinion

[196] See art. 393 para. 1 CCP.

direct taking of evidence is not necessary. On the basis of this provision a family court is allowed to read informal notes made by the police before the institution of juvenile proceedings by the court.

From the point of view of effective protection of juvenile suspects' rights it means that in practice the police can opt out of interrogation of a juvenile under provisions of the Code of Criminal Procedure and settle for the preparation of an informal note on what the juvenile said without being instructed about his rights. Such regulations can lead to a variety of local practices and reduce the level of protection of the rights of a juvenile suspect at the stage preceding the institution of court proceedings. Finally, the legal complexity of the different proceedings and different safeguards (during different stages of proceedings) might create confusion, which is problematic from the point of view of effective protection of procedural rights.

BIBLIOGRAPHY

Arczewska 2007
M. Arczewska, 'Społeczne role sędziów rodzinnych – wyniki badań własnych', *Rodzina i Prawo*, 2007, 3, p. 9–22

Bieńkowska and Walczak-Żochowska 2003
E. Bieńkowska and A. Walczak-Żochowska, *Postępowanie w sprawach nieletnich. Komentarz*, Warsaw: C.H. Beck, 2003

Bojarski 2009
T. Bojarski, 'Nieletni przed sądem. Uwagi o niektórych założeniach ogólnych oraz praktyce', *Archiwum Kryminologii*, 2009, XXIX-XXX, p. 269–285

Central Statistical Office 2013
Central Statistical Office, *Statistical Yearbook of the Republic of Poland 2012*, Warsaw, 2013

Committee on the Rights of the Child 2007
Committee on the Rights of the Child, *General Comment No. 10 (2007), Children's rights in juvenile justice*, 2007, available at: www2.ohchr.org/english/bodies/crc/docs/GC10_en.doc

Czarnecka-Dzialuk, Drapała and Więcek-Durańska 2011
B. Czarnecka-Dzialuk, K. Drapała and A. Więcek-Durańska, *Analiza postępowań karnych oraz przed sądem dla nieletnich o wybrane czyny karalne popełnione przez osoby w wieku 15–17 lat*, Warsaw: Institute of Justice, 2011, available at: www.iws.org.pl/pliki/files/badania/raporty/raporty11/AR_Czarnecka-Dzialuk%20,Drapa%C5%82a,%20Wi%C4%99cek-Dura%C5%84ska%20Analiza%20post%C4%99powa%C5%84%20_nieletni_%202011.pdf

Czarnecka-Dzialuk and Wójcik 2011
B. Czarnecka-Dzialuk and D. Wójcik, 'Reagowanie na czyny karalne i demoralizację nieletnich – koncepcje teoretyczne, statystyki i opinie sędziów rodzinnych', in: A.

Siemaszko (ed.), *Stosowanie prawa. Księga jubileuszowa z okazji XX-lecia Instytutu Wymiaru Sprawiedliwości*, Warsaw: Wolters Kluwer, 2011

Gaberle and Korcyl-Wolska 2002
A. Gaberle and M. Korcyl-Wolska, *Komentarz do ustawy o postępowaniu w sprawach nieletnich*, Gdańsk: Arche, 2002

Górecki and Stachowiak 2007
P. Górecki and S. Stachowiak, *Ustawa o postępowaniu w sprawach nieletnich. Komentarz*, Warsaw: Wolters Kluwer, 2007

Grześkowiak, Krukowski, Patulski and Warzocha 1991
K. Grześkowiak, A. Krukowski, W. Patulski and E. Warzocha, *Ustawa o postępowaniu w sprawach nieletnich. Komentarz*, Warsaw: Wydawnictwo Prawnicze, 1991

Kanev *et al.* 2010
K. Kanev, D. Furtunova, P. Roussinova and Y. Bekirska, 'Bulgaria', in F. Dünkel, J. Grzywa, P. Horsfield and I. Pruin (eds.), *Juvenile Justice Systems in Europe*, Vol. 1, Mönchengladbach: Forum Verlag Godesberg, 2010

Kmiecik 1988
R. Kmiecik, 'Naczelne zasady karnoprocesowe w postępowaniu w sprawach nieletnich' in T. Bojarski (ed.), *Postępowanie z nieletnimi. Orzekanie i wykonywanie środków wychowawczych i poprawczych*, Lublin: Uniwersytet Marii Curie-Skłodowskiej, 1988

Kobes 2011
P. Kobes, *Prawny system przeciwdziałania demoralizacji i przestępczości nieletnich*, Warsaw: Wydawnictwa Uniwersytetu Warszawskiego, 2011

Komenda Główna Policji 2013
Komenda Główna Policji, 'Koncepcja PID', available at: www.policja.pl/pol/kgp/biuro-prewencji-i-ruch/wydzial-konwojowy/policyjne-izby-dziecka

Komisja Kodyfikacyjna Rzeczypospolitej Polskiej 1921
Komisja Kodyfikacyjna Rzeczypospolitej Polskiej, 'Uzasadnienie projektu ustawy o sądach dla nieletnich', in *Projekt ustawy o sądach dla nieletnich*, Warsaw, 1921

Korcyl-Wolska 2001
M. Korcyl-Wolska, *Postępowanie w sprawach nieletnich*, Zakamycze: Kantor Wydawniczy Zakamycze, 2001

Korcyl-Wolska 2004
M. Korcyl-Wolska, *Postępowanie w sprawach nieletnich*, Zakamycze: Kantor Wydawniczy Zakamycze, 2004

Krajewski 2006
K. Krajewski, 'The Juvenile Justice System in Poland', in E. L. Jensen and J. Jepsen (eds.), *Juvenile Law Violators, Human Rights, and the Development of New Juvenile Justice Systems*, Oxford-Portland: Hart Publishing, 2006

Kwiatkowska-Darul 2007
V. Kwiatkowska-Darul, *Przesłuchanie małoletniego świadka w polskim procesie karnym.* Toruń: Violetta Kwiatkowska- Darul & Wydawnictwo „Dom Organizatora", 2007

Marek 2009
A. Marek, 'Uwagi o reformie prawa dotyczącego nieletnich', *Archiwum Kryminologii*, 2009, XXIX-XXX, p. 383–391

Ministry of Justice 2010
Ministry of Justice, *Analiza statystyczna danych o ewidencji spraw i orzecznictwie w sprawach nieletnich za lata 1999 - 2009*, Warsaw, 2010, available at: http://bip.ms.gov.pl/pl/dzialalnosc/statystyki/statystyki-2010

Ministry of Justice 2013
Ministry of Justice, *Postępowania w sprawach nieletnich (rodzinnych) w sądach powszechnych zakończone w wyniku postępowania mediacyjnego w latach 2004–2012*, Warsaw, 2013, available at: http://ms.gov.pl/pl/dzialalnosc/mediacje

Ministry of Justice, Central Administration of Prison Service 2013
Ministry of Justice, Central Administration of Prison Service, *Roczna informacja statystyczna za rok 2012*, Warsaw, 2013, available at: http://sw.gov.pl/Data/Files/001c169lidz/rok-2012.pdf

Mozgawa and Szumski 2000
M. Mozgawa and J. Szumski, 'Promoting the rule of law & strengthening the criminal justice system', in A. Siemaszko (ed.), *Crime & Law Enforcement in Poland on the threshold of the 21st century*, Warsaw: Oficyna Naukowa, 2000

Nowikowski 2009
I. Nowikowski, 'Wydawanie wyroku uniewinniającego w postępowaniu w sprawach nieletnich (uwagi *de lege lata* i *de lege ferenda*)', in P. Hofmański and S. Waltoś (eds.), *W kręgu prawa nieletnich. Księga pamiątkowa ku czci Profesor Marianny Korcyl-Wolskiej*, Warsaw: Wolters Kluwer, 2009

Patulski 1985
W. Patulski, 'Rola i zadania sądów rodzinnych w wypełnianiu wskazań ustawy o postępowaniu w sprawach nieletnich', *Zeszyty Naukowe Instytutu Badania Prawa Sądowego*, 1985, 23, p. 16–37

Pergataia 2001
A. Pergataia, *Jugendstrafrect in Russland und den baltischen Staaten*, Mönchengladbach: Forum Verlag Godesberg, 2001

Posnow 2009
W. Posnow, 'Udział obrońcy w przygotowawczym stadium procesu –aspekty realizacji niektórych uprawnień', in J. Skorupka (ed.), *Rzetelny proces karny. Księga jubileuszowa Profesor Zofii Świdy*, Warsaw: Wolters Kluwer, 2009

Pruin 2010
I. Pruin, 'The scope of juvenile justice systems in Europe', in F. Dünkel, J. Grzywa, P. Horsfield and I. Pruin (eds.), *Juvenile Justice Systems in Europe*, Vol. 4, Mönchengladbach: Forum Verlag Godesberg, 2010

Rdzanek-Piwowar 1993
G. Rdzanek-Piwowar, 'Granice nieletniości w polskim prawie karnym', *Archiwum Kryminologii*, 1993, XIX, p. 191–231

Sakalauskas 2010
G. Sakalauskas, 'Lithuania', in F. Dünkel, J. Grzywa, P. Horsfield and I. Pruin (eds.), *Juvenile Justice Systems in Europe*, Vol. 2, Mönchengladbach: Forum Verlag Godesberg, 2010

Stańdo-Kawecka 2002
B. Stańdo-Kawecka, 'Community Sanctions in Polish Penal Law', in H.-J. Albrecht and A. van Kalmthout (eds.), *Community Sanctions and Measures in Europe and North America*, Freiburg i. Br.: Max-Planck-Institut für Ausländisches und Internationales Strafrecht, 2002

Stańdo-Kawecka 2007
B. Stańdo-Kawecka, *Prawo karne nieletnich. Od opieki do odpowiedzialności*, Warsaw: Wolters Kluwer Polska, 2007

Stańdo-Kawecka 2010
B. Stańdo-Kawecka, 'Poland', in F. Dünkel, J. Grzywa, P. Horsfield and I. Pruin (eds.), *Juvenile Justice Systems in Europe*, Vol. 2, Mönchengladbach: Forum Verlag Godesberg, 2010

Stańdo-Kawecka and Krajewski 2010
B. Stańdo-Kawecka and K. Krajewski, 'Polen', in F. Dünkel, T. Lappi-Seppälä, C. Morgenstern and D. van Zyl Smit (eds.), *Kriminalität, Kriminalpolitik, strafrechtliche Sanktionspraxis und Gefangenenraten im europäischen Vergleich*, Mönchengladbach: Forum Verlag Godesberg, 2010

Strzembosz 1984
A. Strzembosz, *Postępowanie w sprawach nieletnich w prawie polskim*, Lublin: Redakcja Wydawnictw Katolickiego Uniwersytetu Lubelskiego, 1984

Światłowski 2009
A. Światłowski, 'Czy postępowania w sprawach nieletnich są postępowaniami karnymi szczególnymi?', in P. Hofmański and S. Waltoś (eds.), *W kręgu prawa nieletnich. Księga pamiątkowa ku czci Profesor Marianny Korcyl-Wolskiej*, Warsaw: Wolters Kluwer, 2009

Świda, Ponikowski and Posnow 2008
Z. Świda, R. Ponikowski and W. Posnow, *Postępowanie karne. Część ogólna*, Warsaw: Wolters Kluwer Polska, 2008

Szumski 1990
J. Szumski, 'Struktura i dynamika środków stosowanych wobec nieletnich w latach 1984–1989', in T. Bojarski (ed.), *Orzekanie środków wychowawczych i poprawczych w praktyce sądów rodzinnych*, Lublin: Wydawnictwo Uniwersytetu Marii Curie-Skłodowskiej, 1990, p. 149–171

Taracha 1988
A. Taracha, 'Udział organów ścigania w postępowaniu w sprawach nieletnich (w postępowaniu przygotowawczym)', in T. Bojarski (ed.), *Postępowanie z nieletnimi. Orzekanie i wykonywanie środków wychowawczych i poprawczych*, Lublin: Uniwersytet Marii Curie-Skłodowskiej, 1988

Trocha 2011
O. Trocha, *Praktyka przesłuchiwania dzieci w Polsce. Raport z badań*, Warsaw: Fundacja Dzieci Niczyje, 2011

Wilamowska 2008
B. Wilamowska, 'Poland', in A. M. van Kalmthout and I. Durnescu (eds.), *Probation in Europe*, Nijmegen: Wolf Legal Publishers, 2008

Witkowska 2014
K. Witkowska, 'Tłumacz w postępowaniu karnym', *Prokuratura i Prawo*, 2014, 1, p. 29–42

Witkowski and Kuć 2007
J. Witkowski and A. Kuć, 'Szkolenia policjantów zajmujących się problematyką nieletnich', *Kwartalnik Policyjny*, 2007, 1, available at: http://kwartalnik.csp.edu.pl/kp/archiwum-1/2007/nr-1/1056,SZKOLENIA-POLICJANTOW-ZAJMUJACYCH-SIE-PROBLEMATYKA-NIELETNICH.html

Zoll 2009
A. Zoll, 'Czy nieletniość jest okolicznością wyłączającą winę?', in P. Hofmański and S. Waltoś (eds.), *W kręgu prawa nieletnich. Księga pamiątkowa ku czci Profesor Marianny Korcyl-Wolskiej*, Warsaw: Wolters Kluwer, 2009

CHAPTER 7
TRANSVERSAL ANALYSIS OF THE COUNTRY REPORTS
General Patterns

Michele PANZAVOLTA and Dorris DE VOCHT

1. INTRODUCTION

The legal study underlying this book was set out to explore the level of legal protection offered to juvenile suspects during interrogation in a number of selected Member States. With this aim, the country reports on *Belgium*, *England and Wales*, *Italy*, *the Netherlands* and *Poland* offer a detailed picture of the existing legal frameworks of procedural safeguards for young suspects during interrogation against the background of their respective juvenile justice systems. In this chapter this valuable information will be evaluated by highlighting the similarities and differences between the five jurisdictions and by discussing the general patterns that can be derived from them.

The approach followed by the country reports and the common template[1] according to which they have been written has been to offer a complete overview of all 'normative' levels of applicable rules not only focusing on constitutional and statutory law but also on secondary legislation, case law, doctrine and other relevant legal sources. The reason for focusing on legal rules has been twofold. First of all, there seems to be a gap in existing knowledge on how and to what extent juvenile suspects are currently legally protected during interrogation throughout the EU. The aim of the legal study is to fill at least part of this void.[2] Secondly, insight into this matter is essential for any attempt to harmonise and optimise the level of legal protection at EU level as envisaged in the Roadmap

1 See chapter 1, paragraph 4 and 9.
2 See chapter 1, paragraph 1 and 4.

for strengthening procedural rights of suspected or accused persons in criminal proceedings.[3]

Evaluating the results of a comparative study that focuses primarily on the law requires extreme caution. The actual effect of all laws and legal regulations is highly dependent on whether and how they are actually applied in practice. Furthermore, the interpretation and application of legal rules may be heavily influenced by the professional culture and competence of the relevant actors (police, prosecutors, judges, *et cetera*). This seems to be especially true in the context of juvenile justice where, in principle, the level of 'formalism' will be lower than in adult criminal proceedings. In theory, this may increase the willingness of officials to deviate from applicable rules when this is deemed necessary or appropriate in the interest of the juvenile. Both of these profiles emerge only to a limited extent in a legal study, mostly through the consideration of the case-law (or through practical instructions issued to/by the competent authorities where existent).

It shall also be remembered that the present legal study is carried out within the framework of a larger research project, where an empirical study has also been conducted. Hence, the inner limitations of any legal study should to a certain extent be compensated for by the empirical strand of the research.[4] As mentioned, the empirical study – exploring the current practice of protecting juvenile suspects during interrogation in the five selected Member States – consists of focus group interviews with key actors and juveniles and analysis of records of interrogations (audio-visual or written records). The results of this empirical research, as well as the merging of the legal and the empirical results and the recommendations for minimum rules based upon them, will be published in a separate, second volume.[5]

It was already highlighted in chapter 1 that the juvenile justice systems represented throughout the EU are very different in many ways.[6] This variation is clearly reflected by the five country reports: each of the jurisdictions has chosen its own approach to juvenile 'criminal' justice,[7] with the result that the differences that can be observed between the selected systems are many and significant. For example, although the large majority of countries, if not all, provide for separate rules for juvenile criminal justice from the system in place for adults, the extent to which the juvenile justice system departs from that of

---

3 Resolution of the Council of 30 November 2009 on a Roadmap for strengthening procedural rights of suspected or accused persons in criminal proceeding [2009] OJ C295/01. See also chapter 1, paragraph 5 and 8.

4 See chapter 1, paragraph 4.

5 Vanderhallen *et al.* 2015 (forthcoming).

6 See on this diversity *inter alia* Giostra and Patane 2007 and Dünkel *et al.* For a global perspective see *inter alia*: Junger-Tas and Decker 2006 and Winterdyk 2014.

7 For the meaning of the terms 'criminal (juvenile) justice' as well as 'punitive (juvenile) justice' within the context of this study, see chapter 1, paragraph 2.

adults differs significantly. The difference may lie in the type of adjudicating courts are empowered to do in cases of children's wrongdoing, but it may also affect the legal rules on crimes, punishment and procedure. In the latter case, the degree of departure from the systems applicable to adults may also vary: there can be special rules only for the relevant procedure to be followed (or parts of that procedure) or there can be a more extensive regulation that also extends to the definition of crimes (or punishable behaviour) and the possible punishments. A clear example of the latter may be found in *Poland*, which – together with *Belgium* – represents a system mainly focused on protection and rehabilitation of the juvenile offender by means of educative measures. The amount of 'youth-specific' rules may also differ between the various systems: they can be only few, covering only very specific aspects of the juvenile's involvement in criminal justice, or they can be numerous to the extent that the juvenile justice system takes its own peculiar shape, different from adult criminal justice. Yet in none of the countries surveyed is there an exhaustive codification of criminal law and procedure for juveniles: to a larger or to a lesser extent all statutes concerning juveniles build upon the existing rules for adults and provide for special rules where needed. For example, in *England and Wales* a specialist criminal court deals with defendants under the age of 18 but there is no separate set of rules for juveniles other than an adaption of rules applicable to adult suspects and defendants. *The Netherlands* represents an example of a juvenile justice system that – like *England and Wales* – provides for a wide variety of youth-specific sanctions in contrast with only a few specific procedural law rules regulating the pre-trial stage. In *Italy*, on the other hand, the separation of the youth from the adult justice system takes place in both the courts and the rules of procedure. There is in fact a separate set of rules of procedural law, providing for a distinctive model of criminal procedure. However, there are no special provisions on the rules on criminal liability and even the separate procedural codification often refers to the rules applicable to adults.

When comparing the different country reports, it is difficult to find a lowest common denominator for all countries, except for few very basic safeguards. In any case, a lowest common denominator would probably not be a useful benchmark for a proper harmonisation attempt. In fact, it would only allow the identification of safeguards that are already present in all countries and it would thus offer a picture in which any harmonisation attempt appears either futile or superfluous. Furthermore, the identification of some common minimum (level of) safeguards would be of little significance, since the effective value of a safeguard (or, more specifically, of a legal provision offering some protection to the suspect) is connected to its function, which also depends on the other surrounding rules and on the general context.[8]

---

8 For the importance of the function played by each (provision on) safeguard(s), see chapter 1, paragraph 9.

It is for the aforementioned reasons that the approach followed here has been different. We believe that a more adequate course of action to gain a meaningful overall picture is to look at similarities and differences between countries and identify which general patterns can be extracted across the surveyed jurisdictions. In this context, a 'general pattern' means a trend that pervades the majority of the different legislations. A general pattern could also consist in the identification of a topical notion, a keystone, or a mainstay of the systems, which in each legal system determines the shape of the safeguards (or the rules), although it may do so in different directions according to the way in which it is construed within each jurisdiction.

The function of the general patterns is thus twofold. The patterns should permit us to identify the crucial legal issues concerning the interrogation of juvenile suspects and the variables involved in each issue. They should permit us to reflect upon how each variable intertwines with the others. Furthermore, the other function of the general patterns should be the identification of a line of convergence (or divergence) between systems, a common trend of evolution or on the other hand conflicting development.

The general patterns described below are clustered into two categories: part I contains general patterns concerning the system (i.e. the context) and part II comprises general patterns concerning the safeguards provided for or applicable during the interrogation phase. The former category focuses on general patterns that are – in a broader sense – connected to the structure and characteristics of the juvenile justice system including its underlying juvenile justice policy and its relevant definitions. The latter category not only concerns procedural rights but also encompasses reflections upon concepts such as vulnerability and well-being, which prove to be crucial for a proper understanding of the kind and level of procedural safeguards needed.

I. SYSTEMS

1. ALL THAT PUNISHES IS OF A CRIMINAL NATURE?

1.1. CRIMINAL PROCEEDINGS VERSUS EDUCATIVE OR PROTECTIVE PROCEEDINGS

As repeatedly mentioned, countries provide different frameworks for juvenile criminal justice. These systems can be classified in many different ways.[9] A major divide between countries can be identified with regard to the formal

[9] See chapter 1, paragraph 2.

classification of criminal proceedings. Some countries in fact do not follow a purely criminal approach. Juvenile criminal justice is formally kept outside of the realm of criminal law. Different reasons can be found for taking this approach. One reason may be that countries try to avoid labelling juvenile proceedings as formally criminal in order to protect the juvenile from the stigma associated with criminal proceedings. Another possible explanation is that juveniles are considered incapable of grasping the difference between right and wrong and understanding in its entirety the concept of guilt, thus they cannot be held criminally liable and they should not receive punishment but only appropriate education.

Belgium and *Poland* are two examples of the aforementioned approach. Both countries do not follow a criminal 'path' in the sense that they do not categorise juvenile 'punitive' proceedings as criminal. In both jurisdictions, proceedings against children who are suspected of committing an offence take the form of 'educative' or 'youth protection' proceedings save for limited exceptions connected to the most serious crimes. In *Belgium*, juveniles are dealt with through the Youth Protection Act. Here the departure from the criminal law approach is marked even in terminology. The treatments imposed on juvenile offenders are qualified as 'measures' and not as 'punishments' or 'penalties'. Also in *Poland*, juveniles (below the age of 17) are not criminally liable. Here too measures can be imposed upon them for 'punishable acts' or for behaviour showing 'signs of demoralisation' (i.e. problematic behaviour not prohibited by criminal law). This choice is theoretically tied with a special emphasis on welfarism as the main feature of juvenile justice.[10] Nevertheless, although the primary goal of broadening the types of behaviour which may result in measures being imposed will be protection of the juvenile, it should be stressed that – in fact – it may result in so-called net-widening, with more juveniles being drawn into the juvenile justice system.

It is important to reiterate that the jurisdictions that follow a more formal criminal approach (*England and Wales, Italy* and *the Netherlands*) also contain, though to varying degrees, elements of protection and education. For example, the separate criminal proceedings for juveniles provided for in the Italian system are mainly focused on protecting the juvenile from the stressful impact of the criminal justice system and providing psychological support and educational treatment. Given this ambiguity, the Italian system of juvenile justice could be characterised as being a hybrid between a welfare- and a justice-oriented model.

A common feature of all of the countries is that there is a clear interrelationship between criminal law and other branches of law within the context of juvenile justice. More specifically, countries tend to supplement criminal justice with administrative and civil law.

10 See chapter 1, paragraph 2.

In some cases, civil measures represent an alternative to criminal punishment. The law provides for civil law 'tracks' of sanctions against offending behaviour by juveniles. The juvenile justice system of *England and Wales* represents an example of such civil law tracks. Starting from 1998, a number of orders were introduced addressing criminal behaviour through civil law: anti-social behaviours orders (ASBOs), child safety orders and parenting orders. Breaching such a civil order is a criminal offence, which means that the civil law approach can quite easily be steered onto a criminal law track.

In other cases, the provisions of civil law intertwine with criminal law in a different way. In *Italy*, for instance, civil law is used to offer protection to the juvenile. During the preliminary hearing and the trial, the judge can deliver temporary civil decisions with a view to protecting the juvenile suspect.

In *the Netherlands* there is also a clear connection between civil and criminal law within the context of juvenile justice. This is illustrated *(inter alia)* by combined court sessions which are held in some court districts and during which juvenile judges simultaneously decide on matters of civil and criminal law.

1.2. FORMAL CRIMINAL NATURE VERSUS SUBSTANTIVE CRIMINAL NATURE

The highlighted divide between juvenile justice systems taking a criminal or a non-criminal approach raises a preliminary difficulty: is it possible to compare systems that display such a profound difference in structure and philosophy? More specifically, should the discussions on the safeguards required for juvenile suspects during interrogations consider and be affected by the formal classification of proceedings, whether criminal or not?

There is usually a difference in the quality and quantity of safeguards available in criminal proceedings compared to other non-criminal types of proceedings. Normally, individuals involved in criminal proceedings receive stronger protection. Most constitutions and human rights charters require that individuals be more intensely safeguarded in criminal matters for the obvious reason that it is in the field of criminal law that the state may interfere with the private life and liberty of an individual in the most intrusive way. The country reports illustrate how this difference is reflected in the provision of procedural safeguards. The educative nature of proceedings in *Poland* and *Belgium* tends to minimise the contrast between the juvenile suspect/defendant and the state prosecuting authority and thus reduce the amount of safeguards. The more we move away from welfaristic models in the direction of more punitive systems, and the more criminal proceedings entail an explicit conflict between the public authority and the suspect/defendant, the stronger the emphasis on procedural safeguards becomes.[11]

Comparative reasoning must surely take into account the different domestic classifications but it naturally moves beyond such classifications. It is indeed possible to compare the safeguards of criminal proceedings with those given in non-criminal (administrative or civil) proceedings, provided that the essence of the proceedings is the same, i.e. that the interests at stake are similar.[12] Although comparative analysis is not hindered by a different categorisation, the aforementioned observations could bring into question the feasibility of any harmonisation effort.

When discussing the safeguards required for juvenile suspects, does it matter whether the proceedings are formally 'labelled' as criminal according to national law or whether they have a (substantial) punitive nature? The answer to this question offered by the recent draft Directive on procedural safeguards for children suspected and accused in criminal proceedings[13] seems to be in the affirmative. The draft Directive in fact embraces and follows a formal classification. The safeguards provided for by the draft Directive apply only to 'criminal proceedings and EAW proceedings' with the exclusion of 'other forms of proceedings which may lead to the imposition of certain restrictive measures (for instance protection measures and education measures)'.[14] The rules and safeguards incorporated in the draft Directive would thus not be mandatory in 'educative' or 'youth protection' proceedings, such as are applicable in *Belgium* and *Poland*.

The case law of the European Court of Human Rights (hereafter: ECtHR) firmly takes a different and more substantive approach: when considering whether proceedings constitute a 'criminal charge' in the sense of art. 6 European Convention on Human Rights (hereafter: ECHR), the ECtHR looks beyond the national classification of proceedings applying the so-called 'Engel criteria'. How the proceedings are formally labelled according to national law is only of a formal and relative value, more importance is given to other factors which look beyond the 'appearance' of proceedings: the nature of the offence and the degree of severity of the penalty at stake.[15] Following these criteria, the ECtHR has recognised on several occasions that the fair trial safeguards provided for in art. 6 ECHR also apply to administrative or civil proceedings against

11 See chapter 1 paragraph 2.

12 This is a plain application of the functional method, in contrast to a purely formalistic approach: on these issues, see chapter 1, paragraph 9.

13 Draft Directive on procedural safeguards for children suspected and accused in criminal proceedings (COM(2013) 822/2). For more information on the draft Directive see chapter 1, paragraph 8.2.

14 Part 3 Legal elements of the Proposal (para. 16).

15 ECtHR 8 June 1976, *Engel and others v. the Netherlands*, no. 5100/71, 5101/71, 5102/71, 5354/72 and 5370/72.

juveniles.[16] From the outset, this seems to conflict with the narrow and more formalistic approach taken by the aforementioned draft Directive on procedural safeguards for children.[17]

When taking the latter (formalistic) approach, the analysis must discuss whether non-criminal proceedings against juveniles (whether labelled administrative, civil or educative) are substantively punitive in nature. The examples of *Poland* and *Belgium* illustrate that proceedings formally labelled as 'non-criminal' might lead to the application of a measure that is just as afflictive as a criminal penalty. For instance, in *Poland*, the judge may impose on juveniles both educative measures and correctional measures. The latter category appears to be equivalent to an ordinary criminal penalty in terms of the negative consequences it has for the individual, particularly when correctional measures entail a deprivation of liberty (e.g. placement in a correctional institution) for an indeterminate period of time. Even educative measures can have an afflictive dimension in that they can consist of a significant curtailment of personal liberty. Furthermore, in exceptional cases there is a possibility of imposing the provisional (pre-trial) measure of placing the juvenile in a police institution for children or a youth detention centre, and even of temporarily placing the juvenile in a remand prison. A similar situation occurs under the Belgian system, where some measures – although meant to be protective – may have a punitive effect. This is true, for example, of the possibility of placement in a closed institution, which has a maximum duration of six months but may be prolonged in case of continuous bad or dangerous behaviour. Taking this into account, the obvious 'risk' of the aforementioned formal approach is that sanctions (with punitive consequences) may be imposed without providing the juvenile with the necessary procedural safeguards.

1.2.1. *Relationship between criminal and non-criminal proceedings*

The little influence that the domestic classification of proceedings should have on the comparative and harmonisation discourse also derives from the fact that criminal and non-criminal proceedings are often interconnected in the field of juvenile justice. Juvenile justice systems that deal with delinquent juveniles outside of criminal proceedings often allow for some form of transferral of the most serious cases to ordinary criminal courts/justice or provide for some exceptions to the competence of juvenile courts. For example, in both *Poland* and *Belgium* educative proceedings tend to give way to ordinary criminal justice for more serious offences. In *Belgium*, the Youth Protection Act empowers

16 See for example: ECtHR 2 March 2010, *Adamkiewicz v. Poland*, no. 54729/00 and ECtHR 14 November 2013, *Blokhin v. Russia*, no. 47152/06.

17 For a more in-depth reflection upon the scope and content of the draft Directive: De Vocht *et al.* 2014.

the prosecutor to order a case against a juvenile aged between 16 and 18 to be transferred to an ordinary criminal court when an educational measure is deemed inadequate. Similar exceptions exist in *Poland* where 15- to 16-year-old juveniles can be brought before ordinary criminal courts if charged with some of the most serious crimes. These examples show how non-criminal and criminal juvenile proceedings dealing with juvenile suspects can be intertwined and how the choice of a formally non-criminal approach does not necessarily rule out the possibility of following criminal tracks in certain exceptional circumstances.

1.2.2. Regular criminal proceedings versus diversion proceedings

Another argument in favour of taking a more substantive approach when looking at juvenile criminal justice is related to diversion proceedings. The juvenile justice system naturally tends to move away from traditional criminal proceedings. This is shown by the fundamental role that diversion mechanisms play in most countries: in many juvenile justice systems there is a strong tendency to divert juveniles away from regular court proceedings. In *the Netherlands*, for example, the principle of subsidiarity applies, which means that ordinary court proceedings should be the exception rather than the rule. As far as possible, juvenile suspects should be dealt with by different (and less stigmatising) means than trial proceedings. The same is true in *Belgium* where the law requires that the least intrusive procedural course of action be followed, which in practice means that the judge should first consider the possibility of mediation or group conferencing, a written project, a supervision measure and as a last resort a custodial sentence.[18]

In general, the possibility of diverting juveniles away from regular (criminal) court proceedings exists in all the surveyed countries. The reports clearly illustrate that the strategies of diversion can differ and take many different forms, varying from police cautions and community resolutions (*England and Wales*) to different forms of (conditional and non-conditional) dismissals by the prosecutor or even by the judge (*Italy*).

Generally, it should be noted that the emphasis on diversion is higher in countries that take a punitive approach than in welfare-oriented systems. In *Poland*, for example, mediation represents the only possibility of diversion and the data presently available seem to indicate that it is not often applied. The fact that countries with a punitive approach place greater emphasis on diversion can be quite easily explained: where juvenile criminal proceedings retain their distinctive

18 This subsidiarity-approach is emphasised by supranational instruments dealing with juvenile justice such as the International Convention on the Rights of the Child (hereafter: CRC), which states in art. 40 para. 3 that State Parties shall promote whenever appropriate and desirable, measures for dealing with children (alleged as, accused of, or recognised as having infringed the penal law) without resorting to judicial proceedings, providing that legal human rights and legal safeguards are fully respected. See also chapter 1, paragraph 7.

role of punishment and stigmatisation, it becomes crucial that the juvenile be diverted from the ordinary course of proceedings whenever it is possible. On the contrary, in countries with a greater welfaristic approach, 'normal' proceedings are already aimed at limiting the impact on the juvenile by the course of punitive justice; thus, there is less need for diversion from ordinary proceedings. However, it would be wrong to conclude that diversion has necessarily no or little role in welfaristic systems. Diversion, in fact, is also a way to accelerate the proceedings and reduce the burden placed on judicial bodies. In addition to this, the forms of diversion can minimise even further the impact of justice on the juvenile compared to – for example – educative proceedings. *Belgium* is a good example of this; as mentioned, the system of diversion there is in fact more developed.

Although the aim of diversion is to inflict the least possible harm on the juvenile, the outcome of such proceedings may well have a substantial punitive nature. This is clearly illustrated by the Dutch example. In *the Netherlands*, the public prosecutor may impose a so-called prosecutorial disposition (*strafbeschikking*) on the juvenile without the intervention of a court. Such a prosecutorial disposition may result in the obligation for the juvenile to pay a fine or to perform community service (for a maximum of 60 hours). Therefore, it may be stated that choosing a different track of proceedings and avoiding the regular criminal process does not necessarily exclude the possibility of imposing punitive sanctions on a juvenile suspect. The same is true in *Italy*, where diversion can take the form of community service. In *England and Wales* the array of out-of-court disposals and penalties includes 'community resolution', where the juvenile agrees to participate in activities based on resolving the offence, and 'youth conditional caution', which can also aim at rehabilitation or punishment (unpaid work or a financial penalty which punish the young person for his or her unlawful behaviour).

In this respect, it is important to note that – from the perspective of procedural safeguards – diversion proceedings generally tend to be less formalistic, providing for a much lower degree of explicit legal protection and emphasizing the importance of the first contact between the suspect and the prosecuting authorities. For example, in *the Netherlands*, at the hearings in which the public prosecutor decides on the sanction to be imposed, there are limitations on the right to legal assistance: in principle the right to legal assistance does apply, but the obligation to inform the juvenile of his right to request the appointment of a lawyer is limited to certain cases and information may be provided – at the latest – at the start of the hearing. In *England and Wales*, the main form of procedural protection offered to the juvenile during diversion proceedings consists of the assistance of an appropriate adult: issuing a youth caution or youth conditional order should happen in the presence of the juvenile and his appropriate adult. Assistance of a lawyer, on the other hand, is possible but not mandatory.

What is crucial in this respect, is that the course of proceedings is not rigidly predefined. In other words, during the first interrogation(s) it will often not be clear which exact course the proceedings will take. In many cases, the type of proceedings to be followed will depend on the outcome of the interrogation(s). The decision on how to proceed will often be taken at the end (or in the course) of the investigations after the first interrogations have taken place. This also explains why in most (if not all) countries the initial interrogation of the suspect is considered to be of such fundamental importance for the proceedings.[19]

Furthermore, diversion proceedings often carry a consensual element on the part of the young suspect. First of all, in several countries the possibility of following (certain) diversion proceedings is made conditional upon the juvenile admitting the offence, which adds to the importance of the interrogation. For example in *the Netherlands*, following the so-called Halt diversion program[20] can only be done when the juvenile has admitted to committing the crime. A similar feature exists in *England and Wales*, where all forms of out-of-court disposal require a confession and some of them even the juvenile's explicit agreement. In *Italy*, although there is no express legal requirement to ascertain the juvenile's guilt in order to conduct a probation program, the case law has mostly moved in the direction that the ascertainment of guilt is a necessary prerequisite for the probation order. Regardless of whether diversion in conditional on the juvenile's confession, in many countries out-of-court disposals require the juvenile's consent to undertake a certain activity or undergo certain obligations.

The above considerations make it necessary to ponder even more carefully not only the importance of the first interrogation(s) of the juvenile carried out by public authorities but also the notion of criminal proceedings. All the above arguments in fact encourage us to adopt a very broad notion of 'criminal proceedings' and 'criminal charge', so that it can include all those situations where the juvenile can substantially be 'punished'. The complexity of juvenile justice systems cannot be fully captured within rigid categories. The domestic labels are important to understand the philosophy of each system but they have to be taken in a somewhat looser way. It is for this reason that a substantive approach to what criminal juvenile justice entails, seems to be preferable: not only because it is directly endorsed by the ECtHR, but also because it makes it possible to compare and harmonise situations where the interests at stake are the same. Taking a more substantive approach is also encouraged by a need for general coherence in the procedural system: while different types of proceedings may justify divergent procedural safeguards, if the level of divergence becomes too wide it cannot be justified purely on the ground of a formal categorisation. Otherwise, the risk is that the system becomes imbalanced, more confusing and thus offers less protection to the juvenile. Looking at the countries involved in

[19] See *inter alia* Cape *et al.* 2007, p. 19–20.

[20] Halt is short for *Het ALTernatief* ('the alternative') and represents the possibility of the Dutch police to refer a case to one of the Halt offices where juveniles suspected of having committed certain minor offences can follow a so-called Halt program as a form of alternative punishment.

the study, this risk is illustrated most clearly by *Poland*, where a mixed system of procedural safeguards (rules of civil procedure, rules of criminal procedure and rules contained in the Juvenile Act) applies depending on the stage of proceedings and the relevant actor. As a result, rights of the juvenile suspect could narrow or widen depending on whether the interrogation was conducted by a family judge or the police, in a clear example of how divergent procedural safeguards in different (stages of) proceedings may cause difficulties in practice.[21]

2. THE TWO FACES OF THE JUVENILE SUSPECT: EITHER JUVENILE OR SUSPECT?

2.1. FOCUS ON SUSPECT OR JUVENILE: PROCEDURAL SAFEGUARDS ARE MOSTLY NOT JUVENILE RELATED

As was mentioned in the opening chapter, 'juvenile' and 'suspect' are terms that evoke opposite reactions. It is self-evident that juveniles are vulnerable and for that reason they require protection. In sharp contrast to this, and although individuals should be presumed innocent until proven guilty, suspects are often viewed as 'evil' or dangerous individuals.[22] While many would think of a juvenile confronted by the authorities as a person in need of protection, a suspect is often associated with someone who tries to escape justice by speaking untruthfully or using other subterfuges. This dichotomy is misleading. Just as juveniles are vulnerable, suspects are also vulnerable by definition. For all suspects, regardless of their age, there is an inherent vulnerability connected to their status in the proceedings, which is especially noticeable during interrogation. For juveniles there is an extra vulnerability related to their age and level of development. Thus, juvenile suspects are vulnerable not once but twice, but it seems that all domestic lawmakers experience difficulties in capturing the essence of this double vulnerability. In the juvenile justice systems involved in the study, the safeguards seem to be conceived either around the *suspect* (vulnerability due to his status in the proceedings), regardless of his condition as a minor, or around the *juvenile* (vulnerability due to his age), regardless of his position as a suspect. While the former focus is visible in the more 'justice'-oriented countries, the latter seems to be the case in the more welfare-oriented systems like *Belgium* and *Poland*.

While this distinction in focus (suspect or juvenile) may have implications for the *content* of procedural safeguards available to juveniles, it does not seem to affect

21 Recent amendments to *Poland's* Juvenile Act (2013) – introducing unified court proceedings based mainly on rules of civil procedure – have diminished this diversity to a certain extent but certainly not completely.

22 See chapter 1, paragraph 2.

the *level* or *degree* of explicit youth-specific legal protection provided. In systems focusing on the juvenile being a suspect, the procedural safeguards provided for by law are more or less a transposition of adult procedural safeguards with often only few derogations. Thus, there seems to be a greater focus on the juvenile's status as a suspect/defendant than on his vulnerability due to his young age. This is illustrated by *Italy, England and Wales* and *the Netherlands.* The main exceptions to this rule concern the right to an appropriate adult and – to a more limited extent – the right to a lawyer, which in most countries has some youth-specific content or derogations.[23] The most common juvenile-specific safeguard in the context of interrogation is the right to an appropriate adult, which seems to be most strongly emphasised in *England and Wales.*[24] In systems focusing on the juvenile as a person in need of care, the protective role of people (e.g. judges) seems to make explicit legal procedural safeguards redundant, at least to a certain extent, as is illustrated by the systems of *Belgium* and *Poland.*[25] In summary, when the focus is on the juvenile being a suspect, he tends to be given the safeguards offered to adult suspects with little or no youth-specific adjustments and when the focus is on the juvenile's vulnerability due to his age, the juvenile is generally given fewer safeguards (in terms of procedural rights) than the adult suspect.

2.2. BEING A JUVENILE DOES NOT AFFECT THE MOMENT OF INTERROGATION

It follows from the country reports that the position of the juvenile as a vulnerable person has influence on the overall context of juvenile justice (particularly on penalties, competent judicial authorities and procedural rules) but it does not seem to affect the moment of interrogation. Generally, the status of juvenile has a stronger influence on the rules of trial proceedings than on the provisions concerning the investigative stage, more specifically the phase of the initial interrogations.[26] Furthermore, the status of juvenile seems to have a stronger impact on substantive law than on procedural law. See for example *the Netherlands* and *England and Wales,* where the rules on arresting and detaining juveniles are similar to the rules applicable to adults, but where juvenile criminal law provides for a wide variety of youth-specific sanctions. *Italy* is a wholly different case: separate rules of criminal procedure law exist but no separate sanctions for juveniles are provided for.

---

23 In some systems – such as *Belgium* and *the Netherlands* – the right to legal assistance is given a broader scope in case of juvenile suspects (for example influencing the possibility of waiver). On the right to legal assistance, see *infra* paragraph 3 (part II).

24 On the right to an appropriate adult, see *infra* paragraph 2 (part II).

25 On the protection by people as opposed to the protection by rules, see *supra* paragraph 3 (part I).

26 See *infra* paragraph 6 (part II).

In summary, it can be concluded that the necessity of providing legal, youth-specific procedural safeguards for juveniles during interrogation seems to be mostly 'disregarded' in both types of systems (both justice-oriented and welfare-oriented models) but for different reasons. In justice-oriented models, procedural safeguards for juveniles are mostly a transposition of adult rules (resulting in no or only a few youth-specific rules). In more welfare-oriented systems the focus on protection by people instead of protection by rules seems to make the existence of (youth-specific) procedural safeguards for juveniles redundant.

3. WHAT IS IT THAT PROTECTS JUVENILES: PEOPLE OR RULES?

3.1. PRESUMPTION THAT THE SYSTEM WILL PROTECT THE JUVENILE

There is no doubt that all systems are concerned with the vulnerability of juvenile suspects and defendants and strive to offer them adequate protection. But what is the best way to achieve such 'adequate protection'? Two different philosophies can be identified. According to one philosophy, the legal safeguards spelled out by the law protect the juvenile defendant. According to another approach, the juvenile defendant is best protected by public actors who are appointed to act in the juvenile's best interest and secure his well-being as much as possible. Systems following the latter pattern seem to take a more paternalistic approach, which is directly tied into the greater welfaristic aspiration of the accompanying juvenile justice system. The public authority has the duty to ensure that proceedings are shaped in a way that is compatible with the needs and vulnerability of the young suspect. A clear example of this approach is the (strong and paternalistic) role of the juvenile judge in *Belgium* and *Poland* and the emphasis placed on the informality of proceedings. In *Belgium*, for example, the same juvenile judge normally deals with the entire case, from the investigation to the trial stage. The pivotal role of the juvenile judge and the wide powers that he is given are also justified by the need to ensure a proper and constant educational line to the juvenile. Ideally, this should allow the juvenile judge to become well acquainted with the juvenile and his situation and to take an individual approach tailored to the juvenile's individual educational needs. A similar trend can be seen in *Poland*, although there the handling of the entire case by the same juvenile judge is only a possibility and not a necessity.

3.2. THE MORE PROTECTIVE THE ROLE OF THE JUDGE, THE LESS NEED FOR LEGAL RULES

The paternalistic approach means that protection by people is considered more important – and maybe also more effective – than the protection offered by rules. Or, to put it more strongly, protection by people makes protection by rules redundant, in whole or in part. The Polish approach to formalism is clearly illustrative of this philosophy: proceedings in juvenile cases do not require detailed procedural forms because the judge should be able to establish a 'sincere and direct contact with the juvenile'. The absence of rigid rules provides the family courts with more flexible methods of educational influence. In the field of interrogation, for instance, the choice was made to give the courts large discretionary powers to choose the 'right approach' when dealing with the juvenile, instead of setting fixed legal rules on how the juvenile should be treated and protected during interrogation. This used to be the case in *Belgium* too, but in the past twenty years several strands of reform have injected a larger and more pervasive set of procedural rights to protect the juvenile.

3.3. PROTECTION BY PEOPLE DURING INTERROGATION NOT SYSTEMATIC

The central role of the family judge does not exclude the police from carrying out the interrogation even in welfaristic systems. For example in *Poland*, the police may interrogate juvenile suspects in 'urgent cases' (*w wypadkach niecierpiących zwłoki*), before the formal proceedings are instigated by the family court. After a recent amendment to the Polish Juvenile Act, the powers of the police in this respect have even been broadened. As a result of this amendment the police have the power to collect and preserve evidence of both 'punishable acts' and 'signs of demoralisation'. Furthermore, in the course of Polish juvenile proceedings, the family court may order the interrogation of the juvenile by the police. In *Belgium* too, the police may conduct interrogations aimed at evidence gathering.

3.4. PROTECTION BY PEOPLE DOES NOT ALWAYS IMPLY SPECIALISATION AND TRAINING

For obvious reasons, the effective extent to which a juvenile judge or prosecutor can offer the juvenile the necessary protection depends on their abilities to deal with juveniles in an appropriate manner. If the role played by certain figures in the juvenile justice system is pivotal for the protection of the juvenile, it appears crucial that they are adequately, appropriately and continuously trained. This emphasises the need for specialisation and training in dealing with (different categories) of juvenile suspects.[27] However, from the country reports it becomes clear that, at present, special continuous training for the main actors involved in juvenile proceedings is not always properly guaranteed in both justice- and welfare-oriented countries. For instance, in *Poland* there are separate family and juvenile departments in court but there is the possibility for a civil law judge to deal with juvenile cases. In addition, in *Belgium* there is a specialised juvenile judge with a clear legal basis but without mandatory (continuous) training.

4. THE DIFFERENT MANIFESTATIONS OF INTERROGATION

4.1. FORMAL LEGAL DEFINITIONS OF THE CONCEPT OF INTERROGATION

The concept of 'interrogation' may have different meanings not only when comparing different national juvenile justice systems but also within a single jurisdiction.[28] Fixed legal definitions are not always provided, and even when they do exist they often leave ample room for interpretation.

In some countries, a formal definition of 'interrogation' is provided by law. This is for instance the case of *England and Wales*, where the legal definition can be found in the Police and Criminal Evidence Act 1984. It is defined as 'the questioning of a person regarding their involvement or suspected involvement in a criminal offence or offences, which (...) must be carried out under caution'. In all other countries the notion of interrogation is left implicit in the legal texts. In *Belgium*, the concept is not defined by law but in the explanatory memorandum of the Salduz Act it is described as 'a substantive interrogation related to an alleged offence with the aim of collecting evidence'.

While the law may not define the term 'interrogation', leaving it to the judiciary to offer a proper interpretation, it may indulge in classifications that can guide the interpreters' activity. For instance, in *the Netherlands*, legal texts make a division, though not always in a consistent manner, between activities labelled as 'to hear' (*horen*) and 'to interrogate' (*verhoren*): the latter is a classic case-related interrogation, while the first is an opportunity for the suspect to put forward his defence in relation to restrictive measures that may be taken (for example to ascertain the lawfulness of the arrest or to decide on the application of police detention). In *Italy* the word 'interrogation' covers the questioning of a suspect

---

27 See *infra* paragraph 4 (part II).

28 See for the working definition of the word 'interrogation' used in this study, chapter 1, paragraph 9.

by a magistrate (public prosecutor or judge) or by the police, but in the latter case only if the police act after an order from the prosecutor. In fact when the police question the suspect on their own initiative, the act qualifies as 'summary information taken from the suspect'. On the other hand, in *Italy*, like in *the Netherlands*, there are confrontations that are predominantly aimed at providing the suspect with an opportunity to discharge himself, but they fall under the general heading of 'interrogation' (*interrogatorio*).

A common feature of all of the definitions available in the countries involved in the study is that none of them are youth-specific and that therefore they apply to all categories of suspects – both adults as well as juveniles.

4.2. WIDE VARIATIONS IN TYPES OF PRE-TRIAL INTERROGATIONS

The examples mentioned above and illustrated in depth in the country reports show that in most countries there are different types of interrogations. In *Italy* for example there are interrogations conducted by the prosecutor and the police in the course of investigative activities and interrogations carried out by the judge for *habeas corpus* proceedings; and even the former category can be further subdivided into different groups. The same situation can be seen in *the Netherlands*, where the pre-trial interrogation of the juvenile suspect distinguishes between 'material interrogations' (aimed at obtaining evidence) and 'procedural interrogations' which allow the defence to express its view and/or enable the authorities to ascertain whether prolonging the deprivation of liberty is legitimate.[29] In *Poland*, where there is no single legal definition of the concept of 'interrogation', there are two different modes of questioning a juvenile in order to determine if he committed a 'punishable act' (*wysłuchanie* and *przesłuchanie*). The concept of *wysłuchanie* ('to listen to') mainly concerns the possibility to enable the person who is heard to present his position on the subject matter. Although the term is typical for civil proceedings it is also used in relation to the family judge's 'listening to' the juvenile. The term *przesłuchanie*, which is best translated as 'interrogation', is used in provisions of both the Code of Civil Procedure and the Code of Criminal Procedure with regard to the questioning of different persons by different authorities. In summary, the wide variation in types of pre-trial interrogation visible in the countries involved in the study is caused by the following variables.

---

29 See the distinction between *'horen'* and *'verhoren'* mentioned in the paragraph above.

4.2.1. *Different authorities*

Pre-trial interrogations of juvenile suspects can be conducted by several different authorities, such as the police, the prosecutor or the (juvenile) judge. Despite this variation in authorities, it seems that – especially in more justice-oriented systems – the police play the main role in pre-trial interrogations of juvenile suspects. For example in *England and Wales* only the police are empowered to carry out the interrogation of a juvenile suspect. In *the Netherlands*, as mentioned above, different types of interrogation exist (conducted by different authorities: police, (assistant) public prosecutor and investigative judge) but the most important pre-trial interrogation with the aim of evidence gathering is also conducted by the police.

Furthermore, it should be noted that the more welfaristic a system is, the greater the judicial involvement in the investigative stage seems to be. This correlation is visible in *Belgium* as well as in *Poland*. Nonetheless, this does not rule out the police playing a role. In *Belgium*, a mandatory hearing by the juvenile judge should take place before any measure can be taken, but the most common forms of interrogation (aimed at evidence gathering) are conducted by the King's Prosecutor or the police. In *Poland*, as mentioned above, the central role of the family judge does not prevent the police from carrying out the interrogation of a juvenile suspect during the investigative stage. A recent amendment to the Juvenile Act has even broadened the powers of the police in this respect.[30] The Italian case is only to some extent similar. In *Italy* the predominant role seems to be taken, at least when reading the provisions of the law in the books, by the public prosecutor. Nonetheless, the police are empowered to act autonomously on some occasions and they can always be asked by the prosecutor to interrogate the suspect.

4.2.2. *Different goals*

In addition to evidence gathering, the pre-trial interrogation of juvenile suspects may have different goals such as providing elements for the defence and gathering information on the educational, health and welfare situation of the juvenile. As mentioned before, the variety of information that can be collected is well illustrated by the Italian system, where there is a wide variation of different types of pre-trial interrogation by different actors aimed at evidence gathering, and at providing the juvenile with an opportunity to defend himself or to consider the lawfulness of arrest and/or detention. A similar division in types of interrogation exists in *the Netherlands*. In some jurisdictions, the different types of interrogation are reflected by variations in legal terminology ('hearing',

---

[30] See *supra* paragraph 3.3 (part. I).

'questioning', 'declaring', *et cetera*) but – as is clear from the Dutch and Belgian example – these different terms are often not used in a consistent manner, not even by the legislator.

4.2.3. *Different proceedings*

Pre-trial interrogations of juvenile suspects can take place within the context (or as a starting point) of different types of proceedings. This diversity of proceedings – criminal, non-criminal and diversionary – is a general feature of most juvenile justice systems given their (at least theoretical) aim of choosing an individual approach and inflicting the least possible harm upon the juvenile. Nevertheless, as mentioned earlier, the distinction between these different types of proceedings is not always as strict as it may seem.[31] Different proceedings may intertwine and overlap, to the extent that they may share common procedural moments, particularly at the beginning of the case. More importantly, during the first and usually most important interrogation(s) it is often not clear – or it has not yet been decided – which kind of proceedings (with which possible outcome) will be pursued.

4.3. WIDE VARIATIONS MAY COMPLICATE THE APPLICABILITY OF PROCEDURAL SAFEGUARDS

The many different contexts in which juvenile suspects may be interrogated make it difficult to determine which procedural safeguards (should) apply and when. The countries involved in the study provide different examples of this complexity.

For example, in *Italy* the social services can hear the juveniles on their personality and social/familial background but these 'auditions' do not qualify as 'interrogation' and are not surrounded by any express safeguards (e.g. right to remain silent). Furthermore, in the context of proceedings for probation, the judge carries out an informal interview, which is not assisted by formalities and safeguards.

Similar examples can also be found in the other countries involved in the study. As mentioned before, in *the Netherlands*, it is not clear from the outset which procedural safeguards apply to hearings about the possibility of diversion. The complexity of the matter (which procedural safeguards apply to which kind of interrogations) is probably greatest in *Poland*. As mentioned before, Polish juvenile proceedings are 'hybrid' in the sense that some procedural issues are

31 See *supra* paragraph 1 (part I).

governed by the Juvenile Act while others are regulated by provisions of the Civil Code or the Code of Criminal Procedure. It all depends on the type of crime, the type of proceedings followed and – to a certain extent – the stage of the proceedings. Although a recent amendment of the Juvenile Act has tried to simplify juvenile proceedings by reducing the applicability of the rules of the Code of Criminal Procedure, the current legal framework still remains quite confusing, making it very difficult to determine what exact procedural safeguards should apply during the interrogation of a juvenile suspect conducted by either the police or the juvenile judge.

Finally, it should be noted that the fact of whether the pre-trial interrogation is 'voluntary' or non-voluntary (whether a juvenile has been arrested or not) may influence the legal protection offered to the juvenile in some countries but not in all of them. For example, in *England and Wales* it makes no difference: the same legal safeguards apply (including the mandatory presence of an appropriate adult). In *the Netherlands* a different approach is taken in the context of Salduz rights: the right to legal assistance before and during interrogation in principle only applies to situations where the interrogation(s) follow(s) an arrest.

5. WHO IS A JUVENILE?

The notion of 'juvenile' in the context of criminal proceedings – and consequently in the field of pre-trial interrogations – varies from country to country. In all countries, however, the notion depends on two age thresholds: a minimum and a maximum age. The upper threshold identifies the separation between juveniles (or children) and adults. The lower threshold, which corresponds to the minimum age of criminal liability, marks the division between children who can be prosecuted and those who cannot. Nonetheless, the identification of a juvenile is not always a sharp one. In some cases (*Italy*) the threshold of criminal liability not only has an age requirement but also rests on an assessment of the effective maturity of the child. In *Poland* the legal definition of 'juvenile' is complex because of its direct reference to the dual character of Polish juvenile proceedings and the corresponding (varying) age categories.

Besides the two basic thresholds, further specific thresholds are found in some countries. In principle, children who cannot be prosecuted cannot be questioned either. Nevertheless, there may be cases where the national law allows for the interrogation of juveniles below the age of criminal responsibility. For example, in *the Netherlands*, juveniles below the age of 12 cannot be prosecuted but they can however be interrogated as a suspect and detained for a certain period of time. With regard to the latter category of juveniles (aged between 10 and 12), there is a clear gap in (explicit) legal protection: for example, although the general assumption in *the Netherlands* is that the right to remain silent also applies to juveniles below the age of 12, there is no explicit legal obligation for the authorities to inform this category of suspects of this right.

Another category that sporadically emerges is that of *young adults*. An example of a separate category of young people aged between 18 and 25 years is to be found in *Italy*. However, membership of this category only entails different treatment in the enforcement of sanctions against these individuals (mostly in the sense that they ought to remain separated from adults) but it is not connected to different level of safeguards during the proceedings. A similar set of separate rules for young adults was also recently introduced in *the Netherlands* with the enactment of a law introducing the possibility of applying juvenile law to young adults between the ages of 18 and 23.

Finally, it should be noted that none of the available definitions of the notion of 'juvenile' contains any references to the special needs or characteristics of juveniles in the context of juvenile (criminal) proceedings.[32]

II. INTERROGATIONS

1. RIGHT TO REMAIN SILENT – JUST LIKE AN ADULT

1.1. SCOPE AND CONTENT GENERALLY THE SAME AS WITH ADULT

Generally, the legal basis of the right to remain silent for juvenile suspects does not differ significantly from the right to remain silent awarded to adult suspects. There is a formal obligation to inform the juvenile of the right to remain silent in all countries. Obviously, there are many variations in the scope and content of this right, as well as in the way the juvenile should be informed of it. Inevitably, the communication of the right depends on the exact scope and content of the right.

It is worth noting that in *Italy*, it is expressly stated that the right to remain silent does not include the right to conceal one's own identity; hence the suspect is informed that he has the right to remain silent save for the information concerning his identity. The same clarification is not made in other countries and this leaves the impression that the suspect has a right to remain silent on his name, date of birth and residence. In *the Netherlands*, for example, a (juvenile) suspect indeed has the right to remain silent when asked about his personal data.[33]

32 See in this respect *infra* paragraph 5 (part II).

33 There is however a legal obligation to hand over identification documents when the police ask for it and this is deemed 'necessary for the fulfilment of police tasks'. In practice, this may infringe with a suspect's right to remain silent on any personal data.

1.2. HOW INFORMATION ON THE RIGHT TO REMAIN SILENT IS PROVIDED FOR DIFFERS WIDELY

The way in which the juvenile is informed of his right to remain silent differs widely. In some countries this right is incorporated in a letter of rights, which is handed over to the suspect (*Belgium* and *Poland*). In other countries the information is provided orally, sometimes according to a standard formula (*the Netherlands*). Finally, some countries require that the information be provided both orally and in writing (*England and Wales*). It is worth noting that only exceptionally is there a legal obligation to inform the juvenile of his right to remain silent in the presence of an appropriate adult (as is the case in *England and Wales*).

It is to be expected that the existing differences between national rules will be reduced in the near future by the successful implementation of Directive 2012/13/EU on the right to information. According to this Directive all suspected and accused persons should be promptly informed of specific procedural rights. This information should be given orally or in writing in simple and accessible language.[34] For arrested suspects, however, the Directive sets out the obligation to inform the person both orally and in writing through a letter of rights.[35] The impact that the EU directive may have on domestic rules is well exemplified by the Italian case. The implementation process has resulted in the recent adoption of an amendment to the code of criminal procedure, which has introduced the legal obligation to provide suspects (including juvenile suspects) who are deprived of their liberty with an extensive letter of rights, also including the information on the right to remain silent.

1.3. LACK OF (YOUTH-SPECIFIC) RULES ON INFORMING OF AND EXPLAINING THE RIGHT TO REMAIN SILENT

Generally, national laws do not require public authorities to assess, or take into account, any special needs of juveniles when they are informed of the right to remain silent. For example, in none of the countries involved in the study are there general or youth-specific rules on the wording to be used when informing the juvenile suspect of his right to remain silent, nor on the speed at which the information should be given or on the consequences of invoking the right to remain silent. Furthermore, as a rule, there is no obligation to check whether the juvenile understands the information and/or to provide him with an (additional)

34 Art. 3 of Directive 2012/13/EU.

35 Art. 4 of Directive 2012/13/EU.

explanation when necessary. More specifically, different legal obligations can be distinguished across countries:

1. To inform the juvenile of his right to remain silent in the physical presence of an appropriate adult (*England and Wales*)
2. To explain caution in their own words when the juvenile does not understand (*England and Wales*)
3. To explain to the juvenile the meaning and function of procedural activities including the caution, if necessary with the involvement of a parent, defence lawyer or social services personnel (*Italy*)
4. To inform the juvenile suspect of the fact that if he refuses to answer to questions the proceedings will go on anyway and of the fact that any statements can be used against him (*Italy*)
5. To inform the juvenile of the fact that adverse inferences may be drawn from his silence (*England and Wales*).

1.4. DETRIMENTAL CONSEQUENCES OF INVOKING THE RIGHT TO REMAIN SILENT

With regard to the latter exception (the drawing of adverse inferences), it should be noted that where domestic law provides for the legal possibility of attaching disadvantageous consequences to the exercise of the right to remain silent, this possibility also applies to juvenile suspects.

In the context of normal criminal proceedings, for example in *England and Wales*, drawing of adverse inferences may be possible if in court the juvenile relies on evidence which was not mentioned during his police interrogations. As mentioned above, the juvenile suspect should be informed of this possibility beforehand. More implicitly, relying on the right to remain silent may – in some jurisdictions – be used to make incriminating evidence more believable: this is possible in, for example, *the Netherlands* and *Belgium*. In those countries, there is, however, no explicit legal obligation to inform the (juvenile) suspect of these possible implications of remaining silent.[36]

It should be recalled that, in the context of diversion proceedings, making use of the right to remain silent might block the possibility of accessing some diversionary tracks. As mentioned before, diversionary proceedings often have

[36] In this respect it should be stressed that in these countries a legal obligation to inform the (juvenile) suspect of his general right to remain silent does exist and that the implications of exercising the right to remain silent can only be used by the trial judge to a very limited extent (in the context of evaluating the credibility of other evidence).

a consensual (or cooperative) element and in some countries – such as *England and Wales*, *Italy* and *the Netherlands* – even require some sort of admission of guilt.

2. ASSISTANCE BY ADULTS: APPROPRIATE OR NOT?

2.1. MOST IMPORTANT YOUTH-SPECIFIC SAFEGUARD BUT GREAT VARIATIONS

The involvement of an appropriate adult is the main (sometimes the only) youth-specific procedural safeguard during interrogation provided for in the legal frameworks of the different countries. Despite the fact that the appropriate adult is present in all the juvenile justice systems, ideas on its role and function seem to differ substantially, resulting in diverging rules and practices. One of the keys to making sense of this variability between the different systems lies in the following correlation: the more welfaristic the proceedings are, the less need for an appropriate adult there seems to be. A possible explanation for this correlation can be found in the underlying assumption of welfaristic systems that the protective role of legal professionals involved in juvenile proceedings (such as the judge in *Poland* and *Belgium*) limits the necessity of involving an appropriate adult.[37] In more justice-oriented systems, such as *England and Wales*, the safeguard of an appropriate adult seems to be considered more crucial, since the presence of an adult on the juvenile's side is taken to balance the vulnerability and immaturity of the minor. Nevertheless, the above picture is blurred – as we shall see – by the overlap, sometimes the trade-off, between the role of appropriate adults and that of lawyers.

Looking at the systems involved in the study, the safeguard of the appropriate adult is – without a doubt – most strongly emphasised in *England and Wales* where it is a mandatory legal requirement for all vulnerable suspects including juveniles. A rather important role for the appropriate adult is also visible in the *Italian* system. There the appropriate adult is viewed as someone offering 'affective and psychological support', which should be possible during any stage of the proceedings but the safeguard mainly applies to acts performed by judicial authorities. According to Italian law, their presence can however be excluded in the interests of the juvenile or the proceedings and they should remain passive during the interrogation (not intervening, not asking questions, *et cetera*). No explicit legal right to have an appropriate adult present during the interrogation is

37 See *supra* paragraph 3 (part I).

provided for in the *Belgian* system and the phenomenon also seems to be of limited significance in *the Netherlands* and *Poland.* In *the Netherlands* and *Belgium*, the juvenile does have a right to have his parents/guardian informed of his arrest but they play only a limited role during the interrogation. In *the Netherlands* parents/guardians have a legal possibility to be present during the interrogation but only instead of a lawyer: according to the regulations currently in force, the authorities should inform the juvenile that the presence of a lawyer is to be preferred. In *Poland* the juvenile suspect also has a right to presence of an appropriate adult *or* a lawyer during interrogation by the police meaning that – like in *the Netherlands* – the two safeguards are considered to be interchangeable and not supplementary.[38] From the perspective of effective procedural rights' protection this 'trade-off' between the right to legal assistance and the right to an appropriate adult is questionable because the two safeguards are very different in nature and clearly serve different purposes. After all, it is at least doubtful that parents who have little understanding of legal matters and are untrained in assisting their child during interrogation will be sufficiently able to help their child understand what is going on and take the most appropriate decisions.[39] On the other hand, it is fair to assume that on average a parent will be better suited to provide the juvenile with the necessary emotional and moral support than a defence lawyer.

2.2. THE APPROPRIATE ADULT LACKS A CLEAR FUNCTION

In addition to the foregoing, one difference noticeable between the systems deserves to be further highlighted: the fact that the countries involved in the study represent varying ideas on the possible role(s) and function(s) of the appropriate adult. In some countries the support of an adult is intended to remedy the vulnerability of the juvenile. In this respect, juvenile suspects are considered not to be too different from ordinary (non-vulnerable) suspects when supported by an adult. This is, for example, the case in *England and Wales.* In other countries, the presence of the appropriate adult is mostly considered to offer psychological support, but it is not perceived as sufficient to fully counterbalance the vulnerability of the young suspect. This difference is reflected in the larger or narrower role given to the appropriate adult in the different countries. The latter approach is for example visible in *Italy.*

The variations in the role and function of the appropriate adult are reflected by the many differences in the rights and obligations given to this figure in the current national legal frameworks (such as obligatory presence during caution

38 See *infra* paragraph 7.1 (part II).
39 See *infra* paragraph 7 (part II).

and interrogation, a right to be present during interrogation, a right to intervene and ask questions during interrogation, *et cetera*). In addition, there are varying ideas on whether the appropriate adult should be prepared or even trained for his role in proceedings. In some countries the role of the appropriate adult is – at least in theory – quite extensive. The best example in this respect is provided by *England and Wales*: there the role of the appropriate adult is to advise, support and assist vulnerable suspects at the police station. They are meant to look after the suspect's welfare, explain police procedures, provide them with information about their rights, ensure that these are safeguarded and facilitate communication with the police. In addition, there is an explicit legal obligation to inform the juvenile suspect of certain rights (such as the right to remain silent) in the presence of an appropriate adult, thus giving the appropriate adult a role in making sure that the juvenile understands what is going on. Furthermore, in *England and Wales*, the actual interrogation of the juvenile should take place in the presence of the appropriate adult: a safeguard that can only be waived in case of a so-called urgent interview. As mentioned above, the role of the appropriate adult in the *Italian* system seems to be quite different from the one described above. There, the assistance of the appropriate adult is a safeguard specifically provided for juveniles, aiming to strengthen their position during proceedings by providing affective and psychological support as well as to organise and manage the juvenile's defence. Nevertheless, the role of the appropriate adult/holder of parental authority during the interrogations can be limited in *Italy*, because the authority can proceed without the adult and social services if it is in the interests of the juvenile to do so or if there are specific needs connected to the proceedings. Furthermore, the appropriate adult has no explicit right to intervene during the interrogations: according to the letter of the code, he cannot ask questions and it is forbidden for him to make signs of (dis)approval to any questions or answers. The appropriate adult may also be present during legal consultation between the lawyer and the juvenile suspect, but this form of participation of the appropriate adult lacks sufficient clarity.

2.3. DIFFERENT IDEAS ON WHICH ADULT IS (MOST) APPROPRIATE

Finally, the systems involved in the study take very different approaches as to which adult is most 'suitable' to offer assistance to the juvenile. Between the varying systems, the appropriate adult may be the holder of parental authority (parent or guardian) or a close friend, but the role could also be fulfilled by a professional or a 'repeat player' such as a teacher, priest, practitioner, member of a Youth Offending Team or social services. For example in *England and Wales*, the appropriate adult may be a parent or carer, an experienced criminal justice professional, or a volunteer (with varying degrees of training), while in *Italy* social services personnel play an important role in proceedings and – more specifically

– during interrogation but they do not exclude the simultaneous presence of a familiar adult. As a result of this broad approach to the concept of 'appropriate adult' there are inconsistencies in the level of safeguarding this adult may provide.

From a comparative perspective, it is worth noting that the approaches to the scope and content of the right to an appropriate adult are of course inextricably linked to why the safeguard was introduced to the juvenile justice system in the first place. For example, in *England and Wales* the need for mandatory protection of juvenile (and other vulnerable) suspects by being assisted by an appropriate adult arose out of a miscarriage of justice.[40] As a result, the introduction of this safeguard was mainly based on the assumption that vulnerable suspects were more susceptible to coercion and suggestion and the expectation that the provision of an appropriate adult would be able to effectively compensate for this aspect of vulnerability. The example of *England and Wales* illustrates how the historical and political context of a procedural safeguards origin may be relevant for truly understanding its goal, scope and content and – even more importantly – how the procedural safeguard is eventually perceived in practice.

3. RIGHT TO LEGAL ASSISTANCE FOR JUVENILE SUSPECTS: NECESSITY OR POSSIBILITY?

The right to legal assistance is one of the most fundamental fair trial rights and – in many cases – constitutes an important precondition for realising an effective criminal defence. This is probably especially true for juvenile suspects who, due to their young age and level of development, will often not be able to adequately defend themselves without the assistance of a legal professional.

In principle, the right to legal assistance for juvenile suspects seems to be well established in all five countries since they broadly provide the juvenile with the basic right to assistance of a lawyer in the initial phase of police interrogation. However, when comparing the different legal frameworks in more detail, it becomes clear that important variations exist with regard to the scope and content of the right to legal assistance in this early stage of proceedings.

3.1. SCOPE OF THE RIGHT TO LEGAL ASSISTANCE

Generally, in all five countries, the right to legal assistance for juvenile suspects includes the right to consultation before interrogation as well as the right to have

40 The so-called 'Confait affair' where two juveniles and an 18-year-old with the mental capacities of a 13-year-old were wrongly convicted of murder.

a lawyer present during interrogation. In this respect, the legal protection offered to the juvenile suspect may differ from the protection offered to adult suspects since the right to legal assistance during interrogation is not (yet) awarded to the latter category in all countries. Although the unconditional right to assistance of a lawyer during interrogation has been – and to a certain extent still is – the subject of heated debate in many Member States, the right seems to be less controversial when it concerns juvenile suspects. It should be noted that – in the next few years – significant changes in the existing legal provisions covering the right to legal assistance are to be expected in all EU Member States with the implementation of the Directive on the right to access to a lawyer in criminal proceedings.[41]

In the countries involved in the study, the right of the juvenile suspect to consult a lawyer before interrogation and to have him present during interrogation are provided for at varying levels and in various sources of 'law'. For example, in *the Netherlands*, the right of a juvenile suspect to assistance of a lawyer in the phase of police interrogation is at present mainly covered by an instruction of the Board of Public Prosecutors while new statutory law is being prepared. In the other countries, the juvenile's right to legal assistance is mostly covered by statutory law.

3.2. WHETHER THE RIGHT TO LEGAL ASSISTANCE IS MANDATORY

The five countries in the study take different approaches to whether the assistance of a lawyer before and/or during interrogation is a necessary requirement for the fairness of proceedings against a juvenile suspect. In other words, whether the right to legal assistance is considered as a necessity or as a possibility differs: there are variations not only between Member States but also within national legal systems depending on the circumstances of the case. The matter of making the right to legal assistance mandatory or not is strongly connected to prevailing views on the ability of the juvenile to understand proceedings and to make his own decisions without the assistance of an adult.[42] The diversity within the current legal frameworks clearly shows that these matters may be approached quite differently by Member States.

Of the countries involved in the study, *England and Wales* is an example of a system where it is never a mandatory requirement to be assisted by a lawyer at the police station, not even in the case of very serious offences. In *England and Wales*,

---

41 Directive 2013/48/EU of October 2013.

42 And – just as important – should assistance of an adult be necessary: which adult is best equipped to act in the best interest of the juvenile. See *supra* paragraph 2.3 (part II).

the (juvenile) suspect does have the right to consult a lawyer before interrogation and benefit from the assistance of a lawyer during interrogation. Nevertheless, the juvenile suspect is given a wide discretionary power to decide on the matter: even when the appropriate adult deems it necessary and asks a solicitor to attend at the police station, it is ultimately the juvenile who decides whether he wants to be assisted by a lawyer or not. In this way, *England and Wales* is an important example of a situation in which the juvenile is considered competent to make such fundamental decisions, which may have far-reaching consequences for the course and outcome of the case.[43] In the other systems, rules on mandatory legal assistance are provided for in different ways and to different extents. For example in *Italy*, the right cannot be waived but conducting the interrogation in the presence of a lawyer is not a necessary condition for the validity of the interrogation. In *the Netherlands*, whether the assistance of a lawyer during the initial stages of police interrogation is mandatory (and therefore cannot be waived) will depend on both the suspect's age and the severity of the case. These relevant factors are laid down in a decision scheme that is quite complex and difficult to apply. It should be noted that this part of the Dutch legal framework is one of the few examples of differentiation in age categories in regulating procedural rights for juvenile suspects during interrogation to be found in the countries involved in the study.[44] In *Poland* the assistance of a lawyer is mandatory for juveniles in some situations, for example when the interests of the juvenile and his parents or guardian conflict or when there is reason to have doubts about the juvenile's mental health. The mandatory character of the right to legal assistance seems to be strongest in *Belgium*: here every juvenile who has to appear before a juvenile judge has to be assisted by a lawyer; furthermore, legal assistance during police interrogation cannot be waived.

It goes without saying that the effectiveness of the right to legal assistance for all suspects, including juveniles, will to a large extent depend on the fulfilment of various, more practical preconditions such as a consistent level of quality among lawyers, appropriate funding and the availability at all times of chosen or duty lawyers.[45] As for the availability of legal assistance at all times, it should be noted that the *ex officio* appointment of lawyers to juveniles (and a corresponding duty scheme) is provided for in some countries. For example in *Belgium*, a system of permanently available duty lawyers (*permanentiedienst*) has been established. *England and Wales, Italy* and *the Netherlands* also have a duty solicitor's scheme, which consists of defence lawyers who take turns in providing legal advice.[46]

---

43 See *infra* paragraph 7.1 (part II).

44 See *infra* paragraph 5.1 (part I).

45 As persuasively pointed out in Cape *et al.* 2010, the dependency on practical preconditions is not only relevant for the right to legal assistance but for all defence rights.

46 Although the question whether and how the existing duty schemes are (effectively) put into practice was not dealt with by the country reports in the present study, other comparative

3.3. WHETHER THE RIGHT TO LEGAL ASSISTANCE IS FREE OF CHARGE

Generally, the countries only to a limited extent provide youth-specific rules on when and how legal assistance should be given free of charge. In this respect, *Belgium* seems to have the most far-reaching system of legal aid for juveniles: for a juvenile suspect legal assistance is always free of charge, regardless of his means. In other systems, legal aid seems to be more restricted with a tendency to apply the same (or similar) rules as applicable to adults. For example in *Italy*, the general conditions for legal aid are the same regardless of whether the suspect is an adult or a juvenile. There is however a youth-specific provision that the defence lawyer who is appointed *ex officio* should be paid directly by the state on a presumption of indigence. Nevertheless, it is possible to claim back the costs afterwards. In *England and Wales* too, the same rules as those applicable to adults generally apply: legal aid for juveniles depends on the same 'interest of justice' test as applicable to adults and – for 17-year-olds who are employed – the same financial test applies. In *Poland*, since 1 January 2014, a juvenile may ask the president of the court to appoint a lawyer, provided that he and his parents demonstrate that they are not able to cover the costs without detriment to the necessary maintenance of themselves and their family. The president of the court has a large discretionary power to decide on the matter and will only appoint a lawyer when he deems it necessary. In *the Netherlands*, the right to legal assistance free of charge will generally depend on the severity of the case (the category of the alleged offence).

3.4. LACK OF RULES ON GOAL OF LEGAL ASSISTANCE DURING INTERROGATION

Based on the legal findings, it becomes clear that existing rules on the lawyer's role (the goal of legal assistance) during interrogation mainly applies to all suspect interrogations and are therefore not youth-specific. A clear example of general rules can be found in *England and Wales* where there are quite extensive guidelines on the solicitor's role at police stations. In *Belgium* it is regulated that the lawyer has to ensure that the right not to incriminate oneself and the right to remain silent are respected, that the suspect is not coerced during the interrogation and that the interrogation is conducted lawfully. In *Italy*, the lawyer has the right to give the suspect advice about the option of answering some or all of the questions, and he is allowed to make applications, comments and remarks which have to be recorded. Where the rules mentioned above focus

research seems to suggest that various EU Member States still encounter serious problems in this respect. See Blackstock *et al.* 2014, chapter 6 and 7.

on the possibilities and competences of the lawyer, in *the Netherlands* the focus seems to be more on what the lawyer is *not* allowed to do, with rules stressing that the role of the lawyer is meant to be passive and should not hinder or influence the interrogation.

From the examples provided by the countries, it is clear that provisions on the role of the lawyer during interrogation are of a general nature, mainly stressing the lawyer's responsibilities in ensuring that the interrogation is conducted in a lawful manner and assisting the suspect in understanding questions and the course of proceedings. Without a doubt these tasks are just as important (if not more so) during the interrogation of a juvenile suspect as in the case of an adult, but the fundamental question remains whether – and if so how – assisting a juvenile suspect in this crucial phase of proceedings requires a different approach by the defence lawyer than when assisting an adult suspect. It appears from the legal study that this question is not addressed by the existing legal frameworks. However, youth-specific observations on the tasks of the defence lawyer when assisting a juvenile suspect can sometimes be found in legal literature. For example, in *England and Wales* it is stressed in legal literature that the lawyer is required to intervene in the interrogation to ensure that the police do not use complex language or ploys designed to elicit responses through leading questions, multiple questions and/or hypothetical questions. The solicitor also needs to be alert to any signs that the young suspect may be susceptible to any veiled threat by the police and to ensure that the interrogation is not conducted in an oppressive manner. In addition, the objective for the solicitor in the interview is to ensure that the young suspect 'does his best in the interview', irrespective of whether or not they respond to questions put by the police, and to keep an accurate record of the interview.

3.5. LIMITED OBLIGATIONS FOR DEFENCE LAWYERS TO BE SPECIALISED

As far as the question of whether providing legal assistance to a juvenile requires a different approach is concerned, it can only be answered in a positive way. Juveniles are not simply little adults, and assisting a juvenile suspect will require the defence lawyer to take a different course of action than when dealing with an adult suspect. Obviously, communicating with juveniles is not the same as communicating with an adult: it will require the defence lawyer to use different wording, avoid the use of legal terminology, *et cetera*. In addition, building a relationship of trust is of paramount importance and requires special consideration when the client is a juvenile. Furthermore, during the interrogation of a juvenile the defence lawyer might be faced with other persons (such as the appropriate adult), which may complicate his role and interaction with his client. These are just a few examples of the ways in which assisting a juvenile suspect is a complex matter requiring special skills from the defence lawyer. Whether the defence lawyer possesses these skills and is able to properly use them will undoubtedly depend on many factors, but it goes without saying that the availability of training and specialisation in dealing with juveniles is of paramount importance. In this respect it should be noted that, in the countries involved in the study, specialisation and training of defence lawyers dealing with juvenile suspects is only guaranteed to a limited extent. In *Italy, the Netherlands* and *Belgium*, specialisation requirements do exist to a certain extent but mainly with regard to situations in which the defence lawyer is appointed to the juvenile. For example in *Belgium*, lawyers who want to assist juveniles in youth protection or criminal proceedings must be specialists in order to be enlisted in the duty scheme. In *the Netherlands* too, specialisation requirements apply for legal aid lawyers in juvenile cases in all legal areas including criminal law. The same is true for *Italy* where only a lawyer specialised in juvenile and family matters can be appointed as a duty defence lawyer. Besides these situations, any lawyer who is a member of the bar can generally provide legal assistance. The lack of specialisation requirements is especially visible in *England and Wales* and *Poland* where no special training or specialisation is required to assist juveniles during police interrogation.[47]

Finally, it is worth mentioning that in some countries (*the Netherlands*, *Belgium* and *Italy*) there are specialist professional organisations for juvenile lawyers.

4. THE NEED FOR SPECIALISATION AND TRAINING

Evidently, the importance of specialisation and training concerns not only the defence lawyer: all professional actors involved in juvenile (criminal) proceedings should be aware of the specific needs of juvenile suspects and should be able to adjust their actions accordingly. Since this is a highly complex task – connected to disciplines such as developmental psychology with which the average law professional will probably not be too familiar – some sort of preparation will be required. The fact that professionals involved in juvenile proceedings should be adequately trained, is also underlined by several supranational instruments on juvenile justice.[48] Clearly, these general (supranational) principles oblige countries to provide for some level of training and/or specialisation of juvenile

47 See on specialisation and training *infra* paragraph 4 (part II).

48 See for example rule 22 of the *Beijing Rules* requiring professional and trained personnel in the justice system. For a description of the relevant supranational legal framework, see chapter 1, paragraph 7.

justice personnel but how this obligation should be fulfilled is mainly left to the state's discretion. As illustrated by the countries involved in the study, the relevant legal frameworks show quite significant variation as to whether and how the need for specialisation is legally framed and as to the level of specialisation required of actors involved in juvenile proceedings.

4.1. LEGAL BASIS FOR SPECIALISATION AND TRAINING

Generally, the legal basis for specialisation of actors involved in interrogation of juveniles is limited and fragmented in the countries involved in the study. As a rule, the relevant legal sources do not address the type of (continuous) training needed, especially when it comes to the specific skills or training necessary for conducting the interrogation of a juvenile suspect. To some extent *Italy* may be viewed as an exception to this rule. It presents an example of a country where the principle of specialisation is strongly emphasised as one of the main principles underlying the system of juvenile justice: as provided by law, juvenile judges and prosecutors are assigned to juvenile courts with exclusive functions, lay judges are chosen with special characteristics, police staff must also be specialised and constant involvement of social services personnel is guaranteed.

4.2. ORGANISATIONAL SEPARATION VERSUS TRAINING AND PREPARATION

The goal of specialisation may be achieved in different ways. In this respect, at least a distinction should be made between specialisation through separation in practice (by working only with juveniles) versus specialisation through training. As becomes clear from the legal study, generally the focus seems to be more on the former than on the latter. In most if not all of the jurisdictions, specialisation is conceived more as organisational separation of persons, authorities and agencies dealing with juvenile suspects (special juvenile departments within the police, public prosecution and judiciary separate from adult criminal justice) than as the realisation of continuous training and preparation of these actors.

4.3. EMPHASIS ON SPECIALISATION OF (QUASI-)JUDICIAL AUTHORITIES

Furthermore, the findings from the legal study provide evidence that, generally, there seems to be a greater emphasis on specialisation of judicial authorities (judges) or quasi-judicial authorities (prosecutors) than of police officers and lawyers. With (quasi-)judicial authorities being the main target group of specialisation and training programs, current legal frameworks pay less attention to the needs of police officers in this respect. Although some training for police officers might be provided, in most countries there is no guarantee that the police officer that normally conducts the first interrogation of a juvenile suspect will have received appropriate training let alone be specialised in dealing with juveniles. An illustration of this pattern can be found in *England and Wales* where police officers and defence lawyers are not required to have any special training when dealing with juveniles[49] while such training is on the other hand provided for the judiciary. Another example can be found in *Italy* where specialised police officers carry out the interrogation on the prosecutor's behalf but where the collection of so-called 'summary information' from the juvenile at the start of the proceedings, for example after arrest, is normally led by regular police forces with no specialisation in dealing with juveniles. A similar tendency can be seen in *Belgium* and *the Netherlands* where – despite the existence of some form of specialisation and training for police officials – there is no formal legal requirement that the pre-trial interrogation of a juvenile suspect is carried out by a specialised police officer. For example in *the Netherlands*, training on interrogation of vulnerable suspects including juveniles is available but only provided for a limited group of certain qualified interrogators. It should be noted that the lack of specialisation of police officers in some countries might be compensated for, to some extent, by the involvement of other systems of support and intervention involved in juvenile proceedings, such as the so-called Youth Offending Teams[50] in *England and Wales* and the Child Welfare Council in *the Netherlands*. However, the role of these 'support systems' during the actual interrogation is curtailed, with the exception of those cases in which YOT members attend an interrogation as an appropriate adult.[51]

5. ONE SIZE FITS ALL?

The setting of a minimum age of criminal responsibility could give rise to the impression that all juveniles above this minimum age should be considered as a homogenous group with similar needs from the perspective of procedural rights protection. All juveniles who have reached the age of criminal responsibility might thus be reduced to one and the same lowest common denominator. In this respect, it is important to note that the minimum age of criminal responsibility differs widely throughout Europe. This diversity is also illustrated by the countries involved in the study where the minimum age varies from 10

[49] Although some specialisation through practice exists.
[50] The influence of which may differ between regions.
[51] See *supra* paragraph 2.1 (part II).

(*England and Wales*) to 14 years (*Italy*). In *Belgium* and *Poland* the minimum age of criminal responsibility equals the age of criminal majority. It goes without saying that juveniles between the ages of 10 and 18 fall into a wide range of (age) categories with varying levels of cognitive, emotional and social development, which may have an impact on the necessary level of legal protection. Furthermore, within the group of juveniles who have reached the age of criminal responsibility, many variations may exist depending not only on the most objective parameter of vulnerability – age – but also on other factors influencing the juvenile's vulnerability, such as mental health problems, addictions, other individual characteristics or the circumstances of the case. The legal study seems to suggest that current legal frameworks tend to take these differentiations into account only to a very limited extent.

5.1. UNIFORM APPROACH IN LEGAL FRAMING OF PROCEDURAL SAFEGUARDS

The existing legal procedural safeguards provided to juvenile suspects in the phase of pre-trial interrogation make very little distinction in age, level of maturity and intellectual and emotional capacities of the juvenile. The current national legal frameworks illustrate only very few examples of differentiation in this respect. One of the rare examples can be found in *the Netherlands* where the possibility of waiving the right to consultation with a lawyer before interrogation is connected to the age of the juvenile and the seriousness of the alleged offence. Apart from these few exceptions, juveniles who have reached the minimum age of criminal responsibility are more or less treated as a homogeneous group requiring the same kind and level of procedural protection. This uniform approach seems to be in contrast with the differentiation in age, which some countries apply in substantive juvenile law especially in relation to sanctions. An example of such differentiation can be found in *England and Wales* where clear age restrictions exist concerning certain types of criminal sanctions.

5.2. NO INDIVIDUAL ASSESSMENT IN THE CONTEXT OF INTERROGATION

In addition to the fact that procedural safeguards are mostly awarded to the category of juvenile suspects as a whole without making any relevant distinctions, it should be stressed that – as a rule – an individual assessment of the juvenile suspect is not provided for. In none of the countries studied is there a legal obligation to systematically assess the juvenile's fitness to be interrogated or the juvenile's specific needs during interrogation. In *Italy* a legal obligation to assess the capacity of the juvenile does exist but only to the extent of determining whether they are punishable. According to Italian law, this is the case only if there is evidence that the juvenile is able to understand and to want his actions: the so-called rebuttable presumption of incapacity. This assessment provided for in the Italian system concerns the juvenile's capacity to be held criminally liable but does not entail the identification of any issues that may affect his ability to participate effectively in the police interrogation which does not exist as such in *Italy*.

The lack of rules on assessing the juvenile suspect for the purpose of the pre-trial interrogation seems to be in stark contrast with the assessment for the purpose of proceedings to be followed and/or measures (sanctions) to be applied. In *Belgium*, for example, the interrogating officials are informed about the juvenile's social environment (by social services) and his mental abilities (by a behavioural expert). The same is true for *Poland* where family probation officers prepare social inquiry reports and supervise the implementation of certain measures. Also in *the Netherlands*, the Child Welfare Council (*Raad voor de Kinderbescherming*) will interview a juvenile as soon as possible after arrest and will draw up a report on the personality and the environment of the juvenile. When the juvenile is summoned to appear in court, the prosecutor is obliged to ask the Child Welfare Council to draw up a full report on the juvenile and his social context. Similar tasks are fulfilled by YOT members in *England and Wales* who may, for example, be asked to write a pre-sentence report for the trial stage, and in *Italy* by social services personnel who draw up reports for the court as well.

5.3. NO SPECIAL CONSIDERATION FOR EXTRA-VULNERABLE JUVENILES

As noted above, current legal frameworks seem to be based on the assumption that by determining the juvenile's age, the vulnerability of the juvenile is given. With age being the determining factor, there are no (additional) legal rules on determining whether there are any factors which might make the juvenile 'extra-vulnerable' due to individual characteristics or the circumstances of the case (mental health problems, addictions, severity of the alleged offence, *et cetera*). There also seems to be no special consideration of the sensitivity of the moment at which the juvenile experiences his first contact with law enforcement authorities. Of course, in most (if not all) countries, the authorities have the obligation to take certain actions when there is reason to believe that the (juvenile) suspect has mental health problems. For example, in *England and Wales*, when suspects are booked into police custody, the custody officer first asks them a set of questions concerning their welfare. If the police are concerned that a suspect has a mental health problem, then they must contact a doctor who will carry out an assessment. The doctor will inform the police about whether the suspect is well enough to be questioned about the offence and to remain at the police station. Although important, this assessment 'only' seems to imply a more general assessment of the juvenile's fitness to be interrogated – connected to his ability to understand questions and formulate answers – and not an individual assessment of the juvenile's specific needs during interrogation. At present, none of the countries involved in the study seem to provide a legal basis for a regular individual assessment in the latter sense.

6. A HOLE INSIDE INTERROGATION?

The impact an interrogation may have on a juvenile suspect not only depends on the availability of effective legal rights protection but also on the way the interrogation is carried out. Although defining the vulnerability of the juvenile suspect during interrogation and establishing whether and how this should affect the form and content of the interrogation are highly complex issues, it may be clear that the interrogation of a juvenile suspect cannot be equated with the interrogation of an adult suspect and will therefore require a different approach and extra protection in the form of separate or additional legal safeguards. As becomes clear from the legal study, however, this assumption is not clearly reflected by domestic legislation.

6.1. LACK OF RULES ON HOW TO CONDUCT PRE-TRIAL INTERROGATIONS

In the countries involved in the study, there are virtually no youth-specific legal standards on how the interrogation of a juvenile suspect should be conducted. The interrogations of juvenile suspects are mainly bound by general (not youth-specific) provisions such as the ban on applying pressure. Generally, there are no rules on the duration of the interrogation, necessary breaks, the type of questions that should (or should not) be asked, which interrogation techniques are (not) allowed, *et cetera*. Only few exceptions can be found but most of them are of a rather general nature. For example in *Poland*, the family judge should hear ('listen to') a juvenile, allowing him complete freedom of expression, and this should take place in conditions as similar to the juvenile's natural environment as possible. Since recent changes to the Juvenile Act, a similar obligation applies to the interrogation of a juvenile by the police:[52] the interrogation should be conducted in circumstances similar to natural circumstances and if needed in the place of residence of the juvenile. Polish legislation provides for another example of a rule on how to conduct the interrogation of a juvenile: in the Juvenile Act it is regulated that repeated interrogations of a juvenile on the same circumstances or

52 Which is possible in 'urgent cases'.

circumstances already established by other evidence and not raising doubt should be avoided. An example of a rule on *where* the interrogation of a juvenile suspect should be carried out can be found in *the Netherlands*: there, a juvenile suspect should be interrogated in a child-friendly interrogation studio when the juvenile is below the age of 12 (and therefore not criminally responsible) or when the police considers it appropriate for example because a juvenile aged 12–18 is especially vulnerable given his mental capacities. Another rule can be found in *Italy* where the authorities are legally obliged to explain to the juvenile the meaning of the procedural activities he is participating in, a general rule which applies to all procedural activities including the interrogation. Formally the relevant legal provision of Italian law refers only to the judge, but given the goal of the rule (to help the juvenile understand proceedings and to enable him to effectively take part in them) it is recommended in legal literature that the obligation should be extended to the police and the prosecutor as well. Furthermore, in some countries – such as *Belgium* and *Italy* – there is a formal legal basis for the involvement of a behavioural expert in the interrogation of the juvenile suspect.

6.2. AUDIO OR AUDIO-VISUAL RECORDING AS A POSSIBILITY INSTEAD OF A MANDATORY SAFEGUARD

A general rule, which does not directly affect the way the interrogation is carried out but does concern the conduct of the interrogation, is the possibility (or obligation) to make audio and/or audio-visual recordings of the interrogation. Generally, national legal frameworks tend to give this 'safeguard' more importance when dealing with juvenile suspects than in the case of the interrogation of adult suspects. It appears that all five countries formally recognise the legal possibility to make audio and/or audio-visual recordings of interrogations of juvenile suspects but doing so is only mandatory in some of the systems, such as *England and Wales* (audio) and – under certain conditions – *Italy* and *the Netherlands*. Sometimes authorities are given a wide discretion when deciding which kind of technology or tool is most appropriate. This is clearly illustrated by the Italian system, where the authorities may choose the most appropriate tool, with the result that interrogations are usually recorded by transcript and only very rarely by making videotapes. In *Belgium*, there is a legal possibility, but not an obligation, to record the interrogation of a juvenile suspect. In *the Netherlands* making audio-visual recordings of the interrogation is mandatory in a limited number of cases.[53] In *Poland*, all procedural actions which are recorded in writing may also be recorded by means of audio or audio-visual recording, but this is never mandatory.

---

[53] When the juvenile is below 16 years of age and suspected of a serious crime.

6.3. COMPARISON WITH RULES ON INTERROGATING ADULT SUSPECTS AND JUVENILE WITNESSES

To a certain extent the lack of youth-specific rules for how to conduct the interrogation of a juvenile suspect mirrors the lack of rules for the interrogation of adult suspects. In most systems, pre-trial interrogations are not bound by specific legal standards on duration, pace, interrogation techniques, *et cetera*, but rather only by a limited number of general rules such as the aforementioned ban on coercion. A sharper contrast is visible when comparing the (lack of) regulation of the interrogation of juvenile suspects with the existing rules on how to interview juvenile witnesses. Generally, the legal frameworks involved in the study do provide for more youth-specific rules on how to carry out an interrogation when it concerns juvenile witnesses. For example, in *the Netherlands* there are several instructions (*aanwijzingen*) on how the juvenile should be treated before and during questioning as a witness. The Dutch regulation also creates the obligation to conduct the interview of a juvenile witness in a child-friendly studio; in the interrogation of a juvenile suspect, on the other hand, this is – as mentioned before – only obligatory under certain conditions. Another example can be found in *England and Wales* where special interview arrangements apply when taking a statement from a juvenile witness involving trained interrogators and special locations with video recording equipment. In general, it can be said that the protection offered to child witnesses during interviews in *England and Wales* is wide-ranging and detailed, but that this protection is generally not extended to juvenile suspects. In *Belgium* a separate set of rules in the Code of Criminal Procedure is dedicated to hearing juvenile victims and witnesses (*inter alia* providing for the right to have an appropriate adult present and special child-friendly locations). To a certain extent, the same is true for *Poland* where the Code of Criminal Procedure offers special protection for juveniles who have been the victim of certain (for example sexual) offences. This special protection *inter alia* includes the fact that the interrogation of the juvenile witness may take place only once during the whole proceedings, should be carried out during a court session in the presence of an expert in psychology and should always be audio and audio-visually recorded.

7. THE JUVENILE OVERRATED?

The initial interrogations during the investigative stage usually constitute the juvenile's first contact with law enforcement authorities. At this point in time, the juvenile is faced with several fundamental decisions, which can – and often will– be of paramount importance for the development and the outcome of the case. These decisions concern not only whether and how to respond to questions but also decisions on invoking or waiving other procedural rights such as the right to assistance of a lawyer or an appropriate adult. Of course, an important question is whether the juvenile is able to make such far-reaching decisions, and if not (sufficiently well), whether and how he should be provided with some sort of assistance in doing so. As becomes clear from the legal study, countries to a large extent tend to consider juvenile suspects as being able to make their own decisions.

7.1. NOT TOO YOUNG TO DECIDE

The current legal frameworks clearly illustrate that juveniles are given ample opportunity to exercise and waive procedural rights and to take important decisions. It seems that, in the majority of cases, they can do so independently – without any assistance. The countries involved in the study only provide a few examples of mandatory assistance of a lawyer or appropriate adult. As mentioned in paragraph 2 (part II) the safeguard of the appropriate adult is most strongly emphasised in *England and Wales* where it is a mandatory legal requirement for the interrogation of all vulnerable suspects. In the other systems, the role of the appropriate adult is more limited or even non-existent. Looking at the other countries, the right seems to have the strongest legal basis in *Italy*. As mentioned before, in the Italian system it is stressed that the appropriate adult should offer the juvenile 'affective and psychological support', which implies that this support might help the juvenile suspect to take decisions and understand their consequences. There are however limitations on the appropriate adult's role of: their presence can be excluded and they should remain passive during interrogation.

A similar pattern seems to appear when looking at the right to legal assistance as a safeguard for providing the juvenile suspect with the necessary assistance in the process of decision-making. While the right to legal assistance seems to have the least binding status in *England and Wales* (where it is never a mandatory requirement), the other systems provide for mandatory legal assistance in different ways and to different extents.[54] As a side note, it should be recalled that in this respect the example of *England and Wales* seems to illustrate another pattern, which could be characterised as 'trading off' procedural safeguards, meaning that the mandatory assistance of the appropriate adult seems to 'level out' the non-mandatory presence of a lawyer.[55] Another example of the right to legal assistance and the right to the presence of an appropriate adult being 'interchangeable' to a certain extent can be found in *the Netherlands*, where the juvenile has to choose between the two safeguards: invoking the right to have

54 See *supra* paragraph 3 (part II).
55 See *supra* paragraph 3.2 (part II).

a trusted person present during interrogation, meaning that the lawyer cannot attend, and *vice versa*. These examples show how procedural safeguards may function as communicating vessels with the mandatory character of one right compensating for the more loose (or even non-binding) character of the other.

Turning back to the matter of decision-making, the picture that follows from the legal study shows that throughout the five countries, the right to legal assistance is given a firmer legal basis than the right to be assisted by an appropriate adult. However, it also shows that both rights only have the status of mandatory safeguards in a limited number of countries or – within countries – in a limited number of situations. Aside from the mandatory assistance of the appropriate adult in *England and Wales* and the obligatory presence of a lawyer in *Belgium*, the current legal frameworks result in many situations in which the juvenile will have to decide for himself whether he deems the assistance (of a lawyer and/or an appropriate adult) appropriate. A striking example is provided by *England and Wales* where the juvenile is given a large discretionary power in deciding whether he wants to be assisted by a lawyer: he may refuse the involvement of a lawyer even when the appropriate adult thinks that legal assistance is indispensable.

The legal framing of the right to an appropriate adult and the right to the assistance of a lawyer clearly reflect how much freedom of decision is given to juvenile suspects: important decisions – such as whether or not to invoke the right to remain silent– are left to their discretion, in some cases even without the assistance of a lawyer or an appropriate adult. An important question of course is whether the juvenile is able to make such decisions. Although this question seems difficult – if not impossible – to answer in general, it may be clear that a lot will depend not only on whether and how the juvenile is assisted by third persons but also on his individual characteristics (level of maturity, intelligence, *et cetera*). Also important in this respect is whether the juvenile has any prior experience with the (criminal) justice system.

7.2. PRESUMPTION OF UNDERSTANDING

The juvenile's ability to decide will to a large extent depend on whether he truly understands the importance and the possible consequences and potential risks of the decisions he has to take. Of course, this will require the juvenile to be sufficiently and adequately informed. For the most part, it is the responsibility of authorities to provide the juvenile suspect with the necessary information. As mentioned before, in this respect a lot will depend on how this information is provided.[56] A juvenile suspect's right to information could be considered as being

[56] See in the context of the right to remain silent *supra* paragraph 1.2 and 1.3 (part II).

threefold: it involves not only the right to information on rights (1), but also the right to be informed of the course and content of proceedings (2), and finally the right to be informed about the case (3). Hereafter, all three aspects of the right to information will be discussed in light of the findings of the legal study.

7.2.1. Few rules geared toward proper understanding of rights

Generally, in the five countries studied, the law only provides for a few youth-specific rules on how to inform the juvenile of his procedural rights. For example, as discussed earlier,[57] national law does not provide for rules on the wording to be used when informing a juvenile suspect of his right to remain silent, nor on the pace at which the information should be given or whether to inform the juvenile of the consequences of invoking his right to remain silent.[58] Furthermore, as a rule, there is no obligation to check whether the information is understood or to provide the juvenile with any (additional) explanation. Although a few rules aimed at a proper understanding of rights do exist – for example in *England and Wales* where the juvenile should be cautioned in the physical presence of the appropriate adult and where the authorities are obliged to ask the juvenile to explain the caution in his own words when he appears not to understand, and in *Italy* where there is an explicit legal obligation for authorities to inform the juvenile of the fact that if he refuses to answer to questions the proceedings will go on anyway and of the fact that any statements can be used against him[59] – the issue generally seems to be ignored by national legislation. The lack of youth-specific rules on how to inform the juvenile suspect of his right to remain silent is mirrored by the lack of rules on how to inform the juvenile suspect of other fundamental procedural rights such as the right to legal assistance. Of course, some national laws provide for fixed rules on the way in which a (juvenile) suspect should be informed of certain rights – orally or in writing (in a standardised form or not) – but mostly this is done without creating explicit legal obligations for the authorities to check whether the content of the information has actually been understood. In *Belgium* a general rule aimed at proper understanding of the juvenile can be found in the constitution ('every child has the right to express his opinion in all instances that concern him; the age and the ability to distinguish must be taken into account') but how this general provision should be applied in the context of interrogating juvenile suspects is not specified.

In summary, much is left to the discretion of the interrogator: not only to decide how the information is provided (should the caution be modified to the

57 See *supra* paragraph 1.3 and 1.4 (part II).
58 With the exception of *England and Wales* where there is an obligation to inform the suspect of the drawing of adverse inferences, see *supra* paragraph 1.3 and 1.4 (part II).
59 See *supra* paragraph 1.3 (part I).

juvenile's level and if so how?), but also whether and how the authorities should check whether the juvenile has understood, and finally what should happen if this is clearly not the case. In this respect, it should be recalled that even when proper and sufficient information is provided to the juvenile, it still remains to be seen whether he will actually understand. After all, whether information is understood will depend not only on what information is given and how, but also on the personal characteristics (level of understanding) of the juvenile.[60] As mentioned earlier,[61] the current legal frameworks appear not to contain any rules on whether and how to assess the individual capacity of the juvenile to understand. This means that the interrogator is not legally obliged to 'assess' the level of comprehension of the juvenile suspect before informing him of certain rights, which implies that he can decide for himself whether and how the provision of information should be adapted to the juvenile's personal situation. All in all, the question of course is whether the interrogator is capable of making such an assessment at all.

In addition to the lack of rules on information of rights, it should be stressed that, in general, the countries also do not provide for explicit rules on the conditions for a valid waiver. There are only a very few examples of youth-specific rules on whether and how the juvenile can waive certain rights. One of these examples is provided by *the Netherlands*, where the juvenile's possibility to waive his right to legal assistance will depend on the juvenile's age as well as the seriousness of the alleged offence. The juvenile should also be informed that waiving the right to consultation includes waiving the right to legal assistance during interrogation.

7.2.2. Few rules geared toward proper comprehension of proceedings

To effectively participate in proceedings, a suspect should be able to understand what is going on. Given their (less developed) level of maturity and corresponding intellectual and emotional capacities, this is even more important when dealing with juvenile suspects. Another reason why understanding proceedings is even more important in the case of juveniles than in the case of adults is connected to the complex nature of juvenile justice proceedings. As discussed earlier in paragraph 1.2.2 (part I), most juvenile justice systems provide for various kinds of diversion and in many cases it will not be immediately clear which track is most likely to be followed. It is important that the juvenile is aware of the different procedural possibilities and how he may be substantially affected by them.

60 Of course, this is also true for adult suspects.
61 See *supra* paragraph 5.2 (part II).

The importance of the juvenile's competence to understand the content and course of proceedings has repeatedly been stressed by the ECtHR as a precondition for the juvenile's ability to effectively participate in proceedings.[62] Generally, understanding proceedings will mean that the juvenile should – at the very least – be informed of the different steps of proceedings (what comes next?) and the role of the actors involved. Obviously, providing this kind of information is also one of the tasks of the defence lawyer and to a certain extent even the appropriate adult. With regard to the latter, *England and Wales* is a good example: there, the appropriate adult should explain police procedures to the juvenile and provide him with information about his rights. However, the involvement of the lawyer and/or the appropriate adult does not mean that law enforcement authorities are exempted from all obligations in this respect. This is also the case because the presence of the former during interrogation is not always guaranteed, while the presence of the latter is certain.

In this respect, it is noteworthy that the laws of the countries involved in the study provide only a few examples of rules aimed at stimulating the juvenile's proper comprehension of proceedings. Worth mentioning is the general obligation laid down in Italian law to explain to the juvenile suspect the meaning of procedural activities, when and where necessary with the involvement of a parent, defence lawyer, behavioural expert or social services personnel. Furthermore, in *England and Wales*, all suspects (including juveniles) have the opportunity to consult the PACE codes of practice. Besides these few rules, the current legal frameworks do not seem to oblige authorities to actively ensure that the juvenile suspect understands the content and course of the proceedings he is participating in.

7.2.3. Lack of youth-specific rules on informing the juvenile about the case

The right to be informed about the case could be viewed as being twofold: not only does it concern the right to be informed of the charges but it also includes the right to have access to the materials of the case (right to disclosure). With respect to the first right, it appears from the legal study that a legal obligation to inform the (juvenile) suspect of the charges at the start of the interrogation exists in most countries. However, in none of the five countries are there youth-specific rules on providing the juvenile suspect with this kind of information: the rules are the same as those applicable to adults and the content and scope of the information to be provided varies significantly between the different systems (whether or not relating to the facts, the nature of the offence, containing clear and precise information of the alleged facts, *et cetera*).

---

62 See chapter 1, paragraph 7.2.

With respect to the right to access to the materials of the case, the laws of the countries involved in the study illustrate that this right is generally awarded to the juvenile under the same conditions as those applicable to adults, with the realisation of the right depending on specific conditions such as the consent of authorities and the possibility to deny certain documents during certain parts of the proceedings. In some countries – such as *Belgium* and *Italy* – there is an explicit legal obligation for authorities to inform the (juvenile) suspect of the facts on which he shall be heard or of incriminating evidence. Only in *Poland* does the law provide for rules on access to the case file specifically drafted for juveniles. These rules, however, only cover the right to access the case file during court proceedings and do not apply during interrogations by the police in 'urgent cases'. In *England and Wales*, the police are under no obligation to disclose evidence to the defence prior to the interrogation.[63]

8. WHAT DEFINES THE JUVENILE'S VULNERABILITY?

The fact that juveniles form an important category of vulnerable suspects requiring special consideration seems to be undisputed within the jurisdictions involved in the study. This is reflected by the existence of *inter alia* special (criminal) procedure rules, youth-specific authorities, various special sanctions and diversion mechanisms, and in some cases – such as in *Belgium* and *Poland* – even separate educative or protective proceedings. The underlying assumption of these youth-specific rules and arrangements seems to be that juvenile suspects should be treated differently from their adult counterparts and that – in principle – they require different or additional forms of protection. Moving beyond what appears to be a self-evident assumption, the question arises as to what exactly defines the vulnerability of the juvenile suspect. After all, while it might not be desirable (if at all possible) to have a fixed rigid legal definition of the juvenile's vulnerability, it still appears important to understand what exactly makes a juvenile suspect vulnerable, in order to determine exactly which procedural safeguards are needed to effectively compensate for this vulnerability. This is especially true for the initial phase of pre-trial interrogation, when the vulnerability of the juvenile is probably greatest. Nevertheless, the laws in each of the countries studied do not seem to provide any explicit answers to this question.

63 Nevertheless, it should be recalled that in *England and Wales* there is an obligation to inform the juvenile (of the nature of) the allegations against him, otherwise the drawing of adverse inferences is not possible.

8.1. UNCLEAR NOTION OF VULNERABILITY (DURING INTERROGATION)

Since a clear definition of the juvenile's vulnerability in the context of criminal proceedings cannot be derived from supranational norms,[64] one might expect the national legislator to deal with this. Nonetheless, the legal study shows that the current legal frameworks generally do not take a clear stance on the issue of vulnerability and there seems to be no clear ideas or views on the matter. In the main, the laws of the five countries do not provide for a legal definition or description of the juvenile suspect's vulnerability in criminal proceedings, neither in general nor more specifically during interrogation.

As mentioned earlier, national laws mostly tend to identify the vulnerability of juveniles through the age factor. The national laws in fact provide legal definitions of the concept of 'juvenile' but these definitions are either related to age (limits or categories) or to the applicability of certain types of juvenile proceedings.[65] For example, according to the Belgian Criminal Code a juvenile is any person who has not yet reached the age of 18. Similarly, in *England and Wales* a 'juvenile' within the context of criminal proceedings is anyone between the age of 10 and 17 inclusive. In taking this objective approach of only using age as the determining factor, no explicit reference is made to the specific needs of the juvenile as a suspect in criminal proceedings.

8.2. DIFFERENT VIEWS ON HOW VULNERABILITY SHOULD BE COMPENSATED FOR

From the legal study it has also become clear that countries generally tend to have different views on how the vulnerability of the juvenile suspect is best compensated for. There are differences in approach not only between the more welfare-oriented countries and jurisdictions that follow a more justice-oriented approach, with the latter focusing more on protection by law as opposed to the former which aim at protection by people,[66] but also between the five countries as a whole. For example, they clearly represent different views on whether the appropriate adult is a necessary or 'appropriate' safeguard which may compensate for the juvenile's vulnerability in the pre-trial stage. The same is true for the right to the assistance of a lawyer. These fundamental differences illustrate that – in addition to the fact that current legal safeguards do not seem to be built upon a clear notion of the juvenile's vulnerability – there also appears

---

64 Because it is not provided for: as discussed in chapter 1, supranational standards are mostly of a general nature and make only limited reference to criminal proceedings. See chapter 1, paragraph 7.

65 See *supra* paragraph 5 (part I).

66 See *supra* paragraph 3 (part I).

to be little consensus between Member States on how the juvenile's well-being during interrogation is best protected.

8.3. VULNERABILITY NOT APPARENTLY TRANSLATED INTO PROCEDURAL SAFEGUARDS

The fact that there is not a single, fixed definition of vulnerability provided by the various domestic legislations is probably not very surprising. It could be argued that it is hard – if not impossible – for a national legislature to find a suitable definition of vulnerability beyond the concept conveyed by general common sense. The juvenile's vulnerability is a highly complex matter with many different aspects, which are probably more strongly connected to developmental psychology and other cognate scientific disciplines than to traditional legal issues. With a single legal definition lacking, the question remains whether a notion (of the relevant aspects) of the juvenile's vulnerability can be derived from the existing legal safeguards provided to juvenile suspects during pre-trial interrogation. As may be clear from the general patterns described above, this seems to be a difficult endeavour, especially when focusing on pre-trial interrogations. As mentioned before, most of the safeguards applicable to juveniles during this phase of proceedings are more or less a transposition of the rules applicable to adults with a few youth-specific additions such as – most importantly – the assistance of the appropriate adult. Although the latter safeguard seems to be the most common youth-specific safeguard, a clear legal basis for its role and function is missing in most countries, save for *England and Wales* where the matter is quite extensively regulated. Therefore, one might say that even the rare examples of youth-specific safeguards do not clarify what exactly they intend to compensate for or protect. Certain characteristics of the current legal frameworks might even be seen as proof of the fact that legislatures do not consider the juvenile's vulnerability during interrogation to be 'a big deal' requiring specific attention from the lawmaker. As discussed, youth-specific rules on how to conduct interrogations and how to inform the juvenile suspect of fundamental rights are generally missing and most countries seem to have high expectations of what a juvenile is effectively able to understand and decide upon. Furthermore, most existing rules concerning legal protection in the phase of interrogations make no differentiation in age, in principle treating all juveniles in the same way. This uniform approach to the legal framing of procedural safeguards might also be seen as a symptom of a certain indifference towards the question of what exactly defines the vulnerability of the juvenile suspect during interrogation. Where age differentiation does exist (as is the case of *the Netherlands* where the mandatory character of the right to legal assistance depends on the age of the juvenile and the seriousness of the offence), the only underlying assumption seems to be that the younger the juvenile is, the stronger the protection he needs (whatever that protection may be according to national law). In summary, one might say that the current legal frameworks generally mostly seem to consider the vulnerability of the juvenile suspect to be a given, i.e. the logical consequence of being under a certain age.

III. CONCLUSIONS

The picture emerging from the country reports is mixed in many ways and it is inevitably difficult – if not impossible – to boil it down into one uniform view. Nevertheless, the general patterns described above should offer an overview of the crucial variables involved in all countries and how the different concepts and safeguards intertwine across the different jurisdictions.

In particular, the general patterns described above illustrate some general and fundamental similarities, which clearly exceed formal domestic typologies concerning the structure and underlying philosophy of the systems. It appears that despite the specifics of each system, there are some common philosophies and trends that pervade the different jurisdictions, particularly with regard to the field of interrogations. This could be summarised by saying that – despite the many fundamental differences between the systems – the legal framing of the interrogation is not so different. The goal of the procedural activity seems to prevail over the characteristics of the suspect and of the system.

In our view these similarities between the systems justify taking a substantive instead of a formal approach when focusing on procedural safeguards for juvenile suspects. The complexities and specific characteristics of the juvenile justice system, such as the intertwinement of different fields of law (criminal, civil and administrative) and the many possibilities of diversion, clearly indicate that limiting ourselves to formal criminal (procedure) law is not enough to fully understand the position of the juvenile suspect and, more specifically, protect him during interrogation in an exhaustive way. In any event the juvenile should be given an equivalent – or at least a uniform – level of protection in all cases that may lead to his punishment (for a behaviour contrary to criminal law), regardless of the formal nature of proceedings. In addition to this, the country reports clearly illustrate the many different shapes and forms of juvenile suspect interrogations in the investigative stage. Taking into account the complexity of juvenile proceedings in virtually all of the countries (different tracks and possibilities of diversion) this highlights the need to carefully look at the context of proceedings when thinking about how to shape procedural safeguards for juvenile suspects: when and where is information gathered from the juvenile suspect and what use can be made of it during following steps of the proceedings?

The study also shows that the current level of legal protection in the Member States involved in the study leaves much to be desired. Often, the existing gaps in legal protection seem to be inextricably linked to certain questionable assumptions such as the hypothesis that protection by people obviates the need for protection by rules, or the (sometimes implicit) assumption that the young age of juveniles does not necessarily influence their competence to effectively participate in the proceedings (i.e. understand what is going on, exercise procedural rights and take important decisions). Furthermore, it is striking that the current frameworks of legal protection mainly consist of classical 'adult' procedural safeguards with only a few youth-specific amendments and additions, the right to an appropriate adult being the most important, and virtually no legal rules on how the interrogation of a juvenile suspect should be conducted. In this way, the general patterns justify the conclusion that – to a considerable extent – domestic legislatures seem to disregard the vulnerabilities that the juvenile suspect carries with him into the interrogation room. Whether this happens because these vulnerabilities are being underestimated or because there is insufficient understanding of their exact scope and content is not clear; however, whatever the underlying cause(s) may be, the fact is that there seems to be a lack of an adequate level of clear youth-specific legal protection during the interrogation phase.

As a final remark it can be said that the study does not highlight formal or substantial barriers to a greater harmonisation of rules on interrogation between countries. The difference in the designs of the juvenile justice systems does not suggest or entail that common improvements cannot be made in the direction of a greater protection of juvenile suspects during interrogations – particularly along the lines sketched in the previous pages.

BIBLIOGRAPHY

Blackstock *et al.* 2014

J. Blackstock, E. Cape, J. Hodgson, A. Ogorodova and T. Spronken, *Inside Police Custody – An Empirical Account of Suspects' Rights in Four Jurisdictions*, Cambridge (etc.): Intersentia, 2014

Cape *et al.* 2007

E. Cape, J. Hodgson, T. Prakken and T. Spronken, *Suspects in Europe*, Antwerp: Intersentia, 2007

Cape *et al.* 2010

E. Cape, Z. Namoradze, R. Smith and T. Spronken, *Effective Criminal Defence in Europe*, Antwerp: Intersentia 2010

De Vocht *et al.* 2014
D.L.F. de Vocht, M. Panzavolta, M. Vanderhallen and M. van Oosterhout, 'Procedural Safeguards for Juvenile Suspects in Interrogations: A Look at the Commission Proposal in Light of an EU Comparative Study', *New Journal of European Criminal Law*, 2014, 2014, 4, p. 480–506

Dünkel *et al.* 2011
F. Dünkel, J. Grzywa, P. Horsfield and I. Pruin, *Juvenile Justice Systems in Europe – Current Situation and Reform Developments*, Vol 2 (2nd revised edition), Mönchengladbach: Forum Verlag Godesberg, 2011

Giostra and Patane 2007
G. Giostra and V. Patane, Europ*ean Juvenile Justice Sy*stems, First Volume, Milano: Giuffrè Editore 2007

Junger-Tas and S.H. Decker 2010
J. Junger-Tas and S.H. Decker (eds.), *International handbook of juvenile justice,* Dordrecht: Springer 2006

Vanderhallen *et al.* 2105
M. Vanderhallen, M. van Oosterhout, M. Panzavolta and D. de Vocht, *Interrogating Young Suspects: Procedural Safeguards from an Empirical Perspective*, Cambridge (etc.): Intersentia (forthcoming 2015)

Winterdyk 2014
J.A. Winterdyk, *International Perspectives, Models and Trends*, Boca Raton: CRC Press 2014

ANNEX
TEMPLATE COUNTRY REPORT
Young Suspects in Interrogations

I GENERAL PART: THE NATIONAL JUVENILE JUSTICE SYSTEM

The goal of this part of the report is to provide the general national framework for the interrogation of juveniles. For a better understanding of the rules of interrogation it is essential to have a clear overview of your juvenile punitive system of criminal justice (or equivalent). Besides the topic mentioned below, authors should address all other general topics that are considered relevant/necessary to grasp the rules/dynamics of the interrogation of juveniles. The introductory part should also strive to give a taste of the legal/cultural background of your national system. Rules do not operate in a vacuum but they are affected (in the way they are devised and interpreted) by the predominant legal and social culture(s) of the country. This part should permit to offer the basic cultural coordinates to permit a more appropriate understanding of the different rules and a better comparison with the rules of other countries. In this regard, some brief information on the policies implemented, on the traditional cultural/legal approaches, on the historical development of the juvenile is also extremely useful.

a) BACKGROUND OF THE NATIONAL JUVENILE JUSTICE SYSTEM

Please indicate:

1. Whether the juvenile justice system is separate from the adult justice system (and if so in what way).
2. Main sources of law dealing with juvenile justice and with juvenile criminal (or punitive) justice in particular.
   - Clarify the relationship between the different sources of the law.
3. Relevance of other fields of law (than criminal) in dealing with juvenile justice (e.g. civil law).
4. A brief history of juvenile justice and of juvenile criminal (or punitive) justice and current trends in criminal policy on juvenile justice.
5. Relevant constitutional or general principles of national juvenile law and national juvenile criminal justice (both criminal law and criminal procedure), including those which have/could have an indirect impact.
   - Distinguish principles connected to criminal justice in general from principles related to juvenile criminal justice.

- Highlight relationship between protection of the wellbeing of juveniles and presumption of innocence (indicate on a 'scale' welfare opposed to justice).
- Classify your system according to relevant typologies of juvenile justice systems.

6. What are the needs of juveniles in front of the criminal process (e.g. be protected from the harsh impact of criminal justice, be placed in a position to effectively participate to the process)? List scholarly studies or Parliamentary/Governmental reports on the issue.

b) STRUCTURE AND MAIN CHARACTERISTICS OF THE JUVENILE JUSTICE SYSTEM

This part of the report should (at least) include:

1. Minimum age of liability.
2. Definition of juveniles (legal definition or other definition which is widely agreed upon in literature or case-law) for the purpose of criminal justice or punitive justice.
   - Legal categories of juveniles? (age, "extra-vulnerable", gender, ethnicity *et cetera*).
3. Relevant actors of the juvenile criminal process (competent authorities for investigations and trial) and within the juvenile criminal process (lawyers, social services, *et cetera*):
   - Identify the main features of each actor.
   - Describe the main role/tasks of each actor (illustrate whether or not they are specialised, the type of specialisation and the legal source for it – see *infra*, II.c.1).
4. Main steps of the juvenile criminal process (indicate if and how it distinguishes from the adult criminal process).
   - Focus specifically on relevant rules on arrest, police detention, detention on remand for juvenile suspects (indicate if and how they differ from the rules for adult suspects). Mention facilities available for juveniles at police station.
   - If possible, provide statistics on juveniles in the criminal justices system (e.g. how many juveniles are arrested, detained by the police, interrogated).
5. Sanctions for juveniles (punishments and measures).
6. Alternatives to criminal proceedings (welfare proceedings, administrative proceedings arising out of the commission of an offence) and availability of diversion/probation mechanisms.
   - If possible, provide statistics on alternative (non-criminal) means for dealing with juvenile offenders.
   - When describing relevant diversion mechanisms: please also indicate whether the juvenile should consent to this way of dealing with his case, if so, whether it is guaranteed that the juvenile will give free and voluntary consent and whether it is possible for the juvenile to obtain (free) legal assistance (or other professional advice) in determining the appropriateness and desirability of the diversion mechanism.

II INTERROGATIONS OF JUVENILES IN THE PRE-TRIAL PHASE

The goal of this part of the report is to provide a detailed and exhaustive overview of the legal rules applicable to the different types of questioning of juveniles. We acknowledge that in your system there might be different types of interrogations/interviews (i.e. different occasions in which the suspect is asked/required/allowed to give statements in the case concerning herself). In principle, you should describe each of these forms. However, we kindly encourage you to avoid an excessively schematic approach. In principle, we would suggest you to start from the type of interrogation of juvenile suspects which is the most common and most relevant for gathering evidence during the investigations and then to address the other types of pre-trial interrogations by highlighting the relevant distinction in function, rules, *et cetera*.

a) "WHAT?" CONCEPT AND FUNCTION OF INTERROGATION

1. Definition of interrogation of juvenile suspects in your country in general (legal definition or other definition which is widely agreed upon in literature or case-law). Please indicate if the definition covers more situations than only hearing of juvenile suspects (for example hearing of witnesses).
   - Indicate whether the same definition applies for adults.
2. Definition of charge, suspect and investigative phase in your national system (if several notions of charges, specify each concept in relation to the unfolding of the proceedings).
   - Indicate whether the same definitions apply for adults.
3. Identify the different types of pre-trial interrogations (i.e. all cases in which the suspect is invited/forced/allowed to give statements in the case/investigation against herself regardless of whether the statements are favorable or not to him).
   - Are the investigating authorities allowed to collect statements from juvenile suspects who spontaneously wish to narrate an event? Would this be considered an interrogation? Specify any different types of interrogations/interview of juvenile suspects?
4. Is there a difference between interrogation of juveniles depending on whether an arrest has taken place? (*infra*, II.b.2)
5. Identify the function(s) of the interrogation(s) of juveniles.
6. Is interrogation of juvenile suspects mandatory? If so, in which situations?
7. Can juveniles under the minimum age of criminal liability be interrogated? If so, what is the scope and goal of this interrogation and are these juveniles protected by the same rules and safeguards as juvenile suspects who are criminally liable?
8. Mediation and diversion. Are there forms of diversion or mediation where juvenile suspects can be interrogated?
   1) Interrogations of juvenile suspects in judicial cooperation with foreign states?
   2) Which of those in pre-trial phases?

b) "WHEN?" INTERROGATION AND THE UNFOLDING OF THE PRE-TRIAL PHASE

1. Is there a precise moment within the proceedings (in the chronological sequence of the different steps in the pretrial phase) during which the interrogation of a juvenile suspect takes place? If so, please indicate. If not, please indicate how it may differ.
2. In case of interrogations after an arrest please illustrate the whole sequence (e.g. arrest, questioning, decision on release/bail/discharge, questioning/statements within habeas corpus proceedings).

c) "WHO?" COMPETENT AUTHORITIES

1. Who is empowered to carry out the interrogation of juvenile suspects?
   1) Police forces? (indicate specifically the police forces competent for the interrogation of juveniles and the type of interrogations they can carry out).
      - Is there some kind of specialisation in dealing with juveniles among police officers? If so, what kind? What is the legal source?
      - Are police officers trained in dealing with juveniles? If so, how?
   2) Prosecutor? (briefly identify the status and role of the prosecutors in your country).
      - Is there some kind of specialisation in dealing with juveniles among prosecutors? If so, what kind? What is the legal source?
      - Are prosecutors trained in dealing with juveniles? If so, how?
   3) Judiciary? (investigating judge, family judge, or other).
      - Is there some kind of specialisation in dealing with juveniles among judges? If so, how?
      - Are judges trained in dealing with juveniles? If so, what kind? What is the legal source?
   4) Other relevant actors?
2. Is there a formal way of assessing the capacity of the juvenile suspect to be interrogated? If so, who is responsible for this assessment and how does it work?
3. What is the role of social services before or during the interrogation of the juvenile suspect? Can they question a suspect? (if you have not defined and described social services before, please do so here).

d) "HOW?" RULES FOR INTERROGATIONS

When describing the relevant rules and safeguards for interrogating juvenile suspects please indicate: a) the legal source of the relevant rules and safeguards; b) whether there are distinct rules/safeguards for different (age)categories of juveniles; c) any relevant differences with the rules and safeguards provided for adult suspects.

1. General issues concerning safeguards:
   1) Right to a lawyer
      - Does the juvenile have the right to consult a lawyer before his interrogation? If so, from what exact moment does this right apply?

- If so, when and how should the juvenile be informed of his right to consult a lawyer?
- Does the juvenile have the right to have a lawyer present during interrogation?
- If so, when and how should the juvenile be informed of his right to have a lawyer present during interrogation? (see also, *infra*, II.d.4)
- If so, what is the role of the lawyer during questioning (active/passive, right to interfere/intervene)?
- Is waiver of the right to consult a lawyer allowed? If so, when, how and under what conditions?
- Is waiver of the right to have a lawyer present during interrogation allowed? If so, when, how and under what conditions?
- Is *ex officio* appointment of lawyers foreseen and – if so – in which situations?
- Is the juvenile offered adequate time to consult with a lawyer before interrogation?
- Is the juvenile offered adequate facilities to consult with a lawyer in private before interrogation (for example at the police station)?

2) Legal aid
   - Does the juvenile have the right to free legal assistance? If so, from what exact moment does this right apply?
   - If so, when and how should the juvenile be informed of his right to free legal assistance? (see also, *infra*, II.d.4)
   - How is legal aid structured? Is there some sort of duty scheme for providing legal assistance to juveniles after arrest?
   - Which lawyers may be appointed in juvenile criminal cases? Is there a list of qualified/specialised lawyers?
   - Are lawyers trained in dealing with juveniles? If so, in what way?
   - Is there some form of specialisation in juvenile (criminal) law among lawyers? Is there for example a separate association of lawyers specialised in juvenile (criminal) law?

3) Right to silence
   - Does the juvenile have a right to silence during interrogation? If so, from what exact moment does this right apply?
   - If so, when and how should the juvenile be informed of his right to silence? (see also, *infra*, II.d.4)
   - If so, what is the scope of the right to silence?
     For example:
     - o Does it include a right not to attend the interrogation or leave the interrogation room (if not detained)?
     - o Can one refuse to answer only one question?
   - Are there any (formal) consequences to exercising the right to silence? (e.g. drawing of inferences from it, ban to access probation/diversion mechanisms, factor in sentencing, *et cetera*). If so, is the juvenile informed of these consequences?

- What is the relationship between the right to silence and the privilege against self-incrimination, are they synonyms or not?

4) Caution (right to be informed on rights)
   - Should the juvenile suspect be cautioned before his interrogation?
   - If so, only before the first interrogation or before every interrogation?
   - If so, how: written (in a standardized form?), verbally or both?
   - What is the content of the caution?
   - Who should give the caution and are they obliged to verify whether the juvenile has understood the meaning of the caution and provide (additional) explanation when necessary? Is it guaranteed that the information on legal rights is provided in a manner appropriate to the juvenile's age and maturity?
   - Language of the caution?
   - Is waiver of the right to be cautioned allowed? If so, when, how and under what conditions?

5) Presence of appropriate adult
   - Does the juvenile suspect have the right to have (a) parent(s) and/or other appropriate adults (e.g. social worker) present in his support? If so, from what exact moment does this right apply?
   - If so, when and how should the juvenile be informed of his right to have an appropriate adult present?
   - Can the right to have an appropriate adult present during interrogation be waived?
   - What if the presence of the appropriate adult is in contrast with the interest of the child?
   - Are there any rules on the role/task of the appropriate adult during interrogation? If so, is the appropriate adult informed of this role/task?

6) Other general or specific safeguards?
   - Presence of an interpreter: does the juvenile have the right to (free) assistance of an interpreter of he cannot understand or speak the language used in the interrogation? If so, from what exact moment does this right apply? If so, when and how should the juvenile be informed of his right to an interpreter?
   - Presence of experts (e.g. psychological assistance)?

7) Are there obligations for the juvenile suspect related to interrogation (e.g. obligation to present himself to the police, obligation to answer certain questions)?

2. Carrying out the interrogation:
   1) Should the charges be read to the juvenile (if so, how detailed must the charge be)?
   2) Does the juvenile have a right to access to file or to be verbally informed of prior discovery of (incriminating) evidence?
   3) Are interrogations of juveniles audio- or video-recorded?

4) Are transcripts made of the interrogation of the juvenile? If so, by whom and does the juvenile and/or his defence lawyer have the right to check and/or correct the transcript?
5) Are there any rules for posing questions to juvenile suspects or on specific interrogation techniques (e.g. ban to ask certain types of questions such as forced-choice questions, ban to ask questions on certain issues, obligations to formulate questions in a certain manner, rules on the use of jargon/difficult vocabulary, rules on mediation of psychologists or other experts)?
   - Can/should questions be asked to investigate the family/cultural background of the juveniles and the circumstances in which they live beyond what is strictly necessary for ascertaining the alleged criminal facts? Is this information relevant for the outcome of the defendant's case with regard to his responsibility?
6) Are there other relevant rules for conducting the interrogation? For example on
   - How long the interrogation may take.
   - Whether the juvenile may be interrogated repeatedly.
   - Whether interrogating at night is allowed.
   - Who may be present during the interrogation (besides the interrogating authority and the juvenile suspect).
   - The roles and competences of people who may be present during the interrogation (other than the interrogating authority and the juvenile suspect, e.g. defence lawyer, appropriate adult). For example: if the defence lawyer has a right to be present: what is his role? Are interventions/interferences on his behalf allowed? (if a lawyer is present and you have not done so in other parts, clarify if lawyers are specialized to deal with juvenile suspects and the kind of specialization required)
7) Are there specific safeguards/rules for interrogating juveniles placed in detention?
8) Are there special rules for the interrogation of "extra-vulnerable" juveniles? Who decides whether the juvenile is "extra-vulnerable"?

3. Outputs of the interrogation:
   1) How can the statements obtained be eventually used? (in and outside the criminal process; in the investigation; in the trial phase; in the sentencing stage)
   2) What is the relevance of confessions (are confessions legally relevant? E.g. for accessing diversion/mediation mechanisms?)

4. Remedies and sanctions:
   1) Which remedies does the juvenile/his representative have to enforce relevant rules and safeguards during interrogation?
   2) Does breaching (or not effectuating) the relevant rules and safeguards during interrogation have consequences? If so, please indicate in relation to each flaw (per single rule/safeguard):
      - How and when the flaw is ascertained.
      - Whether it is for the juvenile or his representative to file a claim/motion or whether there is a system of automatic enforcement.

- The possible consequences/sanctions within the trial (e.g. exclusion, stay of proceedings *et cetera*) and outside the trial (criminal measures, disciplinary measures, restitution)

3) Can the interrogation of the juvenile be disseminated outside of the actors involved in the proceedings (e.g. media) and how does this relate to the general rules on the protection of privacy of the juvenile suspect in front of the press?

e) "WHERE?" LOCATION OF JUVENILE INTERROGATIONS

1. Where is the interrogation of the juvenile suspect generally carried out?
2. Are there special locations/facilities for carrying out the interrogation of the juvenile suspect (for example child friendly interrogation rooms/studio's)?
3. Can the juvenile be interrogated in a detention center (for example prison)?

f) RELEVANT COMPARISONS

1. Comparison with relevant rules for questioning juveniles as witnesses and victims:
   1) Describe in detail the rules and safeguards for the hearing of children as witnesses and victims
   2) Identify the differences with the rules concerning the interrogation of juvenile suspects.
2. Identify the differences with questioning of adult suspects unless it is already dealt with in other parts of the report
3. What are the rules applicable to questioning of juveniles within judicial cooperation with foreign states (in particular, European arrest warrant)? To what extent are they different from the rules normally applicable to the questioning of juveniles in domestic proceedings?
4. Identify whether there are any inconsistencies between the rules and safeguards for the pre-trial interrogations on the one hand and other investigative methods (such as taking of photographs, fingerprints, bodily samples *et cetera*) on the other.

III CONCLUSIONS

MAASTRICHT SERIES IN HUMAN RIGHTS

The *Maastricht Centre for Human Rights* facilitates and supports research in the field of human rights at Maastricht University's Faculty of Law. Research conducted at the Centre is interdisciplinary, with a focus on public international law, criminal law and social sciences. Titles appearing in the Maastricht Series in Human Rights have been peer reviewed under the responsibility of the Board of the Centre.

Published titles within the Series:

1. Ineke Boerefijn, Fons Coomans, Jenny Goldschmidt, Rikki Holtmaat and Ria Wolleswinkel (eds.), *Temporary Special Measures. Accelerating de facto Equality of Women under Article 4(1) UN Convention on the Elimination of All Forms of Discrimination against Women* (2003)
   ISBN 90-5095-359-X
2. Fons Coomans and Menno T. Kamminga (eds.), *Extraterritorial Application of Human Rights Treaties* (2004)
   ISBN 90-5095-394-8
3. Koen De Feyter and Felipe Gómez Isa (eds.), *Privatisation and Human Rights in the Age of Globalisation* (2005)
   ISBN 90-5095-422-7
4. Ingrid Westendorp and Ria Wolleswinkel (eds.), *Violence in the domestic sphere* (2005)
   ISBN 90-5095-526-6
5. Fons Coomans (ed.), *Justiciability of Economic and Social Rights* (2006)
   ISBN 978-90-5095-582-9
6. Jan C.M. Willems (ed.), *Developmental and Autonomy Rights of Children: Empowering Children, Caregivers and Communities. 2nd revised edition* (2007)
   ISBN 978-90-5095-726-7
7. Alette Smeulers and Roelof Haveman (eds.), *Supranational Criminology: Towards a Criminology of International Crimes* (2008)
   ISBN 978-90-5095-791-5
8. Hans van Crombrugge, Wouter Vandenhole and Jan C.M. Willems (eds.), *Shared Pedagogical Responsibility* (2008)
   ISBN 978-90-5095-813-4
9. Hildegard Schneider and Peter Van den Bossche (eds.), *Protection of Cultural Diversity from a European and International Perspective* (2008)
   ISBN 978-90-5095-864-6

10. Fons Coomans, Fred Grünfeld and Menno T. Kamminga (eds.), *Methods of Human Rights Research* (2009)
ISBN 978-90-5095-879-0
11. Jan CM Willems (ed.), *Children's Rights and Human Development. A Multidisciplinary Reader* (2010)
ISBN 978-94-000-0032-2
12. Martine Boersma and Hans Nelen (eds.), *Corruption & Human Rights: Interdisciplinary Perspectives* (2010)
ISBN 978-94-000-0085-8
13. Hans Nelen and Jacques Claessen (eds.), *Beyond the Death Penalty* (2012)
ISBN 978-1-78068-060-6
14. Fons Coomans and Rolf Künneman (eds.), *Cases and Concepts on extraterritorial Obligations in the Area of Economic, Social and Cultural Rights* (2012)
ISBN 978-94-000-0046-9
15. Chen Weidong and Taru Spronken (eds.), *Three Approaches to Combating Torture in China* (2012)
ISBN 978-1-78068-088-0